Surveillance in America

Surveillance in America

AN ENCYCLOPEDIA OF HISTORY, POLITICS, AND THE LAW

Volume One: A–Z

Pam Dixon, Consulting Editor

ABC-CLIO™
An Imprint of ABC-CLIO, LLC
Santa Barbara, California • Denver, Colorado

Library of Congress Cataloging-in-Publication Data

Names: Dixon, Pam, 1960– editor.
Title: Surveillance in America : an encyclopedia of history, politics, and the law / Pam Dixon, consulting editor.
Description: Santa Barbara, California : ABC-CLIO, 2016. | Includes bibliographical references and index.
Identifiers: LCCN 2015030411 | ISBN 9781440840548 (set : hardback : alkaline paper) | ISBN 9781440845437 (vol.1 : hardback : alkaline paper) | ISBN 9781440845444 (vol.2 : hardback : alkaline paper) | ISBN 9781440840555 (ebook)
Subjects: LCSH: Electronic surveillance—Law and legislation—United States. | Privacy, Right of—United States—History. | BISAC: HISTORY / Military / United States. | HISTORY / Military / Strategy. | ART / American / Hispanic American.
Classification: LCC KF5399 .S87 2016 | DDC 342.7308/58—dc23
LC record available at http://lccn.loc.gov/2015030411

ISBN: 978-1-4408-4054-8 (set)
978-1-4408-4543-7 (vol. 1)
978-1-4408-4544-4 (vol. 2)
EISBN: 978-1-4408-4055-5

20 19 18 17 16 1 2 3 4 5

This book is also available on the World Wide Web as an eBook.
Visit www.abc-clio.com for details.

ABC-CLIO, LLC
An Imprint of ABC-CLIO, LLC

ABC-CLIO, LLC
130 Cremona Drive, P.O. Box 1911
Santa Barbara, California 93116-1911

This book is printed on acid-free paper ∞

Manufactured in the United States of America

Contents

Reader's Guide to Related Topics and Primary Documents

Agencies and Organizations

Topics

American Civil Liberties Union (ACLU)
Central Intelligence Agency (CIA)
Church Committee
Data Brokers
Federal Bureau of Investigation (FBI)
Five Eyes
Foreign Intelligence Surveillance Court (FISC)
House Un-American Activities Committee (HUAC)
National Security Agency (NSA)
9/11 Commission
Police Militarization
Privacy Advocacy Organizations
Transportation Security Administration (TSA)

Antisurveillance Programs and Activities

Topics

Anonymization and Deidentification
Antiwiretapping Statutes
Crypto Wars
Encryption
Fair Information Practices
Firewall
Freedom of Information Act (FOIA)
Health Information Privacy

Biographies

Topics

Alexander, Keith B. (1951–)
Ashcroft, John (1942–)
Bamford, James (1946–)
Brandeis, Louis (1856–1941)
Clapper, James R. (1941–)
Douglas, William O. (1898–1980)
Greenwald, Glenn (1967–)
Hayden, Michael (1945–)
Hoover, J. Edgar (1895–1972)
Klein, Mark
Leahy, Patrick (1940–)
Orwell, George (1903–1950)
Snowden, Edward (1983–)

Court Rulings

Topics

American Civil Liberties Union v. Clapper (2015)
American Civil Liberties Union v. National Security Agency (2007)

Arizona v. Evans (1995)
Bartnicki v. Vopper (2001)
Boyd v. United States (1886)
California v. Ciraolo (1986)
California v. Greenwood (1988)
Davis v. Mississippi (1969)
Delaware v. Prouse (1979)
Griswold v. Connecticut (1965)
Hepting v. AT&T (2009)
Illinois v. Krull et al. (1987)
Illinois v. Lidster (2004)
Jewel v. National Security Agency (2015)
Klayman v. Obama (2013)
Michigan Department of State Police v. Sitz (1990)
United States v. Davis (2015)
United States v. U.S. District Court (1972)
Vernonia School District v. Acton (1995)

Documents

The Supreme Court Establishes "Clear and Present Danger" Doctrine in *Schenck v. United States*—1919
Ex parte Endo Ruling Paves the Way for Closing of Internment Camps—1944
Miller v. United States Decision Limits Police "Knock and Announce" Powers—1958
The Supreme Court Expands the Exclusionary Rule in *Mapp v. Ohio*—1961
Albertson Supreme Court Decision Weakens the Subversive Activities Control Board—1965
The Supreme Court Finds a Constitutional Right to Privacy in *Griswold v. Connecticut*—1965
The Supreme Court Expands Privacy Rights in *Katz v. United States*—1967
The Supreme Court Bolsters the Exclusionary Rule in *United States v. Leon*—1984
The Supreme Court Rules on Checkpoints in *City of Indianapolis v. Edmond*—2000
The Supreme Court Rules on Thermal-Imaging Surveillance in *Kyllo v. United States*—2001
The Supreme Court Sanctions School Drug Testing—2002
Secret FISA Court Rejects a Justice Department Surveillance Request—2002
The Supreme Court Rules on Searches during Traffic Stops in *Illinois v. Caballes*—2005
District Court Rules NSL Gag Orders Unconstitutional—2006
Supreme Court Ruling in *Berghuis v. Thompkins* Narrows Miranda Rights—2010

Government Oversight

Topics

Church Committee
Executive Order 12333
Fair Information Practices

Documents

The Church Committee Releases Shocking Revelations of Government Surveillance—1976

Secret FISA Court Rejects a Justice Department Surveillance Request—2002
Secret DOJ Inspector General Report on FBI Use of Section 215 Orders—2008
Senator Feinstein Reacts to Revelations of CIA Spying on the Senate—2014

Laws and Regulations

Topics

Alien Registration Act
Antiwiretapping Statutes
Cable Communications Policy Act of 1984
Civil Rights and Liberties during Wartime
Communications Assistance for Law Enforcement Act (CALEA)
Constitutional Protections
Crypto Wars
Electronic Communications Privacy Act (ECPA)
Espionage Act of 1917
Exclusionary Rule
Executive Order 9066
Executive Order 12333
Fair Information Practices
Firearms Registration
Foreign Intelligence Surveillance Act (FISA)
Freedom of Information Act (FOIA)
Internal Security Act of 1950
National Security Letters (NSLs)
Plain View Doctrine
Privacy Act of 1974
Privacy, Informational
Right to Financial Privacy Act (RFPA)
Terrorism, War on
Third-Party Doctrine
USA PATRIOT Act

Documents

The Sedition Act—1798
Supreme Court Establishes the Exclusionary Rule in *Weeks v. United States*—1914
The Sedition Act—1918
Supreme Court Establishes "Clear and Present Danger" Doctrine in *Schenck v. United States*—1919
Justice Brandeis's Dissent in *Olmstead v. United States*—1928
Alien Registration Act—1940
President Roosevelt Orders the Internment of Japanese Americans—1942
Ex parte Endo Ruling Paves the Way for Closing of Internment Camps—1944
President Truman's "Loyalty Program" Executive Order—1947
President Truman Vetoes the Proposed Internal Security Act—1950
Congress Passes the Internal Security Act over Truman's Veto—1950
President Johnson Criticizes Eavesdropping Provisions in Crime Control Act—1968
President Carter Signs the Foreign Intelligence Surveillance Act (FISA)—1978
The Electronic Communications Privacy Act—1986
Congressman Hyde Praises the Communications Assistance for Law Enforcement Act—1994

President Bush Signs the FISA Amendments Act (FAA)—2008
Two Democratic Senators Debate Reauthorization of FISA—2012

Privacy Rights

Topics

Constitutional Protections
Health Information Privacy
Privacy Act of 1974
Privacy Advocacy Organizations
Privacy, Informational

Documents

"The Right to Privacy in America"—1890
Justice Brandeis's Dissent in *Olmstead v. United States*—1928
The Supreme Court Finds a Constitutional Right to Privacy in *Griswold v. Connecticut*—1965
The Supreme Court Expands Privacy Rights in *Katz v. United States*—1967
The Electronic Communications Privacy Act—1986
World Privacy Forum Urges Stronger Privacy Protections for Medical Records—2014

September 11 Terrorist Attacks and USA PATRIOT Act

Topics

9/11 Commission
Terrorism, War on
USA PATRIOT Act

Documents

President Bush Addresses Congress after the September 11 Attacks—2001
President Bush Signs the USA PATRIOT Act—2001
Section 213 and Section 215 of the USA PATRIOT Act—2001
Senator Feingold Speaks Out against the USA PATRIOT Act—2001
President Bush Signs the Homeland Security Act—2002
The American Library Association Issues a Resolution on Privacy and Civil Liberties—2003
Attorney General Ashcroft Defends the PATRIOT Act on Capitol Hill—2003
Representative Sanders Introduces the Freedom to Read Protection Act—2003
A Bush Administration Official Urges Reauthorization of the PATRIOT Act—2005
District Court Rules NSL Gag Orders Unconstitutional—2006
President Bush Defends the NSA and the PATRIOT Act—2006
President Bush Signs a Reauthorization of the PATRIOT Act—2006
Roving Wiretaps and "Sneak and Peek" Warrants—2006
Senator Leahy Lambasts Republican Opposition to PATRIOT Act Reforms—2006
Inspector General's Report Reveals FBI Abuse of National Security Letters—2007
Secret DOJ Inspector General Report on FBI Use of Section 215 Orders—2008
An American Librarian Recalls Receiving a National Security Letter—2013

Snowden's Release of NSA Surveillance Information

Topics

Alexander, Keith B. (1951–)
Bamford, James (1946–)
Clapper, James R. (1941–)
Greenwald, Glenn (1967–)
Hayden, Michael (1945–)
National Security Agency (NSA)
Snowden, Edward (1983–)

Documents

Presidential Task Force Report on *Liberty and Security in a Changing World*—2013
The Secret FISA Verizon Order—2013
President Obama Responds to the Task Force Review of NSA Operations—2014
Three Senators Speak Out against the USA Freedom Act—November 2014
Three Senators Speak Out in Support of the USA Freedom Act—November 2014

Surveillance, Criticism of Practices and Programs

Documents

James Otis Composes "Against the Writs of Assistance"—1761
Justice Brandeis's Dissent in *Olmstead v. United States*—1928
President Truman Vetoes the Proposed Internal Security Act—1950
President Johnson Criticizes Eavesdropping Provisions in Crime Control Act—1968
The Church Committee Releases Shocking Revelations of Government Surveillance—1976
Senator Feingold Speaks Out against the USA PATRIOT Act—2001
The American Library Association Issues a Resolution on Privacy and Civil Liberties—2003
Representative Sanders Introduces the Freedom to Read Protection Act—2003
Senator Leahy Lambasts Republican Opposition to PATRIOT Act Reforms—2006
Inspector General's Report Reveals FBI Abuse of National Security Letters—2007
Secret DOJ Inspector General Report on FBI Use of Section 215 Orders—2008
Two Democratic Senators Debate Reauthorization of FISA—2012
An American Librarian Recalls Receiving a National Security Letter—2013
Presidential Task Force Report on *Liberty and Security in a Changing World*—2013
Privacy and Civil Liberties Oversight Board Condemns the NSA's Section 215 Program—2014
Senator Feinstein Reacts to Revelations of CIA Spying on the Senate—2014
Three Senators Speak Out against the USA Freedom Act—November 2014

Surveillance, Defenses of Practices and Programs

Documents

The FBI Defends Its Library Awareness Program—1988
The Clinton White House Endorses Clipper and Capstone—1994
Congressman Hyde Praises the Communications Assistance for Law Enforcement Act—1994
President Bush Signs the USA PATRIOT Act—2001
Attorney General Ashcroft Defends the PATRIOT Act on Capitol Hill—2003
A Bush Administration Official Urges Reauthorization of the PATRIOT Act—2005
President Bush Defends the NSA and the PATRIOT Act—2006
Two Democratic Senators Debate Reauthorization of FISA—2012
FBI Director Comey Discusses the Dangers of "Going Dark"—October 2014
Three Senators Speak Out in Support of the USA Freedom Act—November 2014

Surveillance–Industrial Complex (Government–Corporate Partnerships)

Topics

Data Brokers
Data Collection, Online
E-Verify
Persistent Online Tracking
Surveillance–Industrial Complex

Documents

A Report on Law Enforcement's "Little Helpers"—Data Aggregators—2004
A Privacy Rights Group Examines Governmental Use of Commercial Data Brokers—2013
The Secret FISA Verizon Order—2013

Surveillance Programs and Initiatives

Topics

Carnivore
Clipper and Capstone Chips
Echelon
E-Verify
Fusion Centers
Hemisphere Project
House Un-American Activities Committee (HUAC)
McCarthyism
President's Surveillance Program (PSP)
PRISM
Stingray Tracking Technology

Documents

President Roosevelt Orders the Internment of Japanese Americans—1942
President Truman's "Loyalty Program" Executive Order—1947
The Supreme Court Rules on Checkpoints in *City of Indianapolis v. Edmond*—2000
Congress Shuts Down "Total Information Awareness" Program—2003
Roving Wiretaps and "Sneak and Peek" Warrants—2006

Surveillance Types and Practices

Topics

Documents

Technology and Equipment

Topics

Documents

U.S. Constitution

Topics

Documents

Preface

Government surveillance as an issue exploded into modern consciousness with the revelations that Edward Snowden made about the activities of the National Security Agency in 2013. But government surveillance is actually an old issue with a long and tangled history reaching back through generations. The competing interests involved in government surveillance create deeply opposing tensions that never seem to get fully resolved or go away.

Government wants to surveil in secrecy to protect home and country, and those being governed for their part want to be safe and protected. But individuals also want to have autonomy, privacy, and freedom from unfair intrusions or other abuses of government power. The nuanced and long-term interaction of this push and pull between the government's legitimate desire for surveillance and the legitimate desire expressed by individuals and society as a whole for civil liberties and autonomy run deeply though America's history, laws, actions, and policies of government surveillance.

More often than not, these deep tensions combined with government secrecy create an environment where finding symmetry between the positions of those conducting surveillance and those being surveilled becomes difficult at best. The balance of power in this area is especially precarious—individuals cannot confront abuses of government surveillance activities when those activities are conducted in secret, and government has little incentive to reveal its secrets. This is a tug-of-war that will not be fully resolved, but there are moments when, due to extraordinary circumstances, the balance corrects toward transparency.

Key events such as Project Shamrock in the 1940s, the Church Committee proceedings in the mid-1970s, and the 2013 whistle-blowing efforts of Edward Snowden stand as important historic markers in the shaping of U.S. government surveillance policy. These were moments when the push and pull between government secrecy and civil liberties brought new facts to light and provided a more public view of hidden surveillance programs. In these historic instances, the general pattern has been that the government, in secret and under the cloak of classification, overreaches in its surveillance or conducts surveillance that is seen as illegal or in some way out of bounds. These acts are later revealed, and then public and legal pushback creates change toward increased transparency.

Project Shamrock was a major U.S. surveillance program that had no judicial oversight. The project, which began in the mid-1940s, intercepted and analyzed all telegraphic data entering or leaving the United States and involved multiple government agencies. The project operated in secret until 1975, when Congress began to investigate the program. The congressional committee that investigated Project Shamrock—among other intelligence activities—was the Church Committee, and its hearings and reports were major news in the 1970s. Many lasting improvements in how intelligence was gathered stemmed from outrage fueled by facts the Church Committee uncovered. The 1978 passage of the Foreign Intelligence Surveillance Act, which created a mechanism for judicial oversight of secret government surveillance known today as the "FISA court," was one such change. Approximately 50,000 pages of formerly classified material were made public in the late 1970s, a result of the Church Committee's impact.

The famed "crypto wars" of the 1990s, which continued through about 2005, centered on the right of individuals to legally use encrypted communications without government "backdoor" access. The win in this particular battle over where to draw the line between privacy and law enforcement/security went to individuals. But while the security experts and civil liberties advocates who had fought that battle basked in their hard-won victory, the government secretly shifted tactics and began focusing surveillance on social graph analysis, bulk traffic analysis, and targeted malware.

This modern shift in surveillance tactics went unchallenged because it was undertaken in secrecy. Although the existence of what is now called "bulk surveillance" was hypothesized by security experts as early as 2008, it took another five years before the revelations of Edward Snowden, a contractor who had access to NSA surveillance program details, unambiguously proved that bulk surveillance was a reality. Beginning in June 2013, Snowden leaked profound amounts of national security and intelligence data to the public. The details that emerged about the scope and policies of the government's secret PRISM program and other secret government programs shocked legal scholars and members of Congress.

Particularly objectionable were the invasive bulk collection programs, bolstered by legal memos from Justice Department lawyers, which relied on new and broader interpretations of existing law to allow for promiscuous collection of digital information, including that of American citizens. The steady stream of revelations from Snowden systemically eroded trust in the U.S. government at home and abroad. While the nation is divided on whether Snowden is a traitor or a hero, his revelations did spark a substantive public dialogue about the new, controversial interpretations of existing law, and Snowden's information did set the government on a course toward more transparency.

Among the most important changes in U.S. government surveillance policy that have occurred since mid-2013 is the sweeping Presidential Policy Directive 28 around signals intelligence surveillance. The directive, known as PPD28, came at the end of a year-long, intensive government-wide review to assess how the government was handling secret surveillance activities. The review, which was completed in January 2014, has resulted in profound changes in how surveillance is conducted at home and abroad, with notable but not complete advances toward government transparency.

As part of the January 2014 PPD28 and related orders, new principles governing the collection of signals intelligence were put forward by the executive branch. The President announced in the directive that the current program of broad "bulk collection" of metadata related to phone calls would be phased out, and a congressional-authorized program would be put in its place that takes into account privacy and civil liberties. Also, crucial to forward momentum has been the declassification of highly secret documents about surveillance activities undertaken by the government.

Since 2013, more than 40 opinions of the secret Foreign Intelligence Surveillance Court have been declassified, and an historic 270 million pages of records from the FBI were declassified on December 31, 2014. These FBI records, which span from 1920 to 1981, also include recent investigations and offer extraordinary glimpses into highly secret intelligence work. These documents, which were formerly kept under extremely high levels of classification, detail the impact of surveillance programs and include in-depth reports of missteps by the government and mark a milestone toward a lifting of government secrecy. The ripples of these important government declassifications have not yet made their full impact, but it is a major step toward transparency in our time.

Another result of all that we know now in the post-Snowden, post-PPD 28 era is that finding a balance between government secrecy on one hand and autonomy on the other has been made more difficult due to rapid advances in technology, which allow for largely undetectable digital mass surveillance. The standard of allowing for no secret surveillance of American citizens on American soil is being eroded as a result, but there is at least a stream now of discussion and dissent based on newly discoverable facts. This discussion would not be nearly as robust or as meaningful without the declassification and release of the FISA court and FBI documents. For the United States, this massive declassification of national secrets is a Perestroika of sorts of U.S. government surveillance secrets. So far, the government-led changes resulting from the Snowden revelations to date are even greater than those changes sparked by the Church Committee.

Yet the tug-of-war between interests will continue. There will not be a permanent resolution between government surveillance, civil liberties, and autonomy. It is woven into the very fabric of a democratic society to achieve balance through vigorous tensions and thoughtful work toward difficult solutions. Course corrections in the midst of wars, threats, and unsure times is a messy endeavor, yet it is this effort to find balance that in part defines a nation's democratic health. While today the pendulum is moving slowly and incrementally toward increased government transparency about its surveillance activities and capabilities, history shows us that it will move back the other way at some point, and the struggle over balancing of interests will continue unabated.

Pam Dixon
Executive Director
World Privacy Forum

Introduction

Surveillance in America: An Encyclopedia of History, Politics, and the Law is a two-volume reference set crafted to explore all the major issues surrounding government surveillance and its impact on privacy and other treasured constitutional freedoms in 21st-century America.

Advances in telecommunications have enabled people to become more connected than ever before. But these jumps in technological capability have coincided with rising fears about terrorism and crime. Many people assert that the imperatives of safety and security necessitate careful monitoring of modern telecommunications networks and resources. But many others insist that such practices, by their very nature, pose significant dangers to civil liberties.

This debate further intensified in 2013, when whistle-blower Edward Snowden, a contractor working for America's National Security Agency (NSA), revealed that the NSA maintained a vast and secret domestic electronic surveillance program that included private information on millions of Americans who were not suspected of any wrongdoing. Snowden's revelations raised new questions regarding the extent of Fourth Amendment protections against warrantless, unreasonable government intrusions into private lives.

This encyclopedia will make clear to readers that setting appropriate parameters for government surveillance has been an ongoing struggle in the United States, dating all the way back to its earliest days as a nation. Since then, Congress and the Supreme Court have passed and interpreted a wide range of laws governing surveillance. But the process of finding the right surveillance balance between security and liberty is a never-ending one, for world events, political changes, and technological advances all influence that equation.

Volume I of *Surveillance in America* contains 115 authoritative, in-depth entries describing important surveillance programs, agencies, legal cases, individuals, legislation, and technological advances that have shaped how U.S. government surveillance is practiced today. Volume II of the set contains illuminating excerpts from 68 primary documents, which trace the history of government surveillance in the United States, with a special focus on primary documents to help readers understand how surveillance practices and priorities have changed since the September 11, 2001, terrorist attacks on American soil. Each of these documents is supplemented with an introductory headnote that provides historical context for understanding the significance of the source in question. Other helpful features of *Surveillance in America* include a detailed chronology and a general bibliography.

Offering a balanced tone that gives equal credence to concerns over security and individual privacy, *Surveillance in America* offers an ideal point of entry for understanding historical and contemporary debates over the nature and extent of surveillance practices carried out by the U.S. government.

Chronology

1761 James Otis writes his "Against the Writs of Assistance" manifesto.

1789 The Bill of Rights to the U.S. Constitution is introduced, and two years later it is ratified and becomes law. Among these ten amendments to the Constitution is the Fourth Amendment, which guarantees "the right of the people to be secure in their persons, houses, papers, and effects, against unreasonable searches and seizures, shall not be violated, and no Warrants shall issue, but upon probable cause, supported by Oath or affirmation, and particularly describing the place to be searched, and the persons or things to be seized."

1798 The Sedition Act is signed into law.

1886 In *Boyd v. United States*, the Supreme Court rules that seizure or compulsory production of a person's personal papers for the purpose of gathering evidence against that person is a form of compelling self-incrimination.

1890 Louis Brandeis and Samuel Warren publish the seminal article "The Right to Privacy" in the *Harvard Law Review.*

1901 New York Civil Service Commission introduces the first systematic use of fingerprint identifiers in the United States.

1914 In *Weeks v. United States*, the Supreme Court rules that warrantless seizure of evidence from private residence violates constitutional protections.

1918 The Sedition Act of 1918 becomes law.

1919 In *Schenck v. United States*, the Supreme Court establishes the "Clear and Present Danger" doctrine.

1920 American Civil Liberties Union founded.

1924	J. Edgar Hoover appointed Director of the Federal Bureau of Investigation (FBI).
1925	In *Carroll v. United States*, the Supreme Court rules that warrantless searches of automobiles by law enforcement officers are constitutional if they have probable cause to suspect that the vehicle contains unlawful materials or evidence of wrongdoing.
1928	The Supreme Court rules in *Olmstead v. United States* that wiretapped private telephone conversations recorded by authorities without warrants are constitutional.
1934	The Federal Communications Act is passed into law, in part to establish legal parameters for the use of the new technology of wiretapping.
1938	The House Un-American Activities Committee convenes for the first time.
1939	Privacy rights champion William O. Douglas is appointed to the Supreme Court.
	The Hatch Act makes loyalty to the United States an explicit condition of federal employment.
1940	Congress passes the Alien Registration Act, also known as the Smith Act, to combat Communist and Nazi influences in the United States.
1942	President Franklin D. Roosevelt issues Executive Order 9066, paving the way for the forcible internment of Japanese-American citizens and Japanese immigrants living in the United States during World War II.
1947	In *Harris v. United States*, the Supreme Court establishes the "plain view" doctrine of admissibility of evidence.
	President Truman signs Executive Order 9835, which establishes a loyalty program for federal employees.
1949	George Orwell's novel *1984* is published.
1950	Republican Senator Joseph McCarthy tells an audience in Wheeling, West Virginia, that he possesses evidence of widespread Communist infiltration of the State Department.
	The Internal Security Act is passed into law over President Truman's veto.

1952 The National Security Agency (NSA) is created.

1954 The so-called Army–McCarthy hearings stretch from April to June, during which time McCarthy's political fortunes decline precipitously.

1956 The FBI launches its Counter Intelligence (COINTELPRO) program.

1961 The Supreme Court expands the scope of the Exclusionary Rule in *Mapp v. Ohio.*

1965 The first e-mail system is created.

In *Griswold v. Connecticut*, the Supreme Court expands legal recognition of individual right to a "zone of privacy."

U.S. law enforcement begins using surveillance cameras in public places.

1966 Freedom of Information Act is passed into law.

In *Miranda v. Arizona*, the U.S. Supreme Court rules that people suspected of criminal actions must be informed of their constitutional rights to have an attorney, to remain silent, and to otherwise guard against self-incrimination before they are questioned by police.

1967 In *Katz v. United States*, the Supreme Court finds that Fourth Amendment protections against unreasonable searches and seizures require police to obtain a search warrant to wiretap a public pay phone.

National Crime Information Center is established.

1968 In *Terry v. Ohio*, the Supreme Court establishes the "stop and frisk" rule.

Congress passes the Omnibus Crime Control and Safe Streets Act, which includes new restrictions on government wiretapping.

1970 Bank Secrecy Act is passed into law.

1971 The FBI's COINTELPRO program is abolished.

1973 In *Roe v. Wade*, the Supreme Court holds that a woman's right to an abortion was within right to privacy protections enshrined in the Fourteenth Amendment.

1974 Privacy Protection Act is passed into law.

	President Richard M. Nixon resigns to avoid impeachment proceedings set in motion by his involvement in the Watergate scandal, which included secret surveillance of political opponents.
1975	The House of Representatives formally abolishes the House Un-American Activities Committee (HUAC).
1975–1976	Church Committee Reports are published, revealing widespread illegal government surveillance by the CIA and FBI, as well as many other incidents of agency malfeasance.
1978	The Foreign Intelligence Surveillance Act is signed into law by President Jimmy Carter.
1979	The Supreme Court upholds the legality of pen registers in *Smith v. Maryland.*
1984	In *Hudson v. Palmer*, the Supreme Court holds that Fourth Amendment proscriptions against unreasonable searches do not extend to prison cells.
	The Supreme Court bolsters the Exclusionary Rule in *United States v. Leon.*
1986	The Electronic Communications Privacy Act becomes law.
	In *California v. Ciraolo*, the Supreme Court rules that warrantless, aerial observation of a home and yard is legally permissible.
1987	In *O'Connor v. Ortega*, the Supreme Court finds that a supervisor's search of a public employee's office does not violate the employee's "reasonable expectation of privacy."
1988	The Video Privacy Protection Act is passed into law.
1993	President Clinton institutes "Don't ask, don't tell" policy in the U.S. military.
1994	The Communications Assistance for Law Enforcement Act becomes law.
	The Electronic Privacy Information Center (EPIC) is founded.
1995	In *Vernonia School District v. Acton*, the Supreme Court finds that the school's student athlete drug policy does not violate the reasonable search and seizure clause of the Fourth Amendment.
1996	Telecommunications Act passed into law.
1997	The Carnivore surveillance program is invented.
2000	In *Lawrence and Garner v. Texas*, the Supreme Court strikes down a Texas statute, making it a crime for two persons of the

same sex to engage in certain sexual conduct as a violation of the Due Process Clause of the Fourteenth Amendment.

2001 In *Bartnicki v. Vopper*, the Supreme Court rules that the First Amendment protects the public disclosure of an illegally intercepted cellular telephone call.

In *Camfield v. City of Oklahoma City*, the Supreme Court finds that the city violated a citizen's rights under the Video Privacy Protection Act by obtaining his video rental records without a warrant.

In *United States v. Kyllo*, the Supreme Court rules that the use of a thermal-imaging device to detect heat emanating from a private home violates Fourth Amendment privacy protections.

September 11—Terrorists hijack commercial airliners to carry out the deadliest terrorist attacks on American soil in U.S. history.

October 26—President Bush signs the Uniting and Strengthening America by Providing Appropriate Tools Required to Intercept and Obstruct Terrorism Act of 2001 (USA PATRIOT Act) into law.

November 26—Bush signs the Homeland Security Act into law, thus creating the Department of Homeland Security.

2002 The Supreme Court sanctions school drug testing in *Board of Education of Pottawatomie County v. Earls.*

2003 AT&T technician Mark Klein discovers NSA data-mining equipment used to conduct secret surveillance of electronic communications carried out through the company's communications systems.

The American Library Association (ALA) issues a statement expressing grave concern about provisions in the USA PATRIOT Act, which allegedly impinges on civil liberties and privacy.

U.S. Representative Bernie Sanders introduces the Freedom to Read Protection Act.

2005 The *New York Times* reveals widespread warrantless wiretapping and other secret surveillance activities carried out by the Bush administration since 2002.

In *Illinois v. Cabelles*, the Supreme Court expands law enforcement's search authority during traffic stops.

2006 The USA PATRIOT Act is renewed despite objections that Section 215 and other provisions extend too much surveillance authority to the federal government.

2007 The FBI's inspector general issues a report on the agency's abuse of National Security Letters.

The Protect America Act, which amends FISA, is signed into law by President Bush.

2008 The FISA Amendments Act becomes law despite strong criticism from privacy rights advocates and civil libertarians.

2010 The Supreme Court decision in *Berghuis v. Thompkins* weakens Miranda Rights.

2011 Congress and President Obama extend the USA PATRIOT Act.

2012 Legislation to extend the FISA Amendments Act for another five years is passed by Congress and signed into law by President Obama.

2013 June 6—Armed with information from whistle-blower Edward Snowden, an NSA contractor, the *Guardian* and the *Washington Post* reveal the existence of sweeping secret electronic surveillance programs targeting people in the United States and around the world. Revelations include the news that the NSA gained access to the personal information of millions of people through the world's leading telecommunications companies.

December 18—A Presidential Advisory Panel recommends sweeping changes to the NSA's surveillance operations.

2014 January 17—President Obama announces reforms to NSA surveillance operations to better protect constitutional rights of Americans, but critics say that the changes are either cosmetic or insufficient.

January 23—The Privacy and Civil Liberties Oversight Board releases a report calling NSA surveillance programs unconstitutional and illegal.

May 13—Glenn Greenwald publishes *No Place to Hide*, which combines his account of meetings with whistle-blower Edward Snowden with perspectives on the impact of the American surveillance state.

May 31—*The New York Times* reveals the existence of a massive NSA program to collect millions of images for, among other things, biometric facial recognition purposes.

September 14—*Der Spiegel* and *The Intercept* reveal that the National Security Agency and its British counterpart, the Government Communications Headquarters (GCHQ), secretly hacked into German companies in an effort to increase surveillance capabilities over the entire Internet.

2015 *The Intercept* reveals that in 2010 and 2011 the NSA and GCHQ collaborated to hack into the computer network of Gemalto, the largest manufacturer of SIM cards in the world, and steal millions of cellular encryption keys.

A

Administrative Searches

Inspections or searches conducted as part of a general regulatory scheme, often but not exclusively to ensure compliance with laws and regulations, are called administrative searches. One of the fundamental principles of administrative searches is that they may not be used as a pretext to search for evidence of criminal activity. Because these searches are justified by "special needs" beyond the normal need for law enforcement, they do not merit the same constitutional protections. Since the 1980s, courts have broadened the special needs exception to permit a variety of warrantless suspicion-less searches, from mandatory drug testing of certain segments of the population to warrantless searches of people, automobiles, and homes, provided law enforcement has "legitimate" cause for such activities. As a result, Americans in the 21st century are subject to administrative searches that in many respects have become a routine part of daily life. "Anyone who has been stopped at a sobriety checkpoint, screened at an international border, scanned by a metal detector at an airport or government building, or drug tested for public employment has been subjected to an administrative search (or seizure)," wrote Eve Brensike Primus in the *Columbia Law Review.* "In other words, the government conducts thousands of administrative searches every day."

In monitoring regulatory compliance of businesses and industries, administrative agencies routinely make inspections, searches, and seizures. Initially, the U.S. Supreme Court took the position that such searches were not subject to the requirements of the Fourth Amendment. In *Frank v. Maryland* (1959), the Supreme Court found no violation of the Fourth Amendment when administrative searches were conducted without notice and search warrants. The Court thus upheld the conviction of a Baltimore man who refused to allow a city health inspector, looking for evidence of rat infestation, enter and inspect his home without a warrant. In his opinion regarding the Court sustaining the constitutionality of that ordinance, Justice William Brennan asserted that "the power to inspect dwelling places . . . is of indispensable importance to the maintenance of community health; a power that would be greatly hobbled by the blanket requirement of the safeguards necessary for a search of evidence of criminal acts."

The *Frank v. Maryland* (1959) decision suggested that administrative searches were outside the prohibitions of the Fourth Amendment. In dissent, Justice William O. Douglas insisted, "The Court misreads history when it relates the Fourth Amendment primarily to searches for evidence to be used in criminal prosecutions." In Douglas's view, the decision of the Court "greatly dilutes the right of privacy which every homeowner had the right to believe was part of our American heritage."

The Supreme Court's *Frank v. Maryland* (1959) decision assumed a fundamental difference between administrative inspections and searches for evidence of crime. However, administrative inspections can lead to criminal charges or serve as a pretext for the gathering of information to assist criminal investigations. In *Camara v. Municipal Court* (1967), the Supreme Court recognized that and overruled *Frank v. Maryland* (1959). The Court held that, as a general rule, warrants must be obtained to permit administrative searches of private residences. Writing for the Court, Justice Byron White observed that administrative searches "are significant intrusions upon the interests protected by the Fourth Amendment" and that "the reasons put forth in *Frank v. Maryland* and in other cases for upholding these warrantless searches are insufficient to justify so substantial a weakening of the Fourth Amendment's protections."

In *See v. City of Seattle* (1967), the Court extended the *Camara* ruling to commercial establishments. In *See*, a Seattle businessman was convicted of a misdemeanor for refusing to allow a fire inspector to enter his locked warehouse without a warrant. Entry to the warehouse was requested as part of a routine citywide program to achieve compliance with fire regulations. Again, Justice White spoke for the Court, noting, "The businessman, like the occupant of a residence, has a constitutional right to go about his business free from unreasonable official entries upon his private commercial property."

Some commentators interpreted the *Camara* and *See* decisions as requiring that administrative searches should be subject to the same Fourth Amendment requirements that apply to criminal searches. In 1970, the Supreme Court invalidated that interpretation when it decided *Colonnade Corporation v. United States* (1970). At issue there was whether agents of the Federal Bureau of Alcohol, Tobacco and Firearms (ATF) needed a warrant before inspecting an establishment they had probable cause to believe was serving liquor from refilled bottles in violation of federal law. The Court held that "Congress has broad authority to fashion standards of reasonableness for searches and seizures" with respect to an industry "long subject to close supervision and inspection."

The Court amplified its *Colonnade* decision in *Biswell v. United States* (1972). In that case, an ATF agent conducted a surprise warrantless inspection of a pawnshop that was federally licensed to sell guns for sporting use. The agent located and seized two sawed-off rifles that the proprietor was not licensed to possess. In reversing a lower court decision invalidating the seizure, the Court observed that "regulation of the interstate traffic in firearms is not as deeply rooted in history as is governmental control of the liquor industry, but close scrutiny of this traffic is undeniably of central importance to federal efforts to prevent violent crime and to assist the States in regulating the firearms traffic within their borders." The Court concluded that "if the law is to be properly enforced and inspection made effective, inspections without warrant must be deemed reasonable official conduct under the Fourth Amendment."

Under the *Colonnade* and *Biswell* decisions, the Fourth Amendment imposes only a general standard of *reasonableness* with respect to searches and inspections of closely regulated industries. The doctrine assumes that businesses that choose to operate in such fields knowingly subject themselves to pervasive regulation and therefore have minimal expectations of privacy. The obvious question left open by these decisions is: What constitutes a "closely regulated industry"?

In *Marshall v. Barlow's, Inc.* (1978), the Supreme Court struck down a provision of the Occupational Health and Safety Act of 1970 that permitted federal officials to conduct warrantless searches of the workplace. The court determined that the mere fact that a business is involved in interstate commerce and is therefore subject to a variety of federal regulations does not make it a "closely regulated industry." Had the Court ruled otherwise, virtually every business in the United States could be so classified. In *Marshall v. Barlow's*, the Court stipulated that agents inspecting establishments not covered by the *Colonnade–Biswell* exception must first obtain administrative search warrants, but the Court was careful to point out that to obtain such warrants inspectors do not have to meet the standards of probable cause that govern the issuance of search warrants in criminal investigations.

In the 1980s, a more conservative Supreme Court appeared to back away from the strict scrutiny of regulatory searches suggested by the *Barlow's* decision. In *Donovan v. Dewey* (1981), the Court refused to invalidate a provision of the Federal Mine Safety and Health Act of 1977 that allowed the Department of Labor to conduct warrantless inspections of mines on a regular basis. Emphasizing the "certainty and regularity" of the inspection regime, the Court held that the Fourth Amendment warrant requirement was inapplicable. "Under these circumstances," observed Justice Thurgood Marshall, "it is difficult to see what additional protection a warrant requirement would provide."

In *New York v. Burger* (1987), in upholding a warrantless inspection of a junkyard by state officials, the Court articulated a framework for determining the legality of warrantless inspections authorized by state laws. Writing for the Court, Justice Harry Blackmun concluded that such inspections should be upheld as long as three conditions are met:

> First, there must be a "substantial" government interest that informs the regulatory scheme pursuant to which the inspection is made. . . . Second, the warrantless inspections must be "necessary to further [the] regulatory scheme.". . . Finally, "the statute's inspection program, in terms of the certainty and regularity of its application, [must] provid[e] a constitutionally adequate substitute for a warrant."

Because this framework allows agencies considerable latitude in conducting warrantless inspections of regulated industries, it has been criticized by commentators sensitive to Fourth Amendment values. In his dissenting opinion in *Burger*, Justice Brennan, whose views in the area had changed dramatically in the thirty years since he wrote *Frank v. Maryland*, claimed:

> The implications of the Court's opinion, if realized, will virtually eliminate Fourth Amendment protection of commercial entities in the context of administrative searches. No State may require, as a condition of doing business, a blanket submission to warrantless searches for any purpose.

As with other constitutional rights, state courts may grant greater protection to business and industries under their respective state constitutions. In this area, state courts have generally followed the approach taken by the U.S. Supreme Court in *New York v. Burger*, but state appellate courts have made differing judgments as to when there is a sufficient governmental interest to justify dispensing with normal warrant requirements.

John M. Scheb II and Otis H. Stephens Jr.

Further Reading

Harawa, Daniel S. 2013. "The Post-TSA Airport: A Constitution-Free Zone?" *Pepperdine Law Review* 41 (1). http://digitalcommons.pepperdine.edu/cgi/viewcontent.cgi?article=2327&context=plr. Accessed September 18, 2015.

Primus, Eve Brensike. 2011. "Disentangling Administrative Searches." *Columbia Law Review* 111 (254): 254–312. http://columbialawreview.org/wp-content/uploads/2011/03/111-2_Primus.pdf. Accessed September 18, 2015.

Scheb, John M., and John M. Scheb II. 2005. *Law and the Administrative Process*. Belmont, CA: Thomson/Wadsworth.

Alexander, Keith B. (1951–)

Keith Alexander spent much of his life at the highest levels of the U.S. military and government, where he worked in a number of national security and surveillance capacities. He is best known for his directorship of the National Security Agency (NSA) from 2005 until his retirement from public service in March 2014. "[The NSA] was already a data behemoth when Alexander took over," according to *Foreign Policy* reporter Shane Harris, "but under his watch, the breadth, scale, and ambition of its mission . . . expanded beyond anything ever contemplated by his predecessors."

Keith Brian Alexander was born on December 2, 1951, in Syracuse, New York. He was the third of five children of Donald Henry Alexander and Charlotte Colvin Alexander. He was raised in the Syracuse suburb of Onondaga Hill, where he earned money as a paperboy, and he ran track at Westhill High School. His father was a marine and was heavily involved in Republican politics. Alexander entered the U.S. Military Academy at West Point in 1970; two of his classmates would go on to fame: future four-star general and CIA Director David Petraeus and future chairman of the Joint Chiefs of Staff Martin Dempsey.

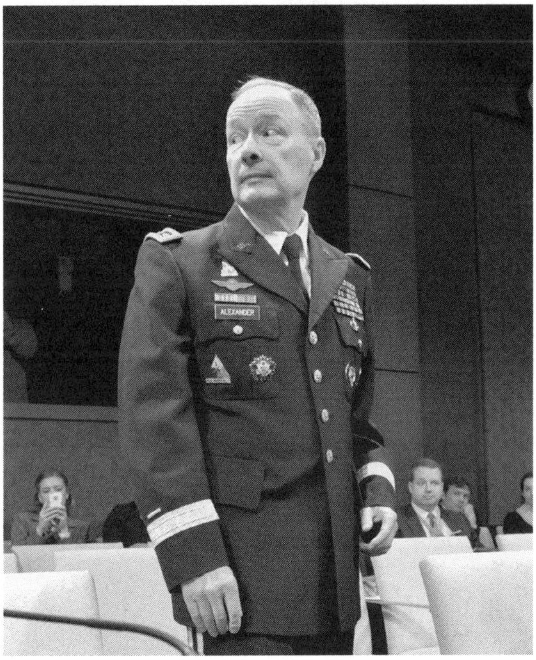

Gen. Keith B. Alexander, director of the National Security Agency and head of the U.S. Cyber Command, arrives to testify before the House Permanent Select Committee on Intelligence on Capitol Hill in Washington, DC, June 2013. Amid revelations that the electronic surveillance agency was sweeping up Americans' phone and Internet records in its quest to investigate terrorist threats, President Barack Obama defended top secret National Security Agency spying programs as legal and called them transparent—even though they are authorized in secret. (AP Photo/J. Scott Applewhite)

Alexander graduated from West Point in 1974, and in 1975 he married Deborah Lynn Douglas, with whom he eventually had four daughters. Alexander has also received four master's degrees: in business administration from Boston University, in electronic warfare and physics from West Point, and in national security strategy from the National Defense University.

Alexander gained expertise in advanced technology and worked in a number of related positions in the military. In his early career, he worked in the area of signals intelligence at a number of secret NSA bases. Other positions included commander of border field office in several locations; deputy director for intelligence for the Joint Chiefs of Staff (1997–1998); director of intelligence, U.S. Central Command (1998–2001); commanding general of the U.S. Army Intelligence and Security Command (2001–2003); and deputy chief of staff for intelligence, army headquarters (2003–2005).

The terrorist attacks of September 11, 2001, occurred while Alexander held his Army Intelligence and Security Command post. Six months earlier, Alexander had said in an interview, "We have to stay out in front of our adversary. It's a chess game, and you don't want to lose this one." The tragedy led to Alexander ordering intercept operators to begin monitoring Americans' phone calls and e-mails, even if they had nothing to do with terrorism. In 2003, when U.S. Secretary of Defense Donald Rumsfeld named Alexander the army's deputy chief of staff for intelligence, he became the army's senior intelligence official. It was during Alexander's time in this role that the human rights abuses at the Abu Ghraib prison in Baghdad, Iraq, occurred. Alexander and other army intelligence officials were heavily criticized for failing to detect—or even tacitly condoning—those acts, but Alexander later described the Abu Ghraib abuses as "totally reprehensible."

In July 2005, after NSA Director Michael V. Hayden moved on to become director of the Central Intelligence Agency, Rumsfeld selected Alexander as Hayden's replacement, making Alexander the agency's sixteenth director. Alexander also became a three-star general.

As director, Alexander oversaw the NSA's warrantless wiretapping program. The George W. Bush administration had approved of the program as part of its "war on terror" efforts in the aftermath of 9/11. The authorization allowed the NSA to monitor phone calls, text messaging, and Internet-related activities without search warrants, a violation of search and seizure laws. Alexander claimed that while "content" was, indeed, gathered via this warrantless wiretapping, data were merely stored for a possible future analysis if a connection to Al Qaeda or other terrorist groups was suspected. It is Alexander's belief, as he stated at a Senate Intelligence Committee hearing in 2013, that "it [was] in the nation's best interest to put all the phone records into a lockbox that we could search when the nation needs to do it."

In June 2009, U.S. Secretary of Defense Robert M. Gates announced the creation of U.S. Cyber Command, an organization that, according to its press release, would "be capable of synchronizing warfighting effects across the global security environment as well as providing support to civil authorities and international partners." The role of NSA director expanded to include the new Cyber Command responsibilities; at the same time Alexander took on the additional post, he was promoted to a four-star general. Alexander expressed great confidence in the need for the Cyber Command initiative: "As our dependence on information networks increases, it will take a team to eliminate vulnerabilities and counter the ever-growing threats to the network. We can succeed in securing it by building strong partnerships between and within the private and public sectors, encouraging information sharing and collaboration, and creating and leveraging the technology that affords us the opportunity to secure cyberspace."

Alexander retired from the NSA in March 2014 and was replaced by Michael S. Rogers. The announcement of his intention to retire came several months after former NSA contractor Edward Snowden leaked documents that revealed the existence and extent of several NSA's surveillance programs. Many of these NSA activities were roundly condemned as illegal violations of privacy rights and other civil liberties. Alexander maintained that the programs were legal, claiming that the PATRIOT Act and the Foreign Intelligence Surveillance Act (FISA) court provided adequate authorization.

Alexander went on to cofound IronNet Cybersecurity Inc., a consulting firm that develops patents and provides companies with intelligence advice, reportedly at anywhere from $600,000 to $1 million per month. Critics have claimed that Alexander's top spot at the NSA means there are risks that his new enterprise would reveal classified information. Alexander has denied such charges, saying, "I've been in government for 40 years; I fully understand the importance and sanctity of classified material. If I retired from the Army as a brain surgeon, wouldn't it be okay for me to go into private practice and make money doing brain surgery? I'm a cyber guy. Can't I go to work and do cyber stuff?" He maintains that his patent ideas have occurred after his retirement from the NSA.

Lawrence W. Baker

Further Reading

Bamford, James. "NSA Snooping Was Only the Beginning. Meet the Spy Chief Leading Us into Cyberwar." *Wired* (June 12, 2013). http://www.wired.com/2013/06/general-keith-alexander-cyberwar/. Accessed May 6, 2015.

"Biography—16th Director." National Security Agency/Central Security Service. https://www.nsa.gov/about/leadership/bio_alexander.shtml. Accessed May 6, 2015.

Dilanian, Ken. "'Cyber Guy' Keith Alexander Defends His Next Big Venture." *Huffington Post* (August 5, 2014). http://www.huffingtonpost.com/2014/08/05/keith-alexander-cybersecurity_n_5652497.html?utm_hp_ref=politics. Accessed May 6, 2015.

Eddlem, Thomas R. "The NSA Domestic Surveillance Lie." *The New American* (September 22, 2013). http://www.thenewamerican.com/usnews/politics/item/16580-the-nsa-domestic-surveillance-lie. Accessed May 6, 2015.

"Embattled NSA Director, Deputy Director Both to Retire." RT.com. http://rt.com/usa/embattled-keith-alexander-deputy-retire-284/. Accessed May 6, 2015.

Friedersdorf, Conor. "Keith Alexander's Unethical Get-Rich-Quick Plan." *The Atlantic* (July 31, 2014). http://www.theatlantic.com/politics/archive/2014/07/keith-alexanders-unethical-get-rich-quick-plan/375367/. Accessed September 18, 2015.

Greenwald, Glen. 2014. *No Place to Hide: Edward Snowden, the NSA, and the Surveillance State*. New York: Metropolitan Books.

Harris, Shane. "The NSA's Cyber-King Goes Corporate." *Foreign Policy* (July 29, 2014). http://foreignpolicy.com/2014/07/29/the-nsas-cyber-king-goes-corporate/. Accessed May 6, 2015.

"Keith B. Alexander." *Public Intelligence* (June 25, 2009). https://publicintelligence.net/keith-b-alexander/. Accessed May 6, 2015.

Stone, Jeff. "Former NSA Director Keith Alexander Denies Revealing U.S. Intelligence Secrets for Massive Salary." *International Business Times* (August 6, 2014). http://www.ibtimes.com/former-nsa-director-keith-alexander-denies-revealing-us-intelligence-secrets-massive-1650662. Accessed May 6, 2015.

Alien Registration Act

The Alien Registration Act of 1940 was proposed by Congressman Howard Smith of Virginia, a poll tax supporter and a leader of the antilabor bloc in Congress, and is generally referred to as the Smith Act. Signed into law by President Franklin Roosevelt, it was the first statute since the Alien and Sedition Acts of 1798 to make mere advocacy of ideas a federal crime. Specifically, the law made it illegal to print, publish, or circulate printed matter advocating or teaching the overthrow of the U.S. government. The act also required all aliens living within the United States to register with the government, be fingerprinted, carry identification cards, and report annually. Individuals found to have ties to "subversive organizations" could be deported.

By acquiring a detailed work history of aliens, the government sought to identify potential problems before they occurred. The other primary objective of the Alien Registration Act was to identify elements of the American Communist Party or other socialist organizations.

Although five million aliens were registered and fingerprinted following its passage, its antisubversive sections were not used until 1943, when a small group of Minneapolis Trotskyites were convicted under its provisions. When the Cold War intensified after the conclusion of World War II, the Truman administration carried out a series of dramatic prosecutions of Communist Party leaders.

Those and subsequent prosecutions eventually forced the Supreme Court to clarify the terms and reach of the Alien Registration Act. In *Dennis v. United States*, 341 U.S. 494 (1951), the Court considered the convictions of eleven Communist

Party leaders on charges of conspiracy to violate the advocacy and organizing sections of the statute. Chief Justice Vinson's plurality opinion for the Court held that there was a distinction between the mere teaching of communist philosophies and the active advocacy of those ideas. The Court applied a revised clear and present danger test and concluded that the evil sought to be prevented by the federal government was serious enough to justify suppression of speech. In 1957, however, several convictions of radical political activists in the United States made under the law were overturned by the U.S. Supreme Court on constitutional grounds. The Smith Act has remained an operative statute since then, but it has been amended on several occasions since its 1940 inception.

Christopher P. Latimer

Further Reading

Cohan, John Alan. 2003. "Seditious Conspiracy, the Smith Act, and Prosecution for Religious Speech Advocating the Violent Overthrow of Government." *St. John's Journal of Legal Commentary* 17. http://scholarship.law.stjohns.edu/cgi/viewcontent.cgi?article=1188&context=jcred. Accessed September 18, 2015.

Fried, Albert. 1996. *McCarthyism: The Great American Red Scare: A Documentary History*. Oxford: Oxford University Press.

American Civil Liberties Union (ACLU)

The American Civil Liberties Union (ACLU) is a nonprofit, nonpartisan organization that works to protect and uphold the U.S. Bill of Rights. Traditionally, the organization has focused primarily on guaranteeing individuals' rights to free expression, equal protection under the law, due process, and privacy.

The ACLU was officially formed in 1920 by a group of social activists that included Roger Baldwin, Crystal Eastman, Jane Addams, Felix Frankfurter, and Albert DeSilver. The organization grew out of the movement to protect conscientious objection and free speech during World War I. "So long as we have enough people in this country willing to fight for their rights, we'll be called a democracy," declared Baldwin.

Since then, the ACLU has held a consistent, prominent position as a defender of constitutional rights against governmental and corporate actors that, according to the group, seek to diminish those rights. Throughout its history, the organization has taken strong public stances on a variety of civil liberty issues, including those related to school prayer, obscene materials, abortion, drug decriminalization, public

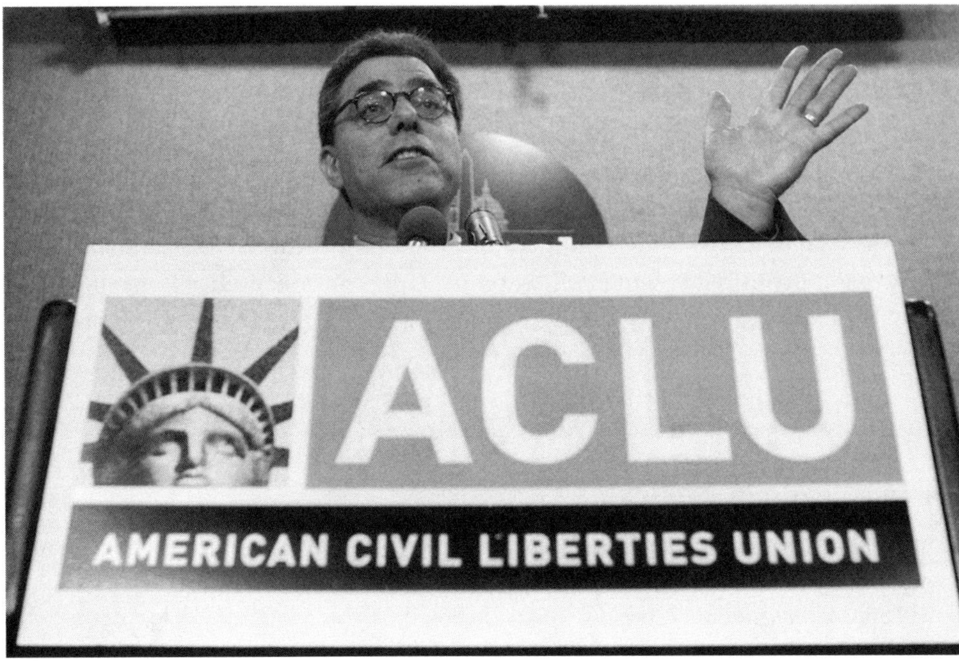

American Civil Liberties Union legal director Steven Shapiro at a news conference in 2004 on Guantanamo detainees. At issue was the indefinite detention of U.S. citizens designated as enemy combatants and of non-citizens at the Guantanamo Bay naval base in Cuba. (Alex Wong/Getty Images)

demonstration, invasion of privacy by government and corporate interests, and alleged civil liberties violations associated with government surveillance programs.

As of 2015, the ACLU claimed more than 500,000 members in state and local chapters nationwide. It is headquartered in New York City, with a sizable national legislative office in Washington, D.C. However, most of the organization's work is conducted by its state and local affiliates. Annual dues and contributions from members provide the ACLU's primary financial support, although it also receives some grants from private foundations and individuals. The ACLU does not receive government funding. Additionally, the organization is politically unaligned; it does not officially support or oppose political candidates or ideologies. It operates under the belief that everyone's rights are threatened if one person's rights are not protected. Maintaining this absolutist approach to civil liberties, the organization has drawn criticism for defending the constitutional rights of such controversial groups as Nazis, Communists, and the Ku Klux Klan.

In its work to protect civil liberties, the ACLU pursues a variety of initiatives, including community-based activism and legislative lobbying. Still, its most prominent and effective efforts have been in the nation's courts, as the organization regularly takes on cases in which civil liberties are possibly threatened. The organization handles close to 6,000 such court cases each year, and it appears before the U.S. Supreme Court more than any other group outside the federal government. In those civil liberty cases where it is not directly involved, the ACLU also frequently submits amicus curiae briefs in support of its position. The ACLU has at times referred to itself as "the nation's largest law firm," a claim that is supported by the organization's national network of local offices and its corps of approximately 5,000 affiliated attorneys.

The ACLU has also been active in the movement to preserve and protect individual privacy. As might be expected, their most notable effects in this area have been recorded in a number of Supreme Court decisions. Perhaps most notably, the ACLU represented the defendant in the 1965 *Griswold v. Connecticut* decision that struck a state ban on contraceptive use. In the decision, the Court cited "marital privacy" and acknowledged that although not clearly stated in the Constitution privacy was protected by "several fundamental constitutional guarantees." Additional cases related to reproductive rights, including *United States v. Vuitch* (1971), *Eisenstadt v. Baird* (1971), *Planned Parenthood v. Casey* (1992), and *Stenberg v. Carhart* (2000), further defined this position. The ACLU has successfully protected privacy rights in other contexts as well. For instance, *Chandler v. Miller* (1997) cited the Fourth Amendment in invalidating a Georgia state statute that required political candidates to submit to a urine test. In *Kitzmiller v. Dover Area School District* (2005), the ACLU, acting on behalf of a group of concerned parents, successfully challenged a public school district's efforts to incorporate "intelligent design" into its biology curricula on the grounds that the initiative violated the Establishment Clause of the First Amendment. The ACLU has also been at the forefront of legal efforts to uncover specifics about various imprisonment and interrogation programs carried out by the U.S. government in the wake of 9/11. According to the group's Web site, "the ACLU's Freedom of Information Act lawsuit compelled the release of critical documents detailing the extent of the Bush torture program, including long-secret legal memos justifying waterboard ing and other abuses and an Inspector General's report highlighting CIA abuses. The ACLU is leading the demand for full accountability for those who authorized or condoned torture."

Since the passage of the PATRIOT Act in 2001 and other national security-oriented legislation, the ACLU also has voiced increasing concern with the growth of a "surveillance society" in which corporate and governmental organizations pose new threats to personal information and privacy. The organization's "Technology and Liberty Project," for instance, currently focuses on myriad privacy issues.

As part of this project, the ACLU has challenged the USA PATRIOT Act, Internet censorship, and breaches of online anonymity.

Steve Munch

Further Reading

Cottrell, Robert C. 2000. *Roger Nash Baldwin and the American Civil Liberties Union.* New York: Columbia University Press.

Kutulas, Judy. 2006. *The American Civil Liberties Union and the Making of Modern Liberalism, 1930–1960.* Chapel Hill: University of North Carolina Press.

Walker, Samuel. 1990. *In Defense of American Liberties: A History of the ACLU.* Carbondale, IL: Southern Illinois University Press.

American Civil Liberties Union v. Clapper (2015)

On May 7, 2015, the case of *American Civil Liberties Union v. Clapper* resulted in a landmark ruling by a federal appeals court about the legality of a mass phone records collection and surveillance program maintained by the National Security Agency (NSA) under the auspices of Section 215 of the USA PATRIOT Act. In the decision, the Second Circuit Court of Appeals unanimously held that the program, which had first been revealed to the public by whistle-blower Edward Snowden, was an illegal violation of Section 215 provisions, for the basic reason that the telephone records of hundreds of millions of Americans are not "relevant" to an "authorized investigation."

The case in question was originally filed by the American Civil Liberties Union (ACLU) and the New York Civil Liberties Union (NYCLU) in the summer of 2013, shortly after Snowden's revelations came to light. When it was first considered at the district court level, a New York court agreed with the federal government's contention that the ACLU and NYCLU lacked "standing" to bring suit because they could not prove that the NSA program had been damaging to them. But the three-judge panel on the appeals court brushed aside that argument, as well as "third-party doctrine" arguments advanced by government lawyers, and unanimously ruled in favor of the civil liberties organizations. According to the court's ruling, the third-party doctrine is not an adequate tool for the "digital age, in which people reveal a great deal of information about themselves to third parties in the course of carrying out mundane tasks."

Privacy and civil rights advocates quickly praised the decision, though they cautioned that the legal fight over the NSA program would almost certainly continue. "The court crushed every argument the Department of Justice invoked in support of the bulk collection program," stated Harley Greiger of the Center for Democracy and Technology. "Members of Congress supporting straight reauthorization of Section 215 of the PATRIOT Act are trying to entrench a useless mass surveillance program that courts deemed illegal, Congress never intended, and the American public does not support. Today's ruling makes the case for bulk collection even flimsier."

On May 13, 2015—less than one week after the appellate court's decision—the House of Representatives passed a bill that would end the NSA's bulk collection of cell phone data from the American public. The measure passed by an overwhelming margin due to broad support from both Republicans and Democrats. Many observers expect similar legislation to pass in the U.S. Senate as well.

Kevin Hillstrom

Further Reading

"Circuit Court Rules Bulk Collection Program Illegal." 2015. Center for Democracy and Technology. https://cdt.org/press/circuit-court-rules-bulk-collection-program-illegal/. Accessed May 13, 2015.

Goitein, Liza. 2015. "How the Second Court's Decision Changes the Legislative Game." Lawfare Blog (May 8). http://www.lawfareblog.com/2015/05/how-the-second-circuits-decision-changes-the-legislative-game/. Accessed May 13, 2015.

Wittes, Lawrence. 2015. "A Few Thoughts on the Second Circuit's 215 Decision and Its Importance." Lawfare Blog (May 9). http://www.lawfareblog.com/2015/05/a-few-thoughts-on-the-second-circuits-215-decision-and-its-importance/. Accessed May 13, 2015.

American Civil Liberties Union v. National Security Agency (2007)

In 2002, several months after the September 11, 2001, terrorist attacks on U.S. soil, President George W. Bush secretly authorized the National Security Agency (NSA), a federal intelligence agency charged with gathering foreign intelligence, to monitor U.S. citizens' international phone calls and e-mails without issuing warrants—all in the interest of national security. This process became known as the Terrorist Surveillance Program (TSP). The intent was to monitor domestic telephone conversations, e-mail, and fax communications of people thought to have contact with members of Al Qaeda or other foreign terrorist groups. A former NSA director, Michael V. Hayden, was quoted in the *Washington Post* as saying that administration officials were concerned that important information could be lost by the time proper warrants were secured from a surveillance court.

When word of the presidential order became public in 2005, many criticized the warrantless surveillance program, calling it a violation of the Constitution and

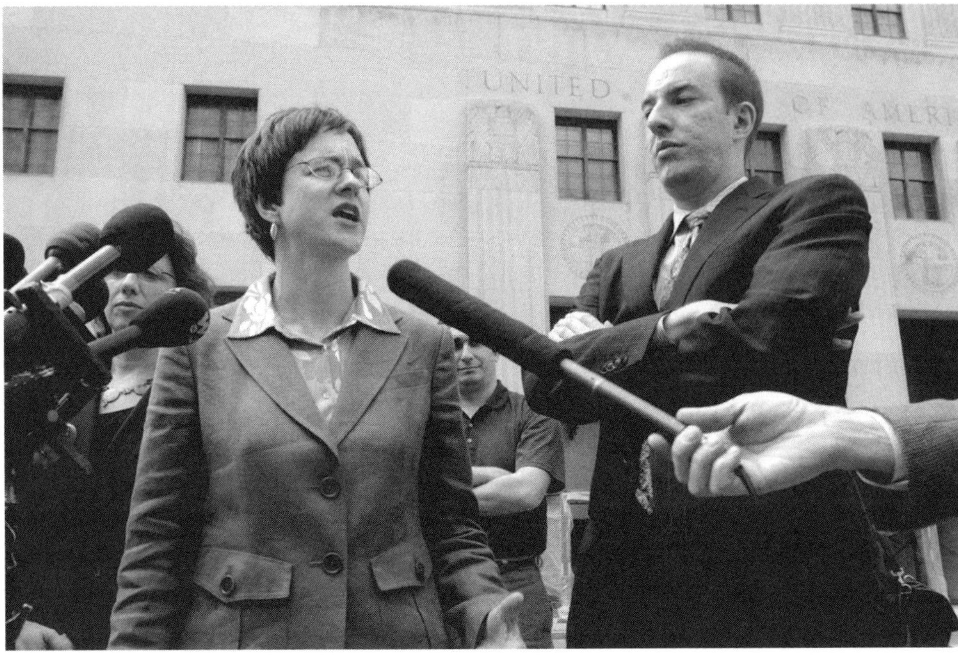

Ann Beeson, the American Civil Liberties Union's associate legal director and the lead attorney for the plaintiffs, addresses the media in Detroit, June 12, 2006, with Anthony Romero, executive director of the ACLU at right. The U.S. government defended warrantless domestic surveillance in court for the first time saying the program is well within the president's authority but that proving that would require revealing state secrets. (AP Photo/Carlos Osorio)

an encroachment on privacy and free speech. For instance, Center for National Security Studies Director Kate Martin claimed that the act by the Bush administration was "the first time a president has authorized government agencies to violate a specific criminal prohibition and eavesdrop on Americans." Caroline Fredrickson, director of the Washington legislative office of the American Civil Liberties Union (ACLU), said, "It's clear that the administration has been very willing to sacrifice civil liberties in its effort to exercise its authority on terrorism, to the extent that it authorizes criminal activity."

But the Bush administration claimed that the NSA's activities were legally defensible, based on a Justice Department legal opinion, which according to the *Washington Post* said that "congressional approval of the war on al Qaeda gave broad authority to the president." They viewed the wiretapping as critical in helping to interrupt terrorist plots and prevent attacks in the United States. Supporters of the TSP assert, for example, that it uncovered a plot by an Ohio naturalized citizen who was planning to destroy the Brooklyn Bridge in New York City; another foiled plot involved planned bomb attacks on British pubs and train stations. Most people in the NSA wiretapping, however, were never charged with a crime.

The *New York Times* reported that the NSA "eavesdrops without warrants on up to 500 people in the United States at any given time"; overseas, that number can reach 7,000. One of the primary critics of the TSP was the ACLU, which describes itself as "our nation's guardian of liberty, working daily in courts, legislatures and communities to defend and preserve the individual rights and liberties that the Constitution and laws of the United States guarantee everyone in this country." The ACLU filed suit against the Bush administration's warrantless wiretapping activities with the U.S. District Court, claiming that the program was in violation of the Constitution and the Foreign Intelligence Surveillance Act (FISA), a law enacted in 1978 that governed how surveillance and collection of foreign intelligence may be handled. According to the law, an agent may gather information if "the electronic surveillance was authorized by and conducted pursuant to a search warrant or court order of a court of competent jurisdiction."

The ACLU was the primary plaintiff; joining the suit were three other organizations—the Council on American–Islamic Relations, Greenpeace, and the National Association of Criminal Defense Lawyers—and five writers who claimed that they had a history of communicating with individuals from the Middle East and were, therefore, targeted by the NSA: James Bamford, Larry Diamond, Christopher Hitchens, Tara McKelvey, and Barnett Rubin.

The ACLU won its suit in U.S. District Court in August 2006 when Judge Anna Diggs Taylor ruled that the NSA program violates the First Amendment, the Fourth Amendment, and the FISA. "It was never the intent of the Framers to give the President such unfettered control," said Taylor, "particularly where his actions blatantly disregard the parameters clearly enumerated in the Bill of Rights."

The NSA, however, appealed the verdict. Beginning in January 2007, the Sixth Circuit of Court of Appeals heard arguments from both the ACLU and the NSA. In July 2007, the Court of Appeals opted to dismiss the case, stating that the plaintiff (NSA) could not claim with certainty that any of its members or interested parties could prove that the NSA had wiretapped them. Because wiretaps are considered privileged information, the government may keep them secret according to the State Secrets Doctrine, so the plaintiff could not provide any evidence. ACLU Legal Director Steve Shapiro claimed that the court's decision "insulates the Bush administration's warrantless surveillance activities from judicial review and deprives Americans of any ability to challenge the illegal surveillance of their telephone calls and e-mails." He further claimed that the ruling "did not uphold the legality of the government's warrantless surveillance activity. Indeed, the only judge to discuss the merits clearly and unequivocally declared that the warrantless surveillance was unlawful."

The ACLU appealed the ruling to the U.S. Supreme Court, but the high court chose in February 2008 not to take the case. ACLU attorney Jameel Jafeer was quoted in a release saying, "Congress enacted the Foreign Intelligence Surveillance Act intending to protect the rights of U.S. citizens and residents, and the president systematically broke that law over a period of more than five years. It's very disturbing that the president's actions will not be reviewed by the Supreme Court. It shouldn't be left to executive branch officials alone to determine what limits apply to their own surveillance activities and whether those limits are being honored. Allowing the executive branch to police itself flies in the face of the constitutional system of checks and balances."

Lawrence W. Baker

Further Reading

"About the ACLU." American Civil Liberties Union. https://www.aclu.org/about-aclu. Accessed September 18, 2015.

"*ACLU v. NSA*, 493 F.3d 644 (6th Cir. 2007)." American Association of University Professors. http://www.aaup.org/brief/aclu-v-nsa-493-f3d-644-6th-cir-2007. Accessed September 18, 2015.

"*ACLU v. NSA:* The Challenge to Illegal Spying." American Civil Liberties Union. https://www.aclu.org/national-security/aclu-v-nsa-challenge-illegal-spying. Accessed September 18, 2015.

Eggen, Dan. 2005. "Bush Authorized Domestic Spying." *Washington Post* (December 16). http://www.washingtonpost.com/wp-dyn/content/article/2005/12/16/AR2005121600021.html. Accessed September 18, 2015.

Landau, Susan. 2010. *Surveillance or Security?: The Risks Posed by New Wiretapping Technologies*. Cambridge, MA: MIT Press.

Risen, James, and Eric Lichtblau. 2005. "Bush Lets U.S. Spy on Callers without Courts." *New York Times* (December 16). http://www.nytimes.com/2005/12/16/politics/16program.html?pagewanted=all&_r=0. Accessed September 18, 2015.

Anonymization and De-identification

Anonymization is an increasingly popular way of protecting the security of data on the Internet. The data anonymization process obscures identifying information, also known as an electronic trail, in order to prevent data from being traced to individuals, organizations, or corporations. The data can still be analyzed and used, but data privacy is maintained. One benefit of anonymization is that the process foils the efforts of large companies or government intelligence agencies to effectively track a source's location or activities. It can also protect individuals from identity theft and targeted marketing on the Internet as well as facilitate the access of information from unauthorized Web sites.

De-identification is a type of anonymization that focuses on removing personal identifiers from electronic health records (EHRs), allowing sensitive patient information to be stored, transmitted, and viewed while keeping the identity of the patient completely confidential. As more large health institutions, medical research firms, private medical practices, health organizations, and U.S. government health agencies adopt the use of EHRs, the process of de-identifying these records is essential to protecting patient confidentiality.

Although anonymization is most commonly used in Web browsing, it is increasingly employed to preserve privacy in other Web activities, including e-mail, instant messaging, and large file transfers, and in mobile devices. In fact, entire operating systems can be configured to utilize anonymizers for every online activity.

Proxy servers are a key tool used in the anonymization process. Anonymous proxy servers are dedicated computer or software systems that function as intermediaries between users and other servers. One type of proxy server, known as a Web-based anonymizer, protects the confidentiality of the user by obscuring identifying information or by replacing a source's real Internet protocol (IP) address with another IP address. In this way, it can also bypass security filters to access restricted Web sites, a feature that allows individuals and organizations to find a way around repressive censorship rules in many parts of the world.

An encrypted tunnel proxy employs encryption in the anonymization process. Hiding, or replacing one variable value with a constant value, is a common encryption technique used to shield data on the Internet. For example, an individual's name, social security number, address, or birth date can be replaced with a 0 in all datasets, effectively hiding valuable information used in identification while keeping other information accessible for analysis.

Other encryption techniques used in data anonymization include hashing, which involves transforming data into a fixed, smaller value known as a hash value; truncation, or shortening a data field; and permutation, or replacing a value, such as a name or phone number, with a unique new value.

Virtual private networks (VPNs) also encrypt data, but do not utilize a proxy server. VPNs create an encrypted connection, or tunnel, between a computer and a host server. All Internet activity—from e-mail to Web browsing—is anonymized with the use of a VPN through this virtual network.

There are a range of anonymizers available commercially or for free on the Internet. One of the best known of these is The Onion Router (Tor), a free software program that routes data and messages through a global volunteer network of servers. Along the way, information is anonymized at several points to ensure that it will be virtually impossible to trace back to its original source.

In a few short years, Tor has grown to become the world's most widespread Internet privacy tool. Developed by the U.S. Naval Research Lab and launched in 2002, it is used by millions of people, many of them working and living in countries with stringent censorship rules. Tor is also used to shield more nefarious activity, including child pornography rings and arms and drug trafficking.

The software's exploding popularity has generated concern from several intelligence agencies around the world, including the NSA. In 2013, a series of leaks by former NSA contractor Edward Snowden revealed that U.S. intelligence authorities had launched an aggressive effort to weaken Tor and identity users of the service by circumventing the service's protections.

Although the anonymization process is supposed to be irrevocable, methods have been developed to reverse it. This process is known as de-anonymizing. One method of de-anonymizing data is by cross-referencing information that is visible and known with anonymized data, which can be analyzed to reveal key identifiers and ultimately the data source.

Margaret Haerens

Further Reading

Chacos, Brad. "How and Why to Surf the Web in Secret." *PC World* (November 7, 2012). http://www.pcworld.com/article/2013534/how-and-why-to-surf-the-web-in-secret.html. Accessed March 16, 2015.

Dredge, Stuart. "What Is Tor? A Beginner's Guide to the Privacy Tool." *The Guardian* (November 5, 2013). http://www.theguardian.com/technology/2013/nov/05/tor-beginners-guide-nsa-browser. Accessed March 16, 2015.

Greenberg, Andy. "How to Anonymize Everything You Do Online." *Wired* (June 17, 2014). http://www.wired.com/2014/06/be-anonymous-online/. Accessed March 16, 2015.

Tucker, Patrick. "Has Big Data Made Anonymity Impossible?" *Technology Review* (May 7, 2013). http://www.technologyreview.com/news/514351/has-big-data-made-anonymity-impossible/. Accessed March 16, 2015.

Antiwiretapping Statutes

In its narrowest sense, wiretapping refers to the interception of telephonic voice communications. This method of eavesdropping has been around for as long as the telephone itself and has historically been strictly legally regulated. As communication methods became more sophisticated, wiretapping methods followed suit, and laws regulating wiretapping had to be updated to cover cellular phones and electronic communications, such as e-mail, fax transmissions, and digital display pagers.

Antiwiretapping laws can be split into two categories: (1) laws that prevent private citizens from intercepting telecommunications and (2) laws that restrict law enforcement officials from doing the same.

The first category of laws is relatively straightforward. Under federal law, it is illegal for any third party to intercept any telephonic or electronic communication between other individuals. However, if one of the parties to the conversation records or consents to the recording of the conversation, the interception of the communication is generally not barred under federal law, as long as the communication is not being intercepted for the purpose of committing a criminal or tortious act. This practice is also permissible under many state laws, but at least 11 states prohibit recording a conversation even if one of the parties consents to the recording.

Laws regulating law enforcement wiretaps are more complicated and controversial. By far the most important federal statute is Title III of the Omnibus Crime and Control Act of 1968. This law states that an order authorizing law enforcement wiretaps (known as a "Title III order") will be issued only if the government can demonstrate (1) probable cause to believe that the interception will reveal evidence of one of a limited list of predicate crimes, with the suspected crime named in the application; (2) probable cause that the communication facility is being used in committing the crime; (3) normal investigative procedures have been tried and failed, are unlikely to succeed, or are dangerous; and (4) surveillance will be conducted in a way that minimizes the interception of irrelevant communications. Every Title III request must be authorized by a U.S. attorney. This constitutes a higher burden on law enforcement than the process for requesting approval for a standard search warrant, but police and other law enforcement agencies' wiretapping requests have historically been granted in most cases.

Title III has undergone two significant amendments since its passage. In 1986, Title III was amended by the Electronic Communications and Privacy Act (ECPA), which extended the Title III restrictions to digital and electronic telecommunication. The USA PATRIOT Act of 2001 and subsequent reauthorizations of that sweeping legislation eased restrictions on wiretapping as well. For example, the PATRIOT Act allowed law enforcement agents to apply for "roving wiretaps," which permit agents to trace calls not just in the jurisdiction in which the authorization was ordered but also anywhere in the United States. It also extended the "pen/trap" rule from telephonic to electronic communications.

Other forms of wiretapping are less invasive because they do not involve intercepting the substance of the communication; thus, they are not as strictly regulated by law. For example, Title III restrictions only apply to intercepting the *content* of the message and do not apply to intercepting the incoming or outgoing *address* of the communication. In the context of telephonic communications, this is commonly known as "tracing" the origin or destination of a call; law enforcement agents use a pen/trap device to determine the number a call is going to or the number that a call came from. In the context of electronic communications, such as e-mail, this might involve intercepting the "To" and "From" line of the message rather than the entire message. In other words, for telephonic intercepts, a different device is used to trace a call, whereas for electronic communications, the same method is used to intercept the addresses and the communication, but the law enforcement agent only looks at the address lines.

Despite this difference, the legal standard for intercepting "addressing" information is the same irrespective of the type of communication that is intercepted. In order to receive authorization to intercept this information, the government must show that "the information likely to be obtained is relevant to an ongoing investigation." This is a far lower standard than is required under Title III and even lower than is required for a traditional search under the Fourth Amendment. (The Supreme Court has held that the Fourth Amendment does not apply to a wiretap that only intercepts addressing information.) Furthermore, if law enforcement officers fail to follow those requirements, the evidence can still be used against the suspect at trial, although the officers could be subject to criminal and civil liability if a court determines that the law enforcement officials did not act in good faith.

There are also separate rules for so-called stored communications, that is, e-mails or voice mails that are stored on a remote server. As with phone traces and intercepting e-mail addresses, recovering stored communications from third parties is not considered a "search" under the Fourth Amendment, so there are no constitutional restrictions on such surveillance. However, federal law creates different legal standards based on the type of communication being sought; for example, a warrant is generally required to recover unopened e-mail, while a subpoena with notice to the party is sufficient to recover opened e-mail or subscriber information.

Ric Simmons

Further Reading

Alberti, Anthony. 2002. *Wiretaps*. Bethesda, MD: Austin & Winfield.

Diffie, Whitfield, and Susan Landau. 1999. *Privacy on the Line: The Politics of Wiretapping and Encryption*. Cambridge, MA: MIT Press.

Wolf, Michelle K. 2012. "Anti-Wiretapping Statutes: Disregarding Legislative Purpose and the Constitutional Pitfalls of Using Anti-Wiretapping Statutes to Prevent the Recording of On-Duty Police Officers." *Journal of Gender Race and Justice* 15 (Winter): 165–201.

Arizona v. Evans (1995)

Arizona v. Evans (1995) is a case that made it all the way to the U.S. Supreme Court in 1995. Issac Evans claimed that he was arrested illegally because of a computer error and that retrieval of evidence pertaining to an unrelated crime should have been thrown out because it was a violation of the Fourth Amendment, which states that "the right of the people to be secure in their persons, houses, papers, and effects, against unreasonable searches and seizures, shall not be violated . . ." The Supreme Court, however, ultimately ruled in favor of the state and created an exclusionary rule exception to the amendment.

On December 19, 1990, Isaac Evans appeared before the Justice of the Peace as a response to a warrant for his arrest, which had been issued six days earlier in connection to his failure to appear in court to address traffic violations. Following Evans's resolution of the matter, the Justice of the Peace "quashed" (nullified) the arrest warrant, but a computer error occurred and the warrant remained on file.

On January 5, 1991, Evans was driving the wrong way on a one-way street in Phoenix, Arizona, when Officer Bryan Sargent pulled him over. Because Evans's driver's license was suspended, Sargent looked up Evans's record in his squad car and confirmed the suspension, but he also noted the still outstanding warrant for his arrest (not knowing, of course, of its invalidity). Sargent promptly arrested Evans and proceeded to search his car, an act that is viewed as constitutional because it is considered "incident" to a lawful arrest. Sargent's search uncovered marijuana. That led to the state of Arizona charging Evans with illegal possession of marijuana.

Soon, the state learned that the warrant for Evans's arrest had not been removed from the system as it should have been. At Evans's trial, his lawyer argued that because the warrant for his arrest was in reality invalid, an arrest should not have been made, and had an arrest not been made, a search and subsequent discovery of the marijuana would not have occurred. The attorney sought an enforcement of the exclusionary rule, which states that the government may not convict a defendant as a result of evidence secured during an arrest or search that violates the Fourth Amendment. (The Fourth Amendment requires police officers to obtain a warrant before arresting or searching a suspect, something they can do only if there is probable cause of a crime having been committed.) Evans claimed that in the absence of any reason to search his vehicle (had he correctly not been arrested) marijuana would not have been discovered, meaning that evidence should be thrown out.

The trial court agreed and dismissed the charges. The state, however, appealed. The Arizona Court of Appeals reversed the lower court's decision, saying that it believed that "the exclusionary rule was not intended to deter justice court employees or Sheriff's office employees who are not directly associated with the arresting officers or the arresting officer's police department." Evans appealed, and the

Arizona Supreme Court reversed again, claiming that the exclusionary rule should force records to be kept organized and maintained more efficiently, regardless of the particular department.

The state of Arizona appealed again, that time to the U.S. Supreme Court. In a 7–2 decision, the Court ruled in favor of Arizona. Chief Justice William Rehnquist explained that the exclusionary rule was designed to discourage police misconduct. In *Arizona v. Evans* (1995), there was no evidence to suggest that Officer Sargent did anything wrong—he searched Evans's car in good faith, based on records he had received. According to Chief Justice Rehnquist, because court employees were responsible for the error, applying the exclusionary rule here would not deter any law enforcement errors in the future. Sargent believed he was correctly following the Fourth Amendment when he arrested Evans, so the exclusionary rule did not have to be applied. The result: The state could proceed with its case against Evans. That 7–2 decision of the U.S. Supreme Court established the "clerical error" exception to the exclusionary rule relating to the Fourth Amendment, which prohibits unreasonable searches and seizures by government actors. In *Arizona v. Evans* (1995), the majority extended the "good faith" exception, holding that the exclusionary rule did not require the suppression of the evidence seized pursuant to mistaken information that resulted from clerical errors of court employees. Relying upon *United States v. Leon* (1984), the Court stated that the exclusionary rule was designed to deter police misconduct—not errors innocently committed by employees in the legal and law enforcement systems. The majority asserted that because the exclusion in the case would not result in any appreciable deterrence (either of police or of court employees), its use in Evans's case was unwarranted. "If court employees were responsible for the erroneous computer record, the exclusion of evidence at trial would not sufficiently deter future errors so as to warrant such a severe sanction," wrote Chief Justice William Rehnquist in his majority opinion.

Two justices dissented: Justice John Paul Stevens believed that the Fourth Amendment and the exclusionary rule did *not* apply only to law enforcement misconduct. Justice Ruth Bader Ginsburg cautioned against police using computer systems that may contain errors, which could result in a person being arrested. Critics believe that so-called good faith exceptions, such as the one used in *Arizona v. Evans* (1995), potentially allow law enforcement to harass citizens; those in favor of the exceptions believe it helps those same officers protect society.

Lawrence W. Baker

Further Reading

"*Arizona v. Evans* (93–1660), 514 U.S. 1 (1995)." Legal Information Institute. https://www.law.cornell.edu/supct/html/93-1660.ZS.html. Accessed September 18, 2015.

Brannen, Daniel E., Richard Clay Hanes, and Rebecca Valentine. 2011. *Supreme Court Drama: Cases That Changed America,* 2nd edition. Detroit: UXL.

"The Exclusionary Rule in a Computer-Driven Society: The Case of *Arizona v. Evans* (1995)." Landmark Cases of the U.S. Supreme Court. http://www.streetlaw.org/en/Page/348/The_Exclusionary_Rule_in_a_ComputerDriven_Society_The_Cae_of_Arizona_v_Evans_1995. Accessed March 19, 2015.

Jackson, Heather A. 1996. "Arizona v Evans: Expanding Exclusionary Rule Exceptions and Contracting Fourth Amendment Protection." *Journal of Criminal Law and Criminology* 86 (4, Summer): 1201–27.

Vile, John R., and David L. Hudson, eds. 2013. *Encyclopedia of the Fourth Amendment.* Thousand Oaks, CA: CQ Press.

Ashcroft, John (1942–)

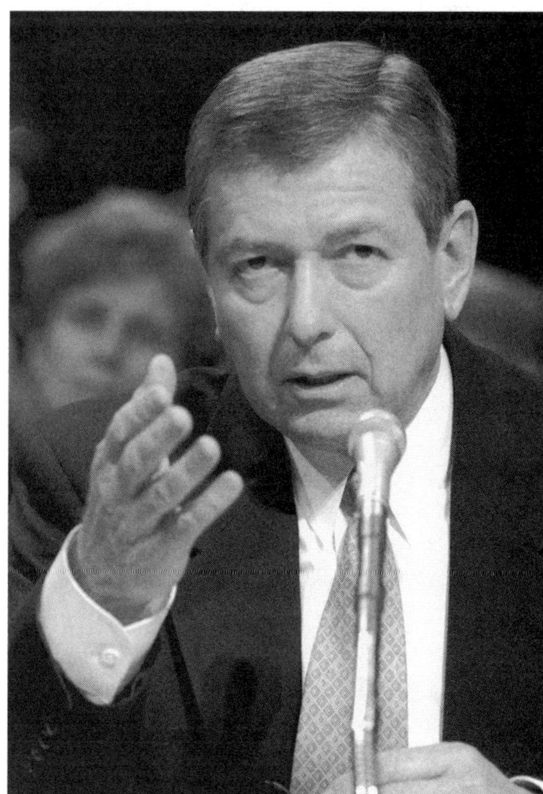

Attorney General-Designate John Ashcroft speaks at his confirmation hearing on January 16, 2001, on Capitol Hill in Washington, D.C. (AP Photo)

John Ashcroft was born on May 9, 1942, in Chicago, Illinois. He attended Yale University and the University of Chicago Law School, where he earned his law degree in 1967. A series of student deferments kept Ashcroft out of the Vietnam War and enabled him to make his mark in Republican politics and state government in Missouri. In 1976, he was elected state attorney general, taking the place of John Danforth. He served in that capacity until 1984, when he won the governorship of Missouri. He formally took office in 1985, and he was reelected in 1988.

During Ashcroft's tenure as governor, he promoted fiscally and socially conservative policies. In 1994, he was elected to the U.S. Senate but was defeated in 2000. Subsequently, he was nominated by George W. Bush as U.S. attorney general. His appointment as head of the Department of Justice was lauded by social and religious conservatives in the Republican Party.

After the September 11, 2001, terrorist attacks on the United States, Ashcroft spearheaded the Justice Department's efforts to combat terrorism, often using controversial initiatives and tactics that, according to critics, violated the constitutional rights of American citizens. The Justice Department, which includes the Federal Bureau of Investigation (FBI), drafted and implemented the USA PATRIOT Act; conducted home and office visits to thousands of Middle Eastern men and Muslim and Arab Americans with no connection to terrorism; required men and boys from 24 Arab and Muslim countries who were living in the United States to register, interview, and reregister with the federal government; in the process (with the Department of Homeland Security) arrested and deported thousands of Arab and Muslim immigrants, often for minor technical violations of complicated immigration and registration requirements; and eliminated internal rules preventing the FBI from using international espionage tactics on U.S. citizens and other suspects in ordinary criminal investigations on U.S. soil.

Ashcroft strongly defended those actions and policies as being vital to United States' national security, and he indicated that excessive privacy concerns too often hindered the ability of law enforcement and national security agencies from combating criminals and terrorists. Ashcroft resigned as attorney general following the reelection of President Bush in 2004. His resignation became effective on February 3, 2005.

After leaving the Bush administration, Ashcroft established a strategic consulting group called The Ashcroft Group in Arlington, Virginia.

Kevin Hillstrom

Further Reading

Altheide, David L. 2006. *Terrorism and the Politics of Fear.* New York: AltaMira Press.

Ashcroft, John. 2006. *Never Again: Securing America and Restoring Justice.* New York: Center Street.

"John Ashcroft Leaves Behind Controversial Legacy as Attorney General." November 11, 2004. PBS NewsHour Web site. http://www.pbs.org/newshour/bb/law-july-dec04-ashcroft_11-11/. Accessed September 18, 2015.

Automobile Stops and Searches

The Fourth Amendment prohibits "unreasonable searches and seizures." Although the amendment states a strong preference for search warrants, courts have long recognized the validity of certain types of warrantless searches. Under the so-called automobile exception, police who have probable cause to believe a motor vehicle contains contraband or evidence of crime may stop and search that vehicle without first obtaining a warrant.

In his majority opinion in *Carroll v. United States* (1925), Chief Justice William Howard Taft wrote that "the guaranty of freedom from unreasonable searches and seizures by the Fourth Amendment has been construed, practically since the beginning of the government, as recognizing a necessary difference between a search of a store, dwelling house, or other structure in respect of which a proper official warrant readily may be obtained and a search of a ship, motor boat, wagon, or automobile for contraband goods, where it is not practicable to secure a warrant, because the vehicle can be quickly moved out of the locality or jurisdiction in which the warrant must be sought." In *Dyke v. Taylor Implement Co.* (1968), Justice Byron White's opinion for the Court stated the doctrine more succinctly: "Automobiles, because of their mobility, may be searched without a warrant upon facts not justifying a warrantless search of a residence or office."

The automobile exception applies not only to cars, but also to all vehicles moving along the public roadways. Thus, in *California v. Carney* (1985), the Supreme Court held that motor homes being used on the road and not in a place regularly used as a residence are subject to the automobile exception.

In *Chambers v. Maroney* (1970), the Supreme Court held that once begun under exigent circumstances a warrantless search of an automobile may continue after the vehicle has been taken to the police station. And in *United States v. Ross* (1982), the Court held that a police officer having probable cause to believe that evidence of crime is concealed within an automobile may conduct a search as broad as one that could be authorized by a search warrant. That ruling effectively allowed police officers to search closed containers found during an automobile search without first having to obtain a warrant, even if those containers were locked in the trunk or otherwise sequestered.

In *United States v. Johns* (1985), the Supreme Court upheld the warrantless search of plastic containers seized during an automobile search, even though the police had waited several days before opening the containers. The Court reasoned that since police legitimately seized the containers during the original search of the automobile, no reasonable expectation of privacy could be maintained once the containers came under police control. The search of the containers, which produced a substantial quantity of marijuana, was therefore not unreasonable simply because it was delayed for several days.

In 1999, the Supreme Court extended the automobile exception by ruling in *Wyoming v. Houghton* (1999) that police officers who have probable cause to search a vehicle may search the belongings of passengers who are capable of concealing objects of the search. The case began in 1998 when a Wyoming highway patrol officer stopped a speeding car. While speaking to the driver, the officer noticed a syringe in the driver's pocket. When questioned about it, the driver admitted using the syringe to inject illegal drugs. Thus having probable cause to search the car, the officer then opened a passenger's purse on the back seat and found contraband. The Wyoming Supreme Court ruled that the search was not within the permissible scope of search of the vehicle. Divided 6–3, the U.S. Supreme Court reversed. In an opinion by Justice Antonin Scalia, the Court justified the search on the following grounds:

> Whereas the passenger's privacy expectations are . . . considerably diminished, the governmental interests at stake are substantial. Effective law enforcement would be appreciably impaired without the ability to search a passenger's personal belongings when there is reason to believe contraband or evidence of criminal wrongdoing is hidden in the car. As in all car-search cases, the "ready mobility" of an automobile creates a risk that the evidence or contraband will be permanently lost while a warrant is obtained. . . . In addition, a car passenger. . . . will often be engaged in a common enterprise with the driver, and have the same interest in concealing the fruits or the evidence of their wrongdoing.

It is important to note that police may stop an automobile without a warrant and temporarily detain the driver as long as they have probable cause to believe that criminal activity is taking place or that traffic laws or automobile regulations are being violated. Sometimes when police stop a vehicle for a traffic violation, evidence of unrelated criminal activity comes into plain view. Such was the case in *Whren v. United States* (1996), when officers patrolling an area of known drug activity stopped a truck for a routine traffic violation. Upon approaching the vehicle, an officer observed a passenger holding plastic bags containing what appeared to be crack cocaine. The driver and the passenger were arrested and several types of illegal drugs were found in the truck. The Supreme Court upheld the search and seizure, saying that "the decision to stop an automobile is reasonable where the police have probable cause to believe that a traffic violation has occurred."

Finally, American courts have allowed brief warrantless stopping of automobiles even in the absence of probable cause, assuming there is "reasonable suspicion" that criminal activity is afoot. In conducting "investigatory stops," police may require a driver to exit the vehicle and produce a driver's license and proof of registration. During the course of that brief encounter, police may develop probable cause to arrest the driver and/or search the automobile. In *Michigan v. Long* (1983), the Supreme Court held that when police stop an automobile based on reasonable suspicion, they may search the passenger compartment for weapons, assuming they have reason to believe that a suspect is dangerous. The search, however, must be limited to those areas in which a weapon may be placed or hidden.

In 2009, though, the U.S. Supreme Court issued a 5–4 ruling in the case of *Gant v. Arizona* (2009) that reined in vehicular searches in certain instances. In *Gant v. Arizona,* officers who arrested a suspect for driving with a suspended license subsequently found drugs in the car while conducting a search for potential weapons or evidence. But the Court majority held that since the suspect had already been handcuffed and secured at that time—and was thus not in any position to destroy evidence or obtain weapons that might have been in the car—a warrantless search on that basis was not permitted.

John M. Scheb II and Otis H. Stephens Jr.

Further Reading

Nisenson, Aaron. "Supreme Court Changes Law on Vehicle Searches." International Union of Police Associations (IUPA) Web site. https://iupa.org/supreme-court-changes-law-on-vehicle-searches/. Accessed March 9, 2015.

Scheb, John M., and John M. Scheb II. 2006. *Criminal Procedure*. Belmont, CA: Thomson/Wadsworth.

Stephens, Otis H., Jr., and Richard A. Glenn. 2006. *Unreasonable Searches and Seizures: Rights and Liberties under the Law*. Santa Barbara, CA: ABC-CLIO.

B

Background Checks (Employment and Volunteerism)

Background checks are investigations into the character or history of an individual. They are performed by government and private sector employers, by purchasers of corporations who are performing due diligence checks on the acquired corporation's leaders, by insurance companies and other litigants who wish to investigate individuals making claims, by charitable organizations who are seeking volunteers, and sometimes by family members or friends who are suspicious of another's activities.

A number of factors have contributed to a dramatic increase in background checks, including fears of terrorism and workplace violence, liability for employee negligence, risks associated with hiring litigious employees, employee fraud and embezzlement, risks associated with volunteers who may abuse the elderly and children, and the low cost and speed with which electronic public records databases can be searched.

Background checks vary greatly in procedure and scope, depending on the purpose for which the check is performed. A background check for a national security position can cost $10,000, involve polygraph testing and an in-depth exploration of the applicant's associations, and may focus on past or current behavior that could subject the applicant to extortion.

Regular employment background checks are much less expensive, ranging in price from a simple and inexpensive electronic records search to in-depth vetting for corporate executives, which can cost thousands of dollars. Regular employment background checks focus on criminal convictions and arrests, history of litigation, history of insurance or workers' compensation claims, driving history, credit card and other debt, military history, interviews with neighbors and other associates, drug and alcohol use (which may be probed by urine analysis, hair, or blood testing), medical problems, and verification of educational status and prior employment. Because of concerns about employee theft, major employers have created cooperative antishoplifting databases that may be queried to see whether an applicant has ever been accused of dishonesty without actually being charged with a crime. Also, in the retail and service sector, background checks often are combined with personality tests designed to gauge an individual's attitudes towards workplace organization, work ethic, and honesty.

In the employment context, background checks are governed by the federal Fair Credit Reporting Act (FCRA) and by state regulations. The FCRA requires employers to obtain consent from the employee before engaging in a background check, specifies procedures to prevent stale and inaccurate information from being provided to the employer, and gives the employee the right to an adverse action notice if the check is used to deny employment. The Federal Equal Employment Opportunity Commission limits employers from solely relying upon criminal conviction information; the conviction must be relevant to the job, or there must be some independent, sound business reason for taking action against the individual. State laws place heightened restrictions, including in some cases prohibitions on considering derogatory information more than seven years old and arrest data that did not result in conviction.

Outside the employment context, investigating the background of another may not be subject to any regulation. For instance, charitable organizations may investigate prospective volunteers to avoid risks of abuse of elders and children.

Chris Jay Hoofnagle

Further Reading

Equal Employment Opportunity Commission (EEOC). n.d. "U.S. Background Checks: What Employers Need to Know." EEOC Web site. http://www.eeoc.gov/eeoc/publications/background_checks_employers.cfm. Accessed March 9, 2015.

Etzioni, Amitai. 1999. *The Limits of Privacy*. New York: Basic Books.

Solove, Daniel J. 2002. "Digital Dossiers and the Dissipation of the Fourth Amendment Privacy." *Southern California Law Review* 75: 1083–167.

Bamford, James (1946–)

James Bamford is an American author known for his in-depth writing about U.S. intelligence gathering activities, most notably the actions of the ultra-secret National Security Agency (NSA). The NSA is a large U.S. intelligence agency created in 1952 and charged with monitoring and collecting signals intelligence (SIGINT)—that is, information and data that are obtained from electronic signals such as communications, radar, and weapons systems.

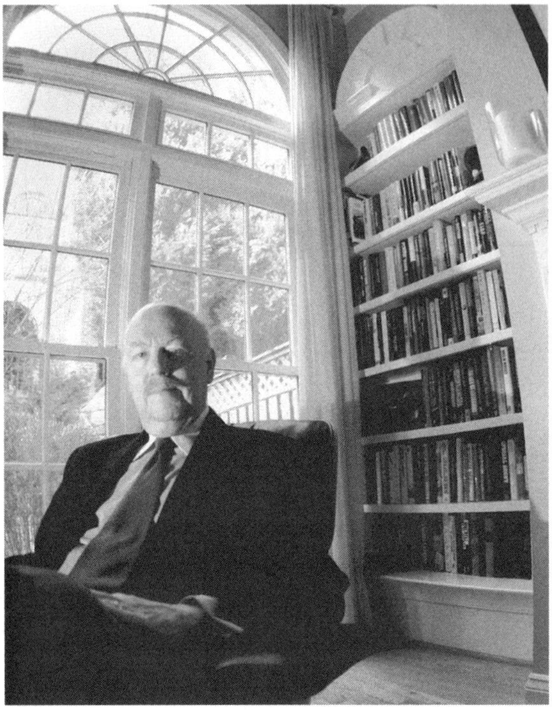

Author James Bamford, who has written several books on the National Security Agency, sits in his Washington home, 2006. (AP Photo)

Born on September 15, 1946, Bamford grew up in Massachusetts and spent three years in the navy, where he worked as an intelligence analyst during the Vietnam War. After leaving the navy, he attended Suffolk University Law School in Boston, Massachusetts, earning a law degree—a juris doctor in international law.

Bamford's career as a journalist was first sparked when he became a whistle-blower on the NSA. While still in law school, Bamford rejoined the Naval Reserve and in 1974 he served two weeks working at a U.S. intelligence intercept site in Sabana Seca, Puerto Rico. During this assignment, he listened to an intercept of a conversation between two Americans. Bamford believed this type of surveillance to be illegal under U.S. law, and he subsequently testified about this incident before the U.S. Senate Select Committee to Study Governmental Operations with Respect to Intelligence Activities—an investigation spearheaded by Senator Frank Church into Operation Chaos, a project by U.S. intelligence agencies to target U.S. citizens involved in antiwar protests.

As a result of Bamford's testimony, committee staffers staged a surprise visit to Puerto Rico and confirmed, despite NSA's claims to the contrary, that the agency was conducting illegal eavesdropping on American citizens. The Church Committee investigation ultimately led to widespread reforms. Meanwhile, the entire experience led Bamford to begin researching a book about the NSA.

In 1982, Bamford published *The Puzzle Palace: Inside the National Security Agency, America's Most Secret Intelligence Organization*, the first book ever written about the NSA. Research for the book was difficult, largely because the highly secretive NSA strongly resisted disclosing any information to Bamford. The agency tried to thwart Bamford's efforts to acquire documents under the Freedom of Information Act (FOIA), and before the book was published, he was threatened by the government with prosecution for revealing classified information and breaching national security. The dispute was related to classified documents released to

Bamford under FOIA during the administration of President Jimmy Carter. When President Ronald Reagan was elected, the new administration sought to reclassify the documents and prevent Bamford from including them in his book. Ultimately, however, Bamford prevailed by showing that he had obtained all his information legally. *The Puzzle Palace* immediately became a national bestseller and is now considered a classic study of the country's largest intelligence agency.

Bamford's career as a journalist continued during the next decade. He worked for most of that time as the Washington investigative producer for ABC's *World News Tonight* with television news anchor Peter Jennings. During that period, Bamford won a number of journalism awards for his coverage of national security issues. In 1997, Bamford left ABC to work on his next book about the NSA. This time, the NSA cooperated with Bamford, granting him wide access to NSA sites and documents. Published in 2001, this book was entitled *Body of Secrets: Anatomy of the Ultra-Secret National Security Agency*. Like Bamford's first book, it also won praise and became a national bestseller. In 2005, Bamford published a third book, *A Pretext for War: 9/11, Iraq and the Abuse of America's Intelligence Agencies*, which focused on events involving the September 11, 2001, terrorist attacks and the Iraq War. In 2008, Bamford returned once again to the subject of the NSA with *The Shadow Factory: The Ultra-Secret NSA from 9/11 to the Eavesdropping on America*. Like earlier books, it too became a bestseller.

Bamford also has written numerous magazine and Internet articles about the NSA, and his articles have appeared in major magazines as well as online. In 2006, he was awarded the Magazine Award for Reporting, one of the highest awards in the magazine industry. In 2014, Bamford conducted a lengthy interview of Edward Snowden, a whistle-blower who garnered worldwide attention by leaking thousands of NSA documents detailing the agency's global surveillance programs, including bulk collection of Americans' telephone data. The interview was published in *Wired* magazine in August 2014 with the title "The Most Wanted Man In the World."

Bamford is considered an expert on the NSA and is a former visiting professor at the Richard and Rhoda Goldman School of Public Policy at the University of California at Berkeley. Today, Bamford lives in Washington, D.C., and London and is reportedly working on his next project, a book titled *Journalism after Snowden: The Future of Free Press in the Surveillance State*, which will be published by Columbia University Press in the Fall of 2015.

Debra Miller

Further Reading

Bamford, James. 1982. *The Puzzle Palace: Inside the National Security Agency, America's Most Secret Intelligence Organization*. Boston, MA: Houghton Mifflin.

Bamford, James. 2001. *Body of Secrets: Anatomy of the Ultra-Secret National Security Agency*. New York: Anchor Books.
Bamford, James. 2005. *A Pretext for War: 9/11, Iraq and the Abuse of America's Intelligence Agencies*. New York: Anchor Books.
Bamford, James. 2008. *The Shadow Factory: The Ultra-Secret NSA from 9/11 to the Eavesdropping on America*. New York: Anchor Books.
Bamford, James. 2013. "They Know Much More Than You Think." *The New York Review of Books* (August 15). http://www.nybooks.com/articles/archives/2013/aug/15/nsa-they-know-much-more-you-think/. Accessed May 12, 2015.
Bamford, James. 2014a. "Edward Snowden: The Untold Story." *Wired* (August). http://www.wired.com/2014/08/edward-snowden/. Accessed May 12, 2015.
Bamford, James. 2014b. "The NSA and Me." *The Intercept* (October 2). https://firstlook.org/theintercept/2014/10/02/the-nsa-and-me/. Accessed May 12, 2015.
Nazaryan, Alexander. 2013. "The N.S.A.'s Chief Chronicler." The New Yorker (June 10). http://www.newyorker.com/books/page-turner/the-n-s-a-s-chief-chronicler. Accessed May 12, 2015.

Banking and Financial Records

Most individuals have high expectations of privacy in their banking records and other financial information, such as credit card transactions. But while the shift from cash to checks and debit and credit cards has made paying for goods and services more convenient, it has resulted in vast amounts of data stored automatically in computerized databases, raising the potential for databases to be linked together to share and combine information obtained from different sources. The result can be a detailed compilation of information about an individual's saving, spending, and even travel habits.

One of the problems raised by the existence of financial information in databases is the increased risk of identity fraud and theft (the assumption of a person's name for financial gain). As more personally identifiable information becomes available, it becomes easier for criminals to access facts that were previously considered private. A second problem is government access to bank and financial records that law-abiding individuals would prefer to keep secret. The possibility of government surveillance of financial activities threatens some of our fundamental freedoms, according to civil liberties organizations and many legal scholars.

Several federal laws have been enacted to protect banking and financial privacy in the United States, but all of the laws contain significant exceptions that allow—or mandate—information to be shared with government authorities and private sector entities for various purposes.

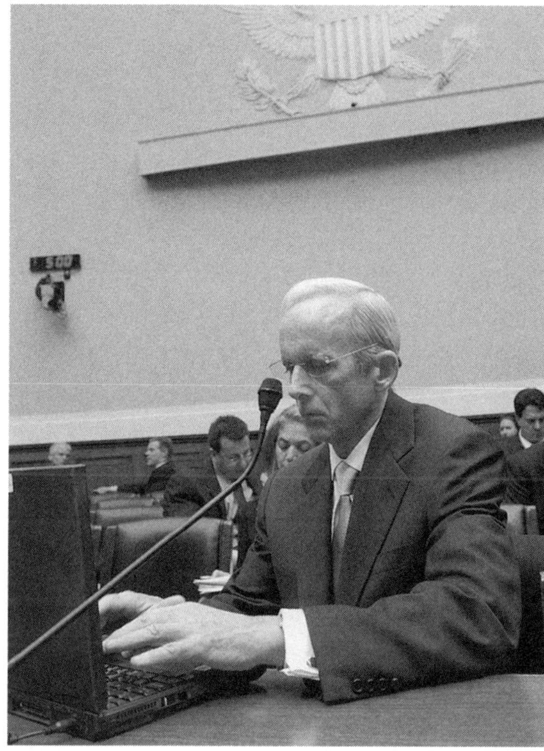

New York Post reporter Christopher Byron testifies on Capitol Hill in Washington, D.C., September 29, 2006, before the House Energy and Commerce Oversight and Investigations subcommittee hearing on Internet data brokers and pretexting. (AP Photo)

The Right to Financial Privacy Act (RFPA) creates a right of privacy in an individual's bank records. It was enacted in response to the Supreme Court's decision in *United States v. Miller* (1976), in which the Court found that bank customers had no legal right to privacy in their banking transactions. The Court concluded that when individuals voluntarily share or develop records in the ordinary course of a business relationship with another entity (as in a bank–customer relationship) they have relinquished their expectation of privacy and therefore have no constitutional protection against government access to it.

The RFPA stipulates that federal government agencies cannot obtain records from a financial institution unless the customer authorizes access; there is an appropriate summons, subpoena, or search warrant; or there is an appropriate written request from a government official who is authorized to obtain the records. Moreover, the government agency must give individuals notice and an opportunity to object before the disclosure can be made. The RFPA only governs disclosures to the federal government, its officers, agents, and departments. It does not govern the sharing of information with private businesses or with state governments.

For sharing financial information in the private sector, the Fair Credit Reporting Act (FCRA) and Financial Services Modernization Act of 1999, also known as the Gramm–Leach–Bliley Act (GLBA), provide some protection for individuals. State laws may provide similar protection against access by state government officials and agencies.

The RFPA has many exceptions, however. The most noteworthy is the Bank Secrecy Act (BSA). The act requires federally insured banks to retain records and create reports that could be useful in tax, criminal, or regulatory investigations.

The law was passed to address concerns that the shift from paper to computerized records would make white-collar law enforcement more complicated. The BSA not only allows banks and other financial institutions (including gambling casinos and dealers in precious metals) to disclose financial records to the federal government in certain circumstances but also the law *requires* them to report the transactions. Moreover, when banks report information to the federal government pursuant to the BSA, they are required *not* to disclose to their customers that reports have been filed about them.

Among other transactions, the law requires the reporting of deposits or withdrawals of more than $10,000 in cash in one day or the purchase of money orders, cashiers' checks, travelers' checks, and similar instruments with more than $3,000 of cash. The bank must report the name, address, occupation, and other information about the transaction in a "currency transaction report" to the Internal Revenue Service. For transactions exceeding $5,000 into or out of the United States, the amount, date, and identity of the recipient must be reported. Moreover, if it appears that the customer is taking action to evade the reporting requirement, the bank must file a suspicious activity report explaining the activity. All of these reports are electronically filed and are immediately available to U.S. attorneys and law enforcement agencies throughout the country. Financial institutions face heavy penalties if they do not comply, and the BSA was strengthened in 2001 by the USA PATRIOT Act, which gave government authorities increased access to bank records in an effort to track financial transactions that could identify terrorists.

The purpose of the BSA is to aid law enforcement in policing money laundering, tax evasion, embezzlers, drug dealers, organized crime, and other criminal behavior. A single report about a customer is usually of no concern to authorities, but multiple reports may signal a need for further investigation. Businesses that routinely deal in large amounts of cash, such as bars and restaurants, can be exempt from having their deposits and withdrawals monitored, although the exemption is not routinely granted.

The BSA covers banks, credit card issuers, retailers and gasoline companies that issue credit cards, travelers' check issuers, the U.S. Postal Service, securities dealers, and casinos. In addition to the mandatory disclosure of the transactions discussed above, some financial information is not protected by the RFPA and therefore can be disclosed to government officials without customer consent: disclosures that do not identify a customer personally; disclosures in connection with the financial institution's own interests (such as the perfection of security interests and information relating to federal government loans); disclosures relating to bank regulatory supervision; disclosure authorized under other federal laws; and emergency disclosure to federal agencies with foreign intelligence or other national security functions.

With respect to the private sector, the GLBA of 1999 imposed limits on the collection and sharing of information in the financial services industry. The GLBA grew out of a movement to reform the financial services industry and eliminate the historical separation of banks, brokerage companies, and insurers. After the collapse of the banking industry in the Great Depression, Congress passed the Glass–Steagall Act, which prohibited national and state banks from affiliating with securities investment companies. In 1956, Congress passed the Bank Holding Company Act, which prohibited a bank from owning nonbank companies in general. The Bank Holding Company Act was later amended in 1982 to prohibit banks from engaging in insurance underwriting activities. As the financial services industry evolved in the 1980s and 1990s, however, Congress repealed these prohibitions in the GLBA, enabling banks to once again engage in a wide range of financial services activities, including insurance and securities investments. (Congress's decision to eliminate these restrictions, carried out with the support of the George W. Bush administration, was widely blamed as a fundamental factor in United States' 2008 financial collapse and subsequent recession.)

Congress perceived significant privacy risks in allowing banks, brokerage firms, and insurers to merge or affiliate, so it included in the GLBA a series of provisions designed to limit the sharing of customer information. Another motivating force was the adoption of the European Union Data Protection Directive in 1995. The directive applies to any entity that maintains personal information on EU citizens. This means that U.S. companies have to ensure that data on EU citizens are treated in accordance with the privacy standards in Europe. Congress fashioned the privacy protections of the GLBA with the idea that compliance with the GLBA would also be compliance with the EU rules.

The privacy protections in the GLBA were far from absolute, however. The GLBA set no limits on the type of information that financial services companies can collect and retain on individuals. Individuals who interact with financial services companies must understand that virtually all information that the business can learn about them can be stored in a database. Moreover, the GLBA expressly authorized banks, insurers, investment companies, and other financial services organizations that are affiliated with each other, through common ownership or otherwise, to share personal financial information without the customer's permission. An affiliate is a company that controls, is controlled by, or is under common control with another company. Although affiliates must tell customers that they are sharing this information, individuals cannot block the sharing of information among affiliated institutions. Because large conglomerates of affiliated entities dominate the financial services industry, sharing of personal information without customer consent is routine.

Customers can choose to opt out of the disclosure of personal data that the conglomerate wishes to share with nonaffiliated third parties. A nonaffiliated company is one that is unrelated to the financial services company that possesses personal information about its customers. Nonaffiliates may include companies that want the information to compile mailing lists for their own marketing purposes.

To opt out of sharing information with nonaffiliated companies, individuals must read the privacy policy of the financial institution to learn how to exercise their opt-out rights. The GLBA does not require affirmative consent from the customer before any data can be distributed to others. To opt out, the customer usually has to call a toll-free number or mail in a response card indicating the consumer's opt-out choice. Even if customers take the initiative and exercise their limited opt-out rights, they must trust the financial services company to honor the request and maintain adequate security procedures to prevent unauthorized sharing and access.

Despite the widespread sharing of financial information allowed by the GLBA, financial institutions cannot disclose customer account numbers or access codes with a nonaffiliated third party for use in marketing activities. Thus, even if customers do not opt out of sharing with nonaffiliates, credit card and debit card numbers, PINs, and account passwords cannot be sold.

In addition to providing a right to opt out of information sharing with nonaffiliated companies, the GLBA requires financial services companies to develop systems to ensure that customer information is secure against hackers and other unauthorized access. The law also prohibits certain kinds of pretexting, the practice of collecting personal information under false pretenses. Pretexters pose as law enforcement officials, social workers, potential employers, banks, and other parties who create convincing stories that elicit information from unsuspecting businesses and consumers. The GLBA criminalizes the use of fraudulent statements to solicit financial information.

To apprise customers of the privacy practices of the business, the GLBA requires financial institutions to provide customers with notices that explain how the company handles personal information and shares it with others. The notice must be clear, conspicuous, and accurately describe the firm's privacy practices. It must explain, in general terms, what information the company collects, with whom it shares the information, and how it safeguards its databases. The notice must be given to customers by mail or through another in-person method of communication. Acceptable ways of communicating depend on the type of business. For example, an online lender may post its privacy policy on its Web site and require that the customer acknowledge receipt before applying for a loan. The disclosure of privacy notices or privacy policies in the financial services industry is now commonplace.

The GLBA exempts several categories of transactions from its privacy protections. Financial institutions can disclose customer information with credit reporting agencies, government regulatory agencies, and a company that is purchasing the business. They can also share information with outside firms that provide essential services, such as data processing, check printing, or mortgage servicing, and with firms that agree to jointly market the company's products and services. These exceptions allow much information to be shared without consumer knowledge or consent.

The GLBA only applies to non-public personal information—data that cannot be obtained from sources in the public domain. Most of the information about customers in a financial institution's database will be nonpublic, but information that is publicly available, such as a mortgage loan that is recorded in the public records, is not restricted by the GLBA.

The FCRA, which protects the privacy of information about consumers held by credit bureaus, also governs certain transactions involving banks and other financial institutions. Under the FCRA, credit reporting agencies (credit bureaus) can release the credit reports of consumers to financial institutions when individuals apply for credit, open bank accounts, or initiate other financial transactions. When a financial company obtains a credit report, it may want to share the report with an affiliated business. Under the FCRA, the credit report cannot be shared with affiliates unless the consumer has first been notified and given an opportunity to opt out. This is similar to the opt-out right under the GLBA, and the opt-out notice is likely to be included in the privacy policy delivered to the customer under the GLBA. It differs, however, because under the GLBA an individual cannot prohibit the sharing of information among affiliated companies. Consumers who exercise their opt-out rights under the FCRA can prevent the sharing of information among affiliates, but only information obtained from a credit report that has been issued by a credit reporting agency.

James P. Nehf

Further Reading

Cate, Fred H., et al. 2003. *Financial Privacy, Consumer Prosperity and the Public Good.* Washington, DC: Brookings Institute.

Fischer, Richard L. 2002. *The Law of Financial Privacy.* Washington, DC: A.S. Pratt & Sons.

Kolodny, Robin, and Sandra Suarez. 2011. "Paving the Road to 'Too Big to Fail': Business Interests and the Politics of Financial Deregulation in the U.S." *Politics and Society* 39 (4): 74–102.

Regan, Priscilla. 1995. *Legislating Privacy: Technology, Social Values, and Public Policy.* Chapel Hill, NC: University of North Carolina Press.

Right to Financial Privacy Act (Online, March 2006). Electronic Privacy Information Center Web site. www.epic.org/privacy/rfpa/. Accessed September 18, 2015.

Smith, Jeff H. 1994. *Managing Privacy: Information Technology and Corporate America.* Chapel Hill, NC: University of North Caroline Press.

Bartnicki v. Vopper (2001)

During contentious collective-bargaining negotiations between a Pennsylvania high school teachers' union and the local school board, Bartnicki, the chief union negotiator, and Kane, the union president, had a conversation on a cellular telephone that was intercepted and recorded by an unidentified person. A nonbinding arbitration proposal, generally favorable to the teachers, had all but settled the dispute when Vopper, a radio commentator critical of the unions, played the tape of the intercepted conversation on his public affairs talk show during a segment dedicated to covering the settlement. The tape was subsequently aired on another station, and a transcript was published in the local newspapers. In the recorded conversation, Bartnicki and Kane discussed the timing of a proposed strike, the difficulties created by public comment on the negotiations, and the need for a dramatic response to the school board's intransigence.

In the aftermath of the tape's release, Bartnicki and Kane filed suit against Vopper and other members of the media. It was subsequently discovered that Vopper obtained the tape from Jack Yocum, the head of a local taxpayers' association opposed to the union's demands. Yocum testified that he had discovered the tape in his mailbox. When he played it, he recognized the voices of Bartnicki and Kane. He played it for the school board and then delivered it to Vopper, as well as to other individuals and media representatives.

Both parties sought summary judgment. Bartnicki alleged that each of the defendants who aired or published the contents of the tape "knew or had reason to know" that the recording of the private phone conversation had been obtained by illegal means in violation of both federal and state wiretapping statutes. Bartnicki sought actual damages, statutory damages, punitive damages, and attorney's fees.

The defendants argued that there was no violation because (1) if the interception was illegal, the defendants had nothing to do with it; (2) the conversation might have been intercepted inadvertently, not illegally, which would make the defendants' actions lawful; and finally, (3) if the defendants had violated the statute by disclosing the conversations, the disclosures were still protected under the First Amendment, thus immunizing the defendants from liability for damages.

The district court found that the defendants had clearly violated the statute because they "knew or had reason to know" that the information was obtained through an illegal interception. Actual involvement in the illegal interception was not required. However, whether the interception was inadvertent was a disputed fact, so summary judgment was denied. The court did, however, grant a motion for an interlocutory appeal, which sought an answer to the following questions of law: "(1) whether the imposition of liability on the media defendants under the [wiretapping] statutes solely for broadcasting the newsworthy tape on [Vopper's] radio news/public affairs program, when the tape was illegally intercepted and recorded by unknown persons who were not agents of [the] defendants, violates the First Amendment; and (2) whether imposition of liability under the [wiretapping] statutes on Defendant Yocum solely for providing the anonymously intercepted and recorded tape to the media violates the First Amendment."

All parties agree that the wiretapping statutes are content-neutral laws of general applicability: They do not seek to discriminate against any particular speech content or single out a particular viewpoint. They seek to protect privacy. A content-neutral regulation is subject to the intermediate scrutiny standard: That is, it will be sustained under a First Amendment challenge if it advances important governmental interests unrelated to the suppression of free speech and does not burden substantially more speech than necessary to further those interests.

The Court of Appeals for the Third Circuit determined that under this standard the wiretapping statues were invalid because they deterred significantly more speech than necessary to protect the privacy interests at stake. Bartnicki appealed, and the U.S. Supreme Court granted certiorari in the case, legally known as *Bartnicki v. Vopper*, 532 U.S. 514.

The Supreme Court accepted the following findings of facts: (1) The conversation was intercepted illegally, that is, in violation of the wiretapping statutes. (2) The defendants violated the wiretapping statutes because they knew or should have known the conversation was intercepted illegally. (3) The defendants played no part in the interception itself; they obtained the information from the tapes lawfully, even though someone else unlawfully intercepted the information. (4) The subject matter of the conversation was a matter of public concern. The Court also accepted (5) that the wiretapping statutes were content-neutral laws of general applicability and that intermediate scrutiny was the appropriate standard to apply. The Court was only required to determine whether the application of these statutes, under these particular facts, violated the First Amendment.

The Court began its analysis of this question by setting out general principles of law from previous cases. *Smith v. Daily Mail* held that "state action to punish the publication of truthful information seldom can satisfy constitutional standards"; *Florida Star v. B.J.F.* held that "if a newspaper lawfully obtains truthful information about a matter of public significance then state officials may not constitutionally punish publication of the information absent a need . . . of the highest order"; *New York Times v. United State*s upheld the publication of documents of great public importance stolen by a third party, focusing primarily on the character of documents' contents and the consequences of the disclosure. That case, however, did not resolve the issue here: whether the government may punish not only unlawful acquisition of information, but also the ensuing publication as well. The Court noted that it had carefully tried to avoid categorically holding whether publication of truthful information may ever be punished under the First Amendment.

The government argued that the statute's provisions against disclosure deterred parties from intercepting private communications, thus minimizing the harm to persons whose private communications have been illegally intercepted. The Court, however, opined that the interest of deterrence was insufficient to justify punishing disclosures in this case. The defendants had published lawfully obtained information of public interest by someone who was not involved in the initial illegality. While illegal interceptors are usually known, and usually disclose intercepted communications for public praise or financial reward, imposing sanctions upon the media in this case would not deter unidentified scanners from such antisocial conduct.

The Court found, however, that the government's interest in minimizing harm from invasions of privacy was a considerably stronger argument. The Court held that as wiretapping statutes encourage uninhibited exchange of ideas and information among private parties and fear of public disclosure might have a chilling effect upon speech. Therefore, the statutes may be applied in most cases without violating the First Amendment: to prevent disclosures of trade secrets or domestic gossip. However, in the case of *Bartnicki v. Vopper*, the Court majority decided that enforcement of the statute imposed unacceptable sanctions on the publication of truthful information of public concern, implicating the core purposes of the First Amendment. By a 6–3 vote, the Supreme Court affirmed the lower court ruling, relying on the general proposition that freedom of expression upon public questions is secured by the First Amendment and that privacy concerns must give way when publishing matters of public importance. The ruling thus established that broadcasters could not be held liable for publishing or broadcasting the truthful contents of materials illegally obtained or intercepted by third parties, providing the information was in the public interest.

Larkin R. Evans

Further Reading

Alberti, Anthony. 2002. *Wiretaps*. Bethesda, MD: Austin & Winfield.

Bartee, Alice Fleetwood. 2006. *Privacy Rights: Cases Lost and Causes Won Before the Supreme Court*. Lanham, MD: Rowman & Littlefield.

Goodale, James C. 1999. *Communications Law*. New York: Practicing Law Institute.

Hargrove-Simon, Elaine. 2009. "U.S. Supreme Court Rules in Historic Bartnicki Case." November 13. University of Minnesota, Silha Center for the Study of Media Ethics and Law Web site. http://www.silha.umn.edu/news/summer2001.php?entry=204126. Accessed March 10, 2015.

Biometrics

Biometrics refers to the field of technology involving the identification, authentication, surveillance, or screening of individuals based on measurable physical and/or behavioral traits. Examples of physical characteristics used in biometrics are fingerprints, facial structure, the eye's iris or retina pattern, and the configuration of veins on the back of a human hand. Other characteristics used in biometrics include handwriting, speech patterns, and the recording of an individual's keystrokes on a keyboard. According to a 2015 study, fingerprinting is the most common trait utilized in biometric analysis.

The use of fingerprints for identification and authentication can be traced back to ancient Babylonian times, where the imprints of human fingers were found on clay tablets as part of business transactions. There is evidence that officials used biometrics to identify and differentiate between early Egyptian traders. In 14th-century China, merchants and officials utilized prints of children's palms and feet as identification.

In the mid-1800s, criminologists developed new investigative and identification systems to address rising crime rates in growing urban centers. One of the most popular of the era was the Bertillon system, developed by French criminologist Alphonse Bertillon in 1879. The Bertillon system was based on anthropometric science, a field of study that entails the meticulous measurement and recording of various components and parts of an individual's body. It also included the photographing of a suspect's face, known commonly as a mug shot. The Bertillon system allowed law enforcement officials to distinguish between suspects and create records for prolific criminals.

By the early 20th century, fingerprint identification became the most popular form of biometric identification. A British administrator working in India named Edward Henry developed a finger-based identification system that analyzed the pattern of folds on a suspect's fingers in 1897. Within four years, Henry's system would replace the Bertillon system of criminal identification by Scotland Yard in London. It is still used today, remaining the most popular form of biometric identification.

The advent of computer technology and the development of the Internet led to key advancements in biometrics: algorithms and databases. An algorithm is a computer program that deconstructs an image, such as a face or the back of an individual's hand, and maps its physical characteristics. This creates quantifiable data that can be used for comparison with millions of other images, which are collected in a computer database.

Increasing security concerns over terrorist activity in the early 21st century spurred growing demand from government security agencies for biometric technology. In the United States, the National Science and Technology Council established a subcommittee to coordinate federal efforts on biometrics in 2003.

The Department of Homeland Security (DHS) established the Automated Biometric Identification System (IDENT) in 2004 to collect and process biometric data to be used for immigration, law enforcement, and intelligence purposes. IDENT links biometric data, including fingerprints, iris scans, digital photographs, and facial images, with biographical information to check for known terrorist suspects, criminals, and immigration violators.

In 2008, the Federal Bureau of Investigation (FBI) launched the Next Generation Identification (NGI) program, which set out to build the world's largest biometric database. The NGI system improved existing capabilities, focusing on the areas of fingerprinting, iris recognition, and palm prints. By 2013, the NGI database had enrolled 73 million fingerprints, 5.7 million palm prints, 8.1 million mug shots, and 8,500 iris scans.

As the government's cache of biometric data grows, so do civil liberty concerns. In 2014, the *Guardian* newspaper reported that GCHQ, the British surveillance agency, and the National Security Agency (NSA) intercepted and enrolled images from Yahoo webcam chats from 2008 to 2010 in their databases for the purpose of scanning the images for potential intelligence targets. Known as the Optic Nerve program, the surveillance enrolled more than 1.8 million images during that period.

Critics of the program were outraged. Charging that the large majority of those people were not legitimate intelligence targets, they asserted that the program violated the privacy of innocent people. Others underscored the need for legislation to regulate and limit the collection, enrollment, and use of biometric data to ensure that the government and private industries do not misuse the technology.

Supporters of the Optic Nerve program assert that biometric surveillance is in accordance with the law in both the United States and Great Britain and is necessary to protect national security.

In recent years, corporations have begun to explore the commercial potential for biometric technology. Leading technology companies are increasingly incorporating biometric modalities into smartphones and other mobile communication devices as authentication systems. Supporters contend that biometric systems offer a higher level of security and are more convenient than traditional authentication methods, such as passwords or codes.

However, critics argue that replacing passwords or codes with fingerprints or iris scans hold many risks. If an imposter or hacker can gain access to an individual's personal data, then they can fully access that person's identity. A compromised password or code can be changed easily; biometric characteristics cannot. Another concern is that biometric systems are not always accurate.

Economic forecasts predict that the overall revenues for the biometrics market will top $13.8 billion in 2015, with increased spending from the business sector. By 2020, it is estimated that the global biometrics industry will top $20 billion as biometric identification systems become more common in many countries.

Margaret Haerens

Further Reading

Ackerman, Spencer, and James Ball. "Optic Nerve: Millions of Yahoo Webcam Images Intercepted by GCHQ." *The Guardian* (February 28, 2014). http://www.theguardian.com/world/2014/feb/27/gchq-nsa-webcam-images-internet-yahoo. Accessed February 28, 2015.

"Biometrics Market to Hit US$13.5 Billion in Revenues in 2015 with Enterprise Catching Up on Government Spending." *ABI Research* (February 9, 2015). https://www.abiresearch.com/press/biometrics-market-to-hit-us138-million-in-revenues. Accessed February 28, 2015.

Chayka, Kyle. "Biometric Surveillance Means Someone Is Always Watching." *Newsweek* (April 17, 2014). http://www.newsweek.com/2014/04/25/biometric-surveillance-means-someone-always-watching-248161.html. Accessed February 28, 2015.

Nadeau, Lauren Katims. "Tracing the History of Biometrics." *Government Technology* (October 23, 2012). http://www.govtech.com/Tracing-the-History-of-Biometrics.html. Accessed February 28, 2015.

"Privacy Impact Assessment for the Automated Biometric Identification System." *U.S. Department of Homeland Security* (December 7, 2012). http://www.dhs.gov/sites/default/files/publications/privacy-pia-nppd-ident-06252013.pdf. Accessed February 28, 2015.

Boyd v. United States (1886)

Boyd v. United States, 116 U.S. 616, is a landmark privacy protection case that established a relationship between the Fourth and Fifth Amendments to the U.S. Constitution. In *Boyd v. United States,* the Supreme Court ruled that seizure or compulsory production of a person's personal papers to be used as evidence against that person is the same as compelling self-incrimination. Ultimately, this broad interpretation of the amendments was severely limited by subsequent Supreme Court cases.

The case centered around the case of E. A. Boyd & Sons, an importing company that was accused of importing 35 cases of plate glass into New York City without paying a duty required under an 1874 customs act. The two partners in Boyd attempted to import the 35 cases to furnish glass needed in the construction of a government building. The glass specified was foreign glass. The partners understood that if part or all of the glass was furnished from the partnership's existing duty-paid inventory it could be replaced by duty-free imports. Pursuant to this arrangement, 29 cases of glass were imported duty free. The partners then claimed they were entitled to duty-free entry of an additional 35 cases that were soon to arrive. The forfeiture action concerned those 35 cases.

The case as filed was civil in nature, but the Supreme Court ruled that the 1874 customs act, which allowed imposition of both fines and prison sentences, was essentially criminal in nature. Boyd was accused of committing fraud under that act. In order to prove his case, the prosecuting attorney needed Boyd's records of a previous shipment involving 29 cases of plate glass. The district attorney obtained an order from the district judge requiring Boyd to produce the invoice for the 29 cases. Boyd produced the invoice. He was subsequently found guilty and the government seized the 35 cases of plate glass. Although he complied with the order, Boyd appealed his conviction, arguing his constitutional rights were denied. The Supreme Court ruled in the partners' favor.

To reach its decision, the Court spent significant time analyzing the origins of the 1874 act at issue. The 1874 act was an amendment to an 1867 act, which itself was an amendment to an 1863 act. The original and first amendments of the act allowed: ". . . [t]he district judge, on complaint and affidavit that any fraud on the revenue had been committed by any person interested or engaged in the importation of merchandise, to issue his warrant to the marshal to enter any premises where any invoices, books, or papers were deposited relating to such merchandise, and to take possession of such books and papers . . ." The Court noted that the act "was the first legislation of the kind" ever enacted. It was "adopted at a period of great national excitement (during the Civil War), when the powers of the government were subjected to a severe strain to protect the national existence." In 1874, the act was amended to allow the Court to order the defendant in the action to produce the books or papers.

The first step in the Court's consideration of Boyd's argument was to find that the requirement that Boyd produce documents in response to a court order was still a "search and seizure" and fell "within the scope of the fourth amendment." The more difficult question for the Court was whether the search was "an 'unreasonable search and seizure' within the meaning of the fourth amendment of the constitution."

The Court distinguished between searches for "stolen or forfeited goods" and "seizure of a man's private books and papers for the purpose of obtaining information therein contained." The simple answer: "[i]n one case, the government is entitled to the possession of the property; in the other it is not," the Court ruled. Using a historical approach, the Court examined the use of writs of assistance in England

and the colonies before the American Revolution. Basically, a writ of assistance allowed a revenue officer collecting taxes for the Crown to search any home or building for smuggled goods. Colonists, who were smuggling a wide variety of goods to avoid taxes imposed by the king, hated the practice. The Court noted that in 1761 Boston resident James Otis called the writs "the worst instrument of arbitrary power, the most destructive of English liberty and the fundamental principles of law, that ever was found in an English law book, since they placed the liberty of every man in the hands of every petty officer." The Supreme Court noted that Otis's comments reflected a sentiment shared by many other colonists, and the Court observed opposition to the writs—and the searches they authorized—was a fundamental contributor to the Revolutionary War.

To show the impropriety of the legislation under consideration in the case, the Supreme Court then discussed two cases that essentially resulted in the end of general warrants in Britain. General warrants, like writs of assistance, allowed officers to seize persons or papers, and more specifically, they were frequently issued to allow searches of private homes for books or papers that could be used to convict the home owner of libel.

The first case was the case of John Wilkes, publisher of the *North Briton,* a newspaper that frequently denounced the Crown and was considered "heinously libelous." The second case was *Entick v. Carrington and Three Other King's Messengers.*

In April 1763, Wilkes published an article in his paper, lambasting the king for a message presented in parliament. After that, Lord Halifax, the British secretary of state, issued a general warrant and Wilkes's home was searched. Wilkes was arrested and temporarily imprisoned in the Tower of London. After charges were dismissed, Wilkes sued for trespass and was victorious. The officer who searched Wilkes's home was ordered to pay £1,000 and Halifax was ordered to pay £4,000.

The second case was decided in 1765. Lord Halifax had again issued a general warrant, and the resulting search of John Entick's home found no libelous materials. In concluding his decision, Lord Camden noted: "It is very certain that the law obligeth no man to accuse himself; because the necessary means of compelling self-accusation, falling upon the innocent as well as the guilty, would be both cruel and unjust; and it should seem, that search for evidence is disallowed upon the same principle. There too the innocent would be confounded with the guilty."

The importance of those old English cases for the Supreme Court in the *U.S. v Brown* case was not in the holdings alone, but also in the fact that "every American statesman, during our revolutionary and formative period as a nation, was undoubtedly familiar" with the principles expressed in those decisions. In other words, when the founding fathers incorporated the right against self-incrimination into the Constitution, they were incorporating the principles that had been decided in British courts almost two decades before the Constitution and the Bill of Rights were drafted. The Court concluded that the drafters of the Constitution would never have approved of the series of statutes that were under consideration in *Boyd*: "The struggles against arbitrary power in which they had been engaged for more than 20 years would have been too deeply engraved in their memories to have allowed them to approve of such insidious disguises of the old grievance which they had so deeply abhorred."

For the Supreme Court, the critical questions addressed by British courts in the cited cases were at the very foundation of the concepts of "constitutional liberty and security." At the conclusion of his review of that history, the Court concluded that "any forcible and compulsory extortion of a man's own testimony, or of his private papers to be used as evidence to convict him of crime, or to forfeit his goods" should be condemned.

The next step in the Court's analysis was to consider the statutory history leading up to the customs act of 1867. The Court found that the first congress, in creating the Judiciary Act of 1789, granted courts the power to compel persons to turn over books or documents in their possession, provided such documents would have been ordered to be produced under the "ordinary rules of chancery." The Court then noted, "Now it is elementary knowledge that one cardinal rule of the court of chancery is never to decree a discovery which might tend to convict the party of a crime, or to forfeit his property. And any compulsory discovery by extorting the party's oath, or compelling the production of his private books and papers, to convict him of crime, or to forfeit his property, is contrary to the principles of a free government."

And then the Court examined the language of the Fourth and Fifth Amendments to the Constitution: "We have already noticed the intimate relation between the two amendments. They throw great light on each other. For the 'unreasonable searches and seizures' condemned in the fourth amendment are almost always made for the purpose of compelling a man to give evidence against himself, which in criminal cases is condemned in the fifth amendment; and compelling a man 'in a criminal case to be a witness against himself,' which is condemned in the fifth amendment, throws light on the question as to what is an 'unreasonable search and seizure' within the meaning of the fourth amendment."

The Court concluded that there was no real distinction between "seizure of a man's private books and papers to be used in evidence against him" and "compelling him to be a witness against himself." The Court subsequently warned that in order to protect against the erosion of "constitutional provisions for the security of person and property" the courts must liberally construe those freedoms rather than apply a strict construction that "deprives them of half their efficacy, and leads to gradual depreciation of the right, as if it consisted more in sound than in substance."

Several of the Court's holdings in *Boyd v. United States* have not stood the test of time, however. The application of the Fourth Amendment to subpoenas was limited by *Hale v. Henkel,* 201 U.S. 43 (1906). In *Warden v. Hayden*, 387 U.S. 294 (1967), the Court ruled that purely evidentiary (but nontestimonial) materials, as well as contraband and fruits and instrumentalities of crime, could be searched for and seized under certain circumstances. In *Katz v. United States*, 389 U.S. 347 (1967), the Court established a reasonable expectation of privacy test for admission of tape recorded conversations, and in *Osborn v. United States*, 385 U.S. 323 (1966), the Court expanded the conditions under which tape recorded conversations could be admissible.

It is also clear that the Fifth Amendment does not independently prohibit the compelled production of every sort of incriminating evidence, but applies only when the accused is compelled to make a *testimonial* communication that is incriminating. The courts have, therefore, declined to extend the protection of the privilege to the giving of blood samples, *Schmerber v. California*, 384 U.S. 757, 763–764 (1966); to the giving of handwriting exemplars, *Gilbert v. California*, 388 U.S. 263, 265–267 (1967); voice exemplars, *United States v. Wade*, 388 U.S. 218, 222–223 (1967); or the donning of a blouse worn by the perpetrator, *Holt v. United States*, 218 U.S. 245 (1910). Furthermore, despite Boyd, neither a partnership nor the individual partners are shielded from compelled production of partnership records on self-incrimination grounds (*Bellis v. United States*, 417 U.S. 85 (1974)).

The language in *Boyd* stipulating that a person may not be forced to produce private papers has nonetheless often appeared as dictum in later Supreme Court decisions. To the extent, however, that the rule against compelling production of private papers rested on the proposition that seizures of or subpoenas for mere evidence, including documents, violated the Fourth Amendment and therefore also transgressed the Fifth, the foundations for the rule have been washed away. In consequence, the prohibition against forcing the production of private papers has long been a rule, searching for a rationale consistent with the proscriptions of the Fifth Amendment against compelling a person to give testimony that incriminates him.

The Supreme Court has noted that the act of producing evidence in response to a subpoena has communicative aspects of its own, wholly aside from the contents of the papers produced. Compliance tacitly concedes the paper's existence and their possession or control by a party. It could also indicate a party's belief that the papers are those sought (*Curcio v. United States*, 354 U.S. 118, 125 (1957)). Elements of compulsion are present, but the more difficult question is whether the tacit averments of the party are both testimonial and incriminating under the Fifth Amendment.

It is unlikely admitting the existence and possession of papers will rise to the level of testimony-afforded protection under the Fifth Amendment. When the existence and location of the papers are a foregone conclusion, a party adds little or nothing to the sum total of the government's information by conceding that he in fact has the papers. Under these circumstances, by enforcement of the summons "no constitutional rights are touched. The question is not of testimony but of surrender" (*In re Harris*, 221 U.S. 274, 279 (1911)).

The historical and statutory history relied upon by the Supreme Court in *Boyd v. United States* is often alluded to by those concerned with finding privacy rights in the Constitution. But with subsequent Supreme Court rulings on specific evidentiary questions, and others that deny any convergence between the Fourth and Fifth Constitutional Amendments, the Supreme Court ruling in *Boyd* has effectively been reversed.

David J. Brown

Further Reading

Bartee, Alice Fleetwood. 2006. *Privacy Rights: Cases Lost and Causes Won Before the Supreme Court*. Lanham, MD: Rowman & Littlefield.

Feinman, Jay M. 2000. *Law 101. Everything You Need to Know about the American Legal System*. New York: Oxford University Press.

Gordley, James. 2003. *Foundations of Privacy Law: Property, Tort, Contract, Unjust Enrichment*. New York: Oxford University Press.

Hall, Kermit L. 2000. *Conscience, Expression and Privacy: The Supreme Court in American Society*. New York: Garland Publishers.

Hubbart, Phillip A. 2005. *Making Sense of Search and Seizure Law: A Fourth Amendment Handbook*. Durham, NC: Carolina Academic Press.

Brandeis, Louis (1856–1941)

Louis Brandeis was a justice of the U.S. Supreme Court from 1916 to 1939 and the first Jewish justice on the Court. Born in Louisville, Kentucky, on November 13, 1856, he graduated from Harvard Law School in 1877 at the top of his class and established a practice in Boston.

In his law practice, Brandeis often represented working people against corporate challenges to minimum age and wage laws, and in 1908, he helped convince the Supreme Court to hold in *Muller v. Oregon* (1908) that such laws were not unconstitutional.

Brandeis also had an enduring impact on legal and cultural understandings of privacy rights in United States. In 1890, he and Samuel Warren published the landmark article "The Right to Privacy" in the *Harvard Law Review*. This collaboration is frequently cited as the first description of an integrated concept of the right to privacy. Brandeis and Warren argued forcefully that the common law should evolve in response to new technology and new business practices to recognize a new right that would protect the right to be let alone. Significantly, the authors focused on the injury caused by private persons and not by government, since tort law is generally concerned with private wrongdoings.

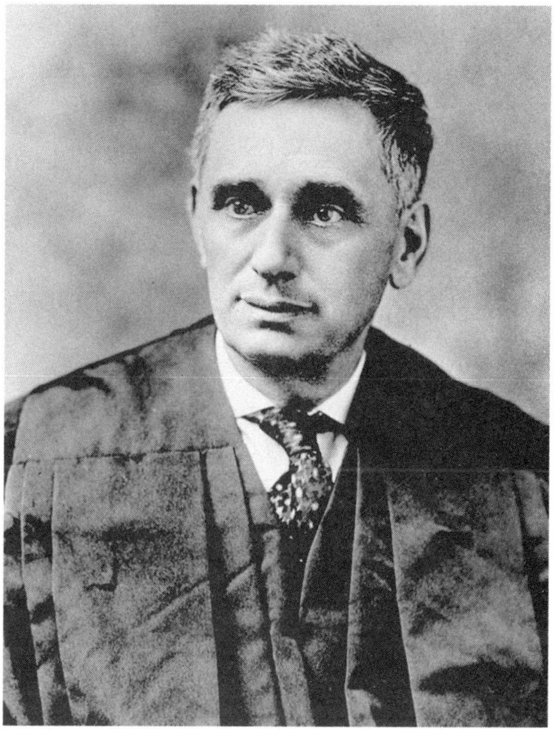

U.S. Supreme Court Justice Louis D. Brandeis is shown in this undated photo. Brandeis served as an associate Justice of the Supreme Court from 1916 to 1939. (AP Photo)

By many accounts, the article is one of the most influential in American law. The article is also a model for legal scholarship. Brandeis and Warren described an emerging social challenge. They discussed how current law failed to provide adequate protection. They examined similar claims in other jurisdictions, including courts in England and France, and they set out an argument for a new approach that eventually transformed the law in the United States. The article is purposeful, ambitious, timely at its publication, and timeless in its ongoing influence.

The Brandeis–Warren article also considered possible limitation on the claim of a right to privacy. They first said the right to privacy "does not prohibit any publication of matter which is of public or general interest." This important qualification anticipated that the claim of privacy would, at times, come in conflict with the freedom of the press and the public's right to know. Brandeis and Warren also suggested limitation that included communications that would otherwise be privileged (such as communications in legislative or judicial proceedings), oral communications, or once the information is published by the individual or with his consent. Brandeis and Warren said that truth would not provide a defense, an important distinction from the law of defamation, nor would the absence of malice.

In 1916, Brandeis was confirmed to the U.S. Supreme Court (despite opposition from corporate interests and anti-Semites) after being nominated by President Woodrow Wilson. After taking his place on the Court, Brandeis continued to take positions that fostered social and economic reform, including President Franklin Roosevelt's New Deal policies. He also remained a dedicated advocate of privacy rights. In 1928, Brandies wrote the dissenting opinion in the landmark decision *Olmstead v. United States*, in which he argued that the Court should recognize and protect a right to privacy against new technologies that threaten it. For the foresight he displayed on this issue, both in his *Olmstead* dissent and "The Right to Privacy," Brandeis is sometimes called the father of privacy.

Brandeis retired from the Court in 1939 and died two years later on October 5, 1941. Brandeis University in Massachusetts is named in his honor.

Kevin M. Keenan

Further Reading

Strum, Philippa. 1984. *Louis D. Brandeis: Justice for the People.* Cambridge: Harvard University Press.

Strum, Philippa. 1993. *Brandeis: Beyond Progressivism.* Lawrence: University Press of Kansas.

Urofsky, Melvin. 2009. *Louis Brandeis: A Life.* New York: Pantheon.

C

Cable Communications Policy Act of 1984

The Cable Communications Policy Act of 1984 (CCPA) was largely crafted to help the powerful industry's growth, but it also contained a variety of relatively toothless privacy protections. The Museum of Broadcast Communications (MBC) has described the CCPA as the fruit of extended negotiations between the cable industry and cities and other municipalities franchising cable systems. "The Act," according to the MBC, "provided substantial comfort to the cable industry's future. Its major provisions created a standard procedure for renewing franchises that gave operators relatively certain renewal, and it deregulated rates so that operators could charge what they wanted for different service tiers as long as there was 'effective competition' to the service."

The CCPA also provided the first significant federal legal provisions regarding the privacy protections that cable companies were mandated to extend to customers, though critics have decried the measures as weak and ineffectual. Under the act, default privacy protections are minimal. For example, although customers must sometimes give consent for their cable company to collect "personally identifiable information," consent is easily obtained and is often not required. Nothing in the act prevents a cable company from obtaining the required consent via the standard cable agreement or via another standardized process such as a click-through agreement on the company's Web site. Even without such consent, cable operators may collect such information in order to "obtain information necessary to render a cable service or other service provided by the cable operator to the subscriber" or to "detect unauthorized reception of cable communications."

Personally identifiable information may include account information such as your name, address, e-mail address, telephone number, driver's license number, social security number, bank account number, and other account information. It may also include information regarding your viewing habits, for example, how much time you spend watching programs, which menu screens you use most often, and which pay-per-view programs you order. Under the act, personally identifiable information does not include "any record of aggregate data which does not identify particular persons." At least one court has ruled that "personally identifiable information" also does not include information stored in the cable converter box. As technology advances and cable companies are able to offer ever more sophisticated program options, privacy advocates have expressed concerns that the amount of personal information collected by cable companies could become enormous.

Beyond collection of personal information, cable companies also have wide latitude to disclose personal information. Even if the customer does not consent, cable companies can disclose customers' personally identifiable information if it is "necessary to render, or conduct a legitimate business activity related to, a cable service or other service provided by the cable operator to the subscriber." Thus, cable operators may disclose your personal information to third parties such as marketing companies, collection agencies, and companies that specialize in warehousing personal information and creating personal profiles; indeed, this legitimate business activity exception means that personal information can be disclosed to almost anyone. Moreover, because of the legitimate business activity provision, cable companies are permitted to combine customers' personal information with personal information obtained from third parties to construct enhanced databases and customer profiles.

Cable companies are required to give customers a privacy notice and policy at the time that the cable agreement is entered into. After this, a privacy policy must also be sent to the customer at least once a year. The policy must inform the customer of what personal information is collected by the cable company, how this information will be used, an explanation of the disclosure practices of the company, how long the customer's personal information will be retained, instructions on how and where to access the personal information that the cable company has collected, and the limitations of the company's legal collection and disclosure of personal information.

If a third party requests a cable subscriber's personally identifiable information pursuant to a court order, the cable company must notify the subscriber. If a governmental entity requests such personal information pursuant to a court order, that entity must show by clear and convincing evidence that the customer is reasonably suspected of engaging in criminal activity and that the information would be material evidence in the case; in addition, the customer must be given the right to appear in court and contest any claims made in support of the court order. However, this notice requirement is deemed inapplicable if the cable operator provides both Internet access and cable access to the customer, because the Electronic Communications Policy Act (enacted after the CCPA) bars companies that provide electronic communications services from notifying customers that their personal information has been requested by a governmental entity via a court order.

Cable customers have the right to access all of the personally identifiable information that the cable operator has collected on the customer at a convenient place designated by the cable company. If the customer finds errors in his or her personal information, the customer must be given a reasonable opportunity to correct any errors. Personally identifiable information must be destroyed by the cable company if the information is no longer necessary for the purpose for which it was collected and there are no pending requests or court orders for such information. The act allows aggrieved customers to collect actual damages; actual damages cannot be less than $100 per day of a violation or $1,000—whichever is higher. The court may also award punitive damages, reasonable attorneys' fees, and reasonable litigation costs. Finally, the act permits states and franchising authorities to enact or enforce laws consistent with the act.

Marcy E. Peek

Further Reading

Cate, Fred H., et al. 2003. *Financial Privacy, Consumer Prosperity, and the Public Good.* Washington, DC: Brookings Institute.

Rubin, Paul H. and Thomas M. Lenard. 2002. *Privacy and the Commercial Use of Information.* Amsterdam: Kluwer Academic Publishers.

Strover, Sharon. n.d. "United States: Cable Television." Museum of Broadcast Communications Web site. http://www.museum.tv/eotv/unitedstatesc.htm. Accessed March 10, 2015.

California v. Ciraolo (1986)

In standard analyses of the Fourth Amendment, which was designed in part to protect individuals' right to privacy, determination about whether a person has a constitutionally protected expectation of privacy in a given situation is based on two levels of inquiry. The first is whether a person has demonstrated an expectation of privacy, and the second is whether society will accept that expectation as reasonable. Although these appear to be straightforward standards, cases such as *California v. Ciraolo*, 476 U.S. 207, illustrate the complexities involved in the analysis of the Fourth Amendment.

In this case, the respondent, Ciraolo, had marijuana growing in his backyard, which was protected from sight at ground level by a ten-foot-high inner fence and a six-foot-high outer fence. The home itself was directly in front of the yard and provided one edge of the fence's perimeter.

That tall barrier, however, was no match for the Santa Clara, California, police department. After receiving an anonymous tip reporting the respondent's illegal activity, the police department dispatched two officers, both of whom were trained in marijuana identification, to fly over the respondent's property in a private plane. The officers, flying at an altitude of 1,000 feet, within publicly navigable airspace, identified and photographed the marijuana growing on the respondent's property. In addition, they photographed the outside of the respondent's house as well as other homes and yards in the surrounding region.

One of the officers subsequently filed an affidavit on the basis of the anonymous tip and his naked eye observations. He attached the photograph of the respondent's home and the surrounding area to the affidavit and obtained a search warrant. As a result of the search, 73 plants were seized from the respondent's property.

The respondent pleaded guilty to cultivating marijuana after the trial court denied his plea to withhold the evidence of the search. The California Court of Appeals, however, reversed the trial court's decision to deny the respondent's motion. It ruled that the aerial observation of the respondent's yard, which occurred without a warrant, violated the Fourth Amendment to the Constitution of the United States. Finally, in May of 1986, the Supreme Court granted a writ of certiorari and again reversed the appellate court's verdict. They ruled in a narrow 5–4 vote that the respondent's motion to withhold the evidence was properly denied and that there had been no violation of the Fourth Amendment in the case.

To properly apply the Fourth Amendment, it was necessary for the court to first decide whether the respondent, Ciraolo, clearly attempted to demonstrate his expectation of privacy with respect to his property. Neither court disagreed that the fences surrounding the yard were obvious evidence that the respondent had demonstrated that expectation.

The Supreme Court, however, addressed the second question, which was whether his expectation to privacy was reasonable. Although the respondent's yard was considered to be part of his home, and the respondent had an expectation of privacy in his home, the Court determined that this did not restrict all police surveillance. While the respondent took measures to prohibit views of his property from ground level, the officers who observed the illegal cultivation of marijuana were in a public area that happened to be in the air, and they possessed every legal right to be there. Therefore, according to the Court, the respondent knowingly exposed his property to public sight. In addition, anyone who flew above the respondent's yard and happened to look down could have viewed what the officers viewed. Therefore, the Court ruled that the respondent's declared expectation that his yard was protected from all observation was not an expectation that society was willing to accept as reasonable.

In his dissent, Justice Lewis F. Powell referred back to the period of the Fourth Amendment's passage and the original intention of the framers of the Constitution to protect citizens' right to security and freedom from surveillance. Powell pointed out that scientific and technological advances had made it possible for police officials to devise strategies for surveillance that did not constitute a physical intrusion of privacy. Thus, the Fourth Amendment gives individuals the right to be in their homes and in the areas directly surrounding their homes, free from any governmental intrusions, yet does not protect these same individuals from intrusions made possible with modern technology. In this instance, police officers observed the respondent's activities by means of a private airplane, a product of modern technology. Powell questioned why this method of surveillance was permitted without a warrant; yet if the officials had climbed a tree or the respondent's fence in order to view the yard, the Court would have deemed this method of search as unreasonable.

The Court's inquiry as to whether society would view the respondent's expectation to privacy as reasonable was also flawed in Powell's opinion. The Court held that the respondent could not expect privacy from aerial observations taken from public airspace and that society would not recognize this expectation as reasonable either. Powell observed that commercial flights are not taken with the purpose of observing one specific home and one specific person's activities as was the case for the officers flying above the respondent's home. At most, people aboard a public aircraft may have only seconds to view what is going on below them as they pass over, and the chances of them connecting what they see to any one specific person are slim to none. Powell thus argued that, contrary to the majority opinion, the respondent did not knowingly expose his property to governmental surveillance any more than any other person who had not constructed a roof to cover his yard.

Since the *California v. Ciraolo* decision was handed down, it has become one of several cases frequently cited in debates about Fourth Amendment implications of drone surveillance. As scholar John Murray argued, "The Supreme Court has held that civilian law enforcement agencies may use manned aircraft for surveillance without engaging in a 'search' under the Fourth Amendment and may do so without a warrant. If this precedent were to apply to drone surveillance, civilian law enforcement agencies would effectively have *carte blanche* to conduct warrantless drone surveillance on citizens."

Sean M. Peek

Further Reading

Bartee, Alice Fleetwood. 2006. *Privacy Rights: Cases Lost and Causes Won Before the Supreme Court*. Lanham, MD: Rowman & Littlefield.

Gordley, James. 2003. *Foundations of Privacy Law: Property, Tort, Contract, Unjust Enrichment*. New York: Oxford University Press.

Hubbart, Phillip A. 2005. *Making Sense of Search and Seizure Law: A Fourth Amendment Handbook.* Durham, NC: Carolina Academic Press.

Murray, John E. 2014. "Ubiquitous Eyes Above: Should Existing Fourth Amendment Precedent Apply to Drone Surveillance?" *Northeastern University Law Journal*, Spring. http://nulj.org/extralegal/spring2014/murray_ubiquitous_eyes_above. Accessed March 11, 2015.

California v. Greenwood (1988)

California v. Greenwood is a case that addresses the issue of privacy and whether a person can expect the contents of garbage bags to remain private. The U.S. Supreme Court ruled that a warrant was not necessary to inspect items in one's garbage because there was no expectation of privacy once items have been discarded as trash.

The case originated in 1984, when Laguna Beach (CA) Police Department investigator Jenny Stracner received information from sources that a man named Billy Greenwood was possibly selling illegal drugs out of his home. A criminal suspect had informed a drug enforcement officer that illegal drugs were being shipped to Greenwood's home; also, a neighbor of Greenwood's had complained about suspicious late-night visits from cars that only stayed a few minutes. Stracner herself then observed the traffic in front of Greenwood's home and also followed one of the vehicles to a suspected drug-dealing location. In April, Stracner asked the local trash collector to pick up the garbage left at Greenwood's curb and turn over the bags to her. When she opened up the bags, she found drug paraphernalia—razor blades and straws that contained cocaine residue—and suspicious phone records.

As a result of what she found in the garbage bags, Stracner obtained a warrant to search Greenwood's home. Officers then discovered marijuana and cocaine. Both Greenwood and Dyanne Van Houten were arrested and released on bail. A month later, the process was repeated—Investigator Robert Rahaeuser looked through more garbage bags, found evidence of drugs, obtained another warrant, and found evidence of drug trafficking in Greenwood's home. Greenwood was again arrested.

Charges of narcotics trafficking were made against Greenwood and Van Houten. The California Superior Court of Orange County, however, dismissed the charges, citing an earlier case, *People v. Krivda* (1971), which ruled that searching the curbside trash without a warrant violated both the Fourth Amendment and the California Constitution. The court reasoned that probable cause to search the house would not have occurred had the evidence not been obtained illegally. The state argued that trash placed by the curb is not protected by the Fourth Amendment because any passerby may have access to it and, therefore, the person leaving the trash there "has no expectation of privacy." The Fourth Amendment generally protects citizens against unreasonable searches and seizures, though the 1914 case *Weeks v. United States* introduced the exclusionary rule, which states that evidence secured in violation of the Fourth Amendment cannot be used in a criminal prosecution.

The Court of Appeals affirmed the lower court's decision. The California Supreme Court opted against hearing an appeal, upholding the lower court's decisions and stating that the California Constitution declared that searches, such as those involving Greenwood's garbage, were unconstitutional. The state then appealed to the U.S. Supreme Court, which agreed to hear the case.

On May 16, 1988, with Justice Anthony M. Kennedy abstaining, the Court ruled 6–2 in favor of the state, saying that a warrant was unnecessary to search trash because Greenwood had no reasonable expectation of privacy once he had place items in the trash. Writing for the Court, Justice Byron R. White stated that garbage is "readily accessible to animals, children, scavengers, snoops, and other members of the public" and that what "a person knowingly exposes to the public, even in his own home or office, is not a subject of Fourth Amendment protection." Furthermore, White wrote, "Respondents placed their refuse at the curb for the express purpose of conveying it to a third party, the trash collector, who might himself have sorted through it or permitted others, such as the police, to do so. The police cannot reasonably be expected to avert their eyes from evidence of criminal activity that could have been observed by any member of the public." The Court had also tended to not enforce the exclusionary rule when it believed law officers had acted in good faith while performing their duties.

Justices William J. Brennan Jr. and Thurgood Marshall dissented. In their dissent, they wrote that having people—be they the police or unwelcome meddlers—go through trash bags "does not negate the expectation of privacy in their contents any more than the possibility of a burglary negates an expectation of privacy in the home." The two justices said, "Scrutiny of another's trash is contrary to commonly accepted notions of civilized behavior. . . . Trash bags can relate intimate details such as professional status, political inclinations, private thoughts, personal relationships and romantic interests . . ." Brennan stated, "Most of us, I believe, would be incensed to discover a meddler—whether a neighbor, a reporter, or a detective—scrutinizing our sealed trash containers to discover some detail of our personal lives."

Supporters praised the decision. Law enforcement officials were free to seek evidence in the same manner as the investigators did in the *Greenwood* case. On the other hand, critics of the ruling expressed concern about citizens' right to privacy being hindered as a result of the *Greenwood* decision. Arthur Spitzer, legal director at the American Civil Liberties Union, said the Court's ruling "is one more step in squeezing the right to privacy to the point where Americans will no longer feel secure against the prying eye of Big Brother."

Lawrence W. Baker

Further Reading

"*California v. Greenwood*." Casebriefs. http://www.casebriefs.com/blog/law/criminal-procedure/criminal-procedure-keyed-to-israel/arrest-search-and-seizure/california-v-greenwood/. Accessed March 15, 2015.

"*California v. Greenwood*—Impact." Law Library—American Law and Legal Information. http://law.jrank.org/pages/24102/California-v-Greenwood-Impact.html. Accessed March 15, 2015.

"*California v. Greenwood*—Should the Fourth Amendment Protect Garbage?" Law Library—American Law and Legal Information. http://law.jrank.org/pages/24101/California-v-Greenwood-Should-Fourth-Amendment-Protect-Garbage.html. Accessed March 15, 2015.

Slobogin, Christopher. 2007. *Privacy at Risk: The New Government Surveillance and the Fourth Amendment*. Chicago: University of Chicago Press.

"U.S. Supreme Court—*California v. Greenwood*." FindLaw. http://caselaw.lp.findlaw.com/scripts/getcase.pl?court=US&vol=486&invol=35. Accessed March 15, 2015.

Carnivore

Carnivore, also referred to as the Carnivore Diagnostic Tool or the Carnivore Electronic Communication Collection System, is the name of a series of suites of software introduced by the Federal Bureau of Investigation (FBI) on July 11, 2000, to carry out court-ordered surveillance of electronic communications over the Internet without the knowledge or consent of individuals being investigated. Specifically, this so-called packet-sniffing software was designed by the FBI to intercept and copy data packets to and from suspects at the site of an Internet service provider (ISP) with the cooperation of the ISP.

The term Carnivore is also commonly used to describe the successors to that series of software, as in 2001 the FBI dropped the name Carnivore to adopt the more neutral name of DCS1000 to describe the intercept suite. Unlike furtively employed and developed tools, Carnivore has been openly discussed by the FBI on its Web site and by other U.S. government institutions. For example, it has been subject to congressional review, and there was even an appraisal of the software under the auspices of the Department of Justice carried out by the Illinois Institute of Technology Research Institute.

Carnivore was a response to the surging popularity of the Internet as a communications network in the 1990s. During that time, it became clear to the FBI that for law enforcement purposes agents would have to use tools to intercept network data traffic in much the same way as phone taps had historically been used to gather evidence of criminal activity.

The FBI is reputed to have developed its first packet capture system in the mid-1990s, but little is publicly known about this first system. The second incarnation, Omnivore, was developed in 1997 for the Solaris x86 platform at a cost of around $900,000. It was designed to give government agencies the ability to capture Internet traffic based on users' identities and to print captured e-mails in real time. In addition, Omnivore was configured to save the captured e-mails to an 8-mm tape backup. In a project named Phiple Troenix, the FBI developed Carnivore to replace Omnivore. This redevelopment was driven by the need for a more modern system that could be run on a personal computer, and this project led to the development of the Carnivore suite at a cost of $800,000 to run on the MicroSoft Windows NT operating system.

From Omnivore to DSC-1000, the Carnivore-type systems seem to have operated in fundamentally the same way. A system is installed in the machine room of an ISP under the administration of an FBI agent. All the transmission control protocol/Internet protocol (TCP/IP) data (the way in which information is coded and packaged to communicate on the Internet) traveling past the Carnivore insertion point is captured as a copy of the data stream. There is no interruption of the data; they are merely mirrored as it flows past. As the TCP/IP data are captured, they are written to a buffer to temporarily store the copies of the packet data, typically to a shared memory area of the system. As the memory area begins to fill, the Carnivore software sifts through the information collected, applying user-defined filters to the buffered packet data. Thus, if Carnivore were configured to collect all e-mails to mperry@uwo.ca, all the packet data to that address would be written from the buffer to a more permanent storage medium (such as a Zip drive or hard drive) while all other data would be flushed from the buffer. In essence, the system replicates all the traffic passing the insertion point, but discards anything that does not meet the search criteria. However, Carnivore was more configurable than simply searching for an e-mail address and could be set to capture sets of data based on fixed or dynamic IP addresses, and it could collect all the packets to/from a particular address or, in pen mode, only the to/from header information. Thus, not only e-mails, but also the Web pages browsed, file transfer protocol, or indeed any transfers from a particular computer or a suspect could be captured by the system.

In the early 2000s, the FBI began moving away from using its own software to using commercially available software. In fact, the FBI's Carnivore/DCS-1000 Report to Congress at the end of 2003 stated that during that year the agency deployed surveillance software eight times during the year, but did not deploy Carnivore or DCS-1000 at all. By 2005, it had been completely mothballed in favor of commercially available software that could be adapted for electronic mass surveillance activities.

Mark Perry

Further Reading

Electronic Privacy Information Center. "Carnivore FOIA Documents." EPIC Web site. https://epic.org/privacy/carnivore/foia_documents.html. Accessed March 11, 2015.

Nabbali, Talitha, and Mark Perry. 2003. "Going for the Throat: Carnivore in an Echelon World. Part 1." *Computer Law and Security Report* 6: 456–67.

Nabbali, Talitha, and Mark Perry. 2004. "Going for the Throat: Carnivore in an Echelon World. Part 2." *Computer Law and Security Report* 20: 84–97.

Cellular Phones

Cell phones, also known as mobile phones or cellular phones, are wireless telephones that employ cellular network technology while allowing users to make and receive calls over an extensive geographical area. Modern cell phones provide a range of services, including text messaging, gaming, taking pictures, making and watching movies, sending and receiving e-mail, and accessing the Internet. In the past few years, cell phones with advanced computing technology, such as the popular iPhone, have become known as smartphones.

The use of cell phones is prevalent on a global scale. In 2015, it is estimated that there are more than 7.5 billion cell phone subscriptions worldwide, meaning that there will be more subscriptions to cell phone service than there are people (7.4 billion). Overall, it is estimated that more than 60 percent of the world's population has a cell phone. In the United States, there are also more cell phone subscriptions than people, and wireless penetration exceeds 100 percent. These statistics are impacted by the trend of many people having more than one cell phone, typically one used for business and another for personal matters.

Cell phones comprise a radio transmitter, a radio receiver, and at least one radio antenna and function like a two-way radio or walkie-talkie. More advanced cell phones contain more than a cellular antenna, such as a GPS, Wi-Fi, or Bluetooth antennas.

When an individual places a call, that person's voice is converted into a radio signal, transmitted over a short range to the nearest cell tower or mast, and eventually relayed by radio waves through the cellular network to its destination.

If the caller is mobile and traveling from the range of one cell tower to another, the call is seamlessly switched between them. The quality of the signal, known as the signal strength, is indicated by the number of bars visible on the cell phone and is determined by a number of factors, most likely the distance between the phone and the cell tower. If the signal strength is weak, service may be interrupted or may not even be available until the caller can move to a more accessible location.

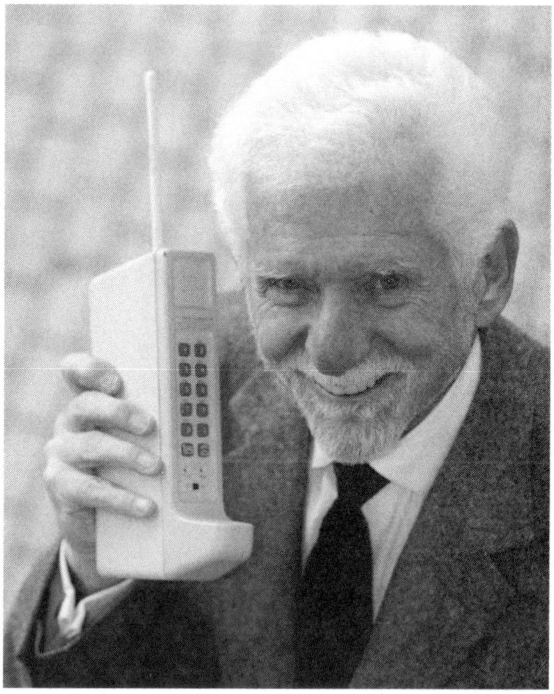

Martin Cooper, chairman and CEO of ArrayComm, holds a Motorola DynaTAC, a 1973 prototype of the first handheld cellular telephone in San Francisco, April 2, 2003. (AP Photo)

The cellular network is made up of cell towers, or masts, operating on a grid that divides cities and large regions into smaller units, known as cells. In major cities, one cell might be made up of only a few city blocks because large buildings can interfere with cell signals. In rural areas, one cell might comprise hundreds of square miles.

In order to optimize service, every cell utilizes a range of radio frequencies and channels so that many people can access the cellular network at one time.

The concept of cellular technology was first proposed in 1947 by Bell Labs' engineers Douglas H. Ring and W. Rae Young, who were working on a prototype of a mobile car phone for AT&T. However, the technology necessary to build a cellular phone system would not be available for several more years.

The first modern mobile phone utilizing cellular technology was invented by Motorola researcher Martin Cooper. On April 3, 1973, he made the first cell phone call to one of the engineers working on the same technology for Bell Labs, Dr. Joel Engel. The handheld mobile phone prototype patented by Cooper, known as the DynaTAC, was much larger and heavier than today's cell phones, took 10 hours to recharge, and allowed only 30 minutes of talk time. It would take almost a decade for the Federal Communications Commission (FCC) to approve the sale of Motorola's phone to the public.

In 1983, the Motorola DynaTAC 8000X was formally introduced on the market at the price of $3,995. Within months, the first commercial cell service was available.

In 1990, cell phones began to utilize digital transmission instead of analog, and the products with that digital technology becoming known as 2G (2nd generation). 2G technology led to added features such as text messaging, downloadable ringtones, Internet browsing, and prepaid phone services. Cell phones become increasingly widespread and a part of daily life for many people around the world. The first commercially successful smartphone was released in 1999 in Japan.

Cell phone technology kept advancing. In 2001, the first 3G network was launched commercially. 3G technology focused on faster data uploading and transmission and higher data storage capacity, which resulted in innovations like radio and television streaming. By 2009, 4G technologies, with even faster data transmission and uploading times, were taking over the cell phone market.

There are several ongoing concerns over the growing popularity of cell phones. One is the impact of frequent cell phone use on human health. A number of studies have investigated the health risks associated with cell phone use, particularly the chances of an increased risk from cancer because of electromagnetic radiation. The environmental impact of cell phone manufacturing and disposal is another long-standing issue.

Privacy and civil liberties groups have also raised concerns over tracking and privacy violations on cell phones. In numerous cases, police have been able to obtain and use data from cell phones to locate and track criminal suspects. Courts have made different rulings regarding the level of privacy that should be afforded to cell phone data. Some states require a warrant to gain access to such data, others do not.

Cell phones are also vulnerable to hacking. In one of the most famous cases of phone hacking, a scandal erupted in 2009 when news broke that several editors and reporters from the British tabloid *News of the World* had hacked the cell phone voice mail of thousands of British celebrities, sport stars, police officials, politicians, crime victims, and even members of the Royal Family to gain secret information it later published in its newspaper. In most countries, phone hacking is illegal unless it is done by official law enforcement with the proper authorization.

Margaret Haerens

Further Reading

Kelly, John, and Susanne Cervenka. "Cell Data Dumps: A Legally Fuzzy Area." *USA Today* (December 8, 2013). http://www.usatoday.com/story/news/nation/2013/12/08/cellphone-data-legal-issues-court/3902859/. Accessed March 20, 2015.

Richtel, Matt. "A Police Gadget Tracks Cell Phones? Shhh! It's Secret." *New York Times* (March 15, 2015). http://www.nytimes.com/2015/03/16/business/a-police-gadget-tracks-phones-shhh-its-secret.html?_r=0. Accessed March 20, 2015.

"Worldwide Cell Phone Subscriptions Forecast to Succeed Worldwide Population in 2015!" *IC Insights* (November 12, 2014). http://www.icinsights.com/news/bulletins/Worldwide-Cellphone-Subscriptions-Forecast-To-Exceed-Worldwide-Population-In-2015/. Accessed March 20, 2015.

Central Intelligence Agency (CIA)

The Central Intelligence Agency (CIA) is part of the American intelligence community, which is led by the director of National Intelligence. Primarily, the CIA is responsible for collecting, analyzing, and reporting information about foreign governments, corporations, individuals, and multinational or para-national groups to U.S. government agencies and branches. The CIA describes its mission as being "the eyes and ears of the nation." The second aspect of the mission of the CIA is to furnish relevant and objective analysis of international intelligence. The third aspect of the agency's mission is to be the government's hidden hand in conducting covert action to preempt threats to U.S. security or to achieve national policy objectives. Those covert operations are conducted at the direction of the president under the supervision of the director of the CIA.

After World War II and in the face of the increasing threat of communism and the beginning of the Cold War, the U.S. Congress created the CIA as the successor to the Office of Strategic Services (OSS), which ceased to exist in October of 1945. The CIA came into existence with the signing of the National Security Act of 1947. While the CIA is authorized to collect intelligence, it has no police power, no power of subpoena, no law enforcement powers, and no internal security functions within the United States. Its focus on foreign governments, businesses, and individuals places its activity *outside* the United States, as Congress created the agency to protect the privacy and security of U.S. citizens from external threats. The areas that are of greatest importance in the work of the CIA include international organized crime, narcotics trafficking, counterterrorism, counterintelligence, nuclear nonproliferation, the environment, and arms control intelligence.

Documentation indicates that at the time of the CIA's creation in 1947 many former Nazi operatives were recruited to be agents. In return, those operatives were promised immunity from prosecution for war crimes committed during World War II (Operation Paperclip). In 1949, Congress passed a law that essentially allowed the CIA to operate in complete secrecy and without the limitations generally applied to the use of federal funds. That law also created a program that permitted defectors from other countries and persons considered essential to national security to be admitted to the United States without going through the normal immigration processes, to be provided with new identities, and to be provided financial support. During the 1950s and 1960s, there existed little oversight of the CIA's activities by Congress or other government agencies.

In the 1970s, however, the eruption of the Watergate scandal and the efforts of Congress to exercise its oversight power over the executive branch of the government began to expose the activities of the CIA. When Watergate became a national issue, President Nixon tried unsuccessfully to have the CIA convince the Federal Bureau of Investigation (FBI) that investigation of Watergate would reveal too much about the involvement of the CIA in such past activities as the Bay of Pigs invasion. At about the same time, James Schlesinger, who was then director of Central Intelligence, authorized a series of reports that brought to light vast wrongdoings by the CIA. Those reports were often referred to as the family jewels.

The general public probably would have known nothing of that sordid history had not a *New York Times* reporter published a story documenting the involvement of the CIA in the assassination of certain foreign leaders. Congressional investigators subsequently confirmed that the CIA had been keeping files on thousands of American citizens who had been involved in the peace movement during the Vietnam War and the period of nuclear proliferation.

In light of these and other revelations concerning CIA involvement in destabilizing foreign governments, plotting assassinations of foreign leaders, and training political radicals later implicated in the murder of innocent civilians, new restrictions were placed on CIA operations and new oversight initiatives were established. After the September 11, 2001, attacks on the World Trade Center and the Pentagon, however, many restrictions on the activities of the CIA were removed. At the same time, the Intelligence Reform and Terrorism Prevention Act of 2004 instituted a number of changes in the structure of the government's management of domestic and foreign intelligence.

During the first decade of the 21st century, the CIA came under heavy criticism for its use of torture and secret prisons against foreign-born prisoners as part of its counterterrorism efforts. More recently, critics have voiced the opinion that many of the intelligence-gathering programs and tools utilized by the CIA, the National Security Agency (NSA), the FBI, and other intelligence agencies abrogate the right to privacy that is constitutionally guaranteed to American citizens. In 2014, members of the U.S. Senate angrily condemned the CIA when it was discovered that the agency had been surreptitiously spying on members of the Senate—the legislative body responsible for oversight of the agency. CIA director John Brennan—who had initially ridiculed the accusation—issued a formal apology, but the gesture failed to mollify many lawmakers who saw the CIA's actions as a grave offense that violated the U.S. Constitution's separation-of-powers provisions.

Gregory M. Duhl

Further Reading

Baer, Robert. 2003. *See No Evil: The True Story of a Ground Soldier in the CIA's War on Terrorism*. New York: Three Rivers Press.

Blum, William. 2003. *Killing Hope: U.S. Military and CIA Interventions since World War II*. Monroe, ME: Common Courage Press.

Darling, Arthur B. 1990. *The Central Intelligence Agency: An Instrument of Government, to 1950*. State College, PA: Pennsylvania State Press.

Risen, James. 2008. *State of War: The Secret History of the CIA and the Bush Administration*. New York: Free Press.

Wallace, Robert, H. Keith Melton, and Henry R. Schlesinger. 2008. *Spycraft: The Secret History of the CIA's Spytechs, from Communism to al-Qaeda*. New York: Dutton.

Church Committee

The Church Committee, technically called the U.S. Senate Select Committee to Study Governmental Operations with Respect to Intelligence Activities, was a temporary U.S. Senate committee created in 1975 and chaired by Senator Frank Church, a Democrat from Idaho. The committee was set up to investigate U.S. intelligence-gathering activities following press reports of illegal spying in the era following Watergate, the political scandal that led to the resignation of President Richard Nixon in August 1974.

Perhaps the most important revelation of illegal spying occurred on December 22, 1974, when investigative reporter Seymour Hersh published an article in *The New York Times* alleging that the Central Intelligence Agency (CIA) had conducted a massive illegal intelligence operation during the Nixon administration, targeting the antiwar movement and other dissident groups in the United States. Secret CIA reports detailing these and other illegal actions conducted during this period, including assassination attempts against foreign leaders, have come to be known as the CIA family jewels.

Directly as a result of these allegations in the press, the Senate on January 27, 1975, voted to create the Church Committee to conduct a broad investigation of intelligence efforts conducted by U.S. agencies such as the CIA, the National Security Agency (NSA), and the Federal Bureau of Investigation (FBI). The committee was made up of six Democratic and five Republican Senators. Democrat members of the group were Frank Church (who served as Chairman),

Philip Hart from Michigan, Walter Mondale from Minnesota, Walter Huddleston from Kentucky, Robert Morgan from North Carolina, and Gary Hart from Colorado. Republican representatives were John Tower from Texas (who served as Vice Chairman), Howard Baker from Tennessee, Barry Goldwater from Arizona, Charles Mathias from Maryland, and Richard Schweiker from Pennsylvania.

Over the next 16 months, after securing a pledge of cooperation from the administration of then President Gerald Ford, the committee completed a careful and thorough examination of intelligence programs. It reviewed tens of thousands of classified and unclassified documents from the CIA, FBI, NSA, and other federal agencies and interviewed hundreds of witnesses, including many CIA and FBI officials and counterintelligence officers. The committee also conducted numerous hearings, many of which were televised to educate the public about intelligence issues and failings.

During this process, the Church Committee issued 14 public reports over the course of 1975 and 1976. These reports alleged serious and various abuses of power by U.S. intelligence agencies along with recommendations for reform. Issued in 1975, the first interim report focused on U.S. attempts to assassinate a number of foreign leaders. The committee issued a final report on April 26, 1976, called the "Final Report of the Select Committee to Study Governmental Operations with Respect to Intelligence Activities." It consisted of six books addressing various topics and concluded that Congress should provide better monitoring of the intelligence community. The committee also released seven volumes of public hearings.

1. Church Committee: Interim Report—Alleged Assassination Plots Involving Foreign Leaders
2. Church Committee: Book I—Foreign and Military Intelligence
3. Church Committee: Book II—Intelligence Activities and the Rights of Americans
4. Church Committee: Book III—Supplementary Detailed Staff Reports on Intelligence Activities and the Rights of Americans
5. Church Committee: Book IV—Supplementary Detailed Staff Reports on Foreign and Military Intelligence
6. Church Committee: Book V—The Investigation of the Assassination of President John F. Kennedy: Performance of the Intelligence Agencies
7. Church Committee: Book VI—Supplementary Reports on Intelligence Activities
8. Church Committee: Volume 1—Hearings on Unauthorized Storage of Toxic Agents
9. Church Committee: Volume 2—Hearings on the Huston Plan
10. Church Committee: Volume 3—Hearings on the Internal Revenue Service

11. Church Committee: Volume 4—Hearings on Mail Opening
12. Church Committee: Volume 5—Hearings on the National Security Agency and Fourth Amendment Rights
13. Church Committee: Volume 6—Hearings on the Federal Bureau of Investigation
14. Church Committee: Volume 7—Hearings on Covert Action

The results of the committee's work were far-reaching. President Gerald Ford responded by issuing Executive Order 11905 to ban U.S. assassinations of foreign leaders. In addition, Congress created permanent intelligence oversight committees in both the Senate and the House of Representatives to supervise the activities of American intelligence agencies such as the NSA and CIA. The two principal oversight committees are the House Permanent Select Committee on Intelligence and the Senate Select Committee on Intelligence: Oversight Subcommittee. Congress also passed the Foreign Intelligence Surveillance Act (FISA) of 1978, a law that created a secret FISA court to issue warrants for domestic wiretapping activity. The committee's overall legacy was to serve warning to the intelligence community that it is not above the law. In light of recent revelations of intelligence and surveillance overreach by the NSA and others, however, civil libertarians and privacy advocates have asserted that a 21st-century Church Committee should be convened to review and reform U.S. intelligence programs and surveillance practices.

Debra Miller

Further Reading

Assassination Archives and Research Center. 2014. "Church Committee Reports." AARC Web site. http://www.aarclibrary.org/publib/church/reports/contents.htm. Accessed February 17, 2015.

Johnson, Loch K. 2011. *National Security Intelligence.* Boston, MA: Polity.

Lee, Timothy B. 2013. "In the 1970s, Congress Investigated Intelligence Abuses. Time to Do It Again?" *The Washington Post* (June 27). http://www.washingtonpost.com/blogs/wonkblog/wp/2013/06/27/in-the-1970s-congress-investigated-intelligence-abuses-time-to-do-it-again/.Accessed September 18, 2015.

Miller, Russell A. 2008. *U.S. National Security, Intelligence and Democracy: From the Church Committee to the War on Terror.* London: Routledge.

Civil Rights and Liberties during Wartime

In time of war, it is tempting for the government to restrict individual rights and liberties for the greater good. Some of these restrictions may be necessary. Other restrictions, however, are counterproductive, offering no benefits for national security and eventually backfiring on the government, at great cost to citizens and noncitizens. Erosions of civil liberties occur whenever the government exercises emergency power and argues that national interests must supersede individual rights.

The first experiment with this theory in the United States came from the Federalist Party during the quasi-war against France, from 1798 to 1800. President John Adams signed the repressive Alien and Sedition Acts of 1798, which deliberately tilted the nation toward England and against Jeffersonian supporters of France. The Sedition Act provided for fines and imprisonment for any person who wrote or spoke anything "false, scandalous and malicious" against the federal government, either House of Congress or the president, with intent to defame those governmental bodies. The statute expired by its own terms on March 3, 1801, but by that time it had energized the Jeffersonian Republicans and helped them gain control of Congress and the presidency in the 1800 elections. Once in office, Thomas Jefferson used his constitutional power to pardon all who had been prosecuted for sedition. So unpopular was the statute and its implementation that it dealt a mortal blow to the Federalist Party.

With the outbreak of the Civil War, President Abraham Lincoln used extraordinary powers to suspend the writ of habeas corpus. Unlike other presidents who claimed broad, unreviewable power in time of emergency, Lincoln conceded that the legality of his actions was uncertain. When Congress returned, he explained that his actions "whether strictly legal or not, were ventured upon under what appeared to be a popular demand and a public necessity, trusting then, as now, that congress would readily ratify them." Congress debated his request at length, with members supporting Lincoln despite the explicit assumption that his acts were illegal. Congress then passed legislation "approving, legalizing, and making valid all the acts, proclamations, and orders of the President, etc., as if they had been issued and done under the previous express authority and direction of the Congress of the United States."

During World War I, the federal government unleashed a campaign against opponents of military action against Germany. Before he asked Congress in 1917 to declare war on Germany, President Woodrow Wilson warned that the "gravest threats against our national peace and safety have been uttered within our own borders." These citizens, he said, "have poured the poison of disloyalty into the very arteries of our national life." With his urging, Congress passed the Espionage Act in June 1917, authorizing fines and imprisonment of anyone who "shall willfully cause or attempt to cause insubordination, disloyalty, mutiny, or refusal of duty, in the military or naval forces of the United States." The statute also categorized as nonmailable any "letter, writing, circular, postal card, . . . newspaper, pamphlet, book, or other publication" that advocated "treason, insurrection, or forcible resistance to any law of the United States."

Several thousand people were prosecuted under the Espionage Act, with their convictions regularly upheld by reviewing courts. The Supreme Court seemed to have no appreciation of the need for free speech during wartime. Challenging that attitude was Zechariah Chafee Jr., whose article in the *Harvard Law Review* in 1919 argued strongly that free speech deserved special protection when the nation was at war. The war clauses of the Constitution, he said, "cannot be invoked to break down freedom of speech." Only through free debate could the government's war policy be "vigorously and constantly cross-examined" to ensure that war is not "diverted to improper ends, or conducted with an undue sacrifice of life and liberty, or prolonged after its just purposes are accomplished." Just as legal proceedings depended on cross-examination, so would it be "a disastrous mistake to limit criticism to those who favor the war."

Unlike the opposition to American involvement in World War I, Nazi aggression in Europe and the Japanese attack on Pearl Harbor generated broad support for U.S. intervention in World War II. In early 1942, President Franklin D. Roosevelt issued an executive order authorizing the military to relocate persons of Japanese descent living on the West Coast, which resulted in more than a hundred thousand Japanese Americans being interned for the duration of the war. Upholding this massive deprivation of liberty in *Korematsu v. United States* (1944), the Supreme Court observed: "Citizenship has its responsibilities as well as its privileges, and in time of war the burden is always heavier."

Political conditions changed after the war when the United States confronted international communism. President Harry Truman issued an executive order to create loyalty review boards to supervise federal employees, and Congress passed a legislation to prohibit aliens from entering the United States if they advocated communist doctrines. The Taft–Hartley Act of 1947 required union officers to file a noncommunist affidavit. This pattern ripened into the McCarthyist period of the 1950s, leading to congressional investigations into communist associations and the loss of jobs by many found guilty by association.

The Vietnam War triggered a number of civil liberties issues, including draft-card burnings, flag burning, and the wearing of black armbands to protest the war. The Supreme Court held in *United States v. O'Brien* (1968) that federal legislation prohibiting the destruction of a draft card did not unconstitutionally abridge free speech. Government, it said, has a legitimate interest in preserving draft cards. On the other hand, in the case of *Tinker v. Des Moines School District* (1969), schoolchildren were permitted to wear black armbands to protest the war. Their conduct had been quiet and nondisruptive.

Flag burning also became a politically explosive issue. In *Texas v. Johnson* (1989), the Court held that a conviction for flag desecration (burning the flag during a protest) was contrary to the First Amendment because it was expressive conduct protected by the First Amendment. Congress responded by passing the Flag Protection Act of 1989, continuing the prohibition on flag burning but deleting from a 1968 statute the words "casts contempt." This change, the sponsors of the legislation argued, made the law content neutral. The Supreme Court, in *United States v. Eichman* (1990), disagreed, holding that the government's interest in protecting the physical integrity of the flag could not justify its infringement on First Amendment Rights. Efforts since that time to pass a constitutional amendment to protect the flag have been unsuccessful.

The terrorist attacks of 9/11 raised again the issue of civil liberties in wartime, but in a war that appears to have no likely termination date. The restoration of civil liberties that typically comes after the cessation of hostilities may not occur because no one knows when or if the war against terrorism will conclude. In terms of its impact on civil liberties, the most significant action that took place in the aftermath of 9/11 was passage of the USA PATRIOT Act on October 26, 2001.

The PATRIOT Act was crafted to strengthen the power of the Bush administration in particular and the U.S. government in general to deter and punish terrorists. Yet the statute goes far beyond the threat of terrorism. It gives the government broad new powers to conduct any criminal investigation. Any increase in the power of the executive branch, especially over law enforcement, inevitably places at risk some constitutional rights and liberties. The risk is even greater when legislation moves through Congress at great speed without the regular care and deliberation of legislative hearings, markups, and floor debates. The House Judiciary Committee held one hearing on September 24, 2001, conducted a markup with amendments offered and agreed to, and issued a lengthy committee report. On the floor, however, that bill was put aside in favor of a substitute measure that few members had seen, with no opportunity for amendment. On the Senate side, there was no committee markup or vote in the judiciary committee, nor was there any opportunity to amend the measure when it reached the floor.

Senator Patrick Leahy (D-Vt.) laid down an early marker after the tragedy of 9/11. He cautioned against tipping the scales to the extent of endangering and jeopardizing civil liberties. "The worst thing that could happen is we damage our Constitution," he said. "If the Constitution is shredded, the terrorists win." Senator Russ Feingold (D-Wis.) issued a similar warning: "Preserving our freedom is the reason we are now engaging in this new war on terrorism. We will lose that war without a shot being fired if we sacrifice the liberties of the American people in the belief that by doing so we will stop the terrorists."

Public support for the PATRIOT Act and the various tools it authorizes has remained fairly strong, however, even in the wake of revelations about various programs of mass surveillance and electronic-intelligence gathering, which have impacted ordinary American citizens not under suspicion of any criminal activity.

In 2011, Congress passed and President Obama signed into law a four-year extension of Section 215 and several other controversial provisions in the PATRIOT Act, citing the provisions as vital tools in ongoing efforts to combat terrorism.

Louis Fisher

Further Reading

Chafee, Zechariah, Jr. 1919. "Freedom of Speech in War Time." *Harvard Law Review* 32: 932.

Rabban, David M. 1997. *Free Speech in Its Forgotten Years*. Cambridge: Cambridge University Press.

Smith, James Norton. 1956. *Freedom's Fetters: The Alien and Sedition Laws and American Civil Liberties*. Ithaca: Cornell University Press.

Smith, Jeffery A. 1999. *War and Press Freedom: The Problem of Prerogative Power*. New York: Oxford University Press.

Tushnet, Mark, ed. 2005. *The Constitution in Wartime: Beyond Alarmism and Complacency*. Durham, NC: Duke University Press.

Clapper, James R. (1941–)

James Clapper has worked in a number of high-ranking intelligence positions and has served as the U.S. director of National Intelligence since 2010. "Nearly every position I have held . . . has focused on intelligence—as a collector, analyst, staff officer, commander, or Director—spanning all phases of the Intelligence cycle," he wrote in his Senate questionnaire during his nomination period.

James Robert Clapper Jr. was born on March 14, 1941, in Fort Wayne, Indiana, the son of James Robert Clapper and Anne Elizabeth Wheatley Clapper. He has a sister, Chris, and a brother, Michael. Clapper initially enlisted in the U.S. Marine Corps Reserve but transferred to the U.S. Air Force Reserve Officer Training Corps. He received his bachelor's degree in government and politics in 1963 from the University of Maryland; his master's degree in political science in 1970 from Saint Mary's University in San Antonio, Texas; and an honorary degree in strategic intelligence from the Joint Military Intelligence College, now known as the National Intelligence University. In 1965, Clapper married Susan Terry, with whom he had one daughter.

Upon completion of school, Clapper was commissioned as a distinguished military graduate from the University of Maryland. He would go on to serve in the U.S. Air Force in a variety of roles. These included a rifleman in the U.S. Marine Corps Reserve; assistant chief staff for intelligence at U.S. Air Force Headquarters during Operations Desert Shield/Desert Storm; commander of signals intelligence units in

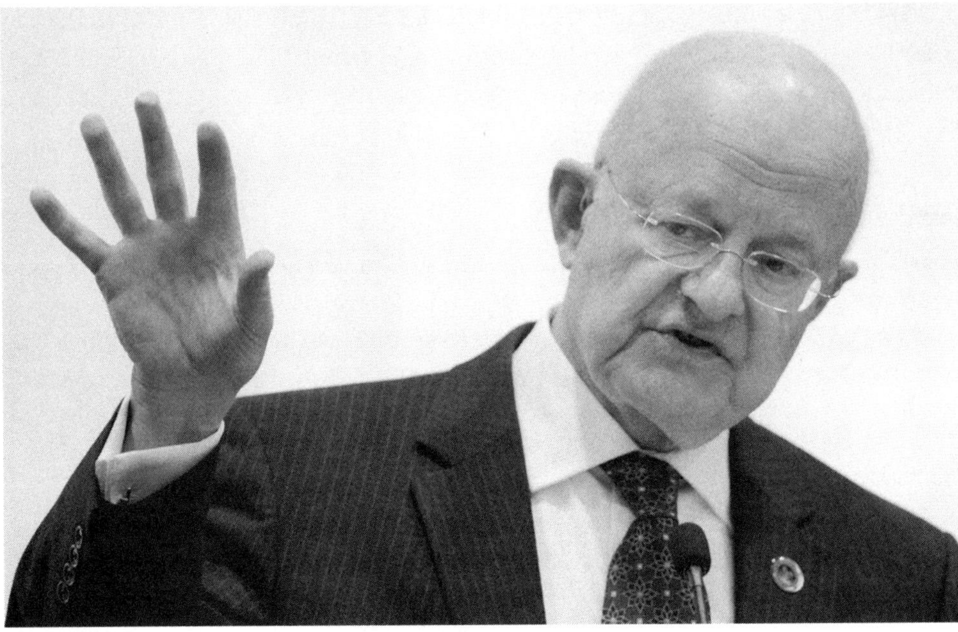

James Clapper, the Director of National Intelligence, speaks at the International Conference on Cyber Security at Fordham University in New York, 2015. (AP Photo)

Thailand, Fort George G. Meade, Maryland, and the Air Force Technical Applications Center, Patrick Air Force Base, Florida; and director of the Defense Intelligence Agency. He served in the latter position from November 1991 to August 1995.

After leaving the directorship of the Defense Intelligence Agency, Clapper worked in the private sector for six years. In September 2001, though, he returned to government service as the director of the National Imagery and Mapping Agency, which later became the National Geospatial-Intelligence Agency, a combat-support agency under the U.S. Department of Defense, and an intelligence agency under the U.S. Intelligence Community. In 2006–2007, he worked again in the private industry, at GeoEye, a satellite imagery company. During the same timeframe, he briefly taught at Georgetown University as the Intelligence and National Security Alliance Distinguished Professor in the Practice of Intelligence. On January 29, 2007, President George W. Bush nominated Clapper as the Under Secretary of Defense for Intelligence, and he was confirmed nearly three months later. He worked in the areas of intelligence, counterintelligence, and security.

On June 5, 2010, President Barack Obama nominated Clapper as the new director of National Intelligence. Obama praised Clapper, saying, "He's improved information sharing, increased intelligence support to our troops in Afghanistan and Iraq, upheld civil liberties, and he played a key role in our effort to update and reorient our intelligence community to meet the threats of our time." He also noted a quality he admired in Clapper—"a willingness to tell leaders what we need to know, even if it's not what we want to hear." Clapper was unanimously approved by the U.S. Senate two months later.

Controversy began to brew around Clapper when accusations were made that the National Security Agency (NSA) was secretly and illegally monitoring the private communication (e-mails, phone calls, etc.) of Americans. On March 12, 2013, Clapper appeared at a U.S. Senate Select Committee on Intelligence. U.S. senator Ron Wyden (D-Oregon) asked Clapper the following: "Last summer the NSA director [Keith Alexander] was at a conference and he was asked a question about the NSA surveillance of Americans. He replied, 'The story that we have millions or hundreds of millions of dossiers on people is completely false.' The reason I'm asking the question is . . . I don't really know what a dossier is in this context. So, what I wanted to see is if you could give me a yes or no answer to the question, Does the NSA collect any type of data at all on millions or hundreds of millions of Americans?" Clapper replied, "No, sir." Wyden followed up: "It does not?" Clapper briefly retorted: "Not wittingly. There are cases where they could inadvertently, perhaps, collect, but not wittingly."

Approximately three months later, former NSA contractor Edward Snowden leaked classified documents that revealed that the NSA was involved in a number of surveillance programs, which included the collection of phone records, with the involvement of various telecommunications companies. Shortly thereafter, Clapper admitted that the NSA collected metadata, which included phone numbers and time and duration of calls, but not the names or addresses of callers.

Clapper later qualified his original answer by saying in a *National Journal* article that "the NSA does not voyeuristically pore through U.S. citizens' e-mails. I stand by that." He was immediately accused of criminal perjury for lying in front of the Senate committee. Clapper apologized for his false answer but claimed that he gave his answer in an attempt to avoid revealing classified information. He also believed that Wyden's question was unfair, so he "responded in what I thought was the most truthful, or least untruthful manner by saying no."

Robert Litt, the general counsel to the Office of the Director of National Intelligence, asserted that Clapper did not lie to Congress but rather replied in a manner in which he "focused his mind on the collection of content of Americans' communications. In that context, his answer was and is accurate." President Obama has continued to support Clapper, stating he had "full faith in Director Clapper's leadership of the intelligence community," despite calls for his resignation.

For his part, Clapper supports the metadata program, which he asserts is misunderstood by the American public. "I view this as an arrangement—a 'lock-box' if you will—for holding data. If we need to look at the data, and can justify that need, we have it available. It was a direct result of 9/11. We had a foreign communicant, a person in Yemen, who was talking to someone in San Diego [one of the 9/11 airplane hijackers]. We had no way legally to 'connect those dots . . .'"

Clapper is enthusiastic about the advances government intelligence has made, especially with regard to advances in technology. "We have a greater diversity of collection capabilitie . . . . A great example is open source intelligence, which now comes to include social media—a hugely important source of intelligence. We've made a lot of investments in open-source capabilities and tools to collect, correlate, and analyze open sources." The career intelligence gatherer once said, "To paraphrase Will Rogers, I never met a collection capability I didn't like."

Lawrence W. Baker

Further Reading

Greenberg, Andy. "Watch Top U.S. Intelligence Officials Repeatedly Deny NSA Spying on Americans over the Last Year." *Forbes* (June 6, 2013). http://www.forbes.com/sites/andygreenberg/2013/06/06/watch-top-u-s-intelligence-officials-repeatedly-deny-nsa-spying-on-americans-over-the-last-year-videos/. Accessed May 6, 2015.

Hirsh, Michael. "James Clapper Clarifies Remarks Over NSA Snooping." *National Journal* (June 6, 2013). http://www.nationaljournal.com/whitehouse/james-clapper-clarifies-remarks-over-nsa-snooping-20130606. Accessed May 6, 2015.

Johnson, Loch K. 2015. "A Conversation with James R. Clapper Jr., the Director of National Intelligence in the United States." *Intelligence and National Security* 30 (1): 1–25. http://www.tandfonline.com/doi/pdf/10.1080/02684527.2014.972613. Accessed May 6, 2015.

Lee, Jesse. "James R. Clapper Jr. as DNI: 'Four Decades of Service.'" *The White House Blog* (June 5, 2010). The White House. https://www.whitehouse.gov/blog/2010/06/05/james-r-clapper-jr-dni-four-decades-service. Accessed May 6, 2015.

Office of the Director of National Intelligence. "Director of National Intelligence: James R. Clapper." http://www.dni.gov/index.php/about/leadership/director-of-national-intelligence. Accessed May 6, 2015.

Pengelly, Martin. "Clapper Did Not Lie to Congress on NSA, Says National Intelligence Counsel." *The Guardian* (January 4, 2014). http://www.theguardian.com/world/2014/jan/04/clapper-lie-congress-nsa-national-intelligence-counsel. Accessed May 6, 2015.

Roberts, Dan, and Spencer Ackerman. "Clapper under Pressure Despite Apology for 'Erroneous' Statements to Congress." *The Guardian* (July 1, 2013). http://www.theguardian.com/world/2013/jul/01/james-clapper-apology-congress-erroneous-response. Accessed May 6, 2015.

Clapper v. Amnesty International USA (2013)

This case involved the unsuccessful challenge by Amnesty International and other parties of the amendments act of the Foreign Intelligence Surveillance Act (FISA) that was enacted in 2008.

According to the U.S. Department of Justice, FISA established "procedures for physical and electronic surveillance and collection of foreign intelligence information." It originally became law in 1978 after "Congress sought to provide judicial and congressional oversight of foreign intelligence surveillance activities while maintaining the secrecy necessary to effectively monitor national security threats." The 1978 FISA legislation established a court, called the U.S. Foreign Intelligence Surveillance Court, or the FISA Court, to oversee requests for surveillance warrants by U.S. law enforcement agencies—most frequently the Federal Bureau of Investigation (FBI) or the National Security Agency (NSA)—against foreign intelligence agents inside the United States.

In 2008, the FISA of 1978 Amendments Act gave the FISA Court the power to authorize surveillance without having to show that the target of the surveillance represents a foreign power. Under this revision of the court's authority, in fact, the target need only dwell outside the United States and be the source of foreign intelligence. Several groups, consisting of journalists, lawyers, and human rights organizations such as the American Civil Liberties Union, claimed that the new procedures violated the Fourth Amendment, the First Amendment, Article III of the Constitution, and the principle of separation of powers. They maintained that the new provisions would result in a fear of being monitored and require them to spend additional time and money to ensure that their international communications remained confidential. Much of their work involved sensitive and privileged communication via telephone and e-mail.

One such group was Amnesty International USA, one of the world's most influential and largest human rights organizations. As the lead plaintiff, it filed suit against the government (*Clapper* refers to James Clapper, director of National Intelligence) in federal court, claiming that the amended act was unconstitutional. Clapper, arguing for the government, maintained that the plaintiffs lacked standing—meaning they could not prove sufficient harm from the government's actions. The district court agreed with the government and dismissed the suit.

The plaintiffs appealed to the Second Circuit Court of Appeals. The court reversed the lower court's ruling, claiming that the plaintiffs had suffered an "injury-in-fact"—Judge Gerard E. Lynch determined that the plaintiffs' claim that they feared being monitored was reasonable based on a "realistic understanding of the world." The government appealed the Second Circuit's decision, saying that the costs the plaintiffs took on were of their own doing. The case was taken on by the U.S. Supreme Court. Arguments took place on October 29, 2012.

On February 26, 2013, the Court ruled in favor of the government by a narrow 5–4 margin, using the same judgment issued by the district court that the plaintiffs did not have sufficient standing to challenge the constitutionality of the government's warrantless wiretapping program. Writing for the majority, Justice Samuel

Alito Jr. said that the plaintiffs could not "demonstrate that the future injury they purportedly fear is certainly impending and because they cannot manufacture standing by incurring costs in anticipation of non-imminent harm." He wrote that the Court was "reluctant to endorse standing theories that require guesswork as to how independent decision-makers will exercise their judgment."

In his dissent, Justice Stephen G. Breyer questioned the speculative nature of the harm referred to by the plaintiffs. "Indeed it is as likely to take place as are most future events that commonsense inference and ordinary knowledge of human nature tell us will happen. This Court has often found the occurrence of similar future events sufficiently certain to support standing."

There was much reaction to the Court's decision. Jameel Jaffer, the deputy legal director of the American Civil Liberties Union and the lawyer for the plaintiffs, was disturbed by the Court's decision, which he believed insulates FISA "from meaningful judicial review and leaves Americans' privacy rights to the mercy of the political branches." Journalist Chris Hedges, one of the plaintiffs in the case, called the ruling "a very depressing decision, but one that has become routine in a court system that when faced with what the government insists are matters of national security writes lengthy opinions about why the courts cannot defend the rule of law."

Lawrence W. Baker

Further Reading

American Civil Liberties Union. "*Amnesty et al. v. Clapper:* FISA Amendments Act Challenge." https://www.aclu.org/national-security/amnesty-et-al-v-clapper. Accessed April 15, 2015.

"*Clapper v. Amnesty International USA.*" *Oyez.* IIT Chicago-Kent College of Law. http://www.oyez.org/cases/2010-2019/2012/2012_11_1025. Accessed April 15, 2015.

"*Clapper v. Amnesty International USA.*" SCOTUSblog. http://www.scotusblog.com/case-files/cases/clapper-v-amnesty-international-usa/. Accessed April 15, 2015.

Dudley, Michaela Chelsea, and Allison Nolan. "*Clapper v. Amnesty International USA* (11–1025)." Legal Information Institute. https://www.law.cornell.edu/supct/cert/11-1025. Accessed April 15, 2015).

Glennon, Michael J. 2015. *National Security and Double Government.* New York: Oxford University Press.

Hedges, Chris. 2015. *Wages of Rebellion.* New York: Nation Books.

Sledge, Matt. 2013. "Clapper v. Amnesty International, Warrantless Wiretapping Challenge, Struck Down By Supreme Court." *Huffington Post* (February 26). http://www.huffingtonpost.com/2013/02/26/clapper-v-amnesty-international-warrantless-wiretapping-supreme-court_n_2765931.html. Accessed April 15, 2015.

Tribe, Laurence H., and Joshua Matz. 2014. *Uncertain Justice: The Roberts Court and the Constitution.* New York: Henry Holt.

Clipper and Capstone Chips

On April 16, 1993, just a few months after President Bill Clinton took office, the White House proposed the Escrowed Encryption Standard (EES) for the encryption of voice, fax, and computer information transmitted over circuit-switched telephone systems. EES was to be used for the protection of sensitive but unclassified information. The standard, which was nominally a National Institute of Standards and Technology (NIST) effort, included a tamper-proof hardware encryption chip (Clipper) and a key-escrow system. Each hardware chip would have its own key; these keys were to be split and registered at birth—escrowed—with two agencies of the U.S. government (NIST and the Department of Treasury Automated Systems Division were the initial escrow agencies). In other words, this was an encryption system in which the federal government held the private keys.

Under this proposal, keys would be released to law-enforcement agents armed with proper authorization. This would enable law enforcement to decrypt intercepted communications. A more advanced chip, Capstone, included additional cryptographic components for authentication and integrity checking: Clipper plus a public key exchange algorithm, the Secure Hashing Algorithm, the Digital Signature Standard, a high-speed exponentiation engine, and a random number generator.

EES—or Clipper as it came to be known—was a method for encrypting voice and fax communications so as to enable the easy decryption of material gathered from legally authorized wiretaps. It reflected a dawning understanding that the world was on the verge of a communications revolution. Protocols for easy access and display of information on the Internet had been developed and were being deployed. This network had been opened for commercial traffic. The World Wide Web was about to burst forth. In very short order, the Internet was transformed from a medium used primarily for scientific communications to a major player in world economic activity. The EES, which provided a government backdoor into encrypted communications, was proposed at a crucial moment.

The Clipper program was voluntary, but there were many objections anyway. In particular, there was public concern that the U.S. government might seek to prevent the usage of nonescrowed systems. In response, the White House stated that there was no intent to require key escrow. Executive branch activities belied that statement. The U.S. Communications for Law Enforcement Act (CALEA), first proposed in 1992 and eventually passed in 1994, required that digitally switched telephone networks be built according to wiretapping standards determined by the U.S. Department of Justice. In 1992, National Security Advisor Brent Scowcroft described the digital telephony bill as a "beachhead [that] we can exploit for the encryption fix."

The government posited that Clipper was an encryption system providing both security and privacy while enabling government access under legal authorization, but there were immediate objections to the government's key-escrow proposal. Of the 320 letters submitted to NIST regarding the Clipper proposal, all but a handful were negative. Civil liberties organizations expressed concerns about threats to privacy. Computer security experts observed that the establishment of escrow agencies was a dangerous concentration of resources and thus Clipper diminished rather than increased security. Business, unhappy with export controls on encryption, did not find EES a useful substitute. Nonetheless in 1994, EES became an official Federal Information Processing Standard.

The EES specified the use of Skipjack, an encryption algorithm developed by the National Security Agency (NSA), and the creation of a Law Enforcement Access Field (LEAF) to be implemented on a tamperproof hardware device. When two participants with Clipper-enabled telephones establish a connection, they set up a session key for that communication (call, fax, etc.). This session key is used to encrypt the communication. This key is passed to the Clipper chip of the device doing the communicating, which encrypts it using the chip's device unique key. This information is combined with the chip's identifier and other information to form the LEAF, or Law Enforcement Access Field, and is shipped to the other participant's device. The system is set up so that only if the LEAF decrypts properly can encrypted communications begin. The communication is encrypted with the session key; because the two participants know the key, they can communicate securely. An eavesdropper would need the device keys in order to decrypt the communication. Of course, given the setup of the system, under authorization law enforcement would have access to the keys.

In a strong algorithm, each additional bit of key length increases the security by a factor of two, so unless one uses the government backdoor-escrowed keys for decryption, data encrypted using Skipjack were vastly more secure than data encrypted using data encryption standard (DES), the 1977 federal standard for protecting secure but unclassified data. The increased security was one reason the government hoped for a strong positive reaction to EES. This was not to be. Just months after EES was made into a standard, Matt Blaze, a researcher at AT&T, discovered a way to defeat law enforcement access to the keys during a Clipper-enabled communication (Blaze's attack did not defeat the EES encryption, just law enforcement access to the encryption keys). The attack was easy to program and demonstrated that Clipper did not fulfill the government's claims of secure communications and easy government access (under proper legal authorization).

Two years after the approval of EES, only AT&T was producing secure telephones with Clipper chips. The company found few purchasers. U.S. business was not interested. Neither were foreign companies; the issue of law enforcement access to keys for devices used outside the U.S. had never been fully worked out and this contributed to foreign unease about Clipper. U.S. law enforcement bought some Clipper-enabled phones, but even they were not particularly enamored of the product. Despite extensive U.S. government efforts to encourage other nations to adopt an escrowed approach for encrypted civilian communications, there was little buy-in from abroad. Few wanted secure communications with the U.S. government holding the keys.

Key escrow was part of a larger effort by the U.S. government to slow civilian deployment of strong encryption. By the end of the decade however, the U.S. government changed its direction. Seeing important advantages to the deployment of strong cryptography throughout civilian infrastructure, the Clinton administration simplified export-control laws and embraced the use of nonescrowed encryption in the civilian sector, including the adoption of the advanced encryption standard, a strong symmetric key algorithm that replaced the aging—and much weaker—DES.

Susan Landau

Further Reading

Diffie, Whitfield, and Susan Landau. 1999. *Privacy on the Line: The Politics of Wiretapping and Encryption.* Cambridge, MA: MIT Press.

Garfinkel, Simson. 2002. *Web Security, Privacy and Commerce,* 2nd Edition. New York: O'Reilly Media Inc.

Landau, Susan. 2010. *Surveillance or Security? The Risks Posed by New Wiretapping Technologies.* Cambridge, MA: Massachusetts Institute of Technology.

Cloud Computing

Cloud computing involves the on-demand delivery of computing resources, such as information technology (IT) services, data storage, or software applications, over the Internet. Cloud-based computing has become increasingly mainstream because it allows consumers—whether they be individuals, small businesses, or large corporations—to more efficiently utilize resources by picking only what services they need from the cloud and paying for only what they use. In recent years, cloud computing has become a lucrative business. McKinsey & Company, an international consulting firm, estimates that 80 percent of the large companies in North America are turning to cloud computing services. Studies have estimated the cloud computing industry to be worth more than $100 billion a year.

There are three types of cloud-based services: Software as a Service (SaaS), Platform as a Service (PaaS), and Infrastructure as a Service (IaaS).

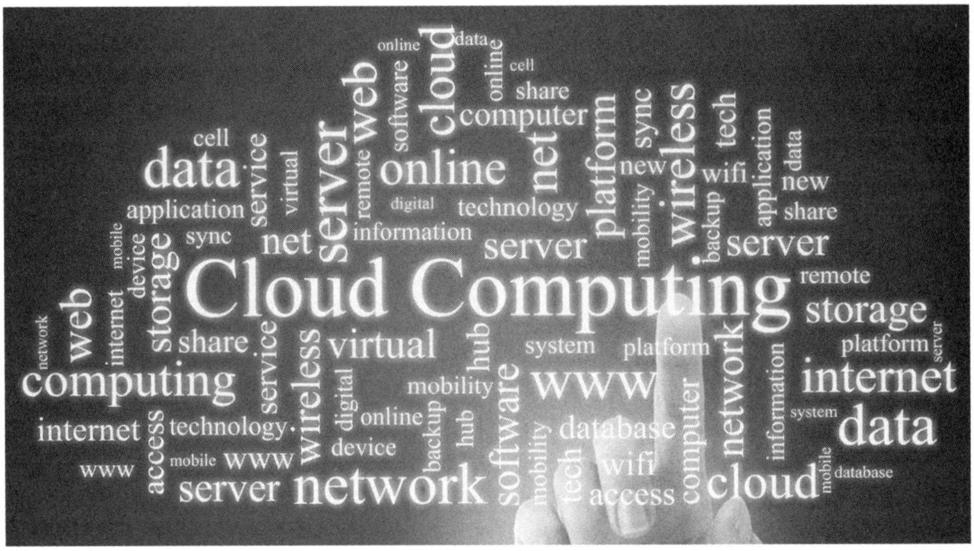

Cloud computing, which brings data and content to servers hosted by third parties like Amazon, Google, and many other companies, has become a popular tool for data storage, file sharing, and data analysis. (Fantasista/Dreamstime.com)

SaaS, also called cloud application services, is the largest cloud market. It offers consumers access to a range of software applications and technical services over the Internet. Some of the most common business applications involve payroll processing, games, e-mail and instant messaging, invoicing, human resources, and customer relations. Examples of SaaS are Twitter, Facebook, QuickBook Online, Microsoft 365, and Salesforce.

In this model, the cloud provider offers technical support and maintains the data center. Usage is scalable, which means it can be increased or decreased if needs change, and access is portable, as long as there is an Internet connection. Disadvantages of the model include the security and confidentiality of personal information and the stability of valuable data. Because the success of SaaS depends on quick access, any significant disruption to service can be detrimental to many individuals and small businesses.

PaaS allows users to utilize their Web browsers to access a cloud-based platform to develop, run, and manage their own software applications and services over the Internet. A number of features can be included in PaaS, such as support, data storage, network access, and tools for design and development. Examples of PaaS include Google App Engine, Windows Azure, and Apprenda.

The advantage of the PaaS model is that users bypass the cost of buying the hardware and software as well as the responsibility for security, storage, and management services. Disadvantages of PaaS include security concerns, limited control and flexibility, and the potential problems associated with being dependent on one PaaS vendor.

The third service model, IaaS, provides computing infrastructure and other resources to corporations and businesses. These services include virtual server space, bandwidth, networking storage, load balancers, and Internet protocol (IP) addresses. Examples of the IaaS model are Amazon Web Service (AWS), Microsoft Azure, and Google Compute Engine (GCE).

Like the other major service models of cloud computing, IaaS is a cost-effective and easily scalable option for consumers. It also places the responsibility and cost of maintaining and replacing hardware and providing support and other services on the IaaS provider. There are also concerns about the security of IaaS, rooted in the belief that data in the cloud are more easily lost or stolen. The possibility of vendor outages is another disadvantage—one that impacts all three cloud computing service models.

Along with choosing from these three basic types of cloud-based service models, individuals, organizations, businesses, and corporations also have several options when it comes to cloud computing infrastructure. There are four main ways that cloud technology is deployed: a public cloud offers services, such as applications and data storage, over the Internet for everyone to access; a private cloud is limited to a specific business or organization, allowing for greater customization when it comes to services, data security and control, and other issues; a community cloud is shared between several related agencies, organizations, or programs that share specific needs related to data security or other issues; and a hybrid cloud is a combination of private, public, and community clouds, depending on the user's needs.

Cloud computing has emerged in the past decade as a growing and lucrative industry, but there are rising concerns, especially about the security of the cloud. With so many organizations, businesses, and large corporations increasingly turning to cloud providers, a wealth of valuable information is vulnerable to hackers and insider attacks, including credit card numbers, intellectual property, medical records, and trade secrets. In one well-publicized incident in 2014, a hacker leaked dozens of nude photos from celebrity iCloud accounts to the press.

Government surveillance is another key concern. In 2013, a series of leaks by former contractor Edward Snowden revealed that the National Security Agency (NSA) had been gathering data from giant cloud providers for surveillance purposes for years. For many organizations, businesses, and corporations, these revelations prompted new questions about security policies, working practices, and data availability when it came to cloud computing. In several countries, consumer and privacy groups called for stronger safeguards against government surveillance and online data gathering as well as fair and transparent rules regarding data access.

Margaret Haerens

Further Reading

Griffith, Eric. 2013. "What Is Cloud Computing?" *PC Mag* (March 13). http://www.pcmag.com/article2/0,2817,2372163,00.asp. Accessed March 14, 2015.

Metz, Cade. 2013. "The World Is Wary of American Cloud Computing, but It Always Was." *Wired* (December 30). http://www.wired.com/2013/12/cloud-us/. Accessed September 18, 2015.

Passary, Sumit. 2014. "Cloud Computing Is the Future but Not If Security Problems Persist." *Tech Times* (June 15). http://www.techtimes.com/articles/8449/20140615/cloud-computing-is-the-future-but-not-if-security-problems-persist.htm. Accessed March 15, 2015.

Pearce, Nathan. 2014. "Can Cloud Computing Overcome Its Crisis of Confidence?" *The Guardian* (February 18). http://www.theguardian.com/media-network/media-network-blog/2014/feb/18/cloud-computing-nsa-privacy-breaches-crisis-confidence. Accessed March 15, 2015.

Communications Assistance for Law Enforcement Act (CALEA)

The Communications Assistance for Law Enforcement Act (CALEA) is a federal law passed in 1994 that created a legal obligation for all private telecommunications carriers to ensure that all of their equipment and networks have the capability to conduct wiretaps if ordered to do so by the appropriate law enforcement agencies. The law did not change the limitations and restrictions on wiretapping procedures originally set out in 1968 by Title III of the Omnibus Crime Control and Safe Streets Act and subsequently amended by other statutes, such as the Electronic Communications and Privacy Act of 1986 and the USA PATRIOT Act. CALEA is codified at 47 U.S.C. 1001–1010.

CALEA was a significant milestone in the evolution of the relationship between law enforcement agencies conducting wiretaps and the telecommunications industry carrying out the communications the agencies seek to intercept. In this context, a wiretap is defined as an interception of a communications' content as well as pen registers and trap and trace devices that seek to trace the destination of outgoing and incoming calls. In 1969, immediately after Congress set out the rules governing wiretapping procedures, a telecommunications company refused to assist the Federal Bureau of Investigation (FBI) in conducting a wiretapping operation. After the legality of this refusal was upheld by a federal appellate court, Congress

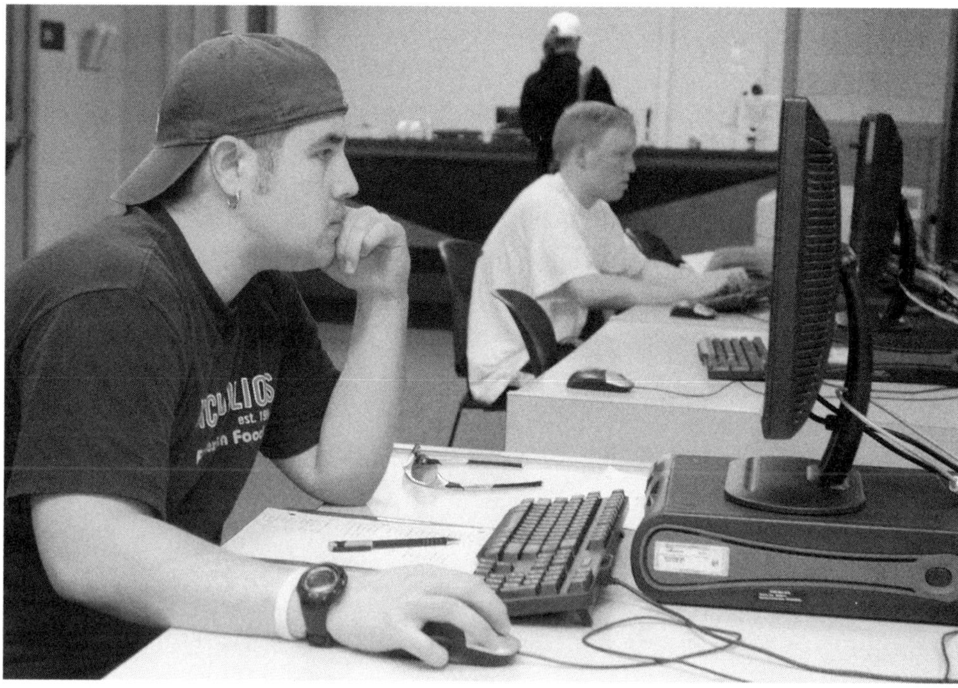

A student at the University of Missouri works on a computer at the university's computer lab on the Columbia campus, July 2006. In 2005, the Federal Communications Commission expanded the Communications Assistance for Law Enforcement Act (CALEA) to allow easier access to e-mails and phone calls on campus computers as a part of antiterrorist efforts. (AP Photo/L.G. Patterson)

amended the federal wiretapping statute to require all telecommunications companies to assist law enforcement with any legal wiretapping activity. The new amendment did not create any duty to these private companies to change or upgrade their equipment or networks, primarily because the existing technology used by the telecommunications companies at the time was able to adequately meet the needs of law enforcement officials when they sought to conduct wiretaps.

This began to change during the revolution of telecommunications technology in the 1980s and early 1990s. This revolution included the gradual switch from analog to digital telephony and the dramatic increase in the use of cellular telephones. These emerging technologies posed new challenges to law enforcement agencies seeking to wiretap telephone communications. For example, many cellular phone networks had a limited capacity to conduct multiple wiretaps at the same time, while speed dialing and voice dialing features sometimes made it impossible to trace the number that had been dialed.

In response, Congress passed CALEA, which required telecommunications companies to retrofit all of their equipment and networks to ensure that the companies could, upon request, isolate and deliver to law enforcement the content of communications as well as the destination and origin of all phone calls for a target telephone. The law also authorized payments to the private companies to reimburse them for the costs of these upgrades, and the companies were given four years to comply with the CALEA requirements.

On August 5, 2005, the Federal Communications Commission (FCC) issued new rules, expanding CALEA's reach to include certain broadband and voice-over Internet protocol (IP) services, even though such networks fall outside the traditional definition of telecommunication carrier. The FCC argued that these networks were increasingly being used as a replacement for the local telephone usage, and so CALEA requirements had to be imposed in order to maintain the ability of law enforcement to conduct effective wiretaps. This move was not without controversy, as numerous privacy groups claimed that CALEA did not and should not be used to cover Internet communications.

Since that time, the FBI and other law enforcement and national security entities have proposed expanding CALEA's reach yet again, by extending its backdoor wiretapping authority to include all online communications services and by establishing mechanisms to levy financial penalties on noncompliant companies. These proposals are fiercely opposed by privacy rights groups like the Electronic Frontier Foundation, which claims that "any government mandate that communications software or services include [CALEA-mandated] backdoors will take away not only developers' right to innovate, but also average users' right to protect their privacy and speak anonymously through the technologies of their choice."

Ric Simmons

Further Reading

Dempsey, James X. 1997. "Communications Privacy in the Digital Age: Revitalizing the Federal Wiretap Laws to Enhance Privacy." *Albany Law Journal of Science and Technology* 8: 70–71.

Electronic Frontier Foundation. "CALEA: The Communications Assistance for Law Enforcement Act (CALEA) of 199." Electronic Frontier Foundation Web site. https://www.eff.org/issues/calea. Accessed March 25, 2015.

Froomkin, A. Michael. 2000. "The Death of Privacy?" *Stanford Law Review* 52: 1461–544.

Consent Searches

These searches, among the exceptions to the warrant requirement, are justified on the grounds that individuals may waive their Fourth Amendment rights. For a consent search to be valid, the consent must be voluntarily given by the individual affected or someone authorized by that person to control access to the place to be searched or the things to be seized.

The question of whether consent to a search is voluntary is determined from the "totality of all the circumstances," including any coercive police tactics and the personal characteristics of the subject giving the consent. A prosecutor seeking to rely upon consent to justify a warrantless search has the burden of proving that the consent was "in fact, freely and voluntarily given" and not the result of implicit or explicit coercion. More recently, the courts have asked, in determining voluntariness, if a reasonable person would feel free to refuse consent. Consent need not be given by the defendant in a criminal proceeding. For example, police may search a bedroom inhabited by two persons so long as they have consent from one of the inhabitants. In other words, the consent of one person who possesses common authority over the premises or effects is valid against the absent, non-consenting person with whom that authority is shared. Additionally, a reasonable belief by an officer that a person has authority to consent to a search—regardless of whether that person actually possesses such authority—is all that is necessary for such a search to be binding on the defendant. Numerous lower courts have held that a person who gives consent may withdraw that consent at any time. When consent is effectively withdrawn, police must discontinue searching.

Otis H. Stephens Jr. and Richard A. Glenn

Further Reading

Rutledge, Devallis. 2013. "Consent Searches: Extracting the Rules from 17 Supreme Court Decisions." *Police: The Law Enforcement Magazine* (February 5). http://www.policemag.com/channel/patrol/articles/2013/02/consent-searches.aspx. Accessed September 18, 2015.

Constitutional Protections

The U.S. Constitution establishes a minimum of privacy to which government officials may add but from which they may not subtract. Louis Brandeis and Samuel Warren, his coauthor and law partner, are generally credited with introducing privacy as a legal concept in their heralded "Right to Privacy" article, published in 1890 in the *Harvard Law Review*. That article focused on tort law, but decades later a Supreme Court justice Brandeis spoke grandly of a constitutional ". . . right to be let alone" in *Olmstead v. U.S.*, 277 U.S. 438 (1928).

Consistent with Brandeis's proclamation, many popular accounts speak of a unitary constitutional right of privacy. Supreme Court jurisprudence since Brandeis

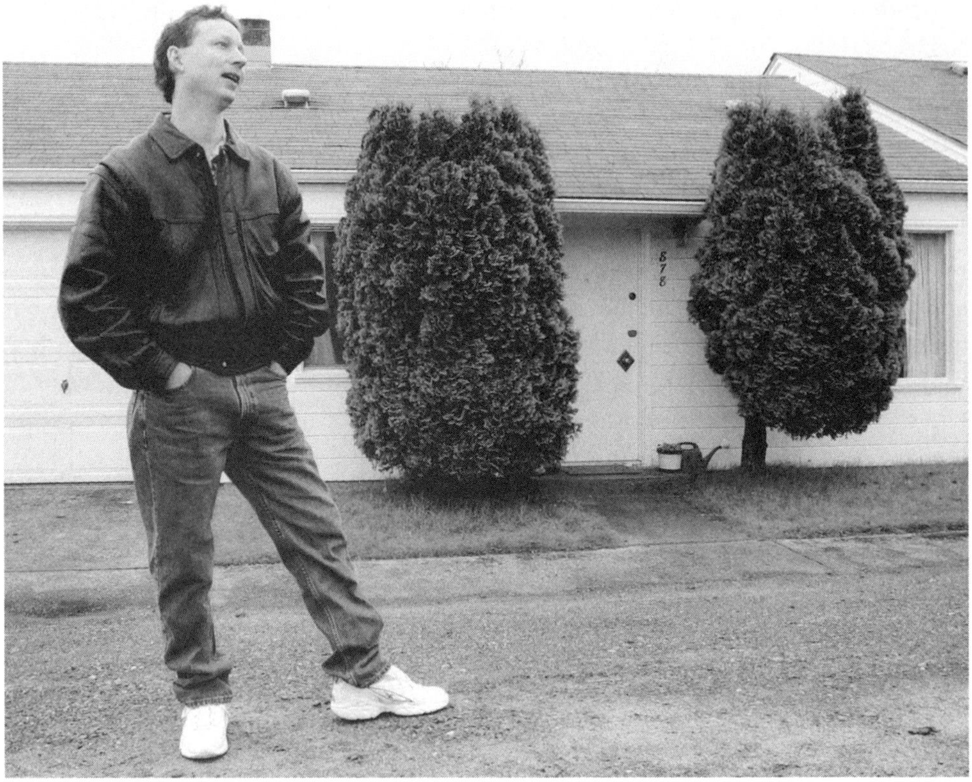

Danny Lee Kyllo stands in front of the house in Florence, Oregon, February 2001, where narcotics agents, using a thermal imaging device, burst in on him to find 100 marijuana plants growing in the attic. The U.S. Supreme Court ruled 5–4 in June 2001 that the thermal imaging of Kyllo's home constituted a search under the Fourth Amendment. (AP Photo)

makes it more accurate and helpful to understand constitutional privacy initially in terms of two distinct sets of rights. One set, which includes the Fourth Amendment's ban against unreasonable searches and seizures, protects what may be called informational privacy and restricts the government's access to information about an individual. Another set of rights, which includes the un-enumerated right of privacy at stake in the Court's highly publicized and controversial abortion decisions, protects individual autonomy by giving individuals freedom to make certain decisions about the course of their lives.

It is true that informational privacy and individual autonomy both entail an individual's "right to be let alone" by the government. But the scope, constitutional basis, and debates over these two principles are sufficiently distinct as to merit separate discussion.

I. Informational Privacy

The Constitution protects informational privacy by regulating the means by which the government collects information. The Fourth Amendment bans unreasonable searches and seizures and the Fifth Amendment's privilege against self-incrimination precludes any person from being "compelled in a criminal case to be a witness against himself."

At the outset, it is important to distinguish the method at work in these provisions from another common method, which protects privacy by focusing on the information's subject matter. A legal regime might choose to designate certain subjects as inherently private and as presumptively beyond government's purview. The government could be prohibited or restricted from accessing or using information about, for instance, an individual's medical treatment, sexual orientation, or religious affiliation. Much is to be said in favor of such an approach. Information pertaining to such highly personal subjects is frequently irrelevant to any legitimate public concern, its public disclosure can be extremely damaging to the individual, and even the threat of disclosure can deter desirable conduct. Although some state and federal privacy laws adopt the approach of designating private subject matters, the Constitution's provisions concerning informational privacy do not.

The Constitution instead restricts the means by which information about any subject may be collected. Provided that it is not obtained through proscribed means, the government may use information everyone would regard as presumptively private. That an individual has a highly embarrassing scar in an intimate area is private in its subject matter. But when the government learns about this fact from the voluntary statement of a third-party witness, the Constitution's protections of informational privacy do not bar the government from using this fact. Conversely, the government may not obtain through proscribed means information that no one would regard as private in its subject matter. The privilege against self-incrimination, for example, permits a criminal suspect to refuse to answer whether she murdered another person on a public street in broad daylight.

It is not clear that any single coherent theory underlies the Constitution's protections of informational privacy. Consider the Fifth Amendment's privilege against self-incrimination. On one hand, the privilege exists because of doubts about the truthfulness of statements obtained through coercion. Even if this is the Fifth Amendment's rationale, it cannot explain the Fourth Amendment. The Fourth Amendment does not rest on doubts over whether, for example, the illegal drugs stashed in an individual's kitchen drawer belong to that individual or whether an individual's authentic beliefs are expressed in the private diary found on the individual's bed stand. If anything, the information's private location actually tends to strengthen rather than weaken its reliability.

It is also problematic to link constitutional protections of informational privacy with the notion that certain subjects are inherently private. The link cannot be a direct one. As mentioned above, constitutional protections restrict access to public information and permit access to private information. As an indirect protection of private subject matters, informational privacy is not very effective. Informational privacy, by itself, permits the government to regulate any subject matter. By regulating subject matters that might reasonably be thought private, the government can generate the justification needed to overcome Fourth Amendment barriers to accessing private areas. The government can obtain information from sources other than a search, a seizure, or compelled statement of a suspect. It may then use such information to establish the probable cause for a violation of law in question that has occurred and, if necessary, acquire a warrant to undertake a search or seizure or make an arrest.

The home is the archetypal private place and is explicitly mentioned in the Third and Fourth Amendments. The government nonetheless remains able to and does enforce prohibitions against violence and abuse in the home, for instance, and this authority is relatively uncontroversial. Informational privacy likewise does not create an effective barrier against regulation of activity occurring in the home that might reasonably be thought private. Consequently, it is difficult to understand the Fourth Amendment's restrictions on gathering information from homes as an indirect means of protecting the private activities that occur there.

If the Fourth Amendment indeed does aim to protect private subject matters, then it would seem that the government must be precluded from regulating certain private matters altogether. The Fourth Amendment, however, has not been so interpreted.

History

Instead of resorting to a unifying theoretical rationale, courts sometimes interpret the Constitution's protections in light of the particular governmental abuses the founders had in mind.

The Fourth Amendment grew out of the colonists' antipathy for the writs of assistance used by the British to enforce revenue laws. These court-issued writs authorized British officials to enter any house or other place to search for and seize prohibited and untaxed goods. Once issued, a writ remained in force throughout the lifetime of the sovereign and six months thereafter.

Construed narrowly as confined to this abuse, the Fourth Amendment condemns only unlimited court-authorized searches. The Fourth Amendment's text explicitly addresses this abuse, requiring that warrants be based "upon probable cause, supported by Oath or affirmation, and particularly describing the place to be searched, and the persons or things to be seized." The first clause of the Fourth Amendment, however, does not confine itself to judicially authorized searches and seizures and speaks more generally of the people's right to be free of "unreasonable searches and seizures . . ." The Supreme Court thus has interpreted the amendment as addressing both warrantless and warrant-based searches and seizures.

The privilege against self-incrimination found in the Fifth Amendment developed as a reaction to the perceived excesses of the British Courts of the Star Chamber, which existed from 1487 to 1641. These courts required that the accused answer any and all questions put to it, and they eventually became a vehicle for the suppression of political dissent.

By the 18th century, British law had rejected the inquisitorial practice of the Star Chamber in favor of the principle that no man should be compelled to accuse himself. Laws were passed, which forbade the use of testimony compelled during trial or obtained before trial through torture. This attitude carried over to the colonies. Nine state constitutions already contained a privilege against self-incrimination when the Fifth Amendment became law in 1791.

In determining the scope of the rights at stake as well as the remedies available for their violation, the Supreme Court has taken explicit account of governmental needs and sought to strike a workable balance between those needs and informational privacy. Whether it has struck the appropriate balance and even used the right methodology for doing so are matters of controversy. The Court's work has been criticized for giving both too much and too little weight to the interest in protecting informational privacy. In the limited space here, only the most basic features of legal doctrine can be summarized. It is important to recognize that the Fourth Amendment and the privilege against self-incrimination apply to governmental officials. They offer no protection whatsoever against invasions of privacy perpetrated by private persons acting at their own behest.

The Fourth Amendment applies only to searches and seizures. In deciding what this phrase comprehends, the Supreme Court generally has asked whether the governmental action frustrates an expectation of privacy that society regards as reasonable. Of course, persons have a justifiable expectation of privacy in the home so that, absent consent, entry into it and the area close by constitutes a search. Persons also have a justifiable expectation in the freedom of movement so that an arrest constitutes a seizure.

One interesting set of issues concerns the use of technology to discern activities in the home. In *Kyllo v. United States*, 533 U.S. 27 (2001), the Supreme Court held that thermal imaging of a home constitutes a search. The Court declared that the use of technology to access information that could not otherwise be obtained without entry into the home constitutes a search, at least when the technology is not in widespread use. It also constitutes a search to eavesdrop electronically on phone conversations originating in the home or even a public phone booth unless one party to the conversation has consented.

In contrast, the Supreme Court has also held that it does not constitute a search for law enforcement personnel to obtain a person's bank records, rummage through her trash, use a pen register that records the phone numbers she has called, or track electronically the location of an automobile driven on public streets. The reasoning of these cases is that because the person has made this information accessible to third parties she has no protectable expectation of privacy regarding that information.

Searches and seizures require justification. The Fourth Amendment's text provides that searches and seizures must be reasonable and that warrants may not be issued without probable cause. As some scholars have argued, this may be read to impose a general requirement of reasonableness and then to specify that reasonableness necessitates a probable cause when a warrant is obtained. So read, the amendment generally requires neither a warrant nor a probable cause for warrantless searches and seizures. The Supreme Court nonetheless has interpreted a probable cause and a warrant as the general benchmark of reasonableness across the board, not just for warrant searches and seizures. The amendment thus embodies a preference for a warrant, which must issue from a neutral magistrate or judge and contains a particularized description of its scope. A warrantless search or seizure may be constitutional only if fits into one of the exceptions that the Court has recognized.

Measured in terms of the real-world conduct they encompass, the exceptions are broad. For instance, warrants are not required of searches and seizures involving automobiles, brief investigatory stops, or exigent circumstances involving a risk of flight or destruction of evidence.

For both warrant-based and warrantless searches, the Fourth Amendment generally requires a probable cause. As with the warrant requirement, the Supreme Court has created exceptions. Some searches and seizures, such as administrative searches of closely regulated businesses and investigatory stops, require only reasonable suspicion. Lesser justification is permissible, the Supreme Court has concluded, in virtue of the more minimal intrusion into privacy or the atypical governmental interests at stake. In a few areas, the Court has dispensed with a requirement of individualized suspicion altogether. For instance, it has upheld random stops near the border to check for aliens who have entered illegally, roadside sobriety checkpoints to prevent drunk driving, and drug testing unrelated to law enforcement in certain school and employment contexts.

A person who believes him or herself to be the victim of Fourth Amendment violations has two principal remedies available. First, if he or she has been charged with crime, evidence obtained as a result of the violation may be excluded. This exclusionary rule has precipitated much criticism due to its effect of withholding relevant evidence of guilt and possibly letting the guilty go free. The Supreme Court has defended the rule as necessary to deter violations or, to put the point somewhat differently, to eliminate an incentive to violate that would otherwise exist. In its core application, the rule precludes the prosecution from introducing illegally obtained evidence as part of its case. Outside of this application, the Supreme Court has established a number of exceptions to rule premised on a judgment that the rule would impose costs in excess of any deterrent benefits in those applications. The exclusionary rule does not apply, for instance, when evidence has been obtained in good-faith reliance on a warrant, when the prosecution seeks to impeach the accused's own trial testimony, or in grand jury and deportation proceedings.

Second, a victim may sue governmental officials responsible for a Fourth Amendment violation for money damages. Litigants seeking such damages must surmount significant hurdles. As a practical matter, a person who in fact is guilty of criminal wrongdoing has great difficulty in winning jury sympathy. In addition, individual governmental officials are legally immune from damage liability unless it can be shown that the law concerning the legality of their conduct was so specific and clearly established that no reasonable person could view their conduct as legitimate.

The Fifth Amendment privilege against self-incrimination prohibits civil and criminal courts from requiring a witness to answer questions that might incriminate her. It also prohibits law enforcement authorities from using coercion to induce a suspect to confess involuntarily. In *Miranda v. Arizona*, 384 U.S. 436 (1966), the Supreme Court concluded that interrogation while in police custody is inherently coercive. To dispel the inherent coercion, the suspect must be informed of his right not to answer questions and to have an attorney if he so desires.

In 2010, however, the Court ruled in *Berghuis v. Thompkins* in an acrimonious 5–4 decision that criminal suspects who do not explicitly invoke their right to remain silent in effect are waiving that right. "A suspect who has received and understood the Miranda warnings, and has not invoked his Miranda rights, waives the right to remain silent by making an uncoerced statement to police," said the Court's majority opinion, written by Justice Anthony Kennedy. In her dissent, Sonia Sotomayor castigated the decision as a severe blow to constitutional protections against self-incrimination. "Criminal suspects must now unambiguously invoke their right to remain silent—which counterintuitively requires them to speak. [Under this decision], suspects will be legally presumed to have waived their rights even if they have given no clear expression of their intent to do so."

The degree to which the privilege protects privacy is limited by the rule that it does not generally allow documents to be withheld. The contents of documents, the Supreme Court has reasoned, are not testimonial in nature and the privilege does not preclude the government from requiring the disclosure of documents, presumably including even private diaries. The privilege permits documents to be withheld only when the government does not know of their existence so that the very act of production, in effect, would constitute an incriminating admission that they exist.

Remedies for violations of the privilege against self-incrimination are similar to those available for Fourth Amendment violations. Money damages may be recovered from the responsible officials subject to the same practical and legal obstacles present in the Fourth Amendment context. Evidence obtained as a result of a confession coerced in violation of the privilege against self-incrimination is subject to exclusion. Statements of the accused in violation of *Miranda* are excluded, but in contrast to the Fourth Amendment context, evidence derived from such statements—the so-called fruits of the violation—are not subject to automatic exclusion. If police illegally seize a map revealing the locus of the murder weapon, which the police then retrieve, the weapon would be subject to exclusion. But the weapon will not be excluded if a suspect reveals the weapon's locus in statements obtained in violation of *Miranda*.

The ongoing war on terror and technological developments raise new issues that the law of informational privacy inevitably will come to address. The war on terror implicates the relationship between informational privacy and national security. The Supreme Court has sought to accommodate the needs of law enforcement through the definition of searches and seizures and through the creation of exceptions to the warrant and probable cause requirements and the exclusionary rule. It is certainly possible that the Supreme Court will further relax normal Fourth Amendment requirements in the name of national security.

Technology threatens to shrink privacy in two sometimes overlapping ways. First, technologies such as electronic tracking, thermal imaging, face recognition, high resolution satellite photography, and information storage and retrieval greatly enhance government's ability to collect information. Second, Internet-based communication such as e-mail, list serves, chats, discussion boards, credit card transactions, and proliferating forms of social media (Facebook, Instagram, etc.) multiply the circumstances in which individuals reveal information about themselves to third parties in a way that may be stored and later accessed by the government. In other contexts, the Supreme Court has reasoned that by voluntarily disclosing information to a third party for one purpose individuals relinquish any legitimate expectation of privacy-respecting disclosure of the information to other third parties for other purposes. A mechanical application of this logic would imply that very little computer-based communication is subject to Fourth Amendment protection. The lower court case law and scholarly commentary is continuing to grapple with how to strike a constitutionally appropriate balance between privacy and governmental needs in a digital world that is evolving at rapid speed.

II. Individual Autonomy

In addition to limiting the government's access to information, the Constitution gives individuals a right to make certain choices about their lives. The First Amendment's protection of freedom of speech grants individuals a right to form and express their own beliefs. The First Amendment's protection of freedom of speech grants individuals a right to form and express their own beliefs and, according to the Supreme Court, implies a "freedom to associate and privacy in one's associations" (*NAACP v. Alabama*, 357 U.S. 449, 462 (1958)). The First Amendment's Religion Clause makes religious belief principally a matter for individuals, not the government, and gives them freedom to exercise their religion as well as freedom from governmental religious establishments. This entry will not focus on these First Amendment rights but will instead address the rights of autonomy the Supreme Court has recognized in the areas of sexuality and family life. It is these rights, which are not enumerated in the Constitution's text, that have come to dominate discussions of and controversies over constitutional privacy.

Like informational privacy, constitutionally protected areas of individual autonomy rely upon the principle of governmental noninterference. Autonomy, however, requires noninterference of significantly greater scope. Constitutional protections of informational privacy inhibit the government's access to certain sources of information. Yet they do not by themselves preclude the government from regulating any activity: Other sources of information remain available. The government may not enforce a criminal prohibition against abortion by coercing an individual to incriminate herself or by searching her home without a warrant for medical bills establishing that a suspect has had one. Insofar as the Constitution's protections of informational privacy are concerned, however, the government may enforce an abortion prohibition by securing the testimony of the physician who performed the abortion. In contrast, rights of autonomy preclude the government from prohibiting the decisions and actions within those rights. The Supreme Court's abortion decisions do not permit the government completely to prohibit women from choosing to have an early abortion.

In addition to denying the government the authority to regulate certain activities, autonomy implies a right of informational privacy as a corollary. Constitutional rights of informational privacy inhibit access to only certain sources of information. In contrast, rights of autonomy tend to render certain subjects of information off limits. Of course, the government may not use sources of information shielded by the Fourth Amendment and the Fifth Amendment privilege against self-incrimination to pry into activity protected by a right of autonomy. But a right autonomy also tends to foreclose inquiry through other sources of information as well. Because women have a constitutional right to abortion, the government may neither obtain a Fourth Amendment warrant nor question witnesses about such a choice unless it is relevant to some other subject that is a permissible object of government regulation. By tending to shield certain subjects from official inquiry, rights of autonomy create an umbrella of privacy that is larger than that established by the Fourth and Fifth Amendments.

In press accounts and popular discussion, one often hears that the constitutional right of privacy is a matter of some controversy. It is important to recognize that there is no controversy over the existence of constitutional protections of informational privacy, which derive almost entirely from the rights specified in the Constitution's text. The scope of these protections is a matter of interpretation and argument, to be sure. But no one challenges their very existence. Similarly, rights of autonomy are not in question insofar as they involve textually specified rights such as the First Amendment's protections of freedom of speech and religion.

In contrast, there is serious controversy over the existence of rights of autonomy that do not derive from any specific right found in the Constitution's text. In its decisions pertaining to contraception, abortion, and homosexuality, the Supreme Court has affirmed rights of individual autonomy that go considerably beyond textually specified rights.

In his majority opinion in *Griswold v. Connecticut*, 381 U.S. 479 (1965), Justice Douglas declared that a constitutional zone of privacy derives indirectly from textually specified guarantees found in the First, Third, Fourth, and Fifth Amendments. These specific guarantees, Justice Douglas opined, "have penumbras, formed by [their] emanations."

In more recent decisions, the Court has not relied upon Justice Douglas's concept of a penumbral right. Instead, it has located rights of autonomy in the Due Process Clause of the Fourteenth Amendment. These rights cannot be derived even indirectly from the text of that clause, which provides that "no State shall deprive any person of life, liberty, or property without due process of law." The text evinces a concern for the process alone. It permits the government to deprive individuals of what is important to them, including life itself, as long as the government provides the process that is due. The Court nonetheless has looked beyond the purely procedural orientation of the Due Process Clause's text to incorporate a concept of ordered liberty, encompassing an individual's right to control certain areas of her life.

In doing so, it has unleashed a vigorous and interesting debate over the existence of un-enumerated constitutional rights generally. The Court's critics maintain the Constitution's text and history provide no warrant for such rights. In their view, the justices who recognize such rights necessarily rely upon their own subjective political and philosophical predilections and engage in illegitimate judicial legislation.

Those who defend the existence of un-enumerated rights can point to the text and history of the Ninth Amendment and the Privileges and Immunities Clause of the Fourteenth Amendment. The Ninth Amendment provides that "the enumeration in the Constitution, of certain rights, shall not be construed to deny or disparage other retained by the people." Its drafting and ratification history suggest that it affirms the existence of unspecified rights. In the debates over ratification of the original Constitution, the antifederalists had argued that the original Constitution should not be ratified because, unlike state constitutions, it did not contain a listing of protected individual rights. In response, the federalists maintained that any such listing would be dangerous. A list, they argued, inevitably would be incomplete and give rise to an inference that unlisted rights are unprotected. The most natural reading of the Ninth Amendment is that it guards against this objectionable inference.

The Privileges and Immunities Clause of the Fourteenth Amendment also can be seen to recognize the existence of constitutional rights going beyond those specifically enumerated in the text. That clause prohibits states from abridging "the privileges or immunities of citizens of the United States" but does not specify those privileges. Senator Jacob Howard, who served as the Fourteenth Amendment's floor manager in the Senate, evidently understood the clause to protect rights not specifically described in the Constitution's text. He declared that the protected privileges encompass "fundamental rights lying at the basis of society," whose content would be "discussed and adjudicated when they should happen practically to arise." Representative John A. Bingham, the principal author of that part of the Fourteenth Amendment containing the Privileges and Immunities Clause, shared this understanding. He told that the "privileges and immunities of citizens of the United States are chiefly defined in the first eight amendments to the Constitution." In other words, the protected privileges include but are not limited to the rights the text enumerates. These views were rooted in natural law philosophy. There were undoubtedly physical laws regulating the universe that scientists had not yet specified but, with scientific progress, would so specify in future. So the moral laws regulating the universe also were incompletely understood. It was important to leave room for progress in our understanding of those and not to forever freeze the list of fundamental rights.

Those who oppose the existence of un-enumerated rights offer alternative explanations of these provisions. The Ninth Amendment, they argue, means only that states remain free to establish rights beyond those protected in the federal constitution as a matter of their own law. As for the Privileges and Immunities Clause of the Fourteenth Amendment, they contend that Senator Howard and Representative Bingham's natural law view was not widely shared enough to give it the force of law.

Although it has chosen the Due Process Clause rather than the Privileges or Immunities Clause or the Ninth Amendment as their source, the Supreme Court has affirmed the existence of un-enumerated constitutional rights in general and the rights of personal autonomy in particular. In so doing, it has opened the door to a controversy over the determination of their scope. Once the existence of un-enumerated rights or a right of autonomy is conceded, how does or should the Supreme Court determine what it encompasses? It obviously cannot determine the scope of an un-enumerated right simply by consulting the Constitution's text. Nor would many modern thinkers contend that fundamental rights are awaiting discovery in a natural moral order accessible through reason or intuition.

In fixing the scope of the un-enumerated right of autonomy, the Supreme Court has used different approaches. Some cases purport to rely on societal tradition. In *Washington v. Glucksberg*, 521 U.S. 702 (1997), for instance, the Court insisted that "fundamental rights and liberties [be] . . . 'deeply rooted in this Nation's history and tradition'. . . ." The Court declined to recognize a fundamental right to physician-assisted suicide, finding no established tradition in support of this practice. The emphasis on tradition often is linked with unease with un-enumerated rights and reflects a strategy for limiting their import. Opponents of un-enumerated rights, such as Justice Antonin Scalia, point to the danger that the unelected Supreme Court justices will give their own subjective notions the force of constitutional law. They seek to limit judicial subjectivity by requiring that any claimed right find overwhelming support in the enactments of legislatures and judicial decisions over the course of time. Using this strategy, Justice Scalia consistently has rejected appeals to un-enumerated rights.

The Supreme Court has not always relied upon tradition, particularly when it has expanded the scope of enumerated rights of autonomy. In *Roe v. Wade*, 410 U.S. 113 (1973), for instance, the Court held that constitutional privacy gives women a right to choose an abortion despite acknowledging that its decision conflicted with laws then in force in a majority of the states. In striking down Texas's law prohibiting consensual adult homosexual sodomy, the Court spoke of an "emerging awareness" that such laws impermissibly invade the control of adults over their private sex lives. It did not, however, purport to derive its holding from tradition. In fact, *Lawrence v. Texas*, 539 U.S. 558 (2003), expressly overrules *Bowers v. Hardwick*, 478 U.S. 186 (1986), an earlier decision that had rejected a claimed constitutional right to consensual homosexual intimacy due to the lack of a supporting societal tradition.

When it does not place exclusive reliance upon tradition, the Supreme Court has referred to its past decisions and the principles it has identified as standing behind them. The Court has not fashioned any precise rules or principles. Its explanations variously invoke the life-shaping character of the choice at stake, its quasi-religious nature, and the absence of demonstrable harm to others. The Court even has relied upon decisions of foreign courts as support. The phrase "reasoned judgment," which some justices have used, captures the imprecision of the method at work.

The uncertain scope of and rationale for its decisions establishing new rights has fueled charges that the Court has engaged in law creation rather than interpretation. It is no doubt true that the Court's cases are susceptible to multiple readings and give the justices a fairly wide berth. However, a method based upon societal tradition likewise gives the Court great latitude. The justices often may select from competing traditions. For example, long-standing proscriptions of sodomy may exist alongside an established practice of nonenforcement and a more general tradition of governmental noninvolvement in the sex lives of consenting adults. The justices' choice of which tradition to emphasize is not itself guided by tradition. It instead can be seen to reflect an undisclosed view of the desirability of the particular right in question or the doctrine of un-enumerated rights. In short, the choice whether to recognize any particular autonomy right or un-enumerated rights generally is not dictated by the Constitution's text or history. It inevitably engages the justices' philosophical beliefs concerning the powers of the government relative to the individual, the role of judicial relative to the legislature and executive branches, and the degree to which government regulation may be based upon religion.

While the Supreme Court's use of an un-enumerated right of autonomy traces back to the 19th century, the focus of the right has shifted from economic to personal matters. In a series of cases in the late 19th and early 20th century, the Court read a kind of economic libertarianism into the Fourteenth Amendment's Due Process Clause. That clause, the Court held, affords strong, although not absolute, protection to an individual's liberty to contract freely with others. It invoked this right of freedom of contract largely against economic regulation, using it to invalidate numerous measures to protect workers, women, and children. In *Lochner v. New York*, 198 U.S. 45 (1905), for instance, the Court struck down a New York ordinance limiting the number of hours bakers could work on the grounds that it violated the liberty of bakers and bakery owners to contract freely.

In the mid-1930s, the Court retreated from the *Lochner*-era doctrine. But the Supreme Court did not forever abandon the idea of an un-enumerated right of autonomy. Beginning in the 1960s, it infused this idea with new content, focusing on rights pertaining to personhood and family life rather than business and property.

This evolution from rights of property to personhood is illustrated by the contrast between the fate of two *Lochner* era decisions and that of *Lochner* itself. In *Meyer v. Nebraska*, 262 U.S. 390 (1923), the Supreme Court overturned a Nebraska law that prohibited the teaching of German in schools. The other decision, *Pierce v. Society of Sisters*, 268 U.S. 510 (1925), struck down an Oregon statute prohibiting parents from sending their children to private schools. Consistent with the general tenor of the *Lochner* era, the *Pierce* Court stressed the property right of private schools to deal freely with customers. The Supreme Court continues to cite *Meyer* and *Pierce* with approval. Their underlying rationale, however, has been subtly recast to accord with modern jurisprudential sensibilities. Instead of focusing on the rights of teachers and schools to sell their wares in a free market, the modern Court has focused on language in those decisions that speak of parents' liberty to direct their children's upbringing. By contrast, the result in *Lochner* could not be explained on the basis of an individual's right to make decisions of a deeply personal nature pertaining to family or self. The result in *Lochner* consequently is no longer regarded as good law and the government now may regulate wages and working conditions without violating a constitutional right of autonomy.

According to Supreme Court case law, the Constitution creates a zone of autonomy that is not limited to and does not derive from the rights specified in the text. In that zone, the government may not dictate the outcome of certain key decisions pertaining to personhood and family life. These broad brush statements conceal considerable diversity in cases over which rights are found in this zone, their basis and scope, and the degree to which the government may impose restrictions.

The Supreme Court long has recognized a fundamental right on the part of parents to direct the upbringing of their children. During the *Lochner* era, it relied upon this right to strike down laws prohibiting parents from sending their children to private schools and authorizing them to be taught foreign languages. More recently, it overturned a state court decision that, without giving any deference to parental objections, had granted grandparents a right to visit children.

Under the Supreme Court precedent, individuals also have a right to decide whether to become parents in the first instance. The Court first recognized a right on the part of married couples to obtain contraceptives and later extended the right to unmarried persons. A much more dramatic extension of the right came with the landmark decision in *Roe v. Wade*, which holds that women have a constitutional right to choose an abortion. Under *Roe's* trimester framework, the government may not regulate abortion as such in the first trimester, may impose only those restrictions that are strictly necessary to promote maternal health in the second trimester, and may generally prohibit abortion altogether after the fetus becomes viable. In *Planned Parenthood v. Casey*, 505 U.S. 833 (1992), the justices by a narrow 5–4 majority reaffirmed *Roe's* central holding that the government may not prohibit abortion altogether before fetal viability. The crucial plurality opinion jointly authored by three justices modified *Roe's* framework in a way that gives the government greater regulatory leeway. So long as it does not unduly burden the right to an abortion, the government may regulate throughout the pregnancy to promote maternal health and to provide pregnant women with truthful information designed to persuade them to choose childbirth over abortion.

Another aspect of what might be described as the right to define one's family is the choice of partner. *Loving v. Virginia,* 388 U.S. 1 (1967), invalidated a Virginia miscegenation statute forbidding persons of different races from marrying. In addition to holding the explicit racial classification a violation of equal protection, the Supreme Court concluded that it violated an un-enumerated due process right to marry. This "fundamental freedom," the Court reasoned, may not be denied on "so unsupportable a basis as" race. More recently, the Court has recognized a right on the part of homosexuals to choose intimate partners and engage in sexual intimacy. *Lawrence v. Texas* overturned a criminal prohibition against consensual homosexual sodomy in the home. Overruling a prior case that had refused to locate such conduct within a fundamental right, the Supreme Court spoke of the liberty of all individuals to choose their personal bonds and accompanying sexual intimacies. The government may not use the criminal law to demean homosexuals for making such choices.

The other prominent issue, which lower courts have begun to address with conflicting results, is whether same-sex couples may claim a constitutional right to marry. One issue is whether laws prohibiting such marriages violate the Equal Protection Clause of the Fourteenth Amendment by unjustifiably discriminating on the basis of homosexuality. The other issue, which is relevant here, concerns whether such laws violate an un-enumerated right of autonomy. *Lawrence v. Texas* and *Loving v. Virginia* furnish considerable support for holding that all adults have a constitutional right to choose their marital partners. A number of the attributes that have prompted the Court to include a choice within a constitutionally protected zone of autonomy are present: The choice involves family; it has a strong bearing on the direction of one's long-term future; a choice to marry a person of the same sex does not inflict any direct or immediate harm on others; and the reasons for denying such a choice are largely religious at the bottom. On the other hand, a tradition-based approach easily could lead the justices to conclude that same-sex marriage is not within a constitutionally protected zone of autonomy.

The legal landscape has changed dramatically regarding this issue since 2012, when President Barack Obama became the first president to express support for same-sex marriage. In *Windsor v. United States* (2013), the Supreme Court struck down Section 3 of the so-called Defense of Marriage Act, a 1996 law that outlawed gay marriage. Same-sex marriage was subsequently legalized in numerous states as lower courts ruled that state bans on gay marriage were unconstitutional. A final decision on the legality and constitutionality of same-sex marriage is expected by the Supreme Court in 2015. The Court could issue a ruling that leaves the issue in the hands of individual states, but many legal experts predict that the decision will legalize gay marriage nationwide.

Finally, the Supreme Court has begun to address whether constitutional protected autonomy includes a right to die. Its cases suggest that while there is some right to voluntary passive euthanasia (the withdrawal or withholding of medical treatment) there is essentially no right to physician-assisted suicide (the provision of the means to end the life of the patient by her physician).

The Supreme Court's case law is not a model of clarity or consistency. Whereas the right to die cases view constitutional autonomy as defined by societal tradition, the cases pertaining to abortion and sexuality do not. In affirming the existence of autonomy rights not based upon tradition, the Court has appealed to a variety of rationales. The cases also vary widely concerning the degree of protection that un-enumerated rights receive. Constitutional analysis typically distinguishes between fundamental and nonfundamental rights. Restrictions on nonfundamental rights receive strict scrutiny. Under this demanding standard of judicial review, regulation survives only if the justices make their own independent determination that it is strictly necessary to further a compelling interest Although *Roe v. Wade* used strict scrutiny, the Court now uses an undue burden standard in its abortion cases. This test deliberately gives the government more regulatory freedom than does strict scrutiny. In addressing regulation of voluntary passive euthanasia and parental rights, the Court has been vague about the standard of review. The Court's opinion in *Lawrence v. Texas* even uses the language of the highly deferential rational basis test applicable to nonfundamental rights.

The existence and scope of an un-enumerated right of autonomy has been a source of political controversy in significant measure because of its connection with abortion. It received attention during the presidential elections and has provided a conspicuous backdrop for presidential appointments and Senate confirmation hearings. It seems quite unlikely that a majority of the justices will repudiate the existence of such a right altogether and overrule established precedents such as *Griswold v. Connecticut* and *Meyer v. Nebraska*. The question for the future is whether a majority of justices will conceive of the right so narrowly that it lacks contemporary significance.

Thomas G. Stacy

Further Reading

Bennett, Colin J., and Grant, Rebecca., eds. 1999. *Visions of Privacy*. Toronto: University of Toronto Press.

Brinn, David. 1999. *The Transparent Society*. New York: Perseus.

Goldberg, Carole. 2002. *Terrorism and the Constitution: Sacrificing Civil Liberties in the Name of National Security*. New York: W.W. Norton.

Kerr, Orin S. 2005. "Searches and Seizures in a Digital World." *Harvard Law Review* 119: 531–79.

Levy, Leonard W. 1968. *Origins of the Fifth Amendment: The Privilege against Self-Incrimination*. New York: Macmillan.

Moore, Adam D. 2010. *Privacy Rights: Moral and Legal Foundations.* University Park, PA: Penn State University Press.
Rappaport, Aaron J. 2002. "Beyond Personhood and Autonomy: Moral Theory and the Premises of Privacy." *Utah Law Review* 441: 507.
Schulhofer, Stephen J. 2012. *More Essential than Ever: The Fourth Amendment in the Twenty-First Century.* New York: Oxford University Press.
Warren, Samuel D., and Louis D. Brandeis. 1890. "The Right to Privacy." *Harvard Law Review 4*: 193.

Crypto Wars

The term Crypto Wars refers to a period of legal challenges and conflict in the 1990s between the U.S. government and civil libertarians, academics, research firms, technology companies, and the public. The battle centered around the public's unfettered access to cryptography, the practice of transforming data into unreadable text for the purpose of private and protected transmission. Cryptography systems are employed to shield e-mail messages, corporate information, credit card data, and intelligence files from hackers, spies, and government agencies.

As Internet and telecommunications technology was advancing by leaps and bounds during the 1990s, electronic security, particularly the use of cryptographic algorithms, became essential in order to protect data. U.S. intelligence agencies, however, fought to gain access to strong cryptography in order to monitor digital threats and better protect the American public and corporations from cyber terrorism and large-scale fraud.

When the U.S. Ninth District Court of Appeals ruled in 1997 that the software source code was protected speech and that the government's attempt to limit the public's access to it was unconstitutional, the Crypto Wars were considered over. Since then, however, it has been revealed that the U.S. government is continuing to sabotage cryptography systems in order to guarantee that intelligence agencies have access to any encrypted transaction or communication in the world.

The origins of the Crypto Wars can be traced back to the 1970s, when the National Bureau of Standards (NBS) identified the need for government-wide standards for encrypting secure communications for the business and private sectors. The NBS subsequently solicited proposals from technology companies and academics to design a data encryption standard (DES). A research group at IBM designed the winning proposal, which was then published in the U.S. *Federal Register* on March 17, 1975. The DES spurred widespread interest in cryptology and digital communication.

Another development in the field was the creation of an algorithm, known as the asymmetric or public key, which allows users to more easily send communications along an insecure channel. Asymmetric keys are considered to be a significant advancement in cryptology and they helped to open up the field to academics, outside governments, research firms, and others interested in encrypting sensitive digital information.

The U.S. government, however, was not enthusiastic about the proliferation of encryption technology. It wanted to maintain access to all kinds of encrypted communication, citing an overriding national security interest. As computer and telecommunication technology exploded, leading to advancements in mobile communication and computing, the U.S. government also struggled to limit the public's access to strong encryption technologies. U.S. authorities began to treat cryptographic software as a munition, which meant it would be regulated under arms trafficking export laws.

In 1991, an American software engineer, Phil Zimmerman, released Pretty Good Privacy (PGP), an e-mail encryption package, on the Internet for free. It quickly became the most widely used encryption software in the world. It also made him the target of a government investigation as to whether Zimmerman's actions had violated U.S. export restrictions for cryptographic software. After three years, the investigation ended without an indictment for Zimmerman.

Another key battle in the Crypto Wars centered on the Clipper Chip, a small computer chip that could allow government intelligence agencies such as the National Security Agency (NSA) to decrypt and monitor encrypted communications from small consumer devices, such as mobile phones and other electronic communication devices. In 1993, the Clinton administration proposed that the Clipper Chip be inserted into every electronic communication device manufactured by U.S. technology firms or sold in the United States.

The backlash was immediate. Civil libertarian and privacy activists protested the government's proposal, arguing that it meant individuals would be subjected to increasing government surveillance. Technology companies and a number of prominent politicians also opposed the proposal, citing concerns over possible technical vulnerabilities as well as increased competition from foreign technology manufacturing companies, who would not be hobbled by such government intrusion. By 1996, the government had abandoned the Clipper Chip proposal and had relaxed export regulations on strong encryption. It seemed that intelligence officials had acknowledged and accepted the trend for open encryption systems.

A key 1997 court decision reinforced that trend. When the U.S. government prohibited Daniel Bernstein, a cryptologist and computer programmer, from publishing a paper on an encryption system that he had developed, he brought suit against the stringent U.S. export regulations on encryption. The court held that software source code was protected speech under the U.S. Constitution.

The Crypto Wars went into a period of dormancy after that ruling. In 2013, however, a series of leaks by former NSA contractor Edward Snowden revealed that U.S. intelligence authorities had aggressively resumed its efforts to exploit strong encryption systems in network communication technologies. The clandestine NSA program, known as Operation Bullrun, involved using supercomputers to break encrypted communication and access bank and medical records; collaborating between the NSA and technology companies to ensure access to strong encryption systems; and weakening encryption standards to more easily exploit secret transmissions.

The NSA and other U.S. government counterintelligence officials argued that programs such as Operation Bullrun were essential to counterterrorism efforts and foreign intelligence gathering. Critics of the program claimed that U.S. government efforts to undermine online security were a violation of online privacy and they made the Internet more vulnerable to criminal hacking, foreign espionage, and illegal surveillance. In light of the Snowden revelations, many technology firms and organizations reassessed their security and encryption processes to protect against government surveillance.

Margaret Haerens

Further Reading

Doctorow, Cory. 2014. "Crypto Wars Redux: Why the FBI's Desire to Unlock Your Private Life Must Be Resisted." *The Guardian* (October 9). http://www.theguardian.com/technology/2014/oct/09/crypto-wars-redux-why-the-fbis-desire-to-unlock-your-private-life-must-be-resisted. Accessed March 7, 2015.

Larson, Jeff, Nicole Perlroth, and Scott Shane. 2013. "Revealed: The NSA's Secret Campaign to Crack, Undermine Internet Security." *ProPublica* (September 5). http://www.propublica.org/article/the-nsas-secret-campaign-to-crack-undermine-internet-encryption. Accessed March 8, 2015.

Wilson, Andi, and Danielle Kehl. 2015. "Remembering the Lessons of the Crypto Wars." *New America* (February 12). http://www.newamerica.org/oti/remembering-the-lessons-of-the-crypto-wars/. Accessed March 7, 2015.

D

Data Brokers

Data brokers are, broadly generalized, companies that collect, sell, package, and analyze data. These kinds of companies, sometimes called "information resellers," have exerted profound influence on government surveillance activities in the United States.

For clarity, data brokers are not the large Internet companies and search engines of today; instead, they are defined more as commercial businesses that act as go-betweens for the purpose of selling or analyzing usually personally identifiable information about individuals to or for third parties. The collection, analysis, and direct sales of the information may be (and often is) invisible to the individuals the data describe, and data broker data may be sold to government and law enforcement. In recent history, data brokers have played a major role in subcontracting data for surveillance activities in the United States. The role of data brokers both historically and in today's surveillance environment is important to trace for these reasons.

Origins of Data Brokers

Data brokers have much of their origins in the marketing activities of the paper-based analog world. As the computer gained broader entry to the marketplace in the 1950s, the technology afforded much easier collection and tracking of information about people, and it created an explosion of new electronic databases that greatly facilitated rapid data analysis.

The types of information that early data brokers gathered tended to be focused on names of individuals, their home address, and other sales-oriented data such as what businesses they frequented. The early data broker companies would copy public information available in courthouses, sometimes by hand, and laboriously digitize it. Retail stores began to understand that they could make money by selling lists of their customers, information about their purchasing histories, and credit data. Magazine publishers also often sold information about their subscribers. By the 1960s, names were selling for one to three cents, and there were more than 250 companies in the business of buying and selling names on lists, according to journalist Vance Packard.

Two events—the increased use of the Social Security number (SSN) as an identifier and the development of zip codes—facilitated increased data broker sophistication in the 1960s. In 1962, the Internal Revenue Service (IRS) began using the SSN to identify people in its computers. Soon, the rest of the U.S. government followed suit. The SSN began its long, slow process of widespread use as a unique identification number in government and business. With the SSN, data brokers were able to disambiguate individuals with similar names. All of a sudden, the multiple Jane Smiths or John Smiths could be identified uniquely. This identification plus computerization assisted the trend of consolidation of small, regional data brokers into large companies that could identify individuals on a national basis.

After the introduction of zip codes in 1963, data broker technology advanced substantially. Instead of just lists of people and their addresses, direct mail marketing companies began to use zip code data to merge a variety of information sets, such as public records like census data, magazine subscription information, and purchasing information. This allowed companies to make assumptions about individuals, such as the kinds of books they might read, the foods they might eat, and possible political affiliations. This kind of geo-demographic analysis was systematized in the 1970s, when Jonathan Robbin created Potential Rating Index for Zip Markets (PRIZM). This system was one of the first to combine zip codes with census data, consumer surveys, and other information to target direct mailing materials.

By the 1980s, the regional credit bureaus had largely consolidated to three major national credit bureaus. TRW (known today as Experian), one of those national credit bureaus, was already compiling the names, addresses, and phone numbers of consumers and creating lists of consumers based on increasingly larger sets of combined information that was now available. Data brokers offered full profiles of people based on where they lived, what they bought, and the cars they drove. The trend in that time was to collect as much data as possible, merge it into a consumer profile, and use it for target marketing. With the advent of national credit bureaus, the use of this data became more systematized and widespread.

Evolution of Data Brokers

The arrival of the Internet transformed data broker activities. The amount of data increased exponentially, and the data analysis and real-time linking of databases grew much more sophisticated. By the late 1980s and early 1990s, data brokers could network troves of data and could conduct advanced artificial intelligence analysis on hundreds and sometimes thousands of bits of information about people. As time went on, data broker analysis could crunch through billions of records and assemble mosaics of people in near-real time. Eventually, data brokers were able to offer sophisticated predictive analysis of consumer behavior. This was a long way from the early sales of lists of consumers. Predictive analysis became an important aspect of the data broker business, with a focus on fraud prevention and detection of subtle anomalies in behavior that might signal problems. Most of this kind of analysis is highly sophisticated and created by networks of supercomputers.

Another change was the relationship between data brokers and the government. Data brokers such as Choicepoint, Acxiom, Lexis Nexis, and others were very active in the post-9/11 period, creating products specifically for government surveillance and antiterrorism use. Massive Web portals that allow for remote desktop searches about individuals are common today, but in that period they were just getting established.

The network of multiple rich databases, plus the remote access design that was refined in the post-9/11 years, is still in use today and has contributed greatly to the shape of the modern surveillance data flow.

The shift of the government to using databases held by nongovernment companies is significant legally and represents perhaps the most important evolution in data brokers and surveillance. Prior to 9/11, the federal government, by and large, had used data held in its own databases, or it had used databases of federal data subcontracted out under strict privacy guidelines, as per the law. But after 9/11, contracts worth millions of dollars were given to data brokers to supply the U.S. government with data held by the brokers themselves about individuals for surveillance purposes. Many federal law enforcement agencies such as the Federal Bureau of Investigation (FBI), National Security Agency (NSA), Secret Service, Transportation Security Administration (TSA), and DHS began to use data broker services. When the government began to use data broker data for surveillance activities, this represented a critical sea change in how government agencies handled data, and this change was controversial.

Modern Practices and Controversies

Currently, there is a sophisticated merging of public and private surveillance activities, and private (nongovernment) data broker information provides the data jet fuel for this activity. Biometric data like voice, video, images; purchase histories; credit histories; histories of whom people associate with; some online habits; travel history; and many other data points are now included in the data brew. These data are collected from many original sources and data feeds, collated through private data brokers, and then accessed by government via contracting arrangements for data use. Often, these data are "scored" by data brokers, which means that risk scores of various types can be associated with individuals. For example, data brokers can generate a terrorist risk score for a person, or a fraud risk score, among many other predictive scores relating to surveillance. The analysis today has become very sophisticated.

The underlying controversy around the way the U.S. government accesses and uses data broker information relates to the relative lack of regulation of this activity. When information about a person is held by the U.S. government in a federal database, the database is subject to a law called the Privacy Act of 1974. This law requires certain levels of accuracy in the data, among other protections such as a means to correct the data. But if the government subcontracts information from a data broker like Acxiom, and the information originated from Acxiom and not the government, then the Privacy Act does not apply and the data will not be covered by that law. Requirements for accuracy and protection of privacy and civil liberties do not have the same force of law in such situations.

In 2003, legal scholar Chris Hoofnagle noted these problems and described data brokers as "big brother's little helpers" in a paper that documented, via numerous government documents and contracts, how data brokers packaged material for the government's use, apart from government due process and privacy laws. In 2005, Robert O'Harrow documented how Acxiom and other data brokers assisted in designing a nongovernment-held network of data broker supercomputers, again pointing out that the network was not subject to the Privacy Act due to the way it was configured.

While some types of data brokers have been regulated—for example, credit bureaus have been regulated by the Fair Credit Reporting Act (FCRA) since the 1970s—the FCRA controls consumer use of credit reporting data, but it does not constrain government surveillance use of the same data. Broadly, a permissive legal structure is in place around surveillance use of data broker data.

As a result, there is scant regulation of the government's use of data broker information, as long as the government does not host the data base itself and as long as the government does not generate the data that is being held by the data broker. There are some exceptions to this, but they are primarily applicable to nonsurveillance-related government uses of data broker data. This is a key issue to understand, because most of the controversies around surveillance use of data about people that are collected, held, analyzed, and sold by data brokers largely stem from this baseline legal issue.

Accuracy of the data used in surveillance activities is an example of this. This issue has been most clearly visible in the screening of airline passengers by the Department of Homeland Security. Passenger screening has been a subject of ongoing controversy for several years. The full details of the system are still not fully publicly known, but O' Harrow chronicled the intense competition between data brokers for the TSA contract after 2001. What is known is that the program collects data about passengers and links the data with other sources of information to establish a risk score for each passenger, which the TSA uses to screen the passengers. Passengers have been put on the No Fly List incorrectly due to errors. These passengers can now get redress for that, but the horror stories of passengers who were incorrectly unable to fly due to errors are plentiful.

A related controversy exists around whether or not data that originate for marketing purposes are used for surveillance and law enforcement activities. Data collected for marketing purposes, such as databases of people who have purchased certain books, can contain many inaccuracies. The concern is that information with lower levels of accuracy could be making its way into potentially high-impact law enforcement databases used by the government. Related to this concern is the issue of what type of data will be accessible for surveillance purposes. As increased amounts of individuals' lives are captured digitally, the potential for government surveillance of the most personal and minute activities of daily life become a real possibility.

Access control to the information has also been controversial. Because of the lack of transparency about access and use of data broker databases by the government for surveillance purposes, it is impossible to know all of the instances when employees of data brokers or the government access the rich personal information improperly. There has been some documentation of unauthorized access, however. For example, two hackers were able to access Acxiom data—Daniel Baas accessed 20 million Acxiom profiles in 2003, and Scott Levine took over 8.2 gigabytes of consumer files around the same time. And ChoicePoint notified individuals that its database was used by a criminal ring in 2005.

Other key controversies are lack of choice about data collection and the shrinking of privacy in the public domain. One current example of this is Automated License Plate Readers (ALPR), which capture images of license plates and store the images in databases for analysis. When mapped out, the ALPR data can reveal home address, known associates, and detailed work and travel patterns, among other information. Data suppliers have collected billions of points of ALPR data nationally, and this information is subcontracted to law enforcement for surveillance and other law enforcement activities. Because people drive cars in public, they do not have a choice about the collection of the ALPR data—other than to not drive a car, which is not a desirable option for most people. While people who travel on airplanes largely understand why biometric face prints may be gathered at the border, capturing day-to-day car location information is not seen in the same way.

A variety of legal scholars and researchers have suggested reforms that would improve the balance of civil liberties with government access to data broker data.

One suggestion is to have the Privacy Act apply to all data, regardless of the source, if those data are used by government. In 2013, the General Accountability Office put limited rules in place for a government system that did just this. The GAO effort did not pertain to surveillance activities, but it was still widely viewed as an important precedent. Another suggested reform is to put in place a framework of rights that limits the collection of information by data brokers.

Pam Dixon

Further Reading

Dempsey, James, and Lara Flint. 2003. "Privacy's Gap: The Largely Non-Existent Legal Framework for Government Mining of Commercial Data." Center for Democracy & Technology. https://cdt.org/files/security/usapatriot/030528cdt.pdf. Accessed May 17, 2015.

Garfinkle, Simson. 2008. *Database Nation*. Sebastopol, CA: O'Reilly Media.

Gellman, Robert, and Pam Dixon. 2013. "Data Brokers and the Federal Government: A New Front in the Battle for Privacy Opens." World Privacy Forum. https://www.worldprivacyforum.org/category/report-data-brokers-and-the-federal-government/. Accessed May 17, 2015.

Hoofnagle, Chris Jay. 2004. "Big Brother's Little Helpers: How ChoicePoint and Other Commercial Data Brokers Collect and Package Your Data for Law Enforcement." *North Carolina Journal of International Law and Commercial Regulation* 29 (595): 595–98. http://scholarship.law.berkeley.edu/facpubs/678. Accessed May 17, 2015.

"Information Resellers: Consumer Privacy Framework Needs to Reflect Changes in Technology and the Marketplace." GAO-13–663: Published: September 25, 2013. Publicly Released: November 15, 2013. http://www.gao.gov/assets/660/658151.pdf. Accessed September 18, 2015.

O'Harrow, Robert. 2005. *No Place to Hide*. New York: Free Press.

Packard, Vance. 1964. *The Naked Society*. New York: IG Publishing.

Smith, Robert Ellis. 2000. *Ben Franklin's Web Site: Privacy and Curiosity from Plymouth Rock to the Internet*.Providence, RI: Privacy Journal.

United States Senate, Committee on Commerce, Science, and Transportation. 2013. "A Review of the Data Broker Industry." http://educationnewyork.com/files/rockefeller_databroker.pdf. Accessed September 18, 2015.

Weiss, Michael J. 1989. *The Clustering of America*. New York: Harper Collins.

Data Collection, Online

Online privacy has been an issue that has steadily grown in urgency and importance since the 1990s, when the Internet truly began transforming American business and culture. Before that time, privacy was the focus of some debate and occasional

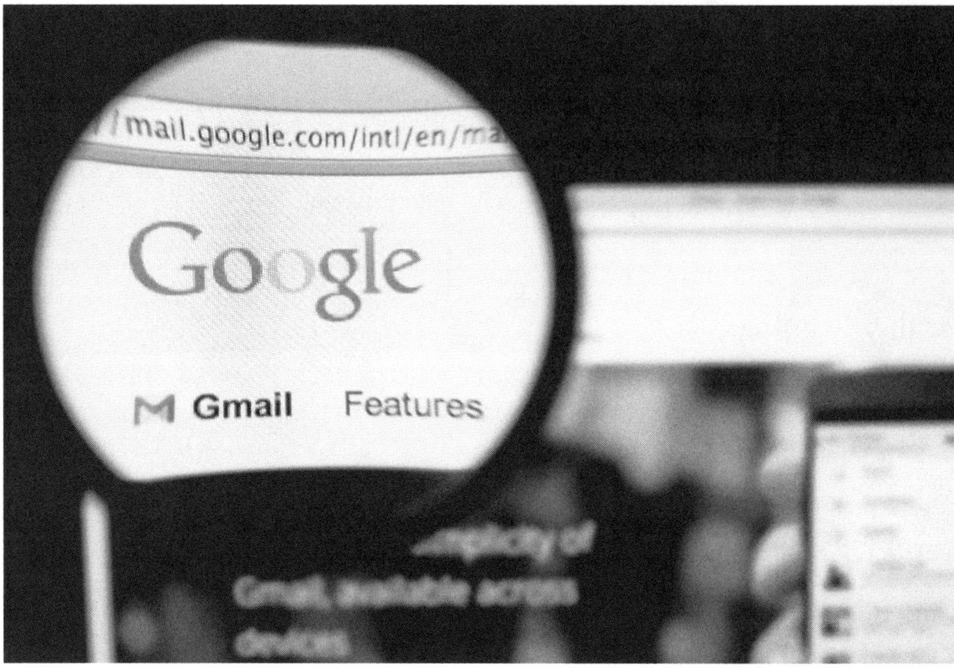

Debate about online privacy has intensified in response to terrorist attacks and advances in surveillance technology. (GilbertC/Dreamstime.com)

legislation. However, these early privacy laws rarely, if ever, recognized the existence of the online world. The growth of interest in online privacy—and to some extent, privacy in general—parallels the growth of the Internet. While Internet technology and its importance to personal and business activities have made online privacy a major subject of concern, debate, and regulation, the history of privacy in the off-line world remains a significant factor in defining online privacy. Online and off-line privacy issues cannot be separated completely or for long.

In its most technical sense, "online" refers to computers or devices that connect to the Internet and the World Wide Web. There are many flavors and varieties of how a device can be online in this sense. Desktop and laptop computers can be online via modems, broadband, cable, digital subscriber line (DSL), or wireless connections. Mobile phones and smart phones can also be online. Additionally, there are open wireless connections that are essentially public online spaces that anyone with a device adapted for wireless connectivity can use to connect. For example, some devices designed primarily to play music come equipped with wireless capability that can connect at wireless hotspots.

Online can also refer to sophisticated proprietary networks that ride on top of the Internet or the Web. For example, hospitals may offer patients the ability to view medical records online over encrypted networks that the hospital tightly controls.

Online may also refer to cloud computing, or the ability to store or work with information on computers owned by third parties with connections via the Internet. Google's Gmail and Yahoo's e-mail are examples of this kind of activity—essentially, people are using Google's and Yahoo's e-mail servers instead of their own to store and manage e-mail. Cloud computing can be used for documents, photos, spreadsheets, music, videos, and anything else that can be stored on a computer. Social networking sites provide another iteration of cloud computing.

Online may also mean the actual activities people undertake. Web sites, blogging, Twittering, Facebooking, e-mailing, geotagging, videoconferencing, voice over Internet phone (VOIP) calls, instant messaging, Skyping, and many other activities are inherently online activities. Over time, the range of these activities will expand and evolve further. It is safe to say that online activities will comprise a greater and greater proportion of peoples' daily lives in the foreseeable future.

Online privacy differs in both broad and narrow ways from off-line privacy under traditional views. As described earlier, privacy is already difficult to quantify and define; online privacy adds another dimension. The boundaries of online privacy are changing as rapidly as technology, which makes it hard to fix on a firm concept of what online privacy looks like or should be. Views of online privacy may be different in some ways now from a few years ago before social networking exploded in use. However, even though online privacy is a moving target, some things are readily discernible.

Online privacy has a different dynamic than off-line privacy. Online activities do not respect traditional national or conceptual borders. Online has a greater capacity for "memory" via longer retention of information. Online activities challenge traditional concepts of information ownership and control, with variable implications for online privacy. Online technologies make it harder to discern or enforce distinctions among individuals (e.g., age) that are clear in person or even on the telephone. Because of these differences in the online space, online privacy poses new, different, and uncertain risks for individuals, businesses, and governments. Most of these new risks have not yet been addressed by any meaningful changes in the law because of the rapidity of the technological advancements and the comparative slowness of policy and legislative processes.

The general pattern of online information persisting for extended periods has led to a phenomenon sometimes called the modern permanent record. The modern permanent record is not a high school paper file maintained on each student in former years. Today's modern permanent record is all of the information that online marketers, social networking sites, online businesses, schools, government agencies, social networks, and others can and do compile on individuals, plus other off-line information. This new kind of record provides a powerful memory of the purchases, Web-browsing activities, physical location, and general history and activities of an individual, a group, or a family. The modern permanent record has the potential to include everything you do, everything you click, everything you see, and every place you go.

The online world introduces a bevy of new privacy risks with consequences of varying types and degrees. Some risks include being exposed to additional criminal activity. For example, phishing and pharming, hacking, data breaches of online information, and other computer intrusions that take advantage of online security flaws, carelessness, and ignorance often fall into this category. Typically, these online attacks seek to gather sensitive information from individuals as they use online tools, such as financially oriented Web pages or sites. Social Security numbers and account numbers are of particular interest to criminals, who use the information for committing identity theft or other forms of fraud. Concerns about identity theft have done much to increase public concern about privacy.

Other online privacy risks do not rise to the level of criminal behavior but still create potential for privacy mischief and other problems. Some privacy challenges relate to the sheer volume of online information being stored and how that information is subsequently used, exchanged, or disclosed. Broadly speaking, as people move more of their lives online, they lose the protection of "privacy through obscurity," which has been a feature of the off-line, paper-based world.

In the past, individuals could live their lives, take action, and make mistakes in relative obscurity due to the limits of paper-based record-keeping systems. Tracking the daily activities of individuals in the predigital age was extremely difficult, expensive, and time-consuming. Paper records were stored in disparate locations, held by independent record keepers, and discarded from time to time. As more and more records are created and stored digitally, and as people live more of their lives through digital mediums, privacy through obscurity is quickly disappearing. The ability to track individuals casually and after-the-fact has increased, and the costs of collecting and retaining information have been reduced dramatically. For example, search engines allow anyone to locate information on a particular individual from a virtually unlimited number of sources. Some limits exist today because old records are still off-line, but that will change over time. We will soon live in a world where some individuals have lived their entire lives in a digital environment, and all of their records may be both digital and online.

This risk can be readily seen in online social networking. For example, recently, the Library of Congress announced that it plans to archive years of Twitter messages, thanks to Twitter's donation of its archive to the Library. (Twitter is an online service that allows users to send very short messages known as tweets to each other through the Twitter Web site.) The Library of Congress announced that every public tweet, since Twitter's inception in March 2006, will be archived digitally at the

Library. The rationale for archiving these messages is to store a slice of history, a snapshot of time that will be invaluable to researchers in the future.

There was an immediate backlash against the planned archive, with some expressing concern about the preservation of private communications. The Library backtracked a bit, restricting its collection to public tweets and limiting the database to researchers. Whether the preservation of these materials is a good or bad idea, it illustrates how easily online information can be saved or repurposed without prior notice to those who posted the information or to data subjects.

Stored data that is sensitive—like health care and financial information—is especially at risk for reuse, misuse, or snooping. Some sensitive data are necessarily shared with insurers, physicians, family members, or as a result of a transaction. Other sensitive information may be disclosed through user groups (e.g., a spina bifida support group). This information may leak out, be inadvertently disclosed, or even be actively sought by commercial interests (marketers or fund-raisers) or government agencies engaged in law enforcement or antiterrorism activities.

Information that individuals share with companies and third-party Web sites online may be eventually requested by government agencies or by civil litigants and used in ways that come as a surprise to a Web site user. A request for information from a Web site may not be focused on a particular user, but that user's information may still be disclosed and perhaps used in a way that is embarrassing or otherwise harmful to that user. Data that are retained online have the risk of also leaking out online or off-line. Data breach laws that have been enacted in many states attempt to address some of the risks introduced by data leakage, but these laws will not protect everyone from all the consequences of disclosures.

Another area of risk is data profiling. As people live more and more of their lives online, it becomes easier and cheaper for government agencies and commercial interests to compile large quantities of data about individuals from their surfing habits, search requests, and other online activities. These compilations are often called profiles. One example is the use of personal information collected and compiled from an individual's Web-browsing habits. Information such as gender, interest areas, career information, and potentially even medical conditions can be gleaned from peoples' Web-surfing patterns. As the data profile grows over time, a more and more detailed picture of that individual can be drawn using information that was never before available for commercial exploitation. One use of this information is for creating targeted marketing and advertising based on that individual's interests as revealed by their Web patterns. This kind of advertising is called behavioral advertising and is controversial because the information may be collected, compiled, stored, used, and disclosed without the knowledge or consent of the consumer. Additionally, this kind of information may be compiled with other information about consumers gleaned from other sources, including off-line sources, to create a rich history of activities and transactions.

Whether or not a data profile compiled from online activities is accurate is one concern. Another is any benefit or harm that might result from someone else's use of a data profile. This is a type of risk that has been around for a long time. In 1970, Congress enacted a law called the Fair Credit Reporting Act (FCRA) because credit reports were inaccurate, incomplete, and used to affect individuals' lives in important ways that were often both unfair and secret. But the potential content and scalability of online data profiles are much greater than for credit reports. A consumer profile may be used to affect an individual's ability to obtain employment, insurance, or housing, or to otherwise affect an individual's opportunities in the general marketplace. No law similar to the FCRA provides defined privacy rights for the broad swaths of data collected about consumers online. These are problems that lawmakers are just now beginning to debate.

Online Privacy and the Modern Permanent Record

Today's modern permanent record looks nothing like the old-fashioned permanent record of the 20th century. In the past, compiled consumer information was largely held by credit bureaus and largely covered adults with a credit history. Interest in consumers has spread beyond the regulated credit reporting system to unregulated consumer data, both online and off-line. These newly evolved data collection and use models merge online data collections and off-line data collections to form an informational picture of the modern consumer that is detailed and comprehensive and may be used to determine a great deal about a consumer's experience and opportunities. This is especially true for today's teens and children, who will be using digital networking technologies for their entire lifetimes.

Consumer data may offer benefits. Advertisers argue that they can serve individuals ads that are more relevant. However, the same information may also be harmful to consumers. In addition, noncredit, unregulated consumer reporting is a well-established business model. Most consumers only find out about these databases accidentally, if at all. These are databases that contain robust and sensitive consumer information, for example financial information or employment information. The information is often supplemented with other nonpersonal data that rely on census tract or neighborhood data. For example, an individual's income can be modeled based on statistics publicly available covering the individual's zip code, neighborhood, or block. Because the information is not used for purposes that fall under the FCRA, the databases are completely unregulated.

In recent years, technological innovations have greatly increased the ease of implementing and expanding this consumer data collection model. Collecting, accessing, and manipulating data has gotten cheaper and faster. In the past, consumer information that was based on noncredit, unregulated reporting was limited to some degree by the expense of obtaining and using the data and the challenge of managing the databases. Technological advances have lowered many of the barriers.

Now there are more noncredit consumer databases in use, the databases are being used in new ways, and they are generally more accessible to more of the population. Individuals can now purchase personal information about almost any individual over the Internet at minimal cost. Often based on public record information, these files or dossiers provide basic identity, location, and history information about individuals (e.g., former addresses, roommates, neighbors, etc.). It is the modern permanent record, with varying degrees of granularity or personalization, now readily available to anyone with a credit card, not just the subject of the record. These databases are one large piece of the consumer data collection picture.

Finding legal remedies for privacy violations has been a constant problem for off-line activities. It is even harder for online activities. In the off-line world, much privacy tort law has derived from work done by William Prosser in 1960. Prosser categorized existing law into four types of privacy torts: (1) intrusion upon an individual's seclusion or solitude; (2) public disclosure of private facts; (3) placing an individual in a false light highly offensive to a reasonable person; and (4) an unpermitted use for private commercial gain of a person's identity. This categorization had a major influence on the law, and many states enacted statutes codifying the so-called Prosser torts.

Many have always doubted the value of these torts as meaningful protection for privacy, and this skepticism has increased in the modern online era. Tort remedies do not necessarily match up with the realities of current online activities or with modern data collection and processing activities. Many online commercial data collection and use activities are hidden, and many consumers are unaware of the extent to which their personal information was obtained, is stored, or is being shared. The need to prove damages is another barrier.

While some class action lawsuits involving violations of online privacy have succeeded, some online companies are often motivated to settle cases to avoid further adverse publicity. Tort actions have some inherent limits. The scope of relief available through lawsuits will often be narrow (i.e., monetary damages) and may not meet or establish substantive privacy standards. Improvements or changes in privacy practices are not directly attainable through litigation. A jury verdict may provide damages, but the classic privacy torts are not likely to induce or force a record keeper to publish descriptions of record systems, limit collection practices, meet data quality standards, allow individual access and correction, or restrict internal uses of data. Some of these results have been achieved through settlements, however.

A second potential shortcoming with current tort remedies relates to their occasional reliance on expectations and reasonableness. Technology can easily erode societal expectations of privacy, and those eroded expectations may not be enforceable through the courts. For example, some point to the popularity of Facebook as evidence that young people no longer care about privacy. While polls suggest otherwise, it is apparent that the technology allows individuals to do things with their information that were impossible a generation ago, and some privacy standards have been changed by technological capabilities.

Finally, the online environment creates additional barriers to legal challenges of commercial privacy practices. Because of its multistate and international environment, the Internet readily brings together companies and consumers from many different jurisdictions. The courts are not nearly as adept in accomplishing the same feat. Consumers may not be able to find privacy remedies because of judicial limits on jurisdiction because, cases may be expensive to pursue, violators may be in other countries, and there is an absence of lawyers willing to represent them.

Robert Gellman and Pam Dixon

Further Reading

Lane, Julia, et al., eds. 2014. *Privacy, Big Data, and the Public Good.* New York: Cambridge University Press.

Nissenbaum, Helen. 2009. *Privacy in Context: Technology, Policy, and the Integrity of Social Life.* Palo Alto, CA: Stanford University Press.

Tanner, Adam. 2014. *What Stays in Vegas: The World of Personal Data—Lifeblood of Big Business—and the End of Privacy as We Know It.* New York: Public Affairs.

Data Mining

Data mining is the use of statistical techniques to unearth previously undiscovered relationships from large volumes of data. A wide range of commercial, governmental, charitable, educational, and medical organizations make use of data-mining applications.

Objectives of data mining include

1. *Security:* Based on the information known about an individual, is she likely to associate with terrorists? Should she be placed on the No Fly List? Should she be targeted for additional investigation and surveillance?
2. *Customer relations management:* How can the information in a firm's database be used to identify products and services in order to increase a firm's bottom line? Say someone just bought the new Harry Potter book

online, for instance. How can that customer's information be used to determine what other products he might be interested in?

3. *Political and charitable fund-raising:* What characteristics make it likely that someone will send a contribution in response to a fund-raiser's mailing?
4. *Credit scoring:* Based on the individual's credit history, would it be a good risk to give an applicant a 30-year mortgage?
5. *Fraud detection:* What characteristics of an insurance claim make it likely to be a fraudulent one? Was it really the cardholder who bought concert tickets on his credit card, or was his card stolen?
6. *Medical:* What group of patients is most likely to benefit from a new treatment? What cities are most at risk of a flu epidemic?

Data mining has exploded in the 21st century due to several factors. First, the amount of information available about individuals and events has expanded rapidly due to the explosion in social media and other digital technology innovations. For example, many grocery stores use frequent-shopper cards to collect information on purchases by individual customers. Digital images collected by surveillance cameras, satellites, and other sources add to the diversity of data available to be mined. Additionally, public records such as property tax assessments, which previously were on paper only, are now commonly found online. Second, the organization of raw data in databases and data warehouses makes the exploration of large data collections feasible. Third, the exponential growth that has occurred in computing power allows firms and governments to run complex algorithms on extremely large databases.

Data mining employs statistical algorithms to detect and explore patterns and relationships. This differs from traditional statistical analysis in which models or hypotheses come first and the researcher asks, "Do the data support my model?"

Some of the statistical techniques used in data mining include regression, decision trees, and neural networks. With any of these techniques, one measure is chosen as a target variable. Other measures or variables are chosen as predictors, such as travel patterns or cell phone use for law enforcement, national security, or other government purposes, and income, past spending patterns, or education, for commercial or political fundraising purposes. Data-mining techniques then attempt to make the most accurate prediction of the target variable.

Regressions try to fit an equation to the available data. The equation has inputs and produces a predicted value. In traditional statistical analysis, the researcher prespecifies which subset of possible inputs should be included in the equation. In a data-mining approach, the researcher puts in all of the information at her disposal and lets the algorithm choose what information actually is important.

Decision tree analysis takes a different approach. This technique divides the data into successively smaller groups, using rules to determine which divisions are best. For example, a tree analysis might find that the most effective rule for predicting the amount spent on books is to divide customers into those who earn over $100,000 and those who do not. The second split might be to divide the under $100,000 group into those who have a college degree versus those who do not.

A neural network is a mathematical model that in some sense simulates a collection of nerve cells (neurons). Each neuron has a set of inputs and one output. The outputs of neurons can connect to the inputs of other neurons. Each neuron "learns" by changing the way it combines input values in proportion to the difference between the actual and predicted values of the target variable.

Data miners usually divide their large datasets into several parts or "samples." Possible relationships are "discovered" using multiple techniques on one sample of data. Another subset of the data is used to establish how well each technique predicts the target variable. Data miners compare alternative techniques to see which one works best on the new data subset. In some cases a regression model might predict best, and in other cases the neural network might be best. These models may also be applied to new samples of data. A financial institution might, for example, develop a model to classify pending credit card purchases as either fraudulent or valid. The model can be applied to new purchases as they happen and can be used to authorize the purchase.

Data mining offers a number of social benefits. The techniques have been used to reveal and then rectify fraudulent Medicare claims. Several states now use data-mining techniques to direct tax audits at those returns that are predicted to contain fraud or error. Pharmaceutical companies have begun to incorporate data mining in the drug discovery process in an effort to predict if a compound will have toxic effects. Hospitals use data mining results to design emergency room protocols to deliver more effective patient care. On the commercial front, businesses have employed data mining to target advertising campaigns and to improve customer service.

Data mining also raises serious privacy concerns in a number of areas, however. For example, people may be misclassified. Even a good model predicts only that people with a certain set of attributes are statistically likely to possess the target attribute. Some people might be denied a mortgage based on a creditworthiness model, even though they actually would make all their payments on time. A larger concern is the misapplication of data-mining techniques. A model that excluded whole neighborhoods from mortgages, for example, would be effectively redlining. Data may also be used for unauthorized purposes that violate constitutional rights to privacy.

Some data are legally protected. Data collected from patients by a health care provider are protected from disclosure by law. Although it might not be illegal, data mining that uses other unprotected data to proxy the protected data certainly violates the spirit of the law.

Because data mining may be effective in the aggregate, however, the very existence of these techniques creates some threat to privacy by creating a demand for data to input to the model. The desire to identify potential terrorists, for example, leads to pressure to supply more personal data to mine for suspects. What can get lost in the face of this pressure is the careful consideration of whether it is good for society in the long run to have public access to personal information such as a person's library records.

Patricia Oslund

Further Reading

American Civil Liberties Union. 2014. *Privacy & S*urveillance. ACLU Web site. https://www.aclu.org/issues/national-security/privacy-and-surveillance. Accessed September 18, 2015.

Custers, Bart, et al., eds. 2012. *Discrimination and Privacy in the Information Society: Data Mining and Profiling in Large Databases*. New York: Springer.

Lane, Julia, et al., eds. 2014. *Privacy, Big Data, and the Public Good*. New York: Cambridge University Press.

Nissenbaum, Helen. 2009. *Privacy in Context: Technology, Policy, and the Integrity of Social Life*. Palo Alto, CA: Stanford University Press.

Davis v. Mississippi (1969)

In *Davis v. Mississippi*, 89 S. Ct. 1394 (1969), the U.S. Supreme Court held that the taking of fingerprints is covered by the Fourth Amendment prohibition against unreasonable searches and seizures. Fourteen-year-old John Davis was fingerprinted during a rape investigation in Meridian, Mississippi. The victim could give no description of her assailant other that that he was a "Negro youth." The police executed a dragnet investigation, interrogating suspects and taking fingerprints. Davis's fingerprints, which were recorded on two occasions, matched latent finger and palm prints taken from the scene of the crime. He was convicted and sentenced to life in prison. The Mississippi Supreme Court upheld the conviction.

On appeal, the state conceded that they did not have probable cause to arrest Davis at the time they took his fingerprints. The majority opinion, written by Justice William Brennan, held that Davis's fingerprint was the fruit of an illegal search, and the evidence, therefore, must be excluded from trial. Davis's conviction was reversed. The court made clear, however, that Fourth Amendment protection applied not to fingerprints themselves, the taking of which was not overly intrusive, but to the arrest in order to take fingerprints. Moreover, the apprehension without probable cause had involved an interrogation and a redundant second request for fingerprints. The Court left open the possibility that the police

> could request or demand fingerprints from citizens with something less than probable cause, using "narrowly circumscribed procedures." Some states subsequently passed statutes authorizing detention for recording physical characteristics based on standards less than probable cause.

Justice Hugo Black dissented, viewing the decision as an excessive expansion of the scope of the Fourth Amendment. Justice Potter Stewart also dissented, calling the reversal a "useless gesture." Stewart argued that fingerprints were not "evidence" in the conventional sense because, even if they were "wrongfully seized," they could be "identically reproduced and lawfully used at any subsequent trial."

Today, the primary importance of *Davis* is in the context of DNA evidence. The legality of "DNA dragnets" has been much discussed, and *Davis* is one of the key precedents in that debate. While some scholars argue that *Davis* makes DNA dragnets unconstitutional, others argue that the decision's apparent allowance of limited detentions to record fingerprints would apply to DNA as well, especially if the DNA recorded were limited to nondiagnostic identifying characteristics, as opposed to the entire genome.

Simon A. Cole

Further Reading

Cole, Simon A. 2001. *Suspect Identities: A History of Fingerprinting and Criminal Identification*. Cambridge, MA: Harvard University Press.

Dilworth, Donald C., ed. 1977. *Identification Wanted: Development of the American Criminal Identification System, 1893–1943*. Gaithersburg, MD: International Association of Chiefs of Police.

Walker, Jeffrey T., and Greg Hemmons. 2015. *Legal Guide for Police: Constitutional Issues*. New York: Routledge.

Deep Packet Inspection (DPI)

Deep Packet Inspection (DPI) is a data processing procedure that scans the contents of e-mails, Web pages, and other forms of Internet traffic for certain digital content. Under DPI, both the header (the "to" and "from" information) and the actual content of the information is examined to look for certain criteria.

In many cases, DPI is employed as a standard tool by network providers to fight viruses and malware and incursions from hackers. But the technology can also be used by government agencies for clandestine eavesdropping (in the United States) and even censorship (in countries like China that censor certain political, cultural, or entertainment content). As the Electronic Privacy Information Center (EPIC) notes, "Deep Packet Inspection has been used in attempts to: build profiles of consumers for marketing purposes; intercept communications at the request of law enforcement (both with and without warrants); enforce copyright laws; prioritize the transmission of some packets over others; and identify computer viruses and spam. DPI also enables non-ISP service providers, such as search engines or webmail providers, to build user profiles based on Internet activity."

Technology writer Duncan Geere compared the procedure of deep packet inspection to "opening up letters in a postal depot and reading the contents. Software is used to scan the contents of each packet (and sometimes log it), and then a packet can be rerouted (or dumped entirely) if it passes certain criteria. Those criteria . . . could be the presence of a virus or just prioritisation of certain types of traffic that are extremely bandwidth-dependent, like YouTube, Netflix, or Skype, over traffic that just needs to arrive eventually, like web browsing or application data." Some users of communications networks use encryption programs and secure communications systems known as Virtual Private Networks (VPNs) to try to keep their content from being scanned by DPIs.

Privacy groups in the United States and Europe have called for strict regulation of DPI technology to ensure that they are used solely to promote Internet service provider (ISP) efficiency (such as through optimizing routing of content) and ward off viruses—not to spy on private correspondence.

Despite the privacy concerns that have been raised about abuses of DPI programs, some cybersecurity experts have cautioned against regulating them so stringently that they cease to become effective tools in fighting viruses, malware, and even cyberterrorism. Richard Clarke and Robert Knake, for example, say that DPI systems, if effectively incorporated into other cybersecurity resources, could prove invaluable in warding off cyber attacks. "Imagine that a new piece of attack software enters into cyberspace, one that no one has ever seen before," they wrote in *Cyberwar: The Next Threat to National Security and What To Do About It*. "The deep-packet inspection system would be tied into Internet security companies, research centers, and government agencies that are looking for zero-day attacks. Within minutes of the malware being seen, its signature would be flashed out to the scanners, which would start blocking it and would contain the attack. A precursor to this kind of deep-packet inspection system is already being deployed. Verizon and AT&T can, at some locations, scan for signatures that they have identified."

Kevin Hillstrom

Further Reading

Aspray, William, and Philip Doty. 2011. *Privacy in America: Interdisciplinary Perspectives*. Lanham, MD: Scarecrow Press.

Clarke, Richard, and Robert Knake. 2010. *Cyberwar: The Next Threat to National Security and What to Do about It*. New York: Ecco.

Geere, Duncan. 2012. "How Deep Packet Inspection Works." *Wired.co.uk* (April 27). http://www.wired.co.uk/news/archive/2012-04/27/how-deep-packet-inspection-works. Accessed September 18, 2015.

House Committee on Energy and Commerce, Subcommittee on Technology and the Internet. 2008. *What Your Broadband Provider Knows about Your Web Use: Deep Packet Inspection and Communications Laws and Policies*. Washington, DC: Government Printing Office.

Delaware v. Prouse (1979)

Delaware v. Prouse is a case that was appealed to the U.S. Supreme Court that resulted in the ruling that law enforcement officials may not stop motorists to check their driver's license or automobile registration without there being suspicion of a crime being committed.

On the evening of November 30, 1976, a New Castle County, Delaware, police officer pulled over a car owned by William Prouse, who was a passenger in a car driven by a second person. The officer had not observed anything suspicious in the manner of the car's operation nor otherwise suspected either Prouse or the driver of any crime. The officer was simply doing a routine check of a driver's automobile registration and driver's license. When he approached Prouse's car, however, he smelled marijuana. He then noticed marijuana lying in plain view on the floor of the car and subsequently arrested Prouse for possession of marijuana.

In court, Prouse and his attorney argued that the evidence of marijuana should be suppressed because the Fourth Amendment said that the police officer had no right to stop him (and, then to search his car) because there was no probable cause of a crime being committed and that Prouse had the right to privacy. The state of Delaware, on the other hand, believed that its police officers should have the right to randomly stop motor vehicles in the interest of road safety. Delaware officials believed such stops gave police officers a "brief opportunity" to detain a vehicle "for a minute"—which it believed constituted nothing more than a simple check of a driver's automobile paperwork rather than a serious intrusion of privacy. It was the state's opinion that increasing traffic road safety outweighed what it believed to be a minor intrusion of privacy at best. The Delaware Supreme Court ruled in favor of Prouse, and the state appealed to the U.S. Supreme Court.

The Court ruled 8–1 that stopping a vehicle without any reasonable suspicion of a crime being committed was a violation of the Fourth and Fourteenth Amendments. It was, therefore, a case of unreasonable search and seizure. "The State's interest in discretionary spot checks as a means of ensuring the safety of its roadways does not outweigh the resulting intrusion on the privacy and security of the persons detained," said the Court. Writing for the Court, Justice Byron White wrote that searching a car can only be done when probable cause is present, otherwise citizens would fear "unfettered governmental intrusion" each time they entered their automobiles. He said it could not "conceive of any legitimate basis upon which a patrolman could decide that stopping a particular driver for a spot check would be more productive than stopping any other driver." Therefore, sanctioning such random stops would, in the Court's opinion, lead to a "grave danger" of abuse. "People are not shorn of all Fourth Amendment protection when they step from the sidewalks into their automobiles."

In fact, the Court believed that such random checks on automobiles contributed only little to road safety. It did, however, acknowledge that there were occasions where spot checks could be deemed legal. Subsequent legal decisions have established that law enforcement has greater flexibility and standing to stop vehicles without probable cause if all vehicles in such "checkpoints"—such as those to catch drunk drivers—are treated the same.

Lawrence W. Baker

Further Reading

Burkoff, John M. "*Delaware v. Prouse,* 440 U.S. 648 (1979)." Civil Liberties. http://uscivilliberties.org/cases/3687-delaware-v-prouse-440-us-648-1979.html. Accessed September 18, 2015.

"*Delaware v. Prouse.*" Oyez. http://www.oyez.org/cases/1970-1979/1978/1978_77_1571. Accessed September 18, 2015.

"*Delaware v. Prouse*—Significance." Law Library—American Law and Legal Information. http://law.jrank.org/pages/24026/Delaware-v-Prouse-Significance.html.

Dempsey, John S., and Linda S. Forst. 2013. *An Introduction to Policing,* 7th Edition. Albany, NY: Delmar, Cengage Learning.

Hagerty, P. 1984. "Sobriety Checkpoint Roadblocks—Constitutional in Light of *Delaware v Prouse*?" *Saint Louis University Law Journal* 28 (3): 813–34.

Douglas, William O. (1898–1980)

William O. Douglas ranks as one of the most unyielding civil libertarians—and one of the most outspoken critics of government and corporate surveillance practices—in the history of the U.S. Supreme Court. Born on October 16, 1898, in Maine, Minnesota, Douglas spent most of his impoverished childhood in the Pacific Northwest. He was able to attend Whitman College in Washington State on an academic scholarship, however, and he graduated from that institution with degrees in economics and English. After briefly teaching high school, he entered Columbia University's law program, graduating in 1925.

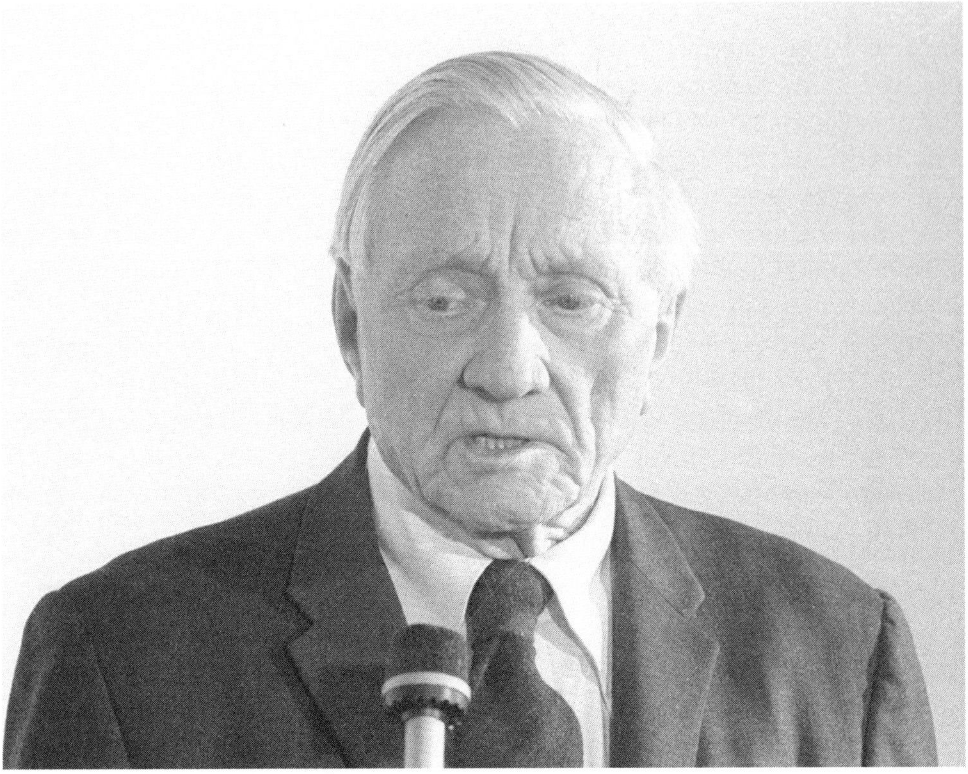

Justice William O. Douglas speaks to a group of students at Seattle Central Community College, Seattle, Washington, 1974. (AP Photo)

Douglas quickly gained a reputation as a talented young lawyer and professor, in large part because of a high-profile position at the Yale Law School. In 1934, he was appointed to the Securities and Exchange Commission (SEC) by President Franklin D. Roosevelt, and over the next several years he became a close advisor and friend to the president. In 1937, he was named chairman of the SEC.

Douglas remained with the SEC until 1939, when Supreme Court Justice Louis Brandeis resigned. Roosevelt nominated Douglas to replace Brandeis, and his nomination was confirmed by the U.S. Senate on April 4, 1939. The 40-year-old Douglas was sworn into office thirteen days later. Douglas kept his seat on the Court for the next 36 years and 209 days, making him the longest-serving Supreme Court justice in American history. He was also one of the most controversial justices ever so serve on the Court—so controversial, in fact, that conservatives in Congress tried to have him impeached and removed from the Court on a number of occasions.

During his long career, Douglas established himself in both his court opinions and his many books and letters as a proud and iconoclastic liberal, a sharp-tongued critic of "the Establishment," and as someone who felt that eternal vigilance was necessary to protect civil liberties against governmental overreach and corporate greed. In 1969, for example, he published *Points of Rebellion,* a book in which Douglas emphasized the importance of dissent in a healthy democratic society and cast a distrustful eye toward governmental attitudes toward the expanding world of electronic surveillance. "Big brother in the form of an increasingly powerful government and in an increasingly powerful private sector will pile the records high with reasons why privacy should give way to national security, to law and order, to efficiency of operations, to scientific advancement, and the like," he wrote. "The cause of privacy will be won or lost essentially in legislative halls and in constitutional assemblies. If it is won, this pluralistic society of ours will experience a spiritual renewal. If it is lost we will have written our own prescription for mediocrity and conformity. The tendency of these mounting invasions of privacy is the creation of a creeping conformity that makes us timid in our thinking at a time when the problems which envelop us demand bold and adventuresome attitudes."

Douglas made his staunch beliefs about free speech rights and civil liberties known in other cases as well, including *Dennis v. United States* (1951), in which Douglas argued vehemently for the free-speech rights of American Communists, and *Griswold v. Connecticut* (1965), in which he castigated state anticontraception laws as blatant violations of the right to privacy. In 1952, he wrote "The Black Silence of Fear," one of the best-known attacks on McCarthyism of that entire era. In that essay, which appeared in *New York Times Magazine,* Douglas opined that "once we had confidence in each other [in America.] Now there is suspicion. Innocent acts become telltale marks of disloyalty. . . . Fear has driven more and more men and women in all walks of life either to silence or to the folds of the orthodox. Fear has mounted: fear of losing one's job, fear of being investigated, fear of being pilloried. This fear has stereotyped our thinking, narrowed the range of free public discussion, and driven many thoughtful people to despair."

Douglas also became known as a strong advocate for the environment, both on the bench and in his essays and memoirs. He served for several years in the 1960s on the board of directors of the Sierra Club, and he was credited with helping gain protected status for several wilderness areas across the United States.

Douglas died on January 19, 1980, of a stroke, four years and two months after he retired from the Court. He was married four times and had two children.

Kevin Hillstrom

Further Reading

Douglas, William O. 1969. *Points of Rebellion.* New York: Random House.

Douglas, William O. 1980. *The Court Years: 1939–1975.* New York: Random House.

Murphy, Bruce Allan. 2003. *Wild Bill. The Legend and Life of William O. Douglas*. New York: Random House.
Theoharis, Athan G. 1998. *Culture of Secrecy: The Government Versus the People's Right to Know*. Lawrence: University Press of Kansas.

Drones

A drone is what is known as an unmanned aerial vehicle (UAV). They are flown remotely with a person on the ground or at a command center controlling the drone's movement. They can stay in the air for varying amounts of time—some for less than an hour, others for upward of thirty hours. Drones are used by the military as well as by commercial and private users. Recently, the cost of production has decreased, and more private individuals have been purchasing and flying drones. As drone technology has advanced, its utility for surveillance and military purposes has been widely recognized. But this recognition has also sparked calls

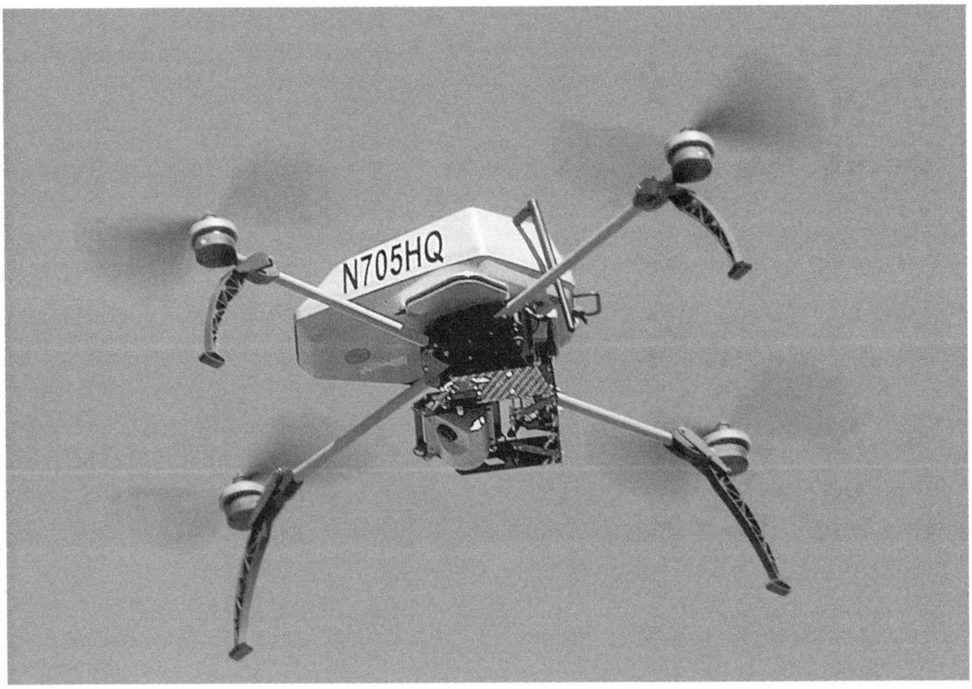

A drone operated by the Alameda County Sheriff's Office flies during a demonstration of a search and rescue operation on August 14, 2015, in Dublin, California. As law enforcement joins the ranks of hobbyists sending drones into American skies, civil liberties advocates are raising the specter of unchecked police surveillance and state lawmakers are drafting limits. (AP Photo/Noah Berger)

for new regulations governing how both government agencies and corporations and private individuals all use drones.

The military uses drones in conflict zones to carry out missions that are too risky for personnel. Using an unmanned vehicle means that there is no danger to the flight crew while conducting dangerous operations. The drone is launched by soldiers from the combat area; control of the drone is then transferred to a command center far from the combat zone. Three people are needed to fly the drone: the pilot commands its flight, the second person operates monitors, cameras, and sensors, while the third person is in contact with ground forces. Hobbyists control their drones via remote controls or from their smartphones. This limits the distance a personal drone can fly; the operator must be within its line of sight in order to fly it.

Drones perform many functions for both military and commercial users. In October 2001, the first drones flew missions over Afghanistan, and since then the military has been using drones consistently for surveillance and attack purposes. The cameras and sensors on board are highly sensitive and give detailed images of activity on the ground. This allows operators to monitor movements of enemy forces in real time. Drones are flying over war zones constantly, feeding information to the U.S. military. Devices equipped with laser-guided missiles are also capable of carrying out precision strikes against the enemy by remote control. According to *Time,* drones "represent a revolution in the idea of what combat is: with drones the United States can exert force not only instantly but undeterred by the risk of incurring American casualties or massive logistical bills, and without the terrestrial baggage of geography; the only relevant geography is that of the global communications grid."

Technology companies engaged in drone development have also touted the potential benefits of drones to a wide range of industries and people. Farmers can use drones to monitor their sprawling crops and irrigation systems or for crop dusting their fields. Drones have also been used recently to monitor environmental conditions in undeveloped areas. Fire departments use drones to detect wildfires and track their size and movement. Still other organizations use drones to observe wildlife, especially endangered species. Drones allow people to observe animals in their natural environment without disturbing them with human presence; this allows wildlife preservation teams to see how animals are adapting to changes in their habitat, as well as monitor their population growth and decline. Additionally, oil companies have been using drones to inspect and clean their offshore oil rigs. It is difficult, expensive, and dangerous to send workers to do this job; using drones cuts costs and decreases danger to people.

Despite all their positive uses, drones still cause a lot of concern among the population. There are safety risks; during the summer of 2014, a private drone nearly crashed into a commercial airliner at London Heathrow Airport. Had the collision not been avoided, it could have injured or killed passengers and caused significant damage to the aircraft. Another incident in 2014 involved two men being arrested after their drone nearly collided with a police helicopter in New York. Few regulations govern private operation of drones, and many private operators are unaware of the few laws that are in place.

Another issue raising an uproar is that of drones being used by police for surveillance. Police departments have been campaigning to obtain drones to carry out surveillance operations. In 2011, a SWAT team in Texas deployed a drone for a raid on a drug house; this was the first time a drone was used for domestic surveillance. Law enforcement experts expect that usage of drones by police departments is likely to greatly increase in the future despite questions that have been raised about Fourth Amendment rights to privacy and illegal searches. Privacy advocates have thus urged lawmakers and government officials to implement laws and regulations that firmly establish the kind of information that police and national security agencies can—and can't—gather using drone technology.

Due to the fact that drones are becoming a more popular means of accomplishing tasks, new regulations and safety measures have been called for in commercial applications as well. The Federal Aviation Administration (FAA) restricts drone flights by private companies as well as by government agencies; however, it does not regulate hobbyists. The FAA states that drones cannot be flown above four hundred feet, and the operator must remain in sight of the unmanned vehicle. However, these restrictions will not last long. A law was passed calling for drones to be integrated into the U.S. airspace and the systems that manage that space. Experts believe that as this regulatory regime fills out, it will open the marketplace for further commercial use of drone technology.

Grace Vandemark

Further Reading

Cole, Chris, and Jim Wright. 2010. "What are Drones?" Drone Wars UK Web site (January). http://dronewars.net/aboutdrone/. Accessed May 10, 2015.

"Drones: What Are They and How Do They Work?" *British Broadcasting Corporation* (January 31, 2012). http://www.bbc.com/news/world-south-asia-10713898. Accessed September 18, 2015.

Grossman, Lev. 2013. "Drone Home: They Fight and Spy for America Abroad: But What Happens When They Come Home?" *Time* (February 11).

Horgan, John. 2013. "Unmanned Flight: The Drones Come Home." *National Geographic* (March). http://ngm.nationalgeographic.com/2013/03/unmanned-flight/horgan-text. Accessed September 18, 2015.

Tate, Karl. 2013. "How Unmanned Aircraft Work (Infographic)." Live Science Web site (June 27). http://www.livescience.com/37815-how-unmanned-drone-aircraft-work-infographic.html. Accessed September 18, 2015.

Due Process Clause

The Fourteenth Amendment of the U.S. Constitution states in Section One, "... No State shall make or enforce any law which shall abridge the privileges or immunities of citizens of the United States; nor shall any State deprive any person of life, liberty, or property, without due process of the law; nor deny to any person within its jurisdiction the equal protection of the laws." This is known as the Due Process Clause, and it works in conjunction with the Fourth Amendment, which prohibits unlawful search and seizure. Due process of law requires law enforcement to obtain a warrant to search and seize "persons, houses, papers, and effects."

These amendments were created as a result of British treatment of the colonies prior to the American Revolution. British soldiers were permitted to enter American homes without warrants in search of various illegal goods. The Fourth and Fourteenth Amendments require probable cause before obtaining a warrant and due process of the law when investigating and convicting an individual of a crime. Another rule was subsequently enacted, the Exclusionary Rule, which states that evidence obtained illegally may not be used in court.

These laws work together, through a system of checks and balances, to protect everyone: the alleged criminal from being convicted by evidence that was obtained illegally, and the individuals otherwise unsuspected of criminal activity from being wrongfully searched. These laws also prevent law enforcement agencies from abusing the power granted to them; they have laws they must follow, and without so doing it is difficult for them to secure conviction of crimes.

The problem the judicial system is facing today is that these laws and policies were written when the technology available today had not yet been conceived. How does obtaining information and evidence using electronic surveillance technologies fit into the Due Process Clause? The original precedent set by the Supreme Court came in 1928 in *Olmstead v. The United States*, which concerned the new technology of telephone wiretapping. The Court was charged with deciding if this was within the law. Wiretapping was found to be legal because it did not include physical evidence, nor did it trespass upon the individual's property. The Fourth Amendment only discusses physical property, not intangible conversations. This decision was altered in 1934 when Congress passed the Federal Communications Act, which stated that federal officers could wiretap, but were forbidden from divulging any information that may have been gained. Thus, information gathered from wiretapping was inadmissible in court.

Judicial precedent continued to be set throughout the following decades. In another case, *Berger v. New York* (1967), the Court decided that issuing warrants to allow law enforcement officers to trespass onto private property and install surveillance equipment was unconstitutional under the Due Process Clause. The warrants simply stated whose conversations were to be spied upon; they offered no further information such as the content of the conversations they were seeking to overhear, and no probable cause was required for obtaining a warrant. Additionally, no termination date was given; therefore, theoretically the police could listen for as long as they desired. The statute was also found unconstitutional because the individual being monitored was not made aware of the fact; a traditional warrant is shown to the person to whom it relates.

The Court decided to save the issue of electronic surveillance in matters of national security for a future date. The executive branch has subsequently proclaimed that it has full legal authority to wiretap against domestic subversion and against foreign intelligence operations. This provision does require the federal government to gain a warrant when the subject of its surveillance is a U.S. citizen; however, no warrant is necessary for foreign nationals, or for gathering foreign intelligence. This is where the law becomes quite ambiguous.

Federal agencies are continuously monitoring telephone metadata, as well as e-mail communications and Internet activity. This concept of continuous monitoring rather than seeking out specific information is sometimes called dragnet surveillance. Federal officials may need a warrant to target a specific citizen for electronic surveillance, but if they are scanning all information and they happen to find information of interest, they do not need a warrant as the discovery is considered incidental. Likewise, they may employ electronic surveillance technology against U.S. citizens if the citizen in question is communicating outside the United States. This is problematic because many Web sites, including e-mail providers, have servers outside the United States; therefore, a lot of communication crosses into foreign territory, thus making it vulnerable to warrantless federal search. All of this surveillance conducted by federal officials violates the Due Process Clause; there is no probable cause proven, few warrants are issued, and the surveillance takes place without the knowledge of the affected individual. However, a stream of executive orders and acts passed by Congress has normalized this level of surveillance.

Grace Vandemark

Further Reading

National Paralegal College. 2015. "The Exclusionary Rule." http://nationalparalegal.edu/conLawCrimProc_Public/ProtectionFromSearches&Seizures/ExclusionaryRule.asp. Accessed March 28, 2015.

Orth, John V. 2003. *Due Process of Law: A Brief History.* Lawrence: University Press of Kansas.

Sullivan, E. Thomas, and Toni M. Massaro. 2013. *The Arc of Due Process in American Constitutional Law.* New York: Oxford University Press.

Wasserman, Rhonda. 2004. *Procedural Due Process: A Reference Guide to the U.S. Constitution.* Westport, CT: Greenwood Publishing.

E

Echelon

Echelon is the code name for a surveillance system that eavesdrops on a vast quantity of communications—cellular, fiber optic, satellite, and microwave—from around the world. This network is run cooperatively, and in virtual secrecy, by national security departments of the so-called Five Eyes Alliance, which consists of Australia, Canada, New Zealand, the United Kingdom, and the United States. The primary U.S. agency involved in operating Echelon is the National Security Agency (NSA).

Echelon was first revealed to the world in 1988. Margaret Newsham, a former computer programmer for Lockheed Martin, worked on the expansion of Echelon and, in the process, saw some things she did not like—for instance, eavesdropping on the conversations of a U.S. senator unsuspected of any wrongdoing. She reported the news to the U.S. House Select Committee on Intelligence and then leaked it to a journalist with the British magazine *New Statesman*, which published the first article on Echelon. The intelligence community made no comment on the article, and it failed to spark public interest. Eight years later, Nicky Hagar finished a book about New Zealand intelligence, *Secret Power*, which provided much greater detail about Echelon. Again the intelligence community ignored it, and after an initial splash, it seemed it would have little effect.

However, in 1998, the European Parliament's Science and Technological Options Assessment group authored a report titled *An Appraisal of Technologies of Political Control*, which used Hagar's research on Echelon. Apparently, the official stamp of the European Parliament gave the story credibility, and media coverage was intense. The story suddenly produced a great stir. What proved shocking about Echelon was the amount of communications it intercepted, the sharing of this information among many nations, and the fact that few public officials knew of its existence. It also gained notoriety for its enormous potential for abuse and allegations of actual abuse.

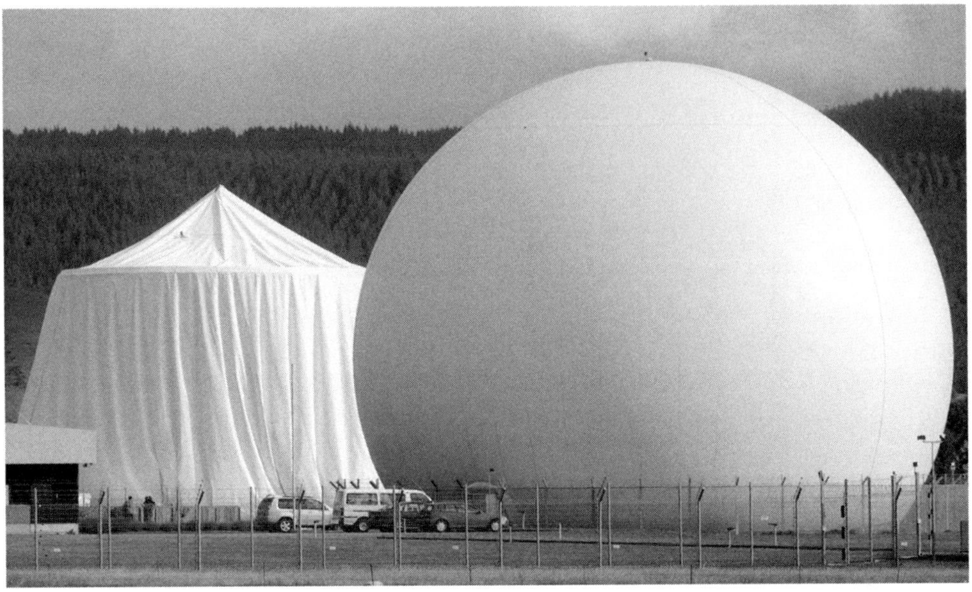

A satellite communications dome at Waihopai satellite communications interception station near Blenheim, New Zealand, 2008. Waihopai satellite communications is part of a surveillance spying alliance known as Five Eyes that groups together five English-speaking democracies—the United States, Britain, Canada, Australia, and New Zealand—a collaboration that began during World War II when the allies were trying to crack German and Japanese naval codes and has endured for more than 70 years. At left is a damaged satellite communications dome covered with a tent. (AP Photo/New Zealand Herald, Tim Cuff)

According to a 2001 European Parliament report, Echelon possesses two unusual features:

> The first . . . is the capacity to carry out quasi-total surveillance. Satellite receiver stations and spy satellites in particular are alleged to give it the ability to intercept any telephone, fax, Internet or e-mail message sent by any individual and thus to inspect its contents.
>
> The second . . . [is that] the states participating in ECHELON . . . can place their interception systems at each other's disposal, share the cost and make joint use of the resulting information.

This international cooperation also allows these nations to circumvent rules about spying on their own citizens. With Echelon, a nation can claim "it wasn't me who did the spying." Ordinarily, these nations' laws prevent them from spying on their own citizens without first obtaining a warrant. A warrant requires the government to show probable cause that the target of the surveillance has committed a crime. But, for example, if Country A conducts surveillance in Country B, then Country B has not broken its own laws on surveillance. (Country A may be guilty of international espionage, but only if Country B wants to do anything about it.) With Echelon, Country B can get the information that Country A collected and pretend it was not responsible for the surveillance. Of course, in reality, Country B has conspired to invade privacy and colluded in the violation of its own laws—and that is the problem with Echelon, according to privacy advocates.

Another problem is the potential use of Echelon for purposes other than national security. It is suspected that the United States uses Echelon to gain an advantage for U.S. businesses bidding on international contracts. On one occasion, the United States scuttled a contract between the European airplane company Airbus and Saudi Arabia by spying on the contracting parties and revealing that European officials were bribing Saudi officials. Other documents reveal that the United States tracks not only bribery, but also other actions it considers aggressive. On another occasion, the United States allegedly gave information acquired through Echelon to a U.S. company, Raytheon, helping it to gain an advantage in negotiations and scoop a billion-dollar contract with Brazil from the hands of the French company Thomson-CSF.

Echelon can be a powerful force for law enforcement. In March 2003, unnamed American authorities reported that Echelon was used to monitor the cell phone calls of several persons suspected of being key Al Qaeda leaders who planned and supported the September 11 attacks. The surveillance helped lead to the capture of two leaders, Khalid Shaikh Mohammed and Mustafa al-Hisawai, by Pakistani intelligence agents.

Privacy advocates worry, though, that Echelon is not bound by any legal guidelines to limit its use to appropriate purposes. With no independent oversight of its activities, history suggests the power of Echelon is likely to be abused. Although not enough is known about Echelon to determine the full extent of such abuse (such as the examples of industrial espionage conducted by the United States mentioned above), there is ample evidence that governments abuse other forms of surveillance.

Kevin M. Keenan

Further Reading

Keefe, Patrick Radden. 2006. *Chatter. Uncovering the Echelon Surveillance Network and the Secret World of Global Eavesdropping*. New York: Random House.

Wright, Steve. 1998. *An Appraisal of Technologies of Political Control.* Science and Technological Options Assessment (STOA). Manchester: Omega Foundation.

Electronic Communications Privacy Act (ECPA)

The 1986 Electronic Communications Privacy Act (ECPA) is a pioneering piece of legislation that addressed the privacy of electronic mail at an early stage of the penetration of the Internet into mainstream commerce and everyday life. ECPA quickly became an outdated law, however, because it relied on a model of electronic mail and Internet activity, which became obsolete as electronic communication practices and technology changed.

ECPA was initially crafted to bring the constitutional and statutory protections against the wiretapping of telephone communications into the computer age. The law reflected a legislative determination that some electronic communication activities should be excludedfrom the era's prevailing legal standard, which stated that there is no reasonable expectation of privacy in records maintained by third parties.

ECPA has three major parts or "titles." Title I amended the Wiretap Act, a criminal statute that seeks to (1) protect the privacy of wire and oral communications and (2) set out the circumstances and conditions under which the interception of wire and oral communications may be authorized. ECPA extended to electronic communications the same protections against unauthorized interceptions that had previously existed for oral and wire communications via common carrier transmissions. Specifically, it prohibited the intentional actual or attempted interception, use, disclosure, or "procure[ment] [of] any other person to intercept or endeavor to intercept any wire, oral, or electronic communication."

Title II of ECPA was the Stored Communications Act, which was intended to protect e-mail and similar electronic communications, including data transfers between businesses and customers.

Distinctions recognized by ECPA include electronic mail in transit; electronic mail in storage for less than or more than 180 days; electronic mail in draft; opened versus unopened electronic mail; electronic communication service; and remote computing service.

Title III of ECPA sets rules in place for state's use of so-called pen register and trap and trace devices. As the Department of Justice summarized, it defined the circumstances under which government authorities could obtain court orders "authorizing the installation and use of a pen register (a device that captures the dialed numbers and related information to which outgoing calls or communications are made by the subject) and/or a trap and trace (a device that captures the numbers and related information from which incoming calls and communications coming to the subject have originated)."

The precise characterization of an activity can make a significant difference to the protections afforded under ECPA. For example, if an electronic communications service holds a text message in electronic storage, then law enforcement needs a probable cause warrant to obtain access. If a remote computing service stores the same text message on behalf of the subscriber, then law enforcement does not need a warrant, and a subpoena is sufficient. Whether a search engine or a social networking site is a remote computing service remains in dispute.

According to privacy advocates, the ECPA provides its strongest protections against individuals who seek to intercept the wire and electronic communications of other individuals. "In general," states the Electronic Privacy Information Center (EPIC), "the statute bars [individuals from] wiretapping and electronic eavesdropping, possession of wiretapping or electronic eavesdropping equipment, and the use or disclosure of information unlawfully obtained through wiretapping or electronic eavesdropping." Violators of ECPA provisions risk heavy financial penalties, up to five years of prison, and exposure to civil suits. Title I of the ECPA also prohibits the government from using illegally obtained communications as evidence in criminal proceedings, but U.S. agencies are not subject to suits for violating the law.

Today, the ECPA is widely regarded as a law that badly lags behind technological developments. "In 1986, there was no World Wide Web, nobody carried a cell phone, and the only 'social networking' two-year-old Mark Zuckerberg was doing was at preschool or on play dates," points out the American Civil Liberties Union (ACLU). "Online privacy law shouldn't be older than the Web, and Americans shouldn't have to choose between new technology and privacy." In addition, surveillance and privacy experts alike agree that in recent years American courts have struggled mightily in applying ECPA to situations not contemplated by the law's drafters. Developments like cloud computing have created models of information transfer and storage that do not fit clearly under any of the law's existing standards.

But while there is considerable support for updating the law, reaching agreement on the particulars of major reforms has been difficult. Although ECPA modifications have been introduced through the Communications Assistance to Law Enforcement Act (1994), the USA PATRIOT Act (2001), the USA PATRIOT reauthorization acts (2006), and the Foreign Intelligence Surveillance Act (FISA) Amendments Act of 2008, these changes have been only incremental. As a result, privacy advocates, telecommunications companies, and government agencies have all lobbied Congress on ECPA—though these parties often disagree on what lawmakers should do. "Technology companies and digital rights groups [are] lobbying for clear standards that are adaptable to technological advances," observed EPIC. "Law enforcement has questioned the need [for] ECPA reform, fearing that reforms could decrease their ability to acquire digital information in a timely manner."

Kevin Hillstrom

Further Reading

American Civil Liberties Union. n.d. "Modernizing the Electronic Communications Privacy Act." ACLU.org Web site. https://www.aclu.org/technology-and-liberty/modernizing-electronic-communications-privacy-act-ecpa. Accessed February 11, 2015.

Electronic Privacy Information Center. n.d. "Electronic Communications Privacy Act." EPIC.org Web site. https://epic.org/privacy/ecpa/. Accessed February 11, 2015.
Helft, Miguel, and Claire Cain Miller. 2011. "1986 Privacy Law Is Outrun by the Web," *New York Times*, January 9.
U.S. Department of Justice. "Electronic Communications Privacy Act of 1986." Justice Information Sharing Web site. https://it.ojp.gov/default.aspx?area=privacy&page=1285. Accessed February 11, 2015.

Electronic Mail

Electronic mail (e-mail) refers to messages transmitted through the Internet or other networks. In modern implementations, e-mail messages are usually delivered very quickly, although not quite in real time, unlike instant messaging (IM) and other similar communication methods. Internet users commonly treat e-mail as an online equivalent of postal mail, often unaware of its implications for privacy and security.

Third-party monitoring of e-mail is commonplace and may occur without the knowledge of either or both parties to a communication. Other privacy issues arise from technical mechanisms employed by marketers and others to monitor reception and treatment of e-mail messages; from the storage and retention of e-mail messages; and as consequences of the actions of individual e-mail users. In addition, e-mail is commonly used to transmit intrusive and unwanted advertisements and other unsolicited messages called spam.

The standard protocol for sending Internet e-mail is the Simple Mail Transfer Protocol (SMTP). The Post Office Protocol version 3 (POP3) and the Internet Message Access Protocol (IMAP) are the most common protocols used for accessing received e-mail messages. Typically, the sender uses e-mail client software to compose a message. That software then transmits the message through an SMTP server, usually one operated by the sender's own Internet access provider, which transmits the message to an SMTP server designated to receive messages on behalf of the recipient. The message is held there until it is retrieved by the recipient.

The header of a message and its envelope both contain addressing information, although most e-mail clients display only the header. The "from" and "to" fields in the header normally contain the e-mail addresses of the sender and recipient, respectively, and sometimes their names as well. However, these fields do not control delivery of a message, and they can easily be altered by the sender. Another means of concealing the address of a recipient (for example, from other recipients) is to place it in the "bcc" (blind carbon copy) field rather than the "to" field. Extensions to the SMTP protocol can be used to authenticate the source of a message or encrypt its content. E-mail messages may be sent pseudonymously or anonymously by routing them through a remailer that strips or alters identifying information before forwarding each message and, optionally, encrypts the message content.

An e-mail message may be sent in plain text or in various enhanced formats such as HTML and may include file attachments and (depending upon the format) embedded images and even program code. Current e-mail clients may disable certain enhanced features due to their privacy and security implications. For example, a sender may embed a link to an image located on the sender's Web server in an HTML e-mail message in order to monitor whether and when the message is opened or previewed by the recipient. If the recipient's e-mail client were to retrieve the image from the sender's Web server in order to display the message, the access log for that server would reveal the date and time that the message was opened, the Internet protocol (IP) address from which the image was requested, and other information that the sender might find useful.

Some e-mail systems provide senders with the ability to track delivery of messages, control message retention or forwarding, and even recall messages after they have been sent. Although standard Internet e-mail does not intrinsically support these functions, they can be implemented by e-mail client software or various work-arounds.

User actions can have many privacy-related consequences, often unintended. For example, an e-mail message can be forwarded by its recipient to a third party without the sender's knowledge or consent. Although such forwarding may be considered a breach of "netiquette," e-mail users may give little thought to the original sender's privacy or other rights in the message content. A related concern arises when a forwarded message contains the e-mail addresses of many other recipients, none of whom may be aware that their addresses are circulating widely.

The "reply to all" function available in many e-mail clients causes the user's reply to be directed at all of the recipients of the original message as well as its sender. Frequently, users will inadvertently reply to all while intending only a private reply. Similarly, subscribers to Internet mailing lists may inadvertently send a reply to the entire list while intending to direct a response to only the individual who posted a particular message, either by using the reply to all function or (if the listserver is configured to direct replies to the entire list) by merely selecting reply without first checking the reply to address in the posted message.

In the United States, there are federal laws that protect the privacy of e-mail. The most important of these, the Electronic Communications Privacy Act (ECPA) of 1986, makes it illegal to intercept an e-mail message. This prohibition applies to law enforcement officials as well as private entities. However, there are many exceptions to this prohibition; for example, an e-mail service provider may view messages when necessary for purposes related to the operation of the service, and government agencies can often monitor e-mail communications under the auspices of national security or law enforcement concerns. The latter has become especially true with the revolution in surveillance-enabling technologies.

Law enforcement officials can access e-mail messages with a warrant or court order, and, in some instances, even without an order or warrant. Such access was expanded under the USA PATRIOT Act, enacted in the aftermath of the September 11, 2001, terrorist attacks by Al Qaeda on American soil. In 2000, it was revealed that the Federal Bureau of Investigation (FBI) had developed an automated system for scanning e-mail messages using hardware and software installed at a suspect's Internet service provider. The system, originally named Carnivore and later renamed DCS1000, was widely criticized by privacy advocates and civil libertarians. Critics charged that the system was capable of broad privacy violations and lacked accountability; the FBI claimed that it protected privacy by intercepting only those communications that were within the scope of a court order. The government effectively abandoned Carnivore by 2003, although other mechanisms for intercepting and monitoring e-mail remain in use.

A seemingly unobjectionable exception to ECPA permits interception of e-mail with the consent of the sender or recipient. Some Internet providers routinely require such consent as a term of service, however, and courts generally have held that an employer has the right to access messages sent or received using its e-mail systems, at least if the employer has informed employees that their e-mail will be monitored. Surveys of employers in the U.S. report that monitoring of employee e-mail has become the rule rather than the exception, especially in larger firms.

Storage and archiving of e-mail messages can greatly increase the likelihood that third parties will gain access to their content. Declining data storage costs have removed much of the incentive to delete unneeded messages, while technological advances have made it easier to recover deleted messages and those that exist only in otherwise obsolete backup archives. Meanwhile, businesses increasingly are adopting consistent policies on electronic document retention, largely in response to changes in the legal environment, and U.S. government agencies have gained increased legal authorization and technological capacity to review e-mail data (as well as other types of electronic communication).

David E. Sorkin

Further Reading

Lane, Julia, et al., eds. 2014. *Privacy, Big Data, and the Public Good.* New York: Cambridge University Press.

Schneier, Bruce. 2015. *Data and Goliath: The Hidden Battles to Collect Your Data and Control Your World.* New York: Norton.

Singer, Peter W., and Allan Friedman. 2014. *Cybersecurity and Cyberwar: What Everyone Needs to Know.* New York: Oxford University Press.

Electronic Surveillance

Historically, the Fourth Amendment's prohibition of unreasonable searches and seizures was limited to physical entries into places. Thus, in *Olmstead v. United States* (1928), the Supreme Court held that wiretapping without a physical entry into the home was beyond the scope of the Fourth Amendment. Writing for the majority in *Olmstead*, Chief Justice William Howard Taft observed that "one who installs in his house a telephone instrument with connecting wires intends to project his voice to those quite outside" and concluded that "that the wires beyond his house, and messages passing over them, are not within the protection of the Fourth Amendment." For Chief Justice Taft, it was irrelevant that federal agents had violated state law by intercepting Mr. Olmstead's conversations: "Whether the state of Washington may prosecute and punish federal officers violating this law, and those whose messages were intercepted may sue them civilly, is not before us." Dissenting, Justice Oliver Wendell Holmes Jr. called wiretapping a "dirty business" and argued that federal courts should not countenance lawbreaking by federal agents. In his oft-quoted dissent, Justice Louis D. Brandeis argued that "every unjustifiable intrusion by the government upon the privacy of the individual, whatever the means employed, must be deemed a violation of the 4th Amendment."

The *Olmstead* decision left the regulation of wiretapping and electronic eavesdropping to the state legislatures and state courts. Most states had statutes prohibiting unauthorized interception of telephone conversations, but these prohibitions were rarely applied to the police. In 1959, Samuel Dash published *The Eavesdroppers*, which showed the extent to which law enforcement agencies at all levels of government were employing wiretapping, often in disregard of state law. Dash's landmark study played an important role in changing judicial and legislative attitudes toward electronic surveillance.

Justice Brandeis's *Olmstead* dissent was vindicated in 1967 when the U.S. Supreme Court held in *Katz v. United States* that the "Fourth Amendment protects people, not places." In *Katz*, the Court ruled that electronic eavesdropping by law agencies without prior judicial authorization is a violation of the Fourth Amendment. Reflecting on *Katz* several years later, the Supreme Court observed in *United States v. United States District Court* (1972) that while "physical entry of the home is the chief evil against which the wording of the Fourth Amendment is directed, its broader spirit now shields private speech from unreasonable surveillance."

In *Berger v. New York* (1967), the Supreme Court struck down a state statute that authorized courts to issue wiretap orders in cases where there was "reasonable ground to believe that evidence of a crime may be thus obtained." Justice Tom Clark's opinion for the Court compared this permissive statute with the infamous general warrants of colonial times. In holding that electronic eavesdropping can be permitted only on the basis of probable cause, Justice Clark insisted that "officers be required to comply with the basic command of the Fourth Amendment before the innermost secrets of one's home or office are invaded."

The upshot of the Court's seminal decisions in *Katz* and *Berger* is that the use of wiretaps, hidden microphones, concealed cameras, and other devices that permit law enforcement agencies to intercept the content of what would otherwise be private communications implicates the Fourth Amendment. Therefore, in order to employ such means of surveillance, agents must obtain prior judicial authorization, which in turn must be based on probable cause.

It is important to understand, however, that for the police to use technology to augment their natural senses does not necessarily trigger Fourth Amendment protections. The question is whether the police use methods that infringe on a person's reasonable expectations of privacy. For example, in *Smith v. Maryland* (1979), the Supreme Court determined that the employment of a pen register (a device that records the phone numbers that are dialed from a particular phone number) is not a search within the meaning of the Fourth Amendment. Writing for the Court, Justice Harry Blackmun observed that merely by using the phone the defendant "voluntarily conveyed numerical information to the telephone company and 'exposed' that information to its equipment in the ordinary course of business." Blackmun concluded that in so doing the defendant "assumed the risk that the company would reveal to police the numbers he dialed." Similarly, in *Dow Chemical Company v. United States* (1986), the Court held that high-altitude photography of a chemical plant was not a search within the meaning of the Fourth Amendment. The Court concluded that the means of surveillance was incapable of revealing intimate activities that would give rise to constitutional concerns.

In the 1980s, police looking for marijuana being grown indoors under artificial light began to use infrared imaging devices, which can provide a strong indication whether marijuana is being grown inside a closed structure. In *Kyllo v. United States* (2001), the U.S. Supreme Court held that when "the Government uses a device that is not in general public use, to explore details of the home that would previously have been unknowable without physical intrusion, the surveillance is a 'search' and is presumptively unreasonable without a warrant."

In the wake of *Katz v. United States*, Congress enacted a legislation governing the interception of electronic communications, both by law enforcement agencies and by private parties. Title III of the Omnibus Crime Control and Safe Streets Act of 1968, known generally as the Wiretap Act, prohibits interception of electronic communications without a court order unless one party to the conversation consents. Interception is defined as "aural or other acquisition of the contents of any wire, electronic or oral communication through the use of any electronic, mechanical, or other device." In 1986, Congress expanded the meaning of wire communications to include conversations through switching stations, thus making the statute applicable to cellular telephones.

Title III permits issuance of wiretap orders by federal and state courts on sworn application authorized by the U.S. attorney general, a specially designated assistant, or a state official at a similar level. To permit the use of electronic surveillance by its own agents, a state must adopt legislation along the lines of the federal act, and most states have done so.

Before a court may issue a wiretap order, it must find the probable cause that the subject of the wiretap has committed or is committing one of a series of enumerated crimes for which wiretapping is authorized and that conventional modes of investigation will not suffice. Court orders permit surveillance for a thirty-day period. At the period's expiration, the recordings made of intercepted communications must be delivered to the judge who issued the order. They are then sealed under the judge's direction.

The Electronic Communications Privacy Act (ECPA) of 1986 established federal standards for access to e-mail and other electronic communications and to transactional records, including subscriber identifying information, call logs, phone bills, etc. The new law established a high standard for access to the contents of electronic communications, but allowed agencies to easily gain access to transactional records. One part of the act governs the use of pen registers and trap and trace devices. It requires judges to issue orders to allow the use of such devices when properly requested by prosecutors. There is no standard of proof that prosecutors have to meet to obtain such orders. The courts have generally taken the position that users of telephones have no reasonable expectation of privacy with regard to numbers associated with incoming or outgoing phone calls. Congress has chosen not to provide significant statutory protection in this area, much to the chagrin of civil libertarians.

Shortly after the terrorist attacks of September 11, 2001, Congress enacted the USA PATRIOT Act to facilitate government counterterrorism efforts. Title II of this controversial Act, entitled "Enhanced Surveillance Procedures," includes a number of provisions expanding the federal government's authority to engage in electronic eavesdropping. Among other things, Title II facilitates use of pen registers and trap and trace surveillance. To secure a pen register or trap and trace order, agents have only to certify that the information they are seeking is relevant to an ongoing investigation of terrorism or various other federal crimes.

Under Title II, agents are authorized to obtain court orders allowing use of technology that records e-mail addresses and URLs of Web sites being accessed from particular computers. Federal courts may issue roving surveillance orders in connection with foreign intelligence matters, enabling investigators to intercept e-mail and cell phone communications where suspects frequently change their account numbers. The act also permits federal agents to seize voice mail messages pursuant to a search warrant instead of a wiretap order.

The USA PATRIOT Act also permits federal agents to use easily obtained administrative subpoenas that require Internet providers to turn over subscriber records and other information without notice to subscribers. Despite strenuous objections by civil libertarians and a flurry of lawsuits attacking various provisions of the act, Congress in the fall of 2005 reauthorized the PATRIOT Act, albeit with some modifications.

Since that time, concerns about government overreach in surveilling activities in the name of national security have intensified, especially in the wake of the revelations by whistle-blower Edward Snowden regarding the extent of electronic surveillance being carried out by the National Security Agency (NSA) and other government agencies on Americans unsuspected of any criminal activity. Examples of these activities range from the U.S. government's current capacity, through orders from the Foreign Intelligence Surveillance Court (FISC), to force telecommunications companies to disclose private information to government investigators, to the Federal Bureau of Investigation's (FBI) use of so-called national security letters to compel individuals and organizations to turn over private records—and to keep silent about doing so.

Changes in technology always create new problems for the legal system. The rapid diffusion of personal computers and the Internet has created an exciting new medium of communication for many millions of law-abiding citizens. It has also provided new opportunities for terrorists, child molesters, and con artists. Law enforcement agencies insist that they need broad powers to monitor Internet communication, but civil liberties advocates worry about the threat to privacy inherent in online surveillance. And with the advent of sweeping new surveillance-enabling technologies at the same time that digital communications capacities are undergoing similarly transformative expansions, U.S. courts and lawmakers will face even greater challenges in terms of striking an appropriate privacy–security balance in years to come.

John M. Scheb II

Further Reading

Dash, Samuel. 1959. *The Eavesdroppers: The Unknown Story of Wiretapping Today-Its Victims, Its Practitioners, The Techniques, and What the Law Says About It.* New Brunswick, NJ: Rutgers University Press.

Freiwald, Susan. 2004. "Online Surveillance: Remembering the Lessons of the Wiretap Act." *Alabama Law Review* 56 (9): 46–52.

President's Review Group on Intelligence and Communications Technologies. 2013. Liberty and Security in a Changing World. https://www.whitehouse.gov/sites/default/files/docs/2013-12-12_rg_final_report.pdf. Accessed September 18, 2015.

Encryption

Encryption is the conversion of electronic data, known as plaintext, into an unreadable form, known as ciphertext, in order to secure the data for transmission. Once it is sent, the ciphertext is then decrypted by authorized parties who hold a cipher key, also known as an encryption key. The processes of encryption and decryption are central elements in the field of cryptology, which is centered around the storage and transmission of secret data. Encryption is the process by which easily comprehended information, such as ordinary text, a photograph, or a motion picture, is converted into a form that can only be understood with the aid of a key.

The method by which the plaintext message is encrypted is called a cipher; it is often incorrectly referred to as a code. While a code also converts information into some other form, this is done for technical reasons rather than to keep the information secret. For example, a code such as the American Standard Code for Information Interchange (ASCII) or Unicode, both used to convert the letters and characters of ordinary text to binary numbers for use in computers, is necessary in order to allow human beings to use binary computers; the usefulness of these

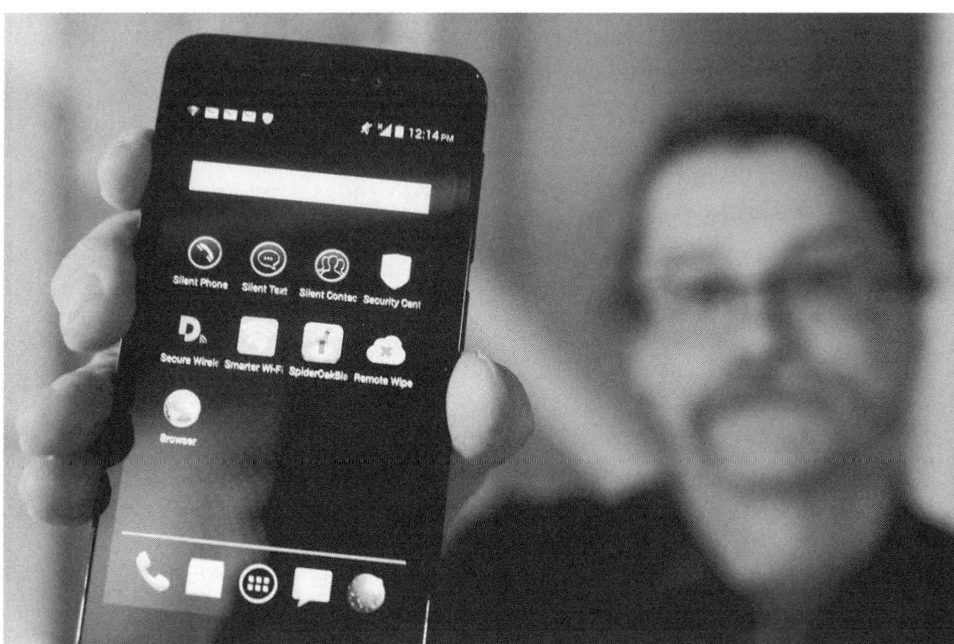

Silicon Valley pioneer and Silent Circle cofounder Jon Callas holds up Blackphone with encryption apps displayed on it at the Computer History Museum in Mountain View, California, 2014. "Snowden's leaks were a real boon for us," said Callas, whose company sells an encryption app that allows users to talk and text in private. (AP Photo/Eric Risberg)

codes would be destroyed if the information was kept secret, however. Encryption, in which the existence of the message is not hidden but the content of the message is rendered incomprehensible, is also sometimes confused with steganography, in which the existence of the message is hidden; encryption and steganography may be combined, of course.

Most encryption methods can be classified as either symmetric or asymmetric key algorithms. The former and much older type requires that the sender and receiver share a key, kept secret from the rest of the world; the key is used both to encrypt and decrypt messages. The key can be very simple or very complex, but the system has two weaknesses: Only persons who know the key can send and receive encrypted messages, and anyone who has the key can decrypt all messages encoded with it. As the number of persons with whom the key is shared increases, the likelihood that one of them will inadvertently or deliberately allow the key to fall into the hands of an unauthorized person increases as well.

Simple and not-so-simple symmetric-key encryption has been in use for millennia. Evidence found on ancient stone tablets and papyrus reveals that a number of ancient civilizations employed cryptography, including Egyptian, Hebrew, and Greek societies. The Assyrians used it to protect trade secrets central to its pottery industry. In China, it was utilized to shield important information about the nation's silk trade.

In the fifth century BC, Spartan warriors relied on a cipher device, a machine designed to encrypt and/or decrypt data, to relay secret messages between military commanders. The cipher device that they used was a scytale, a cylinder with a band of leather or parchment wound around it. A commander would write a message on the band and unwind it from the cylinder and then deliver it to another commander in the field, who would wrap the band of meaningless letters around a scytale of the same diameter to decrypt it.

A scytale is an example of a transposition cipher, which is an encryption method that shifts units of plaintext—usually characters or groups of characters—in order to create ciphertext.

The legendary Roman leader Julius Caesar utilized substitution ciphers to communicate with his military leaders. In this encryption method, messages were manually encrypted by substituting symbols, letters, and pictures for text.

There are several types of substitution ciphers. Some of the most common include the simple substitution cipher, which consists of substituting every character of plaintext for another character; the polyalphabetic substitution cipher, which replaces groups of letters or characters in plaintext; and the homophonic substitution cipher, which entails replacing letters of plaintext with a variety of substitutes, including numbers, and is characterized by higher-frequency letters having a higher number of substitutes in order to make it harder for cryptanalysis.

Another encryption cipher, polygraph substitution ciphers, replaces whole groups of letters or characters instead of single ones.

Around the time of World War I, mechanization led to key advancements in cryptography. In 1915, the first rotor machine was invented by two Dutch inventors. Rotor machines were mechanized cipher devices largely comprising rotors, or drums, which produced complex polyalphabetic substitution ciphers that were very difficult to break by cryptanalysis. The machines also allowed for much faster rates of encryption and decryption.

The legendary Enigma machine is the best-known example of a rotor cipher device. There were several models of the Enigma, the most celebrated version being the one used by the German military during World War II. The Enigma code was eventually broken by Polish and British cryptanalysts during the war.

A new era in cryptology dawned with the development of electronic technology. Computers have allowed for more sophisticated encryption techniques, leading to improvements in security for both public and private industry. Cryptographic systems became common outside of diplomatic, political, and military circles, and today they are used to encrypt everything from credit card transactions to private e-mail correspondence to medical records.

As cryptographic technology advanced, the U.S. National Bureau of Standards (NBS) identified the need for government-wide encryption standard. The data encryption standard (DES) became the algorithm used by the U.S. government in financial transactions and was eventually adopted worldwide. Its popularity made it influential in cryptology and with academics in the field.

The tremendous advances in cryptography for military and intelligence purposes during World War II led to government involvement in and regulation of cryptography. In 1952, during the Korean War, then President Harry Truman created the National Security Agency (NSA). At the time, the primary function of the NSA was cryptography and its counterpart cryptanalysis, or the breaking of codes used by others. The NSA worked to maintain a United States lead in these areas, which it did successfully until the emergence of asymmetric or public-key cryptography (PKC).

PKC avoids the weakness of symmetric cryptography by using two keys: a public key, available to all, used to encrypt the message, and a private key, known only to the recipient, used to decrypt it. Once the public key is made available, anyone who wishes can use it to send encrypted messages to the recipient. The public key may be made available to anyone without increasing the likelihood that the private key will fall into the wrong hands, so anyone can encrypt messages while only the authorized recipient can decrypt them.

The invention of PKC is generally credited to the team of Martin Hellman, a professor at Stanford University, and two graduate students, Whitfield Diffie and Ralph Merkle, and to the slightly later work of three Massachusetts Institute of Technology professors: Ron Rivest, Adi Shamir, and Len Adleman. The latter group patented their encryption method, known as RSA (the initial letters of the surnames of the inventors), and it forms the basis for asymmetric encryption methods in wide use today. The NSA and its British counterpart later claimed to have been aware of the possibility of public-key encryption for some time and to have kept it secret for security reasons.

The NSA initially attempted to prevent the public's use of PKC. Under the Arms Export Control Act (AECA) and the International Traffic in Arms Regulation (ITAR), cryptographic devices were classified as significant military equipment. Exporting public-key encryption outside the United States was, at least in theory, a violation of AECA and ITAR. But privacy pioneers such as Phil Zimmerman, the developer of the popular PKC program Pretty Good Privacy (PGP), made public-key encryption methods available over the Internet (including, inevitably, to people outside the United States) and e-mailed their public keys to persons outside the United States. Providing information on the Internet, however, even for free, may constitute an export; after making PGP available as a free download, Zimmerman was investigated for violation of AECA but never prosecuted.

The NSA is a security agency; perhaps its institutional focus on the potential use of PKC by spies and terrorists blinded it to the commercial possibilities. PKC provides obvious advantages to businesses such as online retailers and financial institutions, who need an easy way to protect the privacy of communications with their customers; without it, Internet commerce could not have expanded to the extent it has. Thus, business interests, as well as privacy advocates, had a strong interest in PKC.

The NSA attempted to address the problem with the Clipper chip. The Clipper chip was intended to be included in all communications devices sold in the United States and would have added a third component to the public/private key pair—a spare key to any encrypted message sent or received with the device. This spare key would be transmitted to a government facility and held in escrow, from which it could be retrieved by court order. This would give the government access, subject to constitutional restraints, to all encrypted communications in the United States (Froomkin 1995, 752–63).

Needless to say, neither businesses nor privacy advocates were enthusiastic. Nor did they trust the integrity or the competence of the government. They feared that the government might use its escrow powers improperly or that the escrow database might be hacked and the spare keys made available to criminals. In addition, critics recognized that no one outside the United States would want to send encrypted communications using a device that made the content available to the U.S. government, and no non-U.S. manufacturer would incorporate the Clipper chip into devices for sale outside the United States. Consumers would presumably prefer devices made without the Clipper chip, which would also be cheaper to manufacture; the effect on U.S. manufacturers of communications equipment would be disastrous. Opposition from nearly all sectors of society ultimately led to the demise of the Clipper chip.

Asymmetric encryption is now an accepted part of Internet commerce, transparent to most users. PKC is incorporated into Web browsers in the form of the secure socket layer (SSL), which encrypts messages between the browser and a Web server. Most users will not be aware that SSL is in use unless the Web page tells them or unless they notice the tiny lock icon on their Web browser or by looking at the URL: Encrypted pages generally have an address starting with "https" rather than "http." SSL can also be used to confirm a server's or user's identity through the use of a digital certificate and can be used to ensure that the content of a message has not been altered in transit (Lessig 1999, 39–40).

Public key encryption is widely available and difficult to break; it has also become an indispensable part of the Internet economy. In addition, PKC has numerous other legitimate uses. It can be used to verify identity through digital certificates and signature; to preserve the confidentiality of business and personal communications; and to protect copyrighted information (such as a movie recorded on a DVD) from unauthorized copying. But PKC can also be used by terrorists, child pornographers, and other criminals. The challenge for lawmakers is to create a set of rules that permits the economically and socially beneficial uses of PKC—encryption of credit card numbers, bank account information, business records, confidential business and personal communications, and the like—while controlling the harmful uses.

The first problem is not easily solved, for the same encryption tool that can be used to conceal a legal but confidential business plan can be used to conceal a dangerous terrorist plot. Encryption can create a virtual private network that can save businesses millions of dollars in infrastructure costs—or provide a hidden marketplace for child pornographers. The encryption technology is merely a tool, and the appropriate legislative approach is to enhance penalties for crimes committed using that tool. A knife that can be used for slicing melons can also be used to commit a robbery; the legislature has responded not by outlawing knives but by providing that the penalty for a crime committed with a knife is more severe than the penalty for a similar crime committed without one.

There seems to be no downside to allowing the use of encryption to verify the identity of Web servers and Internet users. Copy-protection encryption, however, has presented significant legislative difficulties in commercial transactions, aside from privacy concerns. The content industry has lobbied heavily for legislative protection for, and even mandate of, copyright protection encryption technologies.

Yet users and equipment makers resent copy-protection encryption; equipment must be designed to play encrypted material, sometimes with uneven results. And users may want to record protected material to other media for legitimate space-shifting purposes. The use of encryption thus diminishes utility while simultaneously raising the cost: Consumers end up with a more expensive but less useful media player.

Within the United States, the problem is addressed by a combined legislative and technological approach. Movies could easily be recorded with nearly unbreakable encryption. But in order to be make movies that can be played, the recording industry must share the decryption key with the equipment manufacturing industry; the more complex the encryption, the greater the chance of incompatibility, and the greater the number of keys distributed, the greater the chance that a decryption key will be leaked to the general public.

Instead, movies are recorded with relatively simple encryption, and the Digital Millennium Copyright Act (DMCA) provides penalties for the circumvention of this encryption. The combination of encryption to stop the casual user from copying the movie and criminal penalties to deter the more sophisticated user have managed to control, though not eliminate, piracy of movies within the United States.

As digital cryptographic systems have become more prevalent and advanced, new controversies have emerged. In 2013, for example, a government whistleblower named Edward Snowden leaked information that proved that U.S. counterintelligence agencies were continuing to sabotage cryptosystems in order to ensure that intelligence agencies have unhindered access to any encrypted transaction or communication in the world. U.S. government counterintelligence officials argued that such counterterrorism efforts were essential to the country's national security. Critics of the program claimed that U.S. government efforts to undermine online security was a violation of online privacy and made the Internet more vulnerable to criminal hacking, foreign espionage, and illegal surveillance.

Aaron Schwabach; updated by Margaret Haerens

Further Reading

Diffie, Whitfield, and Susan Landau. 2007. *Privacy on the Line: The Politics of Wiretapping and Encryption*. Cambridge, MA: MIT Press.

Ferguson, Niels, Bruce Schneier, and Tadayoshi Kohno. 2010. *Cryptography Engineering*. Indianapolis, IN: John Wiley & Sons.

Froomkin, Michael. 1995. "The Metaphor Is the Key: Cryptography, the Clipper Chip, and the Constitution." *University of Pennsylvania Law Review* 143: 709.

Kahn, David. 1967. *The Codebreakers: The Story of Secret Writing*. New York: Scribner.

Lessig, Lawrence. 2006. *Code and Other Laws of Cyberspace, Version 2.0*. New York: Basic Books.

Lewis, James Andrew. 2014. "2014 as the Year of Encryption: A Very Brief History of Encryption Policy." Center for Strategic and International Studies (January 10). http://csis.org/publication/2014-year-encryption-very-brief-history-encryption-policy. Accessed March 9, 2015.

Mao, Wenbo. 2003. *Modern Cryptography: Theory and Practice.* Upper Saddle River, NJ: Prentice Hall.

Pednekar-Magal, Vandana, and Peter Shields. 2003. "The State and Telecom Surveillance Policy: The Clipper Chip Initiative." *Communication Law and Policy* 8: 429.

Reiman, Phillip E. 1996. "Cryptography and the First Amendment: The Right to Be Unheard." *John Marshall Journal of Computer & Information Law* 14: 325.

Robertson, Cam. 2014. "Encryption: A Brief History of Our Secret Keeping." *SC Magazine* (August 26). http://www.scmagazine.com/encryption-a-brief-history-of-our-secret-keeping/article/368068/. Accessed March 9, 2015.

Solove, Daniel. 2011. *Nothing to Hide: The False Tradeoff between Privacy and Security.* New Haven, CT: Yale University Press.

Stallings, William. 2010. *Cryptography and Network Security: Principles and Practice,* 5th Edition. Upper Saddle River, NJ: Prentice Hall.

Wilson, Andi, and Danielle Kehl. 2015. "Remembering the Lessons of the Crypto Wars." *New America* (February 12). http://www.newamerica.org/oti/remembering-the-lessons-of-the-crypto-wars/. Accessed March 9, 2015.

Espionage Act of 1917

The Espionage Act was passed by Congress in 1917 after the United States entered the First World War. The legislation was passed at the urging of President Woodrow Wilson, who feared any widespread dissent in time of war constituted a real threat to an American victory. It prescribed a $10,000 fine and 20 years in prison for interfering with the recruiting of troops or the disclosure of information dealing with national defense. Additional penalties were included for the refusal to perform military duty and for using the U.S. mail to distribute material urging treason or resistance. In 1918, an amendment to this legislation known as the Sedition Act extended the law to cover a wide range of speech critical of the war or the U.S. government. Specifically, the amendment made it a crime to "willfully utter, print, write, or publish any disloyal, profane, scurrilous, or abusive language about the form of the Government of the United States" or to "willfully urge, incite, or advocate any curtailment of the production" of materials "necessary or essential to the prosecution of the war."

As a result of the Espionage Act, about 75 newspapers either lost their mailing privileges or were pressured to print nothing more about World War I between June 1917 and May 1918. Additionally, the editor of the *Milwaukee Leader* was sentenced to 20 years' imprisonment after being convicted on a charge of conspiracy to violate the Espionage Act. Hundreds of individual Americans were also convicted and sentenced to prison under the act, the most prominent being labor organizer and Socialist leader Eugene Debs.

While some provisions of the Espionage Act were relatively straightforward and noncontroversial, the parts of the legislation that curtailed freedom of speech drew an outcry from civil libertarians. This curtailment of speech rights led to approximately 900 people being convicted under the Espionage Act. This measure was quickly challenged in the courts, but the law was upheld by the Supreme Court in *Schenck v. United States* (1919).

Christopher P. Latimer

Further Reading

Kohn, Stephen M. 1994. *American Political Prisoners: Prosecutions under the Espionage and Sedition Acts*. Westport, CT: Praeger.

Murphy, Paul L. 1979. *World War I and the Origin of Civil Liberties in the United States*. New York: W.W. Norton.

E-Verify

U.S. immigration law prohibits employers from hiring workers who are not authorized to work in the United States. Legal workers include U.S. citizens as well as foreign persons who have permission to work in the country. The federal government established E-Verify in 1997 as a pilot program to help employers judge whether applicants and employees are eligible U.S. workers and to prevent the hiring of unauthorized immigrants. The program was implemented nationwide in 2003.

Run by the U.S. Citizenship and Immigration Services (USCIS) and the Social Security Administration (SSA), E-Verify works through the Internet by allowing employers to enter employee information into a federal database designed to verify whether or not workers are authorized to work in the United States. E-Verify is closely linked with another program, called I-9. Under provisions of the Immigration Reform and Control Act of 1986, all U.S. employers are required to complete an Employment Eligibility Verification Form I-9 for each new employee hired. The I-9 form documents that the prospective employee has shown documentation, such as passports or visa authorizations, to prove identity and work eligibility. E-Verify compares information provided in the I-9 form with millions of other government records and makes a determination about whether the employee can legally work in the country. If the I-9 information matches other government information, the

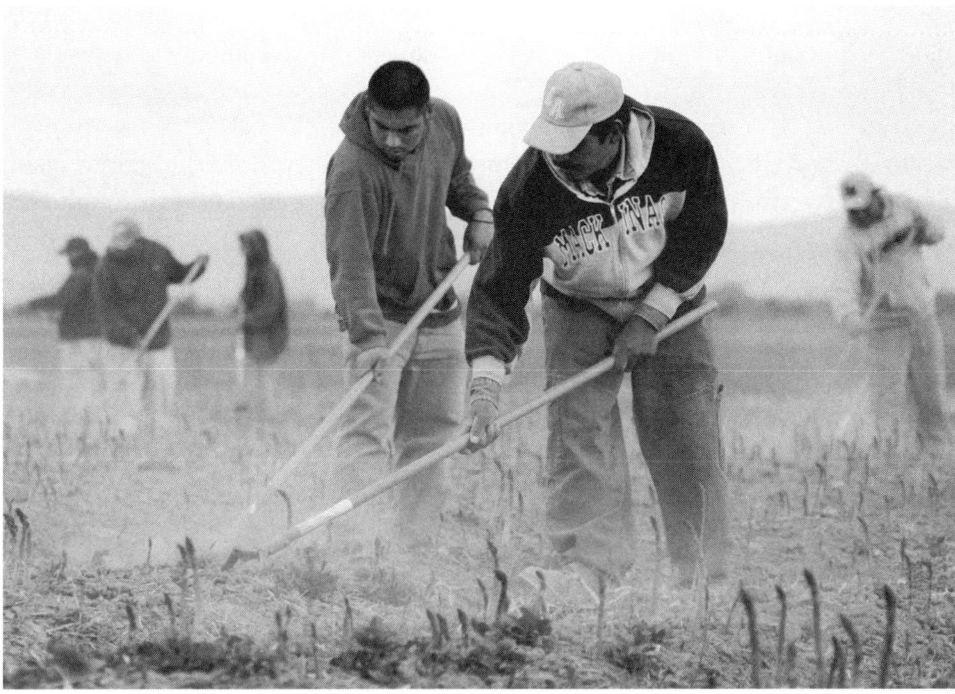

E-Verify is now a widely used program to check for employees' eligibility to work in the United States. In this image, Latino workers till an asparagus field near Toppenish, Washington, 2009. Bringing unlikely allies together, both farmers and immigrant advocacy groups had hoped in the early days of the program to slow down the use of E-Verify to check a worker's eligibility to work in the United States. (AP Photo/Elaine Thompson, File)

employee is deemed to be authorized to work in the United States. If there is a mismatch of information, the employee is given a short period of time to resolve the matter.

Federal agencies and contractors are required to use E-Verify, and it is free and voluntary nationwide for all other U.S. employers. However, a number of states have passed legislation mandating the use of E-Verify statewide for all or certain groups of employees. In 2008, for example, Arizona mandated that all its employers verify the legal status of new employees through the federal E-Verify database. In 2012, the federal E-Verify program was extended by Congress for three years, through September 30, 2015.

Supporters of E-Verify claim that it helps to reduce illegal immigration and gives employers a way to protect themselves and show they are not in violation of laws that prohibit the hiring of undocumented immigrants. Also, according to the Department of Homeland Security (DHS), the home of USCIS, employers are happy with the E-Verify program. The DHS Web site states that in a customer survey of more than 1,300 randomly selected employers who use E-Verify users rated the program exceptionally high in overall customer satisfaction in categories such as registration, the online tutorial, ease of use, technical assistance, and customer service.

Critics of E-Verify, however, point to problems E-Verify poses for both employees and employers. E-Verify is not 100 percent accurate and critics claim that E-Verify errors have already hurt thousands of innocent workers. Employees can be rejected by E-Verify, for example, due to errors resulting from a variety of benign factors, including simple typos, name misspellings, or name changes after marriage. Employees thus rejected by the E-Verify system then are denied employment unless they are able to prove, using their own time and money, that the discrepancy in documentation found by E-Verify is unwarranted. Conversely, E-Verify sometimes makes mistakes that allow illegal, undocumented foreign workers to be considered eligible for work. Critics claim, too, that the E-Verify program fails to prevent illegal immigration or keep employers from hiring illegal workers and instead simply forces workers who are rejected by the program further into the underground economy.

In addition, critics argue that businesses are reluctant to sign up for E-Verify. Certain industries, such as agriculture, have historically been dependent on the use of cheap, illegal workers and do not want the federal government to bar the hiring of those workers. Other employers fear that they will be fined or otherwise sanctioned for hiring illegal workers who manage to beat the E-Verify system. Another complaint against E-Verify is that it creates a huge new federal bureaucracy to track and collect sensitive information on U.S. citizens—a bureaucracy that could pose a significant privacy and security threat by attracting hackers who want to steal identities.

Despite these criticisms, supporters of E-Verify have pushed the Congress in recent years to introduce and pass legislation to mandate that E-Verify be used by all U.S. employers. In February 2015, for example, the U.S. House of Representatives held hearings to consider whether Congress should adopt the Legal Workforce Act (H.R. 2164), a bill that would require the use of E-Verify by all U.S. employers.

Debra Miller

Further Reading

Bier, David. 2012. "Why Everyone Should Fear E-Verify." *The Huffington Post* (July 13). http://www.huffingtonpost.com/david-bier/why-everyone-should-fear-e-verify_b_1610057.html. Accessed September 18, 2015.

Preston, Julia, and Ashley Parker. 2013. "Bill to Expand U.S. Database to Verify Hires." *New York Times*, June 26.

Exclusionary Rule

The Fourth Amendment to the U.S. Constitution protects persons from unreasonable searches and seizures. The amendment is silent, however, as to how this right is to be enforced. In *Weeks v. United States* (1914), the U.S. Supreme Court adopted the so-called exclusionary rule, which held that evidence obtained by police in violation of the Fourth Amendment could not be used against a criminal defendant in a federal trial. In short, because the police had no authority to seize the evidence, the prosecution had no right to introduce the evidence at trial. The *Weeks* decision clearly marked the start of a suppression of evidence doctrine that had not previously existed in the common law.

The exact scope and significance of the decision in *Weeks* have been subjects of much discussion and controversy. This is in large part because the opinion in *Weeks*, though unanimous, was ambiguous about whether the exclusionary rule was a constitutional requirement or simply a judicially created remedy to deter constitutional violations.

On the one hand, the opinion written by Justice William Day observed that to allow the use of illegally seized evidence would be to affirm "a manifest neglect if not an open defiance . . . of the Constitution." Yet the opinion also noted that the exclusion of illegally seized evidence was necessary to deter further police misconduct. Since the case against the defendant would be harmed by the exclusion of relevant evidence, police would be less likely to violate the prohibition against unreasonable searches and seizures. Justice Day further noted that the integrity of trial courts would be undermined if they permitted the introduction of illegally obtained evidence. He emphasized this point by stating: "The efforts of the courts and their officials to bring the guilty to punishment, praise-worthy as they are, are not to be aided by the sacrifice of those great principles established by years of endeavor and suffering which have resulted in their embodiment in the fundamental law of the land."

Almost a century after its adoption, scholars are divided. Some maintain that the Fourth Amendment implicitly requires the exclusion of all illegally seized evidence. Others insist that the exclusionary rule is simply a judicially created remedy applicable only in those situations in which the exclusion of evidence would deter further police misconduct. If the latter interpretation is true, of course, then exceptions to the rule are possible.

The *Weeks* decision explicitly stated that the exclusionary rule did not apply to searches conducted by state police officers. As a result, states were not required to exclude evidence obtained by an unreasonable search and seizure. Some states chose to do so; most did not.

In *Wolf v. Colorado* (1949), the Supreme Court faced the question of whether the Fourth Amendment, and by extension the exclusionary rule, should be applied to the states through the Due Process Clause of the Fourteenth Amendment. While making the Fourth Amendment applicable to the states, the justices specifically rejected the notion that the exclusionary rule should be binding upon the states. In a 5–4 opinion, Justice Felix Frankfurter noted that the rule was a judicial implication without foundation in the Fourth Amendment. Accordingly, states remained free to adopt or ignore the exclusionary rule in state criminal proceedings.

Twelve years later, in *Mapp v. Ohio* (1961), the Supreme Court, again dividing 5–4, overruled this aspect of the *Wolf* decision and extended the federal exclusionary rule to state criminal prosecutions. Justice Tom Clark's opinion for the majority emphasized both the constitutional foundations and the practical necessities of the rule. Reiterating *Weeks*, the opinion called the exclusion doctrine an essential ingredient of the Fourth Amendment and declared it necessary to discourage police misconduct and maintain judicial integrity. As such, all evidence obtained by searches in violation of the Fourth Amendment was inadmissible in state criminal proceedings.

Mapp formally linked the exclusionary rule to the Fourth Amendment. Subsequent decisions of the Supreme Court, however, have deconstitutionalized the rule, redefined its purpose, and limited its application. In *U.S. v. Calandra* (1974), for example, the Court, per Justice Lewis Powell, rejected the notion that the rule was a personal constitutional right. Instead, the six-member majority declared that the exclusionary rule was merely a prophylactic measure designed to deter future unlawful police misconduct. The justices then adopted a cost-benefit approach, concluding that the rule was only to be applied in those settings where the exclusion of evidence would result in the significant deterrence of future police misconduct. In all other settings, the social costs of excluding relevant evidence far outweighed any potential benefits from its application.

This cost-benefit approach has resulted in the curtailment of the operation of the exclusionary rule. In addition, the Supreme Court has formally adopted several exceptions to this rule. The first exception, announced in *Nix v. Williams* (1984), does not require the suppression of evidence that has been seized illegally if the prosecution can establish that the evidence inevitably would have been discovered by lawful means in the course of a continuing investigation. In a companion ruling, *Segura v. United States* (1984), the justices held that the exclusionary rule does not prohibit the use of illegally obtained evidence if the prosecution can establish that the evidence later would have been found as a result of other independent sources.

The most controversial exception was adopted in *United States v. Leon* (1984). The good-faith exception permits the use of illegally seized evidence where police have a search warrant and in good-faith conduct the search on the assumption that the warrant is valid, though the warrant is later found to be unsupported by probable cause. The justices extended this exception in *Illinois v. Krull* (1987), holding that the exclusionary rule does not apply to evidence obtained by police, who acted in objectively reasonable reliance upon a state statute authorizing warrantless searches, but which is subsequently found to violate the Fourth Amendment. *Arizona v. Evans* (1995), meanwhile, held that the exclusionary rule does not require the suppression of evidence seized in violation of the Fourth Amendment where the mistaken information upon which the investigating authorities based their actions resulted from clerical errors of court employees. In each of the aforementioned cases, the Court concluded that no basis existed for believing that the exclusion of evidence would have any deterrent effect upon police (or judicial) misconduct.

The legal parameters of the exclusionary rule were further defined by the Supreme Court in *Herring v. United States* (2009), which upheld the good faith exception to the exclusionary rule in cases of police record-keeping error, and in *Davis v. United States* (2011). In this latter case, the Court determined by a 6–2 vote that the good faith exception to the exclusionary rule applies when the police conduct a search authorized by precedent or statute, even if that precedent or statute is later found to be unconstitutional.

More than a century after its adoption, the exclusionary rule continues to generate controversy. Supporters of the exclusionary rule argue that without the rule the protection of the Fourth Amendment is of no value. In the words of Justice Frank Murphy in dissent in *Wolf*, the rule is the only means of "giving content to the commands of the Fourth Amendment." Without it, nothing will deter the police from heavy-handed tactics and clear violations of individual constitutional rights. Opponents assert that the rule is contrary to justice and leads to the withholding of valuable evidence that could help establish truth in judicial proceedings.

Richard A. Glenn

Further Reading

Maclin, Tracy. 2013. *The Supreme Court and the Fourth Amendment's Exclusionary Rule.* New York: Oxford University Press.

Stephens, Otis H., Jr. and Richard Glenn. 2005. *Unreasonable Searches and Seizures: Rights and Liberties under the Law.* Santa Barbara, CA: ABC-CLIO.

Executive Order 9066

Executive Order 9066 is a presidential order signed by President Franklin D. Roosevelt on February 19, 1942, which authorized the relocation and internment of tens of thousands of Japanese Americans during World War II. The executive order gave the U.S. military the power to remove Japanese American citizens and Japanese

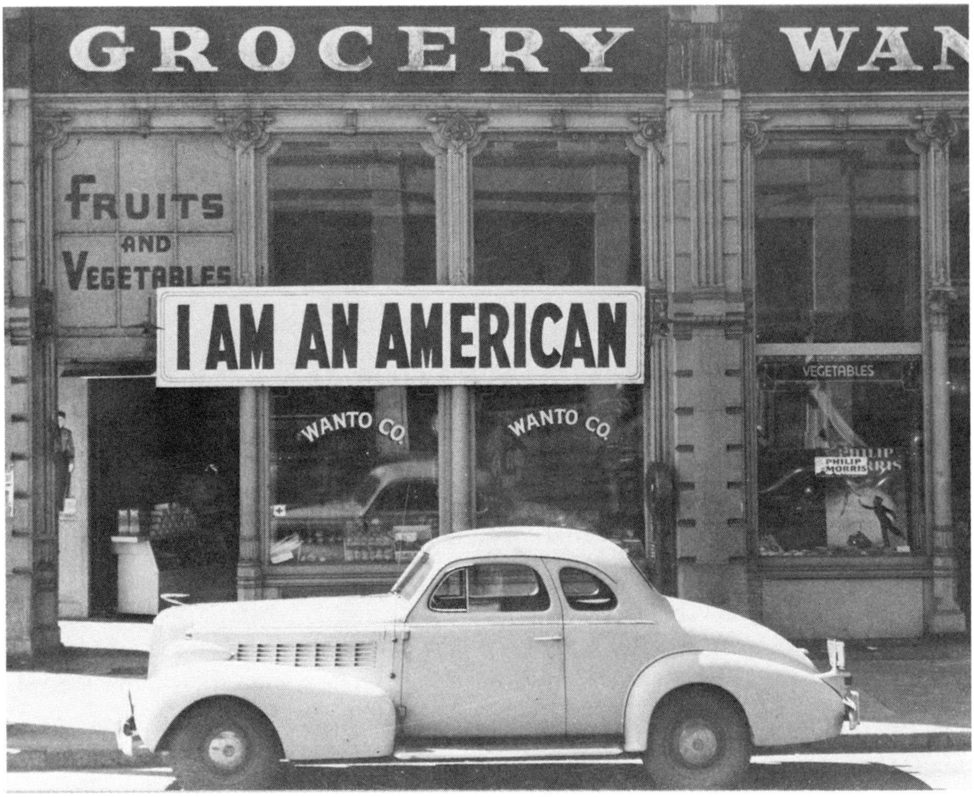

In a dark period of U.S. history, a large sign reading "I am an American" was placed in the window of a store in California. The store was closed following orders to persons of Japanese descent to evacuate from certain West Coast areas. The owner, a University of California graduate, was housed with hundreds of evacuees in War Relocation Authority centers for the duration of World War II. (Library of Congress)

immigrants suspected of being resident enemy aliens from a large stretch of the West Coast from Washington to California as well as inland areas in Southern Arizona. Those citizens were ordered to pack up a few possessions and were transported to hastily constructed detention centers located in remote areas of the West. Although the executive order largely affected Japanese Americans, it also was used to arrest and intern American citizens of German and Italian descent. The U.S. Supreme Court upheld Executive Order 9066 during the war, but since then the order has been widely criticized as a gross violation of Americans' civil liberties.

Historians attribute Executive Order 9066 as a by-product of war hysteria following the Japanese bombing of a U.S. naval base at Pearl Harbor, Hawaii, on December 7, 1941. The Pearl Harbor attack shocked Americans because it came as a complete surprise and did significant damage to American ships and naval forces.

Within days, the United States had formally declared war against both Japan and Germany. During this period, President Roosevelt came under enormous pressure to protect United States from future Japanese aggression. Fears focused on the West Coast, where important military bases, shipping ports, and agriculture were believed to be vulnerable to another Japanese attack.

According to the order, detentions of Japanese Americans were justified because the successful prosecution of the war required every possible protection against espionage and against sabotage to national defense materials and sites. However, these war fears combined with preexisting racism against Japanese Americans in the West to create an environment in which people of Japanese descent could be singled out for persecution without significant opposition from the public or public officials.

Implementation of the order by an agency called the War Relocation Authority (WRA) brought ruination to the lives of as many as 120,000 Japanese Americans, causing them to lose homes, property, farms, and businesses without any type of compensation. Military officers systematically rounded up Japanese immigrants, without regard to whether they were citizens or not, allowing them to take only whatever they could carry and giving them very little time to prepare for moving to internment centers. Many of those detained were second-generation Japanese Americans, who had never been to Japan and who only knew American lifestyles. The detention centers where the evacuees were housed were crudely built in barren areas in Arizona, Utah, California, Arkansas, Idaho, and Colorado. The centers resembled concentration camps, with barbed wire fences, armed guards, and cramped, uninsulated wood buildings that offered little to no privacy or protection from the cold or the elements. Families were forced to adapt to these difficult conditions, and this experience often disrupted traditional roles and broke family bonds between husbands and wives and parents and their children.

The internment program authorized by Executive Order 9066 was challenged by Fred Korematsu, a 23-year-old Japanese American who refused the order to move with his family to a detention camp in Tanforan, California. Instead, he chose to stay with his girlfriend and tried to avoid detection by assuming a new identity and having plastic surgery done to change the appearance of his eyes. Nevertheless, Korematsu was caught by the military and sent into detention. In a test case brought by the American Civil Liberties Union, Korematsu sued the government, alleging race discrimination and violation of his constitutional rights. Eventually, his case reached the U.S. Supreme Court, but on December 18, 1944, in a 6–3 decision, the Court in *Korematsu v. United States* upheld Korematsu's arrest and ruled that the internment of Japanese Americans was constitutional. The Court's majority opinion reasoned that Executive Order 9066 was justified on the basis of military necessity because U.S. military officials feared that Japanese Americans would be disloyal and might assist with a Japanese invasion of the West Coast. Three justices dissented from the majority opinion, however, arguing that the decision validated racial discrimination.

The same day as the *Korematsu* decision, however, the Court also issued a unanimous decision in a case known as ex parte endo that struck a serious blow against internment. In the ex parte endo decision, the Court stated that citizens *believed by the government itself to be loyal to the United States* could not legally be detained. Once this decision was rendered, the U.S. government began taking steps to release detainees and return them to their communities.

It took several decades for the U.S. government to acknowledge that the internment program created by Executive Order 9066 was a mistake—and a violation of core American values.

In 1980, President Jimmy Carter established the Commission on Wartime Relocation and Internment of Civilians (CWRIC) to study the matter, and in 1983 the commission concluded that the incarceration of Japanese Americans was the result of race prejudice, war hysteria, and a failure of political leadership. Also in 1983, Korematsu's conviction was reversed when a group of pro bono attorneys succeeded in reopening the *Korematsu* case. The reversal was based on the discovery of government documents by University of California San Diego political science professor Peter Irons, showing that the government's claim of military necessity was fabricated and unfounded. Finally, in 1988, President Ronald Reagan publicly apologized for the government's treatment of Japanese Americans and authorized reparations to be paid to former internees or their descendants. In 1998, President Bill Clinton awarded Fred Korematsu the Presidential Medal of Freedom. Korematsu died on March 31, 2005.

Debra Miller

Further Reading

Des Jardins, Julie. "From Citizen to Enemy: The Tragedy of Japanese Internment." The Gilder Lehrman Institute of American History. The Gilder Lehrman Institute Web site. http://www.gilderlehrman.org/history-by-era/world-war-ii/essays/from-citizen-enemy-tragedy-japanese-internment. Accessed February 23, 2015.

The Fred T. Korematsu Institute. 2015. "About Fred Korematsu." The Fred T. Korematsu Institute Web site. http://korematsuinstitute.org/institute/aboutfred/. Accessed February 23, 2015.

Goldstein, Richard. 2005. "Fred Korematsu, 86, Dies; Lost Key Suit on Internment." *New York Times* (April 1). http://www.nytimes.com/2005/04/01/national/01korematsu.html?_r=0. Accessed September 18, 2015.

History Matters. "Executive Order 9066: The President Authorizes Japanese Relocation." History Matters Web site. http://historymatters.gmu.edu/d/5154. Accessed February 23, 2015.

Robinson, Greg. 2001. *By Order of the President: FDR and the Internment of Japanese Americans*. Cambridge, MA: Harvard University Press.
Tateishi, John. 1984. *And Justice for All: An Oral History of the Japanese American Detention Camps*. Seattle: University of Washington Press.

Executive Order 12333

Executive Order 12333, entitled "United States Intelligence Activities," is a directive issued on December 4, 1981, by U.S. president Ronald Reagan dealing with the scope of authority given to U.S. intelligence agencies. In part, the executive order continued a ban on U.S. assassinations of foreign leaders, created by previous executive orders signed by President Gerald Ford (Executive Order 11905) and President Jimmy Carter (Executive Order 12036). In addition, however, President Reagan's executive order significantly expanded the ability of U.S. intelligence agencies to collect foreign intelligence data—in part by ordering federal agencies to cooperate with requests for such information.

Executive Order 12333 was amended several times by President George W. Bush as part of a U.S. campaign to target terrorism networks following the terrorist attacks of September 11, 2001, on American soil. It was amended by Executive Order 13284 in 2003, by Executive Order 13555 in 2004, and by Executive Order 13470 in 2008 to reflect changes to the structure of the intelligence community, such as the creation of the Department of Homeland Security (DHS) and the Director of National Intelligence.

Documents released by the federal government in 2014 in response to a lawsuit filed by the American Civil Liberties Union indicated that Executive Order 12333 is heavily relied upon as a legal basis for intelligence activities that American national security agencies undertake outside the United States. The released documents, for example, included a 2007 NSA manual that cited Executive Order 12333 as "the primary source of NSA foreign intelligence-gathering authority." NSA is one of the largest and most secret U.S. intelligence agencies and in recent years has been the focus of public debate because of leaks by Edward Snowden, a former employee of a contractor affiliated with the agency. Documents leaked by Snowden have suggested that the NSA is collecting massive amounts of data on a global basis, often also sweeping up data on American citizens.

Critics of U.S. intelligence activities have charged that surveillance activities, programs, and initiatives carried out under the authority of Executive Order 12333 pose a significant threat to the privacy and security of Americans. Critics explain that Executive Order 12333 allows data collection that would be forbidden under other statutory sources, such as Section 215 of the USA PATRIOT Act and the Foreign Intelligence Surveillance Act (FISA) of 1978. Section 215 of the USA PATRIOT Act, for example, builds in certain protections for U.S. citizens. It only allows the bulk collection of U.S. telephone metadata—that is, lists of phone numbers—and specifically disallows collection of the audio content of telephone conversations of American citizens. In contrast, Executive Order 12333 provides no such protections for data-collecting programs conducted outside the United States. Executive Order 12333 therefore authorizes, as an incidental part of foreign intelligence collection efforts, the broad collection of American citizens' telephone conversations, including the audio content. No limits are placed by the executive order on how much data can be collected, and the order allows the agency to retain this data indefinitely—all without ever showing that U.S. citizens are suspected of any type of crime or wrongdoing.

Dividing data collection into different categories with different rules depending on whether it is collected inside or outside the United States, critics say, does not make sense in today's world, when U.S. citizens travel frequently out of the country and their communications are sent around the globe. Many Americans routinely make cell phone calls overseas or while they are travelling, for example. And e-mail systems like Google and Yahoo utilize servers located in various foreign countries, so e-mails, e-mail contact lists, and other information sent by Americans—even those sent to recipients within the United States—can easily be collected as part of foreign intelligence programs.

Critics also point out that because Executive Order 12333 is not a statute but rather a directive from the executive branch it is not subject to effective oversight by the U.S. Congress like other intelligence activities governed by legislation. The permanent intelligence committees set up in the House and Senate to provide oversight over American intelligence efforts simply have not focused on NSA's broad authority under the executive order. In 2014, however, privacy and open government advocates called upon President Obama and the Privacy and Civil Liberties Oversight Board, an agency in the executive branch of government that advises the president and executive branch officials on privacy and civil liberties issues, to review Executive Order 12333 surveillance, release information about the order's surveillance programs to the public, and improve privacy protections for Americans.

Debra Miller

Further Reading

"Executive Order 12333—United States Intelligence Activities." *Federal Register*. The U.S. National Archives and Records Administration Web site. http://www.archives.gov/federal-register/codification/executive-order/12333.html. Accessed February 18, 2015.

Gorski, Ashley. 2014. "New NSA Documents Shine More Light into Black Box of Executive Order 12333." ACLU Blog of Rights (October 30). https://www.aclu.org/blog/national-security/new-nsa-documents-shine-more-light-black-box-executive-order-12333. Accessed February 18, 2015.

Joel, Alexander W. 2014. "The Truth about Executive Order 12333." *Politico* (August 18). http://www.politico.com/magazine/story/2014/08/the-truth-about-executive-order-12333-110121.html#.VOUv-8o5AVA. Accessed February 18, 2015.

Raymond, Nate, and Aruna Viswanatha. 2014. "New Documents Show Legal Basis for NSA Surveillance Programs." *Reuters* (September 29). http://www.reuters.com/article/2014/09/29/us-nsa-surveillance-idUSKCN0HO1YQ20140929. Accessed February 18, 2015.

Tye, John Napier. 2014. "Meet Executive Order 12333: The Reagan Rule That Lets the NSA Spy on Americans." *The Washington Post* (July 18). http://www.washingtonpost.com/opinions/meet-executive-order-12333-the-reagan-rule-that-lets-the-nsa-spy-on-americans/2014/07/18/93d2ac22-0b93-11e4-b8e5-d0de80767fc2_story.html. Accessed February 18, 2015.

F

Fair Information Practices

Fair Information Practices (FIPs) are a set of internationally recognized principles for addressing the privacy of information about individuals. Although information privacy is a subset of privacy, it is a major focus of much privacy legislation in general and of online privacy in particular. FIPs are important because they provide the underlying policy for many national laws addressing privacy and data protection matters. The FIPs principles set out the elements of what is usually meant by the general term "information privacy."

FIPs originated with a 1973 U.S. Department of Health, Education, and Welfare (HEW) advisory committee. The same concepts were later revised and restated by the Council of Europe and by the Organization for Economic Cooperation and Development (OECD) at the beginning of the 1980s. The eight principles set out by the OECD are the Collection Limitation Principle, Data Quality Principle, Purpose Specification Principle, Use Limitation Principle, Security Safeguards Principle, Openness Principle, Individual Participation Principle, and Accountability Principle.

These principles have been highly influential. The original 1973 HEW principles were enacted into law as the Privacy Act of 1974, a law that regulates privacy practices of federal agencies. The restatement of FIPs by European institutions influenced privacy legislation in the European Union and elsewhere around the world. While there is broad international consensus on the substance of FIPs, different statements of FIPs sometimes are organized differently.

FIPs are not self-implementing or self-enforcing. Actual implementation of FIPs at the statutory, regulatory, or data controller level can vary widely, depending on the country, the data controller, type of data, conflicting goals, and other factors. The actual application of FIPs in any given context requires judgment and skill. Most agree that the principles should be applied more rigorously to medical records than to pizza delivery records.

To illustrate, the accountability principle can be met through many different mechanisms. They include criminal or civil penalties, national or provincial supervisory officials, other administrative enforcement, various forms of self-regulation including industry codes and privacy seals, formal privacy policies, compliance audits, employee training, privacy officers at the data controller level, and other methods. Similarly, providing data subjects with access to their own records may have different exceptions, depending on whether the records are maintained for employment, educational, credit, medical, law enforcement, or national security purposes.

Notwithstanding the worldwide recognition and adoption of FIPs, critics can be found on both sides. Some in the privacy community believe that FIPs are too weak, allow too many exemptions, do not require establishment of a national privacy agency, fail to account for the weaknesses of self-regulation, and have not kept pace with information technology. Critics from a business perspective often prefer to limit FIPs to reduced elements of notice, consent, and accountability. They complain that other elements may be unworkable, expensive, or inconsistent with openness or free speech principles. Some versions of FIPs advocated by business critics leave out or water down principles deemed inconvenient or too costly to implement.

The continuing importance of FIPs in an interconnected or networked environment is underscored by the 2009 Madrid Declaration—a civil society document signed by more than 100 worldwide organizations and by more than 100 experts—published concurrently with the 31st annual meeting of the International Conference of Privacy and Data Protection Commissioners. Among other things, the Madrid Doctrine reaffirms support for a global framework of Fair Information Practices.

Robert Gellman and Pam Dixon

Further Reading

Gellman, Robert. 2015. *Fair Information Practices: A Basic History.* Bobgellman.com Web site. http://bobgellman.com/rg-docs/rg-FIPShistory.pdf. Accessed March 26, 2015.

Solove, Daniel J., Marc Rotenberg, and Paul M. Schwartz. 2006. *Privacy, Information, and Technology.* New York: Aspen Publishing.

Federal Bureau of Investigation (FBI)

The Federal Bureau of Investigation (FBI) is the largest law enforcement agency in the United States. Created in 1908 during the presidency of Theodore Roosevelt as the Bureau of Investigation (BOI), it has conducted surveillance of U.S. citizens

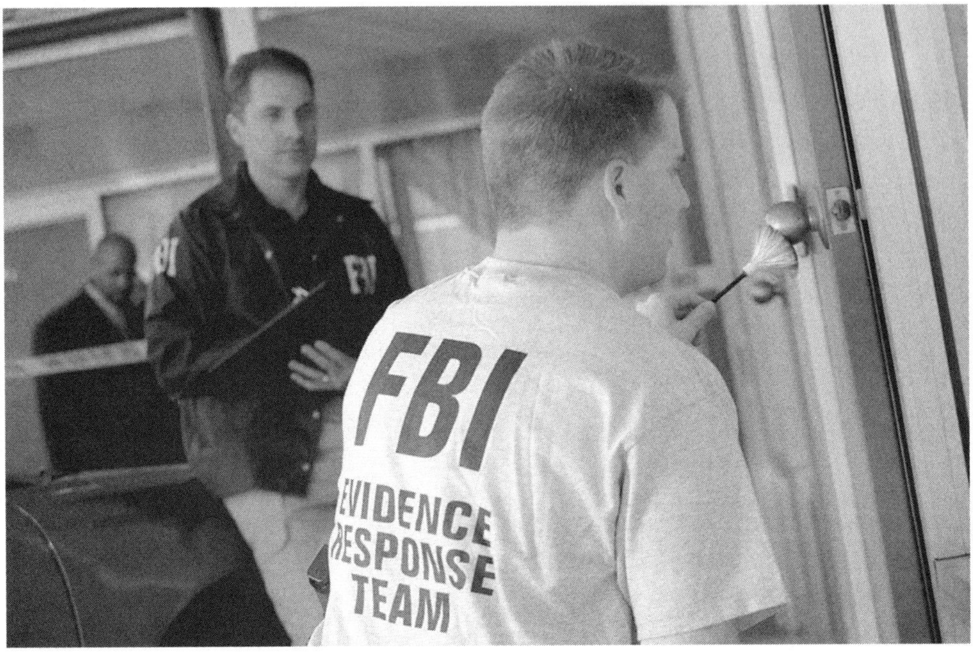

Federal Bureau of Investigation evidence response team dusts for fingerprints at a crime scene. (Federal Bureau of Investigation)

in one form or another since its inception. Although the FBI started out as a very small organization meant to tackle the rare case of interstate crime, it grew during times of war to also protect the nation from foreign threats, and now has a worldwide presence.

During the Progressive Era, innovations in transportation and communication made it easier for criminals to conduct their illegal activities across state borders. These innovations included the mass production of the automobile, extensive train lines, and spread of the telephone. On the other side, citizens demanded that the federal government step into a more protective role because state and local governments were unable to effectively cooperate to fight interstate crime syndicates. The U.S. Department of Justice had a small, scattered force of investigators to fight crime and corruption at the federal level, but it was not until 1908 that Attorney General Charles Bonaparte was able to create a unified organization.

The bureau was initially composed of 34 special agents, including detectives and secret servicemen, but grew quickly. During the 1910s, it expanded to employ over 600 people and took on a greater role during World War I, which included investigation of espionage and other war-related crimes. Its focus turned to organized crime and the enforcement of Prohibition during the 1920s. In response to bootlegging and associated crime that assumed new levels of deadliness with the commercial introduction of machine guns, the FBI set up field offices in 30 cities around the country, started a formal training process for agents, and initiated a countrywide fingerprinting process to help identify criminals and solve cases. The agency began wiretapping in the 1920s to arrest bootleggers. The Supreme Court determined that this was legal as long as agents did not enter a suspect's home to conduct the wiretapping. The bureau also began reporting national crime statistics and standardized crime reporting systems.

During the 1930s, when the organization adopted its present name, the FBI became the most powerful law enforcement agency in the United States under the leadership of J. Edgar Hoover. As this era unfolded, lawmakers increased the FBI agent's power to make arrests, carry weapons, and persecute criminal offenders. The U.S. Congress gave the FBI more power and funding through several federal crime laws, so the organization founded a technical laboratory to process forensic evidence and a national academy to train agents. However, with the start of World War II, the FBI once again turned toward investigations of espionage and sabotage. The agency had a total of over 17,000 employees by the time the war ended.

The FBI took a leading role fighting communism in the United States after World War II. Its civil rights record was mixed. Although agents often carried out orders to support civil rights legislation during the 1960s, Hoover also approved surveillance of Martin Luther King Jr. and other civil rights leaders. The antiwar sentiment that came about during the Vietnam War challenged the FBI's role as protector against protesters who railed against the unpopular war. Some more radical groups turned against the U.S. government, making the possibility of homegrown terrorism a reality. In this turbulent environment, Hoover died and the FBI was without a credible director during the Watergate Scandal. In 1973, Clarence Kelley was appointed director of the FBI. He and Attorney General Edward Levi responded to revelations that the intelligence-gathering operations of the bureau abrogated citizens' constitutional rights by establishing new guidelines to prevent unlawful abuses of domestic surveillance and foreign counterintelligence operations.

In 1984, the FBI established the Computer Analysis and Response Team (CART) to gather evidence from computers. Greater incidence of international crime, including the drug trade, white-collar scandals, and terrorism made establishment of a wider net imperative. The agency continued to grow, reaching over 20,000 employees by 1988. During the 1990s, the introduction of DNA testing revolutionized the accuracy with which criminals could be identified. The 2000s brought the information age, and the FBI responded with the National Infrastructure Protection Center (NIPC) to protect the national Internet infrastructure against malicious attack from cyber threats. The FBI also implemented an electronic surveillance software program called Carnivore under President Bill Clinton.

The 2001 terrorist attacks in New York City and Washington, D.C., reoriented the FBI's mandate to protect the United States from future terrorist attacks. In the

9/11 Commission's report about the terrorist attack, the FBI was blamed for not cooperating with other national security agencies and for maintaining outdated procedures that hindered fruitful investigation. Robert S. Mueller was sworn in as director of the FBI the same year that the PATRIOT Act was passed. This legislation gave the organization sweeping new investigative powers, some of which have been heavily criticized by privacy advocates for eroding civil liberties.

Mary Le Rouge

Further Reading

Ball, Kirstie, and Laureen Snider, eds. 2013. *The Surveillance-Industrial Complex: A Political Economy of Surveillance.* New York: Routledge.

Burrough, Bryan. 2015. *Days of Rage: America's Radical Underground, the FBI, and the Forgotten Age of Revolutionary Violence.* New York: Penguin.

Landau, Susan. 2011. *Surveillance or Security?: The Risks Posed by New Wiretapping Technologies.* Cambridge, MA: MIT Press.

Theoharis, Athan. 2004. *The FBI and American Democracy: A Brief Critical History.* Lawrence: University Press of Kansas.

Weiner, Tim. 2012. *Enemies: A History of the FBI.* New York: Random House.

Firearms Registration

Firearms registration laws mandate that individuals owning guns are legally required to register those weapons with a designated law enforcement agency. There are several reasons for the establishment of a firearms registration system: such laws aid law enforcement in combating the illegal distribution of firearms, allow police to trace the gun ownership of weapons used in criminal activity, and impose accountability on gun owners and dealers.

During the gun registration process, a record is created that includes a weapon's serial number and information about the owner, such as the results of a background check and current address. The record is updated if a gun owner transfers title of the gun to another individual. In the case of a lost or stolen gun, registration laws require gun owners to report the loss.

In the United States, there is no comprehensive national gun registry. Instead, there is a limited registration system that was mandated by the National Firearms Act (NFA) of 1934. Passed right after the repeal of Prohibition, the law was proposed as a response to a wave of organized crime violence, which culminated in the bloody St. Valentine's Day massacre on February 14, 1929, in Lincoln Park, Chicago.

The NFA created a narrow category of weapons frequently used in gangland crimes, which would be registered and taxed. This new category, which came to be

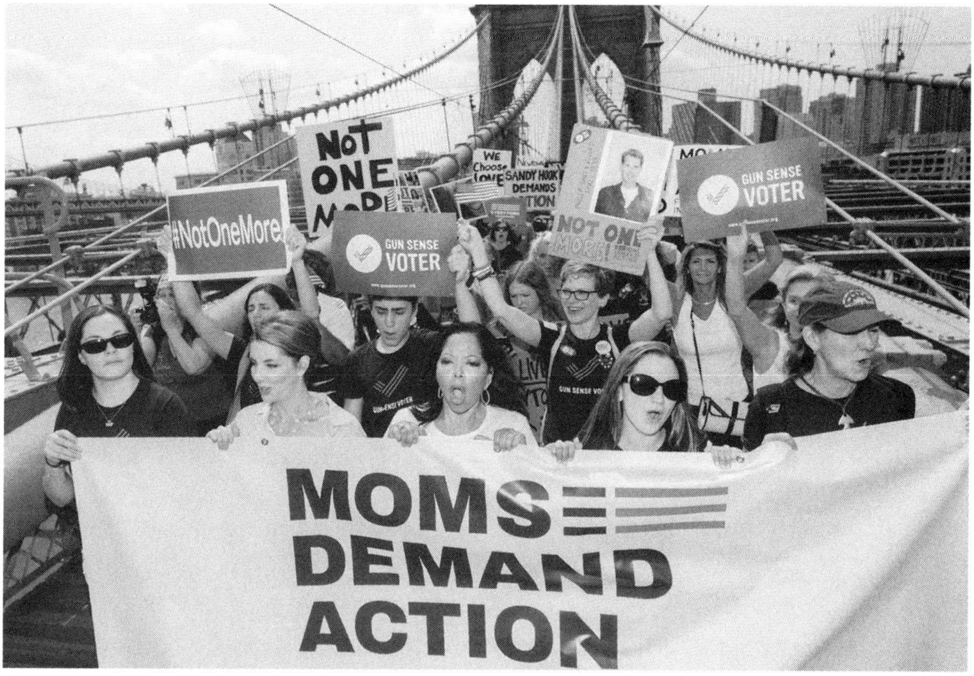

Hundreds of demonstrators march across the Brooklyn Bridge to call for tougher gun control laws, June 14, 2014, in New York. The protest was underwritten by former New York mayor Michael Bloomberg, one of the most visible gun control advocates in the United States, and included relatives of some of those slain in the 2012 shooting rampage at Sandy Hook Elementary School in Newtown, Connecticut. (AP Photo/John Minchillo)

known as NFA firearms, included machine guns, short-barreled shotguns or rifles (having barrels less than 18 inches in length), and mufflers or silencers. The tax to register and transfer titles of NFA firearms totaled $200, which is equivalent to around $3,500 today. The prohibitive tax was designed to discourage the transfer of ownership of these guns.

The NFA was challenged in the late 1960s when a convicted felon, Miles Edward Haynes, was prosecuted for failing to register his firearm under the 1934 law. In *Haynes v. United States,* Haynes argued that requiring him to register his gun was tantamount to self-incrimination, because he was prohibited from owning a weapon because of his felony conviction. The NFA was unconstitutional because it violated the Fifth Amendment of the U.S. Constitution, which protects individuals from being forced to incriminate themselves.

In 1968, the U.S. Supreme Court sided with the petitioner in *Haynes v. United States.* In its decision, the Court held that the registration requirement under the NFA was a violation of an individual's constitutional rights. In effect, the decision made the NFA unenforceable.

The U.S. Congress amended the NFA later that year to reflect the Supreme Court ruling. In the Gun Control Act of 1968, Congress designated the federal government responsible for registering NFA firearms, not the individual. In addition, a provision was added to prohibit the use of any registration information as evidence in a criminal proceeding.

Over the years, Congress, the U.S. Department of Treasury, and the Bureau of Alcohol, Tobacco, and Firearms (ATF) have weakened the NFA through regulations and rulings that more narrowly define the type of firearms covered by the law. There has not been the political will by Congress to create a comprehensive national gun registry in recent years.

Six U.S. states and the District of Columbia have stepped in to create their own gun registry systems. Only two, Hawaii and the District of Columbia, have systems mandating that all firearms be registered with the designated law enforcement authorities.

Eight states prohibit registration of some or all firearms, including Delaware, Florida, Georgia, Idaho, Pennsylvania, Rhode Island, South Dakota, and Vermont. There are exceptions to the registration ban for convicted felons.

In the wake of the 2012 Sandy Hook Elementary School shooting, which resulted in the murder of 20 small schoolchildren and 6 adult staff members in Newtown, Connecticut, there was a renewed push by gun safety advocates for a national gun registry as part of a larger package of gun safety measures. Although the public signaled that it would support some tighter regulation of guns, such as expanded background checks, political pressure applied by gun control opponents such as the National Rifle Association (NRA) kept Congress from taking action.

Margaret Haerens

Further Reading

Bureau of Alcohol, Tobacco and Firearms. *ATF National Firearms Act Handbook.* ATF Web site. https://www.atf.gov/firearms/national-firearms-act-handbook. Accessed March 28, 2015.

Goode, Erica, and Sheryl Gay Stolberg. 2012. "Legal Curbs Said to Hamper ATF in Gun Inquiries." *New York Times* (December 25). http://www.nytimes.com/2012/12/26/us/legislative-handcuffs-limit-atfs-ability-to-fight-gun-crime.html?pagewanted=all. Accessed March 28, 2015.

Kopel, Dave. "The Catastrophic Consequences of Gun Registration." *NRA Publications.* http://www.nrapublications.org/index.php/15162/the-catastrophic-consequences-of-gun-registration/. Accessed March 28, 2015.

Marty, John. 2013. "Regulating Guns Like Cars: Perspective on the Gun Debate after Sandy Hook." *Minneapolis Post* (January 3). http://www.minnpost.com/community-voices/2013/01/regulating-guns-cars-perspective-gun-debate-after-sandy-hook. Accessed March 28, 2015.

Firewalls

A firewall is known as the first line of defense for computers and networks that use the Internet. They can be either hardware or software; most computer operating systems have a firewall built in, and routers also come equipped with a basic firewall. Firewalls are located at the entry point through which information must pass to get into a system. They also protect information that is trying to leave the network. The firewall blocks any data that does not meet specific criteria, set forth by rules in the programming, from entering or exiting the system.

Many different kinds of firewalls exist, and each of these varies in complexity and capability; they also have their own set of limitations, depending upon what they are designed to accomplish. Firewalls can protect networks from viruses that destroy files or cause malfunctions; they can also prevent malicious code from entering the system.

Firewalls do not only filter incoming information, they also scan all outgoing data to be sure nothing of import leaves the network. They make sure that personal information, such as banking and tax data, and passwords remain confidential and are not transmitted outside the system. A firewall also ensures that any unusual behavior on one's computer is not allowed to exit and cause harm to other computers and networks.

Although firewalls provide a successful initial defense for a computer system, they are not infallible. Hackers have developed a variety of ways to circumvent firewalls. Many firewalls can be fooled by files that seem to be from a legitimate source. This means that malicious communications can enter the system, and once a firewall has been compromised, it becomes vulnerable to any number of breaches. Without a good firewall protecting a computer or network, hackers can easily hijack the computer in order to send out viruses.

Firewalls also do nothing to prevent a computer from being physically trespassed upon. If a hacker gains physical access to a computer, they can alter the firewall settings to allow malicious communications to enter, or exit, the system.

Firewalls protect computer and network systems from any number of encroachments from ill-intentioned sources. However, they will not necessarily stop law enforcement from finding a way around them. Police agencies often rely upon evidence retrieved from computers; firewalls and even encrypted information do not stand in their way. In accordance with the Fourth Amendment, warrants must be issued to government agencies and law enforcement bodies to search electronic devices; therefore, government agencies must have a way around encryptions and firewalls to gain access to the information.

Government agencies also utilize firewalls as part of their overall electronic security systems. Indeed, government agencies utilize some of the most advanced security measures, yet hackers are still able to access the sensitive information they possess. According to the Government Accountability Office (GAO), in fact, the so-called cyber incidents involving government agencies increased by 35 percent between 2010 and 2013. Hackers are not only acting as spies seeking government information, but they are also looking for the personal information that government agencies harbor in their databases.

Despite all these hacks on government networks, as well as networks belonging to companies and individuals, firewalls are still the first step that should be taken to secure a network. In conjunction with other security measures, such as antispyware and antimalware, firewalls are very effective in protecting computers from hackers and keeping personal information secure.

Grace Vandemark

Further Reading

Fakhoury, Hanni, and Nadia Kayyali. "Know Your Rights." Electronic Frontier Foundation. Last updated October 2014. https://www.eff.org/issues/know-your-rights. Accessed May 13, 2015.

Frates, Chris, and Curt Devine. 2014. "Government Hacks and Security Breaches Skyrocket." CNN (December 19). http://www.cnn.com/2014/12/19/politics/government-hacks-and-security-breaches-skyrocket/. Accessed May 13, 2015.

Ginter, Andrew. 2013. "13 Ways Your Firewall Could Fail You." Wired Innovation (August 12). http://insights.wired.com/profiles/blogs/do-you-know-the-13-ways-your-firewall-could-fail-you#axzz3VvcsaPgF. Accessed March 30, 2015.

Greenberg, Andy. 2010. "Encryption Can't Stop the Wiretapping Boom." *Forbes* (April 30). http://www.forbes.com/sites/andygreenberg/2014/04/08/darpa-funded-researchers-help-you-learn-to-hack-a-car-for-a-tenth-the-price/. Accessed May 13, 2015.

The University of Texas at Austin. "Firewalls: What They Are, What They Can Do for You." http://www.utexas.edu/its/secure/articles/firewalls.php. Accessed March 30, 2015.

Five Eyes

The "Five Eyes"—sometimes known as the Five Eyes Alliance or the Five Eyes Agreement—refers to a long-standing global surveillance network consisting of the leading intelligence agencies of five primarily English-speaking nations—the United States, the United Kingdom, New Zealand, Australia, and Canada. The member agencies are the U.S. National Security Agency (NSA), the UK's Government Communications Headquarters (GCHQ), New Zealand's Government Communications Security Bureau (GCSB), the Australian Signals Directorate (ASD), and Communications Security Establishment, Canada (CSEC).

Historians trace the origins of the Five Eyes to the World War II era, when American and British intelligence collaborated closely in their efforts to defeat the Axis powers. After the war, in 1946, the United States and United Kingdom decided to continue sharing sensitive intelligence data with one another. The two nations cobbled together a secret British–U.S. Communication Agreement (later known as the UKUSA agreement) that enabled them to share all kinds of secret surveillance intelligence with one another. Their joint operations were explicitly related to "foreign intelligence," which the agreement defined as "all communications of the government or of any military, air, or naval force; faction, party, department, agency, or bureau of a foreign country; or of any person or persons acting or purporting to act therefor, and shall include communications of a foreign country which may contain information of military, political or economic value." Not surprisingly, most of the information shared between the U.S. and British intelligence agencies pertained to the Soviet Union and other Cold War foes in Eastern Europe and Asia.

By 1955, the secret agreement had been expanded to include Australia, Canada, and New Zealand, thus bringing the Five Eyes Alliance to its present membership. Since then, the Five Eyes has adjusted their surveillance operations and information-sharing practices to meet the challenges of—and surveillance opportunities opened by—ever-changing communications technology.

For the rest of the 20th century, the Five Eyes operated under a shroud of secrecy that was so heavy that the prime minister's office of Australia was reportedly unaware of its existence until the early 1970s. According to Privacy International, a UK-based organization devoted to protecting privacy rights around the world, "the existence of the agreement has been noted in history books, and references are often made to it as part of reporting on the intelligence agencies [but] there is little knowledge or understanding outside the services themselves of exactly what the arrangement comprises."

The first formal acknowledgement of the Five Eyes from any of the member nations did not come until 2010, when the GCHQ approved a public release of some of the alliance's early documents from the 1940s and 1950s. This release sparked renewed interest in the group, but fascination and concern about the Five Eyes reached a dramatically higher level after whistle-blower Edward Snowden revealed major, previously unknown, surveillance activities being carried out by the NSA and GCHQ on its own citizens and other ordinary citizens around the globe. Many of the documents released by Snowden showed the extent to which the Five Eyes members routinely shared sensitive, top secret surveillance intelligence with one another.

Since then, officials familiar with the Five Eyes operations have come forward to defend the program's value and practices. "The benefits of membership are immense, say intelligence experts," according to a PBS story on the alliance. "While the U.S. has worldwide satellite surveillance abilities, the club benefits from each member's regional specialty, like Australia and New Zealand's in the Far East. 'We practice intelligence burden sharing,' said one former U.S. official. 'We can say, "that's hard for us cover, so can you?"' The ease and rapidity of information-sharing among the five 'makes it quicker to connect the dots,' said another intelligence veteran. 'You can't underestimate the importance of the common language, legal system and culture,' said another."

Still, the United States is recognized as "first among equals" in the Five Eyes membership, by virtue of the scope of its operations, the sophistication of the technology it can bring to bear, and the financial resources upon which it can draw. As the Australian magazine *The Age* observed, though, the other members do make notable contributions: "Britain is a leader in traditional spying, thanks in part to its reach into countries that were once part of the British Empire. Australia has excelled in gathering regional signals and intelligence, providing a window into the growing might of Asia. Canadians, Australians and New Zealanders can sometimes prove useful spies because they don't come under the same scrutiny as their British and American counterparts."

According to Privacy International and other experts, rumors of a strict "no-spying-on-one-another" provision within the alliance are false. But the group states that "there is a general understanding that citizens will not be directly targeted and where communications are incidentally intercepted there will be an effort to minimize the use and analysis of such communications by the intercepting State."

Kevin Hillstrom

Further Reading

Greenwald, Glen. 2014. *No Place to Hide: Edward Snowden, the NSA, and the Surveillance State*. New York: Metropolitan Books.

Perry, Nick, and Paisley Dodds. 2013. "Five Eyes Spying Alliance Will Survive Edward Snowden: Experts." *The Age* (July 18). http://www.theage.com.au/it-pro/security-it/five-eyes-spying-alliance-will-survive-edward-snowden-experts-20130718-hv0xw.html. Accessed May 8, 2015.

Privacy International. n.d. "What Is the 5 Eyes?" Privacy International Web site. https://www.privacyinternational.org/?q=node/51. Accessed May 8, 2015.

Viotti, Paul R., Michael A. Opheim, and Nicholas Bowen. 2008. *Terrorism and Homeland Security: Thinking Strategically about Policy*. Boca Raton, FL: CRC Press.

Foreign Intelligence Surveillance Act (FISA)

In passing the Foreign Intelligence Surveillance Act (FISA) of 1978, Congress created special rules and procedures affecting foreign intelligence surveillance in

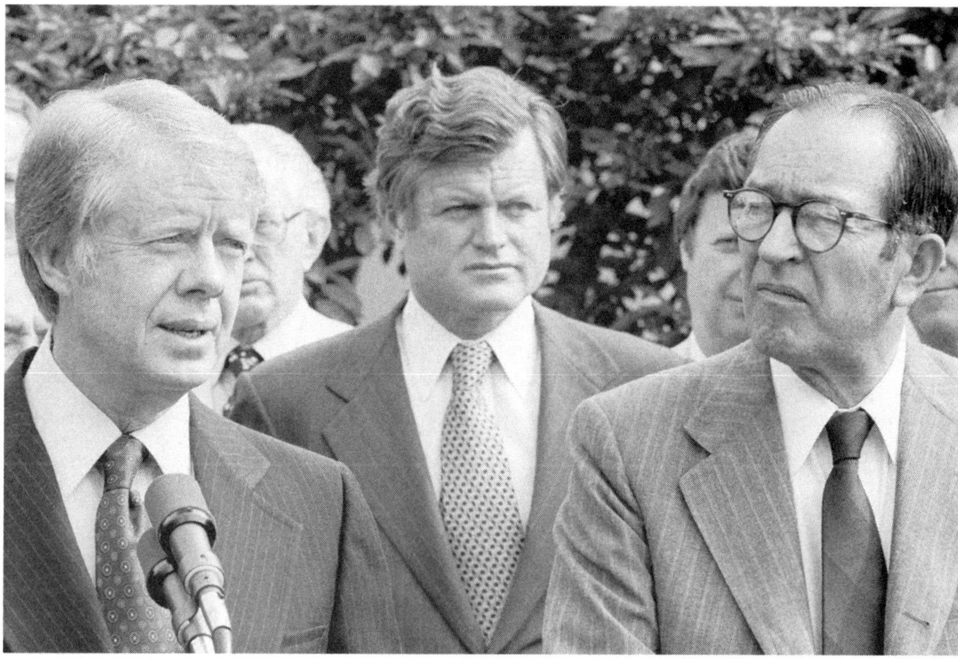

President Jimmy Carter announces the Foreign Intelligence Surveillance Act of 1977 in the White House Rose Garden, May 17, 1977. The proposed plan was aimed at keeping the government from illegally spying on citizens. Standing behind Carter is Sen. Edward M. Kennedy (D-Mass.), one of the sponsors of the bill, with Attorney General Griffin Bell at right. (AP Photo/Bob Daugherty)

the United States. Foreign intelligence surveillance, or "counterintelligence," consists of activities designed to protect the United States against espionage, sabotage, assassinations, and terrorism conducted by or on behalf of foreign governments or organizations. Frequently, these activities include electronic eavesdropping and other means of covert surveillance. Ever since *Katz v. United States* (1967), electronic eavesdropping by law enforcement agents has required prior judicial authorization. In *Katz*, the Supreme Court recognized that the Fourth Amendment protects personal privacy from any means of intrusion by law enforcement. In *Berger v. New York* (1967), the Court recognized that "eavesdropping involves an intrusion on privacy that is broad in scope," and its "indiscriminate use . . . in law enforcement raises grave constitutional questions."

In 1968, Congress enacted the Omnibus Crime Control and Safe Streets Act. Title III of the act, adopted largely in response to the *Berger* and *Katz* decisions, authorized the use of electronic surveillance by federal law enforcement officers but required prior judicial authorization and otherwise limited the conditions for its use. However, Congress included language in the statute making clear that

Title III was not intended to limit "the constitutional power of the President to take such measures as he deems necessary to protect the Nation against actual or potential attack or other hostile acts of a foreign power, to obtain foreign intelligence information deemed essential to the security of the United States, or to protect national security information against foreign intelligence activities."

Invoking this exception and asserting inherent executive power, the Nixon administration conducted extensive wiretapping and other forms of electronic surveillance of U.S. citizens without probable cause or prior judicial approval. In 1973, the Senate Select Committee to Study Governmental Operations with Respect to Intelligence Activities, better known as the "Church Committee," conducted a far-reaching investigation of the activities of intelligence agencies from the early 1960s through the end of the Nixon administration. The Committee's reports, published in 1975 and 1976, documented the extent to which foreign intelligence agencies conducted unauthorized surveillance of domestic groups perceived as security risks. Among them were civil rights, antiwar, and various New Left organizations.

In *United States v. U.S. District Court* (1972), the Supreme Court held that these activities offended the Fourth Amendment prohibition against unreasonable searches and seizures. Writing for the Court, Justice Lewis Powell recognized that

> domestic security surveillance may involve different policy and practical considerations from the surveillance of "ordinary crime." The gathering of security intelligence is often long range and involves the interrelation of various sources and types of information. The exact targets of such surveillance may be more difficult to identify than in surveillance operations against many types of crimes specified in Title III. Often, too, the emphasis of domestic intelligence gathering is on the prevention of unlawful activity or the enhancement of the Government's preparedness for some possible future crisis or emergency. Thus, the focus of domestic surveillance may be less precise than that directed against more conventional types of crime.

In light of these considerations, Powell suggested that Congress consider enacting "protective standards" for the conduct of foreign intelligence surveillance separate and apart from those applicable to domestic law enforcement. The decision in *United States v. U.S. District Court* as well as the Church Committee reports of 1975 and 1976 prompted Congress to enact FISA in 1978. The act established the Foreign Intelligence Surveillance Court (FISC) consisting of seven federal district court judges appointed by the chief justice of the United States. The USA PATRIOT Act of 2001 expanded the number of judges to eleven.

FISC judges are from different federal judicial circuits and serve staggered terms of seven years. Individual judges review applications to conduct surveillance aimed at obtaining information on foreign intelligence activities. Surveillance includes electronic eavesdropping, physical entries, the use of "pen registers" and "trap and trace" devices, as well as access to certain business records.

The FISC court conducts its business in a secret windowless courtroom located inside the Department of Justice building in Washington, D.C. Applications for surveillance are prepared by the Justice Department's Office of Intelligence and are submitted to the FISC on the authority of the attorney general. The procedure for obtaining a FISA warrant is nonadversarial, much like the procedure by which law enforcement officers obtain search warrants. Surveillance is authorized if a FISC judge finds there is probable cause that the target of the surveillance is a foreign power or an agent of a foreign power. There is no requirement that the target be engaged in any unlawful activity.

A "foreign power" is defined by the statute as "a foreign government or a component thereof," "a faction of a foreign nation or nations," "an entity that is openly acknowledged by a foreign government or governments to be directed and controlled by such foreign government or governments," "a group engaged in international terrorism or activities in preparation therefore," "a foreign-based political organization," or "an entity that is directed and controlled by a foreign government." Denials of surveillance orders are reviewable by a Foreign Intelligence Surveillance Court of Review consisting of three federal district or appeals court judges designated by the chief justice.

After the terrorist attacks of 2001, Congress saw a need to revise FISA and expand the power of the government. The passage of the USA PATRIOT Act in 2001 brought about significant changes in the operation of the FISA, envisioned a clear distinction between the areas of criminal investigation and foreign intelligence gathering, as well as a patent separation of the agencies and departments responsible for performing these tasks. The PATRIOT Act eliminated this distinction. After 2001, the institutions of law enforcement and intelligence gathering would engage in the sharing of information. Many situations presented the opportunity for both criminal investigation and intelligence gathering. If the government characterized its actions as the investigation of crime, then more stringent notions of probable cause would dictate their options and set the rules that would be applied by the courts. However, if the government could justify its actions as the gathering of foreign intelligence, the much more accommodating world of FISA would offer greater freedom for agents and fewer procedural restrictions. With the passage of the PATRIOT Act the government has been given much greater opportunity to proceed under the guise of intelligence gathering and the less restrictive FISA while simultaneously gaining information to be used in criminal proceedings, without having to concern itself with the inconvenience of matters such as probable cause.

It was this blurring of the lines between the realm of criminal investigation and foreign intelligence gathering that resulted in the Court of Review meeting for the first time. Prior to 2002 the Court of Review never met because no application for surveillance had ever been denied. In 2002, the FISC rejected the Justice Department's effort to use evidence obtained pursuant to FISA warrants in criminal cases. The court ruled that FISA was intended to create something of a firewall between foreign intelligence surveillance and ordinary law enforcement. The Justice Department appealed to the Court of Review, which vacated the judgment of the FISC in August 2002 and ordered it to approve the Justice Department's request. No doubt influenced by the horrendous terrorist attacks of September 11, 2001, the Court of Review held that FISC may be used to obtain evidence for a criminal prosecution as long as the government also has a "significant nonlaw enforcement foreign intelligence purpose" in making application for the surveillance warrant.

However, even this modified FISA failed to provide enough power in the eyes of many within the executive branch. In late 2005, the *New York Times* revealed that President George W. Bush authorized the National Security Agency (NSA) to bypass the FISC entirely and engage in warrantless eavesdropping on American citizens who were suspected of ties to Al Qaeda.

These revelations were condemned by civil libertarians and privacy advocates who had long objected to the secretive nature of the FISA court. However, defenders of FISA said that the law remained a valuable tool in efforts to bring legal standards and procedures to an area that historically operated outside the law.

In 2007, Bush signed the Protect America Act into Law. This amendment to FISA empowered the attorney general—rather than courts—to approve year-long warrants of surveillance of international communications carried out by targeted individuals "reasonably believed" to be outside of the United States. This measure was praised by the Bush administration and its allies in surveillance policy as an important tool in ferreting out international terrorist plots. Critics like the American Civil Liberties Union (ACLU), however, charged that the "Police America Act" was riddled with potential for abuse of civil liberties. "The 'Police America Act' has no protections for American phone calls and emails that are caught up in the dragnet," asserted the group. "The new program only requires that the surveillance be targeted at people overseas. While this will allow collection of foreign-to-foreign calls, it also allows the government to pick up all international communications where one party is in the United States, so long as no one particular person in the U.S. is being 'targeted.' The law is silent on how to treat these American phone calls and emails—leaving the administration to decide how to collect, store, datamine and use Americans' private communications."

One year later, the FISA was revamped yet again by the Foreign Intelligence Surveillance Act (FISA) Amendments Act (FAA) of 2008. This legislation extended major new surveillance powers to the NSA and other federal agencies through FISA. It expanded their powers to conduct both domestic and foreign warrantless surveillance, provided that the "intent" of the surveillance was to gather foreign intelligence, and it provided retroactive immunity to all telecommunications companies that cooperated with the U.S. government's warrantless eavesdropping program.

The FAA was enacted with bipartisan support at the urging of the Bush administration, which relentlessly framed the bill as a necessary tool to help the NSA and other national security agencies and departments keep America safe from terror threats. Critics such as journalist Glenn Greenwald, however, charged that the 2008 FISA Amendments Act "effectively legalized the crux of Bush's illegal program" of warrantless eavesdropping on law-abiding Americans. "The 2008 FISA law," asserted Greenwald, "sought to institutionalize some of the scheme, not end it."

In 2012, the FISA Amendments Act was renewed for another five years despite continued criticisms that it enshrined civil liberties violations as standard government practice. The measure passed Congress with bipartisan support and was signed into law by President Barack Obama on December 31, 2012.

Anthony Simones and John M. Scheb II

Further Reading

American Civil Liberties Union. n.d. "ACLU Fact Sheet on the 'Police America Act.'" ACLU Web site. https://www.aclu.org/aclu-fact-sheet-police-america-act. Accessed May 5, 2015.

Bazan, Elizabeth B. 2002. *The Foreign Intelligence Surveillance Act*. New York: Novinka Books.

Greenwald, Glenn. 2014. *No Place to Hide: Edward Snowden, the NSA, and the U.S. Surveillance State*. New York: Macmillan.

Risen, James. 2006. *State of War: The Secret History of the CIA and the Bush Administration*. New York: Simon & Schuster.

Foreign Intelligence Surveillance Court (FISC)

The Foreign Intelligence Surveillance Court (FISC) is a U.S. federal court established in 1978 by the Foreign Intelligence Surveillance Act (FISA), a law that created procedures for physical and electronic surveillance and collection of foreign intelligence information. Congress created the FISC, also called the FISA court, to provide judicial oversight of U.S. foreign intelligence surveillance efforts while still keeping these activities secret due to national security concerns. The FISA reforms were largely the result of recommendations by a Senate committee, called the Church Committee, set up to investigate U.S. intelligence-gathering activities in the mid-1970s. FISC is authorized to review applications and issue orders to authorize intelligence activities targeting foreign targets both inside and outside the United States, but the court operates largely in secret and most of its orders are classified and not made available to the public.

Initially, the FISC was given jurisdiction by FISA over four types of traditional intelligence activities: electronic surveillance, physical searches, pen/trap (telephone) surveillance, and production of business records. Anytime a government intelligence agency, such as the National Security Agency (NSA) or the Federal Bureau of Investigation (FBI), wanted to conduct an intelligence action within the country, it first had to apply to the FISC for a judicial warrant and show that the proposed action met FISA requirements to show probable cause—that the target is a foreign power or agent of a foreign power and describing the collection method, the information being sought, and any facility to be searched. In order to give the government more power to track terrorists, however, FISA was amended in 2008 to remove the traditional individual warrant requirement for targets reasonably believed to be outside the United States. This amendment permits the NSA to conduct mass surveillance of unspecified foreign targets without a warrant as long as the agency follows certain targeting and minimization procedures designed to minimize the impact on privacy of Americans. The FISC simply reviews these targeting and minimization procedures to make sure they comply with the FISA statute, as amended in 2008.

The FISC application and hearing process is ex parte—that is, one-sided—with only the government represented. The targets of the surveillance are not told about the application or hearing, nor are they given an opportunity to appear or present evidence. Also, FISC records are kept secret, and FISC has discretion to decide whether to publish its opinions. The only real exception is that electronic service providers and businesses targeted for business record production are permitted to file petitions with FISC asking to end or modify FISC surveillance orders.

The FISC is located in Washington, D.C., and is composed of eleven judges chosen by the chief justice of the U.S. Supreme Court. The judges must be from a minimum of seven U.S. judicial circuits, and at least three FISC judges must live within 20 miles of the District of Columbia. FISC judges take turns serving on the court, with a different judge presiding each week. If the FISC denies an application for surveillance, the agency making the request can appeal to the U.S. Foreign Intelligence Surveillance Court of Review (FISCR), a three-judge review court created by FISA whose only role is to review denials of surveillance by FISC. Like FISC, the FISCR is ex parte and operates in secret. The government rarely needs to appeal FISC orders, however, because the FISC approves almost all applications for surveillance. According to the *Wall Street Journal* and based on reports provided to

Congress by the U.S. Justice Department, in the 33 years between 1979 and 2012, the court rejected only 11 out of more than 33,900 surveillance applications submitted by the government.

Because of this record and the fact that the court operates both ex parte and in secret, critics accused FISC of rubber-stamping the government's intelligence activities and of failing to provide meaningful review. Also, since FISA was amended, critics say FISC surveillance orders are typically overly broad and there is no real judicial oversight by FISC or any other entity after surveillance is authorized. The result, critics claim, is that U.S. intelligence agencies are able to conduct large-scale foreign surveillance that often sweeps up data, such as telephone and e-mail information, on American citizens. Critics charge that this activity violates the privacy and warrant requirements of the Fourth Amendment to the U.S. Constitution as well as First Amendment regarding free speech and association rights.

The issue of the FISC's oversight has become very controversial in recent years following the leak of a series of classified NSA documents by Edward Snowden beginning in June 2013. Documents leaked by Snowden included a copy of a FISC surveillance order that required Verizon Business Network Services to provide its customers' cellphone information—including call dates and times, length of calls, and locations—for all calls made within the United States. Later, the public learned that this Verizon order was part of a much larger government surveillance program that included all the major telephone companies as well as similar surveillance programs collecting e-mails and Internet information.

The American Civil Liberties Union (ACLU) and other critics have claimed that this bulk surveillance on innocent Americans is illegal and should not be conducted in secret. Members of the Obama administration and other government officials, however, have defended bulk surveillance programs as constitutional under recent Supreme Court decisions and because they do not collect the substantive content of calls or e-mails.

Debra Miller

Further Reading

Electronic Privacy Information Center. 2015. "Foreign Intelligence Surveillance Court (FISC)."

Mears, Bill, and Halimah Abdullah. 2014. "What Is the FISA Court?" CNN (January 17). http://www.cnn.com/2014/01/17/politics/surveillance-court/. Accessed September 18, 2015.

Moyer, Bruce. 2015. "The Most Powerful Court You Have Never Heard Of." *Washington Watch*, Federal Bar Association (March). http://www.fedbar.org/Advocacy/Washington-Watch/WW-Archives/2015/March-2015-The-Most-Powerful-Court-You-Have-Never-Heard-Of.aspx. Accessed September 18, 2015.

Stanley, Jay. 2013. "The FISA Court's Problems Run Deep, and More Than Tinkering is Required." *Free Future*, ACLU (November 21). https://www.aclu.org/blog/national-security-technology-and-liberty/fisa-courts-problems-run-deep-and-more-tinkering. Accessed September 18, 2015.
United States Foreign Intelligence Surveillance Court. Foreign Intelligence Surveillance Court Web site. http://www.fisc.uscourts.gov/. Accessed February 26, 2015.

Fourth Amendment

Adopted in 1789 and ratified by the states in 1791 as part of the Bill of Rights, the Fourth Amendment to the U.S. Constitution provides:

> The right of the people to be secure in their persons, houses, papers and effects, against unreasonable searches and seizures, shall not be violated, and no Warrants shall issue but upon probable cause, supported by Oath or affirmation, and particularly describing the place to be searched and the persons or things to be seized.

Limiting the government's powers of search and seizure was a major concern of the founding generation. One of the main grievances of the American colonists in the decades preceding the American Revolution was the power afforded British customs officials under the infamous Writs of Assistance, which "authorized customs officers to search any houses or businesses at their whim" and "permitted virtually unlimited invasions of privacy" (Stephens and Glenn 2006, 35). Arguing before a Boston court in the Writs of Assistance Case of 1761, James Otis called the Writs "the worst instrument of arbitrary power, the most destructive of English liberty and the fundamental principles of law, that ever was found in an English law book" (Stephens and Glenn 2006, 32).

The Fourth Amendment was adopted to ensure that officials of the U.S. government would never be able to exercise such unlimited powers of search and seizure. In his dissenting opinion in *United States v. Rabinowitz* (1950), Justice Felix Frankfurter characterized the adoption of the Fourth Amendment as "a safeguard against recurrence of abuses so deeply felt by the Colonies as to be one of the potent causes of the Revolution. . . ."

A profound distaste for "general warrants" (those authorizing searches of unspecified persons and places) led the framers of the Bill of Rights to write the particularity requirement into the Fourth Amendment. Courts tend to enforce vigorously the Fourth Amendment requirement that search warrants be issued only "upon probable cause, supported by oath or affirmation," and are specific as to "the place to be searched and the persons or things to be seized." In *Maryland v. Garrison* (1987), the Supreme Court recognized that "limiting the authorization to search to the specific areas and things for which there is probable cause to search . . . ensures that the search will be carefully tailored to its justifications, and will not take on the character of the wide-ranging exploratory searches the Framers intended to prohibit."

The Fourth Amendment, like all the protections of the Bill of Rights, was originally conceived as a limitation on the powers of the newly created national government. However, the protection of the Fourth Amendment, along with most of the protections contained in the Bill of Rights, has been extended to state criminal defendants on the basis of the Fourteenth Amendment's broad limitations on state action. In *Wolf v. Colorado* (1949) the Supreme Court held that the freedom from unreasonable searches and seizures is "implicit in 'the concept of ordered liberty' and as such enforceable against the States through the Due Process Clause [of the Fourteenth Amendment]." Clearly, unrestricted powers of search and seizure are anathema to the classical liberal ideals of individual liberty and limited government on which this country was founded. Consequently, the Fourth Amendment limits search and seizure activities by law enforcement agencies at all levels of government, whether federal, state, or local.

When searches are challenged as being unreasonable, courts must first determine if the Fourth Amendment is applicable. Because the Constitution limits government action, the Fourth Amendment protects a person's rights against the police and other government agents, but not against searches and seizures conducted by private individuals. In *United States v. Jacobsen* (1984), the Supreme Court said that the Fourth Amendment "is wholly inapplicable to a search or seizure, even an unreasonable one, effected by a private individual not acting as an agent of the Government or with the participation or knowledge of any government official." Thus, a search by a privately employed security guard or a search of a package by an employee of a common carrier is not considered a violation of the Fourth Amendment unless the search was instigated by government action. Moreover, the Fourth Amendment does not apply to searches at the national border, searches conducted outside the United States, searches of open fields, or searches of abandoned property. Indeed, the Fourth Amendment does not apply to any situation where a person lacks a "reasonable expectation of privacy."

Where it does apply, the Fourth Amendment expresses a decided preference for searches and seizures to be conducted pursuant to a warrant. The warrant requirement is designed to ensure that the impartial judgment of a judge or a magistrate is interposed between the citizen and the state. As the Supreme Court recognized in *McDonald v. United States* (1948), the rights enshrined in the Fourth Amendment are "too precious to entrust to the discretion of those whose job is the detection of crime and the arrest of criminals."

Searches and seizures often entail serious intrusions into the private spheres of individuals, sometimes resulting in personal injury and/or property damage. Law enforcement officers are not permitted to conduct searches and seizures arbitrarily, or even based on their hunches about criminal activity. For a search to be reasonable under the Fourth Amendment, police generally must have probable cause to believe that a search will produce evidence of crime. Yet there are certain instances, for example, "stop-and-frisk" situations, airport searches, and school searches where police may conduct limited searches based on the lesser standard of reasonable suspicion. In addition to searches based on consent or conducted incident to a lawful arrest, a number of exceptions to the warrant requirement are based on the doctrine of exigent circumstances, evanescent evidence, and emergencies that qualify as exigent circumstances allowing warrantless searches.

To enforce the Fourth Amendment courts have adopted an exclusionary rule that provides that evidence obtained through unreasonable searches and seizures is not admissible in criminal prosecutions. As the Supreme Court recognized in *Weeks v. United States* (1914), if illegally obtained evidence "can thus be seized and held and used in evidence against a citizen accused of an offense, the protection of the 4th Amendment, declaring his right to be secure against such searches and seizures, is of no value, and, so far as those thus placed are concerned, might as well be stricken from the Constitution." As Stephens and Glenn (2006, 3) point out, "[t]he federal exclusionary rule, barring the admission of evidence obtained in violation of the Fourth Amendment, departed sharply from the old common law rule that determined the admissibility of evidence based on its reliability without regard to how it was obtained."

In its landmark decision in *Mapp v. Ohio* (1961), the Supreme Court extended the exclusionary rule to the state courts by way of the Due Process Clause of the Fourteenth Amendment. In recent years, a more conservative Court has limited the scope of the exclusionary rule somewhat. For example, in *United States v. Leon* (1984), the Court recognized a limited "good-faith exception" exempting from the exclusionary rule evidence secured by a law enforcement officer pursuant to a presumably valid search warrant that is subsequently invalidated. Circumstances under which evidence may be obtained under this good-faith exception have been broadened by the Supreme Court over the years in cases such as *Herring v. United States* (2009) and *Davis v. United States* (2011).

The Fourth Amendment has applicability beyond the seizure of evidence. Because the arrest of a suspect is considered a "seizure," the Fourth Amendment applies to arrests and various lesser police–citizen encounters, as well as to the use of force by police in making arrests. Writing for the Supreme Court in *Tennessee v. Garner* (1985), Justice Byron White observed, "It is not always clear just when minimal police interference becomes a seizure," but he concluded that "apprehension by the use of deadly force is a seizure subject to the reasonableness requirement of the Fourth Amendment."

Although the Fourth Amendment sets national standards for search and seizure, state constitutions can afford their citizens more protection than the federal constitution. For example, in some states courts do not recognize the good-faith exception adopted by the U.S. Supreme Court in *United States v. Leon*. Another illustration involves the issue of standing to challenge a Fourth Amendment violation. In *Minnesota v. Carter* (1998), the Supreme Court held that a nonovernight visitor has no legitimate expectation of privacy in an apartment, thus no standing to challenge a police search that yielded contraband. In contrast, some state supreme courts hold that in such an instance a defendant has automatic standing to challenge a search on state constitutional grounds. Yet, in an attempt to prevent state courts from granting more protection to defendants than the federal constitution allows, voters in a few states have adopted constitutional amendments requiring their courts to follow the interpretations of the Supreme Court on search and seizure issues.

Technological advances have afforded law enforcement new means to ferret out crime. The use of helicopters and such high-tech devices as infrared sensors, supersensitive microphones, and miniature radio transmitters challenges the traditional right of privacy enjoyed by citizens in a free country. The current war on terrorism creates new demands for law enforcement agencies to conduct surveillance as well as considerable pressures on courts to allow such activities. In turn, these new means of ferreting out crime present new challenges to the courts in interpreting what constitutes an unreasonable search under the Fourth Amendment.

John M. Scheb, John M. Scheb II, and Otis H. Stephens Jr.

Further Reading

Amar, Akhil Reed. 1994. "Fourth Amendment First Principles." *Harvard Law Review* 107: 757.

Davies, Thomas Y. 1999. "Recovering the Original Fourth Amendment." *Michigan Law Review* 98: 547.

Greenhalgh, William. 2003. *The Fourth Amendment Handbook*. Chicago: American Bar Association.

Landynski, Jacob W. 1978. *Search and Seizure and the Supreme Court*. Baltimore: Johns Hopkins University Press.

Lasson, Nelson B. 1937. *The History and Development of the Fourth Amendment to the United States Constitution*. Baltimore: Johns Hopkins Press.

Maclin, Tracy. 1997. "The Complexity of the Fourth Amendment: A Historical Review." *Boston University Law Review* 77: 925.

Maclin, Tracy. 2013. *The Supreme Court and the Fourth Amendment's Exclusionary Rule*. New York: Oxford University Press.

Scheb, John M., and John M. Scheb II. 2005. *Criminal Law and Procedure*, 5th Edition. Belmont, CA: Wadsworth/Thomson Learning.
Stephens, Otis H., Jr., and Richard A. Glenn. 2006. *Unreasonable Searches and Seizures: Rights and Liberties under the Law*. Santa Barbara, CA: ABC-CLIO.

Freedom of Information Act (FOIA)

The Freedom of Information Act (FOIA), codified at 5 U.S.C. § 552, is a federal law that gives people the right to request and obtain information from U.S. federal government agencies. Signed into law by President Lyndon Johnson on July 4, 1066, FOIA's purpose is to promote open government and democracy by giving U.S. citizens and others broad access to government documents and information. FOIA only applies to federal agencies and other parts of the executive branch of the federal government and does not apply to Congress, federal courts, or certain parts of the executive branch that advise the U.S. President. The executive branch, specifically the Department of Justice's Office of Information Policy, administers the FOIA program and oversees and encourages agency compliance.

Under the FOIA law, "any person" can make a FOIA request, including U.S. citizens, citizens of foreign countries, organizations, universities, and others. A FOIA request may ask for documents as well as various other types of information, such as e-mails, photos, videos, maps, and any records either created by a federal agency or within that agency's control. The law requires federal agencies to promptly respond to each FOIA request and release requested records unless they are specifically excluded under one of nine exemptions:

1. Records classified as secret by an executive order due to national security or foreign policy concerns;
2. Internal federal agency personnel rules and practices;
3. Information specifically excluded from FOIA by other laws or statutes;
4. Confidential business information, such as trade secrets and financial information;
5. Inter- or intra-agency communications that would only be available in litigation;
6. Records, such as medical records or personnel information, that could violate personal privacy;
7. Certain information compiled for law enforcement purposes;
8. Records relating to the regulation and supervision of financial institutions; and
9. Geological information relating to wells.

Agencies may charge fees to cover the cost of producing records, and fee amounts are based on five fee categories according to the type of requester—commercial, educational institutions, noncommercial scientific organizations, news media, or others. Because FOIA is supposed to provide information to the public, news media organizations and educational institutions are exempted from some fees. Persons making FOIA requests may also request a waiver of fees if the records requested are likely to contribute significantly to public understanding of the operations or activities of the government and are not primarily in the commercial interest of the requester. In addition, individuals can request that the federal agency declassify and release specified classified documents by filing a Mandatory Declassification Review (MDR)—a process authorized by Executive Order 13526, a presidential order signed by President Barack Obama in 2009. Persons whose FOIA request has been denied can also sue the agency if it is believed the agency is illegally withholding information that should be provided under FOIA.

FOIA has been amended or otherwise modified several times since its enactment. In 1974, following the Watergate political scandal that led to the resignation of President Richard Nixon, the law was amended by the Privacy Act of 1974 to strengthen its provisions and place a greater burden on federal agencies to release information. This amendment, for example, expanded the right of citizens to obtain records about themselves created or maintained by federal agencies, and it included the right to correct records that are inaccurate or incomplete. In 1976, the Government in the Sunshine Act outlined the types of information that could be exempted from FOIA. Ten years later, in the Anti-Drug Abuse Act of 1986, Congress amended FOIA in two areas—fees charged for FOIA requests and access to law enforcement and national security records.

In 2002, following the September 11, 2001, terrorist attacks in the United States, FOIA was amended again by the Intelligence Authorization Act for fiscal year 2003 to limit access by foreign agents to information held by U.S. intelligence agencies. Later in 2007, the Openness Promotes Effectiveness in our National Government Act reformed FOIA and expanded the definition of who is a representative of the news media—a change that helped bloggers and nontraditional journalists become eligible for reduced FOIA fees. Finally in 2010, the Dodd–Frank Wall Street Reform and Consumer Protection Act included a provision to protect the Securities and Exchange Commission (SEC) from FOIA requests, but this provision was quickly repealed. A proposed law, the FOIA Oversight and Implementation Act of 2014 (H.R. 1211), seeks to improve the FOIA process by creating a single FOIA Web site where people could makc FOIA requests and monitor their status.

FOIA also has been affected by presidential actions. In 1982, President Ronald Reagan signed Executive Order 12356 to dramatically expand FOIA's national security exemption and limit the information that would be released relating to national security. Later, President Bill Clinton sought to expand FOIA, issuing a number of directives to address problems with agency delays in responding to FOIA requests, and to encourage the release of national security information relating to the Cold War and other historical events. In October 1996, President Clinton also signed the Electronic Freedom of Information Act Amendments to require that federal agencies make certain types of records available electronically. On November 1, 2001, President George W. Bush again restricted FOIA, issuing Executive Order 13233 to limit access to records of former U.S. presidents. President Bush's directive, however, was revoked by President Barack Obama in Executive Order 13489, basically restoring the previous FOIA rule, which basically permits access to presidential records five years after a president leaves office. A second order from President Obama, Executive Order 13526, allows government agencies to deny FOIA requests for information relating to national security, even where the information is classified as secret after it has been requested.

Debra Miller

Further Reading

Johnson, Lyndon B. "Statement by the President Upon Signing the 'Freedom of Information Act.'" The American Presidency Project Web site (July 4, 1966). http://www.presidency.ucsb.edu/ws/?pid=27700. Accessed February 24, 2015.

National Security Archives. "FOIA Basics." George Washington University Web site. http://www2.gwu.edu/~nsarchiv/nsa/foia/guide.html. Accessed February 24, 2015.

New York Times. 2015. "A Stronger Freedom of Information Act." February 18. http://www.nytimes.com/2015/02/18/opinion/a-stronger-freedom-of-information-act.html. Accessed May 13, 2015.

Fusion Centers

A nationwide network of "fusion centers" was created in the wake of the terrorist attacks of September 11, 2001, in order to more effectively facilitate information gathering, analysis, and dissemination between federal agencies such as the Central Intelligence Agency (CIA), Federal Bureau of Investigation (FBI), the National Security Agency (NSA), all branches of the military, and other federal, state, local, and tribal stakeholders. The central mission of fusion centers is to prevent another terrorist attack on American soil before it occurs.

Created under the authority of the Department of Homeland Security (DHS) and the Department of Justice (DoJ), fusion centers are operated by state and local agencies and designated by the governor of the state in which they are located;

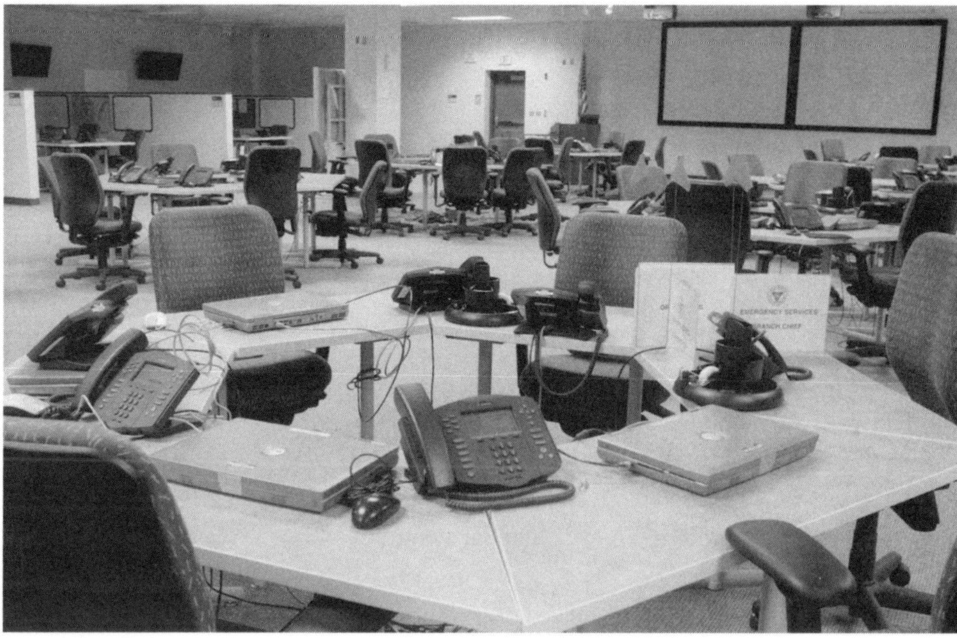

The Department of Homeland Security's Fusion Center at State Police headquarters, shown in 2007, in Midlothian, Virginia. In the event of a major disaster or emergency, the Fusion Center would be used as communication headquarters helping organizations such as FEMA and the Department of Public Safety dispatch aid where most needed. Fusion centers have ignited privacy controversies. (AP Photo/Lisa Billings)

depending on a number of factors, a governor can increase or decrease the number of fusion centers with his or her state. According to the DHS Web site, there were 78 recognized fusion centers around the United States in 2014.

The establishment of a nationwide network of intelligence-sharing centers can be traced back to *The 9/11 Commission Report,* the authoritative study of the events leading up to the 9/11 attacks, which was released by the National Commission on Terrorist Attacks Upon the United States in July 2004. The report concluded that local, state, and federal authorities had failed to share information on potential terrorist threats to the homeland effectively or in a timely manner. It proposed a reform of the national security apparatus that would ensure that threat information would be shared across new networks that transcend individual agencies. Such reforms, the report contended, were essential to protect U.S. national security.

In 2005, the DHS's Homeland Security Advisory Council (HSAC) issued "Intelligence and Information Sharing Initiative: Homeland Security Intelligence and Information Fusion," a plan to implement the 9/11 Commission's recommendations. It introduced the concept of the fusion process as the most effective way to leverage intelligence gathered across tribal, territorial, local, state, and federal governments; identify patterns and trends in criminal and terrorist activity; and provide a state and local context and subject matter expertise to provide a more comprehensive view of any possible threats. The report also proposed the idea of a nationwide network of centers to manage the fusion process.

In July 2005, the DHS and the Global Justice Information Sharing Initiative released the first set of guidelines to assist agencies in launching the network of fusion centers proposed by the HSAC. Although there are basic guidelines for all fusion centers, each one has a different mission statement and operates by its own rules. In 2007, the first fusion centers came online in several states.

That same year, though, criticism began to emerge about the scope and oversight of the fusion center system. Privacy and civil libertarian groups like the American Civil Liberties Union (ACLU) noted that although the scope and mission of fusion centers had changed from strictly counterterrorism to dealing with a broader range of crimes, the system did not have the strong oversight and clearly delineated mission necessary to protect the privacy of American citizens. Reports of local law enforcement groups targeting specific communities without any evidence of wrongdoing and the launch of large-scale data-gathering activities confirmed suspicions that law enforcement and intelligence agencies were abusing civil liberties and violating privacy.

In 2012, a two-year bipartisan investigation by the U.S. Senate Permanent Subcommittee on Investigations found that fusion centers wasted money, violated the civil liberties of American citizens, and had not yielded any noteworthy information on possible terrorist threats to the United States. According to the subcommittee report on the investigation, fusion centers "forwarded 'intelligence' of uneven quality—oftentimes shoddy, rarely timely, sometimes endangering citizens' civil liberties and Privacy Act protections, occasionally taken from already-published sources, and more often than not unrelated to terrorism."

The report revealed that DHS officials knew about the problems with fusion centers but failed to effectively address them. In addition, many of the problems were not reported to the U.S. Congress in a timely manner in an effort to avoid meaningful oversight.

DHS officials point to a number of successes that fusion centers have had in the past several years. For example, the agency reports that the Alabama Fusion Center (AFC) was instrumental in the arrest of dozens of suspected drug traffickers and the disruption of a transnational drug network in the region. Fusion centers have also played a central role in investigating homicides, domestic terrorism plots, and child pornography rings and tracking down wanted fugitives.

Margaret Haerens

Further Reading

ACLU. 2007. "What's Wrong with Fusion Centers?" ACLU Web site (December). https://www.aclu.org/files/pdfs/privacy/fusioncenter_20071212.pdf. Accessed March 19, 2015.

Department of Homeland Security. "State and Major Urban Area Fusion Centers." Department of Homeland Security Web site (December 17, 2014). http://www.dhs.gov/state-and-major-urban-area-fusion-centers. Accessed March 17, 2015.

Isikoff, Michael. 2012. "Homeland Security 'Fusion' Centers Spy on Citizens, Produce 'Shoddy' Work." *NBC News* (October 2). http://investigations.nbcnews.com/_news/2012/10/02/14187433-homeland-security-fusion-centers-spy-on-citizens-produce-shoddy-work-report-says. Accessed March 17, 2015.

U.S. Senate Permanent Subcommittee on Investigations. "Federal Support for and Involvement in State and Local Fusion Centers." *U.S. Senate Permanent Subcommittee on Investigations* (October 3, 2012). http://www.hsgac.senate.gov/subcommittees/investigations/media/investigative-report-criticizes-counterterrorism-reporting-waste-at-state-and-local-intelligence-fusion-centers. Accessed March 19, 2015.

G

"Good-Faith" Exception

Announced in *United States v. Leon* (1984), this exception to the exclusionary rule of the Fourth Amendment permits the use of illegally obtained evidence where police possess an objectively reasonable belief that their warrant is valid, even though the warrant is later found to be unsupported by probable cause or is technically deficient. In this type of situation, because the magistrate erred, declaring the evidence inadmissible would not advance the primary goal of the exclusionary rule—deterring police misconduct.

The Court has extended the "good-faith" exception and thus limited the application of the exclusionary rule in a number of contexts. For example, the exception applies when police obtain evidence by making an honest mistake in the execution of a warrant (police error); when police conduct a warrantless search pursuant to a state statute that is later declared unconstitutional (legislative error); when police obtain evidence in reliance on an erroneous police record indicating the presence of an outstanding warrant (clerical error); and when police conduct a search under the authority of an existing precedent or statute, even if that precedent or statute is later struck down on constitutional grounds.

Otis H. Stephens and Richard A. Glenn

Further Reading

Maclin, Tracy. 2013. *The Supreme Court and the Fourth Amendment's Exclusionary Rule*. New York: Oxford University Press.

Vile, John M., and David L. Hudson Jr. 2012. *Encyclopedia of the Fourth Amendment.* Santa Barbara, CA: ABC-CLIO.

Greenwald, Glenn (1967–)

Glenn Greenwald is a writer and lawyer best known for breaking the story published in *The Guardian*, a British newspaper, about a vast and secret U.S. surveillance program being carried out by United States' National Security Agency (NSA). Greenwald's reports were based on classified document leaks from former NSA contractor Edward Snowden.

Glenn Edward Greenwald was born on March 6, 1967, in New York City, one of two sons of Daniel and Arlene Greenwald. The family eventually moved to Florida, where his parents divorced when Greenwald was in his teens. Greenwald remembers his mother being "a typically 1960s–1970s housewife who married young and never went to college," who took jobs such as cashiering at McDonald's

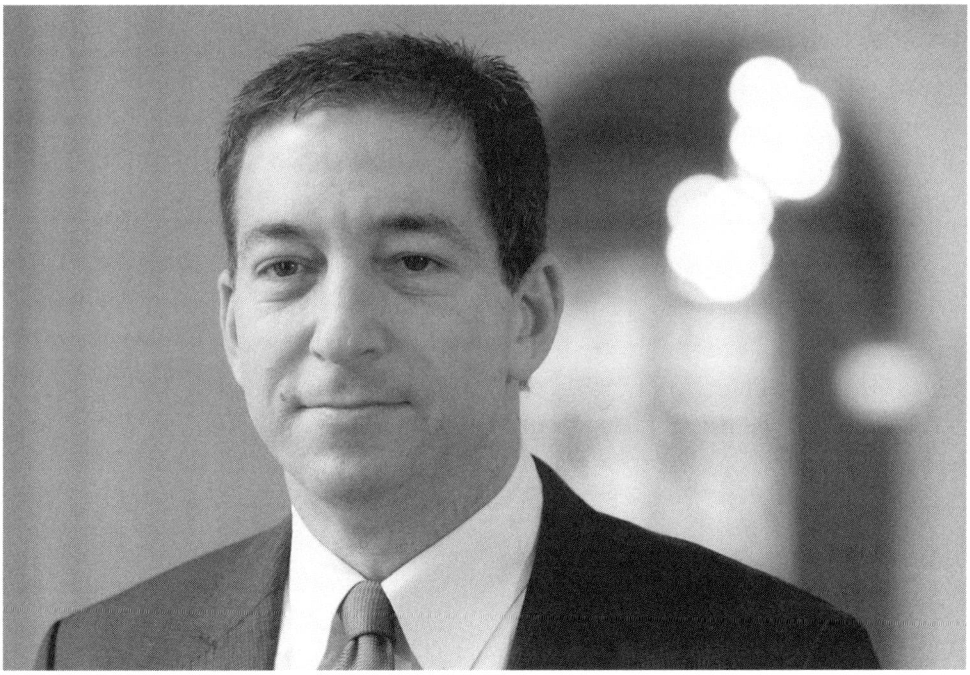

Journalist Glenn Greenwald arrives for a news conference in Munich, southern Germany. Greenwald, who in 2013 helped disclose the National Security Agency's massive surveillance programs, has won a $10,000 Arts and Letters award for "exceptional accomplishment in any genre." His reporting for *The Guardian* helped the paper win a Pulitzer in 2014, and he was featured in the Oscar-winning documentary *Citizen Four*. (AP Photo)

to support her boys. Greenwald looked up to his paternal grandfather, Louis "L. L." Greenwald, who was a local city councilman who worked for the poor and fought against the establishment. The younger Greenwald used his grandfather as a model when he ran for student council. He also took some advice from his grandfather: He taught Greenwald "that the most noble way to use your skills, intellect and energy is to defend the marginalized against those with the greatest power—and that the resulting animosity from those in power is a badge of honor." He found that this was useful advice as a gay teenager. During a time when the fear of AIDS led many to look at homosexuality itself as a disease, Greenwald chose to take the view that "'instead of having you judge me, I'm going to judge you, because I don't accept the fact that you're even in a position to cast judgments upon me.'"

Greenwald received his bachelor's degree in philosophy from George Washington University in 1990, where he excelled in debating. He then enrolled at the New York University of Law, where he started a successful campaign to ban Colorado firms from recruiting on campus after voters in the mountain state passed an amendment that overturned existing antidiscrimination laws. Greenwald earned his law degree in 1994.

Following graduation, he worked for a few years as a litigator at the law firm of Wachtell, Lipton, Rosen & Katz. From there, he began his own law practice, which focused on civil liberties and constitutional law cases. He soon became bored with legal work and found that his background in debating served him well when he became interested in spirited online discussions with conservatives. By 2005, he had left law and travelled to Brazil, where he met his partner, David Miranda. The two of them currently live in Rio de Janeiro.

In October 2005, Greenwald launched a blog called *Unclaimed Territory,* covering such political issues as the Central Intelligence Agency (CIA) leak scandal, which involved CIA officer Valerie Plame and Scooter Libby, an adviser to Vice President Dick Cheney, and the NSA warrantless surveillance program. Greenwald's blog won the Koufax Award in 2006 for the best new blog of 2005.

In February 2007, Greenwald began writing for *Salon.com.* In August 2012, interested in reaching a more international audience, he began working for the *Guardian,* a liberal newspaper based in London. It was with the *Guardian* that Greenwald's public stature reached new heights. Former CIA contractor Edward Snowden contacted Greenwald anonymously in December 2012 to inform him that he had documents of a sensitive nature that he wished to share with Greenwald. Greenwald ignored the communiqué, since he did not want to bother carrying through with the encryption process Snowden required. Eventually, however, Greenwald recognized the potential importance of Snowden's information. Greenwald subsequently joined documentary filmmaker Laura Poitras in Hong Kong to interview Snowden. The whistle-blower turned over countless secret documents related to the U.S. government's security system. "Snowden's archive revealed the technical means used to intercept communications," Greenwald later wrote in *No Place to Hide,* an examination of the U.S. surveillance state that included a detailed account of his meetings with Snowden. "[It revealed] the NSA's tapping of Internet servers, satellites, underwater fiber-optic cables, local and foreign telephone systems, and personal computers. It identified individuals targeted for extremely invasive forms of spying, a list that ranged from alleged terrorists and criminal suspects to the democratically elected leaders of the nation's allies and even ordinary American citizens. And it shed light on the NSA's overall strategies and goals."

In June 2013, Greenwald's first article about Snowden's documents, pertaining to the surveillance system within the NSA under the Obama administration, appeared in the *Guardian*. Snowden later said that he chose Greenwald to partner with to release the documents because "Glenn's writing consistently demonstrated his belief that journalists should serve people rather than governments, and that gives sources the confidence to shoulder great risks to do good."

For his part, Greenwald was happy to be part of the sensitive document release. He was pleased that Snowden chose to forego doing a mass upload of all documents, preferring to have the public research his work on their own and have Snowden and Greenwald focus on what they believed were the most important documents and highlight and write about them. Greenwald also appreciated Snowden's bravado: "He wanted to undermine the culture of fear by saying, 'Yeah . . . not only did I spoil your secrets but here's who I am! I look like every Midwestern son, you can't marginalize me because I'm like you; this is my beautiful girlfriend and my stable career! I'm not some Ted Kaczynski maladjusted maniac living in the forest!' It was a deliberately and provocatively bold thing to do."

Greenwald's bold approach to journalism has received both support and criticism from media counterparts (and the tone of those feelings was often based on whether one thought of Snowden as a heroic whistle-blower or a traitor). For instance, *Newsweek* magazine hailed Greenwald as one of the top ten U.S. opinionists, while NBC newsman David Gregory wondered why Greenwald shouldn't be charged with a crime. Greenwald, for his part, believes that journalists who subscribe to the more traditional way of remaining subjective in their reporting produce "a self-neutering form of journalism that becomes as ineffectual as it is boring." Furthermore, he feels that "a journalist who is petrified of appearing to express any opinions will often steer clear of declarative sentences about what is true, opting instead for a cowardly and unhelpful 'here's-what-both-sides-say-and-I-won't-resolve-the-conflicts' formulation. That rewards dishonesty on the part of political and corporate officials who know they can rely on 'objective' reporters to amplify their falsehoods without challenge. . . ."

Greenwald left the *Guardian* in October 2013 and joined with eBay founder Pierre Omidyar to begin a new news source called First Look Media. Greenwald began serving as editor of First Look Media's *The Intercept*, an online publication that began in February 2014. Upon leaving the *Guardian,* Greenwald said he was not leaving because of any threats. He noted that British prime minister David Cameron was working to stop newspapers from printing what he viewed as damaging leaks from Snowden. Greenwald bristled at this, saying, "There are extremist though influential factions in both [Britain and the United States] which want to criminalize not only whistle-blowing but the act of journalism itself." He believes "it's urgent that everyone who believes in basic press freedoms unite against this."

Greenwald also regularly issues warnings about the dangers of public passivity in the face of government intrusions into private life. Writing in *No Place to Hide,* Greenwald asserted that many governments, including the United States, offer an implicit bargain to citizens:

"Pose no challenge and you have nothing to worry about. Mind your own business, and support or at least tolerate what we do, and you'll be fine. Put differently, you must refrain from provoking the authority that wields surveillance powers if you wish to be deemed free of wrongdoing. This is a deal that invites passivity, obedience, and conformity. . . . In the United States, it was NAACP leaders, Communists, and civil rights and anti-war activists who were targeted with [FBI Director J. Edgar] Hoover's surveillance, not well-behaved citizens who stayed mute about social justice."

In addition to his newspaper and online work, Greenwald is also the author of five books: *How Would a Patriot Act? Defending American Values from a President Run Amok* (2006), *A Tragic Legacy* (2007), *Great American Hypocrites: Toppling the Big Myths of Republican Politics* (2008), *With Liberty and Justice for Some: How the Law Is Used to Destroy Equality and Protect the Powerful* (2011), and *No Place to Hide: Edward Snowden, the NSA, and the U.S. Surveillance State* (2014). Greenwald is the recipient of a number of awards; he was, of course, a key writer for the *Guardian* when it won the 2014 Pulitzer Prize for public service following the NSA/Snowden reports.

Lawrence W. Baker

Further Reading

"Glenn Greenwald." *The Intercept.* https://firstlook.org/theintercept/staff/glenn-greenwald/. Accessed May 6, 2015.

Greenwald, Glenn. 2014. *No Place to Hide: Edward Snowden, the NSA, and the Surveillance State.* New York: Metropolitan Books.

Greenwald, Glenn. 2013. "On Leaving the *Guardian.*" *The Guardian* (October 31). http://www.theguardian.com/commentisfree/2013/oct/31/glenn-greenwald-leaving-guardian. Accessed May 6, 2015.

Keller, Bill. 2013. "Is Glenn Greenwald the Future of News?" *New York Times* (October 27). http://www.nytimes.com/2013/10/28/opinion/a-conversation-in-lieu-of-a-column.html?_r=2. Accessed May 6, 2015.

Reitman, Janet. 2013–2014. "Snowden and Greenwald: The Men Who Leaked the Secrets." *Rolling Stone* (December 4, 2013–January 2, 2014). http://www.rollingstone.com/politics/news/snowden-and-greenwald-the-men-who-leaked-the-secrets-20131204. Accessed May 6, 2015.

Vargas-Cooper, Natasha. 2013. "Glenn Greenwald: Enemy of the State." *Advocate* (November 12). http://www.advocate.com/print-issue/current-issue/2013/11/12/enemy-state. Accessed May 6, 2015.

Griswold v. Connecticut (1965)

In *Griswold v. Connecticut*, 381 U.S. 479, the Supreme Court struck down as unconstitutional a Connecticut law criminalizing the use of contraceptives as inconsistent with a constitutional right of privacy. In so doing, the Court recognized the existence of such a right, navigated an uneasy tension in its prior cases, and laid what became the foundations for constitutional rights to decisional privacy (including abortion) and informational privacy.

Although the U.S. Constitution protects many rights expressly, it does not contain any mention of the word privacy. Nevertheless, prior to *Griswold*, the Supreme Court had recognized in a number of cases that the Constitution protected privacy interests of one form or another. Prior to the New Deal era, the Supreme Court had protected the private sphere from government regulation through a number of related doctrines. Thus, in criminal procedure law, it had held in cases such as *Boyd v. United States*, 116 U.S. 616, 628 (1888), that the Fourth and Fifth Amendments to the Constitution created a form of privacy right protecting a person's private papers from government scrutiny. In *Lochner v. New York,* 198 U.S. 45 (1905) and related cases, it held that the Due Process Clause of the Fourteenth Amendment guaranteed a liberty of contract and state neutrality in economic affairs, which prevented many kinds of state regulation touching private affairs, including workplace safety rules and minimum wage laws. And in *Meyer v. Nebraska,* 262 U.S. 390 (1923), and *Pierce v. Society of Sisters,* 268 U.S. 510 (1925), the Court declared that the Fourteenth Amendment's Due Process Clause denied the states the power to interfere with parents' rights to send their children to private schools and to educate them in languages other than English.

Many of these rules were inconsistent with the needs of the modern regulatory state, and with the notable exception of the *Meyer* and *Pierce* strand of the doctrine, they were gradually whittled away by the Supreme Court. Particularly after the Court comprised a majority of justices appointed by President Franklin D. Roosevelt, the Court's constitutional law jurisprudence shifted to allow significantly greater government regulation of economic activity. Interpretations of the Due Process Clause such as *Lochner*, which appeared to be unmoored from the text of the Constitution, became suspect, and the Court increasingly deferred to modern welfare legislation.

At the same time, however, as it noted in the famous case of *United States v. Carolene Products,* 304 U.S. 144 (1938), the Court began to show a greater willingness to protect First Amendment and other noneconomic civil liberties from government interference. These somewhat divergent impulses—judicial restraint and modern civil libertarianism—would soon come into conflict in contexts relevant to privacy. For example, in *Skinner v. Oklahoma,* 316 U.S. 535 (1942), Justice William O. Douglas, writing for the Court, invalidated under equal protection grounds Oklahoma's law that provided for mandatory sterilization of habitual criminals because it violated a fundamental right to procreate. In *Prince v. Massachusetts,* 321 U.S. 158 (1944), the Court held in the context of children engaged in selling religious materials that the modern state's power to regulate on behalf of child welfare trumped both First Amendment rights and parental rights under *Meyer* and *Pierce*. *Griswold v. Connecticut* (1965) would again place these two guiding principles of post-New Deal constitutional jurisprudence into direct conflict in the context of privacy.

Griswold was the culmination of a series of challenges by birth control advocates to a Connecticut law outlawing contraception. That law, passed in 1879, made it a crime for any person to use or aid any person in using "any drug, medicinal article, or instrument for the purpose of preventing contraception" (*Conn. Gen. Stat.* §§ 53–32, 54–196). The statute had never been enforced, though Abraham Ullman, Connecticut's long-serving attorney general, had threatened to prosecute any violators. Birth control advocates had twice before attempted to challenge the Connecticut statute without first violating it, but in *Tileston v. Ullman,* 318 U.S. 44 (1943), and *Poe v. Ullman*, 367 U.S. 497 (1961), the Supreme Court rejected these challenges on procedural grounds without reaching the issue of the statute's constitutionality.

In 1961, the Planned Parenthood League of Connecticut, guided by Executive Director Estelle Griswold, tried to challenge the statute again by opening a birth control clinic in New Haven. Their goal was for Griswold to be arrested and thus force a decision on the constitutionality of the statute. This time they succeeded. Ten days after the clinic opened, Griswold was arrested along with Charles Lee Buxton, a Yale Medical School Professor and medical director of the clinic. They were found guilty of violating the statute by giving advice to married couples and were fined $100 over their objections that the statute violated the Constitution's

Fourteenth Amendment guarantee of due process of law. The Connecticut state appellate and supreme courts affirmed Griswold and Buxton's convictions.

The U.S. Supreme Court heard Griswold and Buxton's appeal and reversed by a vote of 7–2. The justices recognized that the Constitution includes an unenumerated right of privacy, although they disagreed somewhat about the source and content of that right.

Writing for a majority of the Court, Justice William O. Douglas concluded that state regulation of the use of contraceptives by married couples violated a constitutional right to privacy. However, Douglas had a problem. As a member of the group of justices who had opposed the Court's *Lochner* cases, Douglas was reluctant to merely hold that a broad right of privacy was inherent in the basic notions of due process of law. Indeed, to make such an argument would be to have engaged in the same sort of constitutional interpretation that he and others had been so critical of during the New Deal period, in which they had charged that the earlier cases had essentially made up rights and incorporated them into the Constitution by fiat. His solution to the problem was to locate a right of privacy across a broad spectrum of the protections of the Bill of Rights. Thus, he argued that the First Amendment had been interpreted to include not just the rights protected in *Pierce* and *Meyer* (recasting those cases in the process), but also a right protecting against government intrusion into associations of individuals for a common purpose. Furthermore, other provisions of the Bill of Rights had "penumbras, formed by emanations from those guarantees that help give them life and substance" (p. 484). Thus, the Third Amendment prohibits the quartering of soldiers in private homes, the Fourth Amendment gives people security and privacy in their private homes and papers, the Fifth Amendment's self-incrimination clause creates a zone of privacy that the government could not breach, and the Ninth Amendment recognizes that rights not enumerated by the Constitution might nevertheless be retained by the people. These protections, taken together, he argued, created a broader zone of privacy that while not specifically articulated by any one of these provisions in the Constitution's text was nevertheless protected by all of them acting together. And because marriage was an association of ancient origins and tremendous social importance, its privacy could not be violated by the state intrusion into the marital bedroom for signs of contraceptive use.

Although Justice Douglas's theory garnered the votes of a majority of five of the nine justices, and thus gained the status of binding law, a number of justices articulated alternative theories justifying the outcome. Justice Arthur Goldberg, joined by Chief Justice Earl Warren and Justice William Brennan, joined Douglas's opinion, but also articulated a broader theory of constitutional privacy grounded in the Ninth Amendment, which they argued could be read to protect as against the state's additional rights "so rooted in the traditions and conscience of our people as to be ranked as fundamental." Justice John Harlan, although he rejected Douglas's penumbral theory, agreed with the outcome because the Connecticut law violated basic values "implicit in the concept of ordered liberty," which were protected by the Due Process Clause of the Fourteenth Amendment. Justice Byron White similarly agreed with the outcome, but also rejected Douglas's theory of constitutional privacy. Instead, he argued, the case ought to be resolved by basic principles of due process, because the Connecticut law deprived married people the important liberty of contraceptive use and family planning and did not directly advance the regulatory interests put forward by the state. Justices Potter Stewart and Hugo Black dissented, noting that while they thought the Connecticut statute was a terrible one (Stewart famously called it "an uncommonly silly law") the law did not violate any provision of the Constitution and ought to be upheld by the courts. Black and Stewart were both concerned by the fact that the constitutional text contained no mention of any right of privacy and that for judges to essentially invent such a right would be for them to substitute their own views of morality for that of legislatures. Black, in particular, was troubled by the legacy of *Lochner* and by the Court's reliance on *Meyer* and *Pierce*, which he acknowledged came from that discredited constitutional tradition.

More generally, Black feared for the legitimacy of an unelected judiciary that could so easily substitute its own personal preferences regarding the correctness of laws. In Black's view, such an approach to the judicial role would amount to a shocking departure from the constitutional separation of the judiciary from politics and the political branches of government at all levels.

The Court's opinions in *Griswold* have been read as protecting two distinct varieties of a constitutional right of privacy. On the one hand, *Griswold* can be read as protecting information privacy—a right to keep information secret from the government. Two groups of Supreme Court cases have developed this theme further. First, two cases can be read as explicitly recognizing a constitutional right of informational privacy. Thus, in *Whalen v. Roe,* 429 U.S. 589 (1977), the Court intimated that the *Griswold* right to privacy might include an individual right against government disclosure of certain kinds of sensitive information, such as medical information. This suggestion was confirmed in *Nixon v. Administrator of General Services*, 433 U.S. 425 (1977), in which former President Nixon challenged a federal statute nationalizing his presidential papers as violating his right to privacy with respect to personal papers contained in the archive. The Supreme Court agreed with Nixon that he had a *Whalen*-type privacy interest in, for example, presidential documents relating to his family life or personal legal advice, but held that the act's provisions allowing for archival screening of his papers to separate out the private ones from the public ones sufficiently protected his informational privacy rights given both the government interest in the public papers and the tiny fraction of the total body of papers that were truly private. Further articulation of the constitutional right to informational privacy has been left to lower courts for further development, and although a number of such courts have protected constitutional informational privacy rights, the jurisprudence is neither particularly robust nor consistent.

An alternative reading of *Griswold* as protecting decisional privacy—the right to make reproductive and other intimate decisions without government interference—has received significantly more attention. In *Eisenstadt v. Baird*, 405 U.S. 438 (1972), the Court addressed the contraceptive rights of unmarried persons and confronted the problem that Justice Douglas's rationale for the confidentiality of marital relationships was not as strong outside the marital context. Justice Brennan held for the Court that "if the right of privacy means anything, it is the right of the *individual*, married or single, to be free from unwarranted government intrusion into matters so fundamental as the decision whether to bear or beget a child." In so doing, the Court transformed the constitutional right to privacy from one rooted in the confidentiality of relationships from government scrutiny to an individual liberty interest to make intimate decisions free from government interference. This decisional understanding of the constitutional right to privacy was the basis for *Roe v. Wade*, 410 U.S. 113 (1973), decided the next year, which found the right to privacy to include a right of abortion and located it in the Due Process Clause of the Fourteenth Amendment, thereby abandoning Justice Douglas's penumbral conception of privacy. Subsequent cases, most notably *Planned Parenthood v. Casey* (1992), have confirmed the basic validity of the Court's ruling that abortion rights are constitutionally protected, although numerous challenges have addressed various aspects of this right, prompted in large part by the enormous importance of the abortion issue to the national political landscape. The right to decisional privacy in fundamental decisions has been extended to other areas of the law with mixed results for claimants, with subsequent cases involving such issues as the right to terminate life-sustaining medical care, physician-assisted suicide, parental rights to direct their children's upbringing, and the right to private homosexual conduct.

Griswold v. Connecticut was arguably the most significant of a number of post-*Lochner* Supreme Court decisions in which the Court was called upon to evaluate the constitutionality of regulations of activities and decisions central to personal identity and self-determination. It thus raised one of the central questions to any society in which judges interpret a written Constitution: how to interpret a written text in light of changed times and changed views of morality.

As a general rule, liberals have tended to applaud the Court's willingness in *Griswold* to look beyond a narrow reading of the text of the Constitution to find that the Due Process Clause protects a basic and broad commitment to liberty and individual autonomy. In this regard, they have echoed the arguments of Justices Douglas and Goldberg. Conservatives, on the other hand, have tended to argue that *Griswold*'s right to privacy is unmoored by any limiting principle and that unelected judges interpreting the right to privacy improperly substitute their own elitist morality for the morality of the citizenry acting democratically through its elected representatives. In this regard, conservatives accuse liberals of engaging in the same methodology of constitutional interpretation that was discredited at the end of the *Lochner* era, in an echo of the arguments made by Justices Black and Stewart in dissent.

To this extent, the actual rationale of the decision in *Griswold* has been somewhat obscured by *Roe v. Wade*, as abortion politics have become one of the most long-standing and acrimonious divisions in American politics.

Neil M. Richards

Further Reading

Allen, Anita, and Erin Mack. 1990. "How Privacy Got its Gender." *Northern Illinois University Law Review* 10: 441–54.

Allen, Anita, and Erin Mack. 2003. *Why Privacy Isn't Everything: Feminist Reflections on Accountability for Private Life*. Lanham, MD: Rowman and Littlefield.

Garrow, David J. 1998. *Liberty and Sexuality: The Right to Privacy and the Making of Roe v. Wade.* Berkeley and Los Angeles: University of California Press.

Johnson, John W. 2005. *Griswold v. Connecticut: Birth Control and the Constitutional Right of Privacy*. Lawrence: University Press of Kansas.

Kersch, Ken I. 2004. *Constructing Civil Liberties: Discontinuities in the Development of American Constitutional Law*. New York: Cambridge University Press.

H

Hayden, Michael (1945–)

Michael Hayden is a career military man who rose up the ranks to serve as director of both the National Security Agency (NSA) and the Central Intelligence Agency (CIA).

Michael Vincent Hayden was born on March 17, 1945, in Pittsburgh, Pennsylvania, the son of Harry Hayden Jr. and Sadie Hayden. He has a sister, Debby, and a brother, Harry. Hayden received his Bachelor of Arts degree in history in 1967 from Duquesne University. Upon graduation, he joined the U.S. Air Force (USAF) Reserve Officer Training Corps (ROTC), where he was commissioned as a second lieutenant. Two years later, Hayden earned his Master of Arts degree in modern American history from Duquesne and also entered active military service. Hayden is married to Jeanine Carrier. The couple has three children—Margaret, Michael, and Liam.

Some of the positions Hayden held in his military career included analyst at Headquarters Strategic Air Command at Offutt Air Force Base in Nebraska; chief of Current Intelligence Division at Andersen Air Force Base in Guam; academic ROTC instructor at St. Michael's College in Colchester, Vermont; chief of intelligence for the 51st Tactical Fighter Wing at Osan Air Force Base in South Korea; air attaché at the U.S. Embassy in Sofia, Bulgaria; political-military affairs officer in the USAF Headquarters' Strategy Division in Washington, D.C.; director for defense policy and arms control on the National Security Council; chief for the secretary of the Air Force Staff Group in Washington, D.C.; director of intelligence for U.S. European Command in Stuttgart, Germany; special assistant to the commander of the Air Intelligence Agency (AIA) at Kelly Air Force Base in Texas; commander of the AIA; and deputy chief of staff for the United Nations Command and U.S. Forces Korea, Yongsan Garrison, in South Korea.

In 1999, Hayden became director of the NSA, a position he held until 2005. Early on, he sought to update the technological infrastructure of the agency. Part of the improvement plans included a program called Trailblazer, a system intended to

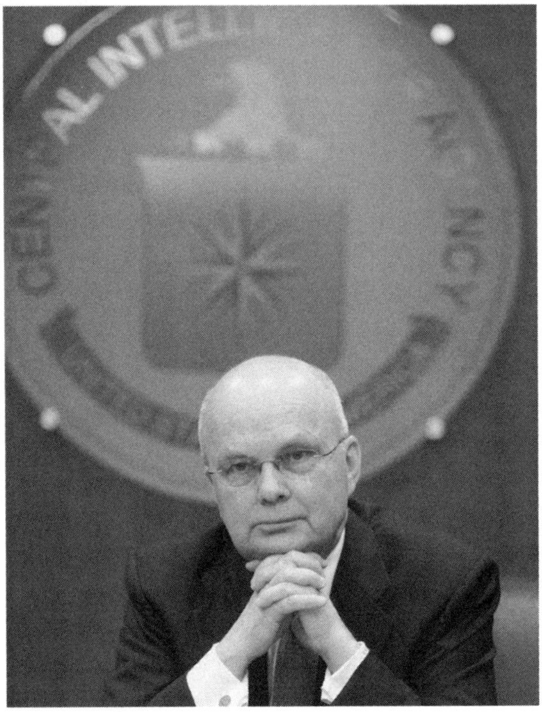

CIA Director Michael Hayden listens to a question during a news conference at CIA headquarters in Langley, Virginia, 2009. (AP Photo)

analyze telecommunications and Internet data, but which wound up hundreds of millions of dollars over budget and was eventually dropped.

Hayden was originally known for seeking more openness in the NSA and being concerned about domestic surveillance. But the terrorist attacks of September 11, 2011, changed much of his thinking. In a speech in 2015, Hayden said that the tone of the Fourth Amendment—which forbids unreasonable search and seizure—changed on 9/11. He said he views the Constitution as a living document and that the issue of reasonableness mentioned in the amendment should be determined by "the totality of circumstances in which we find ourselves in history." He admitted that what he found unreasonable on September 10, 2001, changed to reasonable on September 11, 2001. In response to 9/11, Hayden and the NSA received authorization from President George W. Bush to set up a secret program for monitoring telephony metadata, foreign e-mail, and interceptions of conversations when it was suspected that the communications involved members of Al Qaeda, the group responsible for the 9/11 attacks, or other terrorist groups.

Hayden has bristled at the notion that he and the NSA and other similar agencies capriciously violate civil liberties. "I am not a law enforcement officer. I don't suspect anybody. I am simply going out there to retrieve information that helps keep my countrymen free and safe. This is not about guilt. . . . NSA doesn't just listen to bad people. NSA listens to interesting people. People who are communicating information." He has also discounted criticism that the government monitors its citizens. In an interview, he said, "The NSA doesn't monitor what every American is doing on the Internet. The NSA doesn't check who goes to what Web sites. But you've got these beliefs out there now."

In 2004, Congress passed, and President George W. Bush signed, the Intelligence Reform and Terrorism Prevention Act, a set of complex laws designed to address the issue of terrorism. One part of the act included the creation of a director of national intelligence; Hayden became the principal deputy director of intelligence.

In 2006, President Bush named Hayden director of the CIA. During the post-9/11 era—both before and during Hayden's time as CIA director—the CIA was involved in interrogations of terrorists that some critics believed could be described as torture. Hayden always maintained that any of the interrogations performed were deemed lawful by the U.S. Department of Justice. Such acts included waterboarding (an act that simulates the sensation of drowning) and limiting prisoners' diets. In 2014, five years after Hayden had stepped down from the CIA, the U.S. Senate Intelligence Committee accused the agency of employing torturous interrogation techniques and not being forthcoming about its use of torture. Hayden responded that the CIA provided briefings to Congress about its interrogation methods. He pointed out that U.S. senator Dianne Feinstein (D-CA), a member of the committee, even said, "We have to do some things that historically we have not wanted to do to protect ourselves."

When former NSA contractor Edward Snowden began leaking classified government surveillance documents to the media in June 2013, Hayden condemned Snowden as "the most costly leaker of American secrets in the history of the Republic." Hayden believes Snowden perpetrated "the single greatest hemorrhaging of legitimate American secrets in the history of this country." He believes the leaking hurt the United States in three ways: it provided information about tactics and procedures (he argues that other countries knowing *how* something is done can be more damaging that *what* was done); it damaged the financial health of many American businesses; and it reduced confidence in the government's ability to discreetly keep secrets.

He dismissed talk of allowing Snowden to return to the United States and be granted clemency for his actions. "It is incredibly damaging, and if we give him some sort of clemency or amnesty, all we're doing is teaching the next Edward Snowden that if you do this, make sure you steal a whole bunch of stuff."

Hayden left the CIA in 2009. He moved into the private sector and is currently employed by the Chertoff Group, a consultant group cofounded by former Homeland Security secretary Michael Chertoff.

Lawrence W. Baker

Further Reading

"Eagle Biography: General Michael Vincent Hayden." Gathering of Eagles Foundation. http://www.goefoundation.org/index.php/eagles/biographies/h/hayden-michael-vincent/. Accessed May 12, 2015.

Friedersdorf, Conor. 2015. "Michael Hayden's Hollow Constitution." *The Atlantic* (January 20). http://www.theatlantic.com/politics/archive/2015/01/former-cia-and-nsa-director-nsa-doesnt-just-listen-to-bad-people/385007/. Accessed May 12, 2015.

Hayden, Michael. 2013. "Ex-CIA Chief: What Edward Snowden Did." CNN (July 19). http://www.cnn.com/2013/07/19/opinion/hayden-snowden-impact/. Accessed May 12, 2015.

Hayden, Michael. 2015. "A 'Reasonable' View of Privacy, Security." *Washington Times* (March 18). http://www.washingtontimes.com/news/2015/mar/18/michael-hayden-a-reasonable-view-of-privacy-securi/?page=all. Accessed May 12, 2015.

Hayden, Mike. 2014. "Democrats Define 'Politicization' with So-Called Torture Report." *Washington Times* (December 15). http://www.washingtontimes.com/news/2014/dec/15/michael-hayden-democrats-politicize-cia-torture-re/?page=all. Accessed May 12, 2015.

Hirsh, Michael. 2014. "Michael Hayden Is Not Sorry." *Politico Magazine* (December 9). http://www.politico.com/magazine/story/2014/12/torture-report-michael-hayden-not-sorry-113450.html#.VUkNeyFVhBc. Accessed May 12, 2015.

Hujer, Marc, and Holger Stark. 2014. "Former NSA Director: 'Shame on Us.'" *Spiegel* (March 24). http://www.spiegel.de/international/world/spiegel-interview-with-former-nsa-director-michael-hayden-a-960389.html. Accessed May 12, 2015.

Health Information Privacy

The privacy of health information has been a recognized concern since the dawn of medicine. Privacy issues grew more complex as written record-keeping practices developed and expanded during the first part of the 20th century. The rise of third-party payers (including Medicare and private insurers) during the second part of the 20th century added to the number and type of health records and record keepers as well as to the complexity of health privacy issues.

Interest in and development of electronic health records and electronic networks of health records—now generally referred to as health information technology (HIT)—began in the late-20th-century and has accelerated during the 21st century. The position of the National Health Information Technology Coordinator in the Department of Health and Human Services (DHHS) was initiated by a presidential executive order in 2004 and established by statute in 2009. The formal duties of the coordinator are to support the development of a nationwide health information technology infrastructure that allows for the electronic use and exchange of information to support a wide variety of purposes in the health care system.

As Congress began to pass legislation that supported electronic health information activities, it also recognized the threat that electronic records posed for privacy. The administrative simplification provisions of the 1996 Health Insurance

Portability and Accountability Act (HIPAA) included a requirement for privacy rules that resulted in the issuance of a federal rule on the privacy of health records for paper and electronic records. The DHHS issued an HIPAA health privacy rule at the end of 2002, and the rule took effect in 2003. A separate HIPAA security rule covers electronic records.

While experiments with and implementation of electronic health records and networks accelerates, privacy is trailing the technology. The HIPAA health privacy rule generally covers health care providers and insurers regardless of the technology used for record keeping, but the rule as crafted largely reflects a paper-based record system.

When records were created and maintained by a single provider, roles and responsibilities were relatively clear. As records are centralized and shared between health care providers, responsibility for supporting patient rights loses focus. As actual or potential sharing of patient records expands, the role of consent becomes harder to design and implement. HIPAA largely eliminated the need for consent for all routine health care activities, but that policy may not benefit patients as lifetime records and universal access take hold. As electronic health records are shared more widely among users other than providers and insurers, the lack of privacy rules applicable to third-party users becomes more acute. A 2009 change to the law slightly broadened the scope of HIPAA, but many health record keepers remain outside the privacy and security rules. In short, electronic health records and networks exacerbate privacy shortcomings that were already problematic with paper records.

Another problem has to do with the level of regulation. Prior to HIPAA, health privacy was the topic of state-level legislation, with the exception of federal records and federally funded substance abuse treatment. HIPAA adopted a policy that stronger state laws—that is, those that did a better job of protecting patient privacy—remained in place above the federal floor. That policy works in an environment where we can tell the physical location of the record and the person responsible for maintaining it. In an electronic environment where records are shared electronically across state borders, it is much more difficult to allow state laws to remain in place. Nevertheless, there are so many state laws affecting health record keeping, record keepers, and users that a fully preemptive federal law could create widespread disruptions and an expansion of federal control into areas where the federal government rarely treads. An example is the need of a federal law to replace state court rules that govern the sharing of health records in malpractice or workers' compensation litigation.

Because of some of the complexities of HIPAA and misunderstandings about health care privacy, many people, including health care professionals, believe that health information has better privacy protections than other personal information simply because of its inherently sensitive nature. In the off-line world, however, the privacy protections applicable to health records are often less robust than people believe, and online, the differences between reality and expectation are even greater.

Today, many kinds of nontraditional health activities can take place online that involve the disclosure and maintenance of personal health information outside the familiar health care system. Some examples include

- An individual posts a question on a health Web site that requires users to register. The question may be about a specific health condition, test result, or drug interaction. An individual may utilize many different types of Web sites for this purpose, including general purpose health information Web sites. Even if the individual is not identifiable to other users, the Web site knows who he is.
- An individual participates in discussions on disease-specific or condition-specific Web sites. These crowd-sourced sites allow individuals to share stories, seek support from others, compare treatment methods, or discuss any aspect of health care. Web sites may focus on weight loss, breast cancer, autism, diabetes, and more. Individuals may or may not identify themselves to others, but the Web sites may know who they are.
- A Web user employs tools or "apps" provided by a Web site for assessing the user's weight, cholesterol, fitness, mental health, or any other aspect of well-being. Some may use online-off-line tools, such as a GPS-enabled watch, to upload workout information to a Web site for storage, analysis, and possible sharing with others. Access to the information over time requires the user to register at the Web site.
- A subscriber to a health information Web site, social networking Web site, or other Web sites where the user is identified to the Web site owner participates in a poll, asking what the subscriber ate that day, whether the subscriber cries, or how much exercise the subscriber routinely gets.
- An individual who just received a copy of laboratory test results from her doctor goes to a search engine and enters the results one by onc in order to learn more about what the numbers mean. Users may be known to search engines, many of which retain copies of searches for extended periods.

In general, none of this information shared by users is subject to the privacy protections that apply to health records maintained by a health care provider or a health insurer. While traditional health records may have fewer privacy protections than most people expect, many health records created as a result of Internet interactions have no legal protections at all. Each Web site is likely to have its own terms of service and privacy policy, but the policies established by Web sites are rarely read by consumers, are highly variable, may not offer meaningful privacy protections, and may allow the Web site to use or share identifiable information, allowing the information to slip into consumer data profiles or into the marketing system.

In other cases, the applicability of legal privacy protection may depend on facts or circumstances that are not necessarily transparent to the subject of the record. For example, personal health records (PHRs) are a relatively recent development. A PHR vendor collects a patient's health records with the patient's consent from the health care system or other sources. The PHR vendor stores the information online for use by the patient and the patient's designees through the Internet. There are many types of PHRs today, many different types of PHR vendors, and many different services available. If a health care provider offers PHRs to patients, the PHRs are subject to standard federal health privacy protections. However, if the PHR vendor that is not part of the health care system or working for a health care provider maintains the PHR, then formal privacy protections are scarce because the federal rules and most state health privacy laws do not apply.

This confusing state of affairs is partly the result of rapidly developing technology and partly the result of the way that the law protects health privacy. As discussed in the previous section, the most important health privacy protections derive from the HIPAA. The federal health privacy and security rules issued by the DHHS cover most health care providers and insurers, but little other online health information activity. State health privacy laws remain in effect in addition to HIPAA if the state laws offer better privacy protections. However, few state laws have been amended to apply to nontraditional online health records.

Technically, the HIPAA privacy and security rules apply to "covered entities," which are most health care providers, all health insurance plans, all health care clearinghouses, and the business associates of all of these institutions. Because HIPAA applies only to traditional record keepers within the health care community, nontraditional health record keepers are not subject to the HIPAA rules. For example, schools that have health records are not subject to the HIPAA rules, although they are usually covered by another law called the Family Educational Rights and Privacy Act. Others with health information—including gyms, banks, state motor vehicle departments, landlords, credit bureaus, home testing labs, massage therapists, nutrition counselors, pharmaceutical manufacturers, and transit companies—are generally not covered by HIPAA, by state health privacy laws, or, often, by any privacy law at all. As discussed above, many Web sites that obtain or store health information are not subject to privacy laws. However, some PHR records and some other health records are covered by state or federal breach notification laws.

Robert Gellman and Pam Dixon

Further Reading

Lee, Lisa M., et al. 2010. *Principles and Practices of Public Health Surveillance.* New York: Oxford University Press.

Robichau, Bernard Peter. 2014. *Healthcare Information Privacy and Security: Regulatory Compliance and Data Security in the Age of Electronic Health Records.* New York: Apress.

Hemisphere Project

The Hemisphere Project is the official name for a secret drug interdiction program, maintained by federal, state, and local counternarcotics agencies that made routine use of a massive database maintained by the AT&T telecommunications company containing the records of telephone calls made by American citizens. The existence of the program was revealed by the *New York Times* in September 2013, only three months after whistle-blower Edward Snowden disclosed that the National Security Agency (NSA) had been secretly collecting the metadata of millions of phone calls made by Americans in another surveillance program. Due to the later timing of the *Times* report on the Hemisphere Project, however, and the U.S. government's success in limiting the paper trail of documents concerning the Hemisphere Project, this secret program has never received the notoriety of the other revelations made by Snowden about the NSA.

The *New York Times* story, which was reported by Scott Shane and Colin Moynihan and published on September 1, 2013, revealed that since at least 2007, U.S. drug officials with the Drug Enforcement Administration (DEA) and other agencies had collaborated with AT&T employees to secretly monitor and pore through the contents of an AT&T database containing the records of phone calls made by Americans since as far back as 1987. The legal veneer for gaining access to these records came through "administrative subpoenas," which can be issued directly by law enforcement agencies without approval from prosecutors, judges, or grand juries (unlike search warrants or court subpoenas). According to Shane and Moynihan, the Hemisphere Project provides financial compensation to AT&T for the right to embed AT&T employees in counternarcotics operations in major cities around the country, including Los Angeles, Houston, and Atlanta. These employees navigate the phone records database on behalf of the DEA and other agencies, using their data-mining expertise to help law enforcement agents identify leads for counternarcotics investigations. Reportedly, this database adds four billion phone records on a daily basis. "The scale and longevity of the data storage appears to be unmatched by other government programs, including the N.S.A.'s gathering of phone call logs under the Patriot Act," they wrote. "The N.S.A. stores the data for nearly all calls in the United States, including phone numbers and time and duration of calls, for five years. Hemisphere covers every call that passes through an AT&T switch—not just those made by AT&T customers—and includes calls dating back 26 years, according to Hemisphere training slides bearing the logo of the White House Office of National Drug Control Policy."

The existence of the Hemisphere Project sparked outcries from many civil liberties and privacy groups, lawmakers, and scholars. They pointed out that the Hemisphere Project made no pretense of being involved with national security matters; rather, it was explicitly designed for law enforcement purposes. They also expressed alarm at the fact that other telecommunications giants, including Verizon, Sprint, and T-Mobile, refused to answer questions about whether they also made employees and/or database systems available for the Hemisphere Project or similar programs.

Finally, critics charged that the purported rationale for the program—to neutralize drug traffickers' use of temporary "burner phones" by analyzing calling patterns from multiple telephone numbers—does not compensate for the project's potential for abuse. "To locate the tiny number of people who evade law enforcement agents by using burners, an AT&T-government partnership is sifting through sensitive phone records of vast numbers of people," wrote Catherine Crump, a scholar on surveillance issues who is also a staff attorney with the American Civil Liberties Union (ACLU). "While this may sometimes be justified, today it is happening without any supervision by a judge. And the government is deliberately concealing the origins of all information obtained by the program, making it impossible for criminal defendants to know that they were subjected to scrutiny though the program. As a result, defendants have no opportunity to test the legality of these investigative tactics—and, just as troublingly, no court will have the chance to weigh in on the program's validity."

Officials within the Obama administration and the DEA, however, defended the program. They pointed to several instances in which, they said, the Hemisphere Project had been vital in apprehending drug traffickers and busting up narcotics rings. Officials also emphasized that the AT&T records are still maintained by the telecommunications company, not any government agency. Critics, however, say that this is essentially a distinction without a difference. According to them, technicalities about physical ownership of the data are irrelevant, given the central role that government agencies play in dictating the data-mining activities of the AT&T employees in the project.

Kevin Hillstrom

Further Reading

Boghosian, Heidi. 2013. *Spying on Democracy: Government Surveillance, Corporate Power, and Public Resistance*. San Francisco: City Lights Books.

Crump, Catherine. 2013. "The Vast, Troubling Call Database Drug Agents Use to Identify Burner Phones." Slate.com (September 3). http://www.slate.com/blogs/future_tense/2013/09/03/hemisphere_project_an_aclu_lawyer_on_the_troubling_database_used_to_id_burner.html. Accessed April 29, 2015.

Hsu, Spencer S., and Ellen Nakashima. 2015. "U.S. Kept Secret Law Enforcement Database of Americans' Calls Overseas Until 2013." *Washington Post*, January 16.

Shane, Scott, and Colin Moynihan. 2013. "Drug Agents Use Vast Phone Trove, Eclipsing N.S.A.'s." *New York Times* (September 1). http://www.nytimes.com/2013/09/02/us/drug-agents-use-vast-phone-trove-eclipsing-nsas.html. Accessed April 29, 2015.

Hepting v. AT&T (2009)

This case involved a class action lawsuit that was filed by the Electronic Frontier Foundation (EFF) against AT&T, in which EFF claimed that the telecommunications company illegally helped the National Security Agency (NSA) monitor the phone calls of AT&T customers and other parties whose communication was routed through AT&T's network. The case was ultimately dismissed at the appeal court level, and the U.S. Supreme Court chose not to hear the case.

The EFF, which calls itself "the leading nonprofit organization defending civil liberties in the digital world," filed the lawsuit in response to a December 16, 2005, story in the *New York Times* claiming that President George W. Bush had allowed the NSA to monitor telephone and Internet communications of Americans without court approval and in violation of privacy laws and the First and Fourth Amendments. The president had reportedly disclosed this information to a select few leaders in the Congress and the presiding judge of the Foreign Intelligence Surveillance Court, a federal court that authorizes federal requests for electronic and other types of surveillance for foreign intelligence purposes. A nonpartisan group of legal experts and former government officials expressed their belief that the intent of Congress when it passed the Foreign Intelligence Surveillance Act (FISA) in 1978 was for the U.S. Intelligence Surveillance Court to issue warrants before allowing surveillance to occur. The act was initially passed to allow Congress and the judicial branch to oversee foreign intelligence surveillance activities—both physical and electronic—while maintaining the proper level of secrecy.

The EFF filed a class lawsuit on January 31, 2006, on behalf of AT&T customers who believed AT&T was violating the law and the privacy rights of customers by assisting the NSA in its surveillance. A former AT&T technician, Mark Klein, provided evidence that showed that his former company had routed copies of Internet traffic to a room in San Francisco that was controlled by the NSA. The lead plaintiff in the case, Tash Hepting, was interested in the case because, as a boy, his father had enjoyed using shortwave radios and made contact at one point with a Chinese radio station. This led to him receiving Chinese propaganda, which, in turn, prompted the U.S. government to read his mail. Hepting's stance in the lawsuit, therefore, was a principled one against illegal surveillance.

In June 2006, the U.S. District Court for the Northern District of California rejected both the government and AT&T's attempts to dismiss the case. AT&T had argued that it was merely following the directions of the government, while the government claimed that "state secrets," if revealed, would be a threat to national security. U.S. district judge Vaughn Walker claimed AT&T should have known better—that surely the surveillance activity it was involved in was illegal. And while Judge Walker acknowledged a fine line between "liberty and security," he believed that "dismissing this case at the outset would sacrifice liberty for no apparent enhancement of security."

The government appealed the ruling to the U.S. Court of Appeals. Oral arguments were heard in August 2007, but before a ruling could be made, Congress passed the FISA Amendments Act in July 2008, which said that lawsuits against telecommunication companies should be dismissed if the Bush administration could claim that it requested warrantless surveillance and communicated to these companies that it was legal. Attorney General Michael Mukasey did just that in September 2008, which gave both the government and AT&T retroactive immunity, resulting in *Hepting v. AT&T* being dismissed in June 2009. EFF appealed, but the decision was affirmed. The Supreme Court chose not to take up the case in October 2012.

Lawrence W. Baker

Further Reading

"About the Foreign Intelligence Surveillance Court." United States Foreign Intelligence Surveillance Court. http://www.fisc.uscourts.gov/about-foreign-intelligence-surveillance-court. Accessed April 15, 2015.

"The Foreign Intelligence Surveillance Act of 1978 (FISA)." Justice Information Sharing. U.S. Department of Justice, Office of Justice Programs. https://it.ojp.gov/default.aspx?area=privacy&page=1286. Accessed April 15, 2015.

"Hepting et al. v. AT&T Corp." Electronic Privacy Information Center. *Epic.org*. https://epic.org/privacy/hepting/. Accessed April 15, 2015.

"Hepting v. AT&T." Electronic Frontier Foundation. https://www.eff.org/cases/hepting. Accessed April 15, 2015.

"Tash Hepting: 'It's Not about the Money.'" 2008. Electronic Frontier Foundation. https://www.eff.org/deeplinks/2008/03/tash-hepting-speaks-out. Accessed April 15, 2015.

Hoover, J. Edgar (1895–1972)

J. Edgar Hoover was born on January 1, 1895, in Washington, D.C., the son of a civil servant employed in the U.S. Coast and Geodetic Survey. Hoover grew up and lived his entire life in the nation's capital. Forgoing a traditional college education, he attended night school at George Washington University Law School (working during the day at the Library of Congress), receiving an LLB in 1916 and an LLM in 1917. Having graduated shortly after Congress declared war on Germany in World War I, Hoover did not serve in the military but, instead in July 1917, accepted a draft-deferred appointment in the alien registration section of the Department of Justice. In 1918, he was appointed an assistant to the attorney general, and one year later he was chosen to lead the department's recently created General Intelligence Division. He subsequently compiled dossiers on thousands of social activists and union organizers, and he played a key role in planning and

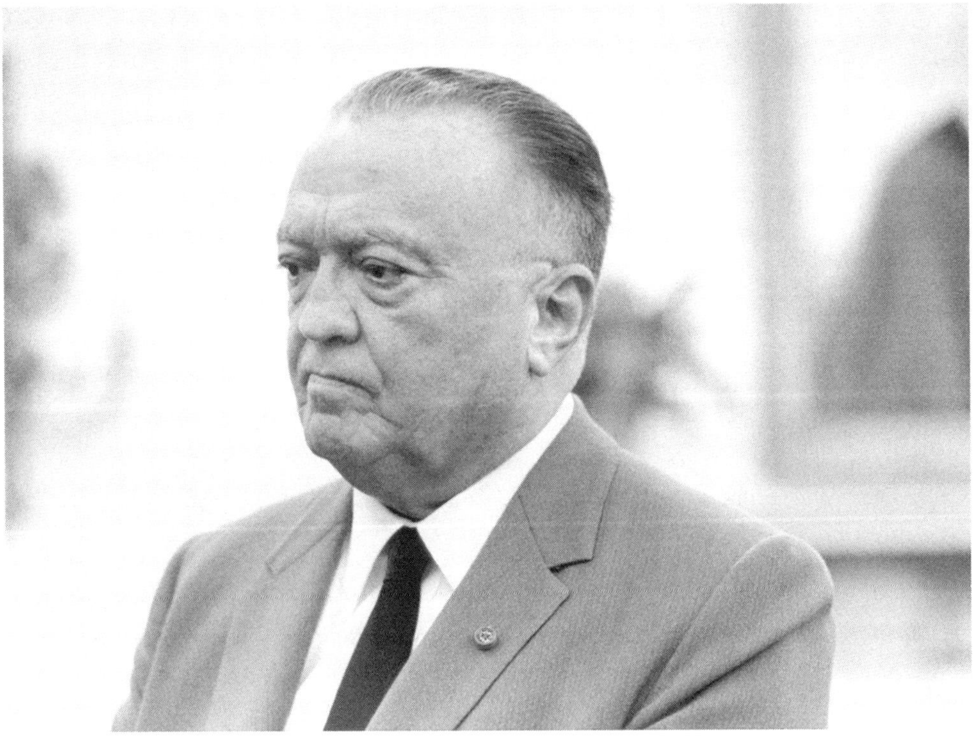

J. Edgar Hoover was director of the Federal Bureau of Investigation and created a powerful federal government crime-fighting agency. He served in that post from 1924 until his death in 1972. Hoover and the FBI drew criticism for a number of surveillance actions in the 1960s, including those against Vietnam War protests. (Yoichi R. Okamoto/Lyndon B. Johnson Presidential Library)

orchestrating the infamous Palmer Raids of January 1920, in which the U.S. government arrested and deported communists and other people identified by authorities as "radical" leftists.

Promoted to Assistant Director of the Bureau of Investigation in 1921, Hoover was appointed Acting Bureau Director in May 1924. The appointment was made permanent seven months later, in December 1924. Hoover served as Bureau Director (renamed as the Federal Bureau of Investigation in 1935) until his death on May 2, 1972.

Hoover's appointment as Bureau Director in May 1924 occurred following a series of highly controversial revelations that Bureau agents and the Bureau's most recent director had abused power during the World War I period and the early-postwar years. These included Bureau monitoring of political and labor union activists and investigating members of Congress who played a key role in triggering a congressional investigation into the Teapot Dome scandal, a scandal that involved senior officials in the Harding administration.

As director, Hoover instituted a series of reforms to improve the quality of Bureau personnel and to preclude future abuses of power. In the process, he refurbished the Bureau's reputation and helped forge a highly professional and respected law enforcement agency. Sensitive to prevailing states' rights fears and to the adverse publicity and congressional inquiries that had tarnished the early Bureau, Hoover acted to project an image of the FBI agent as an apolitical professional. During the 1930s, he purposefully cultivated both the print media and Hollywood to convey the image of the so-called G-Man, the efficient professional who always got his man and respected the law and the Constitution.

This sensitivity to public perceptions, however, did not mean that Hoover had abandoned monitoring "radical activists." Nor, given his own moralistic views, was the director indifferent to the sexual indiscretions of American citizens. Attuned to the moralistic politics of the 1920s (captured in the enforcement of the Prohibition Amendment and the rise of religious fundamentalism), in March 1925 he authorized the creation of a discreet Obscene File to ensure more successful prosecution of purveyors of obscenity and pornography. Creation of this central file ensured a permanent repository of salacious literature and the ability to incur the support of social conservatives. In a companion action, during the late 1930s Hoover himself led highly publicized vice raids in Miami, Florida, to apprehend and prosecute prostitutes and their customers, ostensibly because local police and civic officials protected houses of prostitution.

The combination of Hoover's moralistic and antiradical sentiments underlay his leadership of the FBI and the attendant practice of collecting and maintaining files recording the illicit sexual and political activities of American citizens and alien residents. He devised sophisticated filing procedures to preclude discovery of FBI practices, expanded surveillance activities to include the collection of noncriminal but potentially embarrassing information, approved unlawful investigative practices, and orchestrated leaks of sensitive information about investigative targets and political enemies (and slanted assertions about those targets and enemies) to the media, members of Congress, and officials in the military and the White House. These practices began informally but were refined and expanded during the Cold War years. The FBI director was then able to tap into concerns about ostensible security threats such as subversion and homosexuality without any meaningful oversight. The culmination of these practices came when Hoover launched a mass media program in 1955 and the first of five COINTELPROs in 1956. In the latter program, derogatory information about "radical activists" and suspected "subversives" was publicly leaked to raise doubts about their loyalty and moral character. In the authorization language of the formal COINTELPRO, the purpose was to "harass, disrupt, and discredit." In 1951, Hoover also launched a formal Sex Deviate program to purge homosexuals from federal employment and from influential posts in the private sector. The FBI director's interest in illicit sexual activities was not confined to homosexuals, but it extended to heterosexual conduct. This has been indirectly confirmed by the massive files that he maintained in his office about the sexual activities of civil rights leader Martin Luther King Jr., Senator/President John F. Kennedy, various members of Congress, and First Lady Eleanor Roosevelt. Some information was obtained through illegal wiretaps and bugs, while other information was gleaned from unverified rumors and malicious gossip.

The FBI director was able to finesse any inquiry into his collection of and efforts to act upon such personal information. By creating a secret office file, Hoover could truthfully deny that the FBI maintained derogatory personal information about prominent Americans in its central records system. Hoover also had FBI officials compile summary memoranda detailing information that FBI agents had collected about the "immoral and subversive" activities of members of Congress. These memoranda were also not maintained in the FBI's central records system, but rather in the agency's administrative unit.

During Hoover's tenure as FBI director, many suspected that he collected personal and political information about political activists, including members of Congress, and used this information to advance his own political objectives. Indeed, during an interview in the late 1970s with Ovid Demaris, longtime House Judiciary Committee stalwart Emanuel Celler specifically attributed Hoover's power to the fact that he was the head of an agency that possessed tremendous powers of surveillance over Americans in both public and private life.

Hoover's success in immunizing FBI operations from public scrutiny had a chilling effect on public debate while permitting FBI officials to violate privacy rights.

Hoover's death in May 1972 predated congressional investigations that finally shattered this wall of secrecy. Congressional investigations into Watergate in the 1973–1974 and the 1975 hearings of the Senate Select Committee to Study Governmental Operations with Respect to Intelligence Activities (also known as the Church Committee) uncovered massive illegal surveillance and other unlawful activities by U.S. intelligence agencies.

Responding to these dramatic revelations, Congress enacted the Privacy Act and a series of amendments to the 1966 Freedom of Information Act that permitted citizens to obtain access to FBI records. Over the next few years, Americans came to understand the scope of Hoover's violation of privacy rights and the methods he had employed to preclude discovery. According to the *Washington Post,* Hoover left a "bipolar legacy. For better or worse, he built the FBI into a modern, national organization stressing professionalism and scientific crime-fighting. For most of his life, Americans considered him a hero. But he also stands as a reminder that 48 years of power concentrated in one person is a recipe for abuse. It was mostly after his death that Hoover's dark side became common knowledge—the covert black-bag jobs, the warrantless surveillance of civil rights leaders and Vietnam-era peace activists, the use of secret files to bully government officials, the snooping on movie stars and senators, and the rest."

Athan Theoharis

Further Reading

Ackerman, Kenneth D. 2011. "Five Myths about J. Edgar Hoover." *Washington Post* (November 9). http://www.washingtonpost.com/opinions/five-myths-about-j-edgar-hoover/2011/11/07/gIQASLlo5M_story.html. Accessed September 18, 2015.

Aronson, Marc. 2012. *Master of Deceit: J. Edgar Hoover and America in the Age of Lies.* Somerville, MA: Candlewick.

Johansson, Warren, and William A. Percy. 1994. *Outing: Shattering the Conspiracy of Silence.* New York: Harrington Park Press.

Theoharis, Athan. 2004. *The FBI and American Democracy: A Brief Critical History.* Lawrence: University Press of Kansas.

Weiner, Tim. 2012. *Enemies: A History of the FBI.* New York: Random House.

House Un-American Activities Committee (HUAC)

The House Un-American Activities Committee (HUAC) was formed on May 26, 1938, and abolished in January 1975. The committee was created to investigate disloyalty and "subversive activities." Initially, HUAC's investigations were directed

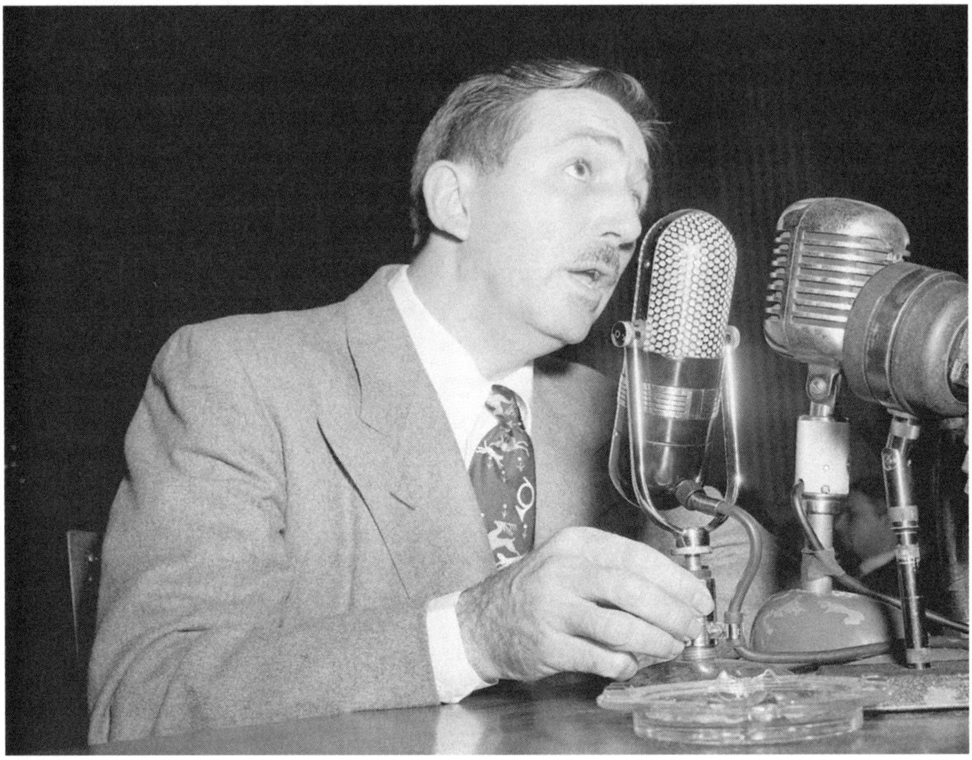

Movie studio executive Walt Disney replies to questions of the House Un-American Activities Committee during a hearing of the Communist probe in Washington, DC, on October 24, 1947. (AP Photo)

primarily at right-wing groups, including a number of profascist organizations and the Ku Klux Klan. However, these investigations were generally short and perfunctory. Under the direction of Chairman Martin Dies Jr., the committee (informally known as the Dies Committee) quickly adopted an anticommunist agenda, investigating the alleged infiltration of American institutions by communists and Soviet sympathizers. Ironically, the committee's founding cochair, Democratic Congressman Samuel Dickstein (NY), would later be revealed as a man who was a paid Soviet operative in the late 1930s and early 1940s.

Today, many consider the HUAC hearings to be the political equivalent of witch hunts. However, HUAC played a crucial role in defining Congress's power to investigate the private associations and activities of American citizens. The committee developed a number of techniques that would later be adopted by Republican Senator Joseph McCarthy (WI) during his own anticommunist crusades of the 1950s. Sweeping allegations of disloyalty were made. Witnesses were pressured to reveal the names of former and current associates, and those who refused were often charged with contempt. Being questioned as an "unfriendly witness" or mentioned during HUAC hearings was considered an indication of guilt. Even the most minor linkage of a person's name to suspect organizations was sufficient "guilt by association" to torpedo careers and marriages.

During the prewar years and the early years of World War II, HUAC's activities were focused on developing legislative policy and investigating the communist influence within labor unions and government programs. The first legislation proposed by the committee was the Voorhis Act, which was signed into law in 1940. The act had two parts. First, it required groups representing foreign governments to be registered with the U.S. Attorney General's office. Second, it required the registration of paramilitary groups and organizations that advocated the forcible overthrow of the U.S. government. The Voorhis Act did not include criminal penalties for membership in these organizations.

The Voorhis Act was quickly followed by the Alien and Registration Act of 1940 (generally referred to as the Smith Act). This legislation was far more sweeping. Not only did the Smith Act make it illegal to organize, join, or affiliate with the groups listed in the Voorhis Act, it also broadened the definition of what was considered subversive activity. Any activities advocating the overthrow of the government—or presenting the overthrow of the government as necessary or desirable—was rendered criminal. Furthermore, those found printing, publishing, teaching, or publicly displaying such material with the intent to overthrow the government could receive a prison sentence of up to 20 years. Although critics argue that the law violates the First Amendment, in cases such as *Yates v. United States* (1957) and *Noto v. United States* (1961), the Supreme Court upheld its constitutionality.

Spurred by a number of sit-down strikes by automobile workers, Dies launched investigations into organized labor beginning in 1938. Among the first organizations to be investigated by the committee were the newly formed Congress of Industrial Organizations (CIO) and a number of its local chapters. These investigations prompted the CIO to change its policies so that unions could be expelled if they were deemed to be "consistently directed toward the achievement of the program purposes of the communist party." By 1950, 11 unions had been expelled from the CIO as "communist dominated." Among these unions was the United Electrical, Radio, and Machine Workers Union of America (UE), which represented every General Electric and Westinghouse plant in the United States.

HUAC began hearings in Chicago to investigate the communist influence within the steel workers union in 1939. Only two years prior, Chicago had been the site of an unprovoked police attack on striking steel workers that resulted in 10 strikers being killed and another 90 injured. HUAC placed the blame of such acts of violence on communists who were undermining union goals. However,

HUAC's claims of communist influence were so sweeping that they acted more as an ideological attack against organized labor than a practical attempt to excise radical revolutionaries from the union ranks.

During this period, HUAC also held a number of investigations into the communist infiltration of government agencies. One of the earliest hearings involved the Federal Theater Project (FTP), a program started by President Franklin D. Roosevelt during the Great Depression to employ out-of-work theater workers. Among those that were brought before the committee as unfriendly witnesses was Project Director Hallie Flanagan. Committee members implied Flanagan herself had communist leanings, citing her support of controversial theatrical productions and her tour of Russian theaters while studying in Europe during the 1920s. The HUAC hearings on the FTP would ultimately lead to the program being shut down in 1939.

Perhaps the pinnacle of HUAC investigations into "red" infiltration of the U.S. government was the case of Alger Hiss. In 1948, President Truman publicly called HUAC's attempts to weed out communists a "red herring." HUAC used its investigation and conviction (on perjury charges) of Alger Hiss, a high-level state department employee, to reaffirm its place within American politics. The Hiss investigation also made HUAC committee member Richard Nixon a major political player on the national scene.

In the late 1940s, HUAC shifted its attention to Hollywood. The committee believed the film industry had a unique capacity to shape public discourse and that it was heavily infiltrated by communists and Soviet sympathizers. For nearly a decade, HUAC subpoenaed members of the film industry (both as friendly and unfriendly witnesses), demanding they disclose any and all knowledge about people in the entertainment industry who might be communists or communist "sympathizers." Among the most famous witnesses were a group of filmmakers and screenwriters, dubbed the Hollywood Ten, who refused to answer questions regarding their union and political affiliations. They argued that the committee's questions violated their constitutional rights. The Hollywood Ten were cited for contempt of court and sentenced to one year in prison. The Supreme Court refused to hear their appeal.

The hearings resulted in the creation of the Hollywood blacklist, which denied people tainted by accusations of being "commies" from working in Hollywood or being a member of one of the industry's labor guilds. Thousands of producers, directors, actors, screenwriters, and technical workers were blacklisted (including the Hollywood Ten). While some were able to continue their careers in the theater, or continued working using nonblacklisted colleagues as cover, many struggled to piece shattered lives back together. The blacklist would remain in place until 1956, when actor/producer Kirk Douglas gave the screenwriting credit for his film *Spartacus* to Dalton Trumbo, one of the Hollywood Ten.

By the 1960s, the committee had shifted its focus from Hollywood to the new wave of social activist movements. Among the groups investigated was the Student Nonviolent Coordinating Committee (SNCC), which pushed for the use of federal intervention in support of the civil rights movement. Representative William Colmer of Mississippi asserted the SNCC was "aiding the Communists to enslave the world."

Other HUAC investigations during this time focused on public school teachers in San Francisco, antiwar protesters in Berkeley, members of the Progressive Labor Party, and even working mothers in California and Ohio. These investigations were increasingly viewed as publicity stunts by the general public, and they were heavily criticized by the media for prying into the private political beliefs and associations of witnesses. HUAC's public standing was further eroded as witnesses made a mockery of hearings. The committee was renamed the Internal Security Committee in 1969 in an attempt to reinvent itself. The committee's influence continued to wane, however, and it was abolished in the beginning of 1975. While often viewed as a dark part of American history, HUAC served as a flashpoint in the debate on privacy, national security, political freedom, and freedom of association.

Brian L. Zirkle

Further Reading

Ceplair, Larry, and Steven Englund. 2003. *The Inquisition in Hollywood: Politics in the Film Community, 1930–1960.* Chicago: University of Illinois Press.

Goldstein, Justin Robert. 2001. *Political Repression in Modern America from 1870 to 1976.* Chicago: University of Illinois Press.

Jacoby, Susan. 2009. *Alger Hiss and the Battle for History.* New Haven, CT: Yale University Press.

Morgan, Ted. 2003. *Reds: McCarthyism in Twentieth-Century America.* New York: Random House.

Navasky, Victor S. 2003. *Naming Names.* New York: Hill and Wang.

Schrecker, Ellen. 1994. *The Age of McCarthyism: A Brief History with Documents.* Boston: St. Martin's Press.

I

Illinois v. Krull et al. (1987)

Illinois v. Krull et al. is a case that centers around the Fourth Amendment exclusionary rule that eventually made its way to the U.S. Supreme Court. The exclusionary rule states that evidence obtained by law enforcement officers who make an unreasonable search and seizure cannot be used against the criminal. The so-called good-faith exception to the exclusionary rule says, however, that such evidence is admissible if officers performed their search with good faith, such as using a warrant that later proves to be legally flawed. The Court ruled that the good-faith exception could also apply to searches that were conducted using state statutes that are later ruled invalid.

At one time, the Illinois Vehicle Code stated that police had the right to search automobile salvage yards without a warrant. On July 5, 1981, Chicago police detective Leilan K. McNally arrived at Action Iron and Metal Company, a Chicago automobile wrecking yard operated by Albert Krull, George Lucas, and Salvatore Mucerino. McNally requested from Lucas the licenses and records of automobiles recently purchased by Action. Lucas was unable to produce this documentation, but he did turn over to McNally a notepad that showed five recent purchases. McNally received permission from Lucas to check the cars. Using a mobile computer, he determined, based on the vehicle identification numbers (VIN), that three were stolen and a fourth had its VIN removed. McNally seized the four cars and arrested Lucas; Krull and Mucerino were arrested later. All were charged with violations of state motor vehicle statutes.

Krull filed a motion in an attempt to suppress the evidence that was uncovered, claiming that the search was warrantless and, therefore, in violation of the Fourth Amendment. McNally admitted that he did not produce a warrant. The Illinois Circuit Court agreed with Krull's motion. The state appealed to the Illinois Appellate Court, which set aside the case after the Illinois state legislature amended the Vehicle Code. The case was sent back to the circuit court for reexamination, after which the circuit judge reaffirmed the original ruling.

The state then appealed the case to the Illinois State Supreme Court, which affirmed the lower court's ruling. The state appealed the case to the U.S. Supreme Court. On March 9, 1987, in a 5–4 vote, the high court reversed the Illinois Supreme Court ruling and applied the good-faith exception to the case, even though the statute had been ruled unconstitutional. The Court believed that applying the exclusionary rule in cases such as *Krull* would not prevent misconduct by law enforcement officials and that withholding such evidence would serve no purpose.

Writing for the majority opinion, Justice Harry Blackmun said the exclusionary rule should not apply "when officers act in objectively reasonable reliance upon a statute authorizing warrantless administrative searches, but where the statute is ultimately found to violate the Fourth Amendment." In her dissent, Justice Sandra Day O'Connor, joined by Justices William Brennan, Thurgood Marshall, and John Paul Stevens, wrote that she disagreed with the expansion of the good-faith exception to the exclusionary rule because she believed that the Fourth Amendment existed to prohibit laws that allowed general searches and to deter legislators from passing suspect laws.

Lawrence W. Baker

Further Reading

Ashley, Jennifer. "*Illinois v. Krull*, 480 U.S. 340 (1987)." Civil Liberties. http://uscivilliberties.org/cases/3950-illinois-v-krull-480-us-340-1987.html. Accessed April 15, 2015.

InsideGov. "*Illinois v. Krull Et Al.*" http://supreme-court-cases.insidegov.com/l/5841/Illinois-v-Krull-Et-Al. Accessed September 18, 2015.

Kerr, Orin. 2011. "Good Faith, New Law, and the Scope of the Exclusionary Rule." *Georgetown Law Journal* 99 (April 14): 1077–118.

McKinnis, Tom. 2009. *The Evolution of the Fourth Amendment.* Lanham, MD: Lexington Books.

McKinnis, Tom. 2013. "*Illinois v. Krull.*" In Vile, John R. and David L. Hudson Jr., eds. *Encyclopedia of the Fourth Amendment.* Santa Barbara, CA: CQ Press.

OpenJurist. "480 U.S. 340—*Illinois v. Krull.*" http://openjurist.org/480/us/340/illinois-v-krull. Accessed September 18, 2015.

Illinois v. Lidster (2004)

Illinois v. Lidster is a case that made it to the U.S. Supreme Court and addressed the subject of the police's use of roadblocks. The Court ruled that law enforcement can use roadblocks as part of its investigations into traffic incidents.

In the early morning hours of August 23, 1997, 70-year-old Joseph L. Pytel was killed in Lombard, Illinois, after a motorist struck him while he was riding his bike home from his place of employment, the U.S. Postal Service, in nearby Carol Stream. The driver did not stop at the scene. The police had no concrete leads other than that the vehicle was a pickup truck, perhaps a Ford Bronco. One week later, Lombard police officers set up roadblocks at the location of the hit-and-run incident. Police cars blocked the lanes of the highway, forcing traffic to slow down and stop. In fact, there was a separate police car parked nearby that was ready to pursue any vehicle that attempted to avoid the roadblock. Police officers spent less than a minute or so with the occupants of each car at what the police termed an "informational checkpoint," asking if they knew anything about the accident that had occurred the week before and handing out flyers about the tragedy.

One driver, Robert S. Lidster, approached the roadblock and accepted a flyer from an officer. As he drove away, he swerved his minivan and narrowly missed hitting Detective Wayne Vasil. Vasil pulled him over to question him and smelled alcohol on his breath and detected slurred speech. Lidster was instructed to leave his car and take a sobriety test with Officer Roy Newton. He was arrested and later charged with driving under the influence of alcohol.

Lidster challenged the arrest in trial court but lost, and he was convicted. He appealed, claiming that the evidence against him was collected as a result of a checkpoint stop that violated the Fourth Amendment. The state argued that there was public interest in seeing the crime solved and that the police took appropriate steps to minimize the intrusion of the motorists' rights. But the appellate court reversed the conviction, finding the roadblock to be a violation of the Fourth Amendment. Judge Robert D. McLaren stated, "If investigating such a crime could be the basis for a roadblock, police could stop all cars entering or leaving town virtually every day on the chance that someone might have seen something that would aid the investigation." The state appealed to the Illinois Supreme Court, but it agreed with the lower court's ruling.

The state then appealed to the U.S. Supreme Court, which did not agree with the state high court's decision and ruled 6–3 in favor of the state. The Court believed that the case upon which the state high court had made its decision, *Indianapolis v. Edmond* (2000), involved a checkpoint set up for the police to search vehicles for possible drugs. The Court had ruled that this went against the Fourth Amendment, because there was no specific, individual suspicion of the drivers and passengers involved in the stops.

On the other hand, the intent of the roadblock and questioning of the occupants of the vehicles in the *Lidster* case was for the police to secure information about a prior crime that did not involve (in all likelihood) any of the cars stopped. The Court, therefore, ruled that the traffic stoppage was constitutional. The Court said that the purpose of setting up the checkpoint in the *Lidster* case "was not to determine whether a vehicle's occupants were committing a crime but to ask vehicle occupants . . . for their help in providing information about a crime . . . committed by others." Furthermore, the police were seeking information about a specific crime with "appropriately tailored . . . checkpoint stops to fit important criminal investigatory needs." They set up the roadblock to fit the circumstances surrounding the crime—that is, the stoppage of vehicles took place on the same day of the week, at the same time, and in the same location as the accident that killed Pytel. The Court ruled that there was no violation of the Fourth Amendment and reversed the Illinois Supreme Court's decision.

The dissenting judges argued that the roadblock required motorists to stop and remain stopped for as long as the police required them to do so. They also questioned whether questioning a "random sample of drivers" would secure information any more meaningfully or successfully than simply placing flyers on the windshields of nearby businesses, whose workers may have been leaving their place of employment around the same time as the hit-and-run accident.

Lawrence W. Baker

Further Reading

CaseBriefs. "*Illinois v. Lidster.*" http://www.casebriefs.com/blog/law/criminal-procedure/criminal-procedure-keyed-to-saltzburg/searches-and-seizures-of-persons-and-things/illinois-v-lidster/. Accessed March 20, 2015.

FindLaw. "*Illinois v. Lidster.*" http://caselaw.lp.findlaw.com/scripts/getcase.pl?court=US&vol=000&invol=02-1060. Accessed March 20, 2015.

Nickelsberg, Jessica E. 2005. "*Illinois v. Lidster:* Continuing to Carve Out Constitutional Vehicle Checkpoints." *Journal of Criminal Law and Criminology* 95 (3) (Spring): 839–70.

Ramsell, Donald J. 2003–2004. "*Illinois v. Lidster*: A View from the Inside." *Journal of the DuPage County Bar Association* 16.

Inevitable Discovery

"Inevitable discovery" is an exception to the exclusionary rule, which states that illegally obtained evidence is inadmissible at trial. The exclusionary rule discourages law enforcement agencies from violating constitutional rights in the course of an investigation. According to inevitable discovery doctrine, however, if evidence would have been found in the course of a normal and customary police investigation, then even if it was illegally obtained, it will be admissible in court.

The concept of inevitable discovery was first accepted by the Supreme Court in the murder case of *Nix v. Williams* (1984), in which the defendant was tricked into revealing the location of the body. The evidence was allowed because the Court reasoned that it would have been found in the course of a normal police search. Although the doctrine was initially used to admit useful evidence found outside the bounds of legality in the course of an investigation, its use has expanded to support the surveillance of ordinary citizens.

The doctrine has given credence to evidence found during warrantless searches, conducted in violation of Fourth Amendment guarantees that the "right of people to be secure in their persons, houses, papers, and effects, against unreasonable searches and seizures, shall not be violated, and no Warrants shall issue, but upon probable cause, supported by Oath or affirmation, and particularly describing the place to be searched, and the persons or things to be seized." Under the inevitable discovery doctrine, a search may be conducted with a hypothetical warrant (claiming that probable cause alone was enough to search), or a prewarrant search (searching and finding evidence, and later obtaining a warrant to seize the evidence).

Use of the inevitable discovery doctrine has increased because it has limited the efficacy of the exclusionary rule in deterring law enforcement officers from illegal search and seizure. Some courts have drawn a distinction, disallowing the admission of primary evidence using the inevitable discovery doctrine, but then have accepted secondary evidence revealed in this way. However, the admission of primary evidence has expanded as the doctrine's usage has grown. Either way, the doctrine allows judgement to be carried out by the police at the scene of a crime, instead of in the courts, where issuance of a warrant would normally be necessary.

The inevitable discovery doctrine has been used to expand the ability of the U.S. government to conduct widespread surveillance of U.S. citizens through electronic means without warrant. The rate of surveillance increased exponentially following the terrorist attacks of September 11, 2001, when the USA PATRIOT Act was signed into law by President George W. Bush. That legislation gave the federal government increased legal authority o wiretap phones, demand cell phone records from telecommunications companies, and access personal e-mails and even library records without a warrant on suspicion of terrorist activity. The PATRIOT Act has been reauthorized, with minor changes, on several occasions since its original passage.

The concept of inevitable discovery has been applied with vigor to new communications technology. In the years since 9/11, technological advances in communication have transformed the lives of Americans. Surveillance was no longer primarily conducted through wired telephone lines when public phone booths and even home phones were becoming obsolete, and it was not even necessary to place tracking devices on vehicles when most cell phones had a GPS device preloaded in their circuitry. In terms of visual evidence, satellite imagery and video cameras in buildings, cities, and on drones provided an easy alternative to the investigative photographer.

The U.S. government has a keen interest in this abundance of electronic information on the activities, relationships, and interests of Americans and other people around the world. Eager to access and analyze this information, choosing targets for further investigation based on suspicion and risk factors, law enforcement and national security actors have been wary of triggering the exclusionary rule, which would normally prevent the use of this evidence in court against a defendant. The inevitable discovery rule has thus been employed with increasing frequency to establish the evidence as legally admissible in a court of law.

Mary Le Rouge

Further Reading

Bloom, Robert. 1992. "Inevitable Discovery: An Exception beyond the Fruits." *American Journal of Criminal Law* 20: 79–104.

Quinn, Gordon D. 1988. "Criminal Law—The Inevitable Discovery Exception to the Exclusionary Rule—The Search for Its Principled Application to Prewarrant Evidence." *Western New England Law Review* 10: 59–98.

Smith, Cary Stacy, and Li-Ching Hung. 2010. *The Patriot Act: Issues and Controversies.* Springfield, IL: Charles C. Thomas Publishing.

Internal Security Act of 1950

The Internal Security Act (ISA) was passed in 1950 during the height of anticommunist hysteria in the United States. The act was aimed at furthering a conservative anticommunist agenda which sought to eliminate the communist influence in American politics and society through coercion. The act is widely regarded by scholars as one of the most egregious attacks on the freedom of speech and association in American history. It was an attempt to criminalize not only a particular ideology, but also private associations that involved no actual criminal activity. The act technically remained part of American law until 1990.

The primary architects of the ISA (also sometimes called the Subversive Activities Control Act) were Congressman John Wood (D-GA), who was chair of the House Un-American Activities Committee at the time, and Senator Pat McCarran (D-NV), one of the Senate's most prominent anticommunists. In fact, the legislation frequently came to be referred to as the McCarran Act.

After the bill sailed through Congress, President Harry S. Truman vetoed the act on September 22, 1950. Truman warned that it would "aid potential enemies by requiring the publication of a complete list of vital defense plants, laboratories, and other installations . . . put the Government of the United States in the thought control business . . . and give Government officials vast powers to harass all of our citizens in the exercise of their right of free speech." The very same day that Truman vetoed the act, however, both the Senate and House overrode his veto to make it the law of the land.

The ISA made it illegal to pursue a communist or "totalitarian" political agenda and required all communist organizations to register with the U.S. attorney general. Any organizations that failed to register could be brought before the Subversive Activities Control Board (SACB) and forced to register as "communist." Registered organizations were required to label their publications and broadcasts as originating from a communist organization. Furthermore, members of registered organizations were denied employment in the government or private firms with federal defense contracts and were prohibited from applying for or using passports.

The act also contained a number of provisions dealing with immigration and naturalization. Aliens who were at any time members of, or affiliated with a communist or totalitarian party were denied entry to the United States. Those already in the United States could be deported without receiving a hearing. Naturalized citizens could have their citizenship revoked if they joined a registered communist organization within five years of becoming a citizen. Additionally, aliens who were members of newly registered communist organizations could be denied naturalization unless they were able to prove they had left the organization within three months of the organization being registered.

Finally, judicial standards for search and seizure, the use of informants, wiretapping, and other forms of surveillance were relaxed. The act also allowed the president to declare an "internal security emergency" during which time the attorney general was empowered to detain anyone who "probably would engage in, or conspire to engage in, acts of espionage or sabotage." The legislation included provisions for administrative hearings, but not court trials. In this way, communist organizations remained formally legal, but mechanisms were institutionalized that allowed for the indefinite detention of their members without any criminal act being committed and with limited judicial oversight.

Anticipating that the law would lead to a wave of arrests (the FBI had compiled a list of 26,000 individuals it considered a threat), Congress earmarked $775,000 to establish six detention camps in Arizona, Florida, Pennsylvania, Oklahoma, and California. However, while several thousand Americans were arrested under the auspices of the act during the 1950s, their numbers never reached the expected level. As a result, an internal security emergency was never declared, and so the provisions that required it were never implemented.

Brian L. Zirkle

Further Reading

Goldstein, Robert J. 2001. *Political Repression in Modern America, from 1870 to 1976.* Chicago: University of Illinois Press.

Morgan, Ted. 2003. *Reds: McCarthyism in Twentieth-Century America.* New York: Random House.

Schrecker, Ellen. 1994. *The Age of McCarthyism: A Brief History with Documents.* Boston: St. Martin's Press.

J

Jewel v. National Security Agency (2015)

This case was a class action lawsuit originally filed by the Electronic Frontier Foundation (EFF) on behalf of AT&T customers against the National Security Agency (NSA) in 2008. The EFF claimed that the NSA and other U.S. government agencies were involved in an "illegal unconstitutional and ongoing dragnet surveillance of [AT&T's] communications and communications records."

On September 18, 2008, the EFF filed a lawsuit on behalf of Carolyn Jewel and other AT&T customers that charged that the NSA was involved in a program of mass surveillance called the Terrorist Surveillance Program (TSP), which was made public in a number of newspaper articles beginning in 2005. A whistleblower, former AT&T telecommunications technician Mark Klein, revealed that AT&T maintained a tap on its fiber-optic system that allowed the NSA to monitor AT&T's Internet traffic, which included bulk telephone records, e-mails, instant messages, and text messages. The plaintiffs alleged that these practices, which had been initiated within months of the terrorist attacks of September 11, 2001, violated both the First and Fourth Amendments to the U.S. Constitution and several other laws pertaining to electronic surveillance, including the Foreign Intelligence Surveillance Act (FISA), the Wiretap Act, the Electronic Communications Privacy Act, and the Administrative Procedure Act.

On January 21, 2010, U.S. chief judge Vaughn Walker of the Northern District of California dismissed the case, saying that the plaintiffs were unable to prove that they were personally affected by the alleged wrongdoings. The plaintiffs appealed to the Ninth Circuit Court. On January 29, 2011, Judge M. Margaret McKeown vacated the lower court's ruling, ruling that the plaintiffs did have standing and questioning whether the government's claim to the state secrets privilege was valid. The case went back to the district court, this time with Judge Jeffrey White overseeing the trial.

The NSA maintained its "state secrets" stance, noting that "the disclosure of sensitive intelligence sources and methods . . . reasonably could be expected to cause exceptionally grave harm to national security," and it urged the public to trust that the agency wasn't abusing any powers. It claimed that "highly classified and properly privileged intelligence sources and methods are at risk of disclosure. The law is clear, however, that where litigation risks or requires the disclosure of information that reasonably could be expected to harm national security, dismissal is required."

On July 8, 2013, however, Judge White agreed with the EFF that the subject matter in the case was not a state secret and that details that should remain classified could do so under the auspices of the FISA. White wrote, "Congress intended for FISA to displace the common law rules such as the state secrets privilege with regard to matter within FISA's purview." This allowed the case to remain active.

Later that year, the court asked the government to discuss the incidents surrounding NSA intelligence leaks, particularly as they pertained to those divulged by Edward Snowden, a former CIA employee who had released classified information to the media in the spring of 2013. The NSA, however, opted to invoke its state secrets privilege in December 2013.

Finally, on February 10, 2015, Judge White ultimately ruled that evidence that was accessible to the public could not provide a complete picture of how the NSA collected its information from AT&T's Internet system and that the public revelation of additional information—which was allowed to be reviewed by the court—"would have to be dismissed on the basis that any possible defenses would require impermissible disclosure of state secret information." White wrote: "Because a fair and full adjudication of the Government Defendants' defenses would require harmful disclosures of national security information that is protected by the state secrets privilege, the Court must exclude such evidence from the case. Addressing any defenses involves a significant risk of potentially harmful effects any disclosures could have on national security."

The court, therefore, ruled that the plaintiffs could not prove that surveillance occurred illegally as alleged, a result that Judge White claimed was frustrating: "The Court is frustrated by the prospect of deciding the current motions without full public disclosure of the Court's analysis and reasoning. However, it is a necessary by-product of the types of concerns raised by this case. Although partially not accessible to the Plaintiffs or the public, the record contains the full materials reviewed by the Court. The Court is persuaded that its decision is correct both legally and factually and furthermore is required by the interests of national security."

The EFF disagreed with White's reasoning, saying that the FISA "allows courts to examine secret evidence that is necessary to determine whether surveillance conducted by the government was done legally."

Lawrence W. Baker

Further Reading

Electronic Frontier Foundation. 2015. "*Jewel v. NSA:* Making Sense of a Disappointing Decision over Mass Surveillance." https://www.eff.org/deeplinks/2015/02/jewel-v-nsa-making-sense-disappointing-decision-over-mass-surveillance. Accessed April 15, 2015.

Electronic Frontier Foundation. "*Jewel v. NSA.*" *NSA Spying on Americans.* https://www.eff.org/cases/jewel. Accessed April 15, 2015.

Kopstein, Joshua. 2013. "No More 'Secrets': An Important Case against NSA Spying Takes a Big Step Forward." *The Verge* (July 9). http://www.theverge.com/2013/7/9/4507088/no-more-secrets-an-important-case-against-nsa-spying-takes-a-big-step. Accessed April 15, 2015.

McAllister, Neil. 2015. "Another U.S. Court Smacks Down EFF's NSA Wiretap Sueball—But Won't Say Why." *The Register* (February 11). http://www.theregister.co.uk/2015/02/11/eff_loses_nsa_wiretap_appeal_again/. Accessed April 15, 2015.

United States Courts. "Case Summary: *Jewel v. NSA*, 08-cv-04373 (N.D. California)." http://www.uscourts.gov/Multimedia/Cameras/NorthernDistrictofCalifornia/08-cv-04373.aspx. Accessed April 15, 2015.

University of Michigan Law School. "Case Profile: *Jewel v. National Security Agency.*" Civil Rights Litigation Clearinghouse. http://www.clearinghouse.net/detail.php?id=12772. Accessed April 15, 2015.

K

Klayman v. Obama (2013)

This case examines whether the U.S. government's collection of bulk phone and Internet records constitutes a violation of the First, Fourth, and Fifth Amendments. A district court judge ruled that the government's actions likely violated the Fourth Amendment. As of April 2015, the case is currently on appeal with the D.C. Circuit Court of Appeals.

On June 6, 2013, the *Washington Post* and the *Guardian* reported that former CIA contractor Edward Snowden had leaked classified information that originated from the National Security Agency (NSA). Shortly thereafter, Larry Klayman, Charles Strange, and Mary Ann Strange filed a suit in which they claimed that the NSA's collection of Verizon Wireless customers' bulk phone records was unconstitutional. They contended that the surveillance violated the "reasonable expectation of privacy, free speech and association, right to be free of unreasonable searches and seizures, and due process rights." Six days later, Michael Ferrari and Matt Garrison filed a similar suit, adding bulk collection of Internet records to the mix.

Though coupled together as part of the same suit, the Klayman/Strange piece was referred to as *Klayman I,* and the Ferrari/Garrison piece was referred to as *Klayman II.* The defendants in *Klayman I* were President Barack Obama, NSA director Keith B. Alexander, Attorney General Eric Holder Jr., Verizon chief executive Lowell McAdam, and U.S. district judge Roger Vinson. The defendants in *Klayman II* were AOL, Apple, AT&T, Facebook, Google, Microsoft, PalTalk, Skype, Sprint, Yahoo!, YouTube, and the government officials from *Klayman I.*

The lead plaintiff in *Klayman I* was Larry Klayman, a former U.S. Justice Department prosecutor and the founder of Freedom Watch, a conservative political advocacy group devoted, among other things, to civil liberties protections. The Stranges, meanwhile, claimed their phone records had been accessed after they had been critical of the Obama administration's handling of a tragedy in which their son was killed in a helicopter crash while he was serving in Afghanistan. Ferrari and Garrison were California private investigators.

On December 16, 2013, Judge Richard J. Leon of the U.S. District Court for the District of Columbia ruled that the surveillance likely violated the Fourth Amendment, calling the NSA's data collection methods "almost-Orwellian." "Plaintiffs have a very significant expectation of privacy in an aggregated collection of their telephone metadata covering the last five years," he said, "and the NSA's Bulk Telephony Metadata Program significantly intrudes on that expectation. I have significant doubts about the efficacy of the metadata collection program as a means of conducting time-sensitive investigations in cases involving imminent threats of terrorism." The judge issued a preliminary injunction that barred the NSA from collecting Verizon data from Klayman and one of his clients, but Leon stayed the order in anticipation of an appeal by the defendants. The defense was pleased with the Fourth Amendment ruling but disappointed in Leon's failure to address First and Fifth Amendment concerns.

The government did, indeed, appeal to the D.C. Circuit Court of Appeals on January 3, 2014. Each side argued in front of a three-judge panel of the court on November 4, 2014. A decision had not yet been reached as of April 2015, and many observers speculated that the case could wind up with the U.S. Supreme Court.

Lawrence W. Baker

Further Reading

Bennett, Wells. 2014. "Recap of Yesterday's Argument in the Section 215 Case." Lawfare (November 5). http://www.lawfareblog.com/2014/11/recap-of-yesterdays-argument-in-the-section-215-case/. Accessed April 15, 2015.

Freedom Watch. "About Us." http://www.freedomwatchusa.org/about. Accessed April 15, 2015.

Nelson, Steven. 2013. "PRISM Class-Action Lawsuit Filed: $20B, Injunction Sought Against 'Complicit' Companies and Officials." U.S. News & World Report (June 12). http://www.usnews.com/news/newsgram/articles/2013/06/12/prism-class-action-lawsuit-filed-20b-injunction-sought-against-complicit-companies-and-officials. Accessed April 15, 2015.

Volz, Dustin. 2014. "The NSA's Mass-Surveillance Program Is about to Go on Trial." *National Journal* (November 3). http://www.nationaljournal.com/tech/the-nsa-s-mass-surveillance-program-is-about-to-go-on-trial-20141103. Accessed April 15, 2015.

Voorhees, Josh. 2013. "Judge Rules NSA Phone Program Likely Unconstitutional." *Slate* (December 16). http://www.slate.com/blogs/the_slatest/2013/12/16/nsa_unconstitutional_judge_richard_leon_rules_phone_spying_program_likely.html. Accessed April 15, 2015.

Klein, Mark

Mark Klein is a retired AT&T whistle-blower who made public his former company's involvement in the National Security Agency's (NSA) illegal warrantless spying on millions of Americans.

Mark Klein was born in the 1940s and grew up in New York City. He received his Bachelor of Arts degree in history at Cornell University in 1966. He also received certificates in electronics and computers from technical schools, and he entered the computer field. In 1981, Klein began his career at AT&T as a communications technician, the first 10 years in New York and then later in California, where he worked until his retirement in May 2004.

Klein rose to public prominence when he alleged that AT&T worked with the NSA to install eavesdropping devices that could monitor the public's e-mail and Internet communications. He prepared a number of documents and identified a secret room in AT&T's Folsom Street office in San Francisco that he said housed equipment that could review large amounts of Internet data. The materials he prepared were used in a class action lawsuit filed by the civil liberties group Electronic Frontier Foundation (EFF) against AT&T. Klein's documents included wiring diagrams and other corporate blueprints, as well as statements about events that he observed when he was employed by AT&T.

Klein's job as a communications technician was to maintain AT&T's computer network in the San Francisco Bay Area, including Internet and telephone communications. In the summer of 2002, he became aware that an NSA representative had visited the Geary Street office in San Francisco where Klein worked. By that fall, Defense Advanced Research Projects Agency (DARPA) Information Awareness Office director John Poindexter proposed the creation of a so-called Total Information Awareness program, which would enable the U.S. government to pull together searchable data from databases of customer information maintained by members of the financial, communications, travel, and health care industries. The overlap of the DARPA news and the appearance of the NSA representative made Klein suspicious.

In early 2003, on a routine tour of the Folsom Street office in advance of some departments being moved, Klein saw the so-called secret room and learned that union technicians were not involved in the setup of equipment—a violation of union rules. In October 2003, Klein moved to the Folsom Street office where his duties took him to the Internet room, where he had to maintain and upgrade the system. When a fellow employee showed Klein some equipment in the Internet room, he confided that the secret room was being used to monitor Internet traffic. Klein learned that there were splitters that copied all signals and fed them into the secret room. Klein confirmed this through wiring documents that he discovered lying around. These documents revealed that the data flow came from the entire network, not just from AT&T's network. Klein also did some research on a piece of equipment he was not familiar with, a semantic traffic analyzer, which he learned was used for spying.

Klein's discovery concerned him on ethical grounds. "They were basically sweeping up, vacuum-cleaning the Internet through all the data, sweeping it all into this secret room. . . . It's the sort of thing that very intrusive, repressive governments would do, finding out about everybody's personal data without a warrant. I knew right away that this was illegal and unconstitutional, and yet they were doing it." Klein also was scared because he "knew this authorization came from very high up—not only high up in AT&T, but high up in the government. So I was in a bit of a quandary as to what to do about it, but I thought this should be halted."

Klein was also angry at what the government was doing. "When the founders wrote the Fourth Amendment," said Klein, "they had a specific antagonism against what were called general warrants. . . . General warrants is when the British troops would come in with a warrant and say: 'We have the right to search your house. We're looking for something. Looking for what? We can't tell you. We're going to ransack your house.' That's a general warrant. They can turn your life upside down, and the colonialists [sic] hated that. So the Fourth Amendment specifically bans general warrants. It calls for specific warrants in which the things to be seized and the persons to be seized are specifically named. There's a reason for that. It's to protect against arbitrary government power. And what they've done is to trample over the Fourth Amendment by basically instituting a general warrant on the Internet."

In January 2004, Klein wrote down his observations and gathered 120 pages of technical documents, materials he pointed out were not classified documents. There were documents that showed how the NSA was installing splitters that would enable domestic and international Internet traffic to be copied. "It's gobs and gobs of information going across the Internet," said Klein.

Klein also learned that there were similar secret "vacuuming" rooms in other locations, including Atlanta, Los Angeles, San Diego, and Seattle. In his younger years in the 1960s, Klein had participated in antiwar marches, so he had some experience in fighting against the establishment. In May 2004, Klein retired from AT&T. At that point he had not yet revealed anything he had learned.

In December 2005, the *New York Times* reported on the government spying without a warrant. The government's retort was to threaten to prosecute anyone who had a security clearance. Klein described the environment as "sort of a witch hunt." He said, "People are afraid of losing their jobs, and it's a rule of thumb that if you become a whistleblower you'll probably lose your job." But since Klein was no longer employed by AT&T, he felt relatively safe; he had no security clearance or job to lose. In early 2006, he began sharing documents with members of Congress and the media—the *Los Angeles Times* and the *New York Times*—but he received little interest. Klein claimed the *Los Angeles Times* had planned on a front-page story until John Negroponte, director of national intelligence, was made aware of Klein's information; Klein was told in March 2006 that the story was killed. The *Times* disputed this, claiming that there was not enough information for a story.

It wasn't until the EFF, a civil liberties group, was working on a lawsuit in an attempt to stop the NSA program that Klein got noticed. He became a witness for EFF in *Hepting v. AT&T*.

Klein received support for what he did. U.S. senator Christopher Dodd (D-Conn.), for example, commended him for his actions: "Had it not been for Mark Klein stepping up, this story might have remained secret for years and years, causing further erosion of our rights."

When Edward Snowden leaked information pertaining to NSA's warrantless surveillance program in June 2013, Klein reacted by saying, "This is complete vindication." A federal appeals court eventually ruled, on May 7, 2015, that the NSA program was illegal. Klein went on to write a book about his experiences that was published in 2009. It is titled *Wiring up the Big Brother Machine . . . And Fighting It.*

Lawrence W. Baker

Further Reading

BBS Radio. "Guest Name: Mark Klein." *The People Speak Radio*. http://bbsradio.com/content/guest-ben-blum-guest-mark-klein-people-speak-many-hosts-may-20–2014. Accessed May 12, 2015.

Klein, Mark. 2009. *Wiring up the Big Brother Machine . . . And Fighting It*. Charleston, SC: BookSurge.

Kravets, David. 2013. "NSA Leak Vindicates AT&T Whistleblower." *Wired* (June 27). http://www.wired.com/2013/06/nsa-whistleblower-klein/. Accessed May 12, 2015.

McMillan, Robert. 2009. "The NSA Wiretapping Story that Nobody Wanted." *PC World* (July 17). http://www.pcworld.com/article/168651/article.html. Accessed May 12, 2015.

Nakashima, Ellen. 2007. "A Story of Surveillance." *Washington Post* (November 7). http://www.washingtonpost.com/wp-dyn/content/article/2007/11/07/AR2007110700006_pf.html. Accessed May 12, 2015.

PBS. 2007. "Interview: Mark Klein." *Spying on the Home Front*. PBS (January 9). http://www.pbs.org/wgbh/pages/frontline/homefront/interviews/klein.html. Accessed May 12, 2015.

PBS. "Whistleblower Mark Klein." *NOW*. http://www.pbs.org/now/shows/307/mark-klein.html. Accessed May 12, 2015.

L

Leahy, Patrick (1940–)

Democratic senator Patrick Leahy of Vermont is known as one of Washington's most outspoken advocates of privacy rights—and as a dogged critic of the National Security Agency (NSA) and various laws and programs that provide the foundation for much of the U.S. government's present surveillance infrastructure.

Born on March 31, 1940, in Montpelier, Vermont, Leahy's childhood home was actually located just across the street from the Vermont Statehouse. After graduating from Saint Michael's College in Colchester in 1961, he received his Juris Doctor from Georgetown University Law Center in 1964. He then served for eight years as state's attorney in Chittenden County before winning election to the U.S. Senate in 1974.

During his more than four decades in the U.S. Senate, Leahy became widely recognized as one of the leading privacy advocates in the Congress (as well as a champion of free-speech rights and the environment). A long-time member of the Senate Judiciary Committee (and sometime chairman), Leahy spoke out, held hearings, and sponsored legislation on many privacy issues. Leahy was the original sponsor of the Senate version of the Electronic Communications Privacy Act of 1986, and he has sponsored legislation on health privacy, security breach notification, and other privacy issues. Leahy was a primary author of the controversial USA PATRIOT Act, but he later objected to its reauthorization and held hearings on abuses of the government's authority to conduct searches and use national security letters. Leahy has also been a long-time proponent of openness in government legislation and the principal congressional sponsor of several Freedom of Information Act amendments seeking to recognize the effect of new technology on information disclosure by federal agencies.

Leahy reacted with outrage to the revelations of government surveillance and data collection activities from NSA whistle-blower Edward Snowden in 2013, and he has repeatedly introduced bills to "reform" these practices, end the legal

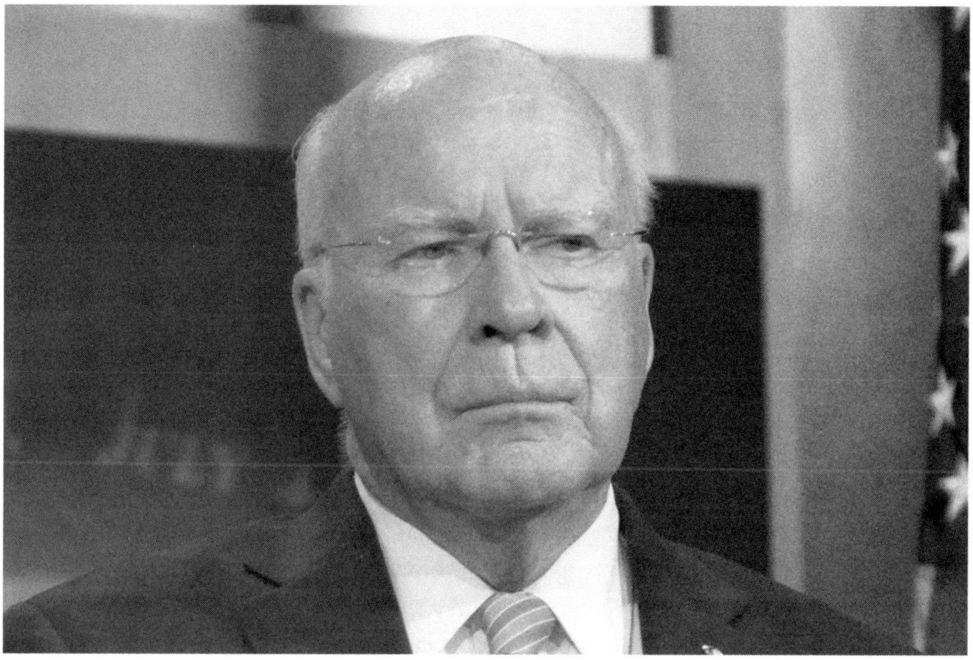

Sen. Patrick Leahy listens during a news conference on Capitol Hill in Washington, DC, 2015. (AP Photo)

authorization for such practices under the Patriot Act, and curb the NSA's powers. "This is a debate about Americans' fundamental relationship with their government," according to Leahy. "[This is a debate] about if the government should be able to create massive data bases about its citizens or about if we are in control of our own government, not the other way around."

Robert Gellman and Pam Dixon

Further Reading

O'Harrow, Robert. 2005. *No Place to Hide: Behind the Scenes of Our Emerging Surveillance Society*. New York: Free Press.

Peterson, Andrea. 2014. "The Senate Has Another Go at NSA Surveillance Reform." *Washington Post* (July 29). http://www.washingtonpost.com/blogs/the-switch/wp/2014/07/29/the-senate-has-another-go-at-nsa-surveillance-reform/. Accessed September 18, 2015.

M

McCarthyism

The term "McCarthyism" was first used in a cartoon by Herbert Bloom published on March 29, 1950, in the *Washington Post.* It initially referred to an extreme form of conservative anticommunism championed by Republican senator Joseph McCarthy of Wisconsin that was purportedly aimed at identifying and eliminating domestic communist threats to the U.S. government. This anticommunist agenda, however, was often pursued at the expense of basic civil liberties such as the freedom of association and the right to privacy. McCarthyism is also used to refer to a more general cultural and political milieu in which concerns about national security and the threat of communism took precedence over the protection of civil liberties and personal privacy—and where paranoia, innuendo, and whisper campaigns were sufficient to ruin the reputations and lives of thousands of Americans. Generally associated with the "Red Scare" of the 1940s and 1950s, the term is still sometimes used pejoratively by political dissenters who believe government policies are encroaching on the basic rights of citizens.

McCarthyism, narrowly defined, began on February 9, 1950, when Senator McCarthy gave a speech in Wheeling, West Virginia, proclaiming he possessed a list of known Communist loyalists that worked in the State Department. This claim quickly took root among the American public, which had become generally suspicious of communism in the 1930s and actively feared it as a threat to their way of life in the post–World War II Cold War years.

The formation of the House Un-American Activities Committee (HUAC) in 1938 marked the arrival of conservative anticommunism on the national political scene. HUAC played a central role in redefining domestic communism from a matter of political opinion to one of national security, and it set the stage for McCarthy's rise to prominence. HUAC was the driving force behind the Alien and Registration Act of 1940 that criminalized the advocacy of revolutionary political ideologies and the association with organizations that engaged in such advocacy.

Furthermore, HUAC initiated a series of highly publicized hearings aimed at exposing the infiltration of communists and Soviet sympathizers into American institutions and organizations (including the federal government and labor unions). Within these hearings, HUAC committee members made sweeping, often unsubstantiated allegations. They offered a conception of American communism that was severely distorted yet plausible enough to be convincing. In this way, the HUAC hearings established a set of strategies that would be adopted by the Permanent Investigating Subcommittee of the Government Operations Committee chaired by McCarthy.

The year 1950 marked the beginning of the McCarthy era proper. In the middle of that year, North Korean military forces invaded South Korea. Though the United States' involvement in the conflict was defined as a "police action," it became a constant reminder that the Cold War was not simply a clash of ideologies, but had tangible costs. On the domestic front, Julius and Ethel Rosenberg were charged as Soviet spies for providing the Soviet Union with highly classified information on the development of atomic weaponry. Their arrests provided the ammunition conservative anticommunists needed to legitimate their attack on domestic communism. In Congress the Internal Security Act of 1950 was passed (over President Truman's veto), further restricting the civil liberties of Americans with unpopular political beliefs. Also during that year, the newsletter *Counterattack* released a list of entertainers believed to be communists or "fellow travelers"—a term used to refer to those with similar opinions and associations as communists.

It was in the beginning of this year that McCarthy made his famous speech in Wheeling, which vaulted him to center stage in the anticommunist movement. McCarthy quickly became the most sought after political spokesperson for the Republican Party, receiving over 2,000 invitations to speak leading up to the November 1950 elections. He, along with many other Republicans, turned communism into a major issue in the elections, labeling many Democratic candidates as "soft" on communism.

Communist charges by McCarthy and other anticommunist extremists escalated during 1951 and 1952. Secretary of Defense and World War II general George Marshall was accused of passively facilitating and even conspiring with communists within the executive branch. Actor/director Charlie Chaplin was publicly accused of being communist by Federal Bureau of Investigation (FBI) director J. Edgar Hoover, and eventually his visa was revoked while he was out of the country on vacation. Extensive hearings by HUAC and the Senate Internal Security Subcommittee (SISS) were held to investigate communist influence within government agencies and labor unions and among high-profile celebrities and artists. During that period of time, HUAC alone spent 108 days in hearings encompassing 34 separate investigations.

Yet the activities of these two committees were overshadowed by McCarthy's Permanent Subcommittee on Investigations (PSI) subcommittee of the Government Operations Committee. Though the PSI was limited to the investigation of government agencies and employees, McCarthy's obstreperous personality and over-the-top tactics attracted a great deal of attention from the media, as did his sweeping claims of communist infiltration.

The overarching purpose of these congressional hearings, which took place in 1953 and 1954, was twofold. Conservative anticommunists used them in order to influence the broader social standards of political orthodoxy and heresy in the United States. Yet they also were aimed at discrediting and marginalizing specific individuals. The hearings themselves could not convict witnesses of any crimes and, in fact, had no practical legislative purpose. However, the hearings were used to condemn individuals without adhering to the standards of due process. Hundreds of witnesses were fired by their employers and blacklisted in their industries. The hysteria spurred by the hearings led to other forms of repression against perceived communists and political dissidents. The most infamous being the Hollywood blacklist which expelled thousands of actors, directors, writers, and technical workers from their labor guilds and denied them employment in Hollywood movie productions.

The response to the anticommunist extremists by Truman and Eisenhower was often inconsistent. Both presidents adopted a conservative anticommunist agenda, though more moderate than that pursued by McCarthy. Truman did cooperate with the Tydings Committee that was set up in order to investigate McCarthy and the validity of his claims and viewed the activities of some "loyalty boards" to be "un-American." Yet he also gave numerous speeches about the threat of domestic communism. His administration continued to emphasize the arrest of communists and pushed for the loyalty standard for the termination of employment to be changed from "reasonable grounds" to "reasonable doubt." The latter resulted in the termination of 565 public employees that had previously been vindicated in hearings by the Loyalty Review Board (LRB).

During the beginning of Eisenhower's term, the president continually appeased McCarthy, refusing to offer even the mildest criticism of his irresponsible threats and wild accusations. The Dwight Eisenhower administration launched investigations for denaturalization of 10,000 citizens and deportation of 12,000 aliens. It also expanded the ability of the executive branch to dismiss federal employees on loyalty issues, resulting in 1,500 more employees being terminated (90 percent of whom were dismissed without receiving any form of hearing).

McCarthy remained a powerful political player for only a few years. As 1953 wore on, he increasingly came across poorly in the national media, particularly in television interviews. Media personalities such as newscaster Edward R. Murrow provided profiles of McCarthy and his hearings that were critical of the senator and warned that anticommunist hysteria was trampling on treasured constitutional rights. Other critics stepped forward as well, including Supreme Court justice William O. Douglas. Writing in *New York Times Magazine,* Douglas charged that "the Communist threat inside the country has been magnified and exalted far beyond its realities. Irresponsible talk by irresponsible people has fanned the flames of fear. . . . Fear has driven more and more men and women in all walks of life either to silence or to the folds of the orthodox. . . . This fear has stereotyped our thinking, narrowed the range of free public discussion, and driven many thoughtful people to despair. . . . [This is] one of the worst witch-hunts we have seen since early days."

The climax of McCarthy's descent into self-destruction came during the nationally televised McCarthy-Army hearings on June 24, 1954. As McCarthy made another of his crass and unsubstantiated accusations of communist leanings, Attorney Joseph Welch interjected: "Have you no sense of decency, sir, at long last? Have you left no sense of decency?" The Senate chamber erupted in applause, and its reverberations were felt by television viewers across the country. McCarthy lost much of the public support he had previously enjoyed, and the Senate voted to formally censure him for his conduct on December 2, 1954.

McCarthyism itself would continue on for another two years. However, it too was crippled in the aftermath of the McCarthy-Army hearings, as television was no longer permitted to air the congressional hearings that had fueled the anticommunist hysteria within the general public. The McCarthy era is generally considered to have ended in 1956, when a series of Supreme Court decisions began to curb the repressive surveillance policies initiated under the guise of national security and reinstate basic civil liberties.

Brian L. Zirkle

Further Reading

Doherty, Thomas Patrick. 2003. *Cold War, Cool Medium: Television, McCarthyism, and American Culture*. New York: Columbia University Press.

Douglas, William O. 1952. "The Black Silence of Fear." *New York Times Magazine*, January 13.

Goldstein, Robert J. 2001. *Political Repression in Modern America, from 1870 to 1976.* Chicago: University of Illinois Press.

Heale, Michael J. 1990. *American Anticommunism: Combating the Enemy Within, 1830–1970.* Baltimore, MD: The John Hopkins University Press.

Schrecker, Ellen. 1998. *Many Are the Crimes: McCarthyism in America.* Boston: Little Brown.

Shogan, Robert. 2009. *No Sense of Decency: The Army-McCarthy Hearings*. Chicago: Ivan R. Dee.

Wicker, Tom. 2006. *Shooting Star: The Brief Arc of Joe McCarthy*. New York: Harcourt.

Michigan Department of State Police v. Sitz (1990)

To some civil libertarians and privacy advocates, the use of sobriety checkpoints by law enforcement has overtones of Orwellian-level state surveillance. These driving-while-intoxicated (DWI) checkpoints, however, were decisively affirmed as constitutional on June 14, 1990, by the U.S. Supreme Court in the case of *Michigan Department of State Police v. Sitz.*

In that case, appellants asserted that a random highway sobriety checkpoint initiative that had been implemented by the Michigan State Police was unconstitutional because the vehicle stops were "unreasonable" searches and seizures under the Fourth and Fourteenth Amendments. The checkpoint program was unreasonable, they said, because they were made without warrants or either of the main exceptions—reasonable suspicion or probable cause—under which warrantless searches were legally permitted.

Ultimately, however, six members of the nine-member Court decided that the sobriety checkpoint program was in fact a "reasonable" response to the threat to surrounding communities posed by drunk driving. "No one can seriously dispute the magnitude of the drunken driving problem or the states' interest in eradicating it," stated the majority opinion, which was penned by Chief Justice William Rehnquist. "Conversely, the weight bearing on the other scale—the measure of the intrusion on motorists stopped briefly at sobriety checkpoints—is slight . . . . In sum, the balance of the state's interest in preventing drunken driving, the extent to which this system can reasonably be said to advance that interest, and the degree of intrusion upon individual motorists who are briefly stopped, weighs in favor of the state program. We therefore hold that it is consistent with the Fourth Amendment."

The Court also took pains to differentiate its *Sitz* decision from a 1979 ruling in *Delaware v. Prouse* that struck down random police stops for the purpose of apprehending unlicensed drivers and vehicles with potential safety issues. The main difference between the two cases, said the Court, was that in *Sitz*, the police could point to empirical data showing that sobriety checkpoints were effective in combating drunk driving. In *Prouse,* by contrast, "we observed no empirical evidence . . . that such stops would be an effective means of promoting roadway safety . . . and that it seems common sense that the percentage of all drivers on the road who are driving without a license is very small and that the number of licensed drivers who will be stopped in order to find one unlicensed operator will be large indeed."

Not all the justices agreed, however. Justice William Brennan charged that "by holding that no level of suspicion is necessary before the police may stop a car for the purpose of preventing drunken driving, the Court potentially subjects the general public to arbitrary or harassing conduct by the police. I would have hoped that before taking such a step, the Court would carefully explain how such a plan fits within our constitutional framework." And in a strongly worded dissent, Justice John Paul Stevens charged that "the most disturbing aspect of the Court's decision today is that it appears to give no weight to the citizen's interest in freedom from suspicionless, unannounced investigatory seizures. . . . The Court is transfixed by the wrong symbol—the illusory prospect of punishing countless intoxicated motorists—when it should keep its eyes on the road plainly marked by the Constitution."

According to Jeremy Byellin, an attorney and a law blogger, "Although Justice Stevens' position ended up being on the losing side of history, he may have been on to something. After all, if a Supreme Court majority can view a police stop of a vehicle as nothing more than a 25 second inconvenience, could a future Supreme Court majority find a brief police search of every house on a certain block to be nothing more than a 45 second inconvenience?"

Kevin Hillstrom

Further Reading

Blade, Bryan Scott. 1991. "Fourth Amendment—The Constitutionality of a Sobriety Checkpoint Program." *Journal of Criminal Law and Criminology* 81 (4) (Winter): 800–818.

Byellin, Jeremy. 2013. "Today in 1990: The Supreme Court Upholds DWI Traffic Checkpoints." ThomsonReuters Legal Solutions blog (June 14). http://blog.legalsolutions.thomsonreuters.com/legal-research/today-in-1990-the-supreme-court-upholds-dwi-traffic-checkpoints/. Accessed April 28, 2015.

"Excerpts from Supreme Court's Decision Upholding Sobriety Checkpoints." 1990. *New York Times*, June 15. http://www.nytimes.com/1990/06/15/us/excerpts-from-supreme-court-s-decision-upholding-sobriety-checkpoints.html. Accessed September 18, 2015.

GHSA. 2015. "State Sobriety Checkpoint Laws." Governors Highway Safety Association (GHSA) Web site. http://www.ghsa.org/html/stateinfo/laws/checkpoint_laws.html. Accessed April 28, 2015.

N

National Identity Cards

In the United States, the creation and implementation of a national system for identification been debated between national security and civil liberties camps for many years—although the lines between the camps are not neatly demarcated. Advocates suggest that a national ID card would provide an effective and simple means to enhance national security, unmask potential terrorists, and guard against illegal immigrants. Critics voice concerns, however, that a national identifier will seriously undermine privacy rights and lurch the United States another step closer to a police state.

Historically, individual autonomy supporters have won this battle. Proposals to extend the Social Security number (SSN) to the status of a universal identifier card have been rejected continuously since its inception in 1936 by both Republican and Democratic presidents (although both George W. Bush and Barack Obama have expressed vague support for the national identifier concept).

The primary concern about national ID card proposals is that access to private information will be sought and gained by unauthorized individuals. In addition, there is the fear that the technology will be used in inappropriate ways to monitor a citizen's movements and to harass and discriminate against minorities or certain suspect categories of people.

Lack of an official national ID system did not stop Congress from passing the REAL ID Act of 2005, which established federal requirements for state driver's licenses and identification cards for those who live or work in the United States. Critics like *Forbes'* Tarun Wadwha believe that the Bush administration thus "instituted a *de facto* national identity system by mandating that records be centralized and state-issued IDs be brought up to a common standard. When the legislation was ultimately implemented, it was done with virtually no public debate or input from important stakeholders (like the state governments who now have to deal with the new requirements)."

Many states have balked at fulfilling the obligations contained in the REAL ID Act on both philosophical and financial grounds. Complaints range from charges that the cards are too invasive of privacy to complaints that technological innovation greatly complicates the process of producing a viable card that won't need continual overhauling. But in a sign of how complex the issue is, conservatives who often raise these points are confronted by fellow conservatives who see beefed-up national ID cards, whether they take the form of REAL ID cards or something else, as necessities for national security and combating illegal immigration. These proponents typically pitch the idea of a system of technologically sophisticated ID cards with tamperproof, unique biometric identifiers that would not allow for centralized collection of sensitive personal information or tracking. The American Civil Liberties Union (ACLU) and other privacy rights organizations have, nonetheless, stood firm against such proposals. Much of their opposition stems from their belief that the U.S. government simply can't be trusted not to turn such systems into tools for unconstitutional surveillance.

Kevin Hillstrom

Further Reading

American Civil Liberties Union. 2010. "Broad Coalition Urges President Obama and Congress to Oppose Biometric National ID." ACLU Web site. https://www.aclu.org/immigrants-rights-technology-and-liberty/broad-coalition-urges-president-obama-and-congress-oppose-b. Accessed March 31, 2015.

Electronic Privacy Information Center. 2014. "National ID and the Real ID Act." EPIC Web site. https://epic.org/privacy/id_cards/. Accessed March 31, 2015.

Wadhwa, Tarun. 2013. "We Don't Need a National ID Card." *Forbes* (February 26). http://www.forbes.com/sites/tarunwadhwa/2013/02/06/the-washington-post-got-it-wrong-we-dont-need-a-national-id-card/. Accessed March 31, 2015.

National Security Letters (NSLs)

National Security Letters (NSLs) have emerged as one of the most controversial law enforcement and counterterrorism tools employed by the U.S. government in the 21st century. The NSL is a type of investigative subpoena, employed primarily by the Federal Bureau of Investigation (FBI), which forces individuals served with NSLs to turn over private data about other people. Typically, NSLs are issued to executives, business owners, and employees at banks and other financial institutions, telecommunications companies, Internet service providers (ISPs), travel agencies, and other entities that maintain information about the practices, habits, and behavior of people under FBI investigation. The subpoenas generally include information about the suspect's name, address, place of employment, telephone and Internet records, credit histories, and other financial data. This quasi-subpoena power is controversial in and of itself, since issuance of NSLs does not require approval from any judge or other legal authority. But perhaps the most contentious element of the FBI's use of NSLs is that the tool includes a so-called gag order. This provision forbids people and companies served with NSLs not only from revealing that they've turned over sensitive information, but also from informing anyone that they've even received an NSL. This gag order extends to friends, colleagues, and family members as well as the targets of FBI investigations.

Critics charge that the gag order provision is a particularly egregious and offensive violation of Americans' free-speech rights. As one anonymous recipient of an NSL told the *Washington Post* in 2007, "Living under the gag order has been stressful and surreal. Under the threat of criminal prosecution, I must hide all aspects of my involvement in the case—including the mere fact that I received an NSL—from my colleagues, my family and my friends. When I meet with my attorneys I cannot tell my girlfriend where I am going or where I have been. I hide any papers related to the case in a place where she will not look. When clients and friends ask me whether I am the one challenging the constitutionality of the NSL statute, I have no choice but to look them in the eye and lie. I resent being conscripted as a secret informer for the government and being made to mislead those who are close to me, especially because I have doubts about the legitimacy of the underlying investigation."

National Security Letters have their roots in a handful of counterterrorism and crime-fighting laws of the late 20th century, including the 1978 Right to Financial Privacy Act (RFPA), 1986 amendments to the RFPA, the Electronic Communications Privacy Act of 1986, and the Fair Credit Reporting Act. But NSLs did not become the powerful surveillance tools they are today until the USA PATRIOT Act—and specifically Section 505 of that legislation—was passed into law in the wake of the terrorist attacks on American soil that took place on September 11, 2001. Section 505 empowered the FBI (and other agencies, under certain circumstances) to issue NSLs when seeking information that is "relevant" to counterterrorism, law enforcement investigations, and other "clandestine intelligence activities." The FBI also made much more extensive use of gag order nondisclosure provisions after 9/11 (Congress eventually cleaned up the language of the law to make it clear that people served with NSLs could still consult with legal counsel about their situations). According to the Electronic Frontier Foundation (EFF), over 300,000 NSLs were issued from 2003 to 2013.

As use of NSLs has proliferated in recent years, so too have legal challenges to the subpoenas—especially in regard to the nondisclosure gag order mandates. Led by individual citizens as well as such civil liberties organizations as the American Civil Liberties Union (ACLU) and the EFF, these challenges have generated considerable political pressure to investigate alleged abuses of the NSL authority. In 2007, the results of an investigation into FBI use of NSLs by the Inspector General's Office of the Department of Justice were published. The audit determined that the FBI had engaged in rampant abuse of its NSL authority from 2003 to 2006, when the agency issued almost 200,000 NSLs, and had misled Congress about the extent of its use of NSLs. Among other findings, the IG report estimated that 60 percent of the NSLs issued by the FBI did not conform to Justice Department guidelines and that more than one in five of them were of questionable legality. According to ACLU lawyers Michael German and Michelle Richardson, the IG report also revealed an epidemic of sloppy use of NSLs that showed disregard for the constitutional rights of Americans. "With no internal controls and with complete disregard for the law, FBI agents soon ignored the minimal process involved in issuing NSLs and instead issued 'exigent letters,' falsely claiming emergencies to obtain records without legal process," wrote German and Richardson. "These illegal requests—sometimes just a phone number written on a Post-it note—were often given to the telecommunications companies with the promise that an NSL or grand jury subpoena would follow, but more often than not these promises went unfulfilled. Some agents found even Post-it notes too burdensome and instead asked company employees to just pull up a person's phone records so they could peek over their shoulder to see whether a formal request such as an NSL was worthwhile."

In the wake of such revelations—related controversies swirling around other government surveillance activities and court decisions that have found NSL gag orders to be unconstitutional on free speech grounds—the FBI and other defenders of NSL have trumpeted various reforms that they say will address those problems. "The FBI has taken numerous steps to improve compliance on the front end of the NSL process and to conduct rigorous self-evaluations after the fact to ensure strict compliance with the various statutes and policies that govern the use of this important tool," stated former FBI lawyers Valerie Caproni and Steven Siegel. "Although NSLs will no doubt remain the national security tool that critics love to hate, when one focuses on reality rather than hyperbole, it is clear that the NSL is a constitutional tool that is reasonably used and is necessary in national security investigations to maintain the safety and security of the American people."

On January 17, 2014, President Barack Obama announced that he was directing the "Attorney General to amend how we use national security letters so that this secrecy will not be indefinite, so that it will terminate within a fixed time unless the government demonstrates a real need for further secrecy. We will also enable communications providers to make public more information than ever before about the orders that they have received to provide data to the government." As of early 2015, however, the Justice Department had not announced any changes to its gag order directives or policies, and civil liberties groups say that NSL nondisclosure requirements remain as all-encompassing and open-ended as ever.

Kevin Hillstrom

Further Reading

Fidler, David P., and Sarah Jane Hughes. 2009. *Responding to National Security Letters: A Practical Guide for Legal Counsel.* Washington, DC: American Bar Association.

German, Michael, et al. 2012. "National Security Letters: Building Blocks for Investigations or Intrusive Tools?" *ABA Journal* (September 1). http://www.abajournal.com/magazine/article/national_security_letters_building_blocks_for_investigations_or_intrusive_t/. Accessed April 29, 2015.

"My National Security Letter Gag Order." 2007. *Washington Post* (March 23). http://www.washingtonpost.com/wp-dyn/content/article/2007/03/22/AR2007032201882.html. Accessed April 29, 2015.

Nieland, Andrew E. 2007. "National Security Letters and the Amended Patriot Act." *Cornell Law Review* 92: 1201–36.

Reuter, Dean, and John Yoo, eds. 2011. *Confronting Terror: 9/11 and the Future of American National Security.* New York: Encounter Books.

National Security Agency (NSA)

The National Security Agency (NSA) was created in 1952 through an executive order issued by President Harry S. Truman to protect the United States from threats to national security. A military branch of the Pentagon, the NSA is considered today to be America's leading code-breaking and surveillance organization. The NSA employs some of the nation's most gifted mathematicians, among others, who use signals intelligence (SIGINT) to decipher electronic transmissions intercepted from satellites. These electronic sources can be communications via the Internet, cellular telephone, fax, radio, and any other means of coded communication. Working in conjunction with the Department of Defense and intelligence agencies of allied governments, the NSA has become one of the largest divisions in government intelligence. It directly employs approximately 30,000 people, but another 60,000 or so people technically employed by private corporations also work primarily on NSA-related tasks.

As suggested by the size of its workforce, the NSA has steadily accrued power over the years. Although the Supreme Court established in the so-called "Keith" case of 1972 (*United States v. United States District Court*) that the U.S. government has no authority to spy, without a warrant, on private citizens within the United States, proponents of robust NSA authority have subsequently contended that this decision only applies to domestic not foreign communication. Consequently, it has been asserted that the president maintains constitutional power to authorize electronic surveillance without consent or warrant to protect national security. In 1978, Congress addressed this debate with the Foreign Intelligence Surveillance Act (FISA), which requires that the government obtain a warrant to conduct surveillance on U.S. soil. Warrants for surveillance have to be issued by the Foreign Intelligence Surveillance Court (FISC). Warrants are justified on probable cause that an individual is affiliated with a foreign power and a threat to national security.

However, presidential authority, justified by an executive order, overrides Congress. Executive authority permits the installing of wiretaps without first obtaining a warrant. In these cases, FISA has authorized surveillance warrants after wiretaps have already been installed and monitored. These procedures have been upheld in court on grounds of national security. In addition, executive orders that authorize eavesdropping for national security have not provided safeguards, guidelines, or limitations on conducting surveillance without consent. Executive orders that avoid judicial scrutiny prevent development of judicial precedent on questions of domestic surveillance.

With restraints on the growth of the NSA virtually absent, individuals such as General Keith B. Alexander, who directed the NSA from 2005 to 2013, were able to greatly expand the agency's size and influence. Journalist Shane Harris, in fact, wrote in 2013 that the "NSA was already a data behemoth when Alexander took over" but that under Alexander's direction, "the breadth, scale, and ambition of [NSA's] mission expanded beyond anything ever contemplated by his predecessors. . . . Today, the agency is routinely scooping up and storing Americans' phone records. It is screening their e-mails and text messages, even though the spy agency can't always tell the difference between an innocent American and a foreign terrorist. The NSA uses corporate proxies to monitor up to 75 percent of Internet traffic inside the United States. And it has spent billions of dollars on a secret campaign to foil encryption technologies that individuals, corporations, and governments around the world had long thought protected the privacy of their communications from U.S. intelligence agencies."

The classified nature of this agency's work, combined with revelations about the extent of its reach, has raised profound concerns that the privacy rights of Americans are often violated by the NSA. Although the word "privacy" is not mentioned explicitly in the U.S. Constitution, privacy rights have been supported based on the First, Fourth, and Fifth Amendments. In relation to the NSA, privacy can be understood to be protection against the disclosure of personal information.

An individual's right to privacy is important because it impedes discrimination and fraud and provides protection from abuses of government power.

Electronic eavesdropping activities carried out by the NSA under the auspices of the USA PATRIOT Act and other national security laws have been particularly contentious—especially in the wake of the information leaked about NSA activities by NSA contractor Edward Snowden.

Proponents of electronic surveillance often highlight the times wiretapping has been used to apprehend terrorists, win wars, and protect national security. Opponents argue electronic surveillance is a violation of civil liberties. Furthermore, of concern is the fact that the NSA's surveillance program violates the separation of powers established in the U.S. Constitution. The top secret nature of the NSA, combined with presidential authority, is a significant privacy concern. The NSA has often been credited with enforcing national security, yet there is strong concern that the capability of the NSA to regulate privacy can simultaneously be a serious threat to civil liberties.

Kevin Hillstrom

Further Reading

Aid, Matthew. 2009. *The Secret Sentry: The Untold History of the National Security Agency*. New York: Bloomsbury.

Bamford, James. 2008. *The Shadow Factory: The Ultra-Secret NSA from 9/11 to the Eavesdropping on America*. New York: Doubleday.

Greenwald, Glenn. 2014. *No Place to Hide: Edward Snowden, the NSA, and the U.S. Surveillance State*. New York: Metropolitan Books.

Harris, Shane. 2013. "The Cowboy of the NSA: Inside General Keith Alexander's All-Out, Barely-Legal Drive to Build the Ultimate Spy Machine." *Foreign Policy* (September 9). http://foreignpolicy.com/2013/09/09/the-cowboy-of-the-nsa/. Accessed April 4, 2015.

Next Generation Identification (NGI)

In 2008, the Federal Bureau of Investigation (FBI) launched the Next Generation Identification (NGI) program, the world's largest biometric database created to help intelligence and law enforcement agencies identify suspected criminals and terrorists and solve crimes. Biometrics is technology that involves the identification, authentication, surveillance, or screening of individuals based on measurable physical and/or behavioral traits. The NGI system was developed to improve the FBI's existing biometric capabilities, focusing on the modalities of fingerprinting, eye recognition, voice identification profiles, photographs, and palm prints. By 2015, the NGI database had enrolled more than a million records.

The FBI has been the largest repository of criminal identification data in the United States since 1924, when the agency consolidated its records with those from Leavenworth Prison in Kansas and the National Bureau of Criminal Identification to create an identification division which worked with the local, state, and federal agencies to identify criminals and help solve crimes. A Civilian Identification Division was established in 1933, allowing the FBI to store thousands of civil fingerprints and screen civil employees applying for high-level positions. The Identification Division became the Criminal Justice Information Services Division (CJISD) in 1992.

Before the advent of computer technology, fingerprint identification was often a very time-consuming and labor-intensive process performed by trained fingerprint analysts. It could often take weeks—sometimes months—to manually conduct a single fingerprint identification or screening. The FBI began to look for ways to automate and improve the process. By 1980, computers were employed by the FBI to aid in fingerprint identification. Computer programmers formulated an algorithm, or computer program, to make the process more efficient. However, it could still take days to process a single request.

The FBI's fingerprint identification capability was greatly improved by the creation of the Integrated Automatic Fingerprint Identification System (IAFIS), a national database of millions of fingerprint records, mug shots, and criminal and terrorist histories submitted voluntarily by state, local, and federal law enforcement agencies. IAFIS also collected and stored the fingerprint records of federal employees and members of the military.

Fully operational in 1999, the IAFIS was the largest database of biometric information in the world, holding the fingerprints and corresponding criminal and terrorist records of more than 70 million subjects in the criminal master file. In addition, it stored more than 73,000 prints from suspected terrorists from around the world.

By the turn of the 21st century, criminal and terrorist threats were evolving and the FBI pressed to update the IAFIS incrementally over several years with a new system that would provide new functionality and improve existing capabilities. One of the main goals with the NGI system was to reduce the margin of error in identifying criminals using new state-of-the-art tools and biometric technology. In September 2014, the FBI announced that the system was fully operational.

The NGI system has implemented several enhancements, including the following:

1. An Interstate Photo System (IPS), which utilizes the FBI's advanced facial recognition capability to search millions of mug shots of convicted criminals for potential matches. The IPS was launched in 2011.
2. The National Palm Prints System (NPPS), which can facilitate the search of millions of palm prints.

3. Rap Back, a feature that provides information to authorized agencies about the existence and extent of criminal records of potential new employees or individuals place on probation or parole.
4. Iris Recognition (IR), a biometric modality that measures various characteristics of the iris of the human eye. The FBI is continuing to hone the biometric capability of the iris, viewing it as a valuable tool for law enforcement and the intelligence community.
5. Advanced Fingerprint Identification Technology (AFIT), a new algorithm that has enhanced fingerprint identification capability and improved the accuracy and speed of fingerprint processing. The FBI asserts that matching accuracy has jumped from 92 percent to over 99.6 percent on account of AFIT, which was deployed in February 2011.
6. Enhanced facial recognition capability, allowing law enforcement agencies to scan large crowds to identify suspected criminal and terrorists and check it against the NGI system.
7. Repository for Individuals of Special Concern (RISC), a feature that allows officers and agents in the field to use a handheld device, known as a Mobile Offender Recognition and Identification System (MORIS) to scan the iris, face, or fingerprints of suspects in the field in order to match them against a database of Wanted Persons, Sex Offenders Registry Subject, Known or Suspected Terrorists and other persons of interest.

Supporters of the NGI system view it as an invaluable tool in efforts to protect Americans from criminal and terrorist activity and a boon to law enforcement and intelligence agencies. Critics charge that there is a major risk that biometric information could be lost or abused, pointing to the fact that a number of private companies have access to it and biometric identification is not foolproof. Others contend that the NGI raises serious privacy and civil liberty concerns. A growing number of voices are calling for meaningful legislation from the U.S. Congress to limit what entities can access the NGI, what kind of information can be enrolled in the system, and how biometric information can be used in the future.

Margaret Haerens

Further Reading

Chayka, Kyle. 2014. "Biometric Surveillance Means Someone Is Always Watching." *Newsweek* (April 17). http://www.newsweek.com/2014/04/25/biometric-surveillance-means-someone-always-watching-248161.html. Accessed March 2, 2015.

"Integrated Automated Fingerprint Identification System." Federal Bureau of Investigation. http://www.fbi.gov/about-us/cjis/fingerprints_biometrics/iafis/iafis. Accessed March 1, 2015.

"Next Generation Identification (NGI)." Federal Bureau of Investigation. http://www.fbi.gov/about-us/cjis/fingerprints_biometrics/ngi. Accessed March 1, 2015.
Whitehead, John W. 2012. "Smile, the Government Is Watching: Next Generation Identification." *The Huffington Post* (September 18). http://www.huffingtonpost.com/john-w-whitehead/the-government-is-watching_b_1890068.html. Accessed March 2, 2015.

9/11 Commission

The 9/11 Commission, formally known as the National Commission on Terrorist Attacks upon the United States, was created by U.S. President George W. Bush and the U.S. Congress on November 22, 2002, to prepare a full and complete account of the circumstances surrounding the September 11, 2001, terrorist attacks. In these attacks, 19 members of the Islamic terrorist group Al Qaeda hijacked four U.S. passenger jets and targeted the World Trade Center in New York City and the Pentagon in Washington, D.C., causing 2,996 deaths and billions of dollars of property damage. The 9/11 Commission was charged with examining the why the nation's intelligence and law enforcement agencies failed to detect the terrorist attack, as well as the immediate response to the attacks. It also was asked to provide recommendations on how the United States might guard against future terrorist attacks.

The commission consisted of five Republicans and five Democrats. Former New Jersey Republican governor Thomas H. Kean was appointed as Chair of the Commission, with Indiana U.S. representative Lee H. Hamilton, a Democrat, as vice chairman. Other members included Richard Ben-Veniste (Democrat), former chief of the Watergate Task Force of the Watergate Special Prosecutor's Office; Fred F. Fielding (Republican), former White House counsel; Jamie Gorelick (Democrat), former deputy attorney general; Slade Gorton (Republican), former U.S. senator from Washington; John F. Lehman (Republican), former secretary of the Navy; Timothy J. Roemer (Democrat), former U.S. representative from Indiana; James R. Thompson (Republican), former governor of Illinois; and Max Cleland (Democrat), former U.S. senator from Georgia—replaced by Bob Kerrey (Democrat), former U.S. senator from Nebraska after Cleland resigned in December 2003.

The commission conducted numerous hearings and interviews and collected millions of pages of both classified and unclassified documents and other evidence. Among those interviewed were many high-level government officials, including President George W. Bush and Vice President Dick Cheney. On July 22, 2004, the commission released a report to the public entitled *The 9–11 Commission Report* (the Report). All 10 members of the commission signed off on the main report and the report was edited for security purposes before it was released. The commission closed on August 21, 2004.

The Report found that although the 9/11 terrorist attacks were certainly a shock, they were not surprising because Islamic terrorism had been a rising threat for over a decade. There had been a number of earlier terrorist attacks on U.S. targets throughout the 1990s. Then in 1998, Al Qaeda leader Osama bin Laden issued a fatwa, an Islamic decree, announcing that Muslims should kill Americans because of the U.S. occupation of Islamic holy places. This was followed by Al Qaeda truck bomb attacks on U.S. embassies in Kenya and Tanzania later in 1998 and by an Al Qaeda attack on the U.S. destroyer USS *Cole* in Yemen in 2000. Despite this history and efforts by the U.S. government to monitor Al Qaeda, the commission found that U.S. analysts were focused on overseas attacks and did not foresee the 9/11 terrorist attack on the homeland.

The commission's report concluded that the 9/11 attack was the result of failures of imagination, policy, capabilities, and management across the government during both the Clinton and Bush administrations. The Report, for example, pointed to a diplomatic failure to evict Al Qaeda from its base in Afghanistan, a failure to conduct effective military strikes against Al Qaeda, a lack of effective intelligence-gathering by the Central Intelligence Agency (CIA), information-sharing problems within the Federal Bureau of Investigation (FBI) and between agencies, a lack of security and preparedness in other government agencies, and a slow response to terrorism by Congress.

Noting that the enemy is not Islam but instead a perversion of Islam, the commission proposed a three-prong strategy: (1) attack terrorists and their organizations; (2) prevent the continued growth of Islamic terrorism; and (3) protect and prepare for terrorist attacks. More specifically, the commission recommended the following:

1. Rooting out terrorist sanctuaries;
2. Strengthening the U.S. and international commitment to stabilizing Afghanistan and Pakistan in order to prevent them from becoming sanctuaries for terrorists;
3. Confronting problems with the U.S.–Saudi Arabia relationship and promoting political, economic, and cultural reform in that country;
4. Offering a U.S. example of moral leadership in the world in order to present an alternative to Muslim youth other than violence and death;
5. Taking a stand with Muslim governments who do not respect the rule of law or tolerance;
6. Communicating and defending American ideals in the Islamic world through stronger diplomacy;

7. Offering an agenda of public education and economic opportunity;
8. Developing a coalition of governments to create a common strategy against Islamic terrorism;
9. Countering the development of weapons of mass destruction;
10. Relying less on drying up tracking terrorist money and more on following the money as an intelligence-gathering and preventive tool;
11. Targeting terrorist travel as another antiterrorism approach;
12. Designing a comprehensive screening system for borders and transportation to intercept terrorists;
13. Creating a biometric entry/exit screening system that also speeds qualified travel;
14. Setting standards for birth certificates, drivers' licenses, and other forms of identification;
15. Developing security strategies for all transportation systems, not only aviation;
16. Improving No Fly and Automatic Selectee lists without delay and prioritizing checkpoint screening;
17. Setting guidelines for collecting and sharing security information while maintaining privacy safeguards;
18. Ensuring that the expansion of government powers is necessary and supervised;
19. Basing federal funding for emergency preparedness on risk and vulnerabilities, putting New York and Washington, D.C., at the top of the list; and
20. Making homeland security funding contingent on the development of an incident command system that promotes teamwork, a regional approach, and improved standards for private sector emergency preparedness.

In 2014, 10 years after the initial 9/11 Commission Report, the commission released an update—*Today's Rising Terrorist Threat and the Danger to the United States: Reflections on the Tenth Anniversary of the 9/11 Commission Report*. The 2014 report said that most of the commission's recommendations have been enacted into law or adopted as policy and that Al Qaeda's leadership and core has been seriously diminished. However, the report found that the threat from Islamic terrorism remains because groups linked with Al Qaeda have dispersed throughout the Middle East, creating large terrorist sanctuaries. The report pointed, for example, to the terrorist group called ISIS, which controls large areas in Iraq and Syria. The report concluded that although the terrorist threat has evolved, it is still extremely dangerous.

Debra Miller

Further Reading

Former 9/11 Commission Commissioners. 2014. "Today's Rising Terrorist Threat and the Danger to the United States: Reflections on the Tenth Anniversary of the 9/11 Commission Report." Bipartisan Policy Center Web site (July). http://bipartisanpolicy.org/library/rising-terrorist-threat-9-11-commission/. Accessed February 12, 2015.

Hulse, Carl. 2015. "Claims against Saudis Cast New Light on Secret Pages of 9/11 Report." *New York Times* (February 4). http://www.nytimes.com/2015/02/05/us/claims-against-saudis-cast-new-light-on-secret-pages-of-9-11-report.html?_r=0. Accessed September 18, 2015.

Kean, Thomas H., and Lee H. Hamilton. 2006. *Without Precedent: The Inside Story of the 9/11 Commission.* New York: Random House.

National Commission on Terrorist Attacks Upon the United States. "9–11 Commission Report." Commission Web site, now a Federal record managed on behalf of the National Archives and Records Administration. http://govinfo.library.unt.edu/911/report/index.htm. Accessed February 11, 2015.

U.S. Department of Homeland Security. "Implementing 9/11 Commission Recommendations, Progress Report 2011." DHS Web site. http://www.dhs.gov/implementing-911-commission-recommendations. Accessed February 11, 2015.

O

Orwell, George (1903–1950)

George Orwell was a British writer best known for the novels *Animal Farm* and *Nineteen Eighty-Four.* The latter work is considered a dystopian novel, one that features a world set in the future, with a government that imposes totalitarian rule. Two terms emerged from Orwell's writing that are still often used to refer to aspects of a surveillance state: "Orwellian," as a description of a situation that goes counter to a free society; and "Big Brother," referring to the government's influence and power on society, especially to civil liberties and surveillance.

George Orwell is the pen name of Eric Arthur Blair, who was born on June 25, 1903, in Mothihari, Bihar, India. He was the middle child of Richard Walmesley Blair and Ida Mabel Limouzin Blair; he had two sisters, Marjorie and Avril. His father was a supervisor in the opium trade in the Indian Civil Service. In 1907, Orwell, his mother, and his sisters moved to England; his father remained in India for a period of time, visiting them when he was on leave, before permanently joining his family in England.

As a boy, Orwell attended boarding school—St. Cyprian's prep school—an experience he did not enjoy. In an essay entitled "Such, Such Were the Joys," which was not published until after his death, he recalled that in "a world where the prime necessities were money, titled relatives, athleticism, tailor-made clothes, neatly-brushed hair, a charming smile, I was no good." He believed that "The future was dark. Failure, failure, failure—failure behind me, failure ahead of me—that was by far the deepest conviction that I carried away." Orwell went on to graduate from Eton College (a secondary school) in 1921. He did not attend university.

Upon leaving Eton, he went to Burma to attend a police training program. He had a family connection there—his maternal grandmother lived in Moulmein, Burma. He became a policeman in Burma until July 1927, when he returned to England on leave due to illness. He decided against returning to Burma, but his experiences in that Southeast Asian nation (now officially known as Myanmar) became

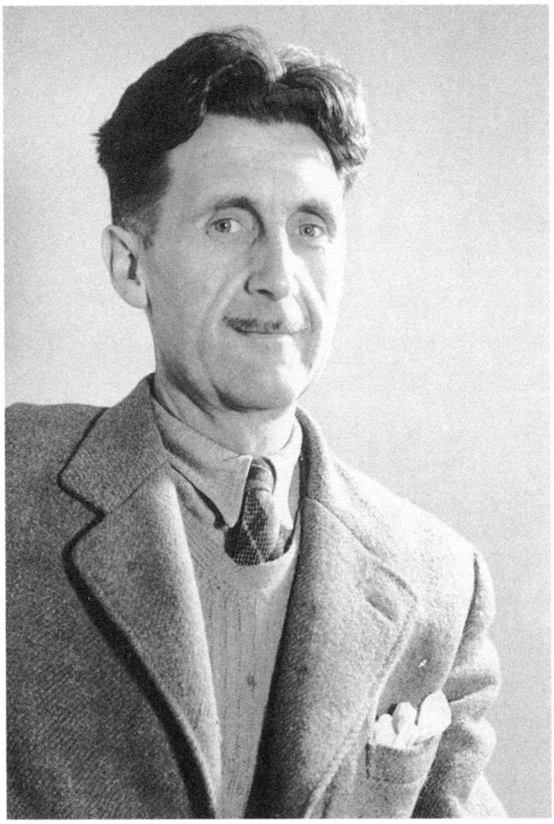

Writer George Orwell was born Eric Arthur Blair in Motihari, India, in 1903, and died in 1950. The terms "Orwellian," "Thought Police," and "Big Brother" came from his dystopian novel *Nineteen Eighty-Four*. (AP Photo)

the source of his first novel, *Burmese Days* (1934).

Orwell began writing in the early 1930s. In the essay "Why I Write" (1946), Orwell said, "From a very early age, perhaps the age of five or six, I knew that when I grew up I should be a writer. Between the ages of about seventeen and twenty-four I tried to abandon this idea, but I did so with the consciousness that I was outraging my true nature and that sooner or later I should have to settle down and write books." And so he did.

In 1949, Orwell published one of his two most famous works: *Nineteen Eighty-Four*. The novel is set in the future, in what used to be Great Britain but what is now called Airstrip One, part of a province called Oceania. Society is controlled by a government that seeks only power for power's sake, and its leader is known as Big Brother. Whether Big Brother is a real person or simply a powerful, invisible symbol is never made clear. But the concept of Big Brother lived on—beyond literature. It became a synonym for all-controlling and all-seeing government, and the term is used often by critics of government surveillance of citizens. "Big Brother is watching you" was a phrase that was commonly employed in the novel as well, and it is a much-used expression when concerns exist that the government is prying too much into citizens' private lives.

The word "Orwellian" also became a commonly used term in society. Because of the themes of government power, surveillance, manipulation, and misinformation contained in *Nineteen Eighty-Four*, Orwellian came to be used to describe instances where such conditions existed. The media frequently used the term Orwellian when reporting on efforts by the U.S. government to re-label terms it viewed as too harsh: for instance, torture (such as that practiced in 2003 by members of the U.S. Army and the Central Intelligence Agency at the Abu Ghraib prison in Iraq) was called "enhanced interrogation techniques," and mass surveillance efforts were dubbed "bulk collection."

Pundits and the government disagree over whether the real government is mimicking the government from *Nineteen Eighty-Four.* President Barack Obama, for instance, claimed he was not Big Brother, in reference to the United States' gathering of telephone and Internet records. "In the abstract, you can complain about Big Brother and how this is a potential program run amok, but when you actually look at the details, then I think we've struck the right balance," said Obama. But many critics, including Orwell's biographer Michael Shelden, claims that "throwing out such a broad net of surveillance is exactly the kind of threat Orwell feared."

When former National Security Agency contractor Edward Snowden turned whistle-blower in June 2013 and revealed classified U.S. documents pertaining to a mass surveillance program, many looked at Orwell's vision of the future in *Nineteen Eighty-Four* as prophetic. According to digital culture expert Mark Pesce, "For 29 years after [the actual year] 1984 we really thought we'd dodged a bullet, that western democracies were safe, powerful and we were all living in freedom. Then . . . when the Snowden revelations came out it started to become clearer and clearer that in fact *1984* wasn't far off the mark; that the NSA and its associated organisations were all colluding in massive wide-scale surveillance of populations and specific targeted surveillance of world leaders." Many argue that Orwell's *Nineteen Eighty-Four* has become more relevant as massive surveillance programs carried out by the United States, Britain, and other countries have come to light.

Orwell died of tuberculosis on January 21, 1950. *Nineteen Eighty-Four* was the final work released before his death. Orwell had married twice: his first wife was Eileen O'Shaughnessy (married from 1936 until her death in 1945); his second wife was Sonia Brownell (married in 1949 until his death in 1950). Orwell had an adopted son, Richard Blair.

Lawrence W. Baker

Further Reading

Funnell, Antony. 2014. "1984 and Our Modern Surveillance Society." *Radio National.* ABC (July 29). http://www.abc.net.au/radionational/programs/futuretense/1984-and-our-modern-surveillance-society/5631512. Accessed May 12, 2015.

"George Orwell." 1991. *Contemporary Authors.* Vol. 132. Detroit, MI: Gale.

Greenblatt, Alan. 2013. "Our Surveillance Society: What Orwell and Kafka Might Say." National Public Radio Online (June 8). http://www.npr.org/2013/06/08/189792140/our-surveillance-society-what-orwell-and-kafka-might-say. Accessed May 12, 2015.

Greenwald, Glenn. 2015. "The Orwellian Re-branding of 'Mass Surveillance' as Merely 'Bulk Collection.'" *The Intercept* (March 13). https://firstlook.org/theintercept/2015/03/13/orwellian-re-branding-mass-surveillance-merely-bulk-collection/. Accessed May 12, 2015.
Orwell, George. 1946. "Why I Write." *Gangrel* (Summer): 1079–85.
Orwell, George. 1949. *Nineteen Eighty-Four.* New York: Harcourt Brace.

P

Persistent Online Tracking

Persistent online tracking is the practice of tracing the online behavior of Web and mobile apps users through the use of cookies and other tools by large technology companies, marketing firms, and social networking Web sites. Individuals can be tracked across multiple Web sites, and companies can compile detailed records of a user's retail preferences, health issues, financial data, and other information. Persistent online tracking raises privacy concerns because the user is often unaware of the practice and cannot easily opt out or stop it once it begins.

One of the more common and best-known tools used by companies to track online behavior is "cookies," a term that refers to a small text string that is sent by a Web site and stored on a user's Web browser. When the user returns to the Web site using the same browser, the browser will then send the cookie back with information on the user. The cookie can fulfill a number of functions: it identifies the user, saves login and credit card information, compiles a record of retail preferences, and tracks the general interests of users in order to customize Web sites to appeal to those interests.

There are two types of cookies: single-session cookies are erased after one visit to a Web site and help with navigation; and persistent cookies, which stay on a computer's hard drive until they are manually erased.

As privacy concerns about cookies emerged, some browser developers began to offer "private browsing," an option that blocked long-term cookies and allowed for more confidentiality on the Internet. In California, legislators passed a bill, the California Online Privacy Protection Act of 2003, that required the operators of Web sites that employ cookies or other online tracking technology to post information about the Web site's privacy policy, including what information is gathered by their cookies and how that data will be used. Some users manually disabled the cookies on their hard drives.

As more users looked for ways to circumvent online tracking, technology companies began to develop more persistent and harder-to-detect methods. These new tools include authenticated tracking, which permanently identifies users through authentication software and follows them across different online devices; device fingerprinting, a method that identifies users by the defining characteristics of their hardware; and browser fingerprinting, which allows companies to recognize users by unique browser configurations, utilizing such identifiers as operating systems, plugins, and even font style.

The latest development in online persistent tracking is canvas fingerprinting. When a user visits a Web site with this technology, the Web site directs the user's Web browser to draw a hidden image, which then generates a unique numerical code used to identify that user in the future.

These new advancements in online tracking methods are much more difficult for users to detect and circumvent. Standard Web-browsing settings cannot be configured to block them, and many antitracking tools are ineffective against fingerprinting technologies. As soon as new methods to block these new online tracking tools are developed, fresh and more sophisticated tracking technologies emerge.

As well as large tech companies, marketing firms, and other companies, governments are also tracking individuals online to identify and monitor criminal and terrorist activity. In 2013, a series of leaks by former National Security Agency (NSA) contractor Edward Snowden revealed that U.S. intelligence authorities have developed the capability to access a wide range of online data from millions of Internet users, both foreign and domestic.

One top secret program, known as XKeyscore, allows NSA analysts to mine vast databases without explicit authorization, according to documents provided by Snowden. With one stroke, an individual's entire browsing history, e-mail archives, online chats, and even metadata can be accessed without the user's knowledge.

The NSA acknowledged the existence of XKeyscore but denied that its analysts could access unlimited information on individuals without authorization. It claimed that the program did not exist to track the ordinary online activity of Americans and that it was employed only to collect legally obtained information on legitimate foreign intelligence targets.

Margaret Haerens

Further Reading

Angwin, Julia. 2014. "Meet the Online Tracking Device That Is Virtually Impossible to Block." ProPublica.org (July 21). http://www.propublica.org/article/meet-the-online-tracking-device-that-is-virtually-impossible-to-block. Accessed March 25, 2015.

Greenwald, Glenn. 2013. "XKeyscore: NSA Tool Collects 'Nearly Everything a User Does on the Internet.'" *The Guardian* (July 31). http://www.theguardian.com/world/2013/jul/31/nsa-top-secret-program-online-data. Accessed March 25, 2015.

Nikiforakis, Nik, and Günes Acar. 2014. "Browser Fingerprinting and the Online-Tracking Arms Race." *IEEE Spectrum* (July 25). http://spectrum.ieee.org/computing/software/browser-fingerprinting-and-the-onlinetracking-arms-race. Accessed March 25, 2015.

Temple, James. 2013. "Stale Cookies: How Companies Are Tracking You Online Today." sfgate.com (October 2.) http://blog.sfgate.com/techchron/2013/10/02/stale-cookies-how-companies-are-tracking-you-online-today/. Accessed March 25, 2015.

Plain View Doctrine

This doctrine allows the admission of evidence seized by law enforcement officers during a warrantless search. It will also allow admission of evidence discovered and seized by police during a search authorized by a warrant when the warrant did not specifically cover the items seized. In some instances, it is also interpreted to allow a warrantless search. In order to seize an item in plain view, there must be probable cause to believe the item is evidence of a crime, the instrumentality of a crime, or contraband. Although the doctrine usually applies to objects that can be seen, it is frequently argued that it may be extended to items that can be smelled, heard, tasted, or felt.

One of the earliest Supreme Court cases to address the question of what an officer can do when contraband is in plain view was *Steele v. United States* (1925). In that case, two federal prohibition agents watched through an open garage door as cases of whisky were unloaded for storage. They had no warrant, but they used their observations as the basis to obtain one. Despite the nature of the primary "search" the court authorized issuance of the subsequent warrant and eventual seizure of more than 200 cases of whiskey and gin, two 50-gallon drums of whiskey, several 5-gallon jugs, and dozens of bottles of whiskey. The violation of privacy, however, was not addressed.

Steele was distinguished by another Prohibition-era case called *Taylor v. United States* (1932), which concerned a case wherein probation agents peering through a garage window saw boxes of liquor. In that instance, rather than get a warrant, they broke into the garage and seized 122 cases of whiskey. The Supreme Court called that seizure a violation because the officers did not first seek a warrant on the basis of their observation of the contraband in the garage.

Looking through a doorway while in a home to see contraband got the Supreme Court's approval in *Ker v. California,* 374 U.S. 23 (1963). In that case, officers were arresting Ker in his living room when they looked through a doorway to the kitchen and saw a brick of marijuana sitting on a scale. Seizure of the drug and the bringing of drug charges against Ker were upheld despite the fact that there was no search warrant for Ker's premises. According to the Court, "The discovery of the brick of marijuana did not constitute a search, since the officer merely saw what was placed before him in full view."

The plain view doctrine has been applied by the courts in many instances of warrantless seizures. An officer who accompanies a student to the student's dorm room to get an identification card may lawfully seize marijuana seeds and a pipe in plain view (*Washington v. Chrisman* (1982)). Officers securing a home after arresting a robbery suspect may seize evidence of the robbery (clothing worn by the robber) when it is on the floor in plain sight (*Maryland v. Buie* (1990)).

The court extended the plain view doctrine to automobiles in *Harris v. United States* (1968). In this case, a police officer opened Harris' car door after the vehicle had been legally impounded to close an open window and thus protect the interior from rain that had begun to fall. In opening the door, however, the officer found a robbery victim's registration card that was later used as evidence against Harris. The court ruled: "Once the door had lawfully been opened, the registration card, with the name of the robbery victim on it, was plainly visible. It has long been settled that objects falling in the plain view of an officer who has a right to be in the position to have that view are subject to seizure and may be introduced in evidence." The same logic was later applied to situations in which an officer stops a car for a traffic violation and sees contraband on a car seat (*Texas v. Brown* (1983)).

What if the item is not exactly in "plain view"? In *New York v. Class* (1986), officers stopped a speeder and needed to locate the vehicle identification number of his car. One officer opened the car door to look on the doorjamb for the number and then realized that the number for that model car was on the dash. To see the number, the officer moved some papers out of the way. In doing so, he uncovered a gun handle. Police seized the gun, and the driver was arrested for illegal possession of a handgun. In allowing the admission of the gun as evidence the Supreme Court stated, "A citizen does not surrender all the protections of the Fourth Amendment by entering an automobile. Nonetheless, the State's intrusion into a particular area, whether in an automobile or elsewhere, cannot result in a Fourth Amendment violation unless the area is one in which there is a 'constitutionally protected reasonable expectation of privacy.'"

For many years, the Supreme Court required an "inadvertent" quality to discoveries to make them legal under the plain view doctrine. The Court noted in *Coolidge v. New Hampshire* (1971), "What the 'plain view' cases have in common is that the police officer in each of them had a prior justification for an intrusion in the course of which he came inadvertently across a piece of evidence incriminating the accused. The doctrine serves to supplement the prior justification—whether it be a warrant for another object, hot pursuit, search incident to lawful arrest, or some other legitimate reason for being present unconnected with a search directed against the accused—and permits the warrantless seizure. Of course, the extension of the original justification is legitimate only where it is immediately apparent to the police that they have evidence before them; the 'plain view' doctrine may not be used to extend a general exploratory search from one object to another until something incriminating at last emerges."

Nevertheless, the Supreme Court did away with the requirement that the discovery be "inadvertent" in *Horton v. California* (1990). In this case, a police officer obtained a warrant to search an armed robbery suspect's home for stolen items. To obtain the warrant, the office had expressed a desire to search for stolen property and weapons used during the crime. For unknown reasons, the warrant allowed a search for only stolen property. While executing the warrant, the officer found none of the stolen items, but found and seized weapons used during the crime. The court held there were no violations of the defendant's privacy rights in this case since a valid warrant had been issued. Therefore, seizure of the guns was authorized under the plain view doctrine, even though it was clear the discovery was not "inadvertent."

In applying the decision in Horton, courts basically adopted a three-part test to determine if the plain view doctrine applies: (1) Was the officer engaged in lawful activity at the time; (2) Was the object's incriminating character obvious and not hidden; and (3) Did the officer have lawful access to the object—was it in plain view?

There have been cases where the courts have refused to extend the plain view doctrine. Most notable is the *Arizona v. Hicks* (1987) case. In that case, police responded to Hicks' apartment after a bullet fired through his floor hit an occupant in an apartment a floor below. Officers arrived to search for the shooter, other possible victims, and weapons used. Upon looking around the squalid living quarters, however, an officer saw an expensive stereo that seemed out of place under the circumstances. The officer moved the stereo equipment to take down serial numbers. Then, upon calling the police station, he learned the turntable had been taken in an armed robbery. Hicks was charged with armed robbery after it was determined that all the equipment had been taken in the same heist.

In the *Hicks* case, the court took a two-step analysis to determine the plain view doctrine did not protect police in this case. First, it ruled that moving the equipment to get the serial number was a search "separate and apart from the search for the shooter, victims, and weapons that was the lawful objective of his entry into the apartment." The second question was whether the search was "reasonable" under the Fourth Amendment. The court found that the search was unreasonable because the officer did not have probable cause to believe the stereo equipment had been stolen. The officer's reasonable suspicion did not equate to probable cause.

David J. Brown

Further Reading

Bartee, Alice Fleetwood. 2006. *Privacy Rights: Cases Lost and Causes Won before the Supreme Court*. Lanham, MD: Rowman & Littlefield.

Hubbart, Phillip A. 2005. *Making Sense of Search and Seizure Law: A Fourth Amendment Handbook*. Durham, NC: Carolina Academic Press.

Pettifor, Bonnie, and Charles E. Petit. 2000. *Weeks v. United States: Illegal Search and Seizure*. Berkeley Heights, NJ: Enslow Publishers.

Rutledge, Devallis. 2006. "Seizing Evidence in Plain View." *Police: The Law Enforcement Magazine*, March 1. http://www.policemag.com/channel/patrol/articles/2006/03/point-of-law.aspx. Accessed September 18, 2015.

Police Militarization

Police militarization is an escalating issue in the United States. It is a phenomenon best understood as the process of civilian police forces becoming increasingly more like the military. In the United States, as well as in most democracies, the military is responsible for external security through violent conflict or the threat thereof. Police officers are responsible for internal security by enforcing the laws set forth by the state or federal legislature. The issue arises when the police become more like the military and treat their communities like war zones—and residents like potential enemy combatants.

The process of police militarization is encompassed in the increased cooperation between military and police forces. There is often a transfer of information, technology, and military weapons and equipment. Police are often given excess military equipment because congressional representatives were concerned that community police departments were outgunned by gangs and wanted the police to be equipped to handle the escalating pressure from these well-armed organizations. The Department of Homeland Security established grants for the purpose of arming civilian police, which offers financial support for arming police forces nationwide.

More evidence of police militarization can be found in the formation of paramilitary police units that are closely modeled after military special operations units. These police units, such as Special Weapons and Tactics (SWAT) teams, are specialized forces meant to respond to extreme situations such as terrorist threats and hostage situations. However, there has been a dramatic increase since 1980 in paramilitary police unit deployments, and many of these deployments have been for highly controversial and violent raids for contraband items such as drugs or illegal weapons. *Mother Jones* reported in 2014 that the number of SWAT raids in the

United States "has increased 20-fold since the 1980s, going from 3,000 per year to at least 60,000. And SWAT teams are no longer limited to large cities: In the mid-1980s, only 20 percent of towns with populations between 25,000 and 50,000 had such teams. By 2007, 80 percent did."

These raids often take place at night and involve quickly storming the residence in question and conducting a rapid search of the property. Many civilians have been killed due to these raids, which has caused outrage in many communities. Drug and weapons searches have traditionally been the responsibility of community police forces rather than special teams.

The fact that community police departments are able to access information from the military as well as military technology is exacerbating the issue of police militarization. Critics of this trend assert that the distinction between the two forces is becoming increasingly more obscure as time progresses. They claim that as a result, unconstitutional behavior that violates the civil liberties of Americans is on the upswing in many communities, especially in poor communities with high minority populations.

The issue of police militarization has been particularly sensitive lately because of the 2014 police shooting of an unarmed black man in Ferguson, Missouri, and the subsequent police response to mass protests of the shooting. The law enforcement response was widely criticized for being so overbearing and intimidating that it further exacerbated tensions.

It is considered beneficial for police departments to have access to some advanced technology and weapons in the event of a hostile situation; with this technology they can respond and be very effective diffusing volatile situations. However, critics contend that the use of special teams and advanced technology has extended beyond simply reacting to hostile situations. They are being used regularly for patrol purposes and scare tactics, which is regarded by many civilians, police, and government personnel as highly inappropriate.

Many are fearful that without measures to stop the trend toward police militarization, communities will increasingly feel as if they are under martial law rather than being patrolled and protected by their community police. "Giving military-grade weapons to every police force and every officer comes with costs," asserted Senator Claire McCaskill (D-MO) "Officers dressed in military fatigues will not be viewed as partners in any community" (Grossman, 2014).

In May 2015, President Barack Obama issued an executive order prohibiting the federal government from providing a variety of military-style equipment to local law enforcement. Obama's order also imposed new restrictions on the distribution of other types of weapons and gear to local police departments. Equipment subject to outright bans as a result of Obama's directive included armored vehicles on tracks, weaponized vehicles (including aircraft), grenade launchers, firearms or ammunition of .50 caliber or higher caliber, bayonets, and camouflage uniforms.

Grace Vandemark

Further Reading

American Civil Liberties Union. 2015. "War Comes Home: The Excessive Militarization of American Policing." https://www.aclu.org/war-comes-home-excessive-militarization-american-policing. Accessed March 28, 2015.

Bauer, Shane. 2014. "The Warrior Cops Suit Up." *Mother Jones,* November–December: 18.

Eichenwald, Kurt. 2014. "Why Militarized Police Departments Don't Work." *Newsweek,* August 18, 2014: 30–38.

Grossman, Andrew. 2014. "Senators Criticize Growing Militarization of Local Police Departments." *Wall Street Journal*, September 9: A4.

Grovum, Jake. 2015. "States Face Uphill Battle Over Growing Militarization of Police." *Huffington Post* (March 24). http://www.huffingtonpost.com/2015/03/24/states-police-militarization_n_6932576.html. Accessed September 18, 2015.

Kraska, Peter B. 2007. "Militarization and Policing—Its Relevance to 21st Century Police." *Policing*: 1-13.

President's Surveillance Program (PSP)

The President's Surveillance Program (PSP) is the umbrella term used to refer to a slate of secret intelligence and surveillance activities and programs authorized by President George W. Bush in the aftermath of the September 11, 2001, terrorist attacks on the United States.

This authorization by Bush, given on October 4, 2001, became the basis for much of the counterterrorism efforts undertaken by the federal government in the years immediately following 9/11. One major element of the PSP was an arrangement whereby United States' major telecommunication companies relinquished "call records"—data on when and where calls had been placed—for tens of millions of customers. The other major element of the PSP, dubbed the Terrorist Surveillance Program (TSP), was a warrantless wiretapping program carried out by the National Security Agency (NSA). Under the TSP, the NSA installed cutting-edge surveillance equipment at telecommunications facilities across the nation and began monitoring and analyzing up to 1.7 billion e-mails a day in "real time"—as the messages were sent.

The existence of the highly classified PSP initiative did not come to public light until 2005, when the *New York Times* broke the story that the Bush administration was engaging in warrantless wiretapping of American communications on a massive scale. These revelations about the TSP arm of the PSP sparked condemnation from privacy advocates as well as Bush's political adversaries. But most Republicans rallied to defend both Bush and the PSP. As journalist Glenn Greenwald noted, "At the time of the 2005 NSA warrantless eavesdropping controversy, liberals and Democrats overwhelmingly viewed the agency's surveillance program as menacing. Part of this, of course, was typical partisan hackery: George W. Bush was president and Democrats saw an opportunity to inflict political harm on him and his party. But a significant part of their fear was genuine: because they considered Bush malicious and dangerous, they perceived that state surveillance under his control was therefore threatening and that they in particular were endangered as political opponents. Accordingly, Republicans had a more benign or supportive view of the NSA's actions."

Greenwald observed, however, that when Democratic President Barack Obama extended many of the surveillance policies first instituted through the PSP during his own two terms in office, Democrats both in Washington and around the country became more supportive of the policies. Meanwhile, support from Republicans for the same policies that they had embraced throughout the Bush years declined considerably with a Democrat in the White House.

In the aftermath of the *New York Times* stories about the PSP, Bush administration officials and supportive lawmakers gradually shifted authorization for PSP activities from the president to congressional bills. The Protect America Act of 2007 and the FISA Amendments Act (FAA) of 2008 were the two main pieces of legislation under which PSP operations continued (although under different names).

In 2009, the inspectors general of five different U.S. intelligence agencies—the Department of Justice (DOJ), the Department of Defense (DOD), the Central Intelligence Agency (CIA), the NSA, and the Office of the Director of National Intelligence—released a report that cast considerable doubt on the efficacy of the PSP during the early 2000s. According to this *Unclassified Report on the President's Surveillance Program*, information gathered as a result of its various initiatives might have contributed in a limited way to counterterrorism successes. But the report stated that most of the leads were "determined not to have any connection to terrorism." The IG report further suggested that the Bush administration was so protective of the program that few CIA or FBI personnel even knew of its existence, further diminishing its effectiveness. Finally, the IGs of the agencies revealed that some Justice Department lawyers were so upset by legal justifications for the PSP made by Deputy Attorney General John Yoo that the program nearly prompted mass resignations.

In light of the IG report, some critics said that the PSP was unconstitutional and didn't even make a meaningful contribution to the so-called War on Terror.

"The surveillance program was overly secret and its importance overblown," said privacy advocate Gregory Nojeim of the Center for Democracy and Technology in the *Washington Post.* "It is now clear that many of [the surveillance programs] could have been conducted just as easily within the law—perhaps more effectively and certainly with far less damage to the justice system," echoed a *New York Times* editorial.

Kevin Hillstrom

Further Reading

Editors of the *New York Times.* 2009. "Illegal, and Pointless." *New York Times,* July 16. http://www.nytimes.com/2009/07/17/opinion/17fri1.html. Accessed September 18, 2015.

Electronic Frontier Foundation. "How the NSA's Domestic Spying Program Works." https://www.eff.org/nsa-spying/how-it-works. Accessed May 11, 2015.

Holtzman, Elizabeth, and Cynthia Cooper. 2012. *Cheating Justice: How Bush and Cheney Attacked the Rule of Law and Plotted to Avoid Prosecution—And What We Can Do about It.* Boston: Beacon Press.

Johnson, Carrie, and Ellen Nakashima. 2009. "Inspector Generals Report Faults Secrecy of Surveillance Program." *Washington Post,* July 11. http://www.washingtonpost.com/wp-dyn/content/article/2009/07/10/AR2009071002536.html. Accessed September 18, 2015.

"Unclassified Report on the President's Surveillance Program, 10 July 2009." Prepared by the Offices of the Inspector General of the Department of Defense, Department of Justice, Central Intelligence Agency, National Security Agency, Office of the Director of National Intelligence. Report No. 2009–0013-AS. http://documents.nytimes.com/federal-report-on-the-president-s-surveillance-program. Accessed September 18, 2015.

Yoo, John C. 2007. "The Terrorist Surveillance Program and the Constitution." *George Mason Law Review* 14.

PRISM

PRISM is a code name for a secret spy program created in 2007 by the National Security Agency (NSA), a U.S. intelligence agency. Authorized as part of U.S. foreign intelligence-gathering efforts under the 2008 Amendments to the Foreign Intelligence Surveillance Act (FISA), PRISM is used by the NSA to collect communications, including e-mails, photos, search histories, audio and video chats, and other data, from nine major U.S. Internet companies—Microsoft, Yahoo, Google, Facebook, AOL, Skype, YouTube, PalTalk, and Apple.

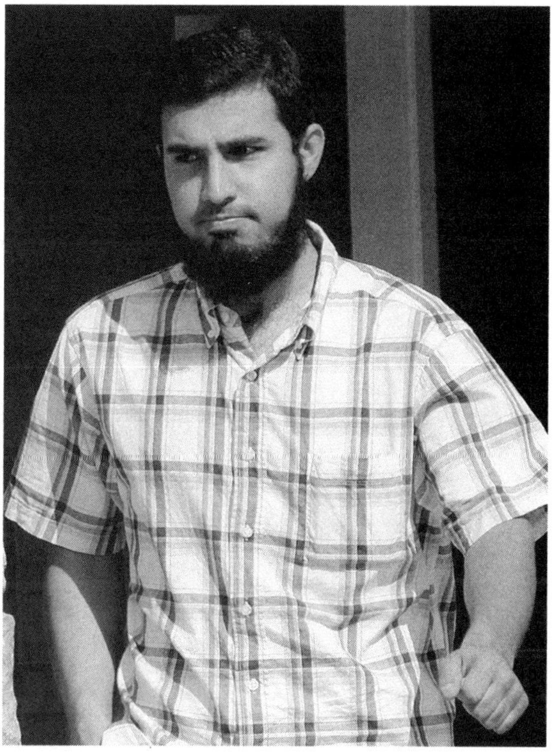

Najibullah Zazi leaves his apartment in Aurora, Colorado, for a meeting with his attorney. The Obama administration declassified a handful of details on June 11, 2013, that credited its PRISM Internet spying program with intercepting a key e-mail that unraveled a 2009 terrorist plot in New York. Zazi's foiled plot to bomb the New York subways has become the centerpiece of that effort. It remains the most serious Al Qaeda plot inside the United States since 9/11. PRISM remains controversial. (AP Photo/Ed Andrieski, File)

The public learned about the existence of PRISM in June 2013, after classified documents were leaked by Edward Snowden, an employee of a defense contractor hired by the NSA. A first set of documents released by Snowden revealed that U.S. intelligence agencies were collecting telephone communication data, including call dates and times, call duration, and numbers called, from customers of Verizon, a U.S. cell phone provider. A few days later, a second set of documents made public by Snowden showed that the government was also conducting mass surveillance of Internet communications, through the PRISM program. These revelations created a public controversy and led to a debate about the extent to which these programs might be spying on Americans.

In April 2014, the NSA released a report on Section 702 of the FISA that described the way in which the PRISM program works. According to the report, NSA analysts first identify the target—which must be a non-U.S. person located outside the United States. Next, analysts identify a telephone number or e-mail address used by the target—called a selector. Contrary to early reports following the Snowden revelations, the NSA report explained that the NSA does not have direct access to Internet servers; rather, data for specified selectors is collected in one of two ways. First, under the PRISM program, the NSA works through the Federal Bureau of Investigation (FBI) to require an Internet service company, such as Google, to produce communications to and from a specific foreign target—for example, an individual who is a member of a foreign terrorist organization. Another method is to require Internet companies to assist with surveillance by lawfully intercepting or tapping Internet information being sent through their networks—a method called "upstream" collection.

The NSA report also explained that once data is provided to the agency, the NSA follows certain minimization procedures outlined in the FISA statute to protect the privacy of Americans. In this process, intelligence analysts review a sample of the data collected, according to the report, once after the data is first provided and then on an annual basis. Analysts check to make sure that the target of the surveillance is a foreign intelligence target—that is, not a U.S. person and not currently located in the United States. If the NSA discovers that it is receiving data unrelated to a specific target, or that the target is not a non-U.S. person or is located in the United States, the report states that the surveillance of selectors associated with that target is terminated. Otherwise, data relating to foreign targets is retained by the NSA for a maximum of five years.

Although the NSA report maintains that PRISM is not used to target U.S. citizens, other U.S. persons, or anyone located within the United States, critics point out that private data belonging to Americans is often collected as an incidental part of foreign intelligence collection. Virtually all information sent by Americans in e-mails or using the Internet, critics say, could be swept up as part of a foreign intelligence search. Critics also worry that once foreign intelligence data is collected and stored, intelligence agencies may be able to search through that data for private information on Americans without a warrant. Such broad intelligence surveillance affects Americans in ways that, according to many observers, violates constitutional guarantees of privacy, search and seizure provisions of the Fourth Amendment to the U.S. Constitution, and First Amendment free speech and association rights.

A July 2, 2014, report by the Privacy and Civil Liberties Oversight Board—an independent agency within the federal government's executive branch charged with reviewing executive branch actions for their effect on privacy and civil liberties—also expressed concerns about how the PRISM program affects privacy rights and civil liberties. The report found no evidence of intentional abuse and said the intelligence efforts were lawful. However, the board also warned that the incidental collection of U.S. persons' communications, as well as the use of queries to search collected data for communications of specific U.S. persons, allows a great deal of private information about Americans to be acquired by the government. The report offered a series of recommendations to ensure that intelligence programs appropriately balance national security concerns with privacy and civil liberties.

Debra Miller

Further Reading

Aid, Matthew. 2009. *The Secret Sentry: The Untold History of the National Security Agency*. New York: Bloomsbury.

Bamford, James. 2008. *The Shadow Factory: The Ultra-Secret NSA from 9/11 to the Eavesdropping on America*. New York: Doubleday.

Greenwald, Glenn. 2014. *No Place to Hide: Edward Snowden, the NSA, and the U.S. Surveillance State*. New York: Metropolitan Books.

Kaminski, Margot. 2013. "PRISM's Legal Basis: How We Got Here, and What We Can Do to Get Back." *The Atlantic* (June 7). http://www.theatlantic.com/national/archive/2013/06/prisms-legal-basis-how-we-got-here-and-what-we-can-do-to-get-back/276667/. Accessed April 11, 2015.

National Security Agency. 2014. "NSA Director of Civil Liberties and Privacy Office Report: NSA's Implementation of Section 702 of the Foreign Intelligence Surveillance Act." April 16. http://icontherecord.tumblr.com/post/83424169816/nsas-implementation-of-foreign-intelligence. Accessed September 18, 2015.

Privacy and Civil Liberties Oversight Board. 2014. "Report on the Surveillance Program Operated Pursuant to Section 702 of the Foreign Intelligence Surveillance Act." July 2. https://www.pclob.gov/library/702-Report.pdf. Accessed September 18, 2015.

Sledge, Matt. 2014. "Government Privacy Board Says Controversial NSA Surveillance Program Is Constitutional." *The Huffington Post* (July 2). http://www.huffingtonpost.com/2014/07/02/pclob-section-702_n_5550010.html. Accessed April 11, 2015.

Privacy Act of 1974

The Privacy Act of 1974 was the first comprehensive privacy law enacted in the world. It regulates the collection, use, maintenance, disclosure, and disposition of personal information by U.S. federal executive branch agencies and provides rights to certain individuals about whom records are maintained. It establishes civil and criminal penalties for violations of the law and assigns the Office of Management and Budget (OMB) as the agency responsible for providing guidance and overseeing implementation by the other agencies. The Privacy Act recognizes that government must collect information necessary to run its programs and carry out its various missions, but it seeks to limit unnecessary intrusions or unfair practices associated with government use of information.

Prior to passage of the Privacy Act (1974), changes in American society generated growing concern about the use of automated data systems to keep records about people, especially by the federal government. At that time, the federal government was one of few organizations that had significant personally identifiable information, access to large data storage and processing capabilities, and the resources to use them. The public concern about the issues posed by automation of personal record-keeping systems prompted the secretary of what was then the Department of Health, Education, and Welfare to convene an Advisory Committee on Automated Personal Data Systems. The Advisory Committee's report recommended passage of a Code of Fair Information Practice comprising five basic principles that became the foundation for the act: (1) there must be no personal data record-keeping systems whose very existence is secret; (2) there must be a way for individuals to find out what data about them are kept and how the data are used; (3) there must be a way for individuals to prevent information about themselves obtained for one purpose from being used or made available for other purposes without their consent; (4) there must be a way for individuals to correct or amend records about themselves; and (5) any organization creating, maintaining, using, or disseminating records of personally identifiable information must assure the reliability of the data for their intended use and must take precautions to prevent misuse of the data.

The Privacy Act was passed on December 31, 1974, in the final week of the 93rd Congress, in the wake of the Watergate scandal. Instead of the usual practice of convening a conference committee of senators and representatives to reconcile differences between bills passed by the two houses of Congress, staff members from the key committees of the House and Senate put together the final bill that ultimately was enacted. In lieu of the traditional accompanying conference report, the staff produced a document entitled, "Analysis of House and Senate Compromise Amendments to the Federal Privacy Act," that was submitted to both Houses and is generally considered more reliable than the original committee reports as legislative history for interpreting the statute.

In passing the Privacy Act, there was a desire to circumscribe the scope of coverage of the law. The law does not cover all personally identifiable information, nor all such information held by the federal government, but only that which falls into the ambit of certain key definitions. In general, the protections extend only to information about an individual maintained by a U.S. federal executive branch agency, connected to an identifier particular to the individual, and retrieved by that identifier. Such information is said to be in a "system of records."

The act explicitly includes as examples of identifiers, in addition to name or identifying number, a fingerprint, voice print, or photograph. For example, a system of records might be a cabinet of files arranged alphabetically or by Social Security number that would allow someone to retrieve the file about a particular person directly. The same information filed chronologically would not be covered, since getting to any particular individual's record would potentially require searching through the entire file cabinet to locate the record.

Only U.S. citizens or lawful, permanent resident aliens enjoy the protections of the act. Neither deceased persons nor organizations or businesses of any kind are covered, although in some cases sole proprietors of businesses may have Privacy Act rights. Likewise, information in the custody of the Congress, the Supreme Court, the immediate office of the White House, or a state or local governments is not covered.

A "system of records" may be composed of paper or electronic files. However, despite the fact that the law emerged due to concerns stemming from developments in automatic data processing, it was not written to accommodate modern, sophisticated electronic records systems. In the era of databases searchable by keyword, data mining, and other innovations, almost anything might be considered a "system of records." This issue was directly addressed by the Court of Appeals for the District of Columbia Circuit in *Henke v. Commerce* (1996) when it held that it is not just the ability to retrieve the records that implicates the Privacy Act, but an agency must actually retrieve records in order for a system of records to exist.

The major responsibility of agencies is to safeguard from improper disclosure the information in its systems of records. The Privacy Act model established the framework for many disclosure laws that succeeded it, setting up the basic rule that an agency may not disclose information by any means without the written consent of the subject individual unless the disclosure falls into one of a number of exceptions. The most often used statutory exception permits disclosures within an agency to other employees who have a need for the information to carry out their duties. Another commonly used exception permits disclosures that are required by the Freedom of Information Act. There are also disclosure exceptions to accommodate law enforcement requests and court orders that meet certain standards: in the case of "compelling circumstances" affecting the health or safety of an individual; for carrying out censuses and other statistical uses; to the Congress or the comptroller general; and to the National Archives and Records Administration (NARA) for managing the process of accessioning permanently valuable records.

In addition to these specific statutory disclosure exceptions, the Congress enacted another provision, the use of which permits agencies to add, via an administrative process, new disclosures that might be necessary to conduct business. This provision accommodates disclosures that were not contemplated and could not be predicted or anticipated at the time of passage of the act. The controversial exception, called a "routine use," is a term of art that refers to a disclosure of a record outside of the custodial agency "for a purpose which is compatible with the purpose for which it was collected." These generally fall into three categories: (1) those where there is a direct nexus to the reason for which the information was collected, e.g., disclosure to a contractor for contracted work; (2) those which are necessary and proper, e.g., disclosure to a law enforcement agency to investigate fraud in an agency's program; or (3) those disclosures required by statute, whether or not related to the program purpose of the system of records. An agency wishing to add a routine use disclosure must publish notice of a new or significantly altered routine use in the *Federal Register*, solicit comment from the public, and report the disclosure to OMB and both houses of the Congress. This ability to add new disclosures and broaden the use of personal information via a simple administrative process has generated considerable criticism.

Although widely thought of as merely an access and disclosure law, the Privacy Act is more properly classified as an information resources management statute in that it regulates how federal agencies collect, use, maintain, and dispose of significant collections of records. The law limits an agency to collecting only information which is "relevant and necessary" to its mission and requires that information be collected "to the greatest extent practicable" from the subjects themselves when it may be used as the basis of any significant decisions about them. It further requires that the agency maintain the records in a manner that is accurate, relevant, timely, and complete and that it review the records for these characteristics prior to disseminating them outside of the agency. Agencies are required to establish rules of conduct for their employees handling Privacy Act records and appropriate safeguards to guard against anticipated threats to the security of the records.

To implement the Code of Fair Information Practice's first principle that there should be no secret record-keeping systems, agencies are required to publish in the *Federal Register* a notice about the existence and character of each system of records. Such notices describe the name, location, and manager of the system of records; the categories of individuals, sources of information, and types of records maintained; the policies of the agency regarding storage, security, retention, and disposal; the routine uses associated with the records; and the agency procedures whereby subjects of the records can gain access or contest the content of the records.

In addition, when collecting information, agencies are required to notify individuals at the time of the collection about the authority for the collection, whether responding is mandatory or voluntary, the purpose of the collection, the routine uses, and the consequences, if any, that would result if the individual failed to respond to the request.

Besides the right to these two types of notices, the Privacy Act affords individuals the right to see and, for a nominal fee, to obtain, a copy of information maintained about themselves. It also affords individuals the right to request an amendment of information that is not accurate, relevant, timely, or complete. In the case of an agency's refusal to amend a record, an individual may request to add a concise statement describing the reasons for disagreement with the agency. If an agency refuses to provide access, make the requested amendment, or simply fails to respond to a request, an individual may appeal for a further review and may seek a civil remedy via judicial review of the reviewing official's determination.

In addition to civil actions related to access or amendment requests, an individual may bring suit against the agency in the district courts of the United States if an agency fails to maintain records in accordance with the standards set forth in the law, or fails to comply with any other provision of the Act, and the individual suffers some adverse consequence. An individual is entitled to actual damages sustained, with a minimum recovery of $1,000, plus costs and reasonable attorney fees. However, it is extremely difficult to prevail in a civil action under the Privacy Act, and not many suits are brought under the law. Success requires a showing of willful and intentional misconduct, a nexus between the agency's failure to comply and the harm done to the individual, and actual out-of-pocket damages.

The Congress established criminal penalties for violation of the Privacy Act as well. It is a crime for an officer or an employee of an agency to willfully disclose Privacy Act records knowing they are protected by the act. It is a crime to maintain a secret system of records—that is, without having published the proper notice in the *Federal Register*. Finally, it is a crime for any person—an employee of an agency, an individual, or a corporate entity—to knowingly and willfully request or obtain a record under false pretenses. Criminal violation of the Privacy Act is a misdemeanor and carries a maximum fine of $5,000. There are only two known prosecutions for criminal violation of the Privacy Act. This is because it is difficult to prove beyond a reasonable doubt that a defendant knowingly and willfully disclosed information and also the penalties are scant compared to other priorities of the Justice Department.

Under some circumstances, an agency may promulgate regulations to exempt itself from certain provisions of the Privacy Act. Two general exemptions permit the Central Intelligence Agency (CIA) or any agency that performs as its principle function the enforcement of criminal laws to exempt itself from most of the requirements of the Act. While the CIA may exempt any system of records under this provision, a criminal law enforcement agency may only exempt those records compiled for a criminal law enforcement purpose. An agency cannot exempt itself from the provisions regarding disclosures; keeping and maintaining an accounting of disclosures; publishing notice in the *Federal Register*; making reasonable efforts to disseminate records that are accurate, relevant, timely, and complete; prohibiting maintenance of records on how an individual exercises rights guaranteed by the First Amendment; establishing rules of conduct for employees and appropriate administrative, technical, and physical safeguards; or establishing routine uses.

Seven specific exemptions apply to particular types of information that an agency may maintain, permitting an agency to exempt itself from the requirement to make the accounting of disclosures available to the subject; grant access, amendment, and appeal rights; limit collection to only information that is relevant and necessary; or describe the sources of categories of records in the *Federal Register* notice. The seven exemptions protect classified information, investigatory material compiled for a law enforcement purpose that does not meet the general exemption's requirements; records of the Secret Service related to protecting the president or other protectees; background investigation records; civil service examination records; and military promotion evaluations. In the case of the law enforcement, background investigation, and military evaluation records, the exemption only extends to information that would reveal the identity of a source who furnished information under a promise that his or her identity would be held in confidence.

Section Seven of the Privacy Act contains provisions regarding the collection of Social Security numbers. Section Seven, unlike the rest of the act, applies to any federal, state or local government agency. It prohibits such an agency from denying an individual any right, benefit, or privilege provided by law because that individual refuses to divulge his or her social security number. It also requires the agency to furnish notice each time it solicits a Social Security number detailing whether the disclosure is mandatory or voluntary, by what authority the information is solicited, and what uses will be made of it.

There are two significant exceptions to the first provision. A government agency may deny an individual a right, benefit, or privilege for failure to divulge an SSN (1) if the disclosure is required by a federal statute, or (2) if the disclosure was required by a statute or regulation adopted before passage of the Privacy Act, and the government entity was actually collecting and maintaining SSNs before that date. Many federal statutes have been passed that permit governments to require the SSN, including for drivers' licensing, applying for federal loans and benefits, and tax administration.

Today, the Privacy Act of 1974 is widely regarded as an important but flawed piece of legislation that is subject to dramatically different interpretations. As a result, debates about applications of the Privacy Act are frequently part of wider discussions about surveillance and personal privacy in modern United States As the Department of Justice acknowledges: "The Act's imprecise language, limited legislative history, and somewhat outdated regulatory guidelines have rendered it a difficult statute to decipher and apply. Moreover, even after more than thirty-five years of administrative and judicial analysis, numerous Privacy Act issues remain unresolved or unexplored."

Maya A. Bernstein

Further Reading

Advisory Committee on Automated Personal Data Systems, U.S. Department of Health, Education & Welfare. 1973. *Records, Computers and the Rights of Citizens: Report of the Secretary's Advisory Committee on Automated Personal Data Systems*. Washington, DC: U.S. Government Printing Office.

Bennett, Colin, and Rebecca Grant, eds. 1999. *Visions of Privacy.* Toronto: University of Toronto Press.

Department of Justice. 2012. *Overview of the Privacy Act of 1974, 2012 Edition.* Department of Justice Web site. http://www.justice.gov/sites/default/files/opcl/docs/1974privacyact-2012.pdf. Accessed September 18, 2015.

Office of Information and Privacy, U.S. Department of Justice. 2006. *Freedom of Information Act Guide & Privacy Act Overview.* Washington, DC: U.S. Government Printing Office.

Office of Management and Budget. 1975. "Privacy Act Implementation: Guidelines and Responsibilities." *Federal Register* 40: 28948–78.

Regan, Priscilla. 1995. *Legislating Privacy: Technology, Social Values, and Public Policy.* Chapel Hill, NC: University of North Carolina Press.

Privacy Advocacy Organizations

The 1980s marked the arrival of the Information Age with an explosion of information and surveillance technologies that fundamentally reconfigured the social, business, and national security landscape. By the end of the decade, the convergence of computer and telecommunications systems had expanded the capacity to collect, process, and disseminate personal information at unprecedented rates. Since that time, a number of privacy advocacy organizations were formed in response to the purported threats to personal privacy these technologies had created. Organizations such as the Electronic Privacy Information Center (EPIC), Privacy International (PI), World Privacy Forum (WPF), and the Electronic Frontier Foundation (EFF) have joined civil liberties groups of longer standing, such as the American Civil Liberties Union (ACLU). All of these groups have mobilized resources on a number of fronts to influence privacy policy at the state, federal, and international levels. Their efforts typically include lobbying for increased privacy protection, legal challenges, and the dissemination of information to the general public. As such, these organizations play an increasingly integral role in the development of privacy policy in the United States and the international community.

One of the first privacy advocacy organizations formed in response to the growth of information technologies was the EFF. The group was founded in 1990 by former Grateful Dead songwriter John Barlow; Mitchell Kapor, the founder of the Lotus software company; and John Gilmore, who was also involved in the creation of Sun Microsystems.

EFF focuses primarily on issues of digital rights, including free speech, privacy, innovation, and consumer rights. Though its efforts are primarily focused

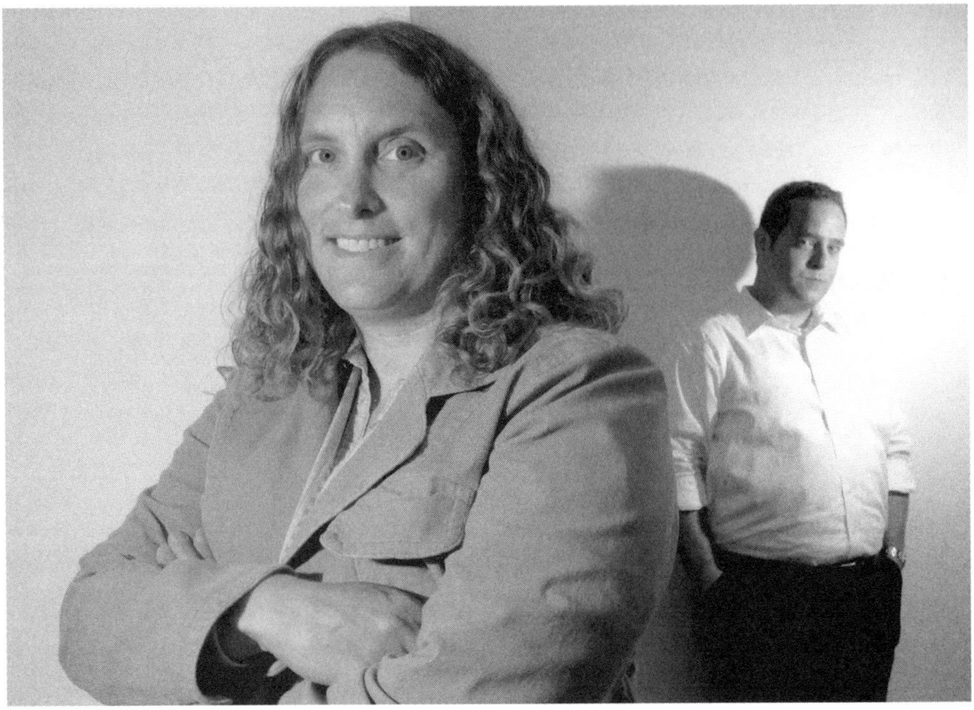

A snapshot in time: a 2006 photo of Shari Steele, Electronic Frontier Foundation's executive director (left), and Kevin Bankston, staff attorney, at their office building in San Francisco. The Electronic Frontier Foundation, as an early digital civil liberties organization, first took on the U.S. Secret Service over raids and seizures of computer equipment from a small games company called Steve Jackson Games. (AP Photo/Jeff Chiu)

in the courts, it also advises policymakers, educates the media and the public, and funds the development of "freedom-enhancing" technologies.

The year 1990 also marked the founding of UK-based Privacy International (PI). It was formed when over 100 privacy experts and human rights organizations joined together to form a worldwide network oriented toward privacy protection. Still one of the leading advocacy groups in the world, PI is composed of a wide range of individuals, including lawyers, academics, journalists, jurists, computer scientists, and human rights activists. Primarily conceived as a watchdog on surveillance by governments and corporations, PI focuses on issues of cyber crime, freedom of information, ID cards, digital money, outsourcing, wiretapping, encryption, and video surveillance.

PI differentiates itself from many other privacy advocacy organizations with its emphasis on an international approach to privacy policy. It has spearheaded public campaigns in a number of countries to push for privacy policy reform. At the same time, PI monitors the activities of international organizations such as the European Union (EU) and the United Nations in order to focus international attention on the policy initiatives of these organizations.

Another leading privacy advocacy organization is the EPIC, which was founded in 1994 by lawyers Marc Rotenberg, David Banisar, and David Sobel. The trio first gained public attention through their successful public relations campaign against Lexis-Nexis in which they were able to force the company to close down a database that contained the Social Security numbers of many individuals. Building on the success of this early effort, the three lawyers established EPIC in order to raise public awareness of the emergent civil liberties issues regarding privacy and freedom of expression associated with the onset of the Information Age. Through advocacy, litigation, policy research, publications, and public education, EPIC has continued to further its program to protect individual privacy rights.

The WPF was founded by Pam Dixon in 2003. Since its inception, WPF has carried out in-depth research and consumer education programs in numerous areas at the intersection of surveillance and privacy rights. Areas of particular focus for Dixon and the WPF include medical identity theft, data mining, new technologies, and corporate invasions of privacy.

In 1994, the Center for Democracy and Technology (CDT) was created by Jerry Berman in order to develop practical solutions to enhance free expression and privacy in global communications technology. Located in Washington, D.C., CDT has worked to build coalitions between corporations and social activist groups (entities that are routinely at odds with each other regarding issues of privacy).

The above organizations are among the most prominent privacy advocacy organizations in the United States. There are, however, hundreds if not thousands of other advocacy groups that deal with privacy issues in the United States and throughout the world, ranging from local grassroots groups to large national and international privacy and civil rights organizations. As privacy rights scholar Colin J. Bennett notes, "There is no concerted worldwide privacy movement that has anything like the scale, resources, or public recognition of organizations in the environmental, feminist, consumer protection, and human rights fields. In the privacy protection sector, there is a diverse, open-ended, and fluid range of groups and individuals, stretching from traditional civil liberties organizations, consumer associations, and groups established to promote freedom in cyberspace to more specialized groups involved with single issues." Together, though, these organizations play an important role in establishing and protecting individual privacy rights, and some observers believe that if perceptions continue to rise that fundamental privacy rights are being sacrificed in the name of national security, these organizations may well gain higher levels of membership and prominence in years to come.

Brian L. Zirkle

Further Reading

American Civil Liberties Union (ACLU). "Rein in the Surveillance State." ACLU Web site. https://www.aclu.org/rein-surveillance-state. Accessed April 2, 2015.

Bennett, Colin J. 2008. *The Privacy Advocates: Resisting the Spread of Surveillance.* Cambridge, MA: Massachusetts Institute of Technology Press.

Privacy, Informational

In the Information Age, government agencies, insurance companies, banks, hospitals, schools, and numerous other public and private institutions collect and maintain enormous quantities of information about individuals. Failure to protect the confidentiality of these records can produce real harm. Without appropriate limits on the disclosure and sharing of personal information, people's reputations, finances, and security can be placed in jeopardy. Over the last several decades, Americans have become increasingly concerned about these issues. Congress and the state legislatures have responded by enacting significant statutory protections of informational privacy.

Informational privacy should, however, be distinguished from constitutional or "decisional" privacy. Whereas the *Stanford Encyclopedia of Philosophy* describes the latter as "the freedom to make one's own decisions without interference by others in regard to matters seen as intimate and personal, such as the decision to use contraceptives or to have an abortion," informational privacy is "concerned with the interest of individuals in exercising control over access to information about themselves. . . . Think here, for instance, about information disclosed on Facebook or other social media."

The Federal Privacy Act of 1974

The seminal legislation in this field is the federal Privacy Act of 1974, which requires that personal information files held by federal agencies are limited to those that are clearly necessary. The Privacy Act prohibits secret record-keeping systems. The law requires that individuals be afforded the opportunity to see what information about them is kept and to challenge the accuracy of such information. It also provides that personal information collected for one purpose will not be used for another purpose without the consent of the affected person. Finally, the Privacy Act requires that if agencies disclose personal information, they must inform the affected person as to whom the disclosure was made, for what purpose, and on what date.

The Privacy Act was amended in 1976 to require that SSNs be kept confidential by the government agencies that collect them. This is of enormous importance today, as criminals often use SSNsto commit "identify theft" or perpetrate fraudulent schemes of various kinds.

State Laws Protecting Informational Privacy

The federal Privacy Act applies only to agencies of the national government. However, most states have adopted laws paralleling the federal protections by limiting record keeping about individuals by state agencies.

Privacy of Educational Records

The Family Educational Rights and Privacy Act (FERPA), better known as the Buckley Amendment, is a 1974 law that was crafted to protect the privacy of students' educational records. The law applies to all state and local educational institutions that receive federal funds and provides that federal funds are to be withheld from school districts that have a policy or practice of permitting the release of education records without the students' written consent, or parental consent of minor students. FERPA defines educational records as "records, files, documents, and other materials" containing information directly related to a student, which "are maintained by an educational agency or institution or by a person acting for such agency or institution." The Family Policy Compliance Office (FPCO) investigates complaints and determines what steps are necessary to insure that violations no longer take place. Federal funds can be withheld unless and until educational institutions comply with these steps.

Financial Privacy

In *United States v. Miller* (1976), the U.S. Supreme Court ruled that bank customers had no legal right to privacy in financial information held by financial institutions because these are the business records of the banks. In order to ameliorate the effect of that decision, Congress enacted the Right to Financial Privacy Act (RFPA) of 1978. The Act defines "financial institution" broadly and states that no government authority may have access to, or obtain copies of, the information contained in the financial records of any customer from a financial institution unless the financial records are reasonably described and the customer authorizes access or there is an appropriate administrative subpoena or summons, a search warrant, or subpoena, or other appropriate written request from an authorized government authority.

RFPA provides exemptions that allow disclosure to a federal agency of information not specifically related to an individual or in regard to a financial institution's interest concerning its loans and loan guarantees, and where federal agencies are conducting supervisory investigations of institutions. In addition the Internal Revenue Service (IRS), which has its own statutory privacy protections, may obtain information from a bank about a customer without a summons or notice. Disclosures may be made pursuant to other federal statutes and, of course, in civil litigation information may be disclosed pursuant to Federal Rules of Civil Procedure. Finally, the federal government can obtain access to personal information if the institution's customer is suspected of terrorist action. The act requires the federal government to give an institution's customer notice when it is seeking disclosure in order to afford a person an opportunity to challenge such a request.

Confidentiality of Health Records

Along with financial records, medical records are an essential element of a person's individual privacy, but historically, the law has not recognized a person's right to privacy in such records. In *Whalen v. Roe* (1977), the U.S. Supreme Court recognized that disclosures of private medical information to doctors, hospital personnel, insurance companies, and to public health agencies are often an essential part of modern medical practice, even when the disclosure may reflect unfavorably on the character of the patient.

In recent years, Congress has recognized this strong desire for privacy in medical records, and when it enacted the Health Insurance Portability and Accountability Act of 1996 (HIPAA), it mandated that the Department of Health and Human Services (HHS) develop privacy standards to protect patients' medical records and other health information furnished to physicians, hospitals, and other health care providers. HHS subsequently promulgated a Privacy Protection Rule that represents the first comprehensive federal protection for the privacy of patients' medical records and other individually identifiable information. The new rule covers such medical information, whether communicated electronically, on paper, or orally, that is used or disclosed by entities subject to the rule. It grants patients access to their records and requires that they consent before release or disclosure of protected information. For example, patients have to grant authorization before an entity subject to the rule can release a patient's medical records to a bank or life insurance company. Affected entities were required to comply with the new rule by April 14, 2003. Those who violate the rule are subject to civil and criminal penalties. HHS has announced that the new federal privacy standards simply set a national "floor" to protect persons and that any state law providing additional protections would continue to apply.

Confidentiality of Library Records

Nearly all the states have also adopted laws protecting the privacy of library records. The New York statute, codified at §4509 of the New York Consolidated Laws, is fairly typical:

> Library records, which contain names or other personally identifying details regarding the users of public, free association, school, college and university libraries and library systems of this state, including but not limited to records related to the circulation of library materials, computer database searches, interlibrary loan transactions, reference queries, requests for photocopies of library materials, title reserve requests, or the use of audio-visual materials, films or records, shall be confidential and shall not be disclosed except that such records may be disclosed to the extent necessary for the proper operation of such library and shall be disclosed upon request or consent of the user or pursuant to subpoena, court order or where otherwise required by statute.

The USA PATRIOT Act of 2001 made it easier for FBI agents to gain access to library records, including circulation records, Internet use records, and registration information. Under Section 215 of the PATRIOT Act, to obtain the necessary surveillance warrant, agents do not have to demonstrate probable cause but only assert before a federal magistrate that the records sought are related to an ongoing investigation related to terrorism or counterintelligence. The American Civil Liberties Union (ACLU), the American Library Association (ALA), and other advocates of "the right to read" have voiced strong opposition to this section of the USA PATRIOT Act. The ALA's "Policy Concerning Confidentiality of Personally Identifiable Information about Library Users Existing ALA Policy" states; "The government's interest in library use reflects a dangerous and fallacious equation of what a person reads with what that person believes or how that person is likely to behave. Such a presumption can and does threaten the freedom of access to information."

Video Privacy

One of the strongest protections of informational privacy is found in the Video Privacy Protection Act of 1988. This federal statute prohibits "any person, engaged in the business . . . of rental, sale or delivery of prerecorded video cassette tapes or similar audiovisual materials" from disclosing "personally identifiably information" to someone other than the consumer without the consumer's written consent. This prevents others from finding out what videos people have been watching, which serves to protect them from embarrassment and abuse from those who disapprove of their private viewing habits. The statute provides a federal civil remedy to consumers whose rights are violated by improper disclosure of video rental information.

The Video Privacy Protection Act does not prohibit the disclosure of information that is subpoenaed by a court of law pursuant to a criminal prosecution or civil suit. However, the statutes provides that the consumer is to be given fair notice and afforded the opportunity to contest the request in court. The act also makes an exception, of course, in cases where law enforcement officers, acting pursuant to judicial authorization, seek such information as part of a legitimate investigation. Under the statute, the consumer whose records are sought is entitled to prior notice that law enforcement agents are seeking to obtain this information (although Section 215 of the USA PATRIOT Act presumably creates an exception to this protection for investigations related to terrorism or counterintelligence).

Computer Privacy

Anyone who uses a computer that is connected to the Internet is well aware of the threats to privacy posed by hackers who find ingenious ways to purloin private information from other parties' computers. Although such activities are prohibited under state and federal laws, perpetrators are often difficult to identify. In most instances, victims do not even realize that they have been victimized. Increasingly, computer users are using antivirus programs, firewalls, and "spam" (junk e-mail) blockers to protect themselves from intruders. And parents are increasingly relying on filtering software to protect their children from Web sites and chat rooms that may harbor hidden dangers. What many computer users still do not realize is how much information is stored on their computer drives without their conscious effort to save such data. Files downloaded from the Internet are stored in caches that must be positively deleted. Even deleted files remain on hard drives unless and until they are overwritten by newly saved files. The only way to "cover one's tracks," as it were, is to employ specialized software designed to expunge deleted files.

Not infrequently, police seize computers and associated media as part of investigations into national security threats, financial fraud, child pornography, and other types of criminal activity. Of course, to make such a seizure from the home or private office, police must have probable cause and, in most instances, a search warrant. However, in most instances employees do not enjoy the same Fourth Amendment protections in the workplace. Employers typically take the position that any computing done on their equipment is their intellectual property. The courts tend to agree and, therefore, are unsympathetic to claims that an employer committed an invasion of privacy by accessing files on an employee's computer. Today many employers routinely monitor their employees' e-mail transmissions and Internet activity. Currently, there are very few laws in effect to regulate this activity or protect workers' electronic privacy in the workplace.

John M. Scheb II

Further Reading

Allen, Anita. 2011. *Unpopular Privacy: What Must We Hide?* Oxford: Oxford University Press.

Branscomb, Anne Wells. 1995. *Who Owns Information? From Privacy to Public Access.* New York: Harper Collins Publishers.

Cate, Fred H. 1997. *Privacy in the Information Age.* Washington, DC: Brookings Institution Press.

Klosek, Jacqueline. 2000. *Data Privacy in the Information Age.* Westport, CT: Quorum Books.

Matheson, David. 2007. "Unknowableness and Informational Privacy." *Journal of Philosophical Research* 32: 251–67.

Stanford Encyclopedia of Philosophy. 2014. "Privacy and Information Technology." http://plato.stanford.edu/entries/it-privacy/. Accessed September 18, 2015.

Profiling

Profiling is a practice of generalizing about individuals based on certain physical or behavioral characteristics. For many Americans, racial profiling is a discriminatory practice used by law enforcement and intelligence agencies to target "suspicious" individuals or groups for additional levels of surveillance and/or investigation based on race, religion, ethnicity, gender, or national origin. Because many civil libertarians and privacy advocates believe that it is a inherently biased practice, it has become controversial and is banned in many jurisdictions across the United States. For supporters, however, racial profiling is viewed as a common sense tool to identify, monitor, and apprehend likely criminals and terrorists.

The racial profiling of minorities, especially African Americans, has long been a divisive topic in the United States. In recent decades, numerous studies have shown that African Americans are more likely to be to be pulled over for traffic stops or detained while walking down the street and questioned by local police officers. As African Americans and other minority groups had some level of success in obtaining equal rights and ending discriminatory practices in the workplace and other arenas, national attention began to focus on the biased practices of many

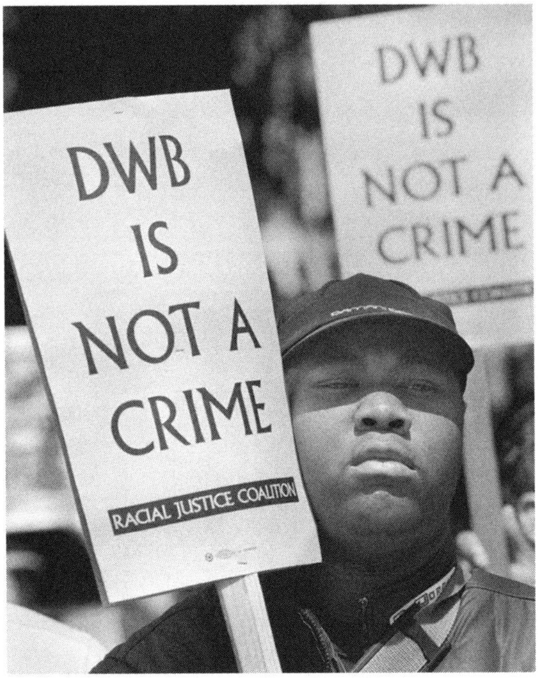

Lonnell McGhee of Oakland, California, listens to speakers at a rally against racial profiling at the state Capitol in Sacramento, California, on April 27, 2000. Organized protests against racial and ethnic profiling continue to be seen in many cities and campuses. (AP Photo/Steve Yeater)

police forces and the unequal treatment of minority populations by the legal system in many communities.

On February 27, 2001, President George W. Bush addressed a joint session of Congress and declared that it was time to eliminate the use of racial profiling by the nation's law enforcement. His announcement was codified in a 2003 directive by the U.S. Department of Justice (DoJ), *Guidance Regarding the Use of Race by Law Enforcement Agencies*. The document stated that "Race-based assumptions in law enforcement perpetuate negative racial stereotypes that are harmful to our rich and diverse democracy, and materially impair our efforts to maintain a fair and just society."

Despite the government's strong stance against racial profiling policies, there have been numerous studies at the local, state, and federal levels that clearly show that the profiling of African Americans and other minorities persists. Several states are now required to report incidents of racial profiling to state agencies or federal authorities.

Arabs and Muslims have also been the targets of racial profiling policies after the September 11, 2001, attacks. The 19 hijackers who perpetrated the attacks were associated with the militant Islamic group Al Qaeda, and all of them hailed from Arab countries: 15 from Saudi Arabia, 2 from the United Arab Emirates, 1 from

Egypt, and the remaining 1 from Lebanon. In response to the attacks, the U.S. government launched an extensive counterterrorism campaign to identify, monitor, and apprehend terrorist suspects and allies in the Arab and Muslim communities.

Critics charged that the counterterrorism campaign led to policies that unfairly profiled many innocent Arabs and Muslims. In one such effort, the New York Police Department (NYPD) used specially trained officers to infiltrate mosques, schools, businesses, and other key institutions in the Muslim community. In the process, the officers collected data on thousands of law-abiding Muslims solely because of their religion, ethnicity, and nation of origin.

NYPD officials defended the program as essential to protecting New York City from another terrorist attack from Al Qaeda or other radical Islamic terrorists. However, in a sweeping investigation of the NYPD program, the Associated Press revealed that the six-year program never generated a lead or triggered a terrorist investigation.

As the federal government has shifted much of the responsibility for immigration enforcement to local and state law enforcement, racial profiling has become a central component of immigration enforcement policy in many states. In an effort to identify, monitor, and detain dangerous undocumented immigrants, racial profiling of Hispanic individuals and entire communities has been employed. Many of the targets of this profiling have been legal aliens or American citizens.

In 2010, Arizona enacted a controversial law, the Support Our Law Enforcement and Safe Neighborhoods Act (SB 1070), which mandated that police officers perform an immigration check of individuals during routine stops if they have a reasonable suspicion that the individual might have violated U.S. immigration laws. Any undocumented immigrant without the proper registration documents with them at the time of the stop would be charged with a misdemeanor crime. The law also prohibited the law enforcement officials from stopping suspects on the basis of race, color, or national origin.

The law generated heated opposition from civil libertarians and immigration reform advocates who were concerned that the policy would lead to increased racial profiling of Hispanic individuals and violate civil rights protections. In 2012, the U.S. Supreme Court struck down three provisions of SB 1070 as unconstitutional, ruling that some sections of the legislation were preempted by federal law.

In December 2014, the Obama administration released new guidelines on the use of racial profiling by federal agents, replacing the 2003 guidelines. The new rules allow the use of racial profiling based on race, ethnicity, gender, sexual orientation, religion, or country of origin for airport screening and border patrol agents but prohibit the practice for all other federal law enforcement personnel.

Margaret Haerens

Further Reading

Apuzzo, Matt, and Michael S. Schmidt. 2014. "U.S. to Continue Racial, Ethnic Profiling in Border Policy." *New York Times*, December 4. http://www.nytimes.com/2014/12/06/us/politics/obama-to-impose-racial-profiling-curbs-with-exceptions.html. Accessed September 18, 2015.

Friedersdorf, Conor. 2013. "The Horrifying Effects of NYPD Ethnic Profiling on Innocent Muslim Americans." *The Atlantic*, March 28. http://www.theatlantic.com/politics/archive/2013/03/the-horrifying-effects-of-nypd-ethnic-profiling-on-innocent-muslim-americans/274434/. Accessed September 18, 2015.

Rushing, Keith. 2013. "Dissecting the Long, Deep Roots of Racial Profiling in America." *The Huffington Post* (May 1). http://www.huffingtonpost.com/keith-rushing/dissecting-racial-profiling_b_2740246.html. Accessed March 15, 2015.

R

Reasonable Expectation of Privacy

The reasonable expectation of privacy test is applied to determine whether or not the Fourth Amendment to the U.S. Constitution will protect against certain searches and seizures by government officials. The reasonable expectation of privacy test was first formulated by the U.S. Supreme Court in *United States v. Katz* (1967). The test actually appeared in a concurring opinion by Justice Harlan, who stated the Fourth Amendment covers a search or seizure if (1) a person exhibits an "actual or subjective expectation of privacy" and (2) "the expectation [is] one that society is prepared to recognize as 'reasonable.'"

What constitutes a reasonable expectation of privacy? The answer is rather difficult because it involves understanding a litany of Supreme Court decisions in particular cases. There is no particular formula for determining when a reasonable expectation of privacy exists. Therefore, one must look at the specific circumstances of each case the Supreme Court decided on the issue and make generalizations and analogies. In *Katz*, the Supreme Court famously stated that "the Fourth Amendment protects people, not places. What a person knowingly exposes to the public, even in his own home or office, is not a subject of Fourth Amendment protection. But what he seeks to preserve as private, even in an area accessible to the public, may be constitutionally protected."

In practice, however, the Court has not always adhered to this approach. In several cases, the Supreme Court has concluded that people lack a reasonable expectation of privacy when they are observed in public. In crafting what is known as the "plain view" doctrine in *Harris v. United States* (1968), the Supreme Court held that "it has long been settled that objects falling in the plain view of an officer who has a right to be in the position to have that view are subject to seizure and may be introduced in evidence." In *Florida v. Riley* (1989), the Supreme Court held that a person lacked a reasonable expectation of privacy in his greenhouse where the roof was partially open to a view from above, thus allowing police flying overhead in a helicopter to peer inside.

People also lack a reasonable expectation of privacy in being overheard when speaking in a public place. In private places, however, if people cannot be seen or heard by others, then generally they will be deemed to have a reasonable expectation of privacy.

Consistent with the view that people lack a reasonable expectation of privacy in public, the Supreme Court has held that a person lacked a reasonable expectation of privacy when law enforcement officials installed a physical tracking device that monitored where he drove in his car. According to the Court in *United States v. Knotts* (1983), a "person traveling in an automobile on public thoroughfares has no reasonable expectation of privacy in his movements from one place to another." In contrast, a tracking device that monitored a person's movements in his home did infringe upon his reasonable expectation of privacy, according to the Court's decision in *United States v. Karo* (1984). While the movements in *Knotts* were in public, the movements within the residence were not, and this amounted to an impermissible search of the residence.

The police can use sensory enhancement technology to enhance what they can see or hear with the naked senses. In *Texas v. Brown* (1983), the Supreme Court held that using a flashlight to "illuminate a darkened area" did not implicate a reasonable expectation of privacy. In *Dow Chemical Co. v. United States* (1986), government officials flew over the defendant's property and used a high-tech aerial mapping camera to take photographs, which could then be magnified to reveal very small objects. The Supreme Court concluded that there was no reasonable expectation of privacy because the "mere fact that human vision is enhanced somewhat, at least to the degree here, does not give rise to constitutional problems."

There are instances, however, when using sensory enhancement technology can implicate a person's reasonable expectation of privacy. In *Kyllo v. United States* (2001), the police used a thermal imaging device to detect heat patterns coming from a person's home. The police did not enter the residence, and the device measured the heat that emanated from the residence. The Supreme Court nevertheless concluded that the defendant had a reasonable expectation of privacy because the device could be used to detect activities within his home.

The Supreme Court has also concluded that people lack a reasonable expectation of privacy in information exposed to third parties. This has become known as the third-party doctrine. For example, in *United States v. Miller* (1976), the Supreme Court held that people lack a reasonable expectation in their bank records because "[a]ll of the documents obtained, including financial statements and deposit slips, contain only information voluntarily conveyed to the banks and exposed to their employees in the ordinary course of business." Employing analogous reasoning in *Smith v. Maryland* (1979), the Supreme Court held that people lack a reasonable expectation of privacy in pen register information (the phone numbers they dial) because people "know that they must convey numerical information to the phone company," and therefore, they cannot "harbor any general expectation that the numbers they dial will remain secret." Similarly, in *California v. Greenwood* (1988), the Supreme Court concluded that people cannot have a reasonable expectation of privacy in trash left for collection on the curb because they "exposed their garbage to the public" and "placed their refuse at the curb for the express purpose of conveying it to a third party, the trash collector."

The third-party doctrine is hard to square with other Fourth Amendment doctrines. If a person is talking on the phone to another person, this does not eliminate either person's reasonable expectation of privacy, even though both are sharing information with each other. One of the parties to the conversation can betray the other, and people do not have a reasonable expectation that their confidantes will not communicate their secrets to the police. However, so long as both parties to the conversation resolve to keep the conversation private, then they will have a reasonable expectation of privacy so long as they do not speak in public or where it is audible to others. Nevertheless, if a person provides information to a bank or a company, then the person has been deemed to have relinquished his reasonable expectation of privacy—even if the bank of company desires to keep the information private. The Court has not explained why exposing information to a bank or company is different from exposing it to another speaker over the telephone.

The third-party doctrine also gives rise to some difficult issues in light of life in the Information Age. Countless companies maintain detailed records of people's personal information: Internet service providers, merchants, bookstores, phone companies, cable companies, and many more. According to the third-party doctrine, a person lacks a reasonable expectation of privacy in this information because it is possessed by third parties.

Taken together, the cases suggest that the Supreme Court believes that people lack a reasonable expectation whenever something is exposed to the public or to third parties. In other words, if a person keeps something a total secret, then he can reasonably expect it to be private. But once something is revealed in public or to others, then he can no longer reasonably expect privacy.

Methodologically, how does the Supreme Court determine whether there is a reasonable expectation of privacy? At first glance, the reasonable expectation test appears to be empirical—a reasonable expectation of privacy is an expectation that a majority of members in society deem reasonable. However, in applying the test, the Supreme Court has rarely looked to empirical evidence or to polls. Instead, the Supreme Court has typically applied its own notions of privacy.

In *Smith v. Maryland*, the Court acknowledged that the reasonable expectation of privacy test has a normative dimension:

> For example, if the Government were suddenly to announce on nationwide television that all homes henceforth would be subject to warrantless entry, individuals thereafter might not in fact entertain any actual expectation of privacy regarding their homes, papers, and effects. Similarly, if a refugee from a totalitarian country, unaware of this Nation's traditions, erroneously assumed that police were continuously monitoring his telephone conversations, a subjective expectation of privacy regarding the contents of his calls might be lacking as well. In such circumstances, where an individual's subjective expectations had been "conditioned" by influences alien to well-recognized Fourth Amendment freedoms, those subjective expectations obviously could play no meaningful role in ascertaining what the scope of Fourth Amendment protection was. In determining whether a "legitimate expectation of privacy" existed in such cases, a normative inquiry would be proper.

Perhaps the reasonable expectation of privacy test should measure whether privacy for a particular matter is normatively desirable, as expectations can erode over time as technology advances. On the other hand, under such an approach, who determines what is normatively desirable?

Even judges recognize that determining what is reasonable can be a vexing exercise and can trigger vehement disagreements between civil libertarians and privacy advocates on the one hand and national security and law enforcement interests on the other. As Jeremy Fogel, a district judge in California who also serves as the director of the Federal Judicial Center in Washington, D.C., wrote, the Fourth Amendment's protections against unreasonable searches and seizures are freighted with both legal and cultural meaning: "Although, from a purely legal standpoint, [Fourth amendment] constraints apply only to actions of the government, its underlying principles and assumptions also inform our common conception of the boundary between the public and private spheres. Today, however, as a result of technological change that continues to outstrip our collective cultural comprehension, defining what constitutes a 'reasonable expectation of privacy' has become enormously difficult. Lay understanding, legal authority, and technological reality often bear little resemblance to each other and frequently are in extreme tension."

Daniel J. Solove

Further Reading

Amsterdam, Anthony G. 1974. "Perspectives on the Fourth Amendment." *Minnesota Law Review* 58: 349–67.

Fogel, Jeremy. 2014. "From the Bench: A Reasonable Expectation of Privacy." *Litigation* 40 (4). http://www.americanbar.org/publications/litigation_journal/2013-14/spring/a_reasonable_expectation_privacy.html. Accessed September 18, 2015.

Slobogin, Christopher, and Joseph E. Schumacher. 1993. "Reasonable Expectations of Privacy and Autonomy in Fourth Amendment Cases: An Empirical Look at 'Understandings Recognized and Permitted by Society.'" *Duke Law Journal* 42: 727.

Solove, Daniel J. 2002. "Digital Dossiers and the Dissipation." *Southern California Law Review* 75: 1083.

Right to Financial Privacy Act (RFPA)

The Right to Financial Privacy Act (RFPA), passed into law in 1978 and made effective in March 1979, was crafted to provide customers of banks and other financial institutions with new privacy protections against government snooping. Its provisions included new regulations governing the actions of authorities seeking private financial records, a variety of mandates on banks and other financial institutions in terms of their handling of private financial records, and established avenues for private individuals whose financial records were being targeted for investigation to file formal objections to turning over such records. However, the RFPA did include a list of exceptional circumstances when official notification to customers was not required.

The RFPA constituted a significant advance in privacy rights. Prior to its passage, private individuals had no legal right to challenge government access to their personal financial information, nor did they have a right to be informed that their records were being examined by authorities. Indeed, private citizens had no legal right to expect privacy for any of their financial information held by financial institutions, according to rulings by the U.S. Supreme Court in *United States v. Miller* (1976) and *Fisher v. United States* (1976). In both of these cases, the Court reasoned that records developed or maintained as part of routine business practice by a third party—a person or institution other than the subject of those records—did not enjoy constitutional protection because the customer should not have any expectation that the record would remain protected from government scrutiny. After all, the records are *already* in the possession of a third party.

These decisions, however, came down at a time in U.S. history when the American public was reeling from Watergate and from Congressional investigations that revealed decades of widespread abuses of government power and violations of civil liberties by the Federal Bureau of Investigation, Central Intelligence Agency, and other intelligence and law enforcement agencies. The political environment in the late 1970s was thus ripe for a backlash against government intrusions into private life, and the architects of the RFPA took full advantage of that. The bipartisan bill, which was signed into law by President Jimmy Carter, included a wide variety of measures to better protect personal financial information from the prying of the government. According to the Electronic Privacy Information Center (EPIC), in fact, the law essentially "creat[ed] a statutory Fourth Amendment protection for bank records."

The RFPA contained three main pillars. First, it mandated that customers be informed before their bank, credit card, or other financial records were handed over to government investigators (in 2002, RFPA was amended to expand the definition of financial institutions from banks, credit unions, and credit card issuers to include money order issuers, securities and futures industries, casinos, and other institutions possessing private financial information). Second, the law gave private individuals the legal standing to challenge the release of their records. And third, it forced government investigators to thoroughly document how they used and distributed the information contained in the records.

When the RFPA first came into effect, some members of the law enforcement community warned that the new privacy protections would make it more difficult to uncover money laundering and other illegal activities by organized crime syndicates and to combat white-collar crime. In the 1980s, however, the law was amended to address some of those concerns. These changes established exceptional circumstances—especially in national security and drug trafficking cases—under which law enforcement could postpone or avoid notifying private citizens that their financial records were being sought.

In addition, from the outset the RFPA included provisions that gave financial institutions immunity from civil liability in return for reporting customers whose financial transactions were indicative of possible criminal behavior. These notifications to the government are made in the form of suspicious activity reports (SARs). Conditions that trigger mandatory reporting of a customer's financial data include any instance in which the financial institution discovers transactions believed to involve funds from illegal activities; hidden funds generated from illegal activities; transactions of no apparent lawful purpose; or funds generated from insider trading of financial knowledge. The RFPA explicitly defines transactions as any deposit, withdrawal, transfer, currency exchange, sale or purchase of investment security, loan, or extension of credit made by the customer. Finally, provisions of the RFPA include a requirement that all transactions involving more than $10,000 in cash be formally reported by the financial institution conducting the transaction, even if the transaction is not regarded as particularly unusual or suspicious for the individual in question.

The last significant revision to the RFPA came in 2001, in the aftermath of the terrorist attacks of September 11. Under Section 358 of the USA PATRIOT Act, financial institutions are legally required to disclose any personal financial information deemed relevant to counterterrorism efforts and investigations being carried out by the federal government.

Kevin Hillstrom

Further Reading

Electronic Privacy Information Center. n.d. "The Right to Financial Privacy Act." EPIC.org Web site. https://epic.org/privacy/rfpa/. Accessed May 5, 2015.

Federal Reserve Board. 2006. "Right to Financial Privacy Act." *Consumer Compliance Handbook.* http://www.federalreserve.gov/boarddocs/supmanual/cch/priv.pdf. Accessed May 5, 2015.

Schneier, Bruce. 2015. *Data and Goliath: The Hidden Battles to Collect Your Data and Control Your World.* New York: W.W. Norton.

S

Search Warrants

A search warrant is a written order issued by a judge (or other officer of a court) authorizing a law enforcement or other government official to search a person or location for illegal material (contraband) or for evidence of involvement in a crime under investigation. Warrants may include special aspects, such as no knock provisions that allow police to execute them without warning. Since searches are likely to be intrusive and disruptive of privacy, the requirement of a search warrant based on probable cause is one of the most important constitutional safeguards of privacy. Indeed, the Fourth Amendment's guarantee against unreasonable searches and seizures was one of the provisions of the Bill of Rights that Supreme Court justice William O. Douglas cited in his majority opinion in *Griswold v. Connecticut* (1965), the decision that made explicit a constitutional right to privacy.

Over the years, the meaning of the warrant clause and other aspects of the Fourth Amendment have been the subject of much interpretation by the courts. Those have dealt with questions such as what constitutes a search, what defines an unreasonable search, when searches may be conducted without warrants, and what satisfies the requirement of probable cause. Interpretation has usually taken place in a context characterized by tension between impatience with aspects of the law that constrain the police and concern that the privacy of the individual be respected.

The constitutional protection of privacy against unreasonable and seizures is grounded in the Fourth Amendment, which states that "the right of the people to be secure in their persons, houses, papers, and effects, against unreasonable searches and seizures, shall not be violated." The amendment further provides that "no Warrants shall issue, but upon probable cause, supported by Oath or Affirmation, and particularly describing the place to be searched, and the person or things to be seized."

The requirement of specificity was especially important to the framers of the Bill of Rights. The events leading to the American Revolution had seen widespread objections to British use of open-ended general warrants, both in United States by customs officials who used them (in the form of writs of assistance) to search for unnamed smuggled goods and in Britain where the government had used general warrants as a means of suppressing opposition journalist John Wilkes. Opposition to such searches had frequently cited the common law right to be left alone, another of the legal bases of the right to privacy.

As with the rest of the Bill of Rights, the Fourth Amendment was originally held to protect Americans from abuse by the federal government but was seen as not applicable to state authorities. During the course of the 20th century, most of the protections of the Bill of Rights were gradually incorporated into the Fourteenth Amendment's Due Process Clause and held to apply also to the states. The Supreme Court held the core of the Fourth Amendment to be applicable to the states in *Wolf v. Colorado* (1948).

A search originally was taken to mean a physical intrusion by an agent of government, particularly into lodging. The definition expanded dramatically during the last third of the 20th century. In the case of *Katz v. United States* (1967), the Supreme Court reversed earlier precedents to include wiretapping of conversations within the meaning of search, opening up a field in which the courts would struggle to stay abreast of proliferating eavesdropping technology. Also, considered searches are physical intrusions into the person, such as those necessary to obtain blood, breath, and DNA samples. However, the action of police who performs a stop and frisk or pat-down of a person deemed to act in a suspicious manner is not considered a search within the meaning of the Fourth Amendment.

One of the difficulties of interpreting the Fourth Amendment is that it has something of a split personality. The first part emphasizes the need to protect the individual from unreasonable searches and seizures, while the second stresses that warrants should issue only for probable cause. Some might argue that any search without a warrant issued for probable cause is unreasonable, but the amendment does not actually say this and the courts have not interpreted it in this fashion. The courts have long recognized that some types of searches do not require warrants. The crucial question thus becomes whether they are reasonable.

Typically, 20th-century courts relied on the standard of probable cause to define reasonableness. Since the 1980s, though, the standard has increasingly become whether an action violates the standard of a reasonable expectation of privacy. The phrase first occurred in the aforementioned *Katz* case in 1967, where it was used to extend the definition of search to include electronic eavesdropping. It has since been used more often to narrow the definition of what might be judged an unreasonable search. In effect, the court evaluates the balance between the weight of the government's interest in the search and the extent to which the individual's privacy interest is affected. In general, the courts tend to look most critically at actions that intrude on the interior of people's homes, while showing greater tolerance for government activities elsewhere. A farmer's fields or even a fenced backyard, for example, have been held not to be entitled to an expectation of privacy.

There is a long list of exceptions to the rule that searches should be based on warrants. In daily practice, many more searches are conducted without warrants than with them. These warrantless searches include (but are not necessarily limited to) a search incident to an arrest, search of a motor vehicle, inventory of personal effects of persons arrested, search of abandoned property (including garbage), evidence in plain view, consensual searches, searches at borders and airports, and searches in exigent circumstances (i.e. those where the delay in obtaining a warrant would make it impossible to conduct the search).

Probable cause is important both to the issuance of search warrants and to the justification for warrantless searches. Since many warrants are based on information supplied by police informants, establishing credibility of the source of information became a major concern. During the 1960s, there was a decided tendency toward tightening requirements for warrants and invoking rules of evidence similar to those used in trials. Police requesting warrants were expected to make clear both the circumstances in which the informant was likely to have gained useful information and the officer's reasons for believing it was true. In 1983, however, the Supreme Court decided in *Illinois v. Gates* that a more holistic judgment of the totality of circumstances was more practical. The Court has also held that administrative searches in workplaces and schools do not have to have warrants or meet the probable cause standard.

The tension between the needs of government and privacy concerns continues to provoke controversies. One of the most controversial aspects of the prohibition of unreasonable searches and seizures has been the exclusionary rule. This excludes from consideration evidence gathered in violation of the Fourth Amendment. This was first adopted by the federal courts in *Weeks v. United States* (1914) and subsequently applied to the states in *Mapp v. Ohio* (1961). The Court has, however, allowed some use of unconstitutionally obtained evidence, for example, in challenging the testimony of witnesses.

While most controversies in this area of privacy have grown out of the criminal justice system, an additional site of controversy has been the area of national security, particularly in the area of electronic surveillance. For example, in the aftermath of the September 11, 2001, attacks, President George W. Bush ordered intercepts of telephonic conversations of American citizens with foreigners suspected of terrorist connections in his authority as commander in chief. Not only did this involve the National Security Agency in spying on American citizens, it also bypassed the procedure set up by the Foreign Intelligence Surveillance Act (FISA) for seeking warrants for national security wiretaps. In such cases, the government argues that the national security requirements outweigh the privacy interests of individuals. When this warrantless wiretapping program became public knowledge, many Americans of various ideological persuasions expressed outrage. But despite condemnation on privacy grounds and warnings that the program had Orwellian overtones, the program was not ended. Instead, warrantless wiretapping belatedly received a veneer of legal cover through provisions in the FISA Amendments Act of 2008.

William C. Lowe

Further Reading

Bodemheimer, Davis J., and James W. Ely Jr., eds. 1993. *The Bill of Rights in Modern America after 200 Years.* Bloomington: Indiana University Press.

Feinman, Jay M. 2000. *Law 101. Everything You Need to Know about the American Legal System.* New York: Oxford University Press.

Sex Offender Registries

Sex offender registries (SORs) are databases of information about persons convicted of sex offenses that have completed their sentence or received probation and now reside in the community. SORs are primarily intended to help law enforcement agencies monitor the whereabouts of known sex offenders, thereby preventing crime as well as providing a pool of suspects to the police when a sex crime is reported. Depending on the jurisdiction, access to SORs may be restricted to criminal justice officials or made available, via formal community notification systems (CNSs), to community organizations and the general public to assist in the managing of risk to children and other vulnerable persons. SORS and CNSs are predicated on the notion that sex offenders, more than other kinds of offenders, have an enduring disposition to offend and should therefore have stringent restrictions placed on their rights to privacy and freedom of movement. SORs and CNSs reflect intense public concern about the risk of serious harm posed by sex offenders, particularly to the most vulnerable persons in society, such as women and children. These concerns also create strong pressure on politicians of all stripes to respond accordingly to public demand for action.

In 1990, the state of Washington passed its Community Protection Act in response to strong media and public reaction to a repeat child sex offender's brutal rape and mutilation of a seven-year-old boy. The SOR component of this legislation requires all convicted sex offenders to register with the police upon release from prison; the CNS component requires dissemination of information about registered offenders to community organizations and the general public. Who specifically receives information depends on a three-tier (high, moderate, and low) system of assessing the degree of risk posed by individual offenders.

Other states soon followed Washington's lead. Some states adopted Washington's systems of tiers of risk; other states treated all sex offenders as a single high-risk class. Of note is that the legislation creating SORs and CNSs took on the names of those child victims that advocates used to mobilize public reaction and governmental response. New Jersey's Megan's Law was triggered by the rape and murder of a seven-year-old girl, named Megan Kanka. Indiana's Zachary's Law, named after a 10-year-old boy murdered by a child molester, established the first SOR that could be accessed by the public via the Internet. Currently over 30 states permit similar online access to SORs.

In 1994, President Bill Clinton signed the Jacob Wetterling Act that required all states to set up SORs or have their criminal justice funding cut by 10 percent. In 1996, this was followed by the federal Megan's Law, which required all states to create CNSs, and the Pam Lychner Act, which created a national SOR linking state database to enable tracking of sex offenders across state lines.

Other countries followed the United States' lead in establishing SORs but declined to link them to CNSs. In 1997, the United Kingdom passed a civil statute, creating a SOR to help police solve sex crimes. In 2000, the Canadian province of Ontario enacted Christopher's Law. This was followed by a federal legislation setting up a national registry (NSOR) in 2004. In Canada's NSOR, strict rules with regard to access and disclosure currently require law enforcement personnel to meet the thresholds established under Section 16 of the Sex Offender Information Registration Act in order to access the registry and disclose information in it.

British and Canadian police and politicians resisted community notification legislation, arguing that it would impede the usefulness of registration as a law enforcement tool because the loss of liberty and privacy and the stigma entailed by community notification would reduce offender compliance with registration requirements.

While the specific characteristics of SORs and CNSs vary by jurisdiction, most share common features. Offenders convicted of identified sexual offences, once outside of prison, must initially provide and regularly update information about themselves to local police. When formally authorized, this information can legitimately be disseminated to community organizations and the general public. The information provided can include the following: home and employment contact information; identifying characteristics such as tattoos and scars; the types of offenses that triggered the need to register; personal information such as age, weight, and place of birth; vehicle make and license number; and recent photographs.

The length of time a released sex offender is required to register varies by jurisdiction, offense type, and offender type. Offenders convicted of multiple counts of child molestation may be required to register for life; those convicted of other offenses, depending on their seriousness, are required to register for shorter, fixed periods of time.

The decision as to whether a sex offender will be subject to registration also depends on the jurisdiction. In the United States, after receiving written notification, offenders who have completed their sentence or are on parole or probation are required to register with local police. In Canada, the decision is made, not at the time of release, but rather by the trial judge immediately after the imposition of sentence. In most circumstances, the prosecutor makes a formal request to the court for inclusion in the registry, and the trial judge then ultimately determines whether the offender will be subject to the registry and how long they will have to register upon release.

Opponents of SORs and CNSs point to the myriad pragmatic and civil libertarian difficulties that they pose. Opponents argue that sex offenders who have paid their debt to society should not have additional measures imposed upon them after sentence completion, should not have to share personal information, and should not be subject to any increased police scrutiny that an otherwise normal offender would avoid.

Opponents further argue that, even if one accepts that police should have access to sex offender information, the public should not have such access. When any interested person, in a jurisdiction with Internet access to its SOR, can access one's personal information by home computer, constitutionally protected privacy rights are seriously eroded. A tertiary concern stems from a slippery slope critique. If society chooses to invade the privacy rights of a particular offender group, what will stop them from invading the privacy of other offender groups? This critique contends that when the rights of one minority group are infringed the rights of all members of society are threatened.

There have been growing legal and political challenges regarding SORs since 2010. Concerns have been raised about how some registries indiscriminately lump dangerous rapists or child molesters with people guilty of nothing more than public urination, "sexting," or in the case of minor teens, consensual sex with boyfriends or girlfriends. "Of course anyone responsible for a sexual assault should be held accountable," says lawyer Nicole Pittman of Human Rights Watch, which reported 747,000 adult and youth sex offenders were registered nationwide on registries as of 2011. "But punishment should fit both the offense and the offender, and placing children who commit sex offenses on a public registry—often for life—can cause more harm than good." These harms can range from difficulty in finding gainful employment to harassment and violence from other members of their communities.

Mihael Cole and Michael Petrunik

Further Reading

Human Rights Watch. 2013. *Raised on the Registry: The Irreparable Harm of Placing Children on Sex Offender Registries in the U.S.* Human Rights Watch Web site. http://www.hrw.org/sites/default/files/reports/us0513_ForUpload_1.pdf. Accessed April 1, 2015.

Kabat, Alan. 1998. "Scarlet Letter Sex Offender Databases and Community Notification: Sacrificing Personal Privacy for a Symbol's Sake." *American Criminal Law Review* 35: 333.

Madden, Sean. 2008. *The Labeling of Sex Offenders: The Unintended Consequences of the Best Intentioned Public Policies*. Lanham, MD: University Press of America.

Petrunik, Michael. 2002. "Managing Unacceptable Risk: Sex Offenders, Community Response, and Social Policy in the United States and Canada." *International Journal of Offender Therapy and Comparative Criminology* 46: 483–511.

Snowden, Edward (1983–)

Edward Snowden is a former computer systems contractor for the National Security Agency (NSA) whose decision in 2013 to leak classified documents concerning a massive NSA surveillance program put him in the eye of a storm of controversy about the size, scope, and intrusiveness of government surveillance of private lives.

Edward Joseph Snowden was born on June 21, 1983, in Elizabeth City, North Carolina. His parents are Lonnie and Elizabeth (Wendy) Snowden; he has an older sister, Jessica. His father worked for the U.S. Coast Guard, and his mother works for the clerk's office at the U.S. District Court for the District of Maryland. They divorced in 2001. When Snowden was in grade school, his family moved to Crofton, Maryland, about 10 miles west of Annapolis. When he was a sophomore at Arundel High School, he suffered from mononucleosis and missed nine months of school. Rather than repeat the tenth grade, he dropped out and eventually passed his General Educational Development (GED) test, which gave him a high school graduation equivalency. He enrolled at Anne Arundel Community College, where he took classes from 1999 to 2005. During this time, he began to develop an interest in computers and technology. He never received a college degree.

Snowden enlisted in the U.S. Army Reserve in the Special Forces unit in May 2004 but was discharged nearly five months later after he broke both legs in a training exercise. In 2005, he worked as a security guard at the Center for Advanced Study of Language at the University of Maryland in College Park. He attended a job fair that focused on intelligence agencies and soon took a job at the Central Intelligence Agency (CIA) in 2006. His interest in computers landed him a job in

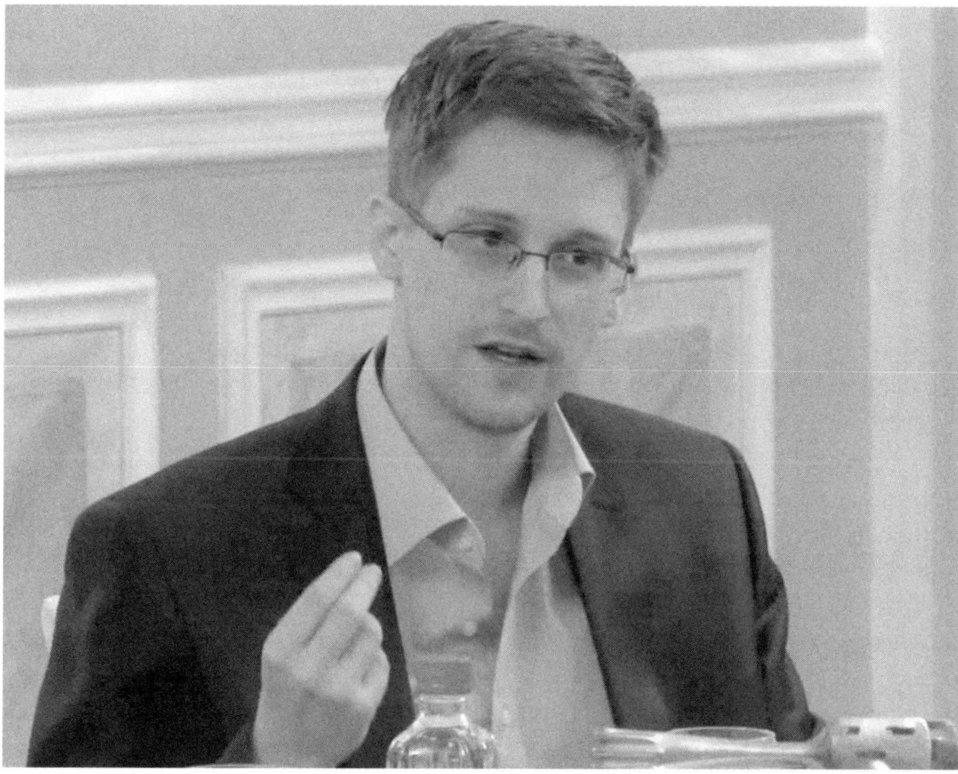

Former National Security Agency systems analyst Edward Snowden speaks in Moscow, Russia, on October 11, 2013. Should Snowden ever return to the United States, he would face criminal charges for leaking information about NSA surveillance programs. The "Snowden Effect" refers to the significant impact his revelations have had on the United States and perceptions of privacy and government surveillance. (AP Photo)

the global communications division. By March 2007, he was moved to a position, under diplomatic cover, in computer network security, based in Geneva, Switzerland. He was exposed to classified documents while in Switzerland and later told the *Guardian* that "much of what I saw in Geneva really disillusioned me about how my government functions and what its impact is in the world." He said he realized that he was "part of something that was doing far more harm than good." He worked in Switzerland for nearly two years before he left the CIA.

In 2009, he moved to Dell, where he worked as a contractor. Dell managed computer systems for various government agencies, including the NSA. He worked in Tokyo, Japan, where he supervised computer upgrading processes and learned about cyber counterintelligence. It was during this time that he learned about the NSA's surveillance programs. Snowden said the NSA was "intent on making every conversation and every form of behaviour in the world known to them."

His opinions about the value of the Internet began to change, as he saw the NSA's surveillance practices invade privacy. "I don't want to live in a world where there's no privacy and therefore no room for intellectual exploration and creativity." He began planning on making public the surveillance practices, because he viewed them as "an existential threat to democracy." He said: "You can't wait around for someone else to act. I had been looking for leaders, but I realized that leadership is about being the first to act."

Snowden moved back to Maryland in 2011 and a year later was transferred to an NSA office in Hawaii. He began downloading secret NSA documents in April 2012. By late 2012 and early 2013, he had made contact first with *Guardian* writer Glenn Greenwald and then with film documentary producer/director Laura Poitros. Snowden left Dell in March 2013 and took a job with Booz Allen Hamilton as a consultant specializing in infrastructure analysis. He later said that he took this job with the intent of obtaining evidence about the NSA's surveillance practices. In May, he took a leave from Booz Allen Hamilton, claiming he needed treatment for epilepsy.

On May 20, 2013, Snowden flew to Hong Kong, where he met with Greenwald, Poitros, and another *Guardian* reporter, Ewen MacAskill, in early June. On June 5, the *Guardian* published the first reports of Snowden's leaks: he claimed that the NSA was collecting phone records of Verizon customers. Two days later, the *Guardian,* as well as the *Washington Post*, published information Snowden had about the NSA's PRISM surveillance program, which captured Internet information from several U.S. telecommunications companies. Three days later, the *Guardian* revealed information about a tool used by the U.S. government called Boundless Informant, which was used to collect and track intelligence data country by country. On June 9, Snowden was revealed as the mystery informant, and two days later he was fired from Booz Allen Hamilton. The company claimed that Snowden's actions represented "a grave violation of the code of conduct and core values of our firm."

On June 14, the U.S. Justice Department announced a variety of criminal charges against Snowden, including "unauthorized communication of national defense information" and "willful communication of classified communications intelligence information to an unauthorized person," both of which constituted violations of the 1917 Espionage Act. Snowden soon left Hong Kong, with the intent of going to Ecuador, but he was stranded in a Moscow airport when his passport was rescinded by the U.S. government. He was granted temporary asylum by Russia.

Reaction to Snowden's actions was, predictably, extremely mixed. James Clapper, the U.S. director of national intelligence, said Snowden's revelations caused "huge, grave damage" to the intelligence efforts of the United States. U.S. secretary of state John Kerry called Snowden a fugitive from justice and said he should "man up" and return to the United States. The *New York Times,* on the other hand, praised Snowden's whistle-blowing and said his efforts had "done his country a great service" for reporting on the NSA's abuses. Indeed, advocates for Snowden insisted that he should not be regarded as a traitor but as a patriot standing up for rights enshrined in the U.S. Constitution.

Snowden has remained low-key in Russia; some say he is working as an information technology specialist. In August 2014, he received a three-year residency permit from Russia, which allows him to live there for up to three years, at which time, according to his lawyer, Anatoly Kucherena, he "will have to decide whether to continue to live in Russia and become a citizen or to return to the United States."

Meanwhile, there are some indications that the NSA bulk phone records collection and surveillance program revealed by Snowden may be coming to an end. On May 7, 2015, a federal appeals court unanimously ruled in *American Civil Liberties Union v. Clapper* that the program, which had always been defended by the Bush and Obama administrations as legal under Section 215 of the USA PATRIOT Act, was in fact blatantly illegal. Less than one week later, the House of Representatives passed a bill that would end the NSA's bulk collection of cell phone data from the American public. The measure passed by an overwhelming margin due to broad support from both Republicans and Democrats.

Lawrence W. Baker

Further Reading

Bamford, James. 2014. "Ed Snowden: The Most Wanted Man in the World." *Wired* (August 13). http://www.wired.com/2014/08/edward-snowden/. Accessed May 13, 2015.

Cole, Matthew, and Mike Brunker. "Edward Snowden: A Timeline." NBC News. http://www.nbcnews.com/feature/edward-snowden-interview/edward-snowden-timeline-n114871. Accessed May 13, 2015.

Friedersdorf, Conor. 2015. "The Vindication of Edward Snowden." *The Atlantic* (May 11). http://www.theatlantic.com/politics/archive/2015/05/the-vindication-of-edward-snowden/392741/. Accessed May 13, 2015.

Greenwald, Glenn, and Ewen MacAskill. 2013. "Boundless Informant: The NSA's Secret Tool to Track Global Surveillance Data." *The Guardian* (June 11). http://www.theguardian.com/world/2013/jun/08/nsa-boundless-informant-global-datamining. Accessed May 13, 2015.

Greenwald, Glenn, Ewen MacAskill, and Laura Poitras. 2013. "Edward Snowden: The Whistleblower behind the NSA Surveillance Revelations." *The Guardian* (June 11). http://www.theguardian.com/world/2013/jun/09/edward-snowden-nsa-whistleblower-surveillance. Accessed May 13, 2015.

Lam, Lana. 2013. "Snowden Sought Booz Allen Job to Gather Evidence on NSA Surveillance." *South China Morning Post* (June 24). http://www.scmp.com/news/hong-kong/article/1268209/snowden-sought-booz-allen-job-gather-evidence-nsa-surveillance?login=1. Accessed May 13, 2015.

Marbella, Jean, Shashank Bengali, and David S. Cloud. 2013. "Details about Edward Snowden's Life in Maryland Emerge." *Baltimore Sun* (June 10). http://articles.baltimoresun.com/2013-06-10/news/bs-md-snowden-profile-20130610_1_anne-arundel-county-arundel-high-the-guardian. Accessed May 13, 2015.

Stingray Tracking Technology

In recent years, police departments and federal agencies have been using technology known as Stingray tracking for surveillance purposes. The device is portable and mimics a cell phone tower. In the area surrounding the device, cell phones connect to the Stingray just as they would connect to a real cellular tower in the area. The Stingray collects information from the cell phones in the area, including incoming and outgoing phone calls and location information. Since the device is portable, officials simply transport it by car to the area they wish to surveil. In some instances, the Stingray is put on a plane and flown over the targeted area to collect information from a broader area.

Law enforcement officials use Stingray technology for a variety of purposes. The reason most often stated for the use of Stingrays is antiterrorism measures. However, it has been used more frequently to collect evidence to arrest and convict members of major drug operations. The technology has also occasionally been used to assist in solving high-profile murders or kidnappings, among other major crimes. Police state that Stingrays are the most useful in any case in which the suspect continually switches cell phones in order to sidestep efforts to wiretap their lines. The Stingray device allows law enforcement to gather information simply by being in the general vicinity of the person whose information they are trying to collect. The technology is also employed in situations where there is not enough evidence for police to obtain a search warrant.

Stingray technology is a highly controversial subject as its constitutionality is questionable. Regulations have not yet been set forth governing the use of Stingrays, and law enforcement often attempts to circumvent the process of obtaining a warrant by wording the technology as if it was a pen register rather than a tracking device collecting information on every cell phone within its radius. In this manner, they do not have to prove probable cause, nor must they specifically state the information they hope to obtain.

Another point of contention regarding Stingray technology is that it collects information on everyone within reach. The agents using the technology are not targeting a specific person. Police ensure that they do not keep the information gathered from people who are not suspects, but their reassurance means little because there is no way to be certain that the information is, in fact, discarded. People are also afraid that the Stingray device is being used to eavesdrop on phone calls or read e-mails and text messages. Again, police assert that this is not the case, but a Stingray model that enables eavesdropping does exist. The Stingray operations are kept in such secrecy that no one can be certain of the ways police are using the technology. Evidence has recently emerged that states that police departments seeking access to Stingray devices must sign a nondisclosure agreement, pledging not to divulge information about the technology and how it is used.

Federal judges seem to be in disagreement about how the technology should be treated. One magistrate judge states that because officials did not actually install the device on someone's private property and because the individual being searched employed the services of a third party (cell phone service provider), no Fourth Amendment rights were violated and the use of the technology could continue without the need for a warrant. Another magistrate judge disagrees, stating that officials need a warrant because the technology is not simply a pen register; it is also a tracking device. He also states that when permission to use Stingrays is requested, the verbiage is so vague that the judges who sign them may not be fully aware of the permissions they are granting.

Many people, proponents and critic alike, are calling for tighter regulations for Stingray technology. Too much is being kept hidden, which could be quite dangerous. Some judges are requiring investigators to reveal the details of the cell phone tracking technology they employ. Other judges are demanding requests for specific permission to utilize Stingrays. Still, there are no uniform regulations, and many think that it is only a matter of time before a case is brought to the Supreme Court, which will force more transparency upon the technology.

Grace Vandemark

Further Reading

Bartley, Lisa. 2014. "Investigation: Law Enforcement Use Secret 'Stingray' Devices to Track Cell Phone Signals." *ABC 7* (December 3). http://abc7.com/news/investigation-law-enforcement-use-secret-devices-to-track-cell-phone-signals/421190/. September 18, 2015.

Stone, Jeff. 2014. "Police Departments in 18 States Use 'Stingray' Tech to Track Cell Phones. But They Won't Talk About It." *International Business Times* (September 24). http://www.ibtimes.com/police-departments-18-states-use-stingray-tech-track-cell-phones-they-wont-talk-about-it-1694552. Accessed September 18, 2015.

Walker, Clarence. 2013. "New Hi-Tech Police Surveillance: The 'Stingray' Cell Phone Spying Device." *Global Research* (April 13). http://www.globalresearch.ca/new-hi-tech-police-surveillance-the-stingray-cell-phone-spying-device/5331165. Accessed September 18, 2015.

Stop and Frisk

Also known as an investigatory detention, a stop and frisk occurs when law enforcement officers stop, question, and pat down a suspicious person. Although the detention is a form of seizure and the pat-down is a form of search, courts do not require police to have probable cause before conducting a stop and frisk. Rather, this tactic is permitted on the lesser standard of reasonable suspicion.

In *Terry v. Ohio* (1968), the Supreme Court upheld the authority of police officers to detain and conduct a limited pat-down search of several men who were acting suspiciously. The Court held that brief detention was justified by the reasonable suspicion of the experienced police officer; the pat-down search was reasonable to protect the officer and others nearby in case the suspects were armed. A decade later, in *Ybarra v. Illinois* (1979), the Court stressed the narrow scope of the pat-down procedure by saying that "nothing in *Terry* can be understood to allow . . . any search whatever for anything but weapons."

Although the original justification of the pat-down search was the need to locate concealed weapons, police often retrieve contraband discovered during pat-downs. In *Minnesota v. Dickerson* (1993), the Supreme Court held that police may seize contraband detected through their sense of touch during a pat-down. Writing for a unanimous Court, Justice Byron White concluded, "If a police officer lawfully pats down a suspect's outer clothing and feels an object whose contour or mass makes its identity immediately apparent, there has been no invasion of the suspect's privacy beyond that already authorized by the officer's search for weapons; if the object is contraband, its warrantless seizure would be justified by the same practical considerations that adhere in the plain-view context."

What Constitutes Reasonable Suspicion?

In *Terry v. Ohio*, the Supreme Court said that in determining whether an officer had reasonable suspicion to conduct a stop and frisk courts must not consider the officer's "inchoate and unparticularized suspicion" but rather "the specific reasonable inferences which he is entitled to draw from the facts in light of his experience." Writing for the Court in *Illinois v. Wardlow* (2000), Chief Justice

William H. Rehnquist observed that although reasonable suspicion "is a less demanding standard than probable cause and requires a showing considerably less than preponderance of the evidence, the Fourth Amendment requires at least a minimal level of objective justification for making the stop." More recently, in *United States v. Arvizu* (2002), the Court said that courts are not to view in isolation the factors upon which police officers develop reasonable suspicion, but rather should consider all of an officer's observations, giving appropriate weight to any inferences drawn by an officer based on his or her training or experience.

Common situations in which officers have been held to have reasonable suspicion include those in which suspects match descriptions of persons who are already wanted by the police, those in which persons appear unusually nervous or agitated when encountering the police, and those where suspects are in possession of unusual items associated with particular crimes (such as burglar's tools). In the *Wardlow* case, the Supreme Court held that the fact that the suspect ran away when approached by the police was grounds for reasonable suspicion, especially in light of the fact that the area was one known for drug trafficking. In *United States v. Sokolow* (1989), the Court held that the police had reasonable suspicion to detain a traveler whose behavior matched a drug courier profile. On the other hand, reasonable suspicion cannot be based on the fact that a person declines to answer questions, refuses to consent to a search, or is a member of a particular racial or ethnic minority.

Investigatory Detention of Automobiles

Courts have routinely applied the stop-and-frisk doctrine to stops of vehicles as well as individuals. In *Delaware v. Prouse* (1979), the Supreme Court implicitly upheld this extension of *Terry*, assuming police have reasonable suspicion that criminal activity is underway. Normally, an officer making an automobile stop will examine the suspect's driver's license, vehicle registration, and license plate. A computer check can reveal whether there are any outstanding warrants on the driver, whether the license has been suspended or revoked, or whether the automobile has been reported stolen. Normally, the officer will also visually scan the driver, any passengers, and any objects in plain view inside the vehicle. Such visual scans sometimes provide probable cause to make an immediate arrest or conduct a warrantless automobile search. Even in the absence of probable cause, an officer may be justified in conducting a limited automobile search based on reasonable suspicion. In *Michigan v. Long* (1983), the Supreme Court held that when police stop an automobile based on reasonable suspicion, they may search the passenger compartment for weapons, assuming they have reason to believe that a suspect is armed and dangerous.

Requests for Identification during So-Called Terry-Stops

The Fifth Amendment prohibits compulsory self-incrimination, which the courts have interpreted as providing a "right to remain silent" in the face of police interrogation (see, e.g., *Miranda v. Arizona* (1966)). In his concurring opinion in *Terry v. Ohio*, Justice Byron White noted that while ". . . nothing in the Constitution . . . prevents a policeman from addressing questions to anyone on the streets, . . . the person stopped is not obliged to answer. . . ."

Many states have long had laws that make it a misdemeanor for persons to refuse to identify themselves when asked to do so by police. In *Brown v. Texas* (1979), the Supreme Court held that such a law could not be constitutionally applied in the absence of reasonable suspicion that the individual who was asked for identification was engaged in or had engaged in criminal conduct. More recently, in *Hiibel v. Sixth Judicial District Court of Nevada* (2004), the Court split 5–4 in upholding a Nevada statute requiring a person detained by police under suspicious circumstances to identify himself. The Court held that, as long as there is reasonable suspicion, requiring identification from a suspect is consistent with the Fourth Amendment as interpreted in *Terry v. Ohio*. The Court also rejected the argument that the law violated the Fifth Amendment, finding that, in most instances, identifying oneself to the police poses no serious threat of self-incrimination. In dissent, Justice John P. Stevens protested that "[a] person's identity obviously bears informational and incriminating worth" and concluded that it should be protected by the Fifth Amendment.

John M. Scheb II

Further Reading

Dudley, Eric C., Jr. 1998. "*Terry v. Ohio*, the Warren Court and the Fourth Amendment: A Law Clerk's Perspective." *St. John's Law Review* 72: 891.

Epps, Charles R., Steven Maynard-Moody, and Donald Haider-Merkel. 2014. *Pulled Over: How Police Stops Define Race and Citizenship*. Chicago: University of Chicago Press.

Scheb, John M., and John M. Scheb II. 2006. *Criminal Procedure*. Belmont, CA: Thomson/Wadsworth.

Stephens, Otis H., Jr., and Richard A. Glenn. 2006. *Unreasonable Searches and Seizures: Rights and Liberties under the Law*. Santa Barbara, CA: ABC-CLIO.

Surveillance

Perhaps it is fitting that the topic of surveillance, so shrouded in intrigue, is often ambiguous and misunderstood. One error involves the common tendency to see surveillance as the opposite of privacy. Another is to associate it only with government and law and order activities in particular. Privacy and surveillance can be interwoven. Viewed in social process terms they are different sides of the same coin. Surveillance may be the means of crossing borders that protect privacy. This is illustrated by strong public concern with the nefarious and multifarious electronic, chemical, and database means of collecting personally identifiable information without the individual's knowledge and consent. Yet surveillance can also be the means of protecting privacy. Consider the passwords and audit trails required to use some databases or various defensive measures such as a perimeter video camera to protect the home. Whether we see surveillance or privacy invasion partly depends on the point of view taken.

Considered in the abstract, it is difficult to reach broad conclusions about the appropriateness of either surveillance or privacy. They can be socially desirable as well as destructive. Surveillance can serve goals of protection, administration, rule compliance, documentation, and strategy, as well as goals involving inappropriate manipulation, restricted life opportunities, social control, and spying. Privacy can not only be central to an individual's dignity and liberty and to intimacy, honest communication, and group borders and democracy, but it can also hide socially destructive behavior (e.g., abuse within families and white-collar crime).

With the development of new communication and computer technologies and new ways of living that increasingly rely on non-face-to-face forms of interaction, questions of personal information have taken on new social significance. The microchip and computer are of course central to surveillance developments and in turn reflect broader social forces set in motion with industrialization involving empirical documentation, rationality, bureaucracy, and capitalism. The increased availability of personal information is one strand in the constant expansion in knowledge witnessed in recent centuries and in the centrality of information to the workings of contemporary society.

The dictionary defines surveillance as "close observation, especially of a suspected person" or persons. Consider an example such as that of an individual suspected of bank robbery who is discreetly followed by police and is apprehended after robbing another bank or the discovery that a leader of an antiglobalization protest movement is a police informer.

The above examples are instances of *traditional surveillance* and the dictionary definition fits. Yet it is too narrow. The focus of surveillance goes beyond suspects, crime, and national security. To varying degrees, surveillance is a property of any social system—from two friends to a workplace to the government. Consider for example a supervisor monitoring an employee's productivity; a doctor assessing the health of a patient; a parent observing a child at play in the park; the driver of a speeding car asked to show a driver's license; or a voyeur. Each of these also involves surveillance.

Information boundaries and contests are found in all societies and beyond that in all living systems. Humans are curious and also seek to protect their informational borders, even as they must also reveal their information. To survive, individuals and groups engage in, and guard against, surveillance. Seeking information about others (whether within or beyond one's group) is characteristic of all societies, as are efforts to protect information.

However, the form, content, and rules about information vary considerably. In the case of surveillance for example, it can take such forms as relying on informers, intercepting smoke signals, taking satellite photographs, gathering information from cookies placed on the computers of Internet users, or mapping the spread of a contagious disease. The traditional forms of surveillance contrast in important ways with what can be called the *new surveillance*, a form that became increasingly prominent toward the end of the 20th century. The new social surveillance can be defined as "scrutiny through the use of technical means to extract or create personal or group data, whether from individuals or contexts." Examples include video cameras; computer matching, profiling, and data mining; work, computer, and electronic location monitoring; DNA analysis; drug tests; brain scans for lie detection; various self-administered tests and thermal and other forms of imaging to reveal what is behind walls and enclosures. The use of technical means to extract and create the information implies the ability to go beyond what is offered to the unaided senses or voluntarily reported. Much new surveillance involves an automated process and extends the senses and cognitive abilities through using material artifacts or software.

Using the broader verb "scrutinize" rather than "observe" in the definition calls attention to the fact that contemporary forms often go beyond the visual image to involve sound, smell, motion, numbers, and words. The eyes do contain the vast majority of the body's sense receptors and the visual is a master metaphor for the other senses (e.g., saying "I see" for understanding). Yet the eye as the major means of direct surveillance is increasingly joined or replaced by other means. The use of multiple senses and sources of data is an important characteristic of much of the new surveillance.

Traditionally, surveillance involved close observation by a person, not a machine. But with contemporary practices, surveillance may be carried out from afar, as with satellite images or the remote monitoring of communications and work. Nor need it be close as in detailed—much initial surveillance involves superficial scans looking for patterns of interest to be pursued later in greater detail. Surveillance has become both farther away and closer than previously. It occurs with sponge-like absorbency and laser-like specificity.

In a striking innovation, surveillance is also applied to contexts (geographical places and spaces, particular time periods, networks, systems, and categories of person), not just to a particular person whose identity is known beforehand.

Moreover, the new surveillance technologies are often applied *categorically* (e.g., all employees are drug-tested or travelers are searched rather than those there is some reason to suspect).

Traditional surveillance often implied a noncooperative relationship and a clear distinction between the object of surveillance and the person carrying it out. In an age of servants listening behind closed doors, binoculars, and telegraph interceptions, that separation made sense. It was easy to distinguish the watcher from the person watched. Yet for the new surveillance with its expanded forms of self-surveillance and cooperative surveillance, the easy distinction between agent and subject of surveillance can be blurred.

In related forms, subjects may willingly cooperate—submitting to personal surveillance in order to have consumer benefits (e.g., frequent flyer and shopper discounts) or for convenience (e.g., fast track lanes on toll roads in which fees are paid in advance). Implanted chips transmitting identity and location, which were initially offered for pets, are now available for their owners (and others) as well. In some work settings, smart badges worn by individuals do the same thing, although not with the same degree of voluntarism.

Beyond the individual forms, surveillance at an aggregate level is central to social management. The careful tracking of behavior through computer records (referred to by Roger Clarke as *dataveillance)* is believed to offer a more rational and efficient approach to social organization and control. The new surveillance relative to traditional surveillance has low visibility or is invisible. Manipulation as against direct coercion has become more prominent. Monitoring may be purposefully disguised as with a video camera hidden in a teddy bear or in a clock. Or it may simply come to be routinized and taken for granted as data collection is integrated into everyday activities (e.g., use of a credit card for purchases automatically conveys information about consumption, time, and location).

With the trend toward ubiquitous computing, surveillance and sensors in one sense disappear into ordinary activities and objects—automobiles, cell phones, toilets, buildings, clothing, and even bodies. The relatively labor-intensive bar code on consumer goods, which requires manually scanning, may soon be replaced with inexpensive embedded radio frequency identification (RFID) computer chips that can be automatically read from short distances. The remote sensing of preferences and behavior offers many advantages such as controlling temperature and lighting in a room or reducing shipping and merchandising costs, while also generating records that can be used for surveillance.

There may be only a short interval between the discovery of the information and the automatic taking of action. The individual as a subject of data collection and analysis may also almost simultaneously become the object of an intervention, whether this involves the triggering of an alarm or the granting (or denial) of some form of access, for example, to enter through a locked door, use a computer, or make a purchase.

The new forms are relatively inexpensive per unit of data collected. Relative to traditional forms, it is easy to combine visual, auditory, text, and numerical data. It is relatively easier to organize, store, retrieve, analyze, send, and receive data. Data are available in real time and data collection can be continuous and offer information on the past, present, and future (à la statistical predictions). Simulated models of behavior are created. The new surveillance is more comprehensive, intensive, and extensive. The ratio of what the individual knows about him or herself relative to what the surveilling organization knows is lower than in the past, even if objectively much more is known.

Surveillance Structures and Processes

Surveillance can be analyzed by breaking it into components. These tell us where to look and what to measure. This can help in identifying the variation that is central to explanation, understanding, and evaluation. We can differentiate structures that are fixed at one point in time (such as a photograph) from processes that involve interaction and developments over time (such as a video). Let us first consider some surveillance structures.

Organizational surveillance is distinct from the *nonorganizational surveillance* carried about by individuals. As James Rules has noted, modern organizations are the driving forces in the instrumental collection of personal data. As organizations increasingly use personal data for what David Lyon calls social sorting, the implications for many aspects of life are profound—whether involving work, consumption, health, travel, or liberty. At the organizational level, formal surveillance involves a *constituency*. This term is used broadly to refer to those with some rule-defined relationship or potential connection to the organization. This may involve formal membership or merely contact with the organization as through renting a video or showing a passport at a border.

Organizations have varying degrees of internal and external surveillance. Erving Goffman has identified many kinds of employee or inmate monitoring, such as within total institutions. These offer examples of the *internal constituency surveillance* found in organizations. Here individuals belong to the organization in a double sense. First, they belong as members. But they also in a sense are belongings of the organization. They are directly subject to its control in ways that nonmembers are not. We can often see a loose analogy to the ownership of property.

External constituency surveillance is present when those who are watched have some patterned contact with the organization, for example, as customers, patients, malefactors, or citizens subject to laws of the state. Those observed do not belong to the organization the way that an employee or inmate does. Credit card companies and banks, for example, monitor client transactions and also seek potential clients by mining and combining databases.

The control activities of a government agency charged with enforcing health and safety regulations is another example. In this case, the organization is responsible for seeing that categories of person subject to its rules are in compliance, even though they are not members of the organization. The same compliance function can be seen with nongovernmental organizations that audit, grant ratings, licenses, and certifications.

In the case of *external nonconstituency surveillance*, organizations monitor their broader environment in watching other organizations and social trends. The rapidly growing field of business intelligence seeks information about competitors, social conditions, and trends that may affect an organization. One variant of this is industrial espionage. Organizational planning (whether by government or the private sector) also requires such data, although this is usually treated in the aggregate instead of in personally identifiable form.

Personal surveillance, in which an individual watches another individual (whether for protection, strategic, or prurient reasons) apart from an organizational role, is another major form. It may involve *role-relationship surveillance* as with family members (parents and children, the suspicious spouse) or friends looking out for and looking at each other (e.g., monitoring location through a cell phone). Or it can involve *non-role-relationship surveillance*—consider the free-floating activities of the voyeur whose watching is unconnected to a legitimate role.

With respect to the roles that are played, we can identify the *surveillance agent* (watcher/observer/seeker). The person about whom information is sought is a *surveillance subject*. All persons of course play both roles, although hardly in the same form or degree. These changes depending on the context and over the life cycle; the roles are sometimes blurred and may overlap.

Within the surveillance agent category, the surveillance function may be *central* to the role, as with police, private detectives, spies, work supervisors, and investigative reporters. Or it may simply be a *peripheral* part of a broader role whose main goals are elsewhere. Illustrative of this are checkout clerks who are trained to look for shoplifters or dentists who are encouraged (or required) to report suspected child abuse when seeing bruises on the face.

A distinction rich with empirical and ethical implications is whether the situation involves those who are a party to the generation and collection of data (*direct participants*) or involves *third parties*. Third parties may legitimately obtain personal information through contracting with the surveillance agent (e.g., to carry out drug tests or to purchase consumer preference lists). Or information may be obtained because confidentiality is violated by the agent or because an outsider illegitimately obtains it (wiretapping, hacking, or corrupting those with the information).

The presence of third parties raises an important secondary use issue—that is, can data collected for one purpose be used without an individual's permission for unrelated purposes? In Europe, the answer generally is no. In the United States, where a much freer market in personal information exists, there are fewer restrictions. Large organizations warehouse and sell vast amounts of very personal information without the consent and with no direct benefit to the subject.

Surveillance can also be analyzed with respect to whether it is *nonreciprocal* or *reciprocal*. Surveillance that is reciprocal may be *asymmetrical* or *symmetrical* with respect to means and goals. In a democratic society, citizens and government engage in reciprocal, but distinct forms of mutual surveillance. Citizens can watch government through Freedom of Information Requests, open hearings and meetings, and conflict of interest and other disclosures required as a condition for running for office. However, citizens cannot legally wiretap, carry out Fourth Amendment searches, or see others' tax returns. In bounded settings, such as a protest demonstration, there may be greater equivalence with respect to particular means; for example, police and demonstrators may videotape each other.

Agent-initiated surveillance, which is particularly characteristic of compliance checks such as an inspection of a truck or a boat, can be differentiated from *subject-initiated surveillance*, such as submitting one's transcript, undergoing osteoporosis screening, or applying for a job requiring an extensive background investigation. In these cases, the individual makes a claim or seeks help and essentially invites or at least agrees to scrutiny.

With agent-initiated surveillance, the goals of the organization are always intended to be served. Yet this need not necessarily conflict with the interests of the subject; consider for example the protection offered by school crossing guards or efficient library service dependent on good circulation records. Public health and medical surveillance have multiple goals, protecting the community as well as the individual. Efficiently run companies provide jobs and services. Providing a limited amount of personal information on a warranty form and having a chip record usage of an appliance such as a lawn mower or a car may serve the interests of both consumers and businesses (e.g., being notified if the manufacturer finds a problem or offering proof of correct usage if the device fails).

Subject-initiated surveillance may reflect goals that serve the interests of the initiator, but they often overlap the goals of the surveilling organization. Consider some protection services that have the capability to remotely monitor home and business interiors (video, audio, heat, gas, motion detection) or health systems for remotely monitory the elderly and ill (e.g., an alarm sent if the refrigerator of a person living alone is not opened after 24 hours). As forms more likely to involve informed consent, these are less controversial than secretly generated agent surveillance. What is good for the organization may also be good for the individual, though that is not always the case and of course depends on the context.

Surveillance Processes

Let us briefly consider several surveillance processes. Rather than being static and fixed at one point in time, surveillance can be viewed as a fluid, ongoing process that involves interaction and strategic calculations over time. Part of the fascination of the study of surveillance lies in its dynamic nature, as groups in conflict relationships reciprocally and continuously adjust their tactics to each other. Here we also see the moral ambivalence that infuses the topic as a result of conflicting values and social interests.

The *myth of surveillance* involves creating and sustaining the belief through the mass media that a technique is omnipresent and omnipotent. As a police officer said, "We want them to think that we are everywhere, all the time and know everything." When such literal watching (whether real or metaphorical) isn't possible, there is an effort to create uncertainty about whether or not surveillance is present. This is presumed to be a deterrent. Of course, in a complex world of conflicting interests, unexpected developments and technology that breaks perfect knowledge and control are rarely possible. New conditions may appear and efforts to resist surveillance are common.

A number of *behavioral techniques of neutralization*—strategic moves by which subjects of surveillance seek to subvert the collection of personal information—can be noted. Among these are direct refusal, discovery, avoidance, switching, distorting, countersurveillance, cooperation, blocking, and masking. Responses to drug testing illustrate most of these.

One type of it is *refusal*—just saying no or feigning an inability to offer the sample in spite of trying. Social systems often leak, and the date of a supposed random or surprise test or search can sometimes be inferred involving a *discovery* move. Employees may receive notice of a test. Such foreknowledge permits *avoidance* moves involving abstinencc, thc hiding or dcstroying of incriminating material, not going to work on that day, or leaving early because one is ill. With *switching*, drug-free urine (whether purchased commercially in liquid or powdered form or obtained from a friend) replaces the person's own. *Distorting responses* (e.g., diuretics and commercially available detox prodcuts) manipulate the surveillance collection process so that while offering technically valid results invalid inferences are drawn. Given the empathy and the multiplicity of actors and interests in complex organizations, various *cooperative* moves in which controllers aid those purportedly controlled may also be seen.

Countersurveillance involves an ironic turning of the tables in which the very technologies used to control others come to be used to advance the interests of those controlled. Thus, while facing a urine drug test, employees can first experiment at home, testing themselves with a variety of readily available products like those used in the official test. The wide availability of new tools, such as covert audio and video recording, offers the surveilled the chance to turn the usual stratification tables. The resulting data can be used defensively or to coerce those in positions of authority. Consider, for example, the potential for the documentation of unwanted sexual advances and police abuse.

Another set of processes involves decisions about whether or not to surveil and if so which technique to use, how to apply it and to whom (e.g., on everyone, randomly, or selectively based on criteria), whether or not the surveilled are informed of and have any say in it, how the data are used, who will have access to it, its degree of security, and how long it will be kept. The social scientist seeks to identify and explain these patterns and their prior correlates.

Such decisions have consequences. Subsequent developments can be contingent on the choices made. For example, some techniques that can be narrowly applied such as DNA for identification purposes will require the creation of large databases against which a sample can be compared. A decision to watch everyone (categorical suspicion) avoids claims of discrimination in targeting, but is more expensive and can lead to a sense of privacy invasion, as there is no predicate for the watching.

Another aspect of process involves the path or "career" of surveillance events. In many, perhaps a majority, of cases no action follows from surveillance, as nothing of interest is discovered. The surveillance is intended to serve a scarecrow function or simply to generate a documentary record. Information may be saved until it is needed or a critical amount has been obtained. Or occasionally too much is discovered to act on or the surveilled can exert counterpressure to prevent action from being taken.

Yet techniques too have careers. The surveillance appetite can be insatiable and often shows a tendency to expand to new goals, agents, subjects, and forms. Awareness of this requires asking of any new tactic, regardless of how benignly it is presented as both means and ends: "Where might it lead?" The expansion of a technology introduced in a limited fashion can often be seen. Extensions beyond the initial use, whether reflecting *surveillance creep* or in many cases *surveillance gallop*, are common. There may be new uses for the data. Consider, for example, the Social Security number that Congress intended only to be used for tax purposes, which has become a de facto national ID number, or the video surveillance cameras, once restricted to prisons and high-security areas, which are now found in offices, shopping malls, homes, public spaces, and over roadways and other transportation corridors.

New surveillance agents and subjects may appear. A common process is a progression from use on animals to prisoners, criminal suspects, noncitizens, the ill, and children and then throughout the society. Tactics developed by government for defense and law enforcement spread to manufacturing and commercial uses and then to uses in interpersonal relations by friends, family, and others. Consider the expansion of drug testing from the military to sensitive categories such as transportation workers to the workforce at large and then even to parents testing their children. Other technological innovations, from global positioning satellites to airborne surveillance drones, have expanded rapidly as well.

We can sometimes note a rarely studied phenomenon of *surveillance contraction.* Widely used tactics may come to be less used as a result of political controversy, the development of regulations and unintended consequences, or as better tactics are developed. For example, congressional legislation in 1988 severely restricted the use of the polygraph for employment purposes.

What Is to Be Done?

Social understanding and moral evaluation require attending to the varied contexts and goals of surveillance. The many settings and forms and processes of surveillance preclude any easy explanations or conclusion.

Two broad contrasting views of the new surveillance can be identified. One view holds that surveillance technology is inherently inhuman, destructive of liberty, and untrustworthy because in the end the technology is controlled by people who are prone to using such data in immoral or illegal ways.

A more optimistic view places great faith in the power of this technology, which is seen to be neutral, to keep people safe and maintain a more secure and ordered society. We want both liberty and order. We seek privacy and often anonymity, but we also know that secrecy can hide dastardly deeds and that visibility can bring accountability and we value freedom of expression. But too much visibility may inhibit experimentation, creativity, and risk taking.

As with any value-conflicted and varied-consequence behavior, particularly those that involve conflicting rights and needs, it is essential to keep the tensions ever in mind. Occasionally, when wending through competing values, the absolutist, no-compromise, don't-cross-this-personal-line, or always-cross-it standard is appropriate. But more often compromise (if rarely a simplistic perfect balance) is required. When privacy and civil liberties are negatively affected, it is vital to acknowledge rather than to deny this, as is so often the case. Such honesty can make for more informed decisions and it also serves an educational function.

Surveillance practices are shaped by manners, organizational policies and laws, and available technologies. These draw on a number of background value principles and tacit assumptions about the empirical world, which need to be analyzed. Whatever action is taken, there is likely costs, gains, and trade-offs. At best, we can hope to find a compass rather than a map and a moving equilibrium rather than a fixed point for decision-making.

Gary T. Marx

Further Reading

Allen, Anita. 2003. *Why Privacy Isn't Everything: Feminist Reflections on Accountability for Private Life*. Lanham, MD: Rowman and Littlefield.

Angwin, Julia. 2014. *Dragnet Nation: A Quest for Privacy, Security, and Freedom in a World of Relentless Surveillance*. New York: Times Books.

Bennett, Colin, and Rebecca Grant, eds. 1999. *Visions of Privacy*. Toronto: University of Toronto Press.

Brinn, David. 1999. *The Transparent Society*. New York: Perseus.

Clarke, Roger. 1988. "Information Technology and Dataveillance." *Communications of the ACM* 31: 498–512.

Diebert, Ronald J. 2013. *Black Code: Inside the Battle for Cyberspace*. Oxford, UK: Signal.

Gandy, Oscar. 1993. *The Panoptic Sort: A Political Economy of Personal Information*. Boulder, CO: Westview Press.

Gilliom, John, and Torin Monahan. 2012. *SuperVision: An Introduction to the Surveillance Society*. Chicago: University of Chicago Press.

Greenwald, Glenn. 2014. *No Place to Hide: Edward Snowden, the NSA, and the U.S. Surveillance State*. New York: Metropolitan Books.

Lyon, David. 2001. *The Electronic Eye: The Rise of Surveillance Society*. Cambridge, UK: Polity/Blackwell.

Marguilis, Steven T. 2003. "Contemporary Perspectives on Privacy: Social, Psychological, Political." *Journal of Social Issues* 59: 243–61.

Solove, Daniel J. 2004. *The Digital Person*. New York: NYU Press.

Staples, William G. 2000. *Everyday Surveillance: Vigilance and Visibility in Postmodern Life*. Lanham, MD: Rowan and Littlefield.

Zureik, Elia, and Mark Salter. 2005. *Global Surveillance and Policing*. Devon, UK: Wilan.

Surveillance Cameras

Surveillance systems that use video cameras to monitor activities in specific locations (both public and private spaces) have become ubiquitous in many parts of the world. Early in its development, this technology, which transfers footage from video cameras to specific monitoring systems, was sometimes also called closed-circuit television (CCTV) in recognition of the fact that the signal carrying these images is not publicly transmitted, unlike broadcast television. First implemented on a widespread basis to monitor public spaces in Great Britain, investments in these systems soared in the United States after the terrorist attacks of September 11, 2001, and the surveillance camera systems are proliferating rapidly in countries such as China and India, where population growth and economic expansion and modernization are feeding demand. "In thirty years camera surveillance grew from an unknown, non-issue to a frequently taken-for-granted 'necessity' on the street, in shopping malls, office buildings and factories, in transit stations and airports," summarized scholars David Lyon, Aaron Doyle, and Randy Lippert:

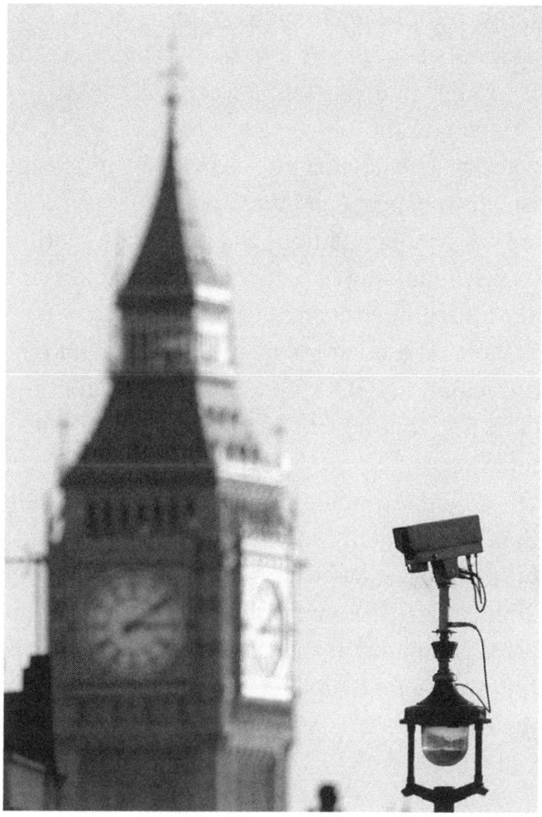

A CCTV camera, with the backdrop of the clock tower containing Big Ben, keeps a watch in central London. After four home-grown suicide bombers killed 52 London commuters on July 7, 2005, Prime Minister Tony Blair vowed that Britain would stop at nothing to defeat terrorism. "Let no one be in any doubt," he said. "The rules of the game are changing." Since the 9/11 attacks in the United States four years earlier, Britain had made its antiterrorism powers among the toughest in the Western world. (AP Photo/Akira Suemori, File)

> A variety of purposes is trumpeted for the cameras—deterrence, retroactive prosecution of criminals, making people feel safer. . . . [But] surveillance camera footage is rarely used for prosecutions, and any possible impact in making people safer is debatable at best. . . . Critics charge that the cameras may serve to place certain groups under greater official scrutiny and to extend the reach of today's "surveillance societies," although their general failure to achieve deterrence or prosecution of offenders suggests that . . . the panoptic effect of the cameras may currently be more dream than reality. Yet surveillance camera technologies are rapidly evolving and we must also consider their potential future functions and effectiveness, for good or ill.

Our modern surveillance camera systems originated in the late 19th century with the invention of the first moving film camera. Equipment for filming and watching moving images became increasingly sophisticated during the early part of the 20th century, but the next major innovation—the development of smaller portable cameras—did not take place until the late 1930s and early 1940s. These devices allowed for operators to film unsuspecting people in ways that had been closed to operators using large and bulky video recorders.

Other innovations followed in the 1940s and 1950s, including the advent of CCTV and the video tape recorder VTR. During the 1960s and 1970s, surveillance systems that employed video cameras gradually became more commonplace. Governments began investing in them to better secure public spaces, especially in crowded urban settings such as train stations, airports, downtown intersections, banks, retail stores (especially convenience stores and gas stations in areas with elevated crime rates), and other places of business came to see them as deterrents to theft. These latter investments were actively cheered on by the insurance industry, which saw the technology as useful not only for suppressing theft, but also for detecting fraudulent workplace injury claims and other events impacting their bottom lines.

Other technological innovations and advances followed in close succession. Small but digitally sophisticated cameras—nanny cams in the parlance of the day—became surveillance tools in many affluent family households, and by the close of the 20th century, Internet protocol (IP) video cameras capable of transmitting footage across computer networks became commonplace. IP cameras and webcams, which followed soon thereafter, rendered CCTV an outdated type of surveillance system, though some such systems are still maintained by business owners without the financial resources to make new investments in next-generation surveillance cameras.

Video surveillance was also revolutionized in the late 1990s and early 2000s by the development of digital recording technology. This evolution made tapes superfluous and made storage of high-quality video surveillance much easier for both government agencies and private businesses. Digital enhancement software (such as biometric recognition programs) soon followed, making digital recording even more valuable. Police departments in New York City and other large metropolitan areas were quick to recognize the utility of this technology, and by the early 2000s, video surveillance cameras were sprouting along subway terminals, housing projects, historic landmarks, parks, highways, and airports. Not surprisingly, the September 2001 terrorist attacks on the Pentagon in Washington, D.C., and the World Trade Center in New York City greatly increased investment in surveillance camera systems at the local, state, and federal levels. Implementation of these new systems was generally supported by the American public, which saw them as unsettling but necessary tools for detecting and thwarting future terrorist attacks.

The combination of the Internet and sophisticated smartphones with built-in camera/video capacities has resulted in an emerging new area of video surveillance as well. "Rather than mounting obtrusive cameras, future law enforcement agencies may begin using these phones as integrated devices, combining video surveillance with public phones in one package for 24/7 public watch dogging," wrote Lucy

Roberts. "Police officers and federal agents may eventually be issued phones with streaming video so that they can immediately send pics of suspects they are tailing back to a database for matching against a face recognition program."

The emergence of drones as a surveillance tool (as well as a weapon for warfare) is also transforming the world of video surveillance. Since they can be outfitted with the latest in video cameras, some of which can closely monitor the movements of targeted people or vehicles from miles away, drones provide another avenue for the state to monitor the activities of unsuspecting people (in addition, drones can also conduct other forms of surveillance, such as interception of cell phone communications). "Many drones, by virtue of their design, their size, and how high they can fly, can operate undetected in urban and rural environments, allowing the government to spy on Americans without their knowledge," summarized the Electronic Frontier Foundation, which fears that drone technology is already infringing on constitutional rights to privacy.

The American Civil Liberties Union (ACLU) shares the same concern about drones, as well as other technologically advanced cameras flooding into American life and society. "Like any intrusive technology, the benefits of deploying public video cameras must be balanced against the costs and dangers," the ACLU stated on its Web site. "This technology (1) has the potential to change the core experience of going out in public in America because of its chilling effect on citizens, (2) carries very real dangers of abuse and 'mission creep,' and (3) would not significantly protect us against terrorism. Given that, its benefits—preventing at most a few street crimes, and probably none—are disproportionately small."

Despite such concerns, however, surveillance cameras and associated hardware and software systems are being purchased and made operational by cities all across the United States. Even relatively small towns are getting into the act, despite the fact that the video cameras installed in their parks and other public spaces rarely capture anything more serious than petty theft or vandalism. But advocates of surveillance camera systems say that security cameras are already proving their worth in tracking down criminals such as the ones who bombed the Boston Marathon race in 2013. In addition, experts acknowledge that as biometric software such as facial-recognition programs get even more sophisticated video footage will become easier to use in identifying suspects or known criminals/terrorists.

Defenders of surveillance camera systems say that, on balance, their security benefits cannot be ignored. "The idea of submitting to constant monitoring feels wrong, nearly un-American, to most of us," acknowledged journalist Farhad Manjoo, who writes frequently about technology and security issues. "Cameras in the sky are the ultimate manifestation of Big Brother." Manjoo also admits that video camera surveillance has a serious potential for abuse. "Once a city is routinely surveilled, the government can turn every indiscretion into a criminal matter. You used to be able to speed down the street when you were in a hurry. Now, in many places around the world, a speed camera will record your behavior and send you a ticket in the mail. Combine cameras with facial-recognition technology and you've got a recipe for governmental intrusion."

Despite these concerns, however, Manjoo believes that surveillance camera systems subject to stringent oversight are when weighed "against other security measures . . . the least costly and most effective choice. In the aftermath of 9/11, we've turned most public spaces into fortresses—now, it's impossible for you to get into tall buildings, airports, many museums, concerts, and even public celebrations without being subjected to pat-downs and metal detectors. When combined with competent law enforcement, surveillance cameras are more effective, less intrusive, less psychologically draining, and much more pleasant than these alternatives."

Kevin Hillstrom

Further Reading

Delgado, Rick. n.d. "From Edison to Internet: A History of Video Surveillance." Yahoo Small Business Web site. https://smallbusiness.yahoo.com/advisor/edison-internet-history-video-surveillance-105000047.html. Accessed April 28, 2015.

Doyle, Aaron, Randy Lippert, and David Lyon, eds. 2012. *Eyes Everywhere: The Global Growth of Camera Surveillance.* New York: Routledge.

Kelly, Heather. 2013. "After Boston: The Pros and Cons of Surveillance Cameras." CNN Web site (April 26). http://www.cnn.com/2013/04/26/tech/innovation/security-cameras-boston-bombings/. Accessed April 28, 2015.

Lynch, Jennifer. 2012. "Are Drones Watching You?" Electronic Frontier Foundation Web site. https://www.eff.org/deeplinks/2012/01/drones-are-watching-you. Accessed April 28, 2015.

Manjoo, Farhad. 2013. "We Need More Cameras, and We Need Them Now." *Slate* (April 18). http://www.slate.com/articles/technology/technology/2013/04/boston_bomber_photos_the_marathon_bombing_shows_that_we_need_more_security.html. Accessed April 28, 2015.

Roberts, Lucy. 2005. "The History of Video Surveillance: From VCRs to Eyes in the Sky." WE * C * U Surveillance Web site. http://www.wecusurveillance.com/cctvhistory. Accessed April 28, 2015.

Surveillance–Industrial Complex

Surveillance–industrial complex is the term that privacy rights activists often use to refer to joint governmental–corporate surveillance efforts, programs, and systems. The term is primarily applied to voluntary corporate contributions to the surveillance state—whether to curry favor with lawmakers and regulators or to secure lucrative contracts. But it is also sometimes employed to refer to efforts by the American government to pressure or legally conscript private corporations and individuals into contributing to government surveillance initiatives.

Defenders of these enlistment practices say that these arrangements, which utilize existing telecommunication networks and systems, elevate the quality of national security and save taxpayers money by saving governments the time and expense of developing their own systems. According to critics such as the American Civil Liberties Union (ACLU), however, this privatization of the national security establishment has Orwellian overtones and adds a dangerous element of unaccountability to government surveillance practices. "It allows the government to carry out privacy-invading practices at 'arm's length' by piggy-backing in or actually cultivating data collection in the private sector that it could not carry out itself without serious legal or political repercussions," stated the ACLU. And while the group notes that some corporate actors actively seek out profitable synergies with governmental surveillance and national security agencies and departments, some of these partnerships are actually costly to private businesses because they "shift costs from government to the private sector by forcing companies to take expensive steps such as hiring additional staff to meet information collection and analysis mandates—in effect, imposing a hidden 'surveillance tax' on those companies."

Although privacy and surveillance experts agree that the September 11 terrorist attacks and the growth in sophisticated telecommunications technology have made corporate–government partnerships more extensive and far-reaching than ever before, historians point out that such partnerships are nothing new in American life. As far back as the 19th century, government officials utilized private security and detective agencies to conduct surveillance against the perceived enemies of the state, most notably radical labor organizers and leaders. During World War II and the subsequent Cold War, manufacturers discovered just how transformative government contracts for planes, trucks, uniforms, weapons, and other military supplies could be to their profitability and growth. They came to recognize that large expenditures for national security were good for business, and they cultivated close relationships with military and civilian leaders throughout the American government.

The mid-20th-century emergence of this so-called military–industrial complex had such a seismic impact on American politics and policy that even some conservative military hawks who typically supported heavy defense spending were troubled. No less a figure than Dwight D. Eisenhower, World War II military hero turned president, urged Americans to be wary of the influence of the corporate–military partnership on Washington, D.C. In his farewell address to the nation in 1961 upon leaving the Oval Office, Eisenhower noted that "we annually spend on military security more than the net income of all United States corporations. This conjunction of an immense military establishment and a large arms industry is new in the American experience. The total influence—economic, political, even spiritual—is felt in every city, every State house, every office of the Federal government . . . We must never let the weight of this combination endanger our liberties or democratic processes . . . Only an alert and knowledgeable citizenry can compel the proper meshing of the huge industrial and military machinery of defense with our peaceful methods and goals, so that security and liberty may prosper together."

The event that triggered the growth of the present-day surveillance–industrial complex—a kind of cousin to the military–industrial complex described by Eisenhower—was the September 11, 2001, terrorist attacks on United States. Prior to that event, national security and law enforcement agencies such as the National Security Agency (NSA), Federal Bureau of Investigation (FBI), and Central Intelligence Agency (CIA) had not made extensive efforts to secure the cooperation of telecommunications companies in their surveillance and counterterrorism activities. But in the aftermath of 9/11, those surveillance and counterterrorism activities spiked enormously—as did efforts to get telecommunications companies to provide access to data and systems that had previously been off-limits. This push for cooperation was greatly aided by legislation such as the USA PATRIOT Act, which gave the NSA and other agencies broad new authority to carry out counterterrorism activities. Rather than greatly expand their own employee rolls, however, government agencies essentially contracted swaths of their surveillance operations out to private companies. Some observers say, in fact, that many government agencies have subcontracted out so many of their activities out to corporate contractors that their surveillance programs would collapse if they were taken away.

By 2013, according to journalist David Rohde, this expansion of government–corporate surveillance has created a world in which more than 4.9 million Americans now have government security clearances. Rohde also cites figures from the Project on Government Oversight, a government watchdog group that estimates that the U.S. government is now paying contractors approximately $300 billion annually.

As the walls have blurred between government and telecommunications companies that provide the backbone of all of our communications and social media resources, groups such as the ACLU worry that privacy laws are now being routinely circumvented. "Our laws have historically protected information held by an individual, while information held by third parties was either assumed to be innocuous or protected by professional codes of confidentiality," noted the group, which says that agencies such as the NSA have turned the third-party rule into a loophole to gain private information from today's telecommunications giants. Privacy advocates also express concern that governmental accountability and transparency is more difficult to pursue under these hazy arrangements, which cell phone companies and other members of the telecommunications industry are loathe to acknowledge, let alone publicize.

Finally, some privacy advocates assert that modern telecommunications companies are too comfortable with the idea of conducting business with the NSA because the companies themselves do not show sufficient respect for the privacy of personal data. In 2014, for example, it was revealed that telecommunications companies such as AT&T and Verizon had been courting advertisers by surreptitiously tracking the Internet activity of more than 100 million cellular customers using secret supercookies. And some of the country's leading media titans have been dismissive of privacy concerns. In 2009, for example, Google CEO Eric Schmidt deflected criticism of the company's user data retention policies by asserting that "if you have something that you don't want anyone to know, maybe you shouldn't be doing it in the first place." Journalist Glenn Greenwald notes, however, that leading figures in the high-tech industry are not as cavalier when it comes to their own privacy. "Internet tycoons who are so willing to devalue our privacy are vehemently protective of their own," wrote Greenwald in *No Place to Hide*. "Mark Zuckerberg purchased the four homes adjacent to his own in Palo Alto, at a cost of $30 million, to ensure his privacy." As CNET put it, "Your personal life is known as Facebook's data. Its CEO's personal life is now known as mind your own business."

Kevin Hillstrom

Further Reading

Ball, Kirstie, and Laureen Snider, eds. 2013. *The Surveillance-Industrial Complex: A Political Economy of Surveillance*. New York: Routledge.

Bamford, James. 2009. *The Shadow Factory: The Ultra-Secret NSA From 9/11 to the Eavesdropping on America*. New York: Doubleday.

Eisenhower, Dwight D. 1961. Farewell address. *Public Papers of the Presidents of the United States: Dwight D. Eisenhower, 1960–1961*. Washington, DC: Office of the Federal Register.

Greenwald, Glenn. 2014. *No Place to Hide: Edward Snowden, the NSA, and the U.S. Surveillance State*. New York: Metropolitan Books.

Rohde, David. 2013. "The Security-Industrial Complex." *The Atlantic*, June 15. http://www.theatlantic.com/politics/archive/2013/06/the-security-industrial-complex/276906/. Accessed September 18, 2015.

Schneier, Bruce. 2015. *Data and Goliath: The Hidden Battles to Collect Your Data and Control Your World*. New York: W.W. Norton.

Stanley, Jay, and the American Civil Liberties Union. 2004. *The Surveillance-Industrial Complex: How the American Government is Enlisting Private Parties in the Construction of a Surveillance Society*. Washington, DC: ACLU (August). https://www.aclu.org/files/FilesPDFs/surveillance_report.pdf. Accessed May 3, 2015.

T

Terrorism, War on

In the immediate aftermath of the terrorist attacks of September 11, 2001, the nation seemed as united as it had ever been in its history. Within a few months, however, the initial unanimity gave way as the debate turned to issues of civil liberties and how they should be balanced against broader issues of national security. Political alliances that might have at first seemed unlikely began to emerge. Staunch conservative Republicans such as former Congressman Bob Barr of Georgia found themselves in agreement with USA PATRIOT Act opponents such as liberal Democrat Russ Feingold of Wisconsin. These new points of agreement between heretofore diametrically opposed political positions demonstrate the limits of viewing the United States as a Manichean polity, split neatly between the coalitions of red and blue.

The debate regarding the place of civil liberties in the aftermath of 9/11 can be roughly divided into three broad categories. The first group, considerably more powerful than the other two in the months just after the attacks, is often labeled as neoconservative. According to the philosophy of this distinct group, while the level of government effectiveness is limited when attempting to redistribute wealth and to ameliorate the more deleterious effects of capitalism, it can actually be quite successful when its power is exercised for the benefit of establishing a national security state. Civil liberties, while important and worthy of protection, must be balanced in relation to the first and primary responsibility of the federal government—providing for the safety of its people. Therefore, measures that might seem excessive to civil libertarian purists are in fact necessary if a free society is to be maintained. Although critics of the neoconservative approach are quick to cite room for abuse should the government become too involved in the personal lives of its citizens, defenders of this position assert that their ultimate goal is the long-term preservation of civil liberty. To achieve this, however, there must be a willingness to sacrifice and to recognize that the world did indeed fundamentally change with the 9/11 terrorist attacks.

The so-called neoconservative approach has been used to justify a host of controversial practices during the War on Terror. The PATRIOT Act, passed with virtual unanimity by both houses of Congress, signed into law by President Bush, and subsequently reauthorized by narrower political margins, has proven to be especially divisive.

Although the neoconservative approach, accepted by many who would not necessarily accept the label, commands support from a strong segment of the American people, two other major positions need to be considered. Libertarianism has long cast a jaundiced eye toward all but the most basic activities of the federal government. Within a year after the terrorist attacks, libertarian conservatives in the country began actively expressing their displeasure with the expansion of federal power brought about by the PATRIOT Act. From their perspective, the government cannot be trusted to gather large quantities of information on average citizens. This violates the narrow parameters that must be shored up and kept in place if a free society is to be maintained. Libertarians tend to come from a position right of center and base their objections on the concentration of federal power. Of particular concern to libertarians is the new right of the government to procure library records and to aggregate and evaluate mass civilian e-mail traffic. In what can at first be mistaken as simple agreement, liberals on the left tend to support the end result of this libertarian thinking but not for the same reasons.

Liberal critics of the PATRIOT Act, the Foreign Intelligence Surveillance Act, and the 2013 revelations of the surveillance activities of the National Security Agency (NSA) frequently express fears that American citizens, officials, and lawmakers are so determined to address the threat of terrorism that they are altering the nation's identity by trampling on basic constitutional freedoms. Much of the outrage on the left in response to the Abu Graib prison scandal, 2005 revelations of warrantless wiretapping by the Bush administration, and Edward Snowden's 2013 whistle-blowing about the nature and extent of NSA surveillance of Americans has centered on the fear that the United States is in some ways putting its own sense of itself as a free society at risk. In the minds of many liberals, the nation has already gone too far in weakening its commitment to human rights and liberties in its effort to maintain its place in the world.

Although by no means an exhaustive taxonomy of the current political environment, the positions associated with the neoconservatives, liberals, and libertarians have tended to be the loudest in reaction to the surveillance measures taken by both the Bush and Obama administrations in the post-9/11 era. After all, the question of civil liberties goes to the heart of the American experiment.

John Wilson Wells

Further Reading

Cohen, David B., and John W. Wells, eds. 2004. *American National Security and Civil Liberties in an Era of Terrorism*. New York: Palgrave Macmillan.

Cole, David, and James X. Dempsey. 2006. *Terrorism and the Constitution: Sacrificing Civil Liberties in the Name of National Security,* Third Edition. New York: New Press.

Darmer, M. Katherine, Robert M. Baird, and Stuart E. Rosenbaum, eds. 2004. *Civil Liberties vs. National Security in a Post 9/11 World.* Amherst, NY: Prometheus Books.

Farber, Daniel. 2008. *Security vs. Liberty: Conflicts between National Security and Civil Liberties in American History*. New York: Russell Sage Foundation.

Gilliom, John, and Torin Monahan. 2012. *SuperVision: An Introduction to the Surveillance Society.* Chicago: University of Chicago Press.

Greenwald, Glenn. 2014. *No Place to Hide: Edward Snowden, the NSA, and the U.S. Surveillance State*. New York: Metropolitan Books.

Schneier, Bruce. 2015. *Data and Goliath: The Hidden Battles to Collect Your Data and Control Your World.* New York: W.W. Norton.

Sidel, Mark. 2004. *More Secure, Less Free?: Antiterrorism Policy and Civil Liberties after September 11.* Ann Arbor: University of Michigan Press.

Third-Party Doctrine

The third-party doctrine is a legal theory that states that an individual can have no reasonable expectation of privacy when they engage the services of a third party, such as the postal service or a telephone, e-mail, or cell phone provider, in disseminating information. The argument for the third-party doctrine is that the Fourth Amendment protection against illegal search and seizure does not apply when third parties are involved.

The third-party doctrine encompasses the idea that technology provided by third parties makes individuals able to do things in private what would otherwise have to be done in public. For example, telephone companies make it possible to call a friend from the privacy of one's home, whereas before the telephone was widely available, a person would have to travel to his friend's house in order to have a conversation. If the individual had to leave his home and physically travel to his friend, this activity could easily be observed by police officers because it would be done publicly. By asserting that individuals can have no expectation to privacy when they use third parties, the third-party doctrine is sometimes described by proponents as an attempt to level the playing field for law enforcement officers. Previously, they had access to much more information, because much more was done in public. The third-party doctrine attempts to bring back into the open what is now being done behind closed doors. Law enforcement officers can obtain information such as telephone and banking data without first obtaining a search warrant through this policy.

It was in 1979, during the *Smith v. Maryland* court case, that the Court set the precedent that the police do not need a warrant to gain access to information from a third party. In Smith's case, the police requested that the telephone company place a pen register—a device that records all the phone numbers dialed from a specific line—on Smith's phone line. Smith petitioned to have the trial court exclude the evidence gathered from the pen register because there had been no warrant and he claimed the register violated his Fourth Amendment rights. The Court denied his motion, ruling that there had been no violation because the pen register did not constitute a search under the Fourth Amendment. When he elected to use the services of the telephone company, stated the Court, Smith accepted the risk that they could turn his information over to the government; he had no reasonable expectation to privacy because he had engaged the services of a third party. The information from the pen register was admissible during the trial, and Smith was convicted.

Another case, *United States v. Jones* (2012), also set precedent for the extent and limitations of the third-party doctrine. Jones had been suspected of drug trafficking, and in an effort to gain evidence against him, law enforcement officials placed a tracking device on Jones' vehicle outside the terms set forth in a search warrant granted for that purpose. The police did not use the GPS data while the car was parked at Jones' house because it was located at his private residence; they did, however, gather evidence while he drove the car because, they reasoned, Jones could not have reasonable expectation of privacy while he was driving on public roads. The district court upheld that there was no violation of the Fourth Amendment through the use of GPS technology. However, the D.C. Circuit reversed the decision, asserting that GPS tracking did, in fact, violate the Fourth Amendment right of Jones and other Americans "to be secure in their persons, houses, papers, and effects, against unreasonable searches and seizures." Jones' car was considered an effect and therefore protected by the Fourth Amendment. Jones had reasonable expectation to privacy, and thus, the third-party doctrine did not apply in the Jones case.

The third-party doctrine is widely acknowledged for its ambiguity. It is difficult to determine in which cases the third-party doctrine applies, when it is lawful to obtain information from a third party without a warrant, and when it is unlawful. The police must have a warrant for anything that would remain private, even with the use of technology and third parties. For example, they may access to whom a telephone call was placed, the time, and the date of the call, but they may not have access to the content of the conversation without a warrant. The third-party doctrine thus remains a point of heated contention. Privacy advocates argue that it is too invasive and gives the government excessive surveillance powers.

Grace Vandemark

Further Reading

Kerr, Orin. 2009. "The Case for the Third Party Doctrine." *Michigan Law Review* 561.

Sacks, Mike. 2012. "Warrantless GPS Tracking Unconstitutional, Supreme Court Rules." *The Huffington Post* (January 23). http://www.huffingtonpost.com/2012/01/23/warrantless-gps-tracking-_n_1224000.html. Accessed September 18, 2015.

Salam, Reihan. 2013. "The Third-Party Doctrine." *National Review*, June 12. http://www.nationalreview.com/agenda/350896/third-party-doctrine-reihan-salam. Accessed September 18, 2015.

Schulhofer, Stephen H. 2012. *More Essential than Ever: The Fourth Amendment in the Twenty-First Century*. New York: Oxford University Press.

Solove, Daniel J. 2004. *The Digital Person: Technology and Privacy in the Information Age*. New York: New York University Press.

Transportation Security Administration (TSA)

The Transportation Security Administration (TSA) is the federal agency responsible for securing the nation's transportation systems, particularly commercial airports. It works with transportation, law enforcement, and intelligence agencies to protect commerce and the public from security threats by employing a layered security strategy.

The TSA was created on November 19, 2001, to assume responsibility for security in the nation's airports after the September 11 terrorist attacks. Today, the agency hires, trains, and manages security officers for more than 450 commercial airports in the United States. These officers screen passengers and luggage; inspect passenger and cargo systems for security flaws; and protect passengers, crews, and cargo from attack. In 2014, the TSA had an annual budget of $7.39 billion and employed more than 55,000 workers.

The evolution of airport security can be traced back to the 1970s, when a spate of airplane hijackings led the Federal Aviation Agency (FAA) to institute measures to protect crews, planes, and passengers. In 1970, sky marshals were introduced on U.S. commercial flights in response to the increasing numbers of hijackings occurring all over the world.

New regulations, procedures, and security strategies were also introduced. In 1972, the FAA instituted screening measures, requiring passengers and their

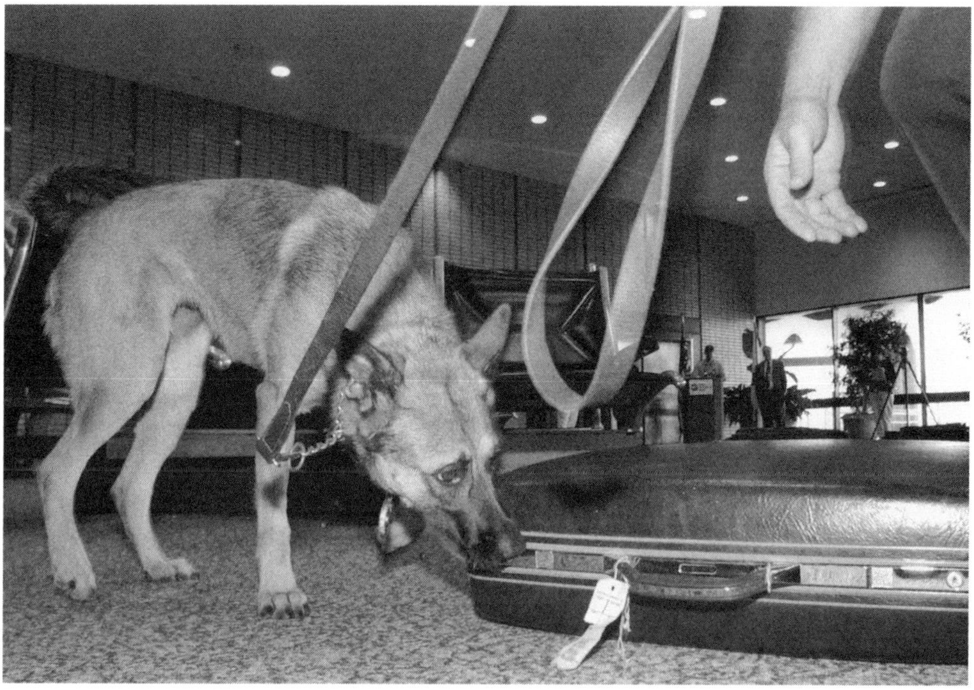

The Transportation Security Administration is using dogs to screen checked baggage at airports across the country. (AP Photo)

carry-on baggage to walk through metal detectors. Airline companies hired private security companies to perform the more stringent screening procedures.

Airline security was tightened again after the 1988 Lockerbie tragedy, when terrorists blew up Pan Am Flight 103 over Lockerbie, Scotland, killing 270 people. The FAA responded by implementing a number of new security measures to address terrorist threats, such as thorough screening procedures for computers, radios, and other electronic equipment.

The September 11, 2001, terrorist attacks exposed major flaws in airport screening procedures and ushered in a new era in airport security. Nineteen hijackers were able to pass passenger screenings in Boston, New Jersey, and Virginia, later taking control over four commercial airliners. The hijackers used the planes to target the World Trade Center in New York City and the Pentagon in Washington, D.C. Nearly 3,000 people were killed in the coordinated terrorist attacks that day.

The events of September 11 generated renewed interest in airport security, leading to significant reforms in the government's entire security strategy and infrastructure. Two months after 9/11, Congress passed the Aviation and Transportation Security Act (ATSA), a measure that federalized airport security and created the

TSA. The ATSA mandated that the newly formed agency would be responsible for hiring and training passenger and baggage screeners and that all checked bags would be screened for explosives.

On March 9, 2003, the TSA was moved from the Department of Transportation to the Department of Homeland Security (DHS), a new cabinet-level agency responsible for protecting the nation against—and carrying out the response to—terrorist attacks, man-made accidents, and natural disasters.

The TSA's security strategy for the nation's commercial airline industry has evolved, changing its focus as new threats emerge. For example, new airline screening procedures were implemented after a British man, Richard Reid, unsuccessfully attempted to detonate plastic explosives he had hidden in his shoes on an international flight on December 21, 2001. As a response to that threat, the TSA required passengers to take off their shoes and run them through the carry-on baggage screener during the passenger screening process. After intelligence surfaced that terrorists might try to hide explosives in liquid containers in order to blow up an American-bound plane, the TSA banned liquids from planes in 2006. Full-body scanners were introduced when a young Nigerian man, Umar Farouk Abdulmatallab, tried to ignite plastic explosives that he had sewn into his underwear right before it was scheduled to land in Detroit on Christmas Day, 2009.

The TSA's tightening security policies have led to growing criticism from the American public. Many critics deride the agency's procedures as ineffectual, invasive, and a violation of civil liberties. Others pointed to security processes that treated every passenger as a threat, which sometimes led to young children being searched or people in wheelchairs being interrogated by TSA agents.

In response to the mounting criticism, the TSA adopted a risk-based approach to airport security in 2011. In this approach, the TSA focused on more effectively identifying possible threats through improved screening techniques and making it easier for experienced travelers, children, the elderly, and the military to fly.

Margaret Haerens

Further Reading

Mann, Charles C. 2011. "Smoke Screening." *Vanity Fair,* December 20. http://www.vanityfair.com/culture/2011/12/tsa-insanity-201112. Accessed September 18, 2015.

Thiessen, Marc A. 2010. "Let's Give Thanks for the TSA." *National Review* (November 23). http://www.nationalreview.com/corner/253829/lets-give-thanks-tsa-marc-thiessen. Accessed March 11, 2015.

TSA. "About TSA." Transportation Security Administration Web site. http://www.tsa.gov/about-tsa. Accessed March 11, 2015.

U

United States v. Davis (2015)

This case involved the U.S. government collecting—without a warrant—information about the location of four people's cell phones during a criminal investigation. The court ruled that the Fourth Amendment gives people reasonable expectation of privacy with regard to their cell phone location information and that a warrant should have been secured first.

In August 2010, Quartavious Davis was part of a group that committed seven armed robberies at a variety of business establishments in Miami, Florida, including two fast food restaurants, a gas station, a drug store, an auto parts store, and a beauty salon. After eyewitnesses identified Davis, his DNA was recovered from a car involved in the robberies, and video footage at one of the stores appeared to show him committing a robbery. In addition, police obtained 67 days' worth of information that identified the location of Davis's cell phone, which totaled 11,000 specific locations. The cell locations helped police pinpoint where Davis was during the crimes, most of which were in the vicinity of the crimes.

Davis objected to the police gaining this information without a search warrant, claiming it was a violation of the Fourth Amendment, and he attempted to have the records suppressed as evidence. The trial court denied Davis's motion and he was subsequently convicted to 162 years in prison without bail.

Davis appealed to the Eleventh Circuit Court of Appeals. Joining Davis in his appeal were the American Civil Liberties Union (ACLU), the Center for Democracy and Technology, the Electronic Frontier Foundation (EFF), and the National Association of Criminal Defense Lawyers. In June 2014, a three-person panel of the appeals court overruled the lower court and stated that the police needed to produce a search warrant before it collected cell phone location records. The panel said, "In short, we hold that cell site location information is within the subscriber's reasonable expectation of privacy. The obtaining of that data without a warrant is a Fourth Amendment violation."

As part of its ruling, the panel referenced a U.S. Supreme Court decision—*United States v. Jones* (2012). In that case, the high court said that the use of a GPS tracking device that was attached to a car in order to detect the vehicle's movements was trespassing and a violation of the Fourth Amendment. The panel stated that under the reasonable expectation of privacy test the data pertaining to cell phone location are protected under the Fourth Amendment, since it could reveal such private matters as "being near the home of a lover, or a dispensary of medication, or a place of worship, or a house of ill repute."

Civil liberties advocates at the time hailed the decision. Jennifer Granick, civil liberties director at the Stanford Center for Internet and Security, praised the court for rejecting "the exceedingly common law enforcement practice of warrantlessly tracking suspects' physical location using cell phone tower data. The opinion . . . is both welcome and overdue. Defendants who have and will be physically tracked without a warrant have new legal support to challenge that surveillance."

Following the panel's decision to vacate the earlier conviction, both sides sought a rehearing. On September 4, 2014, the Eleventh Circuit Court of Appeals opted to vacate the panel's prior ruling, saying it would review the case en banc, meaning the entire collection of circuit judges would participate in a new trial. Arguments were scheduled to be held in front of the en banc court on February 24, 2015.

Lawrence W. Baker

Further Reading

ACLU. 2014. "*United States v. Quartavious Davis*." American Civil Liberties Union (December 17). https://www.aclu.org/technology-and-liberty/united-states-v-quartavious-davis. Accessed April 15, 2015.

"Circuit Split: Eleventh Circuit Creates Division on Standard to Obtain Cell Site Location Information." *Federal Evidence Review* (June 19, 2014). http://federalevidence.com/blog/2014/june/circuit-split-eleventh-circuit-creates-division-standard-obtain-cell-site-location-in. Accessed April 15, 2015.

Granick, Jennifer. 2014. "New Ruling Shows the NSA Can't Legally Justify Its Phone Spying Anymore." *Wired* (June 13). http://www.wired.com/2014/06/davis-undermines-metadata/. Accessed April 15, 2015.

Kerr, Orin. 2014. "The Eleventh Circuit's Novel Approach to the Fourth Amendment in the *Davis* Case." The Volokh Conspiracy (June 19). http://www.washingtonpost.com/news/volokh-conspiracy/wp/2014/06/19/the-eleventh-circuits-novel-approach-to-the-fourth-amendment-in-the-davis-case/. Accessed April 15, 2015.

"Landmark Ruling by 11th Circuit Court on Cell Phone Tracking & Metadata." *Daily Kos* (June 15, 2014). http://www.dailykos.com/story/2014/06/15/1306943/-Landmark-Ruling-by-11th-Circuit-Court-on-Cell-Phone-Tracking-Metadata#. Accessed April 15, 2015.

Ortiz, Erik. 2015. "Quartavious Davis, First-Time Offender With 162-Year Prison Term, Gets Appeal." NBC News (February 21). http://www.nbcnews.com/news/crime-courts/quartavious-davis-first-time-offender-162-year-prison-term-gets-n305776. Accessed April 15, 2015.

United States v. U.S. District Court (1972)

In 1972, the U.S. Supreme Court unanimously ruled in *United States v. U.S. District Court* that wiretaps violated the Fourth Amendment, thereby establishing a precedent that warrants were required before electronic surveillance in domestic cases could begin.

The case originated in 1968 with three members of the White Panther Party living in Ann Arbor, Michigan. The men were John Waterhouse Forrest, Lawrence "Pun" Plamondon, and John Sinclair. They were artists, counterculturists, and writers caught up in the rock-and-roll, drug-induced counterrevolution of the 1960s. They espoused freedom and were disinclined to fall in line with the status quo. The White Panther Party arose after Plamondon had read a newspaper interview in which Black Panther Party cofounder Huey Newton had urged white people to support the Black Panthers by starting a White Panther equivalent. The Black Panthers were a black nationalist group that initially was established to monitor police treatment of African Americans but grew to include social programs. The Federal Bureau of Investigation (FBI) and others, however, believed the Black Panthers—and eventually the White Panthers as well—to be a threat to national security.

On September 29, 1968, a bomb exploded at a Central Intelligence Agency (CIA) recruitment office in Ann Arbor. A year later, the three were charged with conspiring to destroy government property. The case was filed in the U.S. District Court for the Eastern District of Michigan, with Judge Damon J. Keith presiding. The U.S. attorney was Ralph Guy. Forrest's lawyer was Hugh Davis, from the National Lawyers Guild, while Sinclair and Plamondon's attorneys were William Kuntsler and Leonard Weinglass, who had attained some fame when they defended the Chicago Seven following the raucous Democratic National Convention in Chicago in August 1968.

Attorneys for the defendants requested that the government turn over any evidence picked up as a result of electronic surveillance. In its arguments, the United States admitted to wiretapping the defendants without a warrant. The Justice Department's opinion was that a warrant was unnecessary in circumstances where it believed domestic security was at stake. Although the Fourth Amendment required a warrant before a search could be conducted, electronic surveillance was not directly addressed. But the Omnibus Crime Control and Safe Streets Act of

1968 allowed for an exception to the warrant rule when a threat of the overthrowing of the government and "any other clear and present danger to the structure or existence of the Government" were present. The U.S. government claimed the threats were there in the White Panther's case. Furthermore, while it turned over evidence to the court, the government argued that the evidence could not be passed along to the defendants because of national security concerns. The defendants claimed the wiretapping tainted their case.

Judge Keith rejected the government's stance and expressed concern that such a position could extend limitlessly to other situations involving electronic surveillance. He ordered the government to turn over the electronic evidence to the defense. The government appealed to the Court of Appeals for the Sixth Circuit, which also rejected the government's motion and upheld Keith's ruling. The government appealed again, and the U.S. Supreme Court took on the case.

In a unanimous vote of 8–0 (a ninth justice, William Rehnquist, did not participate), the high court turned away the government's argument and ruled in favor of the defense. It viewed the wiretaps in the case as an unconstitutional violation of the Fourth Amendment. Justice Lewis F. Powell Jr. wrote the opinion, in which the Court rejected the government's argument that requiring a warrant would stand in the way of the president's duty to ensure domestic security and protection. The Court expressed concern that too much authority, in the example of using warrantless electronic surveillance, could tempt the executive branch to harass and otherwise persecute political enemies, all in the name of supposed national security. Powell quoted U.S. senator Philip Hart (D-Michigan), who said: "As I read it—and this is my fear—we are saying that the President, on his motion, could declare—name your favorite poison—draft dodgers, Black Muslims, the Ku Klux Klan, or civil rights activists to be a clear and present danger to the structure or existence of the Government." Justice Powell also concluded that the Omnibus Crime Control and Safe Streets Act did not give the president new powers to conduct warrantless searches.

Elsewhere in his opinion, Powell stated that "history abundantly documents the tendency of Government—however benevolent and benign its motives—to view with suspicion those who most fervently dispute its policies. Fourth Amendment protections become the more necessary when the targets of official surveillance may be those suspected of unorthodoxy in their political beliefs. The danger to political dissent is acute where the Government attempts to act under so vague a concept as the power to protect 'domestic security.' Given the difficulty of defining the domestic security interest, the danger of abuse in acting to protect that interest becomes apparent."

Lawrence W. Baker

Further Reading

Center for Constitutional Rights. "*United States v. United States District Court.*" http://ccrjustice.org/ourcases/past-cases/united-states-v.-united-states-district-court. Accessed April 15, 2015.

IIT Chicago-Kent College of Law. "*United States v. United States District Court.*" *Oyez.* http://www.oyez.org/cases/1970-1979/1971/1971_70_153. Accessed April 15, 2015.

Legal Information Institute. "*United States v. United States District Court.*" https://www.law.cornell.edu/supremecourt/text/407/297. Accessed April 15, 2015.

Monday, Mary. 2010. "Unconstitutional Surveillance & *United States v. U.S. District Court:* Who the Winner Is May Be a Secret—Part 1." *Emptywheel* (October 4). http://emptywheel.firedoglake.com/2010/10/04/unconstitutional-surveillance-united-states-v-u-s-district-court-who-the-winner-is-may-be-a-secret-part-1/. Accessed April 15, 2015.

Morrison, Trevor W. 2008. "The Story of *United States v. United States District Court* (Keith): The Surveillance Power." Columbia Public Law & Legal Theory Working Papers. Paper 08155. Columbia Law School, November 20.

Yin, Tung. "*United States v. United States District Court*, 407 U.S. 297 (1972)." Civil Liberties. http://uscivilliberties.org/cases/4647-united-states-v-united-states-district-court-407-us-297-1972.html. Accessed April 15, 2015.

USA PATRIOT Act

The USA PATRIOT Act, or the Uniting and Strengthening America by Providing Appropriate Tools Required to Intercept and Obstruct Terrorism Act, is a law passed by large margins in both houses of Congress and signed into law by President George W. Bush on October 26, 2001. Enacted in the wake of and in response to the September 11, 2001, terrorist attacks, the act was designed to strengthen U.S. security and prevent future terrorist attacks by expanding the powers of law enforcement agencies, such as the Central Intelligence Agency (CIA) and the Federal Bureau of Investigation (FBI), to find and destroy terrorist networks operating both within and outside the United States. An amendment in 2004, the Intelligence Reform and Terrorism Prevention Act (IRTPA), added another provision to the law. The USA PATRIOT Act has been reauthorized twice since then—first in 2005 by the USA PATRIOT and Terrorism Prevention Reauthorization Act and again in 2006 by the USA PATRIOT Act Additional Reauthorizing Amendments Act.

The USA PATRIOT Act, as amended, is composed of several parts, but the main provisions of the law gave the government broad new antiterrorism tools. These tools included enhanced surveillance powers, authority to freeze financial assets of suspected terrorists and terrorist groups, increased border security measures, and new criminal laws that added terrorism-related offenses. Perhaps the

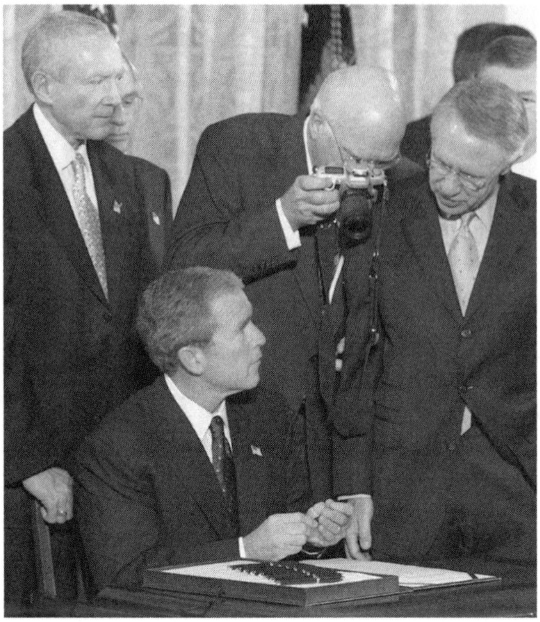

President George W. Bush signs the USA PATRIOT Act during a ceremony in the White House East Room, October 26, 2001; the law gave police unprecedented authority to search people's homes and business records secretly and eavesdrop on telephone and computer conversations. (AP Photo)

most controversial parts of the act, however, were a number of temporary provisions relating to law enforcement's authority to conduct surveillance or spying activities in terrorism cases. These temporary provisions contained sunset clauses that provided for them to expire at the end of 2009.

One surveillance provision, for example, gave federal officials the right to use roving wiretaps to follow suspected terrorists by secretly listening to or recording telephone or Internet communications. Contained in Section 206 of the Act, this power allows officials to use the same warrant to track suspects on whatever communication devices they use, without having to obtain a separate warrant for each phone number, e-mail, or address used. This type of surveillance is said to be roving because it can follow the suspect even if he or she changes phones or e-mails or moves around to different locations. To obtain a warrant for roving wiretaps, the government must apply to the Foreign Intelligence Surveillance Court (FISC) and show that the target is a foreign agent, such as a member of a foreign terrorist organization, and that the target might evade normal surveillance. Roving wiretaps have been used in the past in drug and organized crime cases.

A second surveillance provision, contained in Section 215 of the Act, authorized federal officials to compel third parties to produce business records. The business and other tangible records' provision expanded the ability of investigators to obtain any tangible thing as well as various types of written records—such as business records, phone records, Internet browsing histories, apartment rental records, driver's license records, library records, book sale records, gun sale records, tax return records, educational records, and medical records. Using this authority, investigators can force companies such as telephone providers, banks, and others to release documents pertaining to certain specified persons. This type of surveillance also must be authorized by FISC, after a showing by law enforcement that the records are relevant to an international terrorism or counterintelligence investigation. A slightly higher standard is imposed for certain types of records, including library, book sales, gun sales, and medical records, in order to protect privacy and First Amendment rights.

A third surveillance provision, often called the "lone wolf" provision, was added in 2004. This provision is contained in Section 6001 of the IRTPA. It allows government surveillance of any non-U.S. person who engages or prepares to engage in international terrorism, regardless of whether he or she is affiliated with a foreign power or terrorist group. This new power was believed to be necessary to target so-called lone wolves who become radicalized via the Internet or other ways and who may pose a terrorist threat by themselves and without coordinating with organized terrorist organizations.

These three surveillance provisions were extended for another four years by the PATRIOT Sunsets Extension Act, signed by President Barack Obama on May 29, 2011. The new expiration date is June 1, 2015.

Many parts of the USA PATRIOT Act, especially the three temporary surveillance provisions, have been the subject of significant controversy. The law enforcement community and supporters of the law argue that the law has been vital in the fight against terrorism, but detractors believe that it grants too much power to the government to spy on Americans and violates their privacy and civil liberties. Critics warned that the law could be used to spy on political dissenters and other Americans who have no connection to terrorism. Critics say these fears were realized in June 2013 when classified documents were leaked by Edward Snowden, an employee of a contractor for the U.S. National Security Agency (NSA), showing that U.S. intelligence agencies were conducting mass surveillance of Americans' telephone communications, including call dates and times, call duration, and numbers called, under the authority of Section 215 of the Act.

Debra Miller

Further Reading

American Civil Liberties Union. 2009. "Reclaiming Patriotism: A Call to Reconsider the Patriot Act." https://www.aclu.org/files/pdfs/safefree/patriot_report_20090310.pdf. Accessed September 18, 2015.

Bendix, William, and Paul J. Quirk. 2015. "Secrecy and Negligence: How Congress Lost Control of Domestic Surveillance." *Brookings* (March). http://www.brookings.edu/research/papers/2015/03/02-secrecy-negligence-congres-surveillance-bendix-quirk. Accessed May 4, 2015.

Rosenbach, Eric, and Aki Peritz. 2009. "The USA-PATRIOT Act." Memorandum, "Confrontation or Collaboration? Congress and the Intelligence Community." *Belfer Center for Science and International Affairs*, Harvard Kennedy School (July). http://belfercenter.ksg.harvard.edu/publication/19201/confrontation_or_collaboration_congress_and_the_intelligence_community.html. Accessed May 4, 2015.

U.S. Department of Justice. "Highlights of the USA Patriot Act." U.S. Department of Justice Web site. http://www.justice.gov/archive/ll/highlights.htm. Accessed May 4, 2015.

V

Vernonia School District v. Acton (1995)

This case was the first challenge to mandatory drug testing for high school student athletes to reach the high court. It originated with a decision by officials in Oregon's Vernonia School District to institute a "student athlete drug policy," which included random drug testing by urinalysis of student athletes. The program was described by school officials as both an effort to curb illegal activity and a method for reducing sports-related injuries that were of greater risk of occurring when athletes were under the influence of drugs. A student athlete named James Acton was subsequently dismissed from the football team after refusing to undergo testing. Acton and his parents challenged the policy in court, and the case eventually made its way to the U.S. Supreme Court.

By a 6–3 vote, the Supreme Court found that the drug-testing scheme fit squarely within the "special needs" analysis because the program promoted "legitimate governmental interests." Accordingly, neither warrant nor individualized suspicion was required as long as the search was a reasonable one.

To determine reasonableness, the majority considered the individual privacy interests of the students. They ruled that public school students, because they were in the temporary custody of the state as "schoolmaster," had a lesser expectation of privacy than did adults. Additionally, privacy expectations were even less for student athletes. The justices then considered the government's interest in the drug testing, concluding that the nature of the concern was "important—indeed perhaps compelling."

Having balanced the intrusion on the individual's Fourth Amendment privacy interests against the promotion of a legitimate governmental interest, the Court held the policy to be reasonable and, therefore, constitutional. This case marked the first time the Court had sustained a random, suspicion-less drug-testing program outside the public employment context.

Otis H. Stephens and Richard A. Glenn

Further Reading

Arnold, Tracey L. 1996. "Constitutionality of Random Drug Testing of Student Athletes Makes the Cut . . . but Will the Athletes?" *Journal of Law & Education* 25 (1): 190.

DuPont, Robert L., and Lisa Brady. 2006. *Drug Testing in Schools: Guidelines for Effective Use.* Center City, MN: Hazeldon.

Norton, Amy. 2015. "Doctors Weigh in on Random Drug Testing in Schools." CBS News.com (March 30, 2015). http://www.cbsnews.com/news/doctors-random-drug-testing-in-schools/. Accessed April 2, 2015.

W

Warrantless Searches

In general, the Fourth Amendment requires a law enforcement officer to obtain a warrant before conducting a search or making a seizure of evidence. However, because an absolute warrant requirement would be impractical, courts have upheld the reasonableness of warrantless searches under exigent circumstances. From these decisions has emerged a set of reasonably well-defined exceptions to the warrant requirement.

It is well established in the law that police or other public safety personnel may enter private premises and conduct a warrantless search if they have probable cause to believe that an emergency such as a fire or a ticking time bomb requires their immediate action. As the Supreme Court observed in *Michigan v. Tyler* (1978), "Indeed, it would defy reason to suppose that firemen must secure a warrant or consent before entering a burning structure to put out the blaze." However, in *Welsh v. Wisconsin* (1984), the U.S. Supreme Court made clear that when a warrantless search involves an entry into a person's home "the burden is on the government to demonstrate exigent circumstances that overcome the presumption of unreasonableness that attaches to all warrantless home entries."

A much more controversial exception to the warrant requirement involves a search conducted for the purpose of recovering evanescent or ephemeral evidence—that is, evidence that is about to be lost or destroyed. While there are numerous state and federal court decisions recognizing this exception, the Supreme Court held in *Welsh v. Wisconsin* that destruction of evidence does not constitute exigent circumstances if the underlying offense is relatively minor.

The so-called automobile exception to the warrant requirement is equally controversial. The doctrine is nicely summarized by Justice Byron White's opinion for the Supreme Court in *Chambers v. Maroney* (1970), which states that a warrant is "unnecessary where there is probable cause to search an automobile stopped on the highway; the car is movable, the occupants are alerted, and the car's contents may never be found again if a warrant must be obtained."

There are other situations in which police can lawfully perform warrantless searches. When making a lawful arrest, police can conduct a warrantless search of the person being arrested and the area within his or her immediate grasp or control. When evidence of crime is in plain view of police, they are permitted in most instances to make an immediate seizure, assuming that they have a legal right to be at the place from which the evidence came into plain view. As Justice John Paul Stevens, writing for the Supreme Court in *Horton v. California* (1990), observed: "If an article is already in plain view, neither its observation nor its seizure would involve any invasion of privacy." In 2011, meanwhile, the Supreme Court ruled by an 8–1 margin in *King v. Kentucky* that law enforcement has the right to enter private residences if they are convinced that evidence within that residence is in the process of being destroyed (the *King v. Kentucky* case concerned an incident in which police officers entered a home without a warrant after smelling marijuana being burned).

It is important to understand that all of the aforementioned exceptions to the warrant requirement assume that police officers have probable cause to believe that a particular search is likely to produce evidence of crime. There are exceptions to the probable cause requirement as well. In certain instances, police can detain individuals and subject them to limited pat-down searches on the basis of the lesser standard of reasonable suspicion.

Despite these exceptions, the Fourth Amendment expresses a strong preference for search warrants. The failure of police to obtain a warrant when required to do so places a criminal case in jeopardy, inasmuch as evidence obtained in violation of the Fourth Amendment is subject to the exclusionary rule.

John M. Scheb II and Otis H. Stephens Jr.

Further Reading

Cooke, Jennifer Ison. 2002. "Discretionary Warrantless Searches and Seizures and the Fourth Amendment: A Need for Clearer Guidelines." *South Carolina Law Review* 53: 641.

Scheb, John M., and John M. Scheb II. 2006. *Criminal Procedure*. Belmont, CA: Thomson/Wadsworth.

Stephens, Otis H., Jr., and Richard A. Glenn. 2006. *Unreasonable Searches and Seizures: Rights and Liberties under the Law*. Santa Barbara, CA: ABC-CLIO.

Totenberg, Tina. 2011. "Supreme Court OKs More Warrantless Searches." NPR.org Web site (May 16). http://www.npr.org/2011/05/16/136368744/in-warrantless-search-case-top-court-rules-for-police. Accessed May 5, 2015.

Warrantless Wiretapping

Wiretapping is the covert surveillance of electronic communication on phones, computers, and other electronic devices. Such monitoring is largely done by law enforcement or intelligence agencies for the purposes of obtaining information on criminal or terrorist activity. Since the late 1960s, wiretapping has been permissible in a limited number of cases, but has required a search warrant issued by an authorized court. This check on surveillance powers was put in place to protect the privacy of ordinary Americans and the constitutional rights of criminal or terrorist suspects or individuals associated with criminal activity.

That changed after the terrorist attacks of September 11, 2001, when heightened concerns over U.S. national security led to an aggressive domestic spying program that used wireless wiretapping to monitor the electronic communications of foreign terrorist suspects in the United States. The disclosure of this program has generated a heated debate over the balance between the preservation of civil liberties and U.S. national security.

The practice of wiretapping can be traced back to the late 19th century. However, the practice was questioned by legal scholars, who believed that it violated the U.S. Constitution's prohibition against illegal searches and seizures. The Fourth Amendment reads: "The right of the people to be secure in their persons, houses, papers, and effects, against unreasonable searches and seizures, shall not be violated, and no warrants shall issue, but on probable cause, supported by oath or affirmation, and particularly describing the place to be searched, and the persons or things to be searched."

In 1928, the U.S. Supreme Court held that evidence gathered through the use of warrantless wiretaps was permissible as long as police did not trespass on the property of the surveillance target. That decision was reversed in a landmark 1967 case, *Katz v. the United States*, in which the Supreme Court held that individuals had a reasonable expectation of privacy and that the government and law enforcement were required to get a warrant if wiretapping would violate that expectation.

In 1968, the U.S. Congress further limited the ability of government to wiretap electronic communications without a warrant by passing the Omnibus Crime Control and Safe Street Act, the first federal law to restrict the practice. The legislation mandated that all wiretapping activity must be court approved, be based on probable cause, be concluded after thirty days, and be disclosed to the subject of the investigation after 90 days.

In 1975, a Senate subcommittee investigation, known as the Church Committee, exposed evidence that U.S. intelligence operations, under the aegis of the National Security Agency (NSA), Federal Bureau of Investigation (FBI), and the Central Intelligence Agency (CIA), had illegally wiretapped civil rights leaders, union officials, antiwar activists, journalists, politicians, and student groups.

As a result of the Church Committee findings, the Congress passed the Foreign Intelligence Surveillance Act (FISA) in 1978. The law implemented a new legal review process for foreign intelligence surveillance, featuring a three-judge panel, known as the FISA court, which would review requests to authorize wiretaps involving agents of a foreign power and a person or entity in the United States. The victims of the wiretap do not have to be suspected of a crime—just deemed a threat to national security. Although FISA was regarded as an attempt to restrict the government's power to wiretap American citizens, it raised concerns that it was actually undermining constitutional protections against unreasonable search and seizure.

The Electronic Communications Privacy Act (ECPA) of 1986, also known as the Wiretap Act, extended those protections to private e-mail communications. As the Internet became increasingly popular, government authorities became more concerned about its potential to facilitate criminal and terrorist activity. Intelligence agencies and law enforcement began to develop and utilize technology to surreptitiously monitor chat rooms, Web pages, and other Internet forums.

After the terrorist attacks of September 11, 2001, the U.S. government acted quickly to extend warrantless wiretapping in order to protect U.S. national security. A week after the attacks, the Congress passed the Authorization for Use of Military Force Against Terrorism (AUMF), which gave the president the authorization to use the appropriate force against any nation, individual, or organization that is suspected to be involved with the planning or execution of the 9/11 attacks. AUMF would later be used to justify the government's authorization of widespread warrantless wiretapping and other invasive surveillance methods.

In 2002, President George W. Bush signed an executive order authorizing the NSA to conduct surveillance of electronic communications between international parties and individuals or groups within the United States without a court-approved warrant in order to gather intelligence on possible terrorist activity. When the secret program, code-named Stellar Wind, was revealed in 2005, civil libertarian groups and privacy advocates raised legal challenges. Many filed suit against the telecommunication companies that cooperated with the federal government in illegal wiretapping activities. In response to the growing controversy over civil liberties, the Bush administration announced that Stellar Wind would be overseen by the FISA court instead of U.S. intelligence operations.

In June 2008, the U.S. Congress peeled back some of those protections by passing the FISA Amendments Act, which reinstated and broadened the NSA's authorization to conduct warrantless wiretapping of both foreign and domestic communications. It also provided immunity to telecommunications companies such as AT&T, which complied with government surveillance activities on Americans or individuals in the United States.

In 2012, President Barack Obama signed a five-year extension of the FISA Amendments Act.

Margaret Haerens

Further Reading

Jaffer, Jameel, and Patrick C. Toomey. 2014. "How the Government Misled the Supreme Court on Warrantless Wiretapping." *The Nation* (January 6). http://www.thenation.com/article/177649/how-government-misled-supreme-court-warrantless-wiretapping#. Accessed March 22, 2015.

Mayer, Jane. 2013. "What's the Matter with MetaData?" *New Yorker* (June 6). http://www.newyorker.com/news/news-desk/whats-the-matter-with-metadata. Accessed March 22, 2015.

Nakashima, Ellen. 2014. "Legal Memos Released on Bush-Era Justification for Warrantless Wiretapping." *Washington Post* (September 6). http://www.washingtonpost.com/world/national-security/legal-memos-released-on-bush-era-justification-for-warrantless-wiretapping/2014/09/05/91b86c52-356d-11e4-9e92-0899b306bbea_story.html. Accessed March 22, 2015.

Z

Zero Days

"Zero day" is a term that is most commonly used to refer to a previously unknown hole or security vulnerability in software. This flaw, or zero-day vulnerability, in the product allows hackers or government intelligence agencies to exploit the hole for their own purposes, a strike known as a zero-day attack. The codes formulated and utilized by hackers in these strikes are known as zero-day exploits, and there is a growing and lucrative market for both zero-day vulnerabilities and exploits among hackers, technology firms, large corporations, cyber warriors, and government intelligence agencies all over the world.

The term zero day can be traced back to early digital bulletin boards (BBs), where computer programmers and hackers would refer to soon-to-be released computer programs as zero-day software. The term indicated that the product had been out on the market for zero days. These releases were eagerly anticipated by computer enthusiasts and there was competition among BB users to learn about and obtain copies of zero-day products.

It did not take BB users long to detect flaws in early software programs and to begin to exploit them in various ways. Finding zero-day vulnerabilities became a badge of honor for computer hackers, because it was rare to find one. Once it was found, hackers would use exploit code to embed a virus, malware, or a Trojan horse. The time after a hole was detected and when the software vendor or computer security firm released a patch to fix the flaw became known as zero days. During this period, software vendors raced to come up with a patch to protect its users from potentially destructive attacks.

In some cases, hackers have reported zero-day vulnerabilities to the software company directly. These acts are known as white hat hacking. Several software firms have instituted incentive programs, including financial rewards, to encourage hackers to report flaws in its software.

However, there are many individuals, known as black hat hackers, who are more interested in selling information on zero-day vulnerabilities in a growing and lucrative underground market to criminal enterprises, computer security companies, technology firms, or foreign or U.S. intelligence agencies engaged in espionage activities. Information on zero-day vulnerabilities and exploits can bring up to hundreds of thousands of dollars.

Zero-day attacks come in a number of different attack vectors. One way hackers strike is to target Web browsers, such as Google or Yahoo. Another zero-day exploit is malware sent through e-mail attachments, which is activated when a user opens the attachment. Attacks have also been launched from popular video-sharing Web sites.

One well-known zero-day attack is the Aurora incident of 2010, in which suspected Chinese hackers exploited vulnerabilities in Microsoft's Internet Explorer browser software to target the source code of several companies, including Google and Adobe.

Another is the Sandworm attack. In 2014, computer security experts discovered an insidious strain of malware embedded in PowerPoint files, which would launch a zero-day attack on Microsoft files. Sandworm was traced to a Russian cyber campaign to gain access to NATO, European Union, and telecommunication company systems.

Stuxnet is perhaps the best-known zero-day attack in history. Discovered in 2010, the zero-day exploit was designed to affect industrial programmable logic controllers (PLCs), which manage machinery used in factory assembly lines, amusement parks, and nuclear power plants. In a massive attack on Iran's nuclear capability, Stuxnet destroyed approximately one-fifth of the country's centrifuges, which are used to process nuclear material. In 2012, it was reported that the Stuxnet attacks were developed and launched as part of a U.S.-Israeli intelligence operation known as Operation Olympic Games. Stuxnet reportedly provided valuable information on the structure and workings of Iran's nuclear power program to U.S. intelligence authorities. The operation was exposed when Stuxnet escaped the confines of Iran's nuclear program and made its way to infect PLCs in other countries, including the United States.

Growing concern over government surveillance and intelligence-gathering techniques has led to lawsuits against the National Security Agency (NSA) to force the agency to disclose its decision-making process when it comes to publicizing zero-day exploits. The lawsuits were spurred by reports that U.S. intelligence agencies were hoarding information on zero-day vulnerabilities and exploits to use in case of a cyber conflict. A *Washington Post* report revealed that the NSA spent $25 million in 2013 to obtain zero-day vulnerabilities from hackers.

In light of growing criticism, National Security Director Michael Rogers announced in 2014 that NSA would discontinue the practice and would disclose zero-day vulnerabilities to software vendors in a timely manner.

Margaret Haerens

Further Reading

Fung, Brian. 2013. "The NSA Hacks Other Countries by Buying Millions of Dollars' Worth of Computer Vulnerabilities." *The Washington Post* (August 31). http://www.washingtonpost.com/blogs/the-switch/wp/2013/08/31/the-nsa-hacks-other-countries-by-buying-millions-of-dollars-worth-of-computer-vulnerabilities/. Accessed March 5, 2015.

Peterson, Andrea. 2014. "What Is a Zero-Day Vulnerability?" *The Washington Post* (July 15). http://www.washingtonpost.com/blogs/the-switch/wp/2014/07/15/what-is-a-zero-day-vulnerability/. Accessed March 5, 2015.

Sanger, David. 2012. "Obama Order Sped Up Wave of Cyberattacks against Iran." *New York Times* (June 1). http://www.nytimes.com/2012/06/01/world/middleeast/obama-ordered-wave-of-cyberattacks-against-iran.html?_r=0. Accessed March 5, 2015.

Ungerleider, Neal. 2013. "How Spies, Hackers, and the Government Bolster a Booming Software Exploit Market." *Fast Company* (May 1). http://www.fastcompany.com/3009156/the-code-war/how-spies-hackers-and-the-government-bolster-a-booming-software-exploit-market. Accessed March 5, 2015.

Zetter, Kim. 2014. "Hacker Lexicon: What Is a Zero Day?" *Wired* (November 11). http://www.wired.com/2014/11/what-is-a-zero-day/. Accessed March 4, 2015.

Surveillance in America

Surveillance in America

AN ENCYCLOPEDIA OF HISTORY, POLITICS, AND THE LAW

Volume Two: Primary Documents

Pam Dixon, Consulting Editor

ABC-CLIO™

An Imprint of ABC-CLIO, LLC
Santa Barbara, California • Denver, Colorado

Library of Congress Cataloging-in-Publication Data

Names: Dixon, Pam, 1960– editor.
Title: Surveillance in America : an encyclopedia of history, politics, and the law / Pam Dixon, consulting editor.
Description: Santa Barbara, California : ABC-CLIO, 2016. | Includes bibliographical references and index.
Identifiers: LCCN 2015030411 | ISBN 9781440840548 (set : hardback : alkaline paper) | ISBN 9781440845437 (vol.1 : hardback : alkaline paper) | ISBN 9781440845444 (vol.2 : hardback : alkaline paper) | ISBN 9781440840555 (ebook)
Subjects: LCSH: Electronic surveillance—Law and legislation—United States. | Privacy, Right of—United States—History. | BISAC: HISTORY / Military / United States. | HISTORY / Military / Strategy. | ART / American / Hispanic American.
Classification: LCC KF5399 .S87 2016 | DDC 342.7308/58—dc23
LC record available at http://lccn.loc.gov/2015030411

ISBN: 978-1-4408-4054-8 (set)
978-1-4408-4543-7 (vol. 1)
978-1-4408-4544-4 (vol. 2)
EISBN: 978-1-4408-4055-5

20 19 18 17 16 1 2 3 4 5

This book is also available on the World Wide Web as an eBook.
Visit www.abc-clio.com for details.

ABC-CLIO, LLC
An Imprint of ABC-CLIO, LLC

ABC-CLIO, LLC
130 Cremona Drive, P.O. Box 1911
Santa Barbara, California 93116-1911

This book is printed on acid-free paper ∞

Manufactured in the United States of America

Contents

VOLUME ONE

Reader's Guide to Related Topics and Primary Documents

Arizona v. Evans (1995)
Bartnicki v. Vopper (2001)
Boyd v. United States (1886)
California v. Ciraolo (1986)
California v. Greenwood (1988)
Davis v. Mississippi (1969)
Delaware v. Prouse (1979)
Griswold v. Connecticut (1965)
Hepting v. AT&T (2009)
Illinois v. Krull et al. (1987)
Illinois v. Lidster (2004)
Jewel v. National Security Agency (2015)
Klayman v. Obama (2013)
Michigan Department of State Police v. Sitz (1990)
United States v. Davis (2015)
United States v. U.S. District Court (1972)
Vernonia School District v. Acton (1995)

Documents

The Supreme Court Establishes "Clear and Present Danger" Doctrine in *Schenck v. United States*—1919
Ex parte Endo Ruling Paves the Way for Closing of Internment Camps—1944
Miller v. United States Decision Limits Police "Knock and Announce" Powers—1958
The Supreme Court Expands the Exclusionary Rule in *Mapp v. Ohio*—1961
Albertson Supreme Court Decision Weakens the Subversive Activities Control Board—1965
The Supreme Court Finds a Constitutional Right to Privacy in *Griswold v. Connecticut*—1965
The Supreme Court Expands Privacy Rights in *Katz v. United States*—1967
The Supreme Court Bolsters the Exclusionary Rule in *United States v. Leon*—1984
The Supreme Court Rules on Checkpoints in *City of Indianapolis v. Edmond*—2000
The Supreme Court Rules on Thermal-Imaging Surveillance in *Kyllo v. United States*—2001
The Supreme Court Sanctions School Drug Testing—2002
Secret FISA Court Rejects a Justice Department Surveillance Request—2002
The Supreme Court Rules on Searches during Traffic Stops in *Illinois v. Caballes*—2005
District Court Rules NSL Gag Orders Unconstitutional—2006
Supreme Court Ruling in *Berghuis v. Thompkins* Narrows Miranda Rights—2010

Government Oversight

Topics

Church Committee
Executive Order 12333
Fair Information Practices

Documents

The Church Committee Releases Shocking Revelations of Government Surveillance—1976

Secret FISA Court Rejects a Justice Department Surveillance Request—2002
Secret DOJ Inspector General Report on FBI Use of Section 215 Orders—2008
Senator Feinstein Reacts to Revelations of CIA Spying on the Senate—2014

Laws and Regulations

Topics

Alien Registration Act
Antiwiretapping Statutes
Cable Communications Policy Act of 1984
Civil Rights and Liberties during Wartime
Communications Assistance for Law Enforcement Act (CALEA)
Constitutional Protections
Crypto Wars
Electronic Communications Privacy Act (ECPA)
Espionage Act of 1917
Exclusionary Rule
Executive Order 9066
Executive Order 12333
Fair Information Practices
Firearms Registration
Foreign Intelligence Surveillancc Act (FISA)
Freedom of Information Act (FOIA)
Internal Security Act of 1950
National Security Letters (NSLs)
Plain View Doctrine
Privacy Act of 1974
Privacy, Informational
Right to Financial Privacy Act (RFPA)
Terrorism, War on
Third-Party Doctrine
USA PATRIOT Act

Documents

The Sedition Act—1798
Supreme Court Establishes the Exclusionary Rule in *Weeks v. United States*—1914
The Sedition Act—1918
Supreme Court Establishes "Clear and Present Danger" Doctrine in *Schenck v. United States*—1919
Justice Brandeis's Dissent in *Olmstead v. United States*—1928
Alien Registration Act—1940
President Roosevelt Orders the Internment of Japanese Americans—1942
Ex parte Endo Ruling Paves the Way for Closing of Internment Camps—1944
President Truman's "Loyalty Program" Executive Order—1947
President Truman Vetoes the Proposed Internal Security Act—1950
Congress Passes the Internal Security Act over Truman's Veto—1950
President Johnson Criticizes Eavesdropping Provisions in Crime Control Act—1968
President Carter Signs the Foreign Intelligence Surveillance Act (FISA)—1978
The Electronic Communications Privacy Act—1986
Congressman Hyde Praises the Communications Assistance for Law Enforcement Act—1994

President Bush Signs the FISA Amendments Act (FAA)—2008
Two Democratic Senators Debate Reauthorization of FISA—2012

Privacy Rights

Topics

Constitutional Protections
Health Information Privacy
Privacy Act of 1974
Privacy Advocacy Organizations
Privacy, Informational

Documents

"The Right to Privacy in America"—1890
Justice Brandeis's Dissent in *Olmstead v. United States*—1928
The Supreme Court Finds a Constitutional Right to Privacy in *Griswold v. Connecticut*—1965
The Supreme Court Expands Privacy Rights in *Katz v. United States*—1967
The Electronic Communications Privacy Act—1986
World Privacy Forum Urges Stronger Privacy Protections for Medical Records—2014

September 11 Terrorist Attacks and USA PATRIOT Act

Topics

9/11 Commission
Terrorism, War on
USA PATRIOT Act

Documents

President Bush Addresses Congress after the September 11 Attacks—2001
President Bush Signs the USA PATRIOT Act—2001
Section 213 and Section 215 of the USA PATRIOT Act—2001
Senator Feingold Speaks Out against the USA PATRIOT Act—2001
President Bush Signs the Homeland Security Act—2002
The American Library Association Issues a Resolution on Privacy and Civil Liberties—2003
Attorney General Ashcroft Defends the PATRIOT Act on Capitol Hill—2003
Representative Sanders Introduces the Freedom to Read Protection Act—2003
A Bush Administration Official Urges Reauthorization of the PATRIOT Act—2005
District Court Rules NSL Gag Orders Unconstitutional—2006
President Bush Defends the NSA and the PATRIOT Act—2006
President Bush Signs a Reauthorization of the PATRIOT Act—2006
Roving Wiretaps and "Sneak and Peek" Warrants—2006
Senator Leahy Lambasts Republican Opposition to PATRIOT Act Reforms—2006
Inspector General's Report Reveals FBI Abuse of National Security Letters—2007
Secret DOJ Inspector General Report on FBI Use of Section 215 Orders—2008
An American Librarian Recalls Receiving a National Security Letter—2013

Snowden's Release of NSA Surveillance Information

Topics

Alexander, Keith B. (1951–)
Bamford, James (1946–)
Clapper, James R. (1941–)
Greenwald, Glenn (1967–)
Hayden, Michael (1945–)
National Security Agency (NSA)
Snowden, Edward (1983–)

Documents

Presidential Task Force Report on *Liberty and Security in a Changing World*—2013
The Secret FISA Verizon Order—2013
President Obama Responds to the Task Force Review of NSA Operations—2014
Three Senators Speak Out against the USA Freedom Act—November 2014
Three Senators Speak Out in Support of the USA Freedom Act—November 2014

Surveillance, Criticism of Practices and Programs

Documents

James Otis Composes "Against the Writs of Assistance"—1761
Justice Brandeis's Dissent in *Olmstead v. United States*—1928
President Truman Vetoes the Proposed Internal Security Act—1950
President Johnson Criticizes Eavesdropping Provisions in Crime Control Act—1968
The Church Committee Releases Shocking Revelations of Government Surveillance—1976
Senator Feingold Speaks Out against the USA PATRIOT Act—2001
The American Library Association Issues a Resolution on Privacy and Civil Liberties—2003
Representative Sanders Introduces the Freedom to Read Protection Act—2003
Senator Leahy Lambasts Republican Opposition to PATRIOT Act Reforms—2006
Inspector General's Report Reveals FBI Abuse of National Security Letters—2007
Secret DOJ Inspector General Report on FBI Use of Section 215 Orders—2008
Two Democratic Senators Debate Reauthorization of FISA—2012
An American Librarian Recalls Receiving a National Security Letter—2013
Presidential Task Force Report on *Liberty and Security in a Changing World*—2013
Privacy and Civil Liberties Oversight Board Condemns the NSA's Section 215 Program—2014
Senator Feinstein Reacts to Revelations of CIA Spying on the Senate—2014
Three Senators Speak Out against the USA Freedom Act—November 2014

Surveillance, Defenses of Practices and Programs

Documents

The FBI Defends Its Library Awareness Program—1988
The Clinton White House Endorses Clipper and Capstone—1994
Congressman Hyde Praises the Communications Assistance for Law Enforcement Act—1994
President Bush Signs the USA PATRIOT Act—2001
Attorney General Ashcroft Defends the PATRIOT Act on Capitol Hill—2003
A Bush Administration Official Urges Reauthorization of the PATRIOT Act—2005
President Bush Defends the NSA and the PATRIOT Act—2006
Two Democratic Senators Debate Reauthorization of FISA—2012
FBI Director Comey Discusses the Dangers of "Going Dark"—October 2014
Three Senators Speak Out in Support of the USA Freedom Act—November 2014

Surveillance–Industrial Complex (Government–Corporate Partnerships)

Topics

Data Brokers
Data Collection, Online
E-Verify
Persistent Online Tracking
Surveillance–Industrial Complex

Documents

A Report on Law Enforcement's "Little Helpers"—Data Aggregators—2004
A Privacy Rights Group Examines Governmental Use of Commercial Data Brokers—2013
The Secret FISA Verizon Order—2013

Surveillance Programs and Initiatives

Topics

Carnivore
Clipper and Capstone Chips
Echelon
E-Verify
Fusion Centers
Hemisphere Project
House Un-American Activities Committee (HUAC)
McCarthyism
President's Surveillance Program (PSP)
PRISM
Stingray Tracking Technology

Documents

President Roosevelt Orders the Internment of Japanese Americans—1942
President Truman's "Loyalty Program" Executive Order—1947
The Supreme Court Rules on Checkpoints in *City of Indianapolis v. Edmond*—2000
Congress Shuts Down "Total Information Awareness" Program—2003
Roving Wiretaps and "Sneak and Peek" Warrants—2006

Revelations of SIM Card Spying by the NSA and GCHQ—2015

See also: September 11 Terrorist Attacks and USA PATRIOT Act; Snowden's Release of NSA Surveillance Information

Surveillance Types and Practices

Topics

Administrative Searches
Background Checks (Employment and Volunteerism)
Banking and Financial Records
Consent Searches
Data Collection, Online
Data Mining
Deep Packet Inspection (DPI)
Electronic Surveillance
"Good-Faith" Exception
National Identity Cards
National Security Letters (NSLs)
Next Generation Identification (NGI)
Persistent Online Tracking
Plain View Doctrine
Profiling
Search Warrants
Sex Offender Registries
Stop and Frisk
Surveillance
Warrantless Searches
Warrantless Wiretapping

Documents

Roving Wiretaps and "Sneak and Peek" Warrants—2006

Technology and Equipment

Topics

Biometrics
Cell Phones
Clipper and Capstone Chips
Cloud Computing
Data Collection, Online
Drones
Electronic Mail
Firewall
National Identity Cards
Surveillance Cameras
Zero Day

Documents

The Supreme Court Upholds the Use of Pen Registers in *Smith v. Maryland*—1979
The Clinton White House Endorses Clipper and Capstone—1994

U.S. Constitution

Topics

Constitutional Protections
Due Process Clause
Exclusionary Rule
Fourth Amendment
Inevitable Discovery
Reasonable Expectation of Privacy

Documents

James Otis Composes "Against the Writs of Assistance"—1761
The Bill of Rights—1791
The Supreme Court Expands the Exclusionary Rule in *Mapp v. Ohio*—1961
The Supreme Court Bolsters the Exclusionary Rule in *United States v. Leon*—1984

Primary Documents

1761: JAMES OTIS COMPOSES "AGAINST THE WRITS OF ASSISTANCE"

In the mid-eighteenth century, British officials became frustrated by the colonies' rampant smuggling of molasses, sugar, and other goods to avoid paying duties. In 1760, they convinced the governor of Massachusetts to approve "writs of assistance"—warrants that authorized customs officials to search for contraband material on ships or in buildings. These warrants came under fire from outraged Bostonians. A group of the city's merchants subsequently approached James Otis, one of the most prominent members of Boston's legal profession, to represent them in a legal challenge to the writs. Otis quickly agreed, waving aside offers of compensation for his efforts. In February 1761, he issued his famous "Against the Writs of Assistance" before the Superior Court of Massachusetts. Citing rights guaranteed in English common law, he condemned the writs as clearly unconstitutional. The court ultimately ruled against Otis and his clients, but his fiery and eloquent oratory added fuel to the revolutionary fervor simmering across the colonies, and his speech is frequently cited as a foundational document in the development and passage of the Fourth Amendment to the Constitution.

MAY it please your Honors: I was desired by one of the court to look into thc books, and consider the question now before them concerning Writs of Assistance. I have accordingly considered it, and now appear not only in obedience to your order, but likewise in behalf of the inhabitants of this town, who have presented another petition, and out of regard to the liberties of the subject. And I take this opportunity to declare that whether under a fee or not (for in such a cause as this I despise a fee) I will to my dying day oppose, with all the powers and faculties God has given me, all such instruments of slavery on the one hand and villainy on the other as this Writ of Assistance is.

It appears to me the worst instrument of arbitrary power, the most destructive of English liberty and the fundamental principles of law, that ever was found in an English law-book. I must therefore beg your Honors' patience and attention to the whole range of an argument that may perhaps appear uncommon in many things, as well as to points of learning that are more remote and unusual, that the whole tendency of my design may the more easily be perceived, the conclusions better descend, and the force of them be better felt. I shall not think much of my pains in this cause, as I engaged in it from principle. I was solicited to argue this cause as Advocate-General; and, because I would not, I have been charged with desertion from my office. To this charge I can give a very sufficient answer. I renounced that office and I argue this cause from the same principle; and I argue it with the greater pleasure, as it is in favor of British liberty, at a time when we hear the greatest monarch upon earth declaring from his throne that he glories in the name of Briton and that the privileges of his people are dearer to him than the most valuable prerogatives of his crown; and as it is in opposition to a kind of power, the exercise of which in former periods of history cost one king of England his head and another his throne. I have taken more pains in this cause than I ever will take again, although my engaging in this and another popular cause has raised much resentment. But I think I can sincerely declare that I cheerfully submit myself to every odious name for conscience' sake; and from my soul I despise all those whose guilt, malice, or folly has made them my foes. Let the consequences be what they will, I am determined to proceed. The only principles of public conduct that are worthy of a gentleman or a man are to sacrifice estate, ease, health, and applause, and even life, to the sacred calls of his country.

These manly sentiments, in private life, make good citizens; in public life, the patriot and the hero. I do not say that, when brought to the test, I shall be invincible. I pray God I may never be brought to the melancholy trial; but, if ever I should, it will then be known how far I can reduce to practice principles which I know to be founded in truth. In the meantime I will proceed to the subject of this writ.

Your Honors will find in the old books concerning the office of a justice of the peace precedents of general warrants to search suspected houses. But in more modern books you will find only special warrants to search such and such houses, specially named, in which the complainant has before sworn that he suspects his goods are concealed; and will find it adjudged that special warrants only are legal. In the same manner I rely on it, that the writ prayed for in this petition, being general, is illegal. It is a power that places the liberty of every man in the hands of every petty officer. I say I admit that special Writs of Assistance, to search special places, may be granted to certain persons on oath; but I deny that the writ now prayed for can be granted, for I beg leave to make some observations on the writ itself, before I proceed to other Acts of Parliament. In the first place, the writ is universal, being directed "to all and singular justices, sheriffs, constables, and all other officers and subjects"; so that, in short, it is directed to every subject in the King's dominions. Every one with this writ may be a tyrant; if this commission be legal, a tyrant in a legal manner, also, may control, imprison, or murder any one within the realm. In the next place, it is perpetual; there is no return. A man is accountable to no person for his doings. Every man may reign secure in his petty tyranny, and spread terror and desolation around him, until the trump of the Archangel shall excite different emotions in his soul. In the third place, a person with this writ, in the daytime, may enter all houses, shops, etc., at will, and command all to assist him. Fourthly, by this writ not only deputies, etc., but even their menial servants, are allowed to lord it over us. What is this but to have the curse of Canaan with a witness on us: to be the servants of servants, the most despicable of God's creation? Now one of the most essential branches of English liberty is the freedom of one's house. A man's house is his castle; and whilst he is quiet, he is as well guarded as a prince in his castle. This writ, if it should be declared legal, would totally annihilate this privilege. Custom-house officers may enter our houses when they please; we are commanded to permit their entry. Their menial servants may enter, may break locks, bars, and everything in their way; and whether they break through malice or revenge, no man, no court can inquire. Bare suspicion without oath is sufficient. This wanton exercise of this power is not a chimerical suggestion of a heated brain. I will mention some facts. Mr. Pew had one of these writs, and, when Mr. Ware succeeded him, he endorsed this writ over to Mr. Ware; so that these writs are negotiable from one officer to another; and so your Honors have no opportunity of judging the persons to whom this vast power is delegated. Another instance is this: Mr. Justice Walley had called this same Mr. Ware before him, by a constable, to answer for a breach of the Sabbath-day Acts, or that of profane swearing. As soon as he had finished, Mr. Ware asked him if he had done. He replied, "Yes." "Well then," said Mr. Ware, "I will show you a little of my power. I command you to permit me to search your house for uncustomed goods"—and went on to search the house from the garret to the cellar; and then served the constable in the same manner! But to show another absurdity in this writ: if it should be established, I insist upon it every person, by the 14th Charles Second, has this power as well as the custom-house officers. The words are: "It shall be lawful for any person or persons authorized," etc. What a scene does this open! Every man prompted by revenge, ill-humor, or wantonness to inspect the inside of his neighbor's house, may get a Writ of Assistance. Others will ask it from self-defence; one arbitrary exertion will provoke another, until society be involved in tumult and in blood. . . .

Source: Otis, James. 1906. *James Otis's Speech on the Writs of Assistance.* American History Leaflets, Colonial and Constitutional. Hart, Albert Bushnell and Edward Channing, eds. New York: Parker P. Simmons, pp. 14–18.

1791: THE BILL OF RIGHTS

The Bill of Rights is the collective name given to the first ten amendments to the U.S. Constitution, all of which were ratified on December 15, 1791. When adoption of the Constitution was first being debated by the nation's Founding Fathers, critics such as Virginia delegate George Mason (author of the Virginia Declaration of Rights, *which Thomas Jefferson drew upon in composing the* Declaration of Independence*) argued that it gave far too much authority to the central government. They asserted that without additional language guaranteeing basic liberties the American people would live under the shadow of potential tyranny. These concerns gained so much traction that several state conventions ratified the Constitution only with the understanding that amendments to the Constitution specifying various civil rights would be introduced shortly thereafter.*

On September 25, 1789—fifteen months after the Constitution was ratified—United States' first ever Congress delivered twelve proposed amendments to state legislatures across the nation. The first two of these proposed amendments, which dealt with congressional representation and compensation issues, were not ratified. The next ten articles, however, were ratified by three-fourths of the state legislatures and became part of the U.S. Constitution.

The U.S. Bill of Rights

Preamble to the Bill of Rights

Congress of the United States begun and held at the City of New-York, on Wednesday the fourth of March, one thousand seven hundred and eighty nine.

THE Conventions of a number of the States, having at the time of their adopting the Constitution, expressed a desire, in order to prevent misconstruction or abuse of its powers, that further declaratory and restrictive clauses should be added: And as extending the ground of public confidence in the Government, will best ensure the beneficent ends of its institution.

RESOLVED by the Senate and House of Representatives of the United States of America, in Congress assembled, two thirds of both Houses concurring, that the following Articles be proposed to the Legislatures of the several States, as amendments to the Constitution of the United States, all, or any of which Articles, when ratified by three fourths of the said Legislatures, to be valid to all intents and purposes, as part of the said Constitution; viz.

ARTICLES in addition to, and Amendment of the Constitution of the United States of America, proposed by Congress, and ratified by the Legislatures of the several States, pursuant to the fifth Article of the original Constitution.

Amendment I

Congress shall make no law respecting an establishment of religion, or prohibiting the free exercise thereof; or abridging the freedom of speech, or of the press; or the right of the people peaceably to assemble, and to petition the Government for a redress of grievances.

Amendment II

A well regulated Militia, being necessary to the security of a free state, the right of the people to keep and bear Arms, shall not be infringed.

Amendment III

No Soldier shall, in time of peace be quartered in any house, without the consent of the Owner, nor in time of war, but in a manner to be prescribed by law.

Amendment IV

The right of the people to be secure in their persons, houses, papers, and effects, against unreasonable searches and seizures, shall not be violated, and no Warrants shall issue, but upon probable cause, supported by Oath or affirmation, and particularly describing the place to be searched, and the persons or things to be seized.

Amendment V

No person shall be held to answer for a capital, or otherwise infamous crime, unless on a presentment or indictment of a Grand Jury, except in cases arising in the land or naval forces, or in the Militia, when in actual service in time of War or public danger; nor shall any person be subject for the same offence to be twice put in jeopardy of life or limb; nor shall be compelled in any criminal case to be a witness against himself, nor be deprived of life, liberty, or property, without due process of law; nor shall private property be taken for public use, without just compensation.

Amendment VI

In all criminal prosecutions, the accused shall enjoy the right to a speedy and public trial, by an impartial jury of the State and district wherein the crime shall have been committed, which district shall have been previously ascertained by law, and to be informed of the nature and cause of the accusation; to be confronted with the witnesses against him; to have compulsory process for obtaining witnesses in his favor, and to have the Assistance of Counsel for his defence.

Amendment VII

In Suits at common law, where the value in controversy shall exceed twenty dollars, the right of trial by jury shall be preserved, and no fact tried by a jury, shall be otherwise re-examined in any Court of the United States, than according to the rules of the common law.

Amendment VIII

Excessive bail shall not be required, nor excessive fines imposed, nor cruel and unusual punishments inflicted.

Amendment IX

The enumeration in the Constitution, of certain rights, shall not be construed to deny or disparage others retained by the people.

Amendment X

The powers not delegated to the United States by the Constitution, nor prohibited by it to the States, are reserved to the States respectively, or to the people.

Source: National Archives.

1798: THE SEDITION ACT

Approved by Congress on July 14, 1798, the Sedition Act is regarded by historians as a significant early failure to protect the constitutional liberties of Americans against governmental intimidation and prosecution.

The Sedition Act was passed against the backdrop of significant hostilities between the young United States and France, which was wracked by revolutionary upheaval at the time. With hostility and anxiety about the French on the rise, the Federalist-controlled Congress passed (and Federalist President John Adams signed) the Alien and Sedition Acts. The first three acts imposed various limits on the rights of immigrants arriving on United States' shores and made it more arduous for them to gain U.S. citizenship. The fourth act, known as the Sedition Act, empowered the government to prosecute individuals who criticized the government or president of the United States. Federalist advocates of the act claimed that it would help neutralize traitors and French agents operating on American soil, but opponents decried it as an unconscionable violation of the First and Tenth Amendments and charged (accurately) that it was at least partially aimed at muzzling critics of the government in Vice President Thomas Jefferson's Republican Party. The Sedition Act of 1798 expired on March 3, 1801, the last day of Adams's presidency.

An Act in addition to the act, entitled "An act for the punishment of certain crimes against the United States."

SEC. I Be it enacted by the Senate and House of Representatives of the United States of America, in Congress assembled, That if any persons shall unlawfully combine or conspire together, with intent to oppose any measure or measures of the government of the United States, which are or shall be directed by proper authority, or to impede the operation of any law of the United States, or to intimidate or prevent any person holding a place or office in or under the government of the United States, from undertaking, performing or executing his trust or duty; and if any person or persons, with intent as aforesaid, shall counsel, advise or attempt to procure any insurrection, riot, unlawful assembly, or combination, whether such conspiracy, threatening, counsel, advice, or attempt shall have the proposed effect or not, he or they shall be deemed guilty of a high misdemeanor, and on conviction, before any court of the United States having jurisdiction thereof, shall be punished by a fine not exceeding five thousand dollars, and by imprisonment during a term not less than six months nor exceeding five years; and further, at the discretion of the court may be holden to find sureties for his good behaviour in such sum, and for such time, as the said court may direct.

SEC. 2. And be it further enacted, That if any person shall write, print, utter or publish, or shall cause or procure to be written, printed, uttered or publishing, or shall knowingly and willingly assist or aid in writing, printing, uttering or publishing any false, scandalous and malicious writing or writings against the government of the United States, or either house of the Congress of the United States, or the President of the United States, with intent to defame the said government, or either house of the said Congress, or the said President, or to bring them, or either of them, into contempt or disrepute; or to excite against them, or either or any of them, the hatred of the good people of the United States, or to excite any unlawful combinations therein, for opposing or resisting any law of the United States, or any act of the President of the United States, done in pursuance of any such law, or of the powers in him vested by the constitution of the United States, or to resist, oppose, or defeat any such law or act, or to aid, encourage or abet any hostile designs of any foreign nation against the United States, their people or government, then such person, being thereof convicted before any court of the United States having jurisdiction thereof, shall be punished by a fine not exceeding two thousand dollars, and by imprisonment not exceeding two years.

SEC. 3. And be it further enacted, and declared, That if any person shall be prosecuted under this act, for the writing or publishing any libel aforesaid, it shall be lawful for the defendant, upon the trial of the cause, to give in evidence in his defence, the truth of the matter contained in the publication charged as a libel. And the jury who shall try the cause, shall have a right to determine the law and the fact, under the direction of the court, as in other cases.

SEC. 4. And be it further enacted, That this act shall continue and be in force until the third day of March, one thousand eight hundred and one, and no longer: Provided. That the expiration of the act shall not prevent or defeat a prosecution and punishment of any offence against the law, during the time it shall be in force.

JONATHAN DAYTON, Speaker of the House of Representatives.

THEODORE SEDGWICK, President of the Senate, pro tempore.

APPROVED, July 14, 1798:

JOHN ADAMS, President of the United States.

Source: The Alien and Sedition Acts, July 6, 1798; Fifth Congress; Enrolled Acts and Resolutions; General Records of the United States Government; Record Group 11; National Archives.

1890: "THE RIGHT TO PRIVACY IN AMERICA"

In December 1890, law partners Louis Brandeis (a future U.S. Supreme Court justice) and Samuel Warren published a landmark essay championing privacy rights. This essay, which was published in the prestigious Harvard Law Review, *identified privacy as an implicit concept running throughout Anglo-American common law. At the time, there was no explicit constitutional right to privacy, and even if one could discern such a right in the Fourth or Ninth Amendment, the Bill of Rights did not apply to the states.*

The conventional wisdom is that Warren and Brandeis constructed the legal foundations for a right to privacy out of a very modest body of law. In particular, Warren and Brandeis framed their article around the intersection of the news media and new technology. The newspaper industry had experienced incredible growth during the second half of the nineteenth century. Between 1850 and 1890, the number of newspaper readers grew from approximately 800,000 to more than 8 million. Warren and Brandeis complained, however, that journalism had become sensationalistic and that the press was violating commonly understood boundaries of privacy and decency. Given the increasing capacity of government, the press, and other agencies and institutions to invade previously inaccessible aspects of personal activity, they argued that the law must evolve in response to technological change.

Warren and Brandeis were particularly concerned about the new technology of instant photography. In 1884, the Eastman Kodak Company introduced the "snap camera," a small inexpensive camera that the general public could afford en masse. Before the snap camera, cameras had been expensive and heavy; they had to be set up and people would have to pose to have pictures taken. The snap camera enabled people to take candid pictures and created an obsession for amateur photography among thousands of people who had previously not been able to afford a camera. These developments prompted Warren and Brandeis "to consider whether the existing law affords a principle which can properly be invoked to protect the privacy of the individual; and, if it does, what the nature and extent of such protection is." Warren and Brandeis contended that the law currently did not provide sufficient protection to privacy, but they demonstrated how a right to privacy could be derived using common law reasoning.

Warren and Brandeis adopted the "right to be let alone" language from jurist Thomas B. Cooley's 1888 treatise The Law of Torts. *Cooley's "right to be let alone" was a passing observation in a discussion of why tort law protected against not only batteries but also assaults where there was no physical contact. Cooley observed that in assaults victims endured "a shock to the nerves and the peace and quiet of the individual is disturbed for a period of greater or lesser duration."*

Warren and Brandeis utilized Cooley's recognition of psychological injury as a basis for tort recovery. In essence, they suggested a new tort that allowed people to recover damages for unwarranted intrusion into their private affairs. Today, this essay is widely acknowledged as one of the first arguments in defense of a distinctive identifiable right to privacy, and it became a seminal force in the development of a right to privacy in American jurisprudence.

That the individual shall have full protection in person and in property is a principle as old as the common law; but it has been found necessary from time to time to define anew the exact nature and extent of such protection. Political, social, and economic changes entail the recognition of new rights, and the common law, in its eternal youth, grows to meet the new demands of society.

Thus, in very early times, the law gave a remedy only for physical interference with life and property, for trespasses vi et armis. Then the "right to life" served only to protect the subject from battery in its various forms; liberty meant freedom from actual restraint; and the right to property secured to the individual his lands and his cattle. Later, there came a recognition of man's spiritual nature, of his feelings and his intellect. Gradually the scope of these legal rights broadened; and now the right to life has come to mean the right to enjoy life,—the right to be let alone; the right to liberty secures the exercise of extensive civil privileges; and the term "property" has grown to comprise every form of possession—intangible, as well as tangible.

Thus, with the recognition of the legal value of sensations, the protection against actual bodily injury was extended to prohibit mere attempts to do such injury; that is, the putting another in fear of such injury. From the action of battery grew that of assault. Much later there came a qualified protection of the individual against offensive noises and odors, against dust and smoke, and excessive vibration. The law of nuisance was developed. So regard for human emotions soon extended the scope of personal immunity beyond the body of the individual. His reputation, the standing among his fellow-men, was considered, and the law of slander and libel arose. Man's family relations became a part of the legal conception of his life, and the alienation of a wife's affections was held remediable. Occasionally the law halted, as in its refusal to recognize the intrusion by seduction upon the honor of the family. But even here the demands of society were met. A mean fiction, the action per quod servitium amisit, was resorted to, and by allowing damages for injury to the parents' feelings, an adequate remedy was ordinarily afforded. Similar to the expansion of the right to life was the growth of the legal conception of property. From corporeal property arose the incorporeal rights issuing out of it; and then there opened the wide realm of intangible property, in the products and processes of the mind, as works of literature and art, goodwill, trade secrets, and trademarks.

This development of the law was inevitable. The intense intellectual and emotional life, and the heightening of sensations which came with the advance of civilization, made it clear to men that only a part of the pain, pleasure, and profit of life lay in physical things. Thoughts, emotions, and sensations demanded legal recognition, and the beautiful capacity for growth which characterizes the common law enabled the judges to afford the requisite protection, without the interposition of the legislature.

Recent inventions and business methods call attention to the next step which must be taken for the protection of the person, and for securing to the individual what Judge Cooley calls the right "to be let alone." Instantaneous photographs and newspaper enterprise have invaded the sacred precincts of private and domestic life; and numerous mechanical devices threaten to make good the prediction that "what is whispered in the closet shall be proclaimed from the house-tops." For years there has been a feeling that the law must afford some remedy for the unauthorized circulation of portraits of private persons; and the evil of invasion of privacy by the newspapers, long keenly felt, has been but recently discussed by an able writer. The alleged facts of a somewhat notorious case brought before an inferior tribunal in New York a few months ago, directly involved the consideration of the right of circulating portraits; and the question whether our law will recognize and protect the right to privacy in this and in other respects must soon come before our courts for consideration.

Of the desirability—indeed of the necessity—of some such protection, there can, it is believed, be no doubt. The press is overstepping in every direction the obvious bounds of propriety and of decency. Gossip is no longer the resource of the idle and of the vicious, but has become a trade, which is pursued with industry as well as effrontery. To satisfy a prurient taste the details of sexual relations are spread broadcast in the columns of the daily papers. To occupy the indolent, column upon column is filled with idle gossip, which can only be procured by intrusion upon the domestic circle. The intensity and complexity of life, attendant upon advancing civilization, have rendered necessary some retreat from the world, and man, under the refining influence of culture, has become more sensitive to publicity, so that solitude and privacy have become more essential to the individual; but modern enterprise and invention have, through invasions upon his privacy, subjected him to mental pain and distress, far greater than could be inflicted by mere bodily injury. Nor is the harm wrought by such invasions confined to the suffering of those who may be the subjects of journalistic or other enterprise. In this, as in other branches of commerce, the supply creates the demand. Each crop of unseemly gossip, thus harvested, becomes the seed of more, and, in direct proportion to its circulation, results in the lowering of social standards and of morality. Even gossip apparently harmless, when widely and persistently circulated, is potent for evil.

It both belittles and perverts. It belittles by inverting the relative importance of things, thus dwarfing the thoughts and aspirations of a people. When personal gossip attains the dignity of print, and crowds the space available for matters of real interest to the community, what wonder that the ignorant and thoughtless mistake its relative importance. Easy of comprehension, appealing to that weak side of human nature which is never wholly cast down by the misfortunes and frailties of our neighbors, no one can be surprised that it usurps the place of interest in brains capable of other things. Triviality destroys at once robustness of thought and delicacy of feeling. No enthusiasm can flourish, no generous impulse can survive under its blighting influence.

It is our purpose to consider whether the existing law affords a principle which can properly be invoked to protect the privacy of the individual; and, if it does, what the nature and extent of such protection is.

Owing to the nature of the instruments by which privacy is invaded, the injury inflicted bears a superficial resemblance to the wrongs dealt with by the law of slander and of libel, while a legal remedy for such injury seems to involve the treatment of mere wounded feelings, as a substantive cause of action. The principle on which the law of defamation rests, covers, however, a radically different class of effects from those for which attention is now asked. It deals only with damage to reputation, with the injury done to the individual in his external relations to the community, by lowering him in the estimation of his fellows. The matter published of him, however widely circulated, and however unsuited to publicity, must, in order to be actionable, have a direct tendency to injure him in his intercourse with others, and even if in writing or in print, must subject him to the hatred, ridicule, or contempt of his fellowmen,—the effect of the publication upon his estimate of himself and upon his own feelings nor forming an essential element in the cause of action. In short, the wrongs and correlative rights recognized by the law of slander and libel are in their nature material rather than spiritual. That branch of the law simply extends the protection surrounding physical property to certain of the conditions necessary or helpful to worldly prosperity. On the other hand, our law recognizes no principle upon which compensation can be granted for mere injury to the feelings. However painful the mental effects upon another of an act, though purely wanton or even malicious, yet if the act itself is otherwise lawful, the suffering inflicted is dannum absque injuria. Injury of feelings may indeed be taken account of in ascertaining the amount of damages when attending what is recognized as a legal injury; but our system, unlike the Roman law, does not afford a remedy even for mental suffering which results from mere contumely and insult, but from an intentional and unwarranted violation of the "honor" of another.

It is not however necessary, in order to sustain the view that the common law recognizes and upholds a principle applicable to cases of invasion of privacy, to invoke the analogy, which is but superficial, to injuries sustained, either by an attack upon reputation or by what the civilians called a violation of honor; for the legal doctrines relating to infractions of what is ordinarily termed the common-law right to intellectual and artistic property are, it is believed, but instances and applications of a general right to privacy, which properly understood afford a remedy for the evils under consideration.

The common law secures to each individual the right of determining, ordinarily, to what extent his thoughts, sentiments, and emotions shall be communicated to others. Under our system of government, he can never be compelled to express them (except when upon the witness stand); and even if he has chosen to give them expression, he generally retains the power to fix the limits of the publicity which shall be given them. The existence of this right does not depend upon the particular method of expression adopted. It is immaterial whether it be by word or by signs, in painting, by sculpture, or in music. Neither does the existence of the right depend upon the nature or value of the thought or emotions, nor upon the excellence of the means of expression. The same protection is accorded to a casual letter or an entry in a diary and to the most valuable poem or essay, to a botch or daub and to a masterpiece. In every such case the individual is entitled to decide whether that which is his shall be given to the public. No other has the right to publish his productions in any form, without his consent. This right is wholly independent of the material on which, the thought, sentiment, or emotions is expressed. It may exist independently of any corporeal being, as in words spoken, a song sung, a drama acted. . . .

If the invasion of privacy constitutes a legal injuria, the elements for demanding redress exist, since already the value of mental suffering, caused by an act wrongful in itself, is recognized as a basis for compensation.

The right of one who has remained a private individual, to prevent his public portraiture, presents the simplest case for such extension; the right to protect one's self from pen portraiture, from a discussion by the press of one's private affairs, would be a more important and far-reaching one. If casual and unimportant statements in a letter, if handiwork, however inartistic and valueless, if possessions of all sorts are protected not only against reproduction, but also against description and enumeration, how much more should the acts and sayings of a man in his social and domestic relations be guarded from ruthless publicity. If you may not reproduce a woman's face photographically without her consent, how much less should be tolerated the reproduction of her face, her form, and her actions, by graphic descriptions colored to suit a gross and depraved imagination.

It remains to consider what are the limitations of this right to privacy, and what remedies may be granted for the enforcement of the right. To determine in advance of experience the exact line at which the dignity and convenience of the individual must yield to the demands of the public welfare or of private justice would be a difficult task; but the more general rules are furnished by the legal analogies already developed in the law of slander and libel, and in the law of literary and artistic property.

1. The right to privacy does not prohibit any publication of matter which is of public or general interest. In determining the scope of this rule, aid would be afforded by the analogy, in the law of libel and slander, of cases which deal with the qualified privilege of comment and criticism on matters of public and general interest. There are of course difficulties in applying such a rule; but they are inherent in the subject-matter, and are certainly no greater than those which exist in many other branches of the law,—for instance, in that large class of cases in which the reasonableness or unreasonableness of an act is made the test of liability. The design of the law must be to protect those persons with whose affairs the community has no legitimate concern, from being dragged into an undesirable and undesired publicity and to protect all persons, whatsoever; their position or station, from having matters which they may properly prefer to keep private, made public against their will. It is the unwarranted invasion of individual privacy which is reprehended, and to be, so far as possible, prevented. The distinction, however, noted in the above statement is obvious and fundamental. There are persons who may reasonably claim as a right, protection from the notoriety entailed by being made the victims of journalistic enterprise. There are others who, in varying degrees, have renounced the right to live their lives screened from public observation. Matters which men of the first class may justly contend, concern themselves alone, may in those of the second be the subject of legitimate interest to their fellow-citizens. Peculiarities of manner and person, which in the ordinary individual should be free from comment, may acquire a public importance, if found in a candidate for public office. Some further discrimination is necessary, therefore, than to class facts or deeds as public or private according to a standard to be applied to the fact or deed per se. To publish of a modest and retiring individual that he suffers from an impediment in his speech or that he cannot spell correctly, is an unwarranted, if not an unexampled, infringement of his rights, while to state and comment on the same characteristics found in a would-be congressman could not be regarded as beyond the pale of propriety.

The general object in view is to protect the privacy of private life, and to whatever degree and in whatever connection a man's life has ceased to be private, before the publication under consideration has been made, to that extent the protection is likely to be withdrawn.[43] Since, then, the propriety of publishing the very same facts may depend wholly upon the person concerning whom they are published, no fixed formula can be used to prohibit obnoxious publications. Any rule of liability adopted must have in it an elasticity which shall take account of the varying circumstances of each case,—a necessity which unfortunately renders such a doctrine not only more difficult of application, but also to a certain extent uncertain in its operation and easily rendered abortive. Besides, it is only the more flagrant breaches of decency and propriety that could in practice be reached, and it is not perhaps desirable even to attempt to repress everything which the nicest taste and keenest sense of the respect due to private life would condemn.

In general, then, the matters of which the publication should be repressed may be described as those which concern the private life, habits, acts, and relations of an individual, and have no legitimate connection with his fitness for a public office which he seeks or for which he is suggested, or for any public or quasi public position which he seeks or for which he is suggested, and have no legitimate relation to or bearing upon any act done by him in a public or quasi public capacity. The foregoing is not designed as a wholly accurate or exhaustive definition, since that which must ultimately in a vast number of cases become a question of individual judgment and opinion is incapable of such definition; but it is an attempt to indicate broadly the class of matters referred to. Some things all men alike are entitled to keep from popular curiosity, whether in public life or not, while others are only private because the persons concerned have not assumed a position which makes their doings legitimate matters of public investigation.

2. The right to privacy does not prohibit the communication of any matter, though in its nature private, when the publication is made under circumstances which would render it a privileged communication according to the law of slander and libel. Under this rule, the right to privacy is not invaded by any publication made in a court of justice, in legislative bodies, or the committees of those bodies; in municipal assemblies, or the committees of such assemblies, or practically by any communication in any other public body, municipal or parochial, or in any body quasi public, like the large voluntary associations formed for almost every purpose of benevolence, business, or other general interest; and (at least in many jurisdictions) reports of any such proceedings would in some measure be accorded a like privilege. Nor would the rule prohibit any publication made by one in the discharge of some public or private duty, whether legal or moral, or in conduct of one's own affairs, in matters where his own interest is concerned.

3. The law would probably not grant any redress for the invasion of privacy by oral publication in the absence of special damage. The same reasons exist for distinguishing between oral and written publications of private matters, as is afforded in the law of defamation by the restricted liability for slander as compared with the liability for libel. The injury resulting from such oral communications would ordinarily be so trifling that the law might well, in the interest of free speech, disregard it altogether.

4. The right to privacy ceases upon the publication of the facts by the individual, or with his consent.

This is but another application of the rule which has become familiar in the law of literary and artistic property. The cases there decided establish also what should be deemed a publication,—the important principle in this connection being that a private communication of circulation for a restricted purpose is not a publication within the meaning of the law.

5. The truth of the matter published does not afford a defence. Obviously this branch of the law should have no concern with the truth or falsehood of the matters published. It is not for injury to the individual's character that redress or prevention is sought, but for injury to the right of privacy. For the former, the law of slander and libel provides perhaps a sufficient safeguard. The latter implies the right not merely to prevent inaccurate portrayal of private life, but to prevent its being depicted at all.

6. The absence of "malice" in the publisher does not afford a defence. Personal ill-will is not an ingredient of the offence, any more than in an ordinary case of trespass to person or to property. Such malice is never necessary to be shown in an action for libel or slander at common law, except in rebuttal of some defence, e.g., that the occasion rendered the communication privileged, or, under the statutes in this State and elsewhere, that the statement complained of was true. The invasion of the privacy that is to be protected is equally complete and equally injurious, whether the motives by which the speaker or writer was actuated are taken by themselves, culpable or not; just as the damage to character, and to some extent the tendency to provoke a breach of the peace, is equally the result of defamation without regard to motives leading to its publication. Viewed as a wrong to the individual, this rule is the same pervading the whole law of torts, by which one is held responsible for his intentional acts, even though they are committed with no sinister intent; and viewed as a wrong to society, it is the same principle adopted in a large category of statutory offences.

It would doubtless be desirable that the privacy of the individual should receive the added protection of the criminal law, but for this, legislation would be required. Perhaps it would be deemed proper to bring the criminal liability for such publication within narrower limits; but that the community has an interest in preventing such invasions of privacy, sufficiently strong to justify the introduction of such a remedy, cannot be doubted. Still, the protection of society must come mainly through a recognition of the rights of the individual. Each man is responsible for his own acts and omissions only. If he condones what he reprobates, with a weapon at hand equal to his defence, he is responsible for the results. If he resists, public opinion will rally to his support. Has he then such a weapon? It is believed that the common law provides him with one, forged in the slow fire of the centuries, and to-day fitly tempered to his hand. The common law has always recognized a man's house as his castle, impregnable, often, even to his own officers engaged in the execution of its command. Shall the courts thus close the front entrance to constituted authority, and open wide the back door to idle or prurient curiosity?

Source: Warren, Samuel D. and Louis D. Brandeis. 1890. "The Right to Privacy." *Harvard Law Review* IV (5), December 15. http://faculty.uml.edu/sgallagher/Brandeisprivacy.htm. Accessed September 21, 2015.

1914: THE SUPREME COURT ESTABLISHES THE EXCLUSIONARY RULE IN *WEEKS v. UNITED STATES*

In December 1911, police officers in Kansas City, Missouri, entered the residence of Fremont Weeks (who was at work at the time) and seized papers and other evidence that he had been unlawfully transporting lottery tickets through the mail. Weeks filed a petition for the return of his property, noting that the police had entered his home without a warrant. His petition was denied and he was subsequently convicted in federal district court. Upon appeal, however, his conviction was reversed by the U.S. Supreme Court in a unanimous decision on February 24, 1914. According to the Court, the warrantless seizure of his property violated Weeks' constitutional rights and authorities' refusal to return his materials amounted to a clear violation of his rights under the Fourth Amendment. The justices thus established the "exclusionary rule," which holds that evidence gathered in operations that flout the Fourth Amendment are inadmissible in court. Without the exclusionary rule, declared the Court, privacy protections enshrined through the Fourth Amendment are "of no value" and the amendments itself "might as well be stricken from the Constitution."

MR. JUSTICE DAY delivered the opinion of the Court.

. . . [T]he question presented involves the determination of the duty of the court with reference to the motion made by the defendant for the return of certain letters, as well as other papers, taken from his room by the United States Marshal, who, without authority of process, if any such could have been legally issued, visited the room of the defendant for the declared purpose of obtaining additional testimony to support the charge against the accused, and having gained admission to the house took from the drawer of a chiffonier there found certain letters written to the defendant, tending to show his guilt. These letters were placed in the control of the District Attorney and were subsequently produced by him and offered in evidence against the accused at the trial. The defendant contends that such appropriation of his private correspondence was in violation of rights secured to him by the Fourth and Fifth Amendments to the Constitution of the United States. We shall deal with the Fourth Amendment.

The history of this Amendment is given with particularity in the opinion of Mr. Justice Bradley, speaking for the court in *Boyd* v. *United States* [1884]. . . . As was there shown, it took its origin in the determination of the framers of the Amendments to the Federal Constitution to provide for that instrument a Bill of Rights, securing to the American people, among other things, those safeguards which had grown up in England to protect the people from unreasonable searches and seizures, such as were permitted under the general warrants issued under authority of the Government by which there had been invasions of the home and privacy of the citizens and the seizure of their private papers in support of charges, real or imaginary, made against them. Such practices had also received sanction under warrants and seizures under the so-called writs of assistance, issued in the American colonies. Resistance to these practices had established the principle which was enacted into the fundamental law in the Fourth Amendment, that a man's house was his castle and not to be invaded by any general authority to search and seize his goods and papers. . . .

The effect of the Fourth Amendment is to put the courts of the United States and Federal officials, in the exercise of their power and authority, under limitations and restraints as to the exercise of such power and authority, and to forever secure the people, their persons, houses, papers and effects against all unreasonable searches and seizures under the guise of law. This protection reaches all alike, whether accused of crime or not, and the duty of giving to it force and effect is obligatory upon all entrusted under our Federal system with the enforcement of the laws. The tendency of those who execute the criminal laws of the country to obtain conviction by means of unlawful seizures and enforced confessions, the latter often obtained after subjecting accused persons to unwarranted practices destructive of rights secured by the Federal Constitution, should find no sanction in the judgments of the courts which are charged at all times with the support of the Constitution and to which people of all conditions have a right to appeal for the maintenance of such fundamental rights. What then is the present case? Before answering that inquiry specifically, it may be well by a process of exclusion to state what it is not. It is not an assertion of the right on the part of the Government, always recognized under English and American law, to search the person of the accused when legally arrested to discover and seize the fruits or evidences of crime. . . . Nor is it the case of testimony offered at a trial where the court is asked to stop and consider the illegal means by which proofs, otherwise competent, were obtained—of which we shall have occasion to treat later in this opinion. Nor is it the case of burglar's tools or other proofs of guilt found upon his arrest within the control of the accused. The case in the aspect in which we are dealing with it involves the right of the court in a criminal prosecution to retain for the purposes of evidence the letters and correspondence of the accused, seized in his house in his absence and without his authority, by a United States Marshal holding no warrant for his arrest and none for the search of his premises. The accused, without awaiting his trial, made timely application to the court for an order for the return of these letters, as well as other property. This application was denied, the letters retained and put in evidence, after a further application at the beginning of the trial, both applications asserting the rights of the accused under the Fourth and Fifth Amendments to the Constitution. If letters and private documents can thus be seized and held and used in evidence against a citizen accused of an offense, the protection of the Fourth Amendment declaring his right to be secure against such searches and seizures is of no value, and, so far as those thus placed are concerned, might as well be stricken from the Constitution. The efforts of the courts and their officials to bring the guilty to punishment, praiseworthy as they are, are not to be aided by the sacrifice of those great principles established by years of endeavor and suffering which have resulted in their embodiment in the fundamental law of the land. The United States Marshal could only have invaded the house of the accused when armed with a warrant issued as required by the Constitution, upon sworn information and describing with reasonable particularity the thing for which the search was to be made. Instead, he acted without sanction of law, doubtless prompted by the desire to bring further proof to the aid of the Government, and under color of his office undertook to make a seizure of private papers in direct violation of the constitutional prohibition against such action. Under such circumstances, without sworn information and particular description, not even an order of court would have justified such procedure, much less was it within the authority of the United States Marshal to thus invade the house and privacy of the accused. . . . To sanction such proceedings would be to affirm by judicial decision a manifest neglect if not an open defiance of the prohibitions of the Constitution, intended for the protection of the people against such unauthorized action. . . .

We therefore reach the conclusion that the letters in question were taken from the house of the accused by an official of the United States acting under color of his office in direct violation of the constitutional rights of the defendant; that having made a seasonable application for their return, which was heard and passed upon by the court, there was involved in the order refusing the application a denial of the constitutional rights of the accused, and that the court should have restored these letters to the accused. In holding them and permitting their use upon the trial, we think prejudicial error was committed. . . .

It results that the judgment of the court below must be reversed, and the case remanded for further proceedings in accordance with this opinion. *Reversed.*

Source: Weeks v. United States, 232 U.S. 383 (1914).

1918: THE SEDITION ACT

The Sedition Act of 1918 was enacted in May as a set of amendments to the Espionage Act of 1917. Both of these acts were passed after the United States had entered World War I and exhortations to rally around the flag and support the war were commonplace. The Sedition Act made it a federal crime to "willfully utter, print, write, or publish any disloyal, profane, scurrilous, or abusive language about the form of the Government of the United States" or to "willfully urge, incite, or advocate any curtailment of the production" of materials necessary for the war effort. Surveillance and censorship of the mail intensified in the wake of the act's passage. In addition, hundreds of Americans holding antiwar views were convicted over the next few years under this law, which was upheld as constitutional by the U.S. Supreme Court in both Debs v. United States *(1919) and* Abrams v. United States *(1919). In 1920, Congress repealed the Sedition Act, but despite its short duration it remains one of the most notorious government-sanctioned attacks on civil liberties in U.S. history.*

Be it enacted by the Senate and Home of Representatives of the United States of America in Congress assembled, That section three of title one of the [Espionage] Act entitled "An Act to punish acts of interference with the foreign relations, the neutrality, and. the foreign commerce of the United States, to punish espionage, and better to enforce the criminal laws of the United States, and for other purposes," approved June fifteenth, nineteen hundred and seventeen, be, and the same is hereby, amended so as to read as follows:

Sec. 3. Whoever, when the United States is at war, shall willfully make or convey false reports or false statements with intent to interfere with the operation or success of the military or naval forces of the United States, or to promote the success of its enemies, or shall willfully make or convey false reports or false statements, or say or do anything except by way of bona fide and not disloyal advice to an investor or investors, with intent to obstruct the sale by the United States of bonds or other securities of the United States or the making of loans by or to the United States, and whoever when the United States is at war, shall willfully cause or attempt to cause, or incite or attempt to incite, insubordination, disloyalty, mutiny, or refusal of duty, in the military or naval forces of the United States, or shall willfully obstruct or attempt to obstruct the recruiting or enlistment services of the United States, and whoever, when the United States is at war, shall willfully utter, print, write or publish any disloyal, profane, scurrilous, or abusive language about the form of government of the United States or the Constitution of the United States, or the military or naval forces of the United States, or the flag of the United States, or the uniform of the Army or Navy of the United States into contempt, scorn, contumely, or disrepute, or shall willfully utter, print, write, or publish any language intended to incite, provoke, or encourage resistance to the United States, or to promote the cause of its enemies, or shall willfully display the flag of any foreign enemy, or shall willfully by utterance, writing, printing, publication, or language spoken, urge, incite, or advocate any curtailment of production in this country of any thing or things, product or products, necessary or essential to the prosecution of the war in which the United States may be engaged, with intent by such curtailment to cripple or hinder the United States in the prosecution of war, and whoever shall willfully advocate, teach, defend, or suggest the doing of any of the acts or things in this section enumerated, and whoever shall by word or act support or favor the cause of any country with which the United States is at war or by word or act oppose the cause of the United States therein, shall be punished by a fine of not more than $10,000 or the imprisonment for not more than twenty years, or both: Provided, That any employee or official of the United States Government who commits any disloyal act or utters any unpatriotic or disloyal language, or who, in an abusive and violent manner criticizes the Army or Navy or the flag of the United States shall be at once dismissed from the service. . . .

Sec. 4. When the United States is at war, the Postmaster General may, upon evidence satisfactory to him that any person or concern is using the mails in violation of any of the provisions of this Act, instruct the postmaster at any post office at which mail is received addressed to such person or concern to return to the postmaster at the office at which they were originally mailed all letters or other matter so addressed, with the words "Mail to this address undeliverable under Espionage Act" plainly written or stamped upon the outside thereof, and all such letters or other matter so returned to such postmasters shall be by them returned to the senders thereof under such regulations as the Postmaster General may prescribe.

Source: Sedition Act of 1918. *United States Statutes at Large.* Vol. 40. Washington, DC: Government Printing Office, April 1917–March 1919.

1919: THE SUPREME COURT ESTABLISHES "CLEAR AND PRESENT DANGER" DOCTRINE IN *SCHENCK v. UNITED STATES*

During World War I, American socialist Charles Schenck, who opposed U.S. involvement in the conflict, produced a flyer for distribution to recently drafted American servicemen. Schenk's circular alleged that the war was being orchestrated by monied interests, argued that the draft amounted to "involuntary servitude," and urged servicemen to demand an end to conscription. Schenck was subsequently arrested and charged by the U.S. government with violating the Espionage Act, which President Woodrow Wilson had signed into law in 1917. Schenck was convicted of trying to foment insubordination in the U.S. Armed Forces, but he appealed, asserting that the Espionage Act violated his First Amendment rights of free speech.

The case eventually reached the U.S. Supreme Court, which unanimously upheld Schenk's conviction. The Court, in an opinion written by Justice Oliver Wendell Holmes, stated that (1) the Espionage Act did not violate the U.S. Constitution and (2) Schenck was guilty because the statements in his flyer constituted a "clear and present danger" to American interests that overrode his free speech rights—which were extensive but not limitless. In explaining the latter finding, Holmes famously asserted that statements had to be understood in their full context. For example, he wrote, a man who cried "Fire!" in his own home or in a quiet park would be within his constitutional rights to do so, but "the most stringent protection of free speech would not protect a man in falsely shouting fire in a theatre and causing a panic." Excerpts from Holmes's opinion are reprinted below.

Holmes's "clear and present danger" standard lasted for a half century, when it gave way to the "imminent lawless action" standard enshrined in Brandenburg v. Ohio *(1969). According to the* Brandenburg *standard, speech limitations apply only when they "incite" unlawful acts carried out before authorities can prevent them from taking place.*

This is an indictment in three counts. The first charges a conspiracy to violate the Espionage Act of June 15, 1917, by causing and attempting to cause insubordination, &c., in the military and naval forces of the United States, and to obstruct the recruiting and enlistment service of the United States, when the United States was at war with the German Empire, to-wit, that the defendants willfully conspired to have printed and circulated to men who had been called and accepted for military service under the Act of May 18, 1917, a document set forth and alleged to be calculated to cause such insubordination and obstruction. The count alleges overt acts in pursuance of the conspiracy, ending in the distribution of the document set forth. The second count alleges a conspiracy to commit an offence against the United States, to-wit, to use the mails for the transmission of matter declared to be nonmailable by Title XII, § 2 of the Act of June 15, 1917, to-wit, the above mentioned document, with an averment of the same overt acts. The third count charges an unlawful use of the mails for the transmission of the same matter and otherwise as above. The defendants were found guilty on all the counts. They set up the First Amendment to the Constitution forbidding Congress to make any law abridging the freedom of speech, or of the press, and bringing the case here on that ground have argued some other points also of which we must dispose.

It is argued that the evidence, if admissible, was not sufficient to prove that the defendant Schenck was concerned in sending the documents. According to the testimony, Schenck said he was general secretary of the Socialist party, and had charge of the Socialist headquarters from which the documents were sent. He identified a book found there as the minutes of the Executive Committee of the party. The book showed a resolution of August 13, 1917, that 15,000 leaflets should be printed on the other side of one of them in use, to be mailed to men who had passed exemption boards, and for distribution. Schenck personally attended to the printing. On August 20, the general secretary's report said "Obtained new leaflets from printer and started work addressing envelopes" &c., and there was a resolve that Comrade Schenck be allowed $125 for sending leaflets through the mail. He said that he had about fifteen or sixteen thousand printed. There were files of the circular in question in the inner office which he said were printed on the other side of the one sided circular, and were there for distribution. Other copies were proved to have been sent through the mails to drafted men. Without going into confirmatory details that were proved, no reasonable man could doubt that the defendant Schenck was largely instrumental in sending the circulars about. As to the defendant Baer, there was evidence that she was a member of the Executive Board, and that the minutes of its transactions were hers. The argument as to the sufficiency of the evidence that the defendants conspired to send the documents only impairs the seriousness of the real defence.

It is objected that the documentary evidence was not admissible because obtained upon a search warrant, valid so far as appears. The contrary is established. *Adams v. New York, 192 U.S. 585; Weeks v. United States, 232 U.S. 383,* 395, 396. The search warrant did not issue against the defendant, but against the Socialist headquarters at 1326 Arch Street, and it would seem that the documents technically were not even in the defendants' possession. *See Johnson v. United States,* 228 U.S. 457. Notwithstanding some protest in argument, the notion that evidence even directly proceeding from the defendant in a criminal proceeding is excluded in all cases by the Fifth Amendment is plainly unsound. *Holt v. United States, 218 U.S. 245,* 252, 253.

The document in question, upon its first printed side, recited the first section of the Thirteenth Amendment, said that the idea embodied in it was violated by the Conscription Act, and that a conscript is little better than a convict. In impassioned language, it intimated that conscription was despotism in its worst form, and a monstrous wrong against humanity in the interest of Wall Street's chosen few. It said "Do not submit to intimidation," but in form, at least, confined itself to peaceful measures such as a petition for the repeal of the act. The other and later printed side of the sheet was headed "Assert Your Rights." It stated reasons for alleging that anyone violated the Constitution when he refused to recognize "your right to assert your opposition to the draft," and went on.

"If you do not assert and support your rights, you are helping to deny or disparage rights which it is the solemn duty of all citizens and residents of the United States to retain."

It described the arguments on the other side as coming from cunning politicians and a mercenary capitalist press, and even silent consent to the conscription law as helping to support an infamous conspiracy. It denied the power to send our citizens away to foreign shores to shoot up the people of other lands, and added that words could not express the condemnation such cold-blooded ruthlessness deserves, &c., &c., winding up, "You must do your share to maintain, support and uphold the rights of the people of this country." Of course, the document would not have been sent unless it had been intended to have some effect, and we do not see what effect it could be expected to have upon persons subject to the draft except to influence them to obstruct the carrying of it out. The defendants do not deny that the jury might find against them on this point.

But it is said, suppose that that was the tendency of this circular, it is protected by the First Amendment to the Constitution. Two of the strongest expressions are said to be quoted respectively from well known public men. It well may be that the prohibition of laws abridging the freedom of speech is not confined to previous restraints, although to prevent them may have been the main purpose, as intimated in *Patterson v. Colorado,* 205 U.S. 454, 462. We admit that, in many places and in ordinary times, the defendants, in saying all that was said in the circular, would have been within their constitutional rights. But the character of every act depends upon the circumstances in which it is done. *Aikens v. Wisconsin,* 195 U.S. 194, 205, 206. The most stringent protection of free speech would not protect a man in falsely shouting fire in a theatre and causing a panic. It does not even protect a man from an injunction against uttering words that may have all the effect of force. *Gompers v. Bucks Stove & Range Co., 221 U.S. 418,* 439. The question in every case is whether the words used are used in such circumstances and are of such a nature as to create a clear and present danger that they will bring about the substantive evils that Congress has a right to prevent. It is a question of proximity and degree. When a nation is at war, many things that might be said in time of peace are such a hindrance to its effort that their utterance will not be endured so long as men fight, and that no Court could regard them as protected by any constitutional right. It seems to be admitted that, if an actual obstruction of the recruiting service were proved, liability for words that produced that effect might be enforced. The statute of 1917, in § 4, punishes conspiracies to obstruct, as well as actual obstruction. If the act (speaking, or circulating a paper), its tendency, and the intent with which it is done are the same, we perceive no ground for saying that success alone warrants making the act a crime. *Goldman v. United States, 245 U.S. 474,* 477. Indeed, that case might be said to dispose of the present contention if the precedent covers all *media concludendi.* But, as the right to free speech was not referred to specially, we have thought fit to add a few words.

It was not argued that a conspiracy to obstruct the draft was not within the words of the Act of 1917. The words are "obstruct the recruiting or enlistment service," and it might be suggested that they refer only to making it hard to get volunteers. Recruiting heretofore usually having been accomplished by getting volunteers, the word is apt to call up that method only in our minds. But recruiting is gaining fresh supplies for the forces, as well by draft as otherwise. It is put as an alternative to enlistment or voluntary enrollment in this act. The fact that the Act of 1917 was enlarged by the amending Act of May 16, 1918, c. 75, 40 Stat. 553, of course, does not affect the present indictment, and would not even if the former act had been repealed. Rev.Stats., § 13.

Judgments affirmed.

Source: Justice Holmes, Oliver Wendell. Opinion of the Court. *Schenck v. United States,* 249 U.S. 47. Decided March 3, 1919. United States Reports, Volume 249, March–April 1919.

1928: JUSTICE BRANDEIS'S DISSENT IN *OLMSTEAD v. UNITED STATES*

Roy Olmstead was convicted in the federal district court of transporting and selling liquor in violation of the National Prohibition Act. The evidence used to convict Olmstead was secured by a warrantless wiretap placed by federal agents on telephone lines between Olmstead's home and office. Olmstead challenged the admission of this evidence on the grounds that it was obtained in violation of the Fourth Amendment's guarantee against unreasonable searches and seizures. The U.S. Supreme Court held on June 4, 1928, that because the interception of telephone conversations occurred without "trespass" on private property there was no "search" of a constitutionally protected area. Moreover, conversations were not tangible items that could be "seized." As Chief Justice William H. Taft stated in his majority opinion, "The reasonable view is that one who installs in his house a telephone instrument with connecting wires intends to project his voice to those quite outside, and that the wires beyond his house and messages while passing over them are not within the protection of the Fourth Amendment."

In dissent, Justice Louis Brandeis made an argument for a broader construction of the Fourth Amendment, which has become one of the most famous defenses of privacy in American history. He contended that the amendment conferred upon each individual a general right to privacy, one not confined to traditional categories of searches involving actual trespass on private property or seizures of tangible items. This dissent foreshadowed the Court's holding in Katz v. United States *(1967), which overturned* Olmstead.

MR. JUSTICE BRANDEIS, dissenting. . . . By objections seasonably made and persistently renewed, the defendants objected to the admission of the evidence obtained by wire-tapping, on the ground that the Government's wire-tapping constituted an unreasonable search and seizure, in violation of the Fourth Amendment; and that the use as evidence of the conversations overheard compelled the defendants to be witnesses against themselves, in violation of the Fifth Amendment.

The Government makes no attempt to defend the methods employed by its officers. Indeed, it concedes that if wire-tapping can be deemed a search and seizure within the Fourth Amendment, such wire-tapping as was practiced in the case at bar was an unreasonable search and seizure, and that the evidence thus obtained was inadmissible. But it relies on the language of the Amendment; and it claims that the protection given thereby cannot properly be held to include a telephone conversation. . . .

When the Fourth and Fifth Amendment were adopted, "the form that evil had theretofore taken," had been necessarily simple. Force and violence were then the only means known to man by which a Government could directly effect self-incrimination. It could compel the individual to testify—a compulsion effected, if need be, by torture. It could secure possession of his papers and other articles incident to his private life—a seizure effected, if need be, by breaking and entry. Protection against such invasion of "the sanctities of a man's home and the privacies of life" was provided in the Fourth and Fifth Amendments by specific language. . . . But "time works changes, brings into existence new conditions and purposes." Subtler and more far-reaching means of invading privacy have become available to the Government. Discovery and invention have made it possible for the Government, by means far more effective than stretching upon the rack, to obtain disclosure in court of what is whispered in the closet.

Moreover, "in the application of a constitution, our contemplation cannot be only of what has been but of what may be." The progress of science in furnishing the Government with means of espionage is not likely to stop with wire-tapping. Ways may someday be developed by which the Government, without removing papers from secret drawers, can reproduce them in court, and by which it will be enabled to expose to a jury the most intimate occurrences of the home. Advances in the psychic and related sciences may bring means of exploring unexpressed beliefs, thoughts and emotions. "That places the liberty of every man in the hands of every petty officer" was said by James Otis of much lesser intrusions than these. To Lord Camden, a far slighter intrusion seemed "subversive of all the comforts of society." Can it be that the Constitution affords no protection against such invasions of individual security? . . .

In *Ex parte Jackson*, 96 U.S. 727, it was held that a sealed letter entrusted to the mail is protected by the Amendments. The mail is a public service furnished by the Government. The telephone is a public service furnished by its authority. There is, in essence, no difference between the sealed letter and the private telephone message. As Judge Rudkin said below: "True, the one is visible, the other invisible; the one is tangible, the other intangible; the one is sealed, and the other unsealed, but these are distinctions without a difference." The evil incident to invasion of the privacy of the telephone is far greater than that involved in tampering with the mails. Whenever a telephone line is tapped, the privacy of the persons at both ends of the line is invaded and all conversations between them upon any subject, and, although proper, confidential and privileged, may be overheard. Moreover, the tapping of one man's telephone line involves the tapping of the telephone of every other person whom he may call or who may call him. As a means of espionage, writs of assistance and general warrants are but puny instruments of tyranny and oppression when compared with wire-tapping.

Time and again, this Court in giving effect to the principle underlying the Fourth Amendment, has refused to place an unduly literal construction upon it. This was notably illustrated in the *Boyd* case itself. Taking language in its ordinary meaning, there is no "search" or "seizure" when a defendant is required to produce a document in the orderly process of a court's procedure. "The right of the people to be secure in their persons, houses, papers, and effects, against unreasonable searches and seizures," would not be violated, under any ordinary construction of language, by compelling obedience to a subpoena. But this Court holds the evidence inadmissible simply because the information leading to the issue of the subpoena has been unlawfully secured. . . . The provision against self-incrimination in the Fifth Amendment has been given an equally broad construction. . . .

Decisions of this Court applying the principle of the *Boyd* case have settled these things. Unjustified search and seizure violates the Fourth Amendment, whatever the character of the paper; whether the paper when taken by the federal officers was in the home, in an office, or elsewhere; whether the taking was effected by force, by fraud, or in the orderly process of a court's procedure. From these decisions, it follows necessarily that the Amendment is violated by the officer's reading the paper without a physical seizure, without his even touching it; and that use, in any criminal proceeding, of the contents of the paper so examined—as where they are testified to by a federal officer who thus saw the document, or where, through knowledge so obtained, a copy has been procured elsewhere—any such use constitutes a violation of the Fifth Amendment.

The protection guaranteed by the Amendments is much broader in scope. The makers of our Constitution undertook to secure conditions favorable to the pursuit of happiness. They recognized the significance of man's spiritual nature, of his feelings, and of his intellect. They knew that only a part of the pain, pleasure and satisfactions of life are to be found in material things. They sought to protect Americans in their beliefs, their thoughts, their emotions and their sensations. They conferred, as against the Government, the right to be let alone—the most comprehensive of rights and the right most valued by civilized men. To protect that right, every unjustifiable intrusion by the Government upon the privacy of the individual, whatever the means employed, must be deemed a violation of the Fourth Amendment. And the use, as evidence in a criminal proceeding, of facts ascertained by such intrusion must be deemed a violation of the Fifth.

Applying to the Fourth and Fifth Amendments the established rule of construction, the defendants' objections to the evidence obtained by wire-tapping must, in my opinion, be sustained. It is, of course, immaterial where the physical connection with the telephone wires leading into the defendants' premises was made. And it is also immaterial that the intrusion was in aid of law enforcement. Experience should teach us to be most on our guard to protect liberty when the Government's purposes are beneficent. Men born to freedom are naturally alert to repel invasion of their liberty by evil-minded rulers. The greatest dangers to liberty lurk in insidious encroachment by men of zeal, well meaning but without understanding.

Independently of the constitutional question, I am of opinion that the judgment should be reversed. By the laws of Washington, wire-tapping is a crime. . . . To prove its case, the Government was obliged to lay bare the crimes committed by its officers on its behalf. A federal court should not permit such a prosecution to continue. . . .

The evidence obtained by crime was obtained at the Government's expense, by its officers, while acting on its behalf; the officers who committed these crimes are the same officers who were charged with the enforcement of the Prohibition Act; the crimes of these officers were committed for the purpose of securing evidence with which to obtain an indictment and to secure a conviction. The evidence so obtained constitutes the warp and woof of the Government's case. The aggregate of the Government evidence occupies 306 pages of the printed record. More than 210 of them are filled by recitals of the details of the wire-tapping and of facts ascertained thereby. . . .

When these unlawful acts were committed, they were crimes only of the officers individually. The Government was innocent, in legal contemplation; for no federal official is authorized to commit a crime on its behalf. When the Government, having full knowledge, sought, through the Department of Justice, to avail itself of the fruits of these acts in order to accomplish its own ends, it assumed moral responsibility for the officers' crimes. . . . And if this Court should permit the Government, by means of its officers' crimes, to effect its purpose of punishing the defendants, there would seem to be present all the elements of a ratification. If so, the Government itself would become a lawbreaker. . . .

Decency, security and liberty alike demand that government officials shall be subjected to the same rules of conduct that are commands to the citizen. In a government of laws, existence of the government will be imperilled if it fails to observe the law scrupulously. Our Government is the potent, the omnipresent teacher. For good or for ill, it teaches the whole people by its example. Crime is contagious. If the Government becomes a lawbreaker, it breeds contempt for law; it invites every man to become a law unto himself; it invites anarchy. To declare that in the administration of the criminal law the end justifies the means—to declare that the Government may commit crimes in order to secure the conviction of a private criminal—would bring terrible retribution. Against that pernicious doctrine this Court should resolutely set its face.

Source: Olmstead v. United States, 277 U.S. 438 (1928).

1940: THE ALIEN REGISTRATION ACT

The 1940 Alien Registration Act is also known as the Smith Act because it was proposed by conservative Democratic Congressman Howard Smith of Virginia, a poll tax supporter and a leader of the antilabor bloc in Congress. Signed into law by President Franklin D. Roosevelt, it was the first statute since the Alien and Sedition Acts of 1798 to make mere advocacy of ideas a federal crime. In particular, the Alien Registration Act made it illegal to print, publish, or circulate printed matter advocating or teaching the overthrow of the U. S. government. The act also required all alien residents over the age of fourteen living within the United States to register on an annual basis with the government. Registration requirements included fingerprinting, the carrying of identification cards, and the submission of a comprehensive statement of their personal and occupational status and political beliefs. Individuals found to have ties to "subversive organizations" could be deported.

Although five million aliens were registered and fingerprinted following passage of the Smith Act, its antisubversive sections were not used until 1943, when a small group of Minneapolis Trotskyites were convicted under the law. When the Cold War intensified in the late 1940s, the Truman administration launched dramatic prosecutions of Communist party leaders. These and subsequent prosecutions eventually forced the Supreme Court to clarify the act's terms and reach. In Dennis v. United States, *341 U.S. 494 (1951), the Court considered the convictions of eleven Communist Party leaders on charges of conspiracy to violate the advocacy and organizing sections of the statute. Chief Justice Vinson's plurality opinion for the Court held that there was a distinction between the mere teaching of communist philosophies and the active advocacy of those ideas. The Court applied a revised clear and present danger test and concluded that the evil sought to be prevented by the federal government was serious enough to justify suppression of speech. The statute remains in force today, although it has been amended several times over the years.*

An Act

To prohibit certain subversive activities; to amend certain provisions of law with respect to the admission and deportation of aliens; to require the fingerprinting and registration of aliens; and for other purposes.

Be it enacted by the Senate and House of Representatives of the United States of America in Congress assembled,

Title I

Section 1. (a) It shall be unlawful for any person, with intent to interfere with, impair, or influence the loyalty, morale, or discipline of the military or naval forces of the United States—

(1) to advise, counsel, urge, or in any manner cause insubordination, disloyalty, mutiny, or refusal of duty by any member of the military or naval forces of the United States; or

(2) to distribute any written or printed matter which advises, counsels, or urges insubordination, disloyalty, mutiny, or refusal of duty by any member of the military or naval forces of the United States.

(b) For the purposes of this section, the term "military or naval forces of the United States" includes the Army of the United States, as defined in section 1 of the National Defense Act of June 3, 1916, as amended (48 Stat. 153; U.S.C., title 10, sec. 2), the Navy, Marine Corps, Coast Guard, Naval Reserve, and Marine Corps Reserve of the United States; and, when any merchant vessel is commissioned in the Navy or is in the service of the Army or the Navy, includes the master, officers, and crew of such vessel.

Sec. 2. (a) It shall be unlawful for any person—

(1) to knowingly or willfully advocate, abet, advise, or teach the duty, necessity, desirability, or propriety of overthrowing or destroying any government in the United States by force or violence, or by the assassination of any officer of any such government;

(2) with the intent to cause the overthrow or destruction of any government in the United States, to print, publish, edit, issue, circulate, sell, distribute, or publicly display any written or printed matter advocating, advising, or teaching the duty, necessity, desirability, or propriety of overthrowing or destroying any government in the United States by force or violence.

(3) to organize or help to organize any society, group, or assembly of persons who teach, advocate, or encourage the overthrow or destruction of any government in the United States by force or violence; or to be or become a member of, or affiliate with, any such society, group, or assembly of persons, knowing the purposes thereof.

(b) For the purposes of this section, the term "government in the United States" means the Government of the United States, the government of any State, Territory, or possession of the United States, the government of the District of Columbia, or the government of any political subdivision of any of them.

Sec. 3. It shall be unlawful for any person to attempt to commit, or to conspire to commit, any of the acts prohibited by the provisions of this title.

Sec. 4. Any written or printed matter of the character described in section 1 or section 2 of this Act, which is intended for use in violation of this Act, may be taken from any house or other place in which it may be found, or from any person in whose possession it may be, under a search warrant issued pursuant to the provisions of title XI of the Act entitled "An Act to punish acts of interference with the foreign relations, the neutrality and the foreign commerce of the United States, to punish espionage, and better to enforce the criminal laws of the United States, and for other purposes", approved June 15, 1917 (40 Stat. 228; U.S.C., title 18, ch. 18).

Sec. 5. (a) Any person who violates any of the provisions of this title shall, upon conviction thereof, be fined not more than $10,000 or imprisoned for not more than ten years, or both.

(b) No person convicted of violating any of the provisions of this title shall, during the five years next following his conviction, be eligible for employment by the United States, or by any department or agency thereof (including any corporation the Stock of which is wholly owned by the United States).

Title II

Sec. 20. Section 19 of the Immigration Act of February 5, 1917 (39 Stat. 889; U.S.C., title 8, sec. 155), as amended, is amended by inserting, after "Sec. 19.", the letter "(a)", and by adding at the end of such section the following new subsections:

"(b) Any alien of any of the classes specified in this subsection, in addition to aliens who are deportable under other provisions of law, shall, upon warrant of the Attorney General, be taken into custody and deported:

"(1) Any alien who, at any time within five years after entry, shall have, knowingly and for gain, encouraged, induced, assisted, abetted, or aided any other alien to enter or to try to enter the United States in violation of law.

"(2) Any alien who, at any time after entry, shall have on more than one occasion, knowingly and for gain, encouraged, induced, assisted, abetted, or aided any other alien or aliens to enter or to try to enter the United States in violation of law.

"(3) Any alien who, at any time after entry, shall have been convicted of possessing or carrying in violation of any law any weapon which shoots or is designed to shoot automatically or semi-automatically more than one shot without manual reloading, by a single function of the trigger, or a weapon commonly called a sawed-off shotgun.

"(4) Any alien who, at any time within five years after entry, shall have been convicted of violating the provisions of title I of the Alien Registration Act, 1940.

"(5) Any alien who, at any time after entry, shall have been convicted more than once of violating the provisions of title I of the Alien Registration Act, 1940.

"No alien who is deportable under the provisions of paragraph (3), (4), or (5) of this subsection shall be deported until the termination of his imprisonment or the entry of an order releasing him on probation or parole.

"(c) In the same of any alien (other than one to whom subsection (d) is applicable) who is deportable under any law of the United States and who has proved good moral character for the preceding five years, the Attorney General may (1) permit such alien to depart the United States to any country of his choice at his own expense, in lieu of deportation, or (2) suspend deportation of such alien if not racially inadmissible or ineligible to naturalization in the United States if he finds that such deportation would result in serious economic detriment to a citizen or legally resident alien who is the spouse, parent, or minor child of such deportable alien. If the deportation of any alien is suspended under the provisions of this subsection for more than six months, all of the facts and pertinent provisions of law in the case shall be reported to the Congress within ten days after the beginning of its next regular session, with the reasons for such suspension. The Clerk of the House shall have such report printed as a public document. If during that session the two Houses pass a concurrent resolution stating in substance that the Congress does not favor the suspension of such deportation, the Attorney General shall thereupon deport such alien in the manner provided by law. If during the session the two Houses do not pass such a resolution, the Attorney General shall cancel deportation proceedings upon the termination of such session, except that such proceedings shall not be canceled in the case of any alien who was not legally admitted for permanent residence at the time of his last entry into the United States, unless such alien pays to the Commissioner of Immigration and Naturalization a fee of $18 (which fee shall be deposited in the Treasury of the United States as miscellaneous receipts). Upon the cancelation of such proceedings in any case in which such fee has been paid, the Commissioner shall record the alien's admission for permanent residence as of the date of his last entry into the United States and the Secretary of State shall, if the alien was a quota immigrant at the time of entry and was not charged to the appropriate quota, reduce by one the immigration quota of the country of the alien's nationality as defined in section 12 of the Act of May 26, 1924 (U.S.C., title 8, sec. 212), for the fiscal year then current or next following.

"(d) The provisions of subsection (c) shall not be applicable in the case of any alien who is deportable under (1) the Act of October 16, 1918 (40 Stat. 1008; U.S. C., title 8, sec. 137), entitled 'An Act to exclude and expel from the United States aliens who are members of the anarchist and similar classes', as amended; (2) the Act of May 26, 1922, entitled 'An Act to amend the Act entitled "An Act to prohibit the importation and use of opium for other than medicinal purposes", approved February 9, 1909, as amended' (42 Stat. 596; U.S.C., title 21, sec. 175); (3) the Act of February 18, 1931, entitled 'An Act to provide for the deportation of aliens convicted and sentenced for violation of any law regulating traffic in narcotics', as amended (46 Stat. 1171; U.S.C., title 8, sec. 156a); (4) any of the provisions of so much of subsection (a) of this section as relates to criminals, prostitutes, procurers, or other immoral persons, the mentally and physically deficient, anarchists, and similar classes; or (5) subsection (b) of this section."

Sec. 21. The Act entitled "An Act to provide for the deportation of aliens convicted and sentenced for violation of any law regulating traffic in narcotics", approved February 18, 1931, is amended—

(1) By striking out the words "and sentenced";

(2) By inserting after the words "any statute of the United States" the following: "or of any State, Territory, possession, or of the District of Columbia,"; and

(3) By inserting after the word "heroin" a comma and the word "marihuana".

Sec. 22. No alien shall be deportable by reason of the amendments made by section 20 or 21 on account of any act committed prior to the date of enactment of this Act.

Sec. 23. (a) The first paragraph of section 1 of the Act entitled "An Act to exclude and expel from the United States aliens who are members of the anarchistic and similar classes", approved October 16, 1918, as amended, is amended to read as follows:

"That any alien who, at any time, shall be or shall have been a member of any one of the following classes shall be excluded from admission into the United States:".

(b) Section 2 of such Act of October 16, 1918, as amended, is amended to read as follows:

"Sec. 2. Any alien who was at the time of entering the United States, or has been at any time thereafter, a member of any one of the classes of aliens enumerated in section 1 of this Act, shall, upon the warrant of the Attorney General, be taken into custody and deported in the manner provided in the Immigration Act of February 5, 1917. The provisions of this section shall be applicable to the classes of aliens mentioned in this Act, irrespective of the time of their entry into the United States."

Title III

Sec. 30. No visa shall hereafter be issued to any alien seeking to enter the United States unless said alien has been registered and fingerprinted in duplicate. One copy of the registration and fingerprint record shall be retained by the consul. The second copy shall be attached to the alien's visa and shall be taken up by the examining immigrant inspector at the port of arrival of the alien in the United States and forwarded to the Department of Justice, at Washington, District of Columbia.

Any alien seeking to enter the United States who does not present a visa (except in emergency cases defined by the Secretary of State), a reentry permit, or a border-crossing identification card shall be excluded from admission to the United States.

Sec. 31. (a) It shall be the duty of every alien now or hereafter in the United States, who (1) is fourteen years of age or older, (2) has not been registered and fingerprinted under section 30, and (3) remains in the United States for thirty days or longer, to apply for registration and to be fingerprinted before the expiration of such thirty days.

(b) It shall be the duty of every parent or legal guardian of any alien now or hereafter in the United States, who (1) is less than fourteen years of age, (2) has not been registered under section 30, and (3) remains in the United States for thirty days or longer, to apply for the registration of such alien before the expiration of such thirty days. Whenever any alien attains his fourteenth birthday in the United States he shall, within thirty days thereafter, apply in person for registration and to be fingerprinted.

Sec. 32. Notwithstanding the provisions of sections 30 and 31—

(a) The application for the registration and fingerprinting, or for the registration, of any alien who is in the United States on the effective date of such sections may be made at any time within four months after such date.

(b) No foreign government official, or member of his family, shall be required to be registered or fingerprinted under this title.

(c) The Commissioner is authorized to prescribe, with the approval of the Attorney General, special regulations for the registration and fingerprinting of (1) alien seamen, (2) holders of border-crossing identification cards, (3) aliens confined in institutions within the United States, (4) aliens under order or deportation, and (5) aliens of any other class not lawfully admitted to the United States for permanent residence.

Sec. 33. (a) All applications for registration and fingerprinting under section 31 shall be made at post offices or such other places as may be designated by the Commissioner.

(b) It shall be the duty of every postmaster, with such assistance as shall be provided by the Commissioner, to register and fingerprint any applicant for registration and fingerprinting under such section, and for such purposes to designate appropriate space in the local post office for such registration and fingerprinting. Every postmaster shall forward promptly to the Department of Justice, at Washington, District of Columbia, the registration and fingerprint record of every alien registered and fingerprinted by him. The Commissioner may designate such other places for registration and fingerprinting as may be necessary for carrying out the provisions of this Act, and provide for registration and fingerprinting of aliens at such places by officers or employees of the Immigration and Naturalization Service designated by the Commissioner. The duties imposed upon any postmaster under this Act shall also be performed by any employees at the post office of such postmaster who are designated by the postmaster for such purpose.

Sec. 34. (a) The Commissioner is authorized and directed to prepare forms for the registration and fingerprinting of aliens under this title. Such forms shall contain inquiries with respect to (1) the date and place of entry of the alien into the United States; (2) activities in which he has been and intends to be engaged; (3) the length of time he expects to remain in the United States; (4) the criminal record, if any, of such alien; and (5) such additional matters as may be prescribed by the Commissioner, with the approval of the Attorney General.

(b) All registration and fingerprint records made under the provisions of this title shall be secret and confidential, and shall be made available only to such persons or agencies as may be designated by the Commissioner, with the approval of the Attorney General.

(c) Every person required to apply for the registration of himself or another under this title shall submit under oath the information required for such registration. Any person authorized to register aliens under this title shall be authorized to administer oaths for such purpose.

Sec. 35. Any alien required to be registered under this title who is a resident of the United States shall notify the Commissioner in writing of each change of residence and new address within five days from the date of such change. Any other alien required to be registered under this title shall notify the Commissioner in writing of his address at the expiration of each three months' period of residence in the United States. In the case of an alien for whom a parent or legal guardian is required to apply for registration, the notices required by this section shall be given by such parent or legal guardian.

Sec. 36. (a) Any alien required to apply for registration and to be fingerprinted who willfully fails or refuses to make such application or to be fingerprinted, and any parent or legal guardian required to apply for the registration of any alien who willfully fails or refuses to file application for the registration of such alien shall, upon conviction thereof be fined not to exceed $1,000 or be imprisoned not more than six months, or both.

(b) Any alien, or any parent or legal guardian of any alien, who fails to give written notice to the Commissioner of change of address as required by section 35 of this Act shall, upon conviction thereof, be fined not to exceed $100, or be imprisoned not more than thirty days, or both.

(c) Any alien or any parent or legal guardian of any alien, who files an application for registration containing statements known by him to be false, or who procures or attempts to procure registration of himself or another person through fraud, shall, upon conviction thereof, be fined not to exceed $1,000, or be imprisoned not more than six months, or both; and any alien so convicted within five years after entry into the United States shall, upon the warrant of the Attorney General, be taken into custody and be deported in the manner provided in sections 19 and 20 of the Immigration Act of February 5, 1917, as amended.

Sec. 37. (a) The Commissioner, with the approval of the Attorney General, is authorized and empowered to make the prescribe, and from time to time to change and amend, such rules and regulations not in conflict with this Act as he may deem necessary and proper in aid of the administration and enforcement of this title (including provisions for the identification of aliens registered under this title); except that all such rules and regulations, insofar as they relate to the performance of functions by consular officers or officers or employees in the Postal Service, shall be prescribed by the Secretary of State and the Postmaster General, respectively, upon recommendation of the Attorney General. The powers conferred upon the Attorney General by this Act and all other powers of the Attorney General relating to the administration of the Immigration and Naturalization Service may be exercised by the Attorney General through such officers of the Department of Justice, including officers of the Immigration and Naturalization Service, attorneys, special attorneys, and special assistants to the Attorney General, as he may designate specifically for such purposes.

(b) The Commissioner is authorized to make such expenditures, to employ such additional temporary and permanent employees, and to rent such quarters outside the District of Columbia as may be necessary for carrying out the provisions of this title.

Sec. 38. (a) For the purposes of this title—

(1) the term "United States", when used in a geographical sense, means the States, the Territories of Alaska and Hawaii, the District of Columbia, Puerto Rico, and the Virgin Islands;

(2) the term "Commissioner" means the Commissioner of Immigration and Naturalization.

(b) The provisions of this title shall take effect upon the date of enactment of this Act; except that sections 30 and 31 shall take effect sixty days after the date of its enactment.

Sec. 39. The President is authorized to provide, by Executive order, for the registration and fingerprinting, in a manner as nearly similar to that provided in this title as he deems practicable, of aliens in the Panama Canal Zone.

Approved, June 28, 1940.

Source: Alien Registration Act of 1940. *U.S. Statutes at Large,* 76th Congress, 3rd Session. Washington, DC: Government Printing Office, pp. 670–76.

1942: PRESIDENT ROOSEVELT ORDERS THE INTERNMENT OF JAPANESE AMERICANS

When Japan bombed United States' Pearl Harbor naval base in Hawaii on December 7, 1941, the lives of Japanese immigrants and Japanese Americans living in the western United States were turned upside down. Already victimized by decades of bigotry that had greatly restricted their economic, educational, and citizenship opportunities, the Pearl Harbor attack triggered a fresh upheaval of hostility and suspicion toward people of Japanese descent in United States. Government and military authorities initiated a variety of surveillance programs to track and restrict the activities of people from Japanese-American households and communities. Despite these draconian measures, many Americans felt that more extreme steps needed to be taken to ensure that Japanese Americans did not carry out acts of sabotage or other subversive activities against the United States.

President Franklin D. Roosevelt eventually bowed to this pressure. On February 19, 1942, Roosevelt issued Executive Order 9066, authorizing the establishment of "military areas" from which people designated as potential national security threats could be removed. This order paved the way over the next six months for the internment of more than 120,000 people of Japanese descent—including about 70,000 who were American citizens—in remote detention facilities across the West, where they could be monitored at all times. Several legal challenges to the constitutionality of the government's internment actions subsequently made their way to the U.S. Supreme Court, but each time the Court sided with the government.

Authorizing the Secretary of War to Prescribe Military Areas

Whereas the successful prosecution of the war requires every possible protection against espionage and against sabotage to national-defense material, national-defense premises, and national-defense utilities as defined in Section 4, Act of April 20, 1918, 40 Stat. 533, as amended by the Act of November 30, 1940, 54 Stat. 1220, and the Act of August 21, 1941, 55 Stat. 655 (U.S.C., Title 50, Sec. 104);

Now, therefore, by virtue of the authority vested in me as President of the United States, and Commander in Chief of the Army and Navy, I hereby authorize and direct the Secretary of War, and the Military Commanders whom he may from time to time designate, whenever he or any designated Commander deems such action necessary or desirable, to prescribe military areas in such places and of such extent as he or the appropriate Military Commander may determine, from which any or all persons may be excluded, and with respect to which, the right of any person to enter, remain in, or leave shall be subject to whatever restrictions the Secretary of War or the appropriate Military Commander may impose in his discretion.

The Secretary of War is hereby authorized to provide for residents of any such area who are excluded therefrom, such transportation, food, shelter, and other accommodations as may be necessary, in the judgment of the Secretary of War or the said Military Commander, and until other arrangements are made, to accomplish the purpose of this order. The designation of military areas in any region or locality shall supersede designations of prohibited and restricted areas by the Attorney General under the Proclamations of December 7 and 8, 1941, and shall supersede the responsibility and authority of the Attorney General under the said Proclamations in respect of such prohibited and restricted areas.

I hereby further authorize and direct the Secretary of War and the said Military Commanders to take such other steps as he or the appropriate Military Commander may deem advisable to enforce compliance with the restrictions applicable to each Military area hereinabove authorized to be designated, including the use of Federal troops and other Federal Agencies, with authority to accept assistance of state and local agencies.

I hereby further authorize and direct all Executive Departments, independent establishments and other Federal Agencies, to assist the Secretary of War or the said Military Commanders in carrying out this Executive Order, including the furnishing of medical aid, hospitalization, food, clothing, transportation, use of land, shelter, and other supplies, equipment, utilities, facilities, and services.

This order shall not be construed as modifying or limiting in any way the authority heretofore granted under Executive Order No. 8972, dated December 12, 1941, nor shall it be construed as limiting or modifying the duty and responsibility of the Federal Bureau of Investigation, with respect to the investigation of alleged acts of sabotage or the duty and responsibility of the Attorney General and the Department of Justice under the Proclamations of December 7 and 8, 1941, prescribing regulations for the conduct and control of alien enemies, except as such duty and responsibility is superseded by the designation of military areas hereunder.

Franklin D. Roosevelt
The White House,
February 19, 1942

Source: Roosevelt, Franklin D. "Executive Order 9066: Authorizing the Secretary of War to Prescribe Military Areas, February 19, 1942." *Code of Federal Regulations*, title 3, sec. 1092 (1938–1943).

1944: *EX PARTE ENDO* RULING PAVES THE WAY FOR CLOSING OF INTERNMENT CAMPS

On December 18, 1944, the U.S. Supreme Court issued a unanimous decision that historians regarded as a death knell for the U.S. government's wartime practice of keeping immigrants of Japanese ancestry and Japanese-American citizens in internment camps. In the case, commonly known as Ex Parte Endo*, the Court ruled that citizens believed by the government itself to be loyal to the United States could not legally be detained in camps maintained by the War Relocation Authority or other government agencies: "A citizen who is concededly loyal presents no problem of espionage or sabotage. Loyalty is a matter of the heart and mind not of race, creed, or color. He who is loyal is by definition not a spy or a saboteur. When the power to detain is derived from the power to protect the war effort against espionage and sabotage, detention which has no relationship to that objective is unauthorized."*

The case was named after Mitsuye Endo, a young clerical worker for the California State Department of Motor Vehicles who was involuntarily shipped off to a WRA internment camp after President Franklin D. Roosevelt issued Executive Order 9066.

Although the Court's decision paved the way for the release of Endo and other Japanese Americans from the camps, it did not render a legal judgment about the constitutionality of internment itself. The opinion, authored by Justice William O. Douglas, is excerpted below:

We are of the view that Mitsuye Endo should be given her liberty. In reaching that conclusion we do not come to the underlying constitutional issues which have been argued. For we conclude that, whatever power the War Relocation Authority may have to detain other classes of citizens, it has no authority to subject citizens who are concededly loyal to its leave procedure.

It should be noted at the outset that we do not have here a question such as was presented in Ex parte Milligan, 4 Wall. 2, 18 L.Ed. 281, or in Ex parte Quirin, 317 U.S. 1, 63 S.Ct. 2, 87 L.Ed. 3, where the jurisdiction of military tribunals to try persons according to the law of war was challenged in habeas corpus proceedings. Mitsuye Endo is detained by a civilian agency, the War Relocation Authority, not by the military. Moreover, the evacuation program was not left exclusively to the military; the Authority was given a large measure of responsibility for its execution and Congress made its enforcement subject to civil penalties by the Act of March 21, 1942. Accordingly, no questions of military law are involved.

Such power of detention as the Authority has stems from Executive Order No. 9066. That order is the source of the authority delegated by General De Witt in his letter of August 11, 1942. And Executive Order No. 9102 which created the War Relocation Authority purported to do no more than to implement the program authorized by Executive Order No. 9066.

We approach the construction of Executive Order No. 9066 as we would approach the construction of legislation in this field. That Executive Order must indeed be considered along with the Act of March 21, 1942, which ratified and confirmed it (Kiyoshi Hirabayashi v. United States, supra, 320 U.S. at pages 87–91, 63 S.Ct. at pages 1379–1381, 87 L.Ed. 1774) as the Order and the statute together laid such basis as there is for participation by civil agencies of the federal government in the evacuation program. Broad powers frequently granted to the President or other executive officers by Congress so that they may deal with the exigencies of war time problems have been sustained. And the Constitution when it committed to the Executive and to Congress the exercise of the war power necessarily gave them wide scope for the exercise of judgment and discretion so that war might be waged effectively and successfully. At the same time, however, the Constitution is as specific in its enumeration of many of the civil rights of the individual as it is in its enumeration of the powers of his government. Thus it has prescribed procedural safeguards surrounding the arrest, detention and conviction of individuals. Some of these are contained in the Sixth Amendment, compliance with which is essential if convictions are to be sustained. And the Fifth Amendment provides that no person shall be deprived of liberty (as well as life or property) without due process of law. Moreover, as a further safeguard against invasion of the basic civil rights of the individual it is provided in Art. I, Sec. 9 of the Constitution that "The Privilege of the Writ of Habeas Corpus shall not be suspended, unless when in Cases of Rebellion or Invasion the public Safety may require it." See Ex parte Milligan, supra.

We mention these constitutional provisions not to stir the constitutional issues which have been argued at the bar but to indicate the approach which we think should be made to an Act of Congress or an order of the Chief Executive that touches the sensitive area of rights specifically guaranteed by the Constitution. This Court has quite consistently given a narrower scope for the operation of the presumption of constitutionality when legislation appeared on its face to violate a specific prohibition of the Constitution. We have likewise favored that interpretation of legislation which gives it the greater chance of surviving the test of constitutionality. Those analogies are suggestive here. We must assume that the Chief Executive and members of Congress, as well as the courts, are sensitive to and respectful of the liberties of the citizen. In interpreting a war-time measure we must assume that their purpose was to allow for the greatest possible accommodation between those liberties and the exigencies of war. We must assume, when asked to find implied powers in a grant of legislative or executive authority, that the law makers intended to place no greater restraint on the citizen than was clearly and unmistakably indicated by the language they used.

The Act of March 21, 1942, was a war measure. The House Report (H. Rep. No. 1906, 77th Cong., 2d Sess., p. 2) stated, "The necessity for this legislation arose from the fact that the safe conduct of the war requires the fullest possible protection against either espionage or sabotage to national defense material, national defense premises, and national defense utilities." That was the precise purpose of Executive Order No. 9066, for, as we have seen, it gave as the reason for the exclusion of persons from prescribed military areas the protection of such property "against espionage and against sabotage." And Executive Order No. 9102 which established the War Relocation Authority did so, as we have noted, "in order to provide for the removal from designated areas of persons whose removal is necessary in the interests of national security." The purpose and objective of the Act and of these orders are plain. Their single aim was the protection of the war effort against espionage and sabotage. It is in light of that one objective that the powers conferred by the orders must be construed.

Neither the Act nor the orders use the language of detention. The Act says that no one shall "enter, remain in leave, or commit any act" in the prescribed military areas contrary to the applicable restrictions. Executive Order No. 9066 subjects the right of any person "to enter, remain in, or leave" those prescribed areas to such restrictions as the military may impose. And apart from those restrictions the Secretary of War is only given authority to afford the evacuees "transportation, food, shelter, and other accommodations." Executive Order No. 9102 authorizes and directs the War Relocation Authority "to formulate and effectuate a program for the removal" of the persons covered by Executive Order No. 9066 from the prescribed military areas and "for their relocation, maintenance, and supervision." And power is given the Authority to make regulations "necessary or desirable to promote effective execution of such program." Moreover, unlike the case of curfew regulations (Kiyoshi Hirabayashi v. United States, supra), the legislative history of the Act of March 21, 1942, is silent on detention. And that silence may have special significance in view of the fact that detention in Relocation Centers was no part of the original program of evacuation but developed later to meet what seemed to the officials in charge to be mounting hostility to the evacuees on the part of the communities where they sought to go.

We do not mean to imply that detention in connection with no phase of the evacuation program would be lawful. The fact that the Act and the orders are silent on detention does not of course mean that any power to detain is lacking. Some such power might indeed be necessary to the successful operation of the evacuation program. At least we may so assume. Moreover, we may assume for the purposes of this case that initial detention in Relocation Centers was authorized. But we stress the silence of the legislative history and of the Act and the Executive Orders on the power to detain to emphasize that any such authority which exists must be implied. If there is to be the greatest possible accommodation of the liberties of the citizen with this war measure, any such implied power must be narrowly confined to the precise purpose of the evacuation program.

A citizen who is concededly loyal presents no problem of espionage or sabotage. Loyalty is a matter of the heart and mind not of race, creed, or color. He who is loyal is by definition not a spy or a saboteur. When the power to detain is derived from the power to protect the war effort against espionage and sabotage, detention which has no relationship to that objective is unauthorized.

Nor may the power to detain an admittedly loyal citizen or to grant him a conditional release be implied as a useful or convenient step in the evacuation program, whatever authority might be implied in case of those whose loyalty was not conceded or established. If we assume (as we do) that the original evacuation was justified, its lawful character was derived from the fact that it was an espionage and sabotage measure, not that there was community hostility to this group of American citizens. The evacuation program rested explicitly on the former ground not on the latter as the underlying legislation shows. The authority to detain a citizen or to grant him a conditional release as protection against espionage or sabotage is exhausted at least when his loyalty is conceded. If we held that the authority to detain continued thereafter, we would transform an espionage or sabotage measure into something else. That was not done by Executive Order No. 9066 or by the Act of March 21, 1942, which ratified it. What they did not do we cannot do. Detention which furthered the campaign against espionage and sabotage would be one thing. But detention which has no relationship to that campaign is of a distinct character. Community hostility even to loyal evacuees may have been (and perhaps still is) a serious problem. But if authority for their custody and supervision is to be sought on that ground, the Act of March 21, 1942, Executive Order No. 9066, and Executive Order No. 9102, offer no support. And none other is advanced. To read them that broadly would be to assume that the Congress and the President intended that this discriminatory action should be taken against these people wholly on account of their ancestry even though the government conceded their loyalty to this country. We cannot make such an assumption. As the President has said of these loyal citizens: "Americans of Japanese ancestry, like those of many other ancestries, have shown that they can, and want to, accept our institutions and work loyally with the rest of us, making their own valuable contribution to the national wealth and well-being. In vindication of the very ideals for which we are fighting this war it is important to us to maintain a high standard of fair, considerate, and equal treatment for the people of this minority as of all other minorities." Sen. Doc. No. 96, supra, note 7, p. 2.

Mitsuye Endo is entitled to an unconditional release by the War Relocation Authority.

Second. The question remains whether the District Court has jurisdiction to grant the writ of habeas corpus because of the fact that while the case was pending in the Circuit Court of Appeals appellant was moved from the Tule Lake Relocation Center in the Northern District of California where she was originally detained to the Central Utah Relocation Center in a different district and circuit.

That question is not colored by any purpose to effectuate a removal in evasion of the habeas corpus proceedings. It appears that appellant's removal to Utah was part of a general segregation program involving many of these people and was in no way related to this pending case. Moreover, there is no suggestion that there is no one within the jurisdiction of the District Court who is responsible for the detention of appellant and who would be an appropriate respondent. We are indeed advised by the Acting Secretary of the Interior that if the writ issues and is directed to the Secretary of the Interior or any official of the War Relocation Authority (including an assistant director whose office is at San Francisco, which is in the jurisdiction of the District Court), the corpus of appellant will be produced and the court's order complied with in all respects. Thus it would seem that the case is not moot.

In United States ex rel. Innes v. Crystal, 319 U.S. 755, 63 S.Ct. 1164, 87 L.Ed. 1708, the relator challenged a judgment of court martial by habeas corpus. The District Court denied his petition and the Circuit Court of Appeals affirmed that order. After that decision and before his petition for certiorari was filed here, he was removed from the custody of the Army to a federal penitentiary in a different district and circuit. The sole respondent was the commanding officer. Only an order directed to the warden of the penitentiary could effectuate his discharge and the warden as well as the prisoner was outside the territorial jurisdiction of the District Court. We therefore held the cause moot. There is no comparable situation here.

The fact that no respondent was ever served with process or appeared in the proceedings is not important. The United States resists the issuance of a writ. A cause exists in that state of the proceedings and an appeal lies from denial of a writ without the appearance of a respondent. Hence, so far as presently appears, the cause is not moot and the District Court has jurisdiction to act unless the physical presence of appellant in that district is essential.

We need not decide whether the presence of the person detained within the territorial jurisdiction of the District Court is prerequisite to filing a petition for a writ of habeas corpus. We only hold that the District Court acquired jurisdiction in this case and that the removal of Mitsuye Endo did not cause it to lose jurisdiction where a person in whose custody she is remains within the district.

There are expressions in some of the cases which indicate that the place of confinement must be within the court's territorial jurisdiction in order to enable it to issue the writ. See In re Boles, supra, 48 F. at page 76; Ex parte Gouyet, supra; United States v. Day, supra; United States v. Schlotfeldt, supra. But we are of the view that the court may act if there is a respondent within reach of its process who has custody of the petitioner. As Judge Cooley stated in Matter of Jackson, 15 Mich. 417, 439, 440: "The important fact to be observed in regard to the mode of procedure upon this writ is, that it is directed to, and served upon, not the person confined, but his jailer. It does not reach the former except through the latter. The officer or person who serves it does not unbar the prison doors, and set the prisoner free, but the court relieves him by compelling the oppressor to release his constraint. The whole force of the writ is spent upon the respondent." The statute upon which the jurisdiction of the District Court in habeas corpus proceedings rests (Rev.Stat. § 752, 28 U.S.C. § 452, 28 U.S.C.A. § 452) gives it power "to grant writs of habeas corpus for the purpose of an inquiry into the cause of restraint of liberty." That objective may be in no way impaired or defeated by the removal of the prisoner from the territorial jurisdiction of the District Court. That end may be served and the decree of the court made effective if a respondent who has custody of the prisoner is within reach of the court's process even though the prisoner has been removed from the district since the suit was begun.

The judgment is reversed and the cause is remanded to the District Court for proceedings in conformity with this opinion.

Reversed.

Source: Justice Douglas, William O. Court Opinion in *Ex parte Mitsuyo Endo* 323 U.S. 283, December 18, 1944. United States Reports, Volume 323, November 1944–January 1945.

1947: PRESIDENT TRUMAN'S "LOYALTY PROGRAM" EXECUTIVE ORDER

On March 21, 1947, President Harry S. Truman issued Executive Order 9835, which provided that the head of each department and agency in the executive branch be held personally accountable for a successful program to identify and remove disloyal civilian officers or employees. It directed the establishment within each department or agency of one or more loyalty boards for the purpose of hearing loyalty cases arising within such department or agency and making recommendations with respect to the removal of any employees on grounds relating to loyalty. The order also provided for the establishment of a central Loyalty Review Board in the Civil Service Commission. The board, in addition to various supervisory functions, was authorized to review cases involving persons recommended for dismissal by the loyalty board of any department or agency. The standard for removal prescribed by the order was whether "on all the evidence, reasonable grounds exist for belief that the person involved is disloyal to the Government of the United States." As a quasicriminal law that did not call for criminal penalties, it did not require the customary proof of guilt beyond a reasonable doubt.

Dismissal from employment on disloyalty grounds carried such a stigma that it could destroy reputations, families, personal associations, and professional careers. Usually, dismissal entailed serious economic consequences because a person dismissed under these circumstances could hardly expect to resume his career anywhere in this country. Yet despite these grave consequences, the law provided no protection for the innocent. Although it allowed for a hearing of sorts before an executive loyalty board, little due process was provided. There was no presumption of innocence and the government had no burden of proof to establish disloyalty. On the contrary, the burden of proof to establish innocence was firmly fixed on the accused.

Of the three million government employees who were investigated under this program, 308 were fired as security risks. The president's loyalty order was challenged before the U.S. Supreme Court by discharged employees in Peters v. Hobby, *349 U.S. 331 (1955), and* Cole v. Young, *351 U.S. 536 (1956). Even though the Court ruled in each instance that the employees were unlawfully discharged, it confined its examination to whether statutory guidelines had been followed and not the constitutionality of the orders. By this time, however, Truman's order was no longer in force; on April 27, 1953, President Dwight Eisenhower issued Executive Order 10450, which formally revoked Truman's "loyalty order."*

Executive Order 9835—Prescribing Procedures for the Administration of an Employees Loyalty Program in the Executive Branch of the Government

March 21, 1947

WHEREAS each employee of the Government of the United States is endowed with a measure of trusteeship over the democratic processes which are the heart and sinew of the United States; and

WHEREAS it is of vital importance that persons employed in the Federal service be of complete and unswerving loyalty to the United States; and

WHEREAS, although the loyalty of by far the overwhelming majority of all Government employees is beyond question, the presence within the Government service of any disloyal or subversive person constitutes a threat to our democratic processes; and

WHEREAS maximum protection must be afforded the United States against infiltration of disloyal persons into the ranks of its employees, and equal protection from unfounded accusations of disloyalty must be afforded the loyal employees of the Government:

NOW, Therefore, by virtue of the authority vested in me by the Constitution and statutes of the United States, including the Civil Service Act of 1883 (22 Stat. 403), as amended, and section 9A of the act approved August 2, 1939 (18 U.S.C. 61i), and as President and Chief Executive of the United States, it is hereby, in the interest of the internal management of the Government, ordered as follows:

Part I—Investigation of Applicants

1. There shall be a loyalty investigation of every person entering the civilian employment of any department or agency of the executive branch of the Federal Government.

    a. Investigations of persons entering the competitive service shall be conducted by the Civil Service Commission, except in such cases as are covered by a special agreement between the Commission and any given department or agency.
    b. Investigations of persons other than those entering the competitive service shall be conducted by the employing department or agency. Departments and agencies without investigative organizations shall utilize the investigative facilities of the Civil Service Commission.

2. The investigations of persons entering the employ of the executive branch may be conducted after any such person enters upon actual employment therein, but in any such case the appointment of such person shall be conditioned upon a favorable determination with respect to his loyalty.

    a. Investigations of persons entering the competitive service shall be conducted as expeditiously as possible; provided, however, that if any such investigation is not completed within 18 months from the date on which a person enters actual employment, the condition that his employment is subject to investigation shall expire, except in a case in which the Civil Service Commission has made an initial adjudication of disloyalty and the case continues to be active by reason of an appeal, and it shall then be the responsibility of the employing department or agency to conclude such investigation and make a final determination concerning the loyalty of such person.

3. An investigation shall be made of all applicants at all available pertinent sources of information and shall include reference to:

    a. Federal Bureau of Investigation files.
    b. Civil Service Commission files.
    c. Military and naval intelligence files.
    d. The files of any other appropriate government investigative or intelligence agency.
    e. House Committee on un-American Activities files.
    f. Local law-enforcement files at the place of residence and employment of the applicant, including municipal, county, and State law-enforcement files.
    g. Schools and colleges attended by applicant.
    h. Former employers of applicant.
    i. References given by applicant.
    j. Any other appropriate source.

4. Whenever derogatory information with respect to loyalty of an applicant is revealed a full investigation shall be conducted. A full field investigation shall also be conducted of those applicants, or of applicants for particular positions, as may be designated by the head of the employing department or agency, such designations to be based on the determination by any such head of the best interests of national security.

Part II—Investigation of Employees

1. The head of each department and agency in the executive branch of the Government shall be personally responsible for an effective program to assure that disloyal civilian officers or employees are not retained in employment in his department or agency.

    a. He shall be responsible for prescribing and supervising the loyalty determination procedures of his department or agency, in accordance with the provisions of this order, which shall be considered as providing minimum requirements.

b. The head of a department or agency which does not have an investigative organization shall utilize the investigative facilities of the Civil Service Commission.

2. The head of each department and agency shall appoint one or more loyalty boards, each composed of not less than three representatives of the department or agency concerned, for the purpose of hearing loyalty cases arising within such department or agency and making recommendations with respect to the removal of any officer or employee of such department or agency on grounds relating to loyalty, and he shall prescribe regulations for the conduct of the proceedings before such boards.

   a. An officer or employee who is charged with being disloyal shall have a right to an administrative hearing before a loyalty board in the employing department or agency. He may appear before such board personally, accompanied by counsel or representative of his own choosing, and present evidence on his own behalf, through witnesses or by affidavit.
   b. The officer or employee shall be served with a written notice of such hearing in sufficient time, and shall be informed therein of the nature of the charges against him in sufficient detail, so that he will be enabled to prepare his defense. The charges shall be stated as specifically and completely as, in the discretion of the employing department or agency, security considerations permit, and the officer or employee shall be informed in the notice (1) of his right to reply to such charges in writing within a specified reasonable period of time, (2) of his right to an administrative hearing on such charges before a loyalty board, and (3) of his right to appear before such board personally, to be accompanied by counsel or representative of his own choosing, and to present evidence on his behalf, through witness or by affidavit.

3. A recommendation of removal by a loyalty board shall be subject to appeal by the officer or employee affected, prior to his removal, to the head of the employing department or agency or to such person or persons as may be designated by such head, under such regulations as may be prescribed by him, and the decision of the department or agency concerned shall be subject to appeal to the Civil Service Commission's Loyalty Review Board, hereinafter provided for, for an advisory recommendation.
4. The rights of hearing, notice thereof, and appeal therefrom shall be accorded to every officer or employee prior to his removal on grounds of disloyalty, irrespective of tenure, or of manner, method, or nature of appointment, but

the head of the employing department or agency may suspend any officer or employee at any time pending a determination with respect to loyalty.

5. The loyalty boards of the various departments and agencies shall furnish to the Loyalty Review Board, hereinafter provided for, such reports as may be requested concerning the operation of the loyalty program in any such department or agency.

Part III—Responsibilities of Civil Service Commission

1. There shall be established in the Civil Service Commission a Loyalty Review Board of not less than three impartial persons, the members of which shall be officers or employees of the Commission.

    a. The Board shall have authority to review cases involving persons recommended for dismissal on grounds relating to loyalty by the loyalty board of any department or agency and to make advisory recommendations thereon to the head of the employing department or agency. Such cases may be referred to the Board either by the employing department or agency, or by the officer or employee concerned.
    b. The Board shall make rules and regulations, not inconsistent with the provisions of this order, deemed necessary to implement statutes and Executive orders relating to employee loyalty.
    c. The Loyalty Review Board shall also:

        1. Advise all departments and agencies on all problems relating to employee loyalty.
        2. Disseminate information pertinent to employee loyalty programs.
        3. Coordinate the employee loyalty policies and procedures of the several departments and agencies.
        4. Make reports and submit recommendations to the Civil Service Commission for transmission to the President from time to time as may be necessary to the maintenance of the employee loyalty program.

2. There shall also be established and maintained in the Civil Service Commission a central master index covering all persons on whom loyalty investigations have been made by any department or agency since September 1, 1939. Such master index shall contain the name of each person investigated, adequate identifying information concerning each such person, and a reference to each department and agency which has conducted a loyalty investigation concerning the person involved.

    a. Civil Service Commission all information appropriate for the establishment and maintenance of the central master index.

b. The reports and other investigative material and information developed by the investigating department or agency shall be retained by such department or agency in each case.

3. The loyalty Review Board shall currently be furnished by the Department of Justice the name of each foreign or domestic organization, association, movement, group or combination of persons which the Attorney General, after appropriate investigation and determination, designates as totalitarian, fascist, communist or subversive, or as having adopted a policy of advocating or approving the commission of acts of force or violence to deny others their rights under the Constitution of the United States, or as seeking to alter the form of government of the United States by unconstitutional means.

   a. The Loyalty Review Board shall disseminate such information to all departments and agencies.

Part IV—Security Measures in Investigations

1. At the request of the head of any department or agency of the executive branch an investigative agency shall make available to such head, personally, all investigative material and information collected by the investigative agency concerning any employee or prospective employee of the requesting department or agency, or shall make such material and information available to any officer or officers designated by such head and approved by the investigative agency.
2. Notwithstanding the foregoing requirement, however, the investigative agency may refuse to disclose the names of confidential informants, provided it furnishes sufficient information about such informants on the basis of which the requesting department or agency can make an adequate evaluation of the information furnished by them, and provided it advises the requesting department or agency in writing that it is essential to the protection of the informants or to the investigation of other cases that the identity of the informants not be revealed. Investigative agencies shall not use this discretion to decline to reveal sources of information where such action is not essential.
3. Each department and agency of the executive branch should develop and maintain, for the collection and analysis of information relating to the loyalty of its employees and prospective employees, a staff specially trained in security techniques, and an effective security control system for protecting such information generally and for protecting confidential sources of such information particularly.

Part V—Standards

1. The standard for the refusal of employment or the removal from employment in an executive department or agency on grounds relating to loyalty shall be that, on all the evidence, reasonable grounds exist for belief that the person involved is disloyal to the Government of the United States.
2. Activities and associations of an applicant or employee which may be considered in connection with the determination of disloyalty may include one or more of the following:

   a. Sabotage, espionage, or attempts or preparations therefor, or knowingly associating with spies or saboteurs;
   b. Treason or sedition or advocacy thereof;
   c. Advocacy of revolution or force or violence to alter the constitutional form of government of the United States;
   d. Intentional, unauthorized disclosure to any person, under circumstances which may indicate disloyalty to the United States, of documents or information of a confidential or non-public character obtained by the person making the disclosure as a result of his employment by the Government of the United States;
   e. Performing or attempting to perform his duties, or otherwise acting, so as to serve the interests of another government in preference to the interests of the United States.
   f. Membership in, affiliation with or sympathetic association with any foreign or domestic organization, association, movement, group or combination of persons, designated by the Attorney General as totalitarian, fascist, communist, or subversive, or as having adopted a policy of advocating or approving the commission of acts of force or violence to deny other persons their rights under the Constitution of the United States, or as seeking to alter the form of government of the United States by unconstitutional means.

Part VI—Miscellaneous

1. Each department and agency of the executive branch, to the extent that it has not already done so, shall submit, to the Federal Bureau of Investigation of the Department of Justice, either directly or through the Civil Service Commission, the names (and such other necessary identifying material as the Federal Bureau of Investigation may require) of all of its incumbent employees.

a. The Federal Bureau of Investigation shall check such names against its records of persons concerning whom there is substantial evidence of being within the purview of paragraph 2 of Part V hereof, and shall notify each department and agency of such information.
b. Upon receipt of the above-mentioned information from the Federal Bureau of Investigation, each department and agency shall make, or cause to be made by the Civil Service Commission, such investigation of those employees as the head of the department or agency shall deem advisable.

2. The Security Advisory Board of the State-War-Navy Coordinating Committee shall draft rules applicable to the handling and transmission of confidential documents and other documents and information which should not be publicly disclosed, and upon approval by the President such rules shall constitute the minimum standards for the handling and transmission of such documents and information, and shall be applicable to all departments and agencies of the executive branch.
3. The provisions of this order shall not be applicable to persons summarily removed under the provisions of section 3 of the act of December 17, 1942, 56 Stat. 1053, of the act of July 5, 1946, 60 Stat. 453, or of any other statute conferring the power of summary removal.
4. The Secretary of War and the Secretary of the Navy, and the Secretary of the Treasury with respect to the Coast Guard, are hereby directed to continue to enforce and maintain the highest standards of loyalty within the armed services, pursuant to the applicable statutes, the Articles of War, and the Articles for the Government of the Navy.
5. This order shall be effective immediately, but compliance with such of its provisions as require the expenditure of funds shall be deferred pending the appropriation of such funds.

Executive Order No. 9300 of February 5, 1943, is hereby revoked.
Harry S. Truman

Source: Truman, Harry S. 1947. "Executive Order 9835—Prescribing Procedures for the Administration of an Employees Loyalty Program in the Executive Branch of the Government." *Federal Register* (March 25): p. 12. http://trumanlibrary.org/executiveorders/index.php?pid=502.

1950: PRESIDENT TRUMAN VETOES THE PROPOSED INTERNAL SECURITY ACT

After the conclusion of World War II, fears of Communist aggression and hostility toward United States escalated all across the United States. This tension was felt in Washington as well. A variety of bills were subsequently crafted to identify and weed out Communist agents, saboteurs, and sympathizers. Some of the proposals stemmed from genuine concern about the goals and tactics of the Soviet Union and China, while others were at least partly the product of political opportunism.

One of the most controversial early Cold War laws designed to protect United States from Communist infiltration was the 1950 Internal Security Act, also sometimes known as the Subversive Activities Control Act or the McCarran Act (the latter in recognition of its most prominent sponsor, Democratic Senator Patrick McCarran of Nevada). McCarran and his many allies in Congress and the press touted the bill as a desperately needed weapon to combat the insidious threat of communism, and it easily sailed through both houses of Congress. But President Harry S. Truman vetoed the bill, describing it in his veto message (excerpted here) as a deeply flawed piece of legislation that trampled on basic American freedoms and forced the government into a "thought police" role. Truman's warnings were not heeded by Congress, however. One day after Truman took his stand, Congress overrode his veto and H.R. 9490 became law.

September 22, 1950

To the House of Representatives:

I return herewith, without my approval, H.R. 9490, the proposed "Internal Security Act of 1950."

I am taking this action only after the most serious study and reflection and after consultation with the security and intelligence agencies of the Government. The Department of Justice, the Department of Defense, the Central Intelligence Agency, and the Department of State have all advised me that the bill would seriously damage the security and the intelligence operations for which they are responsible. They have strongly expressed the hope that the bill would not become law.

This is an omnibus bill containing many different legislative proposals with only one thing in common: they are all represented to be "anti-communist." But when the many complicated pieces of the bill are analyzed in detail, a startling result appears.

H.R. 9490 would not hurt the communists. Instead, it would help them.

It has been claimed over and over again that this is an "anti-communist" bill—a "communist control" bill. But in actual operation the bill would have results exactly the opposite of those intended.

It would actually weaken our existing internal security measures and would seriously hamper the Federal Bureau of Investigation and our other security agencies.

It would help the communists in their efforts to create dissension and confusion within our borders.

It would help the communist propagandists throughout the world who are trying to undermine freedom by discrediting as hypocrisy the efforts of the United States on behalf of freedom.

Specifically, some of the principal objections to the bill are as follows:

1. It would aid potential enemies by requiring the publication of a complete list of vital defense plants, laboratories, and other installations.
2. It would require the Department of Justice and its Federal Bureau of Investigation to waste immense amounts of time and energy attempting to carry out its unworkable registration provisions.
3. It would deprive us of the great assistance of many aliens in intelligence matters.
4. It would antagonize friendly governments.
5. It would put the Government of the United States in the thought control business.
6. It would make it easier for subversive aliens to become naturalized as United States citizens.
7. It would give Government officials vast powers to harass all of our citizens in the exercise of their right of free speech.

Legislation with these consequences is not necessary to meet the real dangers which communism presents to our free society. Those dangers are serious, and must be met. But this bill would hinder us, not help us, in meeting them. Fortunately, we already have on the books strong laws which give us most of the protection we need from the real dangers of treason, espionage, sabotage, and actions looking to the overthrow of our Government by force and violence. Most of the provisions of this bill have no relation to these real dangers. . . .

I know that the Congress had no intention of achieving such results when it passed this bill. I know that the vast majority of the members of Congress who voted for the bill sincerely intended to strike a blow at the communists.

It is true that certain provisions of this bill would improve the laws protecting us against espionage and sabotage. But these provisions are greatly outweighed by others which would actually impair our security . . .

H.R. 9490 is made up of a number of different parts. In summary, their purposes and probable effects may be described as follows:

Sections 1 through 17 are designed for two purposes. First, they are intended to force communist organizations to register and to divulge certain information about themselves—information on their officers, their finances, and, in some cases, their membership. These provisions would in practice be ineffective, and would result in obtaining no information about communists that the FBI and our other security agencies do not already have. But in trying to enforce these sections, we would have to spend a great deal of time, effort, and money—all to no good purpose.

Second, those provisions are intended to impose various penalties on communists and others covered by the terms of the bill. So far as communists are concerned, all these penalties which can be practicably enforced are already in effect under existing laws and procedures. But the language of the bill is so broad and vague that it might well result in penalizing the legitimate activities of people who are not communists at all, but loyal citizens.

Thus the net result of these sections of the bill would be: no serious damage to the communists, much damage to the rest of us. Only the communist movement would gain from such an outcome.

Sections 18 through 21 and section 23 of this bill constitute, in large measure, the improvements in our internal security laws which I recommended some time ago. Although the language of these sections is in some respects weaker than is desirable, I should be glad to approve these provisions if they were enacted separately, since they are improvements developed by the FBI and other Government security agencies to meet certain clear deficiencies of the present law. . . .

Sections 22 and 25 of this bill would make sweeping changes in our laws governing the admission of aliens to the United States and their naturalization as citizens.

The ostensible purpose of these provisions is to prevent persons who would be dangerous to our national security from entering the country or becoming citizens. In fact, present law already achieves that objective.

What these provisions would actually do is to prevent us from admitting to our country, or to citizenship, many people who could make real contributions to our national strength. The bill would deprive our Government and our intelligence agencies of the valuable services of aliens in security operations. It would require us to exclude and to deport the citizens of some friendly noncommunist countries. Furthermore, it would actually make it easier for subversive aliens to become United States citizens. Only the communist movement would gain from such actions.

Section 24 and sections 26 through 30 of this bill make a number of minor changes in the naturalization laws. None of them is of great significance—nor are they particularly relevant to the problem of internal security. . . .

Section 31 of this bill makes it a crime to attempt to influence a judge or jury by public demonstration, such as picketing. While the courts already have considerable power to punish such actions under existing law, I have no objection to this section.

Sections 100 through 117 of this bill (Title II) are intended to give the Government power, in the event of invasion, war, or insurrection in the United States in aid of a foreign enemy, to seize and hold persons who could be expected to attempt acts of espionage or sabotage, even though they had as yet committed no crime. It may be that legislation of this type should be on the statute books. But the provisions in H.R. 9490 would very probably prove ineffective to achieve the objective sought, since they would not suspend the writ of habeas corpus, and under our legal system to detain a man not charged with a crime would raise serious constitutional questions unless the writ of habeas corpus were suspended. Furthermore, it may well be that other persons than those covered by these provisions would be more important to detain in the event of emergency. This whole problem, therefore, should clearly be studied more thoroughly before further legislative action along these lines is considered.

In brief, when all the provisions of H.R. 9490 are considered together, it is evident that the great bulk of them are not directed toward the real and present dangers that exist from communism. Instead of striking blows at communism, they would strike blows at our own liberties and at our position in the forefront of those working for freedom in the world. At a time when our young men are fighting for freedom in Korea, it would be tragic to advance the objectives of communism in this country, as this bill would do.

Because I feel so strongly that this legislation would be a terrible mistake, I want to discuss more fully its worst features . . .

Most of the first seventeen sections of H.R. 9490 are concerned with requiting registration and annual reports, by what the bill calls "communist-action organizations" and "communist-front organizations," of names of officers, sources and uses of funds, and, in the case of "communist-action organizations," names of members.

The idea of requiring communist organizations to divulge information about themselves is a simple and attractive one. But it is about as practical as requiring thieves to register with the sheriff. Obviously, no such organization as the Communist Party is likely to register voluntarily.

Under the provisions of the bill, if an organization which the Attorney General believes should register does not do so, he must request a five-man "Subversive Activities Control Board" to order the organization to register. The Attorney General would have to produce proof that the organization in question was in fact a "communist-action" or a "communist-front organization." To do this he would have to offer evidence relating to every aspect of the organization's activities. The organization could present opposing evidence. Prolonged hearings would be required to allow both sides to present proof and to cross-examine opposing witnesses.

To estimate the duration of such a proceeding involving the Communist Party, we need only recall that on much narrower issues the trial of the eleven communist leaders under the Smith Act consumed nine months. In a hearing under this bill, the difficulties of proof would be much greater and would take a much longer time.

The bill lists a number of criteria for the Board to consider in deciding whether or not an organization is a "communist-action" or "communist-front" organization. Many of these deal with the attitudes or states of mind of the organization's leaders. It is frequently difficult in legal proceedings to establish whether or not a man has committed an overt act, such as theft or perjury. But under this bill, the Attorney General would have to attempt the immensely more difficult task of producing concrete legal evidence that men have particular ideas or opinions. This would inevitably require the disclosure of many of the FBI's confidential sources of information and thus would damage our national security.

If, eventually, the Attorney General should overcome these difficulties and get a favorable decision from the Board, the Board's decision could be appealed to the Courts. The Courts would review any questions of law involved, and whether the Board's findings of fact were supported by the "preponderance" of the evidence.

All these proceedings would require great effort and much time. It is almost certain that from two to four years would elapse between the Attorney General's decision to go before the Board with a case, and the final disposition of the matter by the Courts.

And when all this time and effort had been spent, it is still most likely that no organization would actually register.

The simple fact is that when the Courts at long last found that a particular organization was required to register, all the leaders of the organization would have to do to frustrate the law would be to dissolve the organization and establish a new one with a different name and a new roster of nominal officers. The Communist Party has done this again and again in countries throughout the world. And nothing could be done about it except to begin all over again the long dreary process of investigative, administrative, and judicial proceedings to require registration.

Thus the net result of the registration provisions of this bill would probably be an endless chasing of one organization after another, with the communists always able to frustrate the law enforcement agencies and prevent any final result from being achieved. It could only result in wasting the energies of the Department of Justice and in destroying the sources of information of its FBI. To impose these fruitless burdens upon the FBI would divert it from its vital security duties and thus give aid and comfort to the very communists whom the bill is supposed to control.

Unfortunately, these provisions are not merely ineffective and unworkable. They represent a clear and present danger to our institutions.

In so far as the bill would require registration by the Communist Party itself, it does not endanger our traditional liberties. However, the application of the registration requirements to so-called communist-front organizations can be the greatest danger to freedom of speech, press and assembly, since the Alien and Sedition Laws of 1798. This danger arises out of the criteria or standards to be applied in determining whether an organization is a communist-front organization.

There would be no serious problem if the bill required proof that an organization was controlled and financed by the Communist Party before it could be classified as a communist-front organization. However, recognizing the difficulty of proving those matters, the bill would permit such a determination to be based solely upon "the extent to which the positions taken or advanced by it from time to time on matters of policy do not deviate from those" of the communist movement.

This provision could easily be used to classify as a communist-front organization any organization which is advocating a single policy or objective which is also being urged by the Communist Party or by a communist foreign government. In fact, this may be the intended result, since the bill defines "organization" to include "a group of persons * * * permanently or temporarily associated together for joint action on any subject or subjects." Thus, an organization which advocates low-cost housing for sincere humanitarian reasons might be classified as a communist-front organization because the communists regularly exploit slum conditions as one of their fifth-column techniques.

It is not enough to say that this probably would not be done. The mere fact that it could be done shows clearly how the bill would open a Pandora's box of opportunities for official condemnation of organizations and individuals for perfectly honest opinions which happen to be stated also by communists.

The basic error of these sections is that they move in the direction of suppressing opinion and belief. This would be a very dangerous course to take, not because we have any sympathy for communist opinions, but because any governmental stifling of the free expression of opinion is a long step toward totalitarianism.

There is no more fundamental axiom of American freedom than the familiar statement: In a free country, we punish men for the crimes they commit, but never for the opinions they have. And the reason this is so fundamental to freedom is not, as many suppose, that it protects the few unorthodox from suppression by the majority. To permit freedom of expression is primarily for the benefit of the majority, because it protects criticism, and criticism leads to progress.

We can and we will prevent espionage, sabotage, or other actions endangering our national security. But we would betray our finest traditions if we attempted, as this bill would attempt, to curb the simple expression of opinion. This we should never do, no matter how distasteful the opinion may be to the vast majority of our people. The course proposed by this bill would delight the communists, for it would make a mockery of the Bill of Rights and of our claims to stand for freedom in the world.

And what kind of effect would these provisions have on the normal expression of political views? Obviously, if this law were on the statute books, the part of prudence would be to avoid saying anything that might be construed by someone as not deviating sufficiently from the current communist propaganda line. And since no one could be sure in advance what views were safe to express, the inevitable tendency would be to express no views on controversial subjects.

The result could only be to reduce the vigor and strength of our political life—an outcome that the communists would happily welcome, but that free men should abhor.

We need not fear the expression of ideas—we do need to fear their suppression.

Our position in the vanguard of freedom rests largely on our demonstration that the free expression of opinion, coupled with government by popular consent, leads to national strength and human advancement. Let us not, in cowering and foolish fear, throw away the ideals which are the fundamental basis of our free society.

Not only are the registration provisions of this bill unworkable and dangerous, they are also grossly misleading in that all but one of the objectives which are claimed for them are already being accomplished by other and superior methods—and the one objective which is not now being accomplished would not in fact be accomplished under this bill either.

It is claimed that the bill would provide information about the communist party and its members. The fact is, the FBI already possesses very complete sources of information concerning the communist movement in this country. If the FBI must disclose its sources of information in public hearings to require registration under this bill, its present sources of information, and its ability to acquire new information, will be largely destroyed.

It is claimed that this bill would deny income tax exemptions to communist organizations. The fact is that the Bureau of Internal Revenue already denies income tax exemptions to such organizations.

It is claimed that this bill would deny passports to communists. The fact is that the Government can and does deny passports to communists under existing law.

It is claimed that this bill would prohibit the employment of communists by the Federal Government. The fact is that the employment of communists by the Federal Government is already prohibited and, at least in the Executive Branch, there is an effective program to see that they are not employed.

It is claimed that this bill would prohibit the employment of communists in defense plants. The fact is that it would be years before this bill would have any effect of this nature—if it ever would. Fortunately, this objective is already being substantially achieved under the present procedures of the Department of Defense, and if the Congress would enact one of the provisions I have recommended—which it did not include in this bill—the situation would be entirely taken care of, promptly and effectively.

It is also claimed—and this is the one new objective of the registration provisions of this bill—that it would require communist organizations to label all their publications and radio and television broadcasts as emanating from a communist source. The fact is that this requirement, even if constitutional, could be easily and permanently evaded, simply by the continuous creation of new organizations to distribute communist information.

Section 4(a) of the bill, like its registration provisions, would be ineffective, would be subject to dangerous abuse, and would seek to accomplish an objective which is already better accomplished under existing law.

This provision would make unlawful any agreement "to perform any act which would substantially contribute to the establishment within the United States" of a foreign controlled dictatorship. Of course, this provision would be unconstitutional if it infringed upon the fundamental right of the American people to establish for themselves by constitutional methods any form of government they choose. To avoid this, it is provided that this section "shall not apply to the proposal of a constitutional amendment." If this language limits the prohibition of the section to the use of unlawful methods, then it adds nothing to the Smith Act, under which eleven communist leaders have been convicted, and would be more difficult to enforce. Thus, it would accomplish nothing. Moreover, the bill does not even purport to define the phrase, unique in a criminal statute, "substantially contribute." A phrase so vague raises a serious constitutional question.

Sections 22 and 25 of this bill are directed toward the specific questions of who should be admitted to our country, and who should be permitted to become a United States citizen. I believe there is general agreement that the answers to those questions should be: We should admit to our country, within the available quotas, anyone with a legitimate purpose who would not endanger our security, and we should admit to citizenship, any immigrant who will be a loyal and constructive member of the community. Those are essentially the standards set by existing law. Under present law, we do not admit to our country known communists, because we believe they work to overthrow our Government, and we do not admit communists to citizenship, because we believe they are not loyal to the United States.

The changes which would be made in the present law by sections 22 and 25 would not reinforce those sensible standards. Instead, they would add a number of new standards, which, for no good and sufficient reason, would interfere with our relations with other countries and seriously damage our national security.

Section 22 would, for example, exclude from our country anyone who advocates any form of totalitarian or one-party government. We of course believe in the democratic system of competing political parties, offering a choice of candidates and policies. But a number of countries with which we maintain friendly relations have a different form of government.

Until now, no one has suggested that we should abandon cultural and commercial relations with a country merely because it has a form of government different from ours. Yet section 22 would require that. As one instance, it is clear that under the definitions of the bill the present government of Spain, among others, would be classified as "totalitarian." As a result, the Attorney General would be required to exclude from the United States all Spanish businessmen, students, and other non-official travelers who support the present government of their country. I cannot understand how the sponsors of this bill can think that such an action would contribute to our national security.

Moreover, the provisions of section 22 of this bill would strike a serious blow to our national security by taking away from the Government the power to grant asylum in this country to foreign diplomats who repudiate communist imperialism and wish to escape its reprisals. It must be obvious to anyone that it is in our national interest to persuade people to renounce communism, and to encourage their defection from communist forces. Many of these people are extremely valuable to our intelligence operations. Yet under this bill the Government would lose the limited authority it now has to offer asylum in our country as the great incentive for such defection.

In addition, the provisions of section 22 would sharply limit the authority of the Government to admit foreign diplomatic representatives and their families on official business. Under existing law, we already have the authority to send out of the country any person who abuses diplomatic privileges by working against the interests of the United States. But under this bill a whole series of unnecessary restrictions would be placed on the admission of diplomatic personnel. This is not only ungenerous for a country which eagerly sought and proudly holds the honor of being the seat of the United Nations, it is also very unwise, because it makes our country appear to be fearful of "foreigners," when in fact we are working as hard as we know how to build mutual confidence and friendly relations among the nations of the world.

Section 22 is so contrary to our national interests that it would actually put the Government into the business of thought control by requiring the deportation of any alien who distributes or publishes, or who is affiliated with an organization which distributes or publishes, any written or printed matter advocating (or merely expressing belief in) the economic and governmental doctrines of any form of totalitarianism. This provision does not require an evil intent or purpose on the part of the alien, as does a similar provision in the Smith Act. Thus, the Attorney General would be required to deport any alien operating or connected with a well-stocked bookshop containing books on economics or politics written by supporters of the present government of Spain, of Yugoslavia, or any one of a number of other countries. Section 25 would make the same aliens ineligible for citizenship. There should be no room in our laws for such hysterical provisions. The next logical step would be to "burn the books."

This illustrates the fundamental error of these immigration and naturalization provisions. It is easy to see that they are hasty and ill-considered. But far more significant—and far more dangerous—is their apparent underlying purpose. Instead of trying to encourage the free movement of people, subject only to the real requirements of national security, these provisions attempt to bar movement to anyone who is, or once was, associated with ideas we dislike, and in the process, they would succeed in barring many people whom it would be to our advantage to admit.

Such an action would be a serious blow to our work for world peace. We uphold—or have upheld till now, at any rate—the concept of freedom on an international scale. That is the root concept of our efforts to bring unity among the free nations and peace in the world.

The communists, on the other hand, attempt to break down in every possible way the free interchange of persons and ideas. It will be to their advantage, and not ours, if we establish for ourselves an "iron curtain" against those who can help us in the fight for freedom. . . .

Earlier this month, we launched a great Crusade for Freedom designed, in the words of General Eisenhower, to fight the big lie with the big truth. I can think of no better way to make a mockery of that crusade and of the deep American belief in human freedom and dignity which underlie it than to put the provisions of H.R. 9490 on our statute books.

I do not undertake lightly the responsibility of differing with the majority in both Houses of Congress who have voted for this bill. We are all Americans; we all wish to safeguard and preserve our constitutional liberties against internal and external enemies. But I cannot approve this legislation, which instead of accomplishing its avowed purpose would actually interfere with our liberties and help the communists against whom the bill was aimed.

This is a time when we must marshal all our resources and all the moral strength of our free system in self-defense against the threat of communist aggression. We will fail in this, and we will destroy all that we seek to preserve, if we sacrifice the liberties of our citizens in a misguided attempt to achieve national security.

There is no reason why we should fail. Our country has been through dangerous times before, without losing our liberties to external attack or internal hysteria. Each of us, in Government and out, has a share in guarding our liberties. Each of us must search his own conscience to find whether he is doing all that can be done to preserve and strengthen them.

No considerations of expediency can justify the enactment of such a bill as this, a bill which would so greatly weaken our liberties and give aid and comfort to those who would destroy us. I have, therefore, no alternative but to return this bill without my approval, and I earnestly request the Congress to reconsider its action.

HARRY S. TRUMAN

Source: Truman, Harry S. 1965. "Veto of the Internal Security Bill," September 22, 1950. *Harry S. Truman: 1950: Containing the Public Messages, Speeches, and Statements of the President, January 1 to December 31, 1950.* Washington, DC: Government Printing Office, Document 254.

1950: CONGRESS PASSES THE INTERNAL SECURITY ACT OVER TRUMAN'S VETO

On September 23, 1950—one day after President Harry S. Truman vetoed the proposed Internal Security Act as a dangerous and misguided "step toward totalitarianism"—the U.S. Congress overrode his veto and passed the bill into law by a decisive margin. Dispensing with any debate, the House overrode the veto by a vote of 286–48 on the very same day that Truman issued his veto. One day later, the Senate followed suit after a long and passionate debate by a 57–10 vote.

The Internal Security Act required the registration of Communist organizations with the U.S. attorney general, established the Subversive Activities Control Board to investigate individuals suspected of engaging in subversive activities or otherwise promoting Communist ideologies, and granted authorities other broad powers to suppress activities or statements in support of communism and other subversive views. In the decades following its passage, however, several pillars of the law were struck down as unconstitutional by the U.S. Supreme Court or amended by other legislation. Following are several sections of the act that explained the rationale for the legislation and directly affected American civil liberties.

An Act

To protect the United States against certain un-American and subversive activities by requiring registration of Communist organizations, and for other purposes.

SEC. 2. As a result of evidence adduced before various committees of the Senate and House of Representatives, the Congress hereby finds that—

(1) There exists a world Communist movement which, in its origins, its development, and its present practice, is a world-wide revolutionary movement whose purpose it is, by treachery, deceit, infiltration into other groups (governmental and otherwise), espionage, sabotage, terrorism, and any other means deemed necessary, to establish a Communist totalitarian dictatorship in the countries throughout the world through the medium of a world-wide Communist organization. . . .

(4) The direction and control of the world Communist movement is vested in and exercised by the Communist dictatorship of a foreign country.

(15) The Communist movement in the United States is an organization numbering thousands of adherents, rigidly and ruthlessly disciplined. Awaiting and seeking to advance a moment when the United States may be so far extended by foreign engagements, so far divided in counsel, or so far in industrial or financial straits, that overthrow of the Government of the United States by force and violence may seem possible of achievement, it seeks converts far and wide by an extensive system of schooling and indoctrination. Such preparations by Communist organizations in other countries have aided in supplanting existing governments.

The Communist organization in the United States, pursuing its stated objectives, the recent successes of Communist methods in other countries, and the nature and control of the world Communist movement itself, present a clear and present danger to the security of the United States and to the existence of free American institutions, and make it necessary that Congress, in order to provide for the common defense, to preserve the sovereignty of the United States as an independent nation, and to guarantee to each State a republican form of government, enact appropriate legislation recognizing the existence of such World-wide conspiracy and design to prevent it from accomplishing its purpose in the United States. . . .

SEC. 4. (a) It shall be unlawful for any person knowingly to combine, conspire, or agree with any other person to perform any act which would substantially contribute to the establishment within the United States of a totalitarian dictatorship, as defined in paragraph (15) of section 3 of this title, the direction and control of which is to be vested in, or exercised by or under the domination or control of, any foreign government, foreign organization, or foreign individual: Provided, however, That this subsection shall not apply to the proposal of a constitutional amendment. . . .

(f) Neither the holding of office nor membership in any Communist organization by any person shall constitute per se a violation of subsection (a) or subsection (c) of this section or of any other criminal statute. The fact of the registration of any person under section 7 or 8 of this title as an officer or member of any Communist organization shall not be received in evidence against such person in any prosecution for any alleged violation of subsection (a) or subsection (c) of this section or for any alleged violation of any other criminal statute. . . .

SEC.7. (a) Each Communist-action organization (including any organization required, by a final order of the Board, to register as a Communist-action organization) shall, within the time specified in subsection (c) of this section, register with the Attorney General, on a form prescribed by him by regulations, as a Communist-action organization.

(b) Each Communist-front organization . . . shall . . . register with the Attorney General, on a form prescribed by him by regulations, as a Communist-front organization. . . .

(d) Upon the registration of each Communist organization under the provisions of this title, the Attorney General shall publish in the Federal Register the fact that such organization has registered as a Communist-action organization, or as a Communist-front organization, as the case may be, and the publication thereof shall constitute notice to all members of such organization that such organization has so registered. . . .

SEC. 12. (a) There is hereby established a board, to be known as the Subversive Activities Control Board, which shall be composed of five members, who shall be appointed by the President, by and with the advice and consent of the Senate.

Not more than three members of the Board shall be members of the same political party. Two of the original members shall be appointed for a term of one year, two for a term of two years, and one for a term of three years, but their successors shall be appointed for terms of three years each, except that any individual chosen to fill a vacancy shall be appointed only for the unexpired term of the member whom he shall succeed. The President shall designate one member to serve as Chairman of the Board. Any member of the Board may be removed by the President, upon notice and hearing, for neglect of duty or malfeasance in office, but for no other cause. . . .

(e) It shall be the duty of the Board—

(1) upon application made by the Attorney General under section 13 (a) of this title, or by any organization under section 13 (b) of this title, to determine whether any organization is a communist-action organization within the meaning of paragraph (3) of section 3 of this title, or a Communist-front organization within the meaning of paragraph (4) of section 3 of this title; and

(2) upon application made by the Attorney General under section 13 (a) of this title, or by any individual under section 13 (b) of this title, to determine whether any individual is a member of any Communist-action organization registered, or by final order of the Board required to be registered, under section 7 (a) of this title. . . .

SEC. 22. This Act of October 16, 1918 . . . is hereby amended to read as follows: That any alien who is a member of any one of the following classes shall be excluded from admission into the United States:

(1) Aliens who seek to enter the Unites States whether solely, principally, or incidentally, to engage in activities which would be prejudicial to the public interest, or would endanger the welfare or safety of the Unites States;

(2) Aliens who, at any time, shall be or shall have been members of any of the following classes:

(A) Aliens who are anarchists;

(B) Aliens who advocate or teach, or who are members of or affiliated with any organization that advocates or teaches, opposition to all organized government;

(C) Aliens who are members of or affiliated with (i) the Communist Party of the United States, (ii) any other totalitarian party of the United States, (iii) the Communist Political Association, (iv) the Communists or other totalitarian party of any State of the United States, of any foreign state, or of any political or geographical subdivision of any foreign state; (v) any section, subsidiary, branch, affiliate, or subdivision of any such association or party; or (vi) the direct predecessors or successors of any such association or party, regardless of what name such group or organization may have used, may now bear, or may hereafter adopt;

(D) Aliens not within any of the other provisions of this paragraph (2) who advocate the economic, international, and governmental doctrines of world communism or the economic and governmental doctrines of any other form of totalitarianism, or who are members of or affiliated with any organization that advocates the economic, international, and government doctrines of world communism, or the economic and governmental doctrines of any other form of totalitarianism, either through its own utterances or through any written or printed publications issued or published by or with the permission or consent of or under the authority of such organization or paid for by the funds of such organization .

(F) Aliens who advocate or teach or who are members of or affiliated with any organization that advocates or teaches (i) the overthrow by force or violence or other unconstitutional means of the Government of the United States or of all forms of law; or (ii) the duty, necessity, or propriety of the unlawful assaulting or killing of any officer or officers (either of specific individuals or of officers generally) of the Government of the United States or of any other organized government, because of his or their official character; or (iii) the unlawful damage, injury, or destruction of property; or (iv) sabotage;

(G) Aliens who write or publish, or cause to be written or published, or who knowingly circulate, distribute, print, or display, or knowingly cause to be circulated, or displayed, or who knowingly have in their possession for the purpose of circulation, publication, or display any written or printed matter, advocating or teaching opposition to all – organized government, or advocating (i) the overthrow by force or violence or other unconstitutional means of the Government of the United States or of all forms of law; or (ii) the duty, necessity, or propriety of the unlawful assaulting or killing of any officer or officers (either of specific individuals or officers generally) of the Government of the United States or of any other organized government; or (iii) the unlawful damage, injury, or destruction of property; or (iv) sabotage; or (v) the economic, international, and governmental doctrines of world communism or the economic and governmental doctrines of any other form of totalitarianism. . . .

SEC. 102. (a) In the event of any one of the following:

(1) Invasion of the territory of the Unites States or its possessions,

(2) Declaration of war by Congress, or

(3) Insurrection within the United States in aid of a foreign enemy, and if, upon the occurrence of one or more of the above, the President shall find that the proclamation of an emergency pursuant to this section is essential to the preservation, protection and defense of the Constitution, and to the common defense and safety of the territory and people of the United States, the President is authorized to make public proclamation of the existence of an Internal Security Emergency. (b) A state of Internal Security Emergency (hereinafter referred to as the emergency so declared) shall continue in existence until terminated by proclamation of the President or by concurrent resolution of the Congress. . . .

SEC. 103. (a) Whenever there shall be in existence such an emergency, the President, acting through the Attorney General, is hereby authorized to apprehend and by order detain, pursuant to the provisions of this title, each person as to whom there is reasonable ground to believe that such person probably will engage in, or probably will conspire with others to engage in, acts of espionage or of sabotage.

Source: "Internal Security Act of 1950 (McCarran Act)." *U.S. Statutes at Large,* 81st Congress, II Sess., Chp. 1024, pp. 987–1031.

1958: *MILLER v. UNITED STATES* DECISION LIMITS POLICE "KNOCK AND ANNOUNCE" POWERS

This landmark Supreme Court ruling concerned an incident wherein police officers in the District of Columbia, operating without a search warrant, knocked on the apartment door of a William Miller. When Miller asked, "Who's there?" the officers replied, "Police," in a low voice. After the officers completed this standard "knock and announce" procedure, Miller opened the door, but then quickly tried to close it again. At that point, the officers broke the door down, arrested Miller and two other people in the apartment, and collected evidence that was later used in bringing criminal charges against Miller.

The Supreme Court ruled by a 7–2 vote that the officers had not given sufficient notice of their authority and purpose to make a lawful arrest. As a result, the evidence seized in the apartment was also deemed inadmissible and Miller's conviction was reversed. Following are excerpts from the majority opinion penned by Justice William J. Brennan Jr., which was issued on June 23, 1958.

Petitioner, William Miller, together with Bessie Byrd and her brother, Arthur R. Shepherd, was tried and convicted in the District Court for the District of Columbia for conspiracy to commit violations, and violations, of the federal narcotics laws. The Court of Appeals for the District of Columbia Circuit affirmed, one judge dissenting. We granted certiorari, to determine whether evidence seized at the time of petitioner's arrest was properly admitted against the petitioner. The evidence was $100 of marked currency which was seized by the federal officers who arrested the petitioner and Bessie Byrd at their apartment.

On March 25, 1955, at 1:35 A.M., Clifford Reed was arrested, under an arrest warrant, on a Washington, D.C., street on suspicion of narcotics offenses. Reed revealed to Wilson, a federal narcotics agent, that he purchased heroin in 100-capsule quantities from the petitioner through Shepherd. Agent Wilson knew of the petitioner as one who had trafficked in narcotics and had been convicted for a narcotics offense in 1953. Reed said that he was to meet Shepherd later that morning to make a purchase. Agent Wilson enlisted his aid to apprehend Shepherd and the petitioner. About 3 A.M. another federal narcotics agent, Lewis, carrying $100 of marked currency, went with Reed in a taxicab to Shepherd's home. Reed introduced Lewis to Shepherd as a buyer. Shepherd accepted the $100 and agreed to secure 100 capsules of heroin from the petitioner and deliver them to Lewis at Reed's apartment. Shepherd proceeded alone in the taxicab to the petitioner's apartment.

The taxicab was followed by agent Wilson, officer Wurms of the Metropolitan Police Department, and other officers in police cars. Shepherd was seen to leave the taxicab in front of the apartment house where the petitioner and Bessie Byrd occupied a two-room-and-bath basement apartment. The taxicab waited. Shepherd entered the basement but agent Wilson, who looked into the basement hall, could not see where he went. Shepherd came out of the basement within a few minutes and reentered the taxicab. The taxicab was proceeding toward Reed's apartment when the officers following in the police cars intercepted it. Shepherd was arrested and searched. He did not have the marked bills on his person but admitted to agent Wilson and officer Wurms that a package of 100 capsules of narcotics found under the taxicab's front seat was put there by him when the police cars stopped the taxicab. He said that he had taken the package from behind a fire extinguisher in the basement hall where he had been sent by a "fellow" with Reed who had promised him $10 for getting it.

The federal officers returned immediately to the apartment building. About 3:45 A.M. agent Wilson and officer Wurms went to the door of the petitioner's apartment. Officer Wurms knocked and, upon the inquiry from within—"Who's there?"—replied in a low voice, "Police." The petitioner opened the door on an attached door chain and asked what the officers were doing there. Before either responded, he attempted to close the door. Thereupon, according to officer Wurms, "We put our hands inside the door and pulled and ripped the chain off, and entered." The officers had no arrest or search warrant. They did not expressly demand admission or state their purpose for their presence, nor did they place the petitioner under arrest until after they entered the apartment.

Bessie Byrd was also arrested in the apartment and turned over the cash she had in her housecoat. The cash included $34 of the marked currency. After an extended search the remaining $66 of marked currency was found, some in a hatbox in a closet, and the rest within the covers of a bed in the bedroom.

The Government contends that there was probable cause for arresting the petitioner and that the marked currency was properly admitted in evidence because it was seized as an incident to a lawful arrest. *Harris v. United States, 331 U.S. 145, 67 S.Ct. 1098, 91 L.Ed. 1399.* The petitioner's argument breaks down into three contentions: (1) that the officers had no probable cause to arrest the petitioner without a warrant; (2) that the search was not justified as being an incident of a lawful arrest; (3) that the arrest, and therefore the search, was in any event unlawful because the officers broke the door of petitioner's home without first giving notice of their authority and purpose in demanding admission. If any one of these contentions prevails, it is agreed that the marked money was inadmissible in evidence. In the view we take, we need consider only petitioner's third contention.

The lawfulness of the arrest of petitioner depends upon the power of the arresting officers to "break" the doors of a home in order to arrest without warrant persons suspected of having committed narcotics offenses. Agent Wilson did not have statutory authority to arrest without a warrant although officer Wurms, as a member of the Metropolitan Police Department, did have such authority. This Court has said, in the similar circumstance of an arrest for violation of federal law by state peace officers, that the lawfulness of the arrest without warrant is to be determined by reference to state law. By like reasoning the validity of the arrest of petitioner is to be determined by reference to the law of the District of Columbia.

In making reference to that law we are mindful of our policy of not interfering with local rules of law fashioned by the courts of the District of Columbia. *Fisher v. United States, 328 U.S. 463, 476, 66 S.Ct. 1318, 1324, 90 L.Ed. 1382; Griffin v. United States, 336 U.S. 704, 715, 69 S.Ct. 814, 819, 93 L.Ed. 993*. But the Government agrees with petitioner that the validity of the entry to execute the arrest without warrant must be tested by criteria identical with those embodied in 18 U.S.C. § 3109, 18 U.S.C.A. § 3109, which deals with entry to execute a search warrant. That section provides that an officer, executing a search warrant, may break open a door only if, "after notice of his authority and purpose," he is denied admittance. The Government states in its brief that, "where an arrest is made on probable cause rather than a warrant, these statutory requirements must be met before an officer can force entry into an apartment." These statutory requirements are substantially identical to those judicially developed by the Circuit Court of Appeals for the District of Columbia in *Accarino v. United States, 85 U.S.App.D.C. 394, 403, 179 F.2d 456, 465*. Since the rule of Accarino bears such a close relationship to a statute which is not confined in operation to the District of Columbia, we believe that review is warranted here.

From earliest days, the common law drastically limited the authority of law officers to break the door of a house to effect an arrest. Such action invades the precious interest of privacy summed up in the ancient adage that a man's house is his castle. As early as the 13th Yearbook of Edward IV (1461–1483), at folio 9, there is a recorded holding that it was unlawful for the sheriff to break the doors of a man's house to arrest him in a civil suit in debt or trespass, for the arrest was then only for the private interest of a party. Remarks attributed to William Pitt, Earl of Chatham, on the occasion of debate in Parliament on the searches incident to the enforcement of an excise on cider, eloquently expressed the principle:

"The poorest man may in his cottage bid defiance to all the forces of the Crown. It may be frail; its roof may shake; the wind may blow through it; the storm may enter; the rain may enter; but the King of England cannot enter—all his force dares not cross the threshold of the ruined tenement!"

But the common law recognized some authority in law officers to break the door of a dwelling to arrest for felony. The common-law authorities differ, however, as to the circumstances in which this was the case. . . .

Whatever the circumstances under which breaking a door to arrest for felony might be lawful, however, the breaking was unlawful where the officer failed first to state his authority and purpose for demanding admission. The requirement was pronounced in 1603 in Semayne's Case, 5 Coke Co. Rep. 91a, 11 E.R.C. 629, 77 Eng.Repr. 194, at 195: "In all cases where the King is party, the sheriff (if the doors be not open) may break the party's house, either to arrest him, or to do other execution of the K(ing)'s process, if otherwise he cannot enter. But before he breaks it, he ought to signify the cause of his coming, and to make request to open doors * * *." (Emphasis supplied.)

The requirement stated in Semayne's Case still obtains. It is reflected in 18 U.S.C. § 3109, 18 U.S.C.A. § 3109, in the statutes of a large number of States, and in the American Law Institute's proposed Code of Criminal Procedure, § 28. It applies, as the Government here concedes, whether the arrest is to be made by virtue of a warrant, or when officers are authorized to make an arrest for a felony without a warrant. There are some state decisions holding that justification for noncompliance exists in exigent circumstances, as, for example, when the officers may in good faith believe that they or someone within are in peril of bodily harm, *Read v. Case, 4 Conn. 166,* or that the person to be arrested is fleeing or attempting to destroy evidence. *People v. Maddox,* 46 Cal.2d 301, 294 P.2d 6.

But whether the unqualified requirements of the rule admit of an exception justifying noncompliance in exigent circumstances is not a question we are called upon to decide in this case. The Government makes no claim here of the existence of circumstances excusing compliance. The Government concedes that compliance was required but argues that "compliance is evident from the events immediately preceding the officers' forced entry."

The rule seems to require notice in the form of an express announcement by the officers of their purpose for demanding admission. The burden of making an express announcement is certainly slight. A few more words by the officers would have satisfied the requirement in this case. It may be that, without an express announcement of purpose, the facts known to officers would justify them in being virtually certain that the petitioner already knows their purpose so that an announcement would be a useless gesture. *Cf. People v. Martin, 45 Cal.2d 755, 290 P.2d 855; Wilgus, Arrest Without a Warrant, 22 Mich.L.Rev. 541, 798, 802 (1924).* But even by that test the evidence upon which the Government relief was not sufficient to justify the officers' failure expressly to notify the petitioner that they demanded admission to his apartment for the purpose of arresting him.

The single fact known to the officers upon which the Government relies is the "split-second" occurrence in which the petitioner evinced "instantaneous resistance to their entry," an "almost instinctive attempt to bar their entry after they (the officers) had identified themselves as police * * *." It is argued that this occurrence "certainly points up that he knew their purpose immediately * * * (and), at once, realized that he had been detected and that the officers were there to arrest him";

that "(i)t would be wholly unrealistic to say that the officers had not made their purpose known because they did not more formally announce that they were there to arrest him."

But, first, the fact that petitioner attempted to close the door did not of itself prove that he knew their purpose to arrest him. It was an ambiguous act. It could have been merely the expected reaction of any citizen having this experience at that hour of the morning, particularly since it does not appear that the officers were in uniform, *cf. Accarino v. United States, supra, 85 U.S.App.D.C. at page 403, 179 F.2d at page 465,* and the answer "Police" was spoken "in a low voice" and might not have been heard by the petitioner so far as the officers could tell.

Second, petitioner's reaction upon opening the door could only have created doubt in the officers' minds that he knew they were police intent on arresting him. On the motion to suppress, Agent Wilson testified that 'he wanted to know what we were doing there.' This query, which went unanswered, is on its face inconsistent with knowledge. The majority of the Court of Appeals denied the import of the query by inferring that Miller knew Wilson and Wurms personally and recognized them as soon as he opened the door. That inference has no support in the record. But even if this inference were supportable, Miller's recognition of Wilson and Wurms as police officers would not have justified them, in light of other facts known to them, in being virtually certain that Miller actually knew the reason for their presence. The officers knew that petitioner was unaware of Shepherd's arrest; they knew that he was unaware that the currency was marked; they knew that he was unaware that their presence was pursuant to a plan, initiated by Reed's disclosures, to catch the petitioner in a criminal act. Moreover, they did not actually know that petitioner had made a sale to Shepherd and received the marked money, for Shepherd had not talked and had not been seen to enter petitioner's apartment. The fact that the marked money was found in the apartment has no bearing upon the petitioner's knowledge of the officers' purpose since he did not know that the money was marked. This Court said in *United States v. Di Re, supra, 332 U.S.* at page 595, 68 S.Ct. at page 229: "We have had frequent occasion to point out that a search is not to be made legal by what it turns up. In law it is good or bad when it starts and does not change character from its success." The most that can be said is that the petitioner's act in attempting to close the door might be the basis for the officers being virtually certain that the petitioner knew there were police at his door conducting an investigation. This, however, falls short of a virtual certainty that the petitioner knew of their purpose to arrest him. The requirement is not met except by notice of that purpose, for the Government admits that the officers had no authority to break the petitioner's door except to arrest him. We must, therefore, conclude that the petitioner did not receive the required notice of authority and purpose.

We are duly mindful of the reliance that society must place for achieving law and order upon the enforcing agencies of the criminal law. But insistence on observance by law officers of traditional fair procedural requirements is, from the long point of view, best calculated to contribute to that end. However much in a particular case insistence upon such rules may appear as a technicality that inures to the benefit of a guilty person, the history of the criminal law proves that tolerance of shortcut methods in law enforcement impairs its enduring effectiveness. The requirement of prior notice of authority and purpose before forcing entry into a home is deeply rooted in our heritage and should not be given grudging application. Congress, codifying a tradition embedded in Anglo-American law, has declared in § 3109 the reverence of the law for the individual's right of privacy in his house. Every householder, the good and the bad, the guilty and the innocent, is entitled to the protection designed to secure the common interest against unlawful invasion of the house. The petitioner could not be lawfully arrested in his home by officers breaking in without first giving him notice of their authority and purpose. Because the petitioner did not receive that notice before the officers broke the door to invade his home, the arrest was unlawful, and the evidence seized should have been suppressed.

Reversed.

Source: Justice Brennan, William. 1958. Opinion of the Court. *Miller v. United States. Illinois v. Cabelles,* 357 U.S. 301. Decided June 23, 1958. United States Reports, Volume 357, June.

1961: THE SUPREME COURT EXPANDS THE EXCLUSIONARY RULE IN *MAPP v. OHIO*

Mapp v. Ohio *is one of the Supreme Court's most important contributions to the field of criminal justice. In this landmark decision, the Court held that evidence obtained in violation of the Fourth Amendment prohibition against unreasonable searches and seizures is inadmissible in state criminal trials. Since* Weeks v. United States *(1914), the federal courts had observed this rule.* Mapp v. Ohio *is significant because it extended the Fourth Amendment exclusionary rule to the state courts via the Due Process Clause of the Fourteenth Amendment.*

The case concerned Dollree Mapp, who was convicted in an Ohio state court for possession of obscene literature on the basis of evidence seized from her home during a warrantless search. Both the Ohio Court and Appeals and Supreme Court of Ohio affirmed her conviction, the latter ruling that under Ohio law evidence obtained by an unlawful search was admissible in a criminal prosecution and that under Wolf v. Colorado *(1949) a state was not prevented by the U.S. Constitution from adopting the rule as it prevailed in Ohio. On June 19, 1961, the U.S. Supreme Court held by a 6–3 vote that the exclusionary rule limited the states as well as the federal government. The majority opinion, penned by Justice Tom C. Clark and excerpted below, emphasized both the constitutional foundations and the practical necessities of the rule. The dissenting minority opinion, also excerpted here, was written by John M. Harlan.*

Majority Opinion: Appellant stands convicted of knowingly having had in her possession and under her control certain lewd and lascivious books, pictures, and photographs in violation of [state law]. . . . [T]he Supreme Court of Ohio found that her conviction was valid though "based primarily upon the introduction in evidence of lewd and lascivious books and pictures unlawfully seized during an unlawful search of defendant's home. . . ."

The State says that even if the search were made without authority, or otherwise unreasonably, it is not prevented from using the unconstitutionally seized evidence at trial, citing *Wolf v. Colorado* (1949), in which this Court did indeed hold "that in a prosecution in a State court for a State crime the Fourteenth Amendment does not forbid the admission of evidence obtained by an unreasonable search and seizure." [I]t is urged once again that we review that holding. . . .

Today we once again examine *Wolf's* constitutional documentation of the right to privacy free from unreasonable state intrusion, and, after its dozen years on our books, are led by it to close the only courtroom door remaining open to evidence secured by official lawlessness in flagrant abuse of that basic right, reserved to all persons as a specific guarantee against that very same unlawful conduct. We hold that all evidence obtained by searches and seizures in violation of the Constitution is, by that same authority, inadmissible in a state court. Since the Fourth Amendment's right of privacy has been declared enforceable against the States through the Due Process Clause of the Fourteenth, it is enforceable against them by the same sanction of exclusion as is used against the Federal Government. Were it otherwise, then just as without the *Weeks* rule the assurance against unreasonable federal searches and seizures would be "a form of words," valueless and undeserving of mention in a perpetual charter of inestimable human liberties, so too, without that rule the freedom from state invasions of privacy would be so ephemeral and so neatly severed from its conceptual nexus with the freedom from all brutish means of coercing evidence as not to merit this Court's high regard as a freedom "implicit in the concept of ordered liberty." . . . [T]he admission of the new constitutional right by *Wolf* could not consistently tolerate denial of its most important constitutional privilege, namely, the exclusion of the evidence which an accused had been forced to give by reason of the unlawful seizure. To hold otherwise is to grant the right but in reality to withhold its privilege and enjoyment. . . .

Indeed, we are aware of no restraint, similar to that rejected today, conditioning the enforcement of any other basic constitutional right. The right to privacy, no less important than any other right carefully and particularly reserved to the people, would stand in marked contrast to all other rights declared as "basic to a free society." This Court has not hesitated to enforce as strictly against the States as it does against the Federal Government the rights of free speech and of a free press, the rights to notice and to a fair, public trial, including, as it does, the right not to be convicted by use of a coerced confession, however logically relevant it be, and without regard to its reliability. And nothing could be more certain than that when a coerced confession is involved, "the relevant rules of evidence" are overridden without regard to "the incidence of such conduct by the police," slight or frequent. Why should not the same rule apply to what is tantamount to coerced testimony by way of unconstitutional seizure of goods, papers, effects, documents, etc.? . . .

There are those who say, as did Justice (then Judge) Cardozo, that under our constitutional exclusionary doctrine "the criminal is to go free because the constable has blundered." In some cases this will undoubtedly be the result. But, . . . "there is another consideration—the imperative of judicial integrity." The criminal goes free, if he must, but it is the law that sets him free. Nothing can destroy a government more quickly than its failure to observe its own laws, or worse, its disregard of the charter of its own existence. As Mr. Justice Brandeis, dissenting, said in *Olmstead* v. *United States* (1928): "Our Government is the potent, the omnipresent teacher. For good or for ill, it teaches the whole people by its example. . . . If the Government becomes a lawbreaker, it breeds contempt for law; it invites every man to become a law unto himself; it invites anarchy." Nor can it lightly be assumed that, as a practical matter, adoption of the exclusionary rule fetters law enforcement. Only last year this Court expressly considered that contention and found that "pragmatic evidence of a sort" to the contrary was not wanting. . . .

The ignoble shortcut to conviction left open to the State tends to destroy the entire system of constitutional restraints on which the liberties of the people rest. Having once recognized that the right to privacy embodied in the Fourth Amendment is enforceable against the States, and that the right to be secure against rude invasions of privacy by state officers is, therefore, constitutional in origin, we can no longer permit that right to remain an empty promise. Because it is enforceable in the same manner and to like effect as other basic rights secured by the Due Process Clause, we can no longer permit it to be revocable at the whim of any police officer who, in the name of law enforcement itself, chooses to suspend its enjoyment. Our decision, founded on reason and truth, gives to the individual no more than that which the Constitution guarantees him, to the police officer no less than that to which honest law enforcement is entitled, and, to the courts, that judicial integrity so necessary in the true administration of justice. *Reversed and remanded.*

Dissenting Opinion: In overruling the *Wolf* case the Court, in my opinion, has forgotten the sense of judicial restraint which, with due regard for stare decisis, is one element that should enter into deciding whether a past decision of this Court should be overruled. Apart from that I also believe that the *Wolf* rule represents sounder Constitutional doctrine than the new rule which now replaces it. . . .

At the heart of the majority's opinion in this case is the following syllogism: (1) the rule excluding in federal criminal trials evidence which is the product of an illegal search and seizure is "part and parcel" of the Fourth Amendment; (2) *Wolf* held that the "privacy" assured against federal action by the Fourth Amendment is also protected against state action by the Fourteenth Amendment; and (3) it is therefore "logically and constitutionally necessary" that the *Weeks* exclusionary rule should also be enforced against the States.

This reasoning ultimately rests on the unsound premise that because *Wolf* carried into the States, as part of "the concept of ordered liberty" embodied in the Fourteenth Amendment, the principle of "privacy" underlying the Fourth Amendment, it must follow that whatever configurations of the Fourth Amendment have been developed in the particularizing federal precedents are likewise to be deemed a part of "ordered liberty," and as such are enforceable against the States. For me, this does not follow at all. . . .

I would not impose upon the States this federal exclusionary remedy. The reasons given by the majority for now suddenly turning its back on *Wolf* seem to me notably unconvincing.

First, it is said that "the factual grounds upon which *Wolf* was based" have since changed, in that more States now follow the *Weeks* exclusionary rule than was so at the time *Wolf* was decided. While that is true, a recent survey indicates that at present one-half of the States still adhere to the common-law non-exclusionary rule, and one, Maryland, retains the rule as to felonies. . . . Our concern here, as it was in *Wolf*, is not with the desirability of that rule but only with the question whether the States are Constitutionally free to follow it or not as they may themselves determine, and the relevance of the disparity of views among the States on this point lies simply in the fact that the judgment involved is a debatable one. . . .

The preservation of a proper balance between state and federal responsibility in the administration of criminal justice demands patience on the part of those who might like to see things move faster among the States in this respect. Problems of criminal law enforcement vary widely from State to State. . . . For us the question remains, as it has always been, one of state power, not one of passing judgment on the wisdom of one state course or another. In my view this Court should continue to forbear from fettering the States with an adamant rule which may embarrass them in coping with their own peculiar problems in criminal law enforcement. . . .

Source: U.S. Supreme Court, 367 U.S. 643, *Mapp v Ohio* (No. 236), Opinion (Clark) and Dissent (Harlan), June 19, 1961.

1965: *ALBERTSON* SUPREME COURT DECISION WEAKENS THE SUBVERSIVE ACTIVITIES CONTROL BOARD

The Internal Security Act of 1950 included provisions that created the Subversive Activities Control Board (SACB), an agency charged with enforcing the statute's requirements that communist organizations register with the U.S. government. This registration process mandated disclosure of all sources of organization funding and names of people in leadership positions, even though such disclosures triggered a variety of penalties. When the Communist Party of the United States of America defied this registration order, asserting that it violated Fifth Amendment protections against self-incrimination, the Justice Department went to court. The case, known as Albertson v. Subversive Activities Control Board, *eventually reached the U.S. Supreme Court, where the U.S. Attorney General and the SACB received a strong rebuke. By an 8–0 vote, the Court agreed that the registration requirements were unconstitutional because they could be used as evidence in criminal proceedings. The unanimous opinion, delivered on November 15, 1965, and excerpted here, was written by Justice William J. Brennan Jr.*

The Court's decision in Albertson v. Subversive Activities Control Board *triggered a swift slide into political oblivion for the SACB. A mere three years later, Congress voted to repeal the Subversive Activities Control Act (SACA), the statute in the Internal Security Act that had authorized the SACB. "SACA is an example of a statute that had outlived its usefulness," wrote political scientist J. Mitchell Pickerill in* Constitutional Deliberation in Congress: The Impact of Judicial Review *(Duke University Press, 2004). With antiwar sentiment on the rise and McCarthyism in retreat, "the statute [became] so unpopular that many members of Congress viewed a vote to repeal the SACA as being on the 'right side' of the issue."*

The Communist Party of the United States of America failed to register with the Attorney General as required by the order of the Subversive Activities Control Board sustained in Communist Party of the United States v. SACB, 367 U.S. 1, 81 S.Ct. 1357, 6 L.Ed.2d 625. Accordingly, no list of Party members was filed as required by § 7(d)(4) of the Subversive Activities Control Act of 1950, 64 Stat. 993–994, 50 U.S.C. § 786(d)(4) (1964 ed.). Sections 8(a) and (c) of the Act provide that, in that circumstance, each member of the organization must register and file a registration statement; in default thereof, § 13(a) authorizes the Attorney General to petition the Board for an order requiring the member to register. The Attorney General invoked § 13(a) against petitioners, and the Board, after evidentiary hearings, determined that petitioners were Party members and ordered each of them to register pursuant to §§ 8(a) and (c). Review of the orders was sought by petitioners in the Court of Appeals for the District of Columbia Circuit under § 14(a). The Court of Appeals affirmed the orders [and] we granted certiorari. . . . We reverse.

Petitioners address several constitutional challenges to the validity of the orders, but we consider only the contention that the orders violate their Fifth Amendment privilege against self-incrimination.

The Court of Appeals affirmed the orders without deciding the privilege issue, expressing the view that under our decision in Communist Party, 367 U.S., at 105–110, 81 S.Ct., at 1415–1417, the issue was not ripe for adjudication and would be ripe only in a prosecution for failure to register if the petitioners did not register. We disagree. In Communist Party the Party asserted the privilege on behalf of unnamed officers—those obliged to register the Party and those obliged "to register for" the Party if it failed to do so. The self-incrimination claim asserted on behalf of the latter officers was held premature because the Party might choose to register and thus the duty of those officers might never arise. Here, in contrast, the contingencies upon which the members' duty to register arises have already matured; the Party did not register within 30 days after the order to register became final and the requisite 60 days since the order became final have elapsed. As to the officers obliged to register the Party, Communist Party held that the self-incrimination claim asserted on their behalf was not ripe for adjudication because it was not known whether they would ever claim the privilege or whether the claim, if asserted, would be honored by the Attorney General. But with respect to the orders in this case, addressed to named individuals, both these contingencies are foreclosed. Petitioners asserted the privilege in their answers to the Attorney General's petitions; they did not testify at the Board hearings; they again asserted the privilege in the review proceedings in the Court of Appeals. In each instance the Attorney General rejected their claims. Thus, the considerations which led the Court in Communist Party to hold that the claims on behalf of unnamed officers were premature are not present in this case.

There are other reasons for holding that petitioners' self-incrimination claims are ripe for decision. Specific orders requiring petitioners to register have been issued. The Attorney General has promulgated regulations requiring that registration shall be accomplished on Form IS-52a and that the accompanying registration statement shall be a completed Form IS-52, 28 CFR §§ 11.206, 11.207, and petitioners risk very heavy penalties if they fail to register by completing and filing these forms. For example, each day of failure to register constitutes a separate offense punishable by a fine of up to $10,000 or imprisonment of up to five years, or both. Petitioners must either register without a decision on the merits of their privilege claims, or fail to register and risk onerous and rapidly mounting penalties while awaiting the Government's pleasure whether to initiate a prosecution against them. To ask, in these circumstances, that petitioners await such a prosecution for an adjudication of their self-incrimination claims is in effect, to contend that they should be denied the protection of the Fifth Amendment privilege intended to relieve claimants of the necessity of making a choice between incriminating themselves and risking serious punishments for refusing to do so.

Indeed the Government concedes in its brief in this Court that the Court of Appeals' holding of prematurity was erroneous insofar as petitioners' claims of privilege relate to the Board's power to compel the act of registration and the submission of an accompanying registration statement. The brief candidly acknowledges that, since, § 14(b) provides for judicial review of a Board order to register, petitioners' claims in that regard, like any other contention that an order is invalid, may be heard and determined by the reviewing court—thus distinguishing orders that are not similarly reviewable. Nevertheless, the Government argues that petitioners' claims are premature insofar as they relate to "any particular inquiry" on Forms IS-52a and IS-52. Two contingencies are hypothesized in support of this contention: (1) that the Attorney General might alter the present forms or (2) that he might accept less than fully completed forms.

The distinction upon which this argument is predicated is illusory. Neither the statute nor the regulations draw any distinction between the act of registering and the submission of a registration statement, on the one hand, and, on the other hand, the answering of the inquiries demanded by the forms; the statute and regulations contemplate rather that the questions asked on the forms are to be fully and completely answered. Moreover, the contingencies hypothesized are irrelevant. Petitioners are obliged to register and to submit registration forms in accordance with presently existing regulations; the mere contingency that the Attorney General might revise the regulations at some future time does not render premature their challenge to the existing requirements. Nor can these requirements be viewed as requiring that petitioners answer—at the risk of criminal prosecution for error—only those items which will not incriminate petitioners; full compliance is required. Finally, the Government's argument would do violence to the congressional scheme. The penalties are incurred only upon failure to register as required by final orders and, under § 14(b), orders become final upon completion of judicial review. In so providing, Congress plainly manifested an intention to afford alleged members, prior to criminal prosecution for failure to register, an adjudication of all, not just some, of the claims addressed to the validity of the Board's registration orders. We therefore proceed to a determination of the merits of petitioners' self-incrimination claims.

The risks of incrimination which the petitioners take in registering are obvious. Form IS-52a requires an admission of membership in the Communist Party. Such an admission of membership may be used to prosecute the registrant under the membership clause of the Smith Act, 18 U.S.C. § 2385 (1964 ed.) or under § 4(a) of the Subversive Activities Control Act, 64 Stat. 991, 50 U.S.C. § 783(a) (1964 ed.), to mention only two federal criminal statutes. Accordingly, we have held that mere association with the Communist Party presents sufficient threat of prosecution to support a claim of privilege. Patricia Blau v. United States, 340 U.S. 159, 71 S.Ct. 223, 95 L.Ed. 170; Irving Blau v. United States, 340 U.S. 332, 71 S.Ct. 301, 95 L.Ed. 306; Brunner v. United States, 343 U.S. 918, 72 S.Ct. 674, 96 L.Ed. 1332; Quinn v. United States, 349 U.S.155, 75 S.Ct. 668, 99 L.Ed. 964. These cases involved questions to witnesses on the witness stand, but if the admission cannot be compelled in oral testimony, we do not see how compulsion in writing makes a difference for constitutional purposes. . . . It follows that the requirement to accomplish registration by completing and filing Form IS-52a is inconsistent with the protection of the Self-Incrimination Clause.

The statutory scheme, in providing that registration "shall be accompanied" by a registration statement, clearly implies that there is a duty to file Form IS-52, the registration statement, only if there is an enforceable obligation to accomplish registration by completing and filing Form IS-52a. Yet, even if the statute and regulations required petitioners to complete and file Form IS-52 without regard to the validity of the order to register on Form IS-52a, the requirement to complete and file Form IS-52 would also invade the privilege. Like the admission of Party membership demanded by Form IS-52a, the information called for by Form IS-52—the organization of which the registrant is a member his aliases, place and date of birth, a list of offices held in the organization and duties thereof—might be used as evidence in or at least supply investigatory leads to a criminal prosecution. The Government, relying on United States v. Sullivan, 274 U.S.259, 47 S.Ct. 607, 71 L.Ed. 1037, argues that petitioners might answer some questions and appropriately claim the privilege on the form as to others, but cannot fail to submit a registration statement altogether. Apart from our conclusion that nothing in the Act or regulations permits less than literal and full compliance with the requirements of the form, the reliance on Sullivan is misplaced. Sullivan upheld a conviction for failure to file an income tax return on the theory that "(i)f the form of return provided called for answers that the defendant was privileged from making he could have raised the objection in the return, but could not on that account refuse to make any return at all." That declaration was based on the view, first, that a self-incrimination claim against every question on the tax return, or based on the mere submission of the return, would be virtually frivolous, and second, that to honor the claim of privilege not asserted at the time the return was due would make the taxpayer rather than a tribunal the final arbiter of the merits of the claim. But neither reason applies here. A tribunal, the Board, had an opportunity to pass upon the petitioners' self-incrimination claims; and since, unlike a tax return, the pervasive effect of the information called for by Form IS-52 is incriminatory, their claims are substantial and far from frivolous. In Sullivan the questions in the income tax return were neutral on their face and directed at the public at large, but here they are directed at a highly selective group inherently suspect of criminal activities. Petitioners' claims are not asserted in an essentially noncriminal and regulatory area of inquiry, but against an inquiry in an area permeated with criminal statutes, where response to any of the form's questions in context might involve the petitioners in the admission of a crucial element of a crime.

Section 4(f) of the Act, the purported immunity provision, does not save the registration orders from petitioners' Fifth Amendment challenge. In Counselman v. Hitchcock, 142 U.S.547, 12 S.Ct. 195, 35 L.Ed. 1110, decided in 1892, the Court held "that no (immunity) statute which leaves the party or witness subject to prosecution after he answers the criminating question put to him, can have the effect of supplanting the privilege * * *," and that such a statute is valid only if it supplies "a complete protection from all the perils against which the constitutional prohibition was designed to guard * * *" by affording "absolute immunity against future prosecution for the offence to which the question relates." Measured by these standards, the immunity granted by § 4(f) is not complete. . . . It does not preclude any use of the information called for by Form IS-52, either as evidence or as an investigatory lead. With regard to the act of registering on Form IS-52a, § 4(f) provides only that the admission of Party membership thus required shall not per se constitute a violation of §§ 4(a) and (c) or any other criminal statute, or "be received in evidence" against a registrant in any criminal prosecution; it does not preclude the use of the admission as an investigatory lead, a use which is barred by the privilege.

The Government does not contend that the shortcoming of § 4(f) is remedied in regard to information called for on the registration statement Form IS-52. With respect to Form IS-52a, however, the argument is made that, since an order to register is preceded by a Board finding or Party membership, the admission of membership required on that form would be of no investigatory value and thus is not 'incriminatory' within the meaning of the Fifth Amendment privilege. On this view the incompleteness of the § 4(f) grant of immunity would be rendered immaterial and the admission of Party membership could be compelled without violating the privilege. We disagree. The judgment as to whether a disclosure would be "incriminatory" has never been made dependent on an assessment of the information possessed by the Government at the time of interrogation; the protection of the privilege would be seriously impaired if the right to invoke it was dependent on such an assessment, with all its uncertainties. The threat to the privilege is no less present where it is proposed that this assessment be made in order to remedy a shortcoming in a statutory grant of immunity. The representation that the information demanded is of no utility is belied by the fact that the failure to make the disclosure is so severely sanctioned; and permitting the incompleteness of § 4(f) to be cured by such a representation would render illusory the Counselman requirement that a statute in order to supplant the privilege, must provide "complete protection from all the perils against which the constitutional prohibition was designed to guard."

The judgment of the Court of Appeals is reversed and the Board's orders are set aside.

It is so ordered.

Source: Justice Brennan, William J., Jr. Opinion of the Court. *William Albertson and Roscoe Quincy Proctors, Petitioners v. Subversive Activities Control Board,* No. 3, Decided November 15, 1965. United States Reports, Volume 382, October 1965–January 1966.

1965: THE SUPREME COURT FINDS A CONSTITUTIONAL RIGHT TO PRIVACY IN *GRISWOLD v. CONNECTICUT*

This landmark decision centered on Estelle T. Griswold, who was the executive director of the Planned Parenthood League of Connecticut. Both she and the medical director for the League gave information, instruction, and other medical advice to married couples concerning birth control. Griswold and her colleague were convicted under a Connecticut law that criminalized counseling about contraception to married persons. On June 7, 1965, however, the U.S. Supreme Court struck down the law by a 7–2 vote, calling it a violation of the right to privacy between a husband and wife.

Although the Bill of Rights does not explicitly mention a broad right to privacy, Justice William O. Douglas wrote for the majority that the right was to be found in the "penumbras" and "emanations" from the Bill of Rights. This literally means the shadows cast by the Bill of Rights, including the First Amendment (free speech), Third Amendment (prohibition on the forced quartering of troops), Fourth Amendment (freedom from searches and seizures), Fifth Amendment (freedom from self-incrimination), and Ninth Amendment (other rights not specifically listed), as applied against the states by the Fourteenth Amendment.

This seminal decision established a basic sphere or zone of personal privacy to which all individuals are entitled. As a precedent, it placed the burden squarely on the government to justify in interfering with a citizen's life rather than requiring the citizen to demonstrate that the text of the Constitution specifically and narrowly prohibits the government's actions. Fifty years later, Griswold *continues to function as a key legal basis for judicial rulings involving issues of sexual intimacy, reproductive rights, family life, privacy, and the limitations of government power.*

Appellant Griswold is Executive Director of the Planned Parenthood League of Connecticut. Appellant Buxton is a licensed physician and a professor at the Yale Medical School who served as Medical Director for the League at its Center in New Haven—a center open and operating from November 1 to November 10, 1961, when appellants were arrested. They gave information, instruction, and medical advice to married persons as to the means of preventing conception. They examined the wife and prescribed the best contraceptive device or material for her use. Fees were usually charged, although some couples were serviced free.

The statutes whose constitutionality is involved in this appeal are 53–32 and 54–196 of the General Statutes of Connecticut (1958 rev.). The former provides: "Any person who uses any drug, medicinal article or instrument for the purpose of preventing conception shall be fined not less than fifty dollars or imprisoned not less than sixty days nor more than one year or be both fined and imprisoned."

Section 54–196 provides: "Any person who assists, abets, counsels, causes, hires or commands another to commit any offense may be prosecuted and punished as if he were the principal offender."

The appellants were found guilty as accessories and fined $100 each, against the claim that the accessory statute as so applied violated the Fourteenth Amendment. . . .

Coming to the merits, we are met with a wide range of questions that implicate the Due Process Clause of the Fourteenth Amendment. Overtones of some arguments suggest that Lochner v. New York, 198 U.S. 45, should be our guide. But we decline that invitation. We do not sit as a super-legislature to determine the wisdom, need, and propriety of laws that touch economic problems, business affairs, or social conditions. This law, however, operates directly on an intimate relation of husband and wife and their physician's role in one aspect of that relation.

The association of people is not mentioned in the Constitution nor in the Bill of Rights. The right to educate a child in a school of the parents' choice—whether public or private or parochial—is also not mentioned. Nor is the right to study any particular subject or any foreign language. Yet the First Amendment has been construed to include certain of those rights.

By Pierce v. Society of Sisters, the right to educate one's children as one chooses is made applicable to the States by the force of the First and Fourteenth Amendments. By Meyer v. Nebraska, the same dignity is given the right to study the German language in a private school. In other words, the State may not, consistently with the spirit of the First Amendment, contract the spectrum of available knowledge . . . And so we reaffirm the principle of the Pierce and the Meyer cases.

In NAACP v. Alabama we protected the "freedom to associate and privacy in one's associations," noting that freedom of association was a peripheral First Amendment right. Disclosure of membership lists of a constitutionally valid association, we held, was invalid "as entailing the likelihood of a substantial restraint upon the exercise by petitioner's members of their right to freedom of association." In other words, the First Amendment has a penumbra where privacy is protected from governmental intrusion. The right of "association," like the right of belief is more than the right to attend a meeting; it includes the right to express one's attitudes or philosophies by membership in a group or by affiliation with it or by other lawful means. Association in that context is a form of expression of opinion; and while it is not expressly included in the First Amendment its existence is necessary in making the express guarantees fully meaningful.

The foregoing cases suggest that specific guarantees in the Bill of Rights have penumbras, formed by emanations from those guarantees that help give them life and substance. Various guarantees create zones of privacy. The right of association contained in the penumbra of the First Amendment is one, as we have seen.

The Third Amendment in its prohibition against the quartering of soldiers "in any house" in time of peace without the consent of the owner is another facet of that privacy. The Fourth Amendment explicitly affirms the "right of the people to be secure in their persons, houses, papers, and effects, against unreasonable searches and seizures." The Fifth Amendment in its Self-Incrimination Clause enables the citizen to create a zone of privacy which government may not force him to surrender to his detriment. The Ninth Amendment provides: "The enumeration in the Constitution, of certain rights, shall not be construed to deny or disparage others retained by the people."

The Fourth and Fifth Amendments were described . . . as protection against all governmental invasions "of the sanctity of a man's home and the privacies of life."

We have had many controversies over these penumbral rights of "privacy and repose." These cases bear witness that the right of privacy which presses for recognition here is a legitimate one.

The present case, then, concerns a relationship lying within the zone of privacy created by several fundamental constitutional guarantees. And it concerns a law which, in forbidding the use of contraceptives rather than regulating their manufacture or sale, seeks to achieve its goals by means having a maximum destructive impact upon that relationship. Such a law cannot stand in light of the familiar principle, so often applied by this Court, that a "governmental purpose to control or prevent activities constitutionally subject to state regulation may not be achieved by means which sweep unnecessarily broadly and thereby invade the area of protected freedoms." Would we allow the police to search the sacred precincts of marital bedrooms for telltale signs of the use of contraceptives? The very idea is repulsive to the notions of privacy surrounding the marriage relationship.

We deal with a right of privacy older than the Bill of Rights—older than our political parties, older than our school system. Marriage is a coming together for better or for worse, hopefully enduring, and intimate to the degree of being sacred. It is an association that promotes a way of life, not causes; a harmony in living, not political faiths; a bilateral loyalty, not commercial or social projects. Yet it is an association for as noble a purpose as any involved in our prior decisions.

Reversed.

Source: Justice Douglas, William O. Opinion of the Court. *Estelle T. Griswold et al, Appellants v. State of Connecticut,* No. 496, Decided June 7, 1965. United States Reports, Volume 381, May–October 1965.

1967: THE SUPREME COURT EXPANDS PRIVACY RIGHTS IN *KATZ v. UNITED STATES*

Charles Katz was convicted in federal district court of placing bets and wagers in violation of federal law. The evidence used to convict Katz was obtained by an electronic listening device placed outside a public telephone booth in Los Angeles, California. The device was placed outside the booth by agents of the Federal Bureau of Investigation, who did not have a warrant. Katz unsuccessfully challenged the admission of this evidence on the grounds that it was obtained in violation of the Fourth Amendment. A federal appellate court affirmed his conviction.

When the case reached the U.S. Supreme Court on appeal, however, the justices ruled for Katz by a decisive 7–1 margin. In arguably the most important Fourth Amendment case of the last half century, the Katz *majority rejected the legal doctrine enshrined in* Olmstead v. United States (1928), *a ruling that had given government authorities latitude to engage in warrantless searches outside of homes and other "constitutionally protected" physical locations. In his majority opinion, released on December 18, 1967, Justice Potter Stewart explained that the majority ruled in favor of Katz because "[T]he Fourth Amendment protects people not places." Justice John Marshal Harlan's concurrence was also noteworthy because it established the practice of examining Fourth Amendment protections through the standard of "reasonable" expectations of privacy. The lone dissent, penned by Justice Hugo Black, took up the broader question of the role of history in interpreting the Fourth Amendment. By distorting the amendment "to bring it into harmony with the times," Justice Black asserted, the Court had assumed the improper role of a "continuously functioning constitutional convention."*

MR. JUSTICE STEWART delivered the opinion of the Court.

. . . [T]he parties have attached great significance to the characterization of the telephone booth from which the petitioner placed his calls. The petitioner has strenuously argued that the booth was a "constitutionally protected area." The Government has maintained with equal vigor that it was not. But this effort to decide whether or not a given "area," viewed in the abstract, is "constitutionally protected" deflects attention from the problem presented by this case. For the Fourth Amendment protects people, not places. What a person knowingly exposes to the public, even in his own home or office, is not a subject of Fourth Amendment protection. But what he seeks to preserve as private, even in an area accessible to the public, may be constitutionally protected. . . .

The Government stresses the fact that the telephone booth from which the petitioner made his calls was constructed partly of glass, so that he was as visible after he entered it as he would have been if he had remained outside. But what he sought to exclude when he entered the booth was not the intruding eye—it was the uninvited ear. He did not shed his right to do so simply because he made his calls from a place where he might be seen. No less than an individual in a business office, in a friend's apartment, or in a taxicab, a person in a telephone booth may rely upon the protection of the Fourth Amendment. One who occupies it, shuts the door behind him, and pays the toll that permits him to place a call is surely entitled to assume that the words he utters into the mouthpiece will not be broadcast to the world. To read the Constitution more narrowly is to ignore the vital role that the public telephone has come to play in private communication. The Government contends, however, that the activities of its agents in this case should not be tested by Fourth Amendment requirements, for the surveillance technique they employed involved no physical penetration of the telephone booth from which the petitioner placed his calls. It is true that the absence of such penetration was at one time thought to foreclose further Fourth Amendment inquiry. . . . Thus, although a closely divided Court supposed in *Olmstead* that surveillance without any trespass and without the seizure of any material object fell outside the ambit of the Constitution, we have since departed from the narrow view on which that decision rested. Indeed, we have expressly held that the Fourth Amendment governs not only the seizure of tangible items, but extends as well to the recording of oral statements, overheard without any "technical trespass under . . . local property law." Once this much is acknowledged, and once it is recognized that the Fourth Amendment protects people—and not simply "areas"—against unreasonable searches and seizures, it becomes clear that the reach of that Amendment cannot turn upon the presence or absence of a physical intrusion into any given enclosure.

We conclude that the underpinnings of *Olmstead* and *Goldman* have been so eroded by our subsequent decisions that the "trespass" doctrine there enunciated can no longer be regarded as controlling. The Government's activities in electronically listening to and recording the petitioner's words violated the privacy upon which he justifiably relied while using the telephone booth and thus constituted a "search and seizure" within the meaning of the Fourth Amendment. The fact that the electronic device employed to achieve that end did not happen to penetrate the wall of the booth can have no constitutional significance. The question remaining for decision, then, is whether the search and seizure conducted in this case complied with constitutional standards. In that regard, the Government's position is that its agents acted in an entirely defensible manner: They did not begin their electronic surveillance until investigation of the petitioner's activities had established a strong probability that he was using the telephone in question to transmit gambling information to persons in other States, in violation of federal law. Moreover, the surveillance was limited, both in scope and in duration, to the specific purpose of establishing the contents of the petitioner's unlawful telephonic communications.

The agents confined their surveillance to the brief periods during which he used the telephone booth, and they took great care to overhear only the conversations of the petitioner himself.

Accepting this account of the Government's actions as accurate, it is clear that this surveillance was so narrowly circumscribed that a duly authorized magistrate, properly notified of the need for such investigation, specifically informed of the basis on which it was to proceed, and clearly apprised of the precise intrusion it would entail, could constitutionally have authorized, with appropriate safeguards, the very limited search and seizure that the Government asserts in fact took place. . . .

It is apparent that the agents in this case acted with restraint. Yet the inescapable fact is that this restraint was imposed by the agents themselves, not by a judicial officer. They were not required, before commencing the search, to present their estimate of probable cause for detached scrutiny by a neutral magistrate. They were not compelled, during the conduct of the search itself, to observe precise limits established in advance by a specific court order. Nor were they directed, after the search had been completed, to notify the authorizing magistrate in detail of all that had been seized. In the absence of such safeguards, this Court has never sustained a search upon the sole ground that officers reasonably expected to find evidence of a particular crime and voluntarily confined their activities to the least intrusive means consistent with that end. . . .

The Government. . . . argues that surveillance of a telephone booth should be exempted from the usual requirement of advance authorization by a magistrate upon a showing of probable cause. We cannot agree. Omission of such authorization "bypasses the safeguards provided by an objective predetermination of probable cause, and substitutes instead the far less reliable procedure of an after-the-event justification for the. . . . search, too likely to be subtly influenced by the familiar shortcomings of hindsight judgment." . . .

And bypassing a neutral predetermination of the *scope* of a search leaves individuals secure from Fourth Amendment violations "only in the discretion of the police.". . . .

Wherever a man may be, he is entitled to know that he will remain free from unreasonable searches and seizures. The government agents here ignored "the procedure of antecedent justification. . . . that is central to the Fourth Amendment," a procedure that we hold to be a constitutional precondition of the kind of electronic surveillance involved in this case. Because the surveillance here failed to meet that condition, and because it led to the petitioner's conviction, the judgment must be reversed. *It is so ordered.*

MR. JUSTICE HARLAN, concurring.

. . . As the Court's opinion states, "the Fourth Amendment protects people, not places." The question, however, is what protection it affords to those people.

Generally, as here, the answer to that question requires reference to a "place." My understanding of the rule that has emerged from prior decisions is that there is a twofold requirement, first that a person have exhibited an actual (subjective) expectation of privacy and, second, that the expectation be one that society is prepared to recognize as "reasonable." Thus a man's home is, for most purposes, a place where he expects privacy, but objects, activities, or statements that he exposes to the "plain view" of outsiders are not "protected" because no intention to keep them to himself has been exhibited. On the other hand, conversations in the open would not be protected against being overheard, for the expectation of privacy under the circumstances would be unreasonable.

MR. JUSTICE BLACK, dissenting.

. . . . My basic objection is twofold: (1) I do not believe that the words of the Amendment will bear the meaning given them by today's decision, and (2) I do not believe that it is the proper role of this Court to rewrite the Amendment in order "to bring it into harmony with the times" and thus reach a result that many people believe to be desirable. . . . [T]he language of the [Fourth] Amendment is the crucial place to look in construing a written document such as our Constitution. . . .

The first clause protects "persons, houses, papers, and effects, against unreasonable searches and seizures. . . ." These words connote the idea of tangible things with size, form, and weight, things capable of being searched, seized, or both. The second clause of the Amendment still further establishes its Framers' purpose to limit its protection to tangible things by providing that no warrants shall issue but those "particularly describing the place to be searched, and the persons or things to be seized." A conversation overheard by eavesdropping, whether by plain snooping or wiretapping, is not tangible and, under the normally accepted meanings of the words, can neither be searched nor seized. In addition the language of the second clause indicates that the Amendment refers not only to something tangible so it can be seized but to something already in existence so it can be described. Yet the Court's interpretation would have the Amendment apply to overhearing future conversations which by their very nature are nonexistent until they take place. How can one "describe" a future conversation, and, if one cannot, how can a magistrate issue a warrant to eavesdrop one in the future? It is argued that information showing what is expected to be said is sufficient to limit the boundaries of what later can be admitted into evidence; but does such general information really meet the specific language of the Amendment which says "particularly describing"? Rather than using language in a completely artificial way, I must conclude that the Fourth Amendment simply does not apply to eavesdropping. Tapping telephone wires, of course, was an unknown possibility at the time the Fourth Amendment was adopted. But eavesdropping (and wiretapping is nothing more than eavesdropping by telephone) was. . . .

There can be no doubt that the Framers were aware of this practice, and if they had desired to outlaw or restrict the use of evidence obtained by eavesdropping, I believe that they would have used the appropriate language to do so in the Fourth Amendment. They certainly would not have left such a task to the ingenuity of language-stretching judges. . . .

Since I see no way in which the words of the Fourth Amendment can be construed to apply to eavesdropping, that closes the matter for me. In interpreting the Bill of Rights, I willingly go as far as a liberal construction of the language takes me, but I simply cannot in good conscience give a meaning to words which they have never before been thought to have and which they certainly do not have in common ordinary usage. I will not distort the words of the Amendment in order to "keep the Constitution up to date" or "to bring it into harmony with the times." It was never meant that this Court have such power, which in effect would make us a continuously functioning constitutional convention. . . .

Source: Justice Stewart, Potter. Opinion of the Court; Justice Harlan, John Marshall. Concurrence; and Justice Black, Hugo. Dissent. *Charles Katz v. United States,* No. 35, Decided December 18, 1967. United States Reports, Volume 389, October 1967–January 1968.

1968: PRESIDENT JOHNSON CRITICIZES EAVESDROPPING PROVISIONS IN CRIME CONTROL ACT

In 1968, Congress passed and President Lyndon B. Johnson signed a sweeping bill designed to respond to a variety of legal and public concerns in the arena of criminal justice and public safety. The Omnibus Crime Control and Safe Streets Act of 1968 included language imposing new restrictions on gun sales and ownership (support for which owed much to sustained anger about the 1963 assassination of John F. Kennedy); boosting funding to the FBI; providing for the admissibility of "voluntary statements" of defendants who had not received so-called "Miranda Warnings"; and establishing the Law Enforcement Assistance Administration (LEAA) to aid local law enforcement programs and departments.

Johnson supported most of these bill provisions. But he harshly criticized Title III of the bill, which created new opportunities for authorities to engage in wiretapping and eavesdropping activities provided that a court certified that it had "probable cause" to engage in such surveillance. Title III had been crafted in response to Supreme Court decisions in Berger v. New York *(1967) and* Katz v. United States *(1967) that electronic surveillance methods had to be consistent with Fourth Amendment protections. But while the wiretapping provisions had been intended to shore up privacy protections, critics said that the final language, which had been stitched together from House and Senate versions, opened the door to increased electronic surveillance. Johnson shared this concern, as evidenced by his signing statement jab that Title III could create "a nation of snoopers bending through the keyholes of the homes and offices in America." As Johnson's signing statement makes clear, he ultimately felt that the good outweighed the bad in the bill. Still, he used the occasion to make an (unsuccessful) appeal to Congress to go back to Capitol Hill and pass new legislation repealing Title III.*

THE Safe Streets and Crime Control Act of 1968 has had a long journey.

The work behind the principal title of the act began in July 1965 when I appointed the national crime commission. The work of the Congress started more than 16 months ago, in February 1967, when I called upon it to strike a sure and swift blow against crime in America.

Now, almost 500 days later, the legislative process has run its full course. The measure before me carries out many of the objectives I sought. But it also contains several other provisions which are unwise and which will not aid effective law enforcement.

Over the past 10 days, I have given full consideration to this intricate, 110-page bill. I have carefully weighed the good features against the undesirable, the questions of law and policy it raises against the remedial actions I might take to resolve those questions, the immediate crisis of local law enforcement against the bill's response.

My decision has been made only after consulting with the wisest counselors available to the President. I have asked 11 Government departments and agency heads, including those most affected, such as the Attorney General, the Director of the Federal Bureau of Investigation, the Secretary of the Treasury, the Chairman of the Federal Communications Commission, and the Mayor of the District of Columbia, for their views. No department has recommended veto. On the basis of their advice and my own searching examination, I have decided that this measure contains more good than bad and that I should sign it into law.

I sign the bill because it responds to one of the most urgent problems in America today—the problem of fighting crime in the local neighborhood and on the city street.

The program I recommended 16 months ago—the Safe Streets Act—is the heart of this measure.

My program was based on the most exhaustive study of crime ever undertaken in America—the work of the President's national crime commission. The commission—composed of the Nation's leading criminologists, police chiefs, educators, and urban experts—spotlighted the weaknesses in our present system of law enforcement. It concluded that the States and local communities need large-scale Federal financial assistance to help them plan, organize, and mount a concerted and effective attack on crime.

The bill I sign today provides much of that urgently needed assistance. It will give help to the ill-equipped and poorly-trained policeman on the beat, to the overburdened courtroom, to the antiquated correctional institution. The legislation honors the deeply rooted principle that the Federal Government should supplement—but never supplant—local efforts and local responsibility to prevent and control crime.

This measure moves in new directions to fight crime by:

- Authorizing $400 million in Federal grants over a 2-year period for planning and launching action programs to strengthen the sinews of local law enforcement—from police to prisons to parole.
- Creating a National Institute of Law Enforcement and Criminal Justice to begin a modern research and development venture which will put science and the laboratory to work in the detection of criminals and the prevention of crime.
- Establishing a pioneering aid-to-education program of forgivable college loans and tuition grants to attract better law enforcement officers and give them better education and preparation.

- Providing greatly expanded training for State and local police officers at the National Academy of the Federal Bureau of Investigation.
- to encourage the specialized training of community service officers whose mission will be to ease tensions in ghetto neighborhoods.

These are among the prime advantages of this bill I sign today.

The measure also ends three decades of inaction on the problem of gun controls. Interstate traffic in handguns and their sales to minors will now be prohibited by law. The majority of all the murders by firearms in this Nation are committed by these small but deadly weapons.

But as I have told the Nation and the Congress repeatedly, this is only a halfway step toward the protection of our families and homes. We must go further and stop mail order murder by rifle and shotgun. We must close a glaring loophole in the law by controlling the sale of these lethal weapons, as well as the sale of ammunition for all guns.

A week ago I submitted my proposal for more stringent safeguards. I asked, as I had before, "What in the name of conscience will it take to pass a truly effective gun control law?"

In the next few days, the Congress has the opportunity to answer that question. The call for action is compelling. We dare delay no longer. I urge the Congress to act on this bill immediately. I am asking the Attorney General to explore what further steps should be taken in the gun control area so that I may recommend them when the Congress has acted on the legislation I submitted last week.

Title III of this legislation deals with wiretapping and eavesdropping.

My views on this subject are clear. In a special message to Congress in 1967 and again this year, I called—in the Right of Privacy Act—for an end to the bugging and snooping that invade the privacy of citizens.

I urge that the Congress outlaw "all wiretapping and electronic eavesdropping, public and private, wherever and whenever it occurs." The only exceptions would be those instances where "the security of the Nation itself was at stake—and then only under the strictest safeguards."

In the bill I sign today, Congress has moved part of the way by

- banning all wiretapping and eavesdropping by private parties;
- prohibiting the sale and distribution of "listening-in" devices in interstate commerce.

But the Congress, in my judgment, has taken an unwise and potentially dangerous step by sanctioning eavesdropping and wiretapping by Federal, State, and local law officials in an almost unlimited variety of situations.

If we are not very careful and cautious in our planning, these legislative provisions could result in producing a nation of snoopers bending through the keyholes of the homes and offices in America, spying on our neighbors. No conversation in the sanctity of the bedroom or relayed over a copper telephone wire would be free of eavesdropping by those who say they want to ferret out crime.

Thus, I believe this action goes far beyond the effective and legitimate needs of law enforcement. The right of privacy is a valued right. But in a technologically advanced society, it is a vulnerable right. That is why we must strive to protect it all the more against erosion.

I call upon the Congress immediately to reconsider the unwise provisions of Title III and take steps to repeal them. I am directing the Attorney General to confer as soon as possible with the appropriate committee chairmen and warn them of the pitfalls that lie ahead, in the hope that the Congress will move to repeal the dangerous provisions of this title.

Until that can be accomplished we shall pursue—within the Federal Government—carefully designed safeguards to limit wiretapping and eavesdropping. The policy of this administration has been to confine wiretapping and eavesdropping to national security cases only—and then only with the approval of the Attorney General.

This policy, now in its 3d year, will continue in force. I have today directed the Attorney General to assure that this policy of privacy prevails and is followed by all Federal law enforcement officers.

Many States have protected the citizen against the invasion of privacy by making wiretapping illegal. I call upon the State and local authorities in the other States to apply the utmost restraint and caution if they exercise the broad powers of Title III. We need not surrender our privacy to win the war on crime.

Title II of the legislation deals with certain rules of evidence only in Federal criminal trials—which account for only 7 percent of the criminal felony prosecutions in this country. The provisions of Title II, vague and ambiguous as they are, can, I am advised by the Attorney General, be interpreted in harmony with the Constitution, and Federal practices in this field will continue to conform to the Constitution.

Under long-standing policies, for example, the Federal Bureau of Investigation and other Federal law enforcement agencies have consistently given suspects full and fair warning of their constitutional rights. I have asked the Attorney General and the Director of the Federal Bureau of Investigation to assure that these policies will continue.

My overriding concern today, as it has been since the first day I became President, is for safe streets in America. I believe this measure, despite its shortcomings, will help to lift the stain of crime and the shadow of fear from the streets of our communities.

That promise, contained largely in Title I and in the reinforced gun control law I have asked for, must not be deterred.

I believe it is in America's interest that I sign this law today.

Crime will never yield to demagogic lament—only to action. With this measure, we are beginning to act. The Federal Government is taking a long overdue step.

But at a time when crime is on the tip of every American's tongue, we must remember that our protection rests essentially with local and State police officers. For of the 40,000 law enforcement agencies in this Nation, more than 39,750 are local, while some 200 are State and only the remaining 40-plus are Federal. Of the 371,000 full-time law enforcement officers in the Nation, 308,000 are local, while 40,000 are State and only 23,000 are Federal. The essential duties these 23,000 Federal officers are authorized by law to perform are to protect the President, ferret out crime in interstate commerce, investigate crime in interstate commerce, guard our borders, and enforce the tax and customs laws.

Today the Federal Government is acting. But action must now also come from the cities and counties and States across America.

The cities must increase the size of their police forces.

The cities must pay their law enforcement officials more.

The local communities must train them better.

The cities and the States must streamline their courts and correctional institutions.

Both the cities and States must plan with care and imagination to use the new Federal funds we will make available under the act I sign today.

Today, I ask every Governor, every mayor, and every county and city commissioner and councilman to examine the adequacy of their State and local law enforcement systems and to move promptly to support the policemen, the law enforcement officers, and the men who wage the war on crime day after day in all the streets and roads and alleys in America.

Most important of all, I call upon every citizen in this Nation to support their local police officials with respect and with the resources necessary to enable them to do their job for justice in America.

I call upon our church leaders and every parent to provide the spiritual and moral leadership necessary to make this a law-abiding Nation, with respect for the rights of others, respect for their system of government, and support for those charged with the responsibility of protecting our lives, our homes, and our liberties.

Source: President Johnson, Lyndon B. 1970. "Statement by the President Upon Signing the Omnibus Crime Control and Safe Streets Act of 1968." June 19, 1968. In *Lyndon B. Johnson: 1968–1969 (in two books): Containing the Public Messages, Speeches, and Statements of the President. [Book 1].* Washington, DC: Government Printing Office. Document 320.

1976: THE CHURCH COMMITTEE RELEASES SHOCKING REVELATIONS OF GOVERNMENT SURVEILLANCE

In January 1975, the U.S. Senate, acting on behalf of a nation reeling from the Watergate scandal and other revelations of civil liberties transgressions by federal intelligence agencies, established a formal committee to investigate the nature, extent, and legality of various surveillance and other intelligence-gathering activities carried out over the past several decades by the Federal Bureau of Investigation (FBI), the Central Intelligence Agency (CIA), the National Security Agency (NSA), and other intelligence- and defense-related governmental organizations. This committee, officially known as the Select Committee to Study Governmental Operations with Respect to Intelligence Activities, became commonly known as the Church Committee in recognition of Senator Frank Church (D-Idaho), who served as both chairman and as one of its ethical touchstones.

Over the course of the next nine months, the Church Committee held 21 public and 250 executive hearings and conducted interviews with more than 800 individuals in various governmental positions. It ultimately published 14 volumes of reports in 1975–1976 on a wide range of intelligence abuses and activities, examining everything from the U.S. intelligence community's failure to stop the assassination of President John F. Kennedy in 1963 to plots to assassinate foreign leaders to gross violations of the civil liberties of American citizens.

The Church Committee's report on illegal and excessive government surveillance was called Intelligence Activities and the Rights of Americans. *This volume detailed numerous and long-standing surveillance activities carried out by the FBI, CIA, and other agencies that completely disregarded the civil rights of Americans, and it urged Congress to act to provide greater oversight. Excerpts from its introduction and summary (footnotes removed) are featured below. Two years after this report was issued, Congress passed the Foreign Intelligence Surveillance Act (FISA) of 1978, which established a secret FISA court to which government agencies were required to go for approval of domestic wiretapping activity.*

The resolution creating this Committee placed greatest emphasis on whether intelligence activities threaten the "rights of American citizens."

The critical question before the Committee was to determine how the fundamental liberties of the people can be maintained in the course of the Government's effort to protect their security. The delicate balance between these basic goals of our system of government is often difficult to strike, but it can, and must, be achieved. We reject the view that the traditional American principles of justice and fair play have no place in our struggle against the enemies of freedom. Moreover, our investigation has established that the targets of intelligence activity have ranged far beyond persons who could properly be characterized as enemies of freedom and have extended to a wide array of citizens engaging in lawful activity. . . .

We have examined three types of "intelligence" activities affecting the rights of American citizens. The first is intelligence collection—such as infiltrating groups with informants, wiretapping, or opening letters. The second is dissemination of material which has been collected. The third is covert action designed to disrupt and discredit the activities of groups and individuals deemed a threat to the social order. These three types of "intelligence" activity are closely related in the practical world. Information which is disseminated by the intelligence community or used in disruptive programs has usually been obtained through surveillance. Nevertheless, a division between collection, dissemination, and covert action is analytically useful both in understanding why excesses have occurred in the past and in devising remedies to prevent these excesses from recurring.

Intelligence Activity: A New Form of Governmental Power to Impair Citizens' Rights

A tension between order and liberty is inevitable in any society. A Government must protect its citizens from those bent on engaging in violence and criminal behavior, or in espionage and other hostile foreign intelligence activity. Many of the intelligence programs reviewed in this report were established for those purposes. Intelligence work has, at times, successfully prevented dangerous and abhorrent acts, such as bombings and foreign spying, and aided in the prosecution of those responsible for such acts.

But, intelligence activity in the past decades has, all too often, exceeded the restraints on the exercise of governmental power which are imposed by our country's Constitution, laws, and traditions. . . .

It is, of course, proper in many circumstances—such as developing a criminal prosecution—for the Government to gather information about a citizen and use it to achieve legitimate ends, some of which might be detrimental to the citizen. But in criminal prosecutions, the courts have struck a balance between protecting the rights of the accused citizen and protecting the society which suffers the consequences of crime. Essential to the balancing process are the rules of criminal law which circumscribe the techniques for gathering evidence, the kinds of evidence that may be collected, and the uses to which that evidence may be put. In addition, the criminal defendant is given an opportunity to discover and then challenge the legality of how the Government collected information about him and the use which the Government intends to make of that information.

This Committee has examined a realm of governmental information collection which has not been governed by restraints comparable to those in criminal proceedings. We have examined the collection of intelligence about the political advocacy and actions and the private lives of American citizens. That information has been used covertly to discredit the ideas advocated and to "neutralize" the actions of their proponents. As Attorney General Harlan Fiske Stone warned in 1924, when he sought to keep federal agencies from investigating "political or other opinions" as opposed to "conduct . . . forbidden by the laws":

> When a police system passes beyond these limits, it is dangerous to the proper administration of justice and to human liberty, which it should be our first concern to cherish. . . . There is always a possibility that a secret police may become a menace to free government and free institutions because it carries with it the possibility of abuses of power which are not always quickly apprehended or understood.

Our investigation has confirmed that warning. We have seen segments of our Government, in their attitudes and action, adopt tactics unworthy of a democracy, and occasionally reminiscent of the tactics of totalitarian regimes. We have seen a consistent pattern in which programs initiated with limited goals, such as preventing criminal violence or identifying foreign spies, were expanded to what witnesses characterized as "vacuum cleaners," sweeping in information about lawful activities of American citizens.

The tendency of intelligence activities to expand beyond their initial scope is a theme which runs through every aspect of our investigative findings. Intelligence collection programs naturally generate ever-increasing demands for new data. And once intelligence has been collected, there are strong pressures to use it against the target.

The pattern of intelligence agencies expanding the scope of their activities was well described by one witness, who in 1970 had coordinated an effort by most of the intelligence community to obtain authority to undertake more illegal domestic activity:

> The risk was that you would get people who would be susceptible to political considerations as opposed to national security considerations, or would construe political considerations to be national security considerations, to move from the kid with a bomb to the kid with a picket sign, and from the kid with the picket sign to the kid with the bumper sticker of the opposing candidate. And you just keep going down the line.

In 1940, Attorney General Robert Jackson saw the same risk. He recognized that using broad labels like "national security" or "subversion" to invoke the vast power of the government is dangerous because there are no "definite standards to determine what constitutes a 'subversive activity,' such as we have for murder or larceny," Jackson added:

> Activities which seem benevolent or helpful to wage earners, persons on relief, or those who are disadvantaged in the struggle for existence may be regarded as "subversive" by those whose property interests might be burdened thereby. Those who are in office are apt to regard as "subversive" the activities of any of those who would bring about a change of administration. Some of our soundest constitutional doctrines were once punished as subversive. We must not forget that it was not so long ago that both the term "Republican" and the term "Democrat" were epithets with sinister meaning to denote persons of radical tendencies that were "subversive" of the order of things then dominant.

This wise warning was not heeded in the conduct of intelligence activity, where the "eternal vigilance" which is the "price of liberty" has been forgotten. . . .

Summary of the Main Problems

. . . Too many people have been spied upon by too many Government agencies and too much information has been collected. The Government has often undertaken the secret surveillance of citizens on the basis of their political beliefs, even when those beliefs posed no threat of violence or illegal acts on behalf of a hostile foreign power. The Government, operating primarily through secret informants, but also using other intrusive techniques such as wiretaps, microphone "bugs," surreptitious mail opening, and break-ins, has swept in vast amounts of information about the personal lives, views, and associations of American citizens. Investigations of groups deemed potentially dangerous—and even of groups suspected of associating with potentially dangerous organizations—have continued for decades, despite the fact that those groups did not engage in unlawful activity. Groups and individuals have been harassed and disrupted because of their political views and their lifestyles. Investigations have been based upon vague standards whose breadth made excessive collection inevitable. Unsavory and vicious tactics have been employed—including anonymous attempts to break up marriages, disrupt meetings, ostracize persons from their professions, and provoke target groups into rivalries that might result in deaths. . . .

Government officials—including those whose principal duty is to enforce the law—have violated or ignored the law over long periods of time and have advocated and defended their right to break the law.

The Constitutional system of checks and balances has not adequately controlled intelligence activities. Until recently the Executive branch has neither delineated the scope of permissible activities nor established procedures for supervising intelligence agencies. Congress has failed to exercise sufficient oversight, seldom questioning the use to which its appropriations were being put. Most domestic intelligence issues have not reached the courts, and in those cases when they have reached the courts, the judiciary has been reluctant to grapple with them. . . .

The Number of People Affected by Domestic Intelligence Activity

United States intelligence agencies have investigated a vast number of American citizens and domestic organizations. FBI headquarters alone has developed over 500,000 domestic intelligence files, and these have been augmented by additional files at FBI Field Offices. The FBI opened 65,000 of these domestic intelligence files in 1972 alone. In fact, substantially more individuals and groups are subject to intelligence scrutiny than the number of files would appear to indicate, since typically, each domestic intelligence file contains information on more than one individual or group. . . .

The number of Americans and domestic groups caught in the domestic intelligence net is further illustrated by the following statistics:

- Nearly a quarter of a million first class letters were opened and photographed in the United States by the CIA between 1953–1973, producing a computerized index of nearly one and one-half million names. . . .
- Some 300,000 individuals were indexed in a CIA computer system and separate files were created on approximately 7,200 Americans and over 100 domestic groups during the course of CIA's Operation CHAOS (1967–1973).
- Millions of private telegrams sent from, to, or through the United States were obtained by the National Security Agency from 1947 to 1975 under a secret arrangement with three United States telegraph companies.
- An estimated 100,000 Americans were the subjects of United States Army intelligence files created between the mid-1960s and 1971.
- Intelligence files on more than 11,000 individuals and groups were created by the Internal Revenue Service between 1969 and 1973 and tax investigations were started on the basis of political rather than tax criteria.
- At least 26,000 individuals were at one point catalogued on an FBI list of persons to be rounded up in the event of a "national emergency."

Too Much Information Is Collected for Too Long

Intelligence agencies have collected vast amounts of information about the intimate details of citizens' lives and about their participation in legal and peaceful political activities. The targets of intelligence activity have included political adherents of the right and the left, ranging from activist[s] to casual supporters. Investigations have been directed against proponents of racial causes and women's rights, outspoken apostles of nonviolence and racial harmony; establishment politicians; religious groups; and advocates of new lifestyles. The widespread targeting of citizens and domestic groups, and the excessive scope of the collection of information, is illustrated by the following examples:

a) The "Women's Liberation Movement" was infiltrated by informants who collected material about the movement's policies, leaders, and individual members. One report included the name of every woman who attended meetings, and another stated that each woman at a meeting had described "how she felt oppressed, sexually or otherwise." Another report concluded that the movement's purpose was to "free women from the humdrum existence of being only a wife and mother," but still recommended that the intelligence investigation should be continued.
b) A prominent civil rights leader and advisor to Dr. Martin Luther King, Jr., was investigated on the suspicion that he might be a Communist "sympathizer." The FBI field office concluded he was not. Bureau headquarters directed that the investigation continue—using a theory of "guilty until proven innocent" . . .
c) FBI sources reported on the formation of the Conservative American Christian Action Council in 1971. In the 1950s, the Bureau collected information about the John Birch Society and passed it to the White House because of the Society's "scurrilous attack" on President Eisenhower and other high Government officials.
d) Some investigations of the lawful activities of peaceful groups have continued for decades. For example, the NAACP was investigated to determine whether it "had connections with" the Communist Party. The investigation lasted for over twenty-five years, although nothing was found to rebut a report during the first year of the investigation that the NAACP had a "strong tendency" to "steer clear of Communist activities.". . . The Bureau has investigated the Socialist Workers Party for more than three decades on the basis of its revolutionary rhetoric—which the FBI concedes falls short of incitement to violence—and its claimed international links. . . .
e) National political leaders fell within the broad reach of intelligence investigations. For example, Army Intelligence maintained files on Senator Adlai Stevenson and Congressman Abner Mikva because of their participation in peaceful political meetings under surveillance by Army agents. A letter to Richard Nixon, while he was a candidate for President in 1968, was intercepted under CIA's mail opening program. In the 1960s President Johnson

asked the FBI to compare various Senators' statements on Vietnam with the Communist Party line and to conduct name checks on leading antiwar Senators.

f) As part of their effort to collect information which "related even remotely" to people or groups "active" in communities which had "the potential" for civil disorder, Army intelligence agencies took such steps as: sending agents to a Halloween party for elementary school children in Washington, D.C., because they suspected a local "dissident" might be present; monitoring protests of welfare mothers' organizations in Milwaukee; infiltrating a coalition of church youth groups in Colorado; and sending agents to a priests' conference in Washington, D.C., held to discuss birth control measures.

g) In the late 1960s and early 1970s student groups were subjected to intense scrutiny. In 1970 the FBI ordered investigations of every member of the Students for a Democratic Society and of "every Black Student Union and similar group regardless of their past or present involvement in disorders." Files were opened on thousands of young men and women so that, as the former head of FBI intelligence explained, the information could be used if they ever applied for a government job. In the 1960s Bureau agents were instructed to increase their efforts to discredit "New Left" student demonstrators by tactics including publishing photographs ("naturally the most obnoxious picture should be used"), using "misinformation" to falsely notify members events had been cancelled, and writing "tell-tale" letters to students' parents.

h) The FBI Intelligence Division commonly investigated any indication that "subversive" groups already under investigation were seeking to influence or control other groups. . . .

i) Each administration from Franklin D. Roosevelt to Richard Nixon's permitted, and sometimes encouraged, government agencies to handle essentially political intelligence. For example:

- President Roosevelt asked the FBI to put in its files the names of citizens sending telegrams to the White House opposing his "national defense" policy and supporting Col. Charles Lindbergh. . . .
- The Kennedy Administration had the FBI wiretap a Congressional staff member, three executive officials, a lobbyist, and a Washington law firm. Attorney General Robert F. Kennedy received the fruits of a FBI "tap" on Martin Luther King, Jr., and a "bug" on a Congressman, both of which yielded information of a political nature.
- President Johnson asked the FBI to conduct "name checks" of his critics and of members of the staff of his 1964 opponent, Senator Barry

Goldwater. He also requested purely political intelligence on his critics in the Senate, and received extensive intelligence reports on political activity at the 1964 Democratic Convention from FBI electronic surveillance.

- President Nixon authorized a program of wiretaps which produced for the White House purely political or personal information unrelated to national security, including information about a Supreme Court justice.

Covert Action and the Use of Illegal or Improper Means

(a) *Covert Action*—Apart from uncovering excesses in the collection of intelligence, our investigation has disclosed covert actions directed against Americans, and the use of illegal and improper surveillance techniques to gather information: For example:

(i) The FBI's COINTELPRO—counterintelligence program—was designed to "disrupt" groups and "neutralize" individuals deemed to be threats to domestic security. . . . Whatever opinion one holds about the policies of the targeted groups, many of the tactics employed by the FBI were indisputably degrading to a free society. COINTELPRO tactics included:

- Anonymously attacking the political beliefs of targets in order to induce their employers to fire them;
- Anonymously mailing letters to the spouses of intelligence targets for the purpose of destroying their marriages;
- Obtaining from IRS the tax returns of a target and then attempting to provoke an IRS investigation for the express purpose of deterring a protest leader from attending the Democratic National Convention;
- Falsely and anonymously labeling as Government informants members of groups known to be violent, thereby exposing the falsely labeled member to expulsion or physical attack; . . .

(ii) From "late 1963" until his death in 1968, Martin Luther King, Jr., was the target of an intensive campaign by the Federal Bureau of Investigation to "neutralize" him as an effective civil rights leader. In the words of the man in charge of the FBI's "war" against Dr. King, "No holds were barred."

The FBI gathered information about Dr. King's plans and activities through an extensive surveillance program, employing nearly every intelligence-gathering technique at the Bureau's disposal in order to obtain information about the "private activities of Dr. King and his advisors" to use to "completely discredit" them.

The program to destroy Dr. King as the leader of the civil rights movement included efforts to discredit him with Executive branch officials, Congressional leaders, foreign heads of state, American ambassadors, churches, universities, and the press.

The FBI mailed Dr. King a tape recording made from microphones hidden in his hotel rooms which one agent testified was an attempt to destroy Dr. King's marriage. The tape recording was accompanied by a note which Dr. King and his advisors interpreted as threatening to release the tape recording unless Dr. King committed suicide. . . .

- In early 1968, Bureau headquarters explained to the field that Dr. King must be destroyed because he was seen as a potential "messiah" who could "unify and electrify" the "black nationalist movement." Indeed, to the FBI he was a potential threat because he might "abandon his supposed 'obedience' to white liberal doctrines (non-violence)." In short, a non-violent man was to be secretly attacked and destroyed as insurance against his abandoning non-violence.

(b) *Illegal or Improper Means*—This surveillance which we investigated was not only vastly excessive in breadth and a basis for degrading counterintelligence actions, but was also often conducted by illegal or improper means. For example:

(1) For approximately 20 years the CIA carried out a program of indiscriminately opening citizens' first class mail. . . .

(2) From 1947 until May 1975, NSA received from international cable companies millions of cables which had been sent by American citizens in the reasonable expectation that they would be kept private. . . .

(3) Since the early 1930s, intelligence agencies have frequently wiretapped and bugged American citizens without the benefit of judicial warrant. . . .

(4) In several cases, purely political information . . . and purely personal information (such as coverage of the extra-marital social activities of a high-level Executive official under surveillance) was obtained from electronic surveillance and disseminated to the highest levels of the federal government.

(5) Warrantless break-ins have been conducted by intelligence agencies since World War II. During the 1960s alone, the FBI and CIA conducted hundreds of break-ins, many against American citizens and domestic organizations. . . .

(6) The most pervasive surveillance technique has been the informant. . . . Informants have been used against peaceful, law-abiding groups; they have collected information about personal and political views and activities. . . .

4. Ignoring the Law

Officials of the intelligence agencies occasionally recognized that certain activities were illegal, but expressed concern only for "flap potential." Even more disturbing was the frequent testimony that the law, and the Constitution were simply ignored. . . .

5. Deficiencies in Accountability and Control

The overwhelming number of excesses continuing over a prolonged period of time were due in large measure to the fact that the system of checks and balances—created in our Constitution to limit abuse of Government power—was seldom applied to the intelligence community. Guidance and regulation from outside the intelligence agencies—where it has been imposed at all—has been vague. . . .

6. The Adverse Impact of Improper Intelligence Activity

Many of the illegal or improper disruptive efforts directed against American citizens and domestic organizations succeeded in injuring their targets. Although it is sometimes difficult to prove that a target's misfortunes were caused by a counterintelligence program directed against him, the possibility that an arm of the United States Government intended to cause the harm and might have been responsible is itself abhorrent.

The Committee has observed numerous examples of the impact of intelligence operations. Sometimes the harm was readily apparent—destruction of marriages, loss of friends or jobs. Sometimes the attitudes of the public and of Government officials responsible for formulating policy and resolving vital issues were influenced by distorted intelligence. But the most basic harm was to the values of privacy and freedom which our Constitution seeks to protect and which intelligence activity infringed on a broad scale. . . .

In considering its recommendations, the Committee undertook an evaluation of the FBI's claims that domestic intelligence was necessary to combat terrorism, civil disorders, "subversion," and hostile foreign intelligence activity. The Committee reviewed voluminous materials bearing on this issue and questioned Bureau officials, local police officials, and present and former federal executive officials.

We have found that we are in fundamental agreement with the wisdom of Attorney General Stone's initial warning that intelligence agencies must not be "concerned with political or other opinions of individuals" and must be limited to investigating essentially only "such conduct as is forbidden by the laws of the United States." The Committee's record demonstrates that domestic intelligence which departs from this standard raises grave risks of undermining the democratic process and harming the interests of individual citizens. This danger weighs heavily against the speculative or negligible benefits of the ill-defined and overbroad investigations authorized in the past. . . .

The excesses of the past do not, however, justify depriving the United States of a clearly defined and effectively controlled domestic intelligence capability. . . .

The most important reason for the fundamental change in the domestic intelligence operations which our Recommendations propose is the need to protect the constitutional rights of Americans.

In light of the record of abuse revealed by our inquiry, the Committee is not satisfied with the position that mere exposure of what has occurred in the past will prevent its recurrence. Clear legal standards and effective oversight and controls are necessary to ensure that domestic intelligence activity does not itself undermine the democratic system it is intended to protect. . . .

Source: Select Committee to Study Governmental Operations with Respect to Intelligence Activities (Church Committee). 1976. *Intelligence Activities and the Rights of Americans.* Book II. Washington, DC: Government Printing Office, pp. 1–19.

1978: PRESIDENT CARTER SIGNS THE FOREIGN INTELLIGENCE SURVEILLANCE ACT (FISA)

In an attempt to prevent domestic abuse of foreign intelligence surveillance, Congress passed the Foreign Intelligence Surveillance Act of 1978 (FISA), defining broad surveillance authority, but specifying clear limits on such powers. The FISA gave the government broad counterintelligence authority to monitor agents of foreign countries, but its primary purpose was to protect individuals and groups from past abuses by agencies such as the CIA and FBI. The FISA required the government to demonstrate to a super-secret FISA court that the "principal purpose" for their surveillance was foreign intelligence, thus restricting the use of the new surveillance powers in domestic criminal investigations. Following is President Jimmy Carter's formal statement of October 25, 1978, upon signing FISA, which he had strongly supported.

I am pleased to sign into law today the Foreign Intelligence Surveillance Act of 1978. As I said a year and a half ago at the beginning of the process that produced this bill, "one of the most difficult tasks in a free society like our own is the correlation between adequate intelligence to guarantee our Nation's security on the one hand, and the preservation of basic human rights on the other."

This is a difficult balance to strike, but the act I am signing today strikes it. It sacrifices neither our security nor our civil liberties. And it assures that those who serve this country in intelligence positions will have the affirmation of Congress that their activities are lawful.

In working on this bill, the Congress dealt skillfully with sensitive issues. The result shows our country benefits when the legislative and executive branches of Government work together toward a common goal.

The bill requires, for the first time, a prior judicial warrant for all electronic surveillance for foreign intelligence or counterintelligence purposes in the United States in which communications of U.S. persons might be intercepted. It clarifies the Executive's authority to gather foreign intelligence by electronic surveillance in the United States. It will remove any doubt about the legality of those surveillances which are conducted to protect our country against espionage and international terrorism. It will assure FBI field agents and others involved in intelligence collection that their acts are authorized by statute and, if a U.S. person's communications are concerned, by a court order. And it will protect the privacy of the American people.

In short, the act helps to solidify the relationship of trust between the American people and their Government. It provides a basis for the trust of the American people in the fact that the activities of their intelligence agencies are both effective and lawful. It provides enough secrecy to ensure that intelligence relating to national security can be securely acquired, while permitting review by the courts and Congress to safeguard the rights of Americans and others.

This legislation is the first long step toward the goal of establishing statutory charters for our intelligence agencies. I am committed to that goal, and my administration will work with the Congress to achieve it. Many people played important roles in securing passage of this bill.

I am convinced that the bill would not have passed without the leadership of Attorney General Bell; the personal commitment of the Director of Central Intelligence, Admiral Turner; and the work of Admiral Inman of the National Security Agency and Directors Webster and Kelley of the FBI. I extend my personal appreciation to these men and their staffs.

My administration's bill was based on some fine work during the Ford administration under the leadership of Attorney General Levi. His contribution to this legislation was substantial, illustrating the bipartisan nature of this process.

There was strong, effective, and bipartisan leadership in the Congress as well. I particularly want to commend Senators Kennedy, Bayh, and Garn for helping to guide this bill to overwhelming approval in the Senate. Chairman Boland and Congressman Morgan Murphy of the House Intelligence Committee and Chairman Rodino and Congressman Kastenmeier of the House Judiciary Committee undertook the hard work of moving the bill through the House. And, once again, I am indebted to the efforts of Speaker O'Neill and Majority Leader Wright.

I wish as well to express my appreciation to the Vice President, who long supported this foreign intelligence reform in the Senate and who assured the wholehearted commitment of the executive branch to this important legislation.

I have said so often, one of the central goals of my administration is to restore the confidence of the American people in their governmental institutions. This act takes us one more step down that road.

Source: Carter, Jimmy. "Foreign Intelligence Surveillance Act of 1978 Statement on Signing S. 1566 into Law." October 25, 1978. In *Jimmy Carter: 1978 (in two books). [Book 2].* Washington, DC: Government Printing Office, 1979, pp. 1853–1854.

1979: THE SUPREME COURT UPHOLDS THE USE OF PEN REGISTERS IN *SMITH v. MARYLAND*

The case of Smith v. Maryland originated in March 1976, when Patricia McDonough was robbed in Baltimore, Maryland, by an assailant driving a 1975 Monte Carlo automobile. She then received a series of threatening telephone calls, one of which instructed her to go out on her front porch. When she did so, the Monte Carlo drove past her home. Police subsequently spotted the automobile and traced the license plate to Michael Lee Smith. The police then arranged for a "pen register," a device that records the numbers dialed on a telephone, to be placed on Smith's home phone. A short time later, the pen register recorded a call from Smith's residence to McDonough's home. Armed with this information, police obtained a warrant for Smith's home. Incriminating evidence was found in the home, resulting in Smith's arrest. After McDonough positively identified him as her assailant, Smith was brought to trial, convicted, and sentenced to six years in prison. His appeal on Fourth Amendment privacy grounds was turned down by the Maryland Court of Appeals, which ruled that Smith should not have had any expectation of privacy for numbers dialed into a telephone system.

Smith's appeal of the Appeals ruling ultimately reached the U.S. Supreme Court, but in a 5–3 ruling the Court affirmed the Maryland ruling. According to the majority, people had no constitutional right to privacy when voluntarily disclosing information with a third party—such as the numbers that people share with telephone companies when dialing another line. This Smith v. Maryland *decision became a pillar of the legal justification for the NSA domestic surveillance program that was erected in the months and years following 9/11. Following are excerpts from the majority opinion in the case, which was written by Harry A. Blackmun and issued on June 20, 1979.*

The telephone company, at police request, installed at its central offices a pen register to record the numbers dialed from the telephone at petitioner's home. Prior to his robbery trial, petitioner moved to suppress "all fruits derived from" the pen register. The Maryland trial court denied this motion, holding that the warrantless installation of the pen register did not violate the Fourth Amendment. Petitioner was convicted, and the Maryland Court of Appeals affirmed.

Held: The installation and use of the pen register was not a "search" within the meaning of the Fourth Amendment, and hence no warrant was required.

(a) Application of the Fourth Amendment depends on whether the person invoking its protection can claim a "legitimate expectation of privacy" that has been invaded by government action. This inquiry normally embraces two questions: first, whether the individual has exhibited an actual (subjective) expectation of privacy; and second, whether his expectation is one that society is prepared to recognize as "reasonable." *Katz v. United States,* 389 U.S. 347, 88 S.Ct. 507, 19 L.Ed.2d 576. Pp. 2579–2580.

(b) Petitioner in all probability entertained no actual expectation of privacy in the phone numbers he dialed, and even if he did, his expectation was not "legitimate." First, it is doubtful that telephone users in general have any expectation of privacy regarding the numbers they dial, since they typically know that they must convey phone numbers to the telephone company and that the company has facilities for recording this information and does in fact record it for various legitimate business purposes. And petitioner did not demonstrate an expectation of privacy merely by using his home phone rather than some other phone, since his conduct, although perhaps calculated to keep the *contents* of his conversation private, was not calculated to preserve the privacy of the number he dialed. Second, even if petitioner did harbor some subjective expectation of privacy, this expectation was not one that society is prepared to recognize as "reasonable." When petitioner voluntarily conveyed numerical information to the phone company and "exposed" that information to its equipment in the normal course of business, he assumed the risk that the company would reveal the information to the police, cf. *United States v. Miller,* 425 U.S. 435, 96 S.Ct. 1619, 48 L.Ed.2d 71. Pp. 741–746.

283 Md. 156, 389 A.2d 858, affirmed.

Source: Justice Blackmun, Harry A. Opinion of the Court. *Smith v. Maryland,* No. 78–5374, Decided June 20, 1979. United States Reports, Volume 442, May 1979.

1984: THE SUPREME COURT BOLSTERS THE EXCLUSIONARY RULE IN *UNITED STATES v. LEON*

Relying upon a confidential informant, police officers in Burbank, California, instigated surveillance of Alberto Leon and others for suspected drug trafficking activities. Based on an affidavit summarizing police observations, police secured a warrant to search the homes and automobiles of the suspects. When the warrant was executed and large quantities of illegal drugs were discovered, Leon was indicted for violating federal drug laws. However, a federal district court judge subsequently ruled that the affidavit was insufficient to establish probable cause to search all of the residences and automobiles, thus making the warrant illegitimate. The U.S. Court of Appeals for the Ninth Circuit affirmed this decision.

The case of United States v. Leon *ultimately reached the U.S. Supreme Court, which struck down the earlier rulings. Instead, the Court held in a 6–3 ruling that the exclusionary rule should be modified so as not to bar the admission of evidence seized during a reasonable, good-faith execution of a search warrant, even if that warrant was subsequently held to be defective. Equally important, the majority opinion, written by Justice Byron White and decided on July 5, 1984, rejected outright the argument that the Fourth Amendment required the exclusion of illegally obtained evidence. In a dissenting opinion, however, Justice William J. Brennan Jr. criticized the majority for adopting what he saw as an unduly narrow interpretation of the exclusionary rule. Excerpts from both opinions are featured below.*

Opinion of the Court

This case presents the question whether the Fourth Amendment exclusionary rule should be modified so as not to bar the use in the prosecution's case in chief of evidence obtained by officers acting in reasonable reliance on a search warrant issued by a detached and neutral magistrate but ultimately found to be unsupported by probable cause. To resolve this question, we must consider once again the tension between the sometimes competing goals of, on the one hand, deterring official misconduct and removing inducements to unreasonable invasions of privacy and, on the other, establishing procedures under which criminal defendants are "acquitted or convicted on the basis of all the evidence which exposes the truth." . . .

The Fourth Amendment contains no provision expressly precluding the use of evidence obtained in violation of its commands, and an examination of its origin and purposes makes clear that the use of fruits of a past unlawful search or seizure "[works] no new Fourth Amendment wrong." The wrong condemned by the Amendment is "fully accomplished" by the unlawful search or seizure itself, and the exclusionary rule is neither intended nor able to "cure the invasion of the defendant's rights which he has already suffered." The rule thus operates as "a judicially created remedy designed to safeguard Fourth Amendment rights generally through its deterrent effect, rather than a personal constitutional right of the party aggrieved."

Whether the exclusionary sanction is appropriately imposed in a particular case, our decisions make clear, is "an issue separate from the question whether the Fourth Amendment rights of the party seeking to invoke the rule were violated by police conduct." Only the former question is currently before us, and it must be resolved by weighing the costs and benefits of preventing the use in the prosecution's case in chief of inherently trustworthy tangible evidence obtained in reliance on a search warrant issued by a detached and neutral magistrate that ultimately is found to be defective. The substantial social costs exacted by the exclusionary rule for the vindication of Fourth Amendment rights have long been a source of concern. . . . An objectionable collateral consequence of this interference with the criminal justice system's truth-finding function is that some guilty defendants may go free or receive reduced sentences as a result of favorable plea bargains. Particularly when law enforcement officers have acted in objective good faith or their transgressions have been minor, the magnitude of the benefit conferred on such guilty defendants offends basic concepts of the criminal justice system. Indiscriminate application of the exclusionary rule, therefore, may well "[generate] disrespect for the law and administration of justice." Accordingly, "[as] with any remedial device, the application of the rule has been restricted to those areas where its remedial objectives are thought most efficaciously served." Close attention to those remedial objectives has characterized our recent decisions concerning the scope of the Fourth Amendment exclusionary rule. The Court has, to be sure, not seriously questioned, "in the absence of a more efficacious sanction, the continued application of the rule to suppress evidence from the [prosecution's] case where a Fourth Amendment violation has been substantial and deliberate. . . ." Nevertheless, the balancing approach that has evolved in various contexts—including criminal trials—"forcefully [suggests] that the exclusionary rule be more generally modified to permit the introduction of evidence obtained in the reasonable good-faith belief that a search or seizure was in accord with the Fourth Amendment." . . .

Reasonable minds frequently may differ on the question whether a particular affidavit establishes probable cause, and we have thus concluded that the preference for warrants is most appropriately effectuated by according "great deference" to a magistrate's determination.

Deference to the magistrate, however, is not boundless. It is clear, first, that the deference accorded to a magistrate's finding of probable cause does not preclude inquiry into the knowing or reckless falsity of the affidavit on which that determination was based. Second, the courts must also insist that the magistrate purport to "perform his 'neutral and detached' function and not serve merely as a rubber stamp for the police.". . . .

Third, reviewing courts will not defer to a warrant based on an affidavit that does not "provide the magistrate with a substantial basis for determining the existence of probable cause." . . . Even if the warrant application was supported by more than a "bare bones" affidavit, a reviewing court may properly conclude that, notwithstanding the deference that magistrates deserve, the warrant was invalid because the magistrate's probable-cause determination reflected an improper analysis of the totality of the circumstances, or because the form of the warrant was improper in some respect. . . .

Only in the first of these three situations, however, has the Court set forth a rationale for suppressing evidence obtained pursuant to a search warrant; in the other areas, it has simply excluded such evidence without considering whether Fourth Amendment interests will be advanced. To the extent that proponents of exclusion rely on its behavioral effects on judges and magistrates in these areas, their reliance is misplaced. First, the exclusionary rule is designed to deter police misconduct rather than to punish the errors of judges and magistrates. Second, there exists no evidence suggesting that judges and magistrates are inclined to ignore or subvert the Fourth Amendment or that lawlessness among these actors requires application of the extreme sanction of exclusion.

Third, and most important, we discern no basis, and are offered none, for believing that exclusion of evidence seized pursuant to a warrant will have a significant deterrent effect on the issuing judge or magistrate. . . . Judges and magistrates are not adjuncts to the law enforcement team; as neutral judicial officers, they have no stake in the outcome of particular criminal prosecutions. The threat of exclusion thus cannot be expected significantly to deter them. Imposition of the exclusionary sanction is not necessary meaningfully to inform judicial officers of their errors, and we cannot conclude that admitting evidence obtained pursuant to a warrant while at the same time declaring that the warrant was somehow defective will in any way reduce judicial officers' professional incentives to comply with the Fourth Amendment, encourage them to repeat their mistakes, or lead to the granting of all colorable warrant requests. . . .

If exclusion of evidence obtained pursuant to a subsequently invalidated warrant is to have any deterrent effect, therefore, it must alter the behavior of individual law enforcement officers or the policies of their departments. . . .

[E]ven assuming that the rule effectively deters some police misconduct and provides incentives for the law enforcement profession as a whole to conduct itself in accord with the Fourth Amendment, it cannot be expected, and should not be applied, to deter objectively reasonable law enforcement activity. . . .

This is particularly true, we believe, when an officer acting with objective good faith has obtained a search warrant from a judge or magistrate and acted within its scope. In most such cases, there is no police illegality and thus nothing to deter. It is the magistrate's responsibility to determine whether the officer's allegations establish probable cause and, if so, to issue a warrant comporting in form with the requirements of the Fourth Amendment. In the ordinary case, an officer cannot be expected to question the magistrate's probable-cause determination or his judgment that the form of the warrant is technically sufficient. . . . Penalizing the officer for the magistrate's error, rather than his own, cannot logically contribute to the deterrence of Fourth Amendment violations.

We conclude that the marginal or nonexistent benefits produced by suppressing evidence obtained in objectively reasonable reliance on a subsequently invalidated search warrant cannot justify the substantial costs of exclusion. We do not suggest, however, that exclusion is always inappropriate in cases where an officer has obtained a warrant and abided by its terms. . . .

Suppression therefore remains an appropriate remedy if the magistrate or judge in issuing a warrant was misled by information in an affidavit that the affiant knew was false or would have known was false except for his reckless disregard of the truth. . . .

Reversed.

Brennan's Dissent (Joined by Justice Thurgood Marshall)

The majority ignores the fundamental constitutional importance of what is at stake here. While the machinery of law enforcement and indeed the nature of crime itself have changed dramatically since the Fourth Amendment became part of the Nation's fundamental law in 1791, what the Framers understood then remains true today—that the task of combating crime and convicting the guilty will in every era seem of such critical and pressing concern that we may be lured by the temptations of expediency into forsaking our commitment to protecting individual liberty and privacy. It was for that very reason that the Framers of the Bill of Rights insisted that law enforcement efforts be permanently and unambiguously restricted in order to preserve personal freedoms. In the constitutional scheme they ordained, the sometimes unpopular task of ensuring that the government's enforcement efforts remain within the strict boundaries fixed by the Fourth Amendment was entrusted to the courts. . . .

At the outset, the Court suggests that society has been asked to pay a high price—in terms either of setting guilty persons free or of impeding the proper functioning of trials—as a result of excluding relevant physical evidence in cases where the police, in conducting searches and seizing evidence, have made only an "objectively reasonable" mistake concerning the constitutionality of their actions. But what evidence is there to support such a claim?

Significantly, the Court points to none, and, indeed, as the Court acknowledges, recent studies have demonstrated that the "costs" of the exclusionary rule—calculated in terms of dropped prosecutions and lost convictions—are quite low. Contrary to the claims of the rule's critics that exclusion leads to "the release of countless guilty criminals," these studies have demonstrated that federal and state prosecutors very rarely drop cases because of potential search and seizure problems. . . .

What then supports the Court's insistence that this evidence be admitted? Apparently, the Court's only answer is that even though the costs of exclusion are not very substantial, the potential deterrent effect in these circumstances is so marginal that exclusion cannot be justified. The key to the Court's conclusion in this respect is its belief that the prospective deterrent effect of the exclusionary rule operates only in those situations in which police officers, when deciding whether to go forward with some particular search, have reason to know that their planned conduct will violate the requirements of the Fourth Amendment. . . .

The flaw in the Court's argument, however, is that its logic captures only one comparatively minor element of the generally acknowledged deterrent purposes of the exclusionary rule. To be sure, the rule operates to some extent to deter future misconduct by individual officers who have had evidence suppressed in their own cases. But what the Court overlooks is that the deterrence rationale for the rule is not designed to be, nor should it be thought of as, a form of "punishment" of individual police officers for their failures to obey the restraints imposed by the Fourth Amendment. Instead, the chief deterrent function of the rule is its tendency to promote institutional compliance with Fourth Amendment requirements on the part of law enforcement agencies generally. . . .

After today's decisions, however, that institutional incentive will be lost. Indeed, the Court's "reasonable mistake" exception to the exclusionary rule will tend to put a premium on police ignorance of the law. Armed with the assurance provided by today's decisions that evidence will always be admissible whenever an officer has "reasonably" relied upon a warrant, police departments will be encouraged to train officers that if a warrant has simply been signed, it is reasonable, without more, to rely on it. Since in close cases there will no longer be any incentive to error on the side of constitutional behavior, police would have every reason to adopt a "let's-wait-until-it's-decided" approach in situations in which there is a question about a warrant's validity or the basis for its issuance. . . .

Although the Court brushes these concerns aside, a host of grave consequences can be expected to result from its decision to carve this new exception out of the exclusionary rule. A chief consequence of today's decisions will be to convey a clear and unambiguous message to magistrates that their decisions to issue warrants are now insulated from subsequent judicial review. Creation of this new exception for good-faith reliance upon a warrant implicitly tells magistrates that they need not take much care in reviewing warrant applications, since their mistakes will from now on have virtually no consequence: If their decision to issue a warrant was correct, the evidence will be admitted; if their decision was incorrect but the police relied in good faith on the warrant, the evidence will also be admitted. Inevitably, the care and attention devoted to such an inconsequential chore will dwindle. Although the Court is correct to note that magistrates do not share the same stake in the outcome of a criminal case as the police, they nevertheless need to appreciate that their role is of some moment in order to continue performing the important task of carefully reviewing warrant applications. Today's decisions effectively remove that incentive.

Source: Justice White, Byron. Opinion of the Court; Justice Brennan, William J., Jr., Dissent. *United States v. Alberto Antonio Leon et al,* 468 U.S. 897, Decided July 5, 1984. United States Reports, Volume 468, June–October 1984.

1986: THE ELECTRONIC COMMUNICATIONS PRIVACY ACT

The Electronic Communications Privacy Act (ECPA), which sailed through Congress in early October 1986 and was signed into law by President Ronald Reagan on October 21 of that year, was designed to define the government's authority to engage in wiretapping and various electronic surveillance activities and penalize actions by nongovernmental actors that interfered with electronic communications (the latter provisions were written partly in response to an April 1986 "Captain Midnight "incident, in which a disgruntled citizen jammed HBO's satellite signal in Florida to protest their pricing policies).

An amendment to Title III of the Omnibus Crime Control and Safe Streets Act of 1968, the ECPA was widely touted as legislation that would ensure that Americans' personal privacy was not sacrificed in the pursuit of law enforcement goals. The following is a summary of the law prepared by the staff of the Senate Judiciary Committee's Subcommittee on Patents, Copyrights and Trademarks and entered into the Congressional Record *by Senator Pat Leahy (D- Vermont), one of the bill's main sponsors.*

Since its 1986 passage, the ECPA has undergone modest modifications, most recently with the FISA Amendments Act of 2008. According to critics, however, these updates have failed to keep pace with breakthroughs in electronic communications technology, and they charge that the law, as currently constituted, gives law enforcement and other government agencies far too much latitude to monitor private activities and communications. "Since 1986," asserted the American Civil Liberties Union in a statement on its Web site, "technology has advanced at breakneck speed while electronic privacy law remained at a standstill. The outdated ECPA allows the government to intercept and access a treasure trove of information about who you are, where you go, and what you do, which is being collected by cell phone providers, search engines, social networking sites, and other Web sites every day."

The Electronic Communications Privacy Act amends Title III of the Omnibus Crime Control and Safe Streets Act of 1968—the federal wiretap law—to protect against the unauthorized interception of electronic communications. The bill amends the 1968 law to update and clarify federal privacy protections and standards in light of dramatic changes in new computer and telecommunication technologies. Originally introduced in the Senate as S. 1667 by Senators Leahy and Mathias, and H.R. 3378 by Congressmen Kastenmeier and Moorhead, the bill has gone through a substantial revision as a result of negotiations with interested Senators and their staffs, various industry and privacy groups and the Department of Justice.

On June 11, the House Judiciary Committee unanimously reported H.R. 4952. On June 19, Senators Leahy and Mathias introduced that bill as S. 2575. On June 23, the House passed H.R. 4952. On August 12, the Subcommittee on Patents, Copyrights and Trademarks of the Senate Judiciary Committee reported S. 2575. During Subcommittee consideration some Senators expressed concern that the penalties for private viewing of certain satellite transmissions were too severe. Their concerns have been addressed by a reduction of the private and public penalties for home viewing. The bill also addresses the recent Captain Midnight incident by increasing penalties for interfering with satellite transmissions.

The Justice Department strongly supports this bill. The Judiciary Committee reported S. 2575 on September 19.

Highlights of the Leahy-Mathias substitute to amend the Electronic Communications Privacy Act of 1986 follow.

Currently, Title III covers only voice communications. The bill expands coverage to include video and data communications.

Currently, Title III covers only common carrier communications. The bill eliminates that restriction since private carriers and common carriers perform so many of the same functions today that the distinction no longer serves to justify a different privacy standard.

At the request of the Justice Department, the bill continues to distinguish between electronic communications (data and video) and wire or oral communications (voice) for purposes of some of the procedural restrictions currently contained in Title III. For example, court authorization for the interception of a wire or oral communication may only be issued to investigate certain crimes specified in Title III. An interception of an electronic communication pursuant to court order may be utilized during the investigation of any federal felony.

Wire communications in storage, like voice mail, remain wire communications.

To underscore that the inadvertent reception of a protected communication is not a crime, the bill changes the state of mind requirement under Title III from "willful" to "intentional."

Certain electronic communications are exempted from the coverage of the bill including—

The radio portion of a cordless telephone communication that is transmitted between the cordless telephone handset and the base unit;

Tone-only paging devices;

Amateur radio operators and general mobile radio services;

Marine and aeronautical communications systems;

Police, fire, civil defense and other public safety radio communications systems;

Specific transmissions via audio subcarrier;
The satellite transmission of network feeds;
The satellite transmission of satellite cable programming as defined in Section 705 of the Communications Act of 1934;

Any other radio communication which is made through an electronic communications system that is configured so that such communication is "readily accessible to the general public," a defined term in the bill.

The term readily accessible to the general public does not include communications made by cellular radio telephone systems; therefore, the bill continues current restrictions contained in Title III against the interception of telephone calls made on cellular telephone systems. However, the criminal penalty for an unlawful interception of cellular phone call and similar communications is reduced from the current five-year felony.

Under the Simon amendment that criminal penalty is reduced to a $500 fine.

The bill expands the list of felonies for which a voice wiretap may be issued. It also expands the list of Justice Department officials who may apply for a court order to place a wiretap.

The bill creates a limited exception to the requirement that a wiretap order designate a specific telephone to be intercepted where the Justice Department makes a showing that the target of the wiretap is changing telephones to thwart interception of his or her communications.

A telephone company may move to quash an order for such a "roving tap" if compliance would be unduly burdensome.

The bill makes it a crime for a person who has knowledge of a court authorized wiretap to notify any person of the possible interception in order to obstruct, impede or prevent such interception.

Title II of the bill creates parallel privacy protection for the unauthorized access to the computers of an electronic communications system, if information is obtained or altered. It does little good to prohibit the unauthorized interception of information with it is being transmitted, if similar protection is not afforded to the information while it is being stored for later forwarding.

The bill establishes criminal penalties for any person who intentionally accesses without authorization a computer through which an electronic communication service is provided and obtains, alters or prevents authorized access to a stored electronic communication. The offense is punished as a felony if committed for purposes of commercial advantage, malicious destruction or damage, or private commercial gain; otherwise it is punished as a petty offense.

Providers of electronic communication services to the public and providers of remote computing services to the public are prohibited from intentionally divulging the contents of communications contained in their systems except under circumstances specified in the bill.

The contents of messages contained in electronic storage of electronic communications systems which have been in storage for 180 days or less may be obtained by a government entity from the provider of the system only pursuant to a warrant issued under the Federal Rules of Criminal Procedure or with notice to the customer pursuant to an administrative subpoena, a grand jury subpoena, or a court order based on a showing that there is reason to believe that the contents of the communication are relevant to a legitimate law enforcement inquiry. Provisions for delay in notice are also included.

An electronic communications or remote computing service provider may disclose to a non-governmental entity customer information like mailing lists, but not the contents of the communication. Disclosure of such information to the government is required, but only when the government obtains a court order, warrant, subpoena, or customer consent.

At the FCC's request, a section was added to the bill to address problems highlighted by the recent Captain Midnight incident. The bill increases penalties for the intentional or malicious interference with satellite transmissions.

The bill clarifies that telephone companies and other service providers are not civilly or criminally liable for good faith assistance to law enforcement agencies.

Civil penalties are created for users of electronic communications services whose rights under the bill are violated.

The Grassley amendment, which the sponsors have accepted, sets up a reduced penalty structure for the private home viewer whose reception of specified satellite transmissions is not for commercial gain.

The Simon amendment, which the sponsors have accepted sets up the same penalty structure for the interception of radio communications transmitted on frequencies allocated under subpart D of part 74 of the FCC rules.

The penalty structure under the Grassley and Simon amendments is:

A first offender will be subject to a suit by the federal government for injunctive relief. If injunctive relief is granted, the court may use whatever means in its authority, including civil and criminal contempt, to enforce that injunction. It must impose a $500 civil fine. In addition, the penalty for second and subsequent offenses is a $500 fine in a suit brought by the government.

Under the private civil damages provisions of the bill, the first offender may be sued for the greater of actual damages or statutory damages of $50 to $500. The second offender is subject to suit for the greater of actual damages or statutory damages of $100 to $1000. Third and subsequent offenders are subject to full civil damages under the bill.

The bill creates a statutory framework for the authorization and issuance of an order for a pen register or a trap and trace device based on a finding that such installation and use is relevant to an on-going criminal investigation.

Source: "Electronic Communications Privacy Act." Congressional Record-Senate, October 1, 1986, pp. S14450–51.

1988: THE FBI DEFENDS ITS LIBRARY AWARENESS PROGRAM

In the fall of 1987, a news story in the New York Times *revealed the existence of a Federal Bureau of Investigation (FBI) national security initiative aimed at enlisting public libraries in identifying potential security threats. The exposure of the program, known as the Library Awareness Program, triggered a firestorm of controversy. Librarians, civil rights groups, and other detractors asserted that the program amounted to a shocking violation of civil liberties. The FBI and its supporters in Congress and the media defended the program, however. They insisted that if librarians notified the agency of library patrons who engaged in potentially suspicious activities they would be providing another layer of protection to the nation against espionage and terrorism.*

The following defense of the program is excerpted from congressional testimony given by James H. Geer, Assistant Director of the FBI, at a special subcommittee hearing on the agency's Library Awareness Program.

Congressional Testimony of FBI Assistant Director James Geer

FBI investigations since the early 1960s have thoroughly documented SIS [Soviet Intelligence Services] contacts with librarians in specialized science and technology libraries. . . . In response to this SIS effort, the New York Office (NYO) initiated an awareness program which has come to be known as the Library Awareness Program. Interviews of library personnel under this program are patterned after the FBI's "Development of Counterintelligence Awareness" (DECA) program, which seeks to heighten the awareness of corporate executives and their employees to the hostile intelligence services threat. Our library contacts seek to inform selected librarians that they and their libraries are, and have historically been, significant SIS targets for intelligence activities and recruitment. . . .

The proactive approach of this program, which alerts librarians generally of the SIS threat, should not be confused with occasional interviews of librarians in other areas of the United States which are in response to specific investigative leads involving Soviet or other Soviet-bloc nationals. The FBI, within the purview of its Foreign Counterintelligence (FCI) responsibilities, frequently finds it necessary to investigate contacts between Soviet intelligence officers, and other known or suspected hostile intelligence officers and their agents and American citizens. These may include contacts with libraries or librarians. The least intrusive technique available to the FBI to resolve such contacts is direct interview of the person(s) contacted. . . .

The FBI has visited libraries because of the demonstrated need to alert them of the policies and practices of hostile intelligence services and to seek their cooperation. . . . The program is a very measured response to a well planned and organized effort by the SIS and other hostile intelligence services to exploit our specialized scientific and technical libraries and recruit our citizens.

Source: Statement of James H. Geer, Assistant Director, Federal Bureau of Investigation, before the House Subcommittee on Civil and Constitutional Rights, Committee on the Judiciary. U.S. Congress, House Committee on the Judiciary, *FBI Counterintelligence Visits to Libraries*, 100th Congress, 2d Session, July 13, 1988. Washington, DC: Government Printing Office, 1989, pp. 110–20.

1994: THE CLINTON WHITE HOUSE ENDORSES CLIPPER AND CAPSTONE

In the early 1990s, the Clinton administration undertook an encryption technology review, the results of which were announced on February 4, 1994. This statement from the office of the press secretary, reprinted below, discussed the importance of providing digital communications in all of its forms with encryption protection from unauthorized tampering, viewing, or disclosure. But the Clinton White House also emphasized the importance of giving law enforcement and national security agencies the tools to understand the content of encrypted communications as part of legally authorized investigations. It proposed to provide law enforcement with this capability through so-called "key escrow technology" developed by the National Security Agency (NSA) and the National Institute of Standards and Technology (NIST). The cornerstones of this cryptographic arrangement would be "Capstone," a chip for encrypting data transmissions, and "Clipper," which would be used to encrypt voice transmissions. Ultimately, this campaign to create a mandatory encryption standard using key escrow was derailed by legal and political opposition—much of it based on concerns that governmental agencies might abuse such encryption technologies.

Statement of the Press Secretary

Last April, the Administration announced a comprehensive interagency review of encryption technology, to be overseen by the National Security Council. Today, the Administration is taking a number of steps to implement the recommendations resulting from that review.

Advanced encryption technology offers individuals and businesses an inexpensive and easy way to encode data and telephone conversations. Unfortunately, the same encryption technology that can help Americans protect business secrets and personal privacy can also be used by terrorists, drug dealers, and other criminals.

In the past, Federal policies on encryption have reflected primarily the needs of law enforcement and national security. The Clinton Administration has sought to balance these needs with the needs of businesses and individuals for security and privacy. That is why, today the National Institute of Standards and Technology (NIST) is committing to ensure a royalty-free, public-domain Digital Signature Standard. Over many years, NIST has been developing digital signature technology that would provide a way to verify the author and sender of an electronic message. Such technology will be critical for a wide range of business applications for the National Information Infrastructure. A digital signature standard will enable individuals to transact business electronically rather than having to exchange signed paper contracts. The Administration has determined that such technology should not be subject to private royalty payments, and it will be taking steps to ensure that royalties are not required for use of a digital signature. Had digital signatures been in widespread use, the recent security problems with the Internet would have been avoided.

Last April, the Administration released the Key Escrow chip (also known as the "Clipper Chip") that would provide Americans with secure telecommunications without compromising the ability of law enforcement agencies to carry out legally authorized wiretaps. Today, the Department of Commerce and the Department of Justice are taking steps to enable the use of such technology both in the U.S. and overseas. At the same time, the Administration is announcing its intent to work with industry to develop other key escrow products that might better meet the needs of individuals and industry, particularly the American computer and telecommunications industry. Specific steps being announced today include:

- Approval by the Commerce Secretary of the Escrowed Encryption Standard (EES) as a voluntary Federal Information Processing Standard, which will enable government agencies to purchase the Key Escrow chip for use with telephones and modems. The department's National Institute of Standards and Technology (NIST) will publish the standard.
- Publication by the Department of Justice of procedures for the release of escrowed keys and the announcement of NIST and the Automated Services Division of the Treasury Department as the escrow agents that will store the keys needed for decryption of communications using the Key Escrow chip. Nothing in these procedures will diminish the existing legal and procedural requirements that protect Americans from unauthorized wiretaps.
- New procedures to allow export of products containing the Key Escrow chip to most countries.

In addition, the Department of State will streamline export licensing procedures for encryption products that can be exported under current export regulations in order to help American companies sell their products overseas. In the past, it could take weeks for a company to obtain an export license for encryption products, and each shipment might require a separate license. The new procedures announced today will substantially reduce administrative delays and paperwork for encryption exports.

To implement the Administration's encryption policy, an interagency Working Group on Encryption and Telecommunications has been established. It will be chaired by the White House Office of Science and Technology Policy and the National Security Council and will include representatives of the Departments of Commerce, Justice, State, and Treasury as well as the FBI, the National Security Agency, the Office of Management and Budget, and the National Economic

Council. This group will work with industry and public-interest groups to develop new encryption technologies and to review and refine Administration policies regarding encryption, as needed.

The Administration is expanding its efforts to work with industry to improve on the Key Escrow chip, to develop key-escrow software, and to examine alternatives to the Key Escrow chip. NIST will lead these efforts and will request additional staff and resources for this purpose.

We understand that many in industry would like to see all encryption products exportable. However, if encryption technology is made freely available worldwide, it would no doubt be used extensively by terrorists, drug dealers, and other criminals to harm Americans both in the U.S. and abroad. For this reason, the Administration will continue to restrict export of the most sophisticated encryption devices, both to preserve our own foreign intelligence gathering capability and because of the concerns of our allies who fear that strong encryption technology would inhibit their law enforcement capabilities.

At the same time, the Administration understands the benefits that encryption and related technologies can provide to users of computers and telecommunications networks. Indeed, many of the applications of the evolving National Information Infrastructure will require some form of encryption. That is why the Administration plans to work more closely with the private sector to develop new forms of encryption that can protect privacy and corporate secrets without undermining the ability of law-enforcement agencies to conduct legally authorized wiretaps. That is also why the Administration is committed to make available free of charge a Digital Signature Standard.

The Administration believes that the steps being announced today will help provide Americans with the telecommunications security they need without compromising the capability of law enforcement agencies and national intelligence agencies. Today, any American can purchase and use any type of encryption product. The Administration does not intend to change that policy. Nor do we have any intention of restricting domestic encryption or mandating the use of a particular technology.

Source: White House Press Secretary statement on encryption technology, February 4, 1994. Electronic Privacy Information Center (EPIC) Web site. https://epic.org/crypto/clipper/white_house_statement_2_94.html. Accessed February 5, 2015.

1994: CONGRESSMAN HYDE PRAISES THE COMMUNICATIONS ASSISTANCE FOR LAW ENFORCEMENT ACT

On October 25, 1994, the U.S. Congress enacted the Communications Assistance for Law Enforcement Act (CALEA). This legislation mandated that telephone companies design and implement communication network architectures so as to enable law enforcement agencies to wiretap digital telephone calls. As the following excerpt shows, CALEA supporters such as Congressman Henry Hyde (R-IL) championed the bill as a necessary crime-fighting tool, given the dramatic shift in cellular telephone use that was taking place across the country during that time. According to critics such as the Center for Democracy and Technology (CDT), however, the FBI has used CALEA in ways "contrary to Congress' intent," such as by "turning wireless phones into tracking devices, requiring phone companies to collect specific signaling information for the convenience of the government, and allowing interception of packet communications without privacy protections."

These criticisms from the CDT and other privacy advocates intensified after 2005, when the Federal Communications Commission (FCC) expanded CALEA's reach to include Internet service providers (ISPs) as well as Voice over Internet Protocol (VOIP) services. Since that time, the FBI has repeatedly expressed support for legislation that would further expand its surveillance powers under CALEA, but as of 2014, these proposed changes have not received sufficient support for passage.

Mr. Speaker, this legislation, which represents a joint effort by the Committee on the Judiciary and the Committee on Energy and Commerce, is needed to insure that technological advances in the telecommunications industry do not foreclose the ability of law enforcement to conduct court-authorized electronic surveillance. I am pleased to have been an original co-sponsor of this legislation with the chairman of the Subcommittee on Civil on Constitutional Rights, Mr. Edwards.

H.R. 4922, as amended seeks to carefully balance the needs of law enforcement, the interests of the telecommunications industry and the privacy rights of the American public in order to insure that law enforcement can continue to conduct court-authorized wiretaps.

Earlier this year, the Subcommittee on Civil and Constitutional Rights held two joint hearings with the Senate Subcommittee on Technology and the Law. Our hearings revealed that obstacles to court-authorized interceptions are already being encountered. An informal survey conducted by the FBI of Federal, State, and local law enforcement agencies in April of this year revealed 183 technology-based problems encountered in attempts to conduct court-authorized electronic surveillance.

The bill makes it clear that all telecommunications carriers will cooperate and assist in the interception of communications for law enforcement purposes. The definition of "telecommunications carrier" includes such service providers as local exchange carriers, interexchange carriers, competitive access providers [CAPs], cellular carriers, providers of personal communications services (PCS), satellite-based service providers, cable operators, and electric and other utilities that provide telecommunications services for hire to the public, and any other wireline or wireless service for hire to the public.

The bill authorizes an appropriation of $500 million for fiscal years 1995 through 1998, and for subsequent years, such sums as are necessary for telecommunications carriers to retrofit existing facilities to bring them into compliance with law enforcement requirements.

Those covered by the bill have expressed concern that $500 million will not cover the cost of retrofitting existing facilities. Because we do not yet know the exact nature of the technologies that will be needed to satisfy the capability requirements, we cannot know, with certainty, exactly how much money will be needed to retrofit existing services and facilities. According to the GAO, "until capability solutions and capacity requirements are better defined, it is virtually impossible to project a precise estimate of the reimbursement costs of this bill."

If the $500 million authorized in the bill is not appropriated, or if it is not sufficient to cover retrofit costs, any equipment or services that the government cannot pay to retrofit are "grandfathered," and do not have to be brought into compliance until they are replaced or upgraded in the ordinary course of business.

After the 4 year transition period, which may be extended up to two additional years by order of the FCC, industry will pay to insure that new equipment and services meet the legislative requirements as defined by industry standards and specifications to the extent such compliance is reasonably achievable. In the event that compliance is not reasonably achievable, a telecommunications carrier may petition the FCC to determine whether costs of compliance would impose significant difficulty or expense based on 10 enumerated factors including public safety and national security, the impact on rates for basic residential telephone service and the like. If compliance is not reasonably achievable, and the Attorney General does not agree to reimburse, the carrier will not be required to pay to bring its services or features into compliance.

In addition, to the extent that telecommunications carriers must install additional capacity to meet law enforcement needs, the bill requires the Government to pay for the increased capacity requirements.

Court authorized electronic surveillance is one of law enforcement's most important and effective investigative tools. It is often the only means of preventing or solving serious crimes. Failure to pass this legislation will have dire consequences for law enforcement, public safety and our national security.

This legislation is strongly supported by FBI Director Freeh and State and local law enforcement officials. I urge my colleagues to do so as well.

Source: Statement of Henry Hyde (R-IL), *Congressional Record, House,* October 4–5, 1994, 10773–83, p. 109–17.

2000: THE SUPREME COURT RULES ON CHECKPOINTS IN *CITY OF INDIANAPOLIS v. EDMOND*

In 1998, the city of Indianapolis established a checkpoint program under which the police, acting without individualized suspicion, stopped a predetermined number of vehicles at roadblocks in various locations on city roads for the primary purpose of the discovery and interdiction of illegal narcotics. Under the program, at least one officer would (1) approach each vehicle, (2) advise the driver that he or she was being stopped briefly at a drug checkpoint, (3) ask the driver to produce a driver's license and the vehicle's registration, (4) look for signs of impairment, and (5) conduct an open-view examination of the vehicle from the outside. In addition, an officer accompanied by a narcotics-detection dog would walk around the outside of each stopped vehicle.

James Edmond and Joell Palmer, two motorists who had been stopped at such a checkpoint, subsequently filed suit in federal district court asserting that the city's checkpoint program violated the Fourth Amendment. The district court disagreed, but the U.S. Court of Appeals for the Seventh Circuit reversed on the grounds that there was neither probable cause nor articulable suspicion to stop any given driver. The Supreme Court affirmed the appellate court's decision on November 28, 2000, in a 6–3 decision. Justice Sandra Day O'Connor wrote the majority opinion for the Court, which is excerpted here.

JUSTICE O'CONNOR delivered the opinion of the Court. In *Michigan Department of State Police v. Sitz* (1990), . . . we held that brief, suspicionless seizures at highway checkpoints for the purposes of combating drunk driving and intercepting illegal immigrants were constitutional. We now consider the constitutionality of a highway checkpoint program whose primary purpose is the discovery and interdiction of illegal narcotics. . . .

The Fourth Amendment requires that searches and seizures be reasonable. A search or seizure is ordinarily unreasonable in the absence of individualized suspicion of wrongdoing. While such suspicion is not an "irreducible" component of reasonableness, we have recognized only limited circumstances in which the usual rule does not apply. For example, we have upheld certain regimes of suspicionless searches where the program was designed to serve "special needs, beyond the normal need for law enforcement." We have also allowed searches for certain administrative purposes without particularized suspicion of misconduct, provided that those searches are appropriately limited.

We have also upheld brief, suspicionless seizures of motorists at a fixed Border Patrol checkpoint designed to intercept illegal aliens, and at a sobriety checkpoint aimed at removing drunk drivers from the road. In addition, in *Delaware v. Prouse*

(1979), we suggested that a similar type of roadblock with the purpose of verifying drivers' licenses and vehicle registrations would be permissible. In none of these cases, however, did we indicate approval of a checkpoint program whose primary purpose was to detect evidence of ordinary criminal wrongdoing. . . .

In *Sitz*, we evaluated the constitutionality of a Michigan highway sobriety checkpoint program. The *Sitz* checkpoint involved brief suspicionless stops of motorists so that police officers could detect signs of intoxication and remove impaired drivers from the road. Motorists who exhibited signs of intoxication were diverted for a license and registration check and, if warranted, further sobriety tests. This checkpoint program was clearly aimed at reducing the immediate hazard posed by the presence of drunk drivers on the highways, and there was an obvious connection between the imperative of highway safety and the law enforcement practice at issue. The gravity of the drunk driving problem and the magnitude of the State's interest in getting drunk drivers off the road weighed heavily in our determination that the program was constitutional. In *Prouse*, we invalidated a discretionary, suspicionless stop for a spot check of a motorist's driver's license and vehicle registration. The officer's conduct in that case was unconstitutional primarily on account of his exercise of "standardless and unconstrained discretion." We nonetheless acknowledged the States' "vital interest in ensuring that only those qualified to do so are permitted to operate motor vehicles, that these vehicles are fit for safe operation, and hence that licensing, registration, and vehicle inspection requirements are being observed." Accordingly, we suggested that "questioning of all oncoming traffic at roadblock-type stops" would be a lawful means of serving this interest in highway safety. . . .

Not only does the common thread of highway safety thus run through *Sitz* and *Prouse*, but *Prouse* itself reveals a difference in the Fourth Amendment significance of highway safety interests and the general interest in crime control. . . .

We have never approved a checkpoint program whose primary purpose was to detect evidence of ordinary criminal wrongdoing. Rather, our checkpoint cases have recognized only limited exceptions to the general rule that a seizure must be accompanied by some measure of individualized suspicion. . . .

The primary purpose of the Indianapolis narcotics checkpoints is in the end to advance "the general interest in crime control." We decline to suspend the usual requirement of individualized suspicion where the police seek to employ a checkpoint primarily for the ordinary enterprise of investigating crimes. We cannot sanction stops justified only by the generalized and ever-present possibility that interrogation and inspection may reveal that any given motorist has committed some crime. Of course, there are circumstances that may justify a law enforcement checkpoint where the primary purpose would otherwise, but for some emergency, relate to ordinary crime control. For example, as the Court of Appeals noted, the

Fourth Amendment would almost certainly permit an appropriately tailored roadblock set up to thwart an imminent terrorist attack or to catch a dangerous criminal who is likely to flee by way of a particular route. The exigencies created by these scenarios are far removed from the circumstances under which authorities might simply stop cars as a matter of course to see if there just happens to be a felon leaving the jurisdiction. . . .

It goes without saying that our holding today does nothing to alter the constitutional status of the sobriety and border checkpoints that we approved in *Sitz* and *Martinez-Fuerte*, or of the type of traffic checkpoint that we suggested would be lawful in *Prouse*. The constitutionality of such checkpoint programs still depends on a balancing of the competing interests at stake and the effectiveness of the program. When law enforcement authorities pursue primarily general crime control purposes at checkpoints such as here, however, stops can only be justified by some quantum of individualized suspicion. . . .

Because the primary purpose of the Indianapolis checkpoint program is ultimately indistinguishable from the general interest in crime control, the checkpoints violate the Fourth Amendment. The judgment of the Court of Appeals is accordingly affirmed. *It is so ordered.*

Source: Justice O'Connor, Sandra Day. Opinion of the Court. *City of Indianapolis v. James Edmond et al,* 531 U.S. 32, Decided November 28, 2000. United States Reports, Volume 531, October 2000–February 2001.

2001: THE SUPREME COURT RULES ON THERMAL-IMAGING SURVEILLANCE IN *KYLLO v. UNITED STATES*

In the case of Kyllo v. United States, *the U.S. Supreme Court held that government use of sensory enhancing devices not in "general public use" to gather information about a home that would otherwise only be obtainable by entering the premises constitutes a "search" within the meaning of the Fourth Amendment and therefore requires a warrant.*

When a government agent became suspicious that Danny Kyllo, a resident of Florence, Oregon, was illegally growing marijuana, the agent used a thermal-imaging device to scan his triplex. The imaging revealed that the amount of heat emanating from the home was consistent with the high-intensity lamps typically used for indoor marijuana growth. Based on informants, utility bills, and the thermal imaging, a federal magistrate judge issued a warrant to search Kyllo's home. The search unveiled a marijuana-growing operation, and Kyllo was indicted on a federal drug charge. After unsuccessfully moving to suppress the evidence seized from his home, Kyllo entered a conditional guilty plea. But he also appealed to the Ninth Circuit Court, asserting that observations with a thermal-imaging device constituted a search under the Fourth Amendment. At the Court of Appeals, the conviction was upheld and Kyllo petitioned a writ of certiorari to the Supreme Court. The Supreme Court agreed to hear the case and reversed the Circuit Court ruling in a 5–4 decision that the use of a thermal-imaging device not found in general public use to monitor the radiation of heat from a person's home was a "search" within the meaning of the Fourth Amendment and therefore required a warrant.

Justice Antonin Scalia, who wrote the majority opinion, held that a person has a reasonable expectation of privacy, especially in the home, because that was what the Fourth Amendment was adopted to protect. The Court explained that a search occurs when government agents use sense-enhancing technology not available in general public use to collect any information regarding the interior of a home that could not otherwise be obtained without a physical invasion. Scalia's opinion also reflected concern about protecting privacy against more sophisticated surveillance equipment. He asserted that the difference between "off-the-wall" surveillance and "through-the-wall" surveillance was nonexistent because both methods physically intruded upon the privacy of the home.

The Court criticized the Ninth Circuit's rationale by arguing that the appropriate inquiry must not be whether or not the technology reveals intimate details of the subject's life. The Court further held that to limit the prohibition of thermal imaging to "intimate details" would not only have been wrong in principle but would also have been impracticable in application. It argued that this type of standard is impractical in application because the government can never know in advance whether or not the technology will reveal such details. The Fourth Amendment's protection of the home had never been tied to measurement of the quality or quantity of information obtained. In the home, all details were intimate details, because the entire area was held safe from prying government eyes. Excerpts from Scalia's majority opinion are below.

Writing for the dissenters, Justice John P. Stevens argued that using surveillance technology should only be regarded as a "search" if the effort provided its user with the functional equivalent of actual presence in the area being searched. The dissent posited that unlike a device such as an X-ray, which can accomplish a physical penetration, the thermal imaging device only measured heat on the exterior surfaces of the home, failing to reveal any details of the home's interior. Justice Stevens further argued that the heat emissions could have been detected by feeling that some areas in or around the house were warmer than others or observing that snow was melting more quickly on certain sections of the house. Since the public could gather this information without entering the home, Stevens argued there was no need for a warrant and the use of this technique should not be regarded as unconstitutional.

Justice Scalia delivered the opinion of the Court.

This case presents the question whether the use of a thermal-imaging device aimed at a private home from a public street to detect relative amounts of heat within the home constitutes a "search" within the meaning of the Fourth Amendment.

I

In 1991 Agent William Elliott of the United States Department of the Interior came to suspect that marijuana was being grown in the home belonging to petitioner Danny Kyllo, part of a triplex on Rhododendron Drive in Florence, Oregon. Indoor marijuana growth typically requires high-intensity lamps. In order to determine whether an amount of heat was emanating from petitioner's home consistent with the use of such lamps, at 3:20 A.M. on January 16, 1992, Agent Elliott and Dan Haas used an Agema Thermovision 210 thermal imager to scan the triplex. Thermal imagers detect infrared radiation, which virtually all objects emit but which is not visible to the naked eye. The imager converts radiation into images based on relative warmth—black is cool, white is hot, shades of gray connote relative differences; in that respect, it operates somewhat like a video camera showing heat images. The scan of Kyllo's home took only a few minutes and was performed from the passenger seat of Agent Elliott's vehicle across the street from the front of the house and also from the street in back of the house. The scan showed that the roof over the garage and a side wall of petitioner's home were relatively hot compared to the rest of the home and substantially warmer than neighboring homes in the triplex. Agent Elliott concluded that petitioner was using halide lights to grow marijuana in his house, which indeed he was. Based on tips from informants, utility bills, and the thermal imaging, a Federal Magistrate Judge issued a warrant authorizing a search of petitioner's home, and the agents found an indoor growing operation involving more than 100 plants. Petitioner was indicted on one count of manufacturing marijuana, in violation of 21 U.S. C. §841(a)(1). He unsuccessfully moved to suppress the evidence seized from his home and then entered a conditional guilty plea. . . .

II

The Fourth Amendment provides that "[t]he right of the people to be secure in their persons, houses, papers, and effects, against unreasonable searches and seizures, shall not be violated." "At the very core" of the Fourth Amendment "stands the right of a man to retreat into his own home and there be free from unreasonable governmental intrusion." With few exceptions, the question whether a warrantless search of a home is reasonable and hence constitutional must be answered no.

On the other hand, the antecedent question of whether or not a Fourth Amendment "search" has occurred is not so simple under our precedent. The permissibility of ordinary visual surveillance of a home used to be clear because, well into the 20th century, our Fourth Amendment jurisprudence was tied to common-law trespass. We have since decoupled violation of a person's Fourth Amendment rights from trespassory violation of his property, but the lawfulness of warrantless visual surveillance of a home has still been preserved. As we observed, "[t]he Fourth Amendment protection of the home has never been extended to require law enforcement officers to shield their eyes when passing by a home on public thoroughfares."

One might think that the new validating rationale would be that examining the portion of a house that is in plain public view, while it is a "search" despite the absence of trespass, is not an "unreasonable" one under the Fourth Amendment. But in fact we have held that visual observation is no "search" at all—perhaps in order to preserve somewhat more intact our doctrine that warrantless searches are presumptively unconstitutional. . . . As Justice Harlan's oftquoted concurrence described it, a Fourth Amendment search occurs when the government violates a subjective expectation of privacy that society recognizes as reasonable. We have subsequently applied this principle to hold that a Fourth Amendment search does not occur—even when the explicitly protected location of a house is concerned—unless "the individual manifested a subjective expectation of privacy in the object of the challenged search," and "society [is] willing to recognize that expectation as reasonable. . . ."

The present case involves officers on a public street engaged in more than naked-eye surveillance of a home. We have previously reserved judgment as to how much technological enhancement of ordinary perception from such a vantage point, if any, is too much. While we upheld enhanced aerial photography of an industrial complex in Dow Chemical, we noted that we found "it important that this is not an area immediately adjacent to a private home, where privacy expectations are most heightened."

III

It would be foolish to contend that the degree of privacy secured to citizens by the Fourth Amendment has been entirely unaffected by the advance of technology. The question we confront today is what limits there are upon this power of technology to shrink the realm of guaranteed privacy.

The Katz test—whether the individual has an expectation of privacy that society is prepared to recognize as reasonable—has often been criticized as circular, and hence subjective and unpredictable. While it may be difficult to refine Katz when the search of areas such as telephone booths, automobiles, or even the curtilage and uncovered portions of residences are at issue, in the case of the search of the interior of homes—the prototypical and hence most commonly litigated area of protected privacy—there is a ready criterion, with roots deep in the common law, of the minimal expectation of privacy that exists, and that is acknowledged to be reasonable. To withdraw protection of this minimum expectation would be to permit police technology to erode the privacy guaranteed by the Fourth Amendment. We think that obtaining by sense—enhancing technology any information regarding the interior of the home that could not otherwise have been obtained without physical "intrusion into a constitutionally protected area," constitutes a search—at least where (as here) the technology in question is not in general public use. This assures preservation of that degree of privacy against government that existed when the Fourth Amendment was adopted. On the basis of this criterion, the information obtained by the thermal imager in this case was the product of a search.

The Government maintains, however, that the thermal imaging must be upheld because it detected "only heat radiating from the external surface of the house." The dissent makes this its leading point, see post, at 1, contending that there is a fundamental difference between what it calls "off-the-wall" observations and "through-the-wall surveillance." But just as a thermal imager captures only heat emanating from a house, so also a powerful directional microphone picks up only sound emanating from a house—and a satellite capable of scanning from many miles away would pick up only visible light emanating from a house. We rejected such a mechanical interpretation of the Fourth Amendment in Katz, where the eavesdropping device picked up only sound waves that reached the exterior of the phone booth. Reversing that approach would leave the homeowner at the mercy of advancing technology—including imaging technology that could discern all human activity in the home. While the technology used in the present case was relatively crude, the rule we adopt must take account of more sophisticated systems that are already in use or in development. . . . . As for the dissent's extraordinary assertion that anything learned through "an inference" cannot be a search, that would validate even the "through-the-wall" technologies that the dissent purports to disapprove. Surely the dissent does not believe that the through-the-wall radar or ultrasound technology produces an 8-by-10 Kodak glossy that needs no analysis.

The Government also contends that the thermal imaging was constitutional because it did not "detect private activities occurring in private areas." The Fourth Amendment's protection of the home has never been tied to measurement of the quality or quantity of information obtained. In Silverman, for example, we made clear that any physical invasion of the structure of the home, "by even a fraction of an inch," was too much, and there is certainly no exception to the warrant requirement for the officer who barely cracks open the front door and sees nothing but the nonintimate rug on the vestibule floor. In the home, our cases show, all details are intimate details, because the entire area is held safe from prying government eyes.

Limiting the prohibition of thermal imaging to "intimate details" would not only be wrong in principle; it would be impractical in application, failing to provide "a workable accommodation between the needs of law enforcement and the interests protected by the Fourth Amendment." To begin with, there is no necessary connection between the sophistication of the surveillance equipment and the "intimacy" of the details that it observes—which means that one cannot say (and the police cannot be assured) that use of the relatively crude equipment at issue here will always be lawful. The Agema Thermovision 210 might disclose, for example, at what hour each night the lady of the house takes her daily sauna and bath—a detail that many would consider "intimate"; and a much more sophisticated system might detect nothing more intimate than the fact that someone left a closet light on. We could not, in other words, develop a rule approving only that through-the-wall surveillance which identifies objects no smaller than 36 by 36 inches, but would have to develop a jurisprudence specifying which home activities are "intimate" and which are not. And even when (if ever) that jurisprudence were fully developed, no police officer would be able to know in advance whether his through-the-wall surveillance picks up "intimate" details—and thus would be unable to know in advance whether it is constitutional. . . .

We have said that the Fourth Amendment draws "a firm line at the entrance to the house." That line, we think, must be not only firm but also bright—which requires clear specification of those methods of surveillance that require a warrant.

While it is certainly possible to conclude from the videotape of the thermal imaging that occurred in this case that no "significant" compromise of the homeowner's privacy has occurred, we must take the long view, from the original meaning of the Fourth Amendment forward.

Where, as here, the Government uses a device that is not in general public use, to explore details of the home that would previously have been unknowable without physical intrusion, the surveillance is a "search" and is presumptively unreasonable without a warrant.

Since we hold the Thermovision imaging to have been an unlawful search, it will remain for the District Court to determine whether, without the evidence it provided, the search warrant issued in this case was supported by probable cause—and if not, whether there is any other basis for supporting admission of the evidence that the search pursuant to the warrant produced.

The judgment of the Court of Appeals is reversed; the case is remanded for further proceedings consistent with this opinion.

Source: Justice Scalia, Antonin. Opinion of the Court. *Danny Lee Kyllo v. United States,* 533 U.S. 27. Decided June 11, 2001. United States Reports, Volume 533, March–June 2001.

2001: PRESIDENT BUSH ADDRESSES CONGRESS AFTER THE SEPTEMBER 11 ATTACKS

On September 20, 2001, nine days after the worst terrorist attack on the American people in U.S. history, President George W. Bush delivered a nationally televised address to a special joint session of Congress. In this address, Bush lauded the bravery of American civilians and first responders and promised to find and punish the perpetrators of the terrorist attacks. In addition, he discussed the need to harness the capabilities of United States' intelligence community to prevent future terrorist attacks and to combine other agencies into a Department of Homeland Security specifically focused on keeping United States safe. Bush's address, reprinted here, is widely credited with boosting public support for the idea that expanded surveillance by the U.S. government was a necessary and justifiable response to the threat of terrorism.

Mr. Speaker, Mr. President Pro Tempore, members of Congress, and fellow Americans, in the normal course of events, presidents come to this chamber to report on the state of the union. Tonight, no such report is needed; it has already been delivered by the American people.

We have seen it in the courage of passengers who rushed terrorists to save others on the ground. Passengers like an exceptional man named Todd Beamer. And would you please help me welcome his wife Lisa Beamer here tonight?

(APPLAUSE)

We have seen the state of our union in the endurance of rescuers working past exhaustion.

We've seen the unfurling of flags, the lighting of candles, the giving of blood, the saying of prayers in English, Hebrew and Arabic.

We have seen the decency of a loving and giving people who have made the grief of strangers their own.

My fellow citizens, for the last nine days, the entire world has seen for itself the state of union, and it is strong.

(APPLAUSE)

Tonight, we are a country awakened to danger and called to defend freedom. Our grief has turned to anger and anger to resolution. Whether we bring our enemies to justice or bring justice to our enemies, justice will be done.

(APPLAUSE)

I thank the Congress for its leadership at such an important time.

All of America was touched on the evening of the tragedy to see Republicans and Democrats joined together on the steps of this Capitol singing "God Bless America."

And you did more than sing. You acted, by delivering $40 billion to rebuild our communities and meet the needs of our military. Speaker Hastert, Minority Leader Gephardt, Majority Leader Daschle and Senator Lott, I thank you for your friendship, for your leadership and for your service to our country.

(APPLAUSE)

And on behalf of the American people, I thank the world for its outpouring of support.

America will never forget the sounds of our national anthem playing at Buckingham Palace, on the streets of Paris and at Berlin's Brandenburg Gate.

We will not forget South Korean children gathering to pray outside our embassy in Seoul, or the prayers of sympathy offered at a mosque in Cairo.

We will not forget moments of silence and days of mourning in Australia and Africa and Latin America.

Nor will we forget the citizens of 80 other nations who died with our own. Dozens of Pakistanis, more than 130 Israelis, more than 250 citizens of India, men and women from El Salvador, Iran, Mexico and Japan, and hundreds of British citizens.

America has no truer friend than Great Britain.

(APPLAUSE)

Once again, we are joined together in a great cause.

I'm so honored the British prime minister had crossed an ocean to show his unity with America.

Thank you for coming, friend.

(APPLAUSE)

On September the 11th, enemies of freedom committed an act of war against our country. Americans have known wars, but for the past 136 years they have been wars on foreign soil, except for one Sunday in 1941. Americans have known the casualties of war, but not at the center of a great city on a peaceful morning.

Americans have known surprise attacks, but never before on thousands of civilians.

All of this was brought upon us in a single day, and night fell on a different world, a world where freedom itself is under attack.

Americans have many questions tonight. Americans are asking, "Who attacked our country?"

The evidence we have gathered all points to a collection of loosely affiliated terrorist organizations known as al Qaeda. They are some of the murderers indicted for bombing American embassies in Tanzania and Kenya and responsible for bombing the USS Cole.

Al Qaeda is to terror what the Mafia is to crime. But its goal is not making money, its goal is remaking the world and imposing its radical beliefs on people everywhere.

The terrorists practice a fringe form of Islamic extremism that has been rejected by Muslim scholars and the vast majority of Muslim clerics; a fringe movement that perverts the peaceful teachings of Islam.

The terrorists' directive commands them to kill Christians and Jews, to kill all Americans and make no distinctions among military and civilians, including women and children.

This group and its leader, a person named Osama bin Laden, are linked to many other organizations in different countries, including the Egyptian Islamic Jihad, the Islamic Movement of Uzbekistan.

There are thousands of these terrorists in more than 60 countries.

They are recruited from their own nations and neighborhoods and brought to camps in places like Afghanistan where they are trained in the tactics of terror. They are sent back to their homes or sent to hide in countries around the world to plot evil and destruction.

The leadership of Al Qaeda has great influence in Afghanistan and supports the Taliban regime in controlling most of that country. In Afghanistan we see Al Qaeda's vision for the world. Afghanistan's people have been brutalized, many are starving and many have fled.

Women are not allowed to attend school. You can be jailed for owning a television. Religion can be practiced only as their leaders dictate. A man can be jailed in Afghanistan if his beard is not long enough.

The United States respects the people of Afghanistan—after all, we are currently its largest source of humanitarian aid—but we condemn the Taliban regime.

(APPLAUSE)

It is not only repressing its own people, it is threatening people everywhere by sponsoring and sheltering and supplying terrorists.

By aiding and abetting murder, the Taliban regime is committing murder. And tonight the United States of America makes the following demands on the Taliban.

Deliver to United States authorities all of the leaders of Al Quaeda who hide in your land.

(APPLAUSE)

Release all foreign nationals, including American citizens you have unjustly imprisoned. Protect foreign journalists, diplomats and aid workers in your country. Close immediately and permanently every terrorist training camp in Afghanistan. And hand over every terrorist and every person and their support structure to appropriate authorities.

(APPLAUSE)

Give the United States full access to terrorist training camps, so we can make sure they are no longer operating.

These demands are not open to negotiation or discussion.

(APPLAUSE)

The Taliban must act and act immediately.

They will hand over the terrorists or they will share in their fate.

I also want to speak tonight directly to Muslims throughout the world. We respect your faith. It's practiced freely by many millions of Americans and by millions more in countries that America counts as friends. Its teachings are good and peaceful, and those who commit evil in the name of Allah blaspheme the name of Allah.

(APPLAUSE)

The terrorists are traitors to their own faith, trying, in effect, to hijack Islam itself.

The enemy of America is not our many Muslim friends. It is not our many Arab friends. Our enemy is a radical network of terrorists and every government that supports them.

(APPLAUSE)

Our war on terror begins with Al Qaeda, but it does not end there.

It will not end until every terrorist group of global reach has been found, stopped and defeated.

(APPLAUSE)

Americans are asking "Why do they hate us?"

They hate what they see right here in this chamber: a democratically elected government. Their leaders are self-appointed. They hate our freedoms: our freedom of religion, our freedom of speech, our freedom to vote and assemble and disagree with each other.

They want to overthrow existing governments in many Muslim countries such as Egypt, Saudi Arabia and Jordan. They want to drive Israel out of the Middle East. They want to drive Christians and Jews out of vast regions of Asia and Africa.

These terrorists kill not merely to end lives, but to disrupt and end a way of life. With every atrocity, they hope that America grows fearful, retreating from the world and forsaking our friends. They stand against us because we stand in their way.

We're not deceived by their pretenses to piety.

We have seen their kind before. They're the heirs of all the murderous ideologies of the 20th century. By sacrificing human life to serve their radical visions, by abandoning every value except the will to power, they follow in the path of fascism, Nazism and totalitarianism. And they will follow that path all the way to where it ends in history's unmarked grave of discarded lies.

(APPLAUSE)

Americans are asking, "How will we fight and win this war?"

We will direct every resource at our command—every means of diplomacy, every tool of intelligence, every instrument of law enforcement, every financial influence, and every necessary weapon of war—to the destruction and to the defeat of the global terror network.

Now, this war will not be like the war against Iraq a decade ago, with a decisive liberation of territory and a swift conclusion. It will not look like the air war above Kosovo two years ago, where no ground troops were used and not a single American was lost in combat.

Our response involves far more than instant retaliation and isolated strikes. Americans should not expect one battle, but a lengthy campaign unlike any other we have ever seen. It may include dramatic strikes visible on TV and covert operations secret even in success.

We will starve terrorists of funding, turn them one against another, drive them from place to place until there is no refuge or no rest.

And we will pursue nations that provide aid or safe haven to terrorism. Every nation in every region now has a decision to make: Either you are with us or you are with the terrorists.

(APPLAUSE)

From this day forward, any nation that continues to harbor or support terrorism will be regarded by the United States as a hostile regime. Our nation has been put on notice, we're not immune from attack. We will take defensive measures against terrorism to protect Americans.

Today, dozens of federal departments and agencies, as well as state and local governments, have responsibilities affecting homeland security.

These efforts must be coordinated at the highest level. So tonight, I announce the creation of a Cabinet-level position reporting directly to me, the Office of Homeland Security.

And tonight, I also announce a distinguished American to lead this effort, to strengthen American security: a military veteran, an effective governor, a true **patriot,** a trusted friend, Pennsylvania's Tom Ridge.

(APPLAUSE)

He will lead, oversee and coordinate a comprehensive national strategy to safeguard our country against terrorism and respond to any attacks that may come.

These measures are essential. The only way to defeat terrorism as a threat to our way of life is to stop it, eliminate it and destroy it where it grows.

(APPLAUSE)

Many will be involved in this effort, from FBI agents, to intelligence operatives, to the reservists we have called to active duty. All deserve our thanks, and all have our prayers.

And tonight a few miles from the damaged Pentagon, I have a message for our military: Be ready. I have called the armed forces to alert, and there is a reason.

The hour is coming when America will act, and you will make us proud.

(APPLAUSE)

This is not, however, just America's fight. And what is at stake is not just America's freedom.

This is the world's fight. This is civilization's fight. This is the fight of all who believe in progress and pluralism, tolerance and freedom.

We ask every nation to join us.

We will ask and we will need the help of police forces, intelligence service and banking systems around the world. The United States is grateful that many nations and many international organizations have already responded with sympathy and with support—nations from Latin America to Asia to Africa to Europe to the Islamic world.

Perhaps the NATO charter reflects best the attitude of the world: An attack on one is an attack on all. The civilized world is rallying to America's side.

They understand that if this terror goes unpunished, their own cities, their own citizens may be next. Terror unanswered can not only bring down buildings, it can threaten the stability of legitimate governments.

And you know what? We're not going to allow it.

(APPLAUSE)

Americans are asking, "What is expected of us?"

I ask you to live your lives and hug your children.

I know many citizens have fears tonight, and I ask you to be calm and resolute, even in the face of a continuing threat.

I ask you to uphold the values of America and remember why so many have come here.

We're in a fight for our principles, and our first responsibility is to live by them. No one should be singled out for unfair treatment or unkind words because of their ethnic background or religious faith.

(APPLAUSE)

I ask you to continue to support the victims of this tragedy with your contributions. Those who want to give can go to a central source of information, Libertyunites.org, to find the names of groups providing direct help in New York, Pennsylvania and Virginia.

The thousands of FBI agents who are now at work in this investigation may need your cooperation, and I ask you to give it. I ask for your patience with the delays and inconveniences that may accompany tighter security and for your patience in what will be a long struggle.

I ask your continued participation and confidence in the American economy. Terrorists attacked a symbol of American prosperity; they did not touch its source.

America is successful because of the hard work and creativity and enterprise of our people. These were the true strengths of our economy before September 11, and they are our strengths today.

(APPLAUSE)

And finally, please continue praying for the victims of terror and their families, for those in uniform and for our great country. Prayer has comforted us in sorrow and will help strengthen us for the journey ahead.

Tonight I thank my fellow Americans for what you have already done and for what you will do.

And ladies and gentlemen of the Congress, I thank you, their representatives, for what you have already done and for what we will do together.

Tonight we face new and sudden national challenges.

We will come together to improve air safety, to dramatically expand the number of air marshals on domestic flights and take new measures to prevent hijacking.

We will come together to promote stability and keep our airlines flying with direct assistance during this emergency.

(APPLAUSE)

We will come together to give law enforcement the additional tools it needs to track down terror here at home.

(APPLAUSE)

We will come together to strengthen our intelligence capabilities to know the plans of terrorists before they act and to find them before they strike.

(APPLAUSE)

We will come together to take active steps that strengthen America's economy and put our people back to work.

Tonight, we welcome two leaders who embody the extraordinary spirit of all New Yorkers, Governor George Pataki and Mayor Rudolf Giuliani.

(APPLAUSE)

As a symbol of America's resolve, my administration will work with Congress and these two leaders to show the world that we will rebuild New York City.

(APPLAUSE)

After all that has just passed, all the lives taken and all the possibilities and hopes that died with them, it is natural to wonder if America's future is one of fear.

Some speak of an age of terror. I know there are struggles ahead and dangers to face. But this country will define our times, not be defined by them.

As long as the United States of America is determined and strong, this will not be an age of terror. This will be an age of liberty here and across the world.

(APPLAUSE)

Great harm has been done to us. We have suffered great loss. And in our grief and anger we have found our mission and our moment.

Freedom and fear are at war. The advance of human freedom, the great achievement of our time and the great hope of every time, now depends on us.

Our nation, this generation, will lift the dark threat of violence from our people and our future. We will rally the world to this cause by our efforts, by our courage. We will not tire, we will not falter and we will not fail.

(APPLAUSE)

It is my hope that in the months and years ahead life will return almost to normal. We'll go back to our lives and routines and that is good.

Even grief recedes with time and grace.

But our resolve must not pass. Each of us will remember what happened that day and to whom it happened. We will remember the moment the news came, where we were and what we were doing.

Some will remember an image of a fire or story or rescue. Some will carry memories of a face and a voice gone forever.

And I will carry this. It is the police shield of a man named George Howard who died at the World Trade Center trying to save others.

It was given to me by his mom, Arlene (ph), as a proud memorial to her son. It is my reminder of lives that ended and a task that does not end.

(APPLAUSE)

I will not forget the wound to our country and those who inflicted it. I will not yield, I will not rest, I will not relent in waging this struggle for freedom and security for the American people.

The course of this conflict is not known, yet its outcome is certain. Freedom and fear, justice and cruelty, have always been at war, and we know that God is not neutral between them.

(APPLAUSE)

Fellow citizens, we'll meet violence with patient justice, assured of the rightness of our cause and confident of the victories to come.

In all that lies before us, may God grant us wisdom and may he watch over the United States of America.

Thank you.

Source: Bush, George W. 2001. "Address to the Joint Session of the 107th Congress." September 20, 2001. *Public Papers of the Presidents of the United States: George W. Bush (2001, Book II).* Washington, DC: Government Printing Office, pp. 1140–44.

2001: SENATOR FEINGOLD SPEAKS OUT AGAINST THE USA PATRIOT ACT

In the weeks following the terrorist attacks of September 11, 2001, Congress and the administration of President George W. Bush scrambled to pass a bill that would shore up perceived shortcomings in U.S. national security and provide federal agencies with new tools and authority to combat terrorism. When the so-called USA PATRIOT Act came up for consideration in the U.S. Senate after passage in the House of Representatives by a 357–66 vote, however, Senator Russ Feingold (D-WI) spoke out against the legislation. He expressed support for many of its provisions, but voiced grave concerns that some measures in the bill would trample on civil liberties that provided the foundation for American life and values. Feingold attempted to introduce three amendments designed to address perceived civil liberties shortcomings in the bill, but on each occasion, the Senate voted by large margins to table his amendments. Many of the senators who voted against bringing Feingold's proposals up for consideration expressed sympathy with his concerns, but they feared that allowing a vote on his amendments might open the floodgates to other amendment votes capable of scuttling the entire bill.

In the end, Feingold was the only senator in the entire U.S. Senate to vote against the PATRIOT Act when it came up for a vote on October 25, 2001. Since then, many privacy and civil liberties advocates have asserted that Feingold's opposition has been vindicated by revelations of government misconduct carried out under the auspices of the USA PATRIOT Act. Following are excerpts from Feingold's statement in advance of that October 2001 vote.

Mr. President, I have asked for this time to speak about the anti-terrorism bill before us, H.R. 3162. As we address this bill, we are especially mindful of the terrible events of September 11 and beyond, which led to the bill's proposal and its quick consideration in the Congress.

This has been a tragic time in our country. Before I discuss this bill, let me first pause to remember, through one small story, how September 11th has irrevocably changed so many lives. In a letter to *The Washington Post* recently, a man wrote that as he went jogging near the Pentagon, he came across the makeshift memorial built for those who lost their lives there. He slowed to a walk as he took in the sight before him—the red, white and blue flowers covering the structure, and then, off to the side, a second, smaller memorial with a card.

The card read, "Happy Birthday Mommy. Although you died and are no longer with me, I feel as if I still have you in my life. I think about you every day."

After reading the card, the man felt as if he were "drowning in the names of dead mothers, fathers, sons and daughters." The author of this letter shared a moment in his own life that so many of us have had—the moment where televised pictures of the destruction are made painfully real to us. We read a card, or see the anguished face of a grieving loved one, and we suddenly feel the enormity of what has happened to so many American families, and to all of us as a people.

We all also had our own initial reactions, and my first and most powerful emotion was a solemn resolve to stop these terrorists. And that remains my principal reaction to these events. But I also quickly realized that two cautions were necessary, and I raised them on the Senate floor the day after the attacks.

The first caution was that we must continue to respect our Constitution and protect our civil liberties in the wake of the attacks. As the chairman of the Constitution Subcommittee of the Judiciary Committee, I recognize that this is a different world with different technologies, different issues, and different threats. Yet we must examine every item that is proposed in response to these events to be sure we are not rewarding these terrorists and weakening ourselves by giving up the cherished freedoms that they seek to destroy.

The second caution I issued was a warning against the mistreatment of Arab Americans, Muslim Americans, South Asians, or others in this country. Already, one day after the attacks, we were hearing news reports that misguided anger against people of these backgrounds had led to harassment, violence, and even death.

I suppose I was reacting instinctively to the unfolding events in the spirit of the Irish statesman John Philpot Curran, who said: "The condition upon which God hath given liberty to man is eternal vigilance."

During those first few hours after the attacks, I kept remembering a sentence from a case I had studied in law school. Not surprisingly, I didn't remember which case it was, who wrote the opinion, or what it was about, but I did remember these words: "While the Constitution protects against invasions of individual rights, it is not a suicide pact." I took these words as a challenge to my concerns about civil liberties at such a momentous time in our history; that we must be careful to not take civil liberties so literally that we allow ourselves to be destroyed.

But upon reviewing the case itself, *Kennedy v. Mendoza-Martinez,* I found that Justice Arthur Goldberg had made this statement but then ruled in favor of the civil liberties position in the case, which was about draft evasion. He elaborated:

> "It is fundamental that the great powers of Congress to conduct war and to regulate the Nation's foreign relations are subject to the constitutional requirements of due process. The imperative necessity for safeguarding these rights to procedural due process under the gravest of emergencies has existed throughout our constitutional history, for it is then, under the pressing exigencies of crisis, that there is the greatest temptation to dispense with fundamental constitutional guarantees which, it is feared, will inhibit governmental action. The Constitution of the United States is a law for rulers and people, equally in war and peace, and

covers with the shield of its protection all classes of men, at all times, and under all circumstances. . . . In no other way can we transmit to posterity unimpaired the blessings of liberty, consecrated by the sacrifices of the Revolution."

I have approached the events of the past month and my role in proposing and reviewing legislation relating to it in this spirit. I believe we must redouble our vigilance to ensure our security and to prevent further acts of terror. But we must also redouble our vigilance to preserve our values and the basic rights that make us who we are.

The Founders who wrote our Constitution and Bill of Rights exercised that vigilance even though they had recently fought and won the Revolutionary War. They did not live in comfortable and easy times of hypothetical enemies. They wrote a Constitution of limited powers and an explicit Bill of Rights to protect liberty in times of war, as well as in times of peace.

There have been periods in our nation's history when civil liberties have taken a back seat to what appeared at the time to be the legitimate exigencies of war. Our national consciousness still bears the stain and the scars of those events: The Alien and Sedition Acts, the suspension of habeas corpus during the Civil War, the internment of Japanese-Americans, German-Americans, and Italian-Americans during World War II, the blacklisting of supposed communist sympathizers during the McCarthy era, and the surveillance and harassment of antiwar protesters, including Dr. Martin Luther King Jr., during the Vietnam War. We must not allow these pieces of our past to become prologue.

Mr. President, even in our great land, wartime has sometimes brought us the greatest tests of our Bill of Rights. For example, during the Civil War, the government arrested some 13,000 civilians, implementing a system akin to martial law. President Lincoln issued a proclamation ordering the arrest and military trial of any persons "discouraging volunteer enlistments, or resisting militia drafts." Wisconsin provided one of the first challenges of this order. Draft protests rose up in Milwaukee and Sheboygan. And an anti-draft riot broke out among Germans and Luxembourgers in Port Washington, Wisconsin. When the government arrested one of the leaders of the riot, his attorney sought a writ of habeas corpus. His military captors said that the President had abolished the writ. The Wisconsin Supreme Court was among the first to rule that the President had exceeded his authority.

In 1917, the Postmaster General revoked the mailing privileges of the newspaper the *Milwaukee Leader* because he felt that some of its articles impeded the war effort and the draft. Articles called the President an aristocrat and called the draft oppressive. Over dissents by Justices Brandeis and Holmes, the Supreme Court upheld the action.

During World War II, President Roosevelt signed orders to incarcerate more than 110,000 people of Japanese origin, as well as some roughly 11,000 of German origin and 3,000 of Italian origin. . . .

Now some may say, indeed we may hope, that we have come a long way since those days of infringements on civil liberties. But there is ample reason for concern. And I have been troubled in the past six weeks by the potential loss of commitment in the Congress and the country to traditional civil liberties.

As it seeks to combat terrorism, the Justice Department is making extraordinary use of its power to arrest and detain individuals, jailing hundreds of people on immigration violations and arresting more than a dozen "material witnesses" not charged with any crime. Although the government has used these authorities before, it has not done so on such a broad scale. Judging from government announcements, the government has not brought any criminal charges related to the attacks with regard to the overwhelming majority of these detainees.

For example, the FBI arrested as a material witness the San Antonio radiologist Albader Al-Hazmi, who has a name like two of the hijackers, and who tried to book a flight to San Diego for a medical conference. According to his lawyer, the government held Al-Hazmi incommunicado after his arrest, and it took six days for lawyers to get access to him. After the FBI released him, his lawyer said, "This is a good lesson about how frail our processes are. It's how we treat people in difficult times like these that is the true test of the democracy and civil liberties that we brag so much about throughout the world." I agree with those statements.

Now, it so happens that since early 1999, I have been working on another bill that is poignantly relevant to recent events: legislation to prohibit racial profiling, especially the practice of targeting pedestrians or drivers for stops and searches based on the color of their skin. Before September 11th, people spoke of the issue mostly in the context of African-Americans and Latino-Americans who had been profiled. But after September 11, the issue has taken on a new context and a new urgency.

Even as America addresses the demanding security challenges before us, we must strive mightily also to guard our values and basic rights. We must guard against racism and ethnic discrimination against people of Arab and South Asian origin and those who are Muslim. . . .

Some have said rather cavalierly that in these difficult times we must accept some reduction in our civil liberties in order to be secure.

Of course, there is no doubt that if we lived in a police state, it would be easier to catch terrorists. If we lived in a country that allowed the police to search your home at any time for any reason; if we lived in a country that allowed the government to open your mail, eavesdrop on your phone conversations, or intercept your email communications; if we lived in a country that allowed the government to hold people in jail indefinitely based on what they write or think, or based on mere suspicion that they are up to no good, then the government would no doubt discover and arrest more terrorists.

But that probably would not be a country in which we would want to live. And that would not be a country for which we could, in good conscience, ask our young people to fight and die. In short, that would not be America.

Preserving our freedom is one of the main reasons that we are now engaged in this new war on terrorism. We will lose that war without firing a shot if we sacrifice the liberties of the American people.

That is why I found the antiterrorism bill originally proposed by Attorney General Ashcroft and President Bush to be troubling.

The Administration's proposed bill contained vast new powers for law enforcement, some seemingly drafted in haste and others that came from the FBI's wish list that Congress has rejected in the past. You may remember that the Attorney General announced his intention to introduce a bill shortly after the September 11 attacks. He provided the text of the bill the following Wednesday, and urged Congress to enact it by the end of the week. That was plainly impossible, but the pressure to move on this bill quickly, without deliberation and debate, has been relentless ever since.

It is one thing to shortcut the legislative process in order to get federal financial aid to the cities hit by terrorism. We did that, and no one complained that we moved too quickly. It is quite another to press for the enactment of sweeping new powers for law enforcement that directly affect the civil liberties of the American people without due deliberation by the peoples' elected representatives.

Fortunately, cooler heads prevailed at least to some extent, and while this bill has been on a fast track, there has been time to make some changes and reach agreement on a bill that is less objectionable than the bill that the Administration originally proposed.

As I will discuss in a moment, I have concluded that this bill still does not strike the right balance between empowering law enforcement and protecting civil liberties. But that does not mean that I oppose everything in the bill. Indeed many of its provisions are entirely reasonable, and I hope they will help law enforcement more effectively counter the threat of terrorism.

For example, it is entirely appropriate that with a warrant the FBI be able to seize voice mail messages as well as tap a phone. It is also reasonable, even necessary, to update the federal criminal offense relating to possession and use of biological weapons. It made sense to make sure that phone conversations carried over cables would not have more protection from surveillance than conversations carried over phone lines. And it made sense to stiffen penalties and lengthen or eliminate statutes of limitation for certain terrorist crimes.

There are other non-controversial provisions in the bill that I support—those to assist the victims of crime, to streamline the application process for public safety officers benefits and increase those benefits, to provide more funds to strengthen immigration controls at our Northern borders, to expedite the hiring of translators at the FBI, and many others.

In the end, however, my focus on this bill, as Chair of the Constitution Subcommittee of the Judiciary Committee in the Senate, was on those provisions that implicate our constitutional freedoms. And it was in reviewing those provisions that I came to feel that the Administration's demand for haste was inappropriate; indeed, it was dangerous. Our process in the Senate, as truncated as it was, did lead to the elimination or significant rewriting of a number of audacious proposals that I and many other members found objectionable.

For example, the original Administration proposal contained a provision that would have allowed the use in U.S. criminal proceedings against U.S. citizens of information obtained by foreign law enforcement agencies in wiretaps that would be illegal in this country. In other words, evidence obtained in an unconstitutional search overseas was to be allowed in a U.S. court.

Another provision would have broadened the criminal forfeiture laws to permit—prior to conviction—the freezing of assets entirely unrelated to an alleged crime. The Justice Department has wanted this authority for years, and Congress has never been willing to give it. For one thing, it touches on the right to counsel, since assets that are frozen cannot be used to pay a lawyer. The courts have almost uniformly rejected efforts to restrain assets before conviction unless they are assets gained in the alleged criminal enterprise. This proposal, in my view, was simply an effort on the part of the Department to take advantage of the emergency situation and get something that they've wanted to get for a long time.

The foreign wiretap and criminal forfeiture provisions were dropped from the bill that we considered in the Senate. Other provisions were rewritten based on objections that I and others raised about them. For example, the original bill contained sweeping permission for the Attorney General to get copies of educational records without a court order. The final bill requires a court order and a certification by the Attorney General that he has reason to believe that the records contain information that is relevant to an investigation of terrorism.

So the bill before us is certainly improved from the bill that the Administration sent to us on September 19, and wanted us to pass on September 21. But again, in my judgement, it does not strike the right balance between empowering law enforcement and protecting constitutional freedoms. Let me take a moment to discuss some of the shortcomings of the bill.

First, the bill contains some very significant changes in criminal procedure that will apply to every federal criminal investigation in this country, not just those involving terrorism. One provision would greatly expand the circumstances in which law enforcement agencies can search homes and offices without notifying the owner prior to the search. The longstanding practice under the Fourth Amendment of serving a warrant prior to executing a search could be easily avoided in virtually every case, because the government would simply have to show that it has "reasonable cause to believe" that providing notice "may" "seriously jeopardize an investigation." This is a significant infringement on personal liberty.

Notice is a key element of Fourth Amendment protections. It allows a person to point out mistakes in a warrant and to make sure that a search is limited to the terms of a warrant. Just think about the possibility of the police showing up at your door with a warrant to search your house. You look at the warrant and say, "yes, that's my address, but the name on the warrant isn't me." And the police realize a mistake has been made and go away. If you're not home, and the police have received permission to do a "sneak and peak" search, they can come in your house, look around, and leave, and may never have to tell you.

Another very troubling provision has to do with the effort to combat computer crime. The bill allows law enforcement to monitor a computer with the permission of its owner or operator, without the need to get a warrant or show probable cause. That's fine in the case of a so called "denial of service attack" or plain old computer hacking. A computer owner should be able to give the police permission to monitor communications coming from what amounts to a trespasser on the computer.

As drafted in the Senate bill, however, the provision might permit an employer to give permission to the police to monitor the e-mails of an employee who has used her computer at work to shop for Christmas gifts. Or someone who uses a computer at a library or at school and happens to go to a gambling or pornography site in violation of the Internet use policies of the library or the university might also be subjected to government surveillance—without probable cause and without any time limit. With this one provision, fourth amendment protections are potentially eliminated for a broad spectrum of electronic communications.

I am also very troubled by the broad expansion of government power under the Foreign Intelligence Surveillance Act, known as FISA. When Congress passed FISA in 1978 it granted to the executive branch the power to conduct surveillance in foreign intelligence investigations without meeting the rigorous probable cause standard under the Fourth Amendment that is required for criminal investigations. There is a lower threshold for obtaining a wiretap order from the FISA court because the FBI is not investigating a crime, it is investigating foreign intelligence activities. But the law currently requires that intelligence gathering be the primary purpose of the investigation in order for this lower standard to apply.

This bill changes that requirement. The government now will only have to show that intelligence is a "significant purpose" of the investigation. So even if the primary purpose is a criminal investigation, the heightened protections of the Fourth Amendment won't apply.

It seems obvious that with this lower standard, the FBI will try to use FISA as much as it can. And of course, with terrorism investigations that won't be difficult, because the terrorists are apparently sponsored or at least supported by foreign governments. This means that the fourth amendment rights will be significantly curtailed in many investigations of terrorist acts.

The significance of the breakdown of the distinction between intelligence and criminal investigations becomes apparent when you see the other expansions of government power under FISA in this bill. One provision that troubles me a great deal is a provision that permits the government under FISA to compel the production of records from any business regarding any person, if that information is sought in connection with an investigation of terrorism or espionage.

Now we're not talking here about travel records pertaining to a terrorist suspect, which we all can see can be highly relevant to an investigation of a terrorist plot. FISA already gives the FBI the power to get airline, train, hotel, car rental and other records of a suspect.

But under this bill, the government can compel the disclosure of the personal records of anyone—perhaps someone who worked with, or lived next door to, or went to school with, or sat on an airplane with, or has been seen in the company of, or whose phone number was called by—the target of the investigation.

And under this new provision all business records can be compelled, including those containing sensitive personal information like medical records from hospitals or doctors, or educational records, or records of what books someone has taken out of the library. This is an enormous expansion of authority, under a law that provides only minimal judicial supervision.

Under this provision, the government can apparently go on a fishing expedition and collect information on virtually anyone. All it has to allege in order to get an order for these records from the court is that the information is sought for an investigation of international terrorism or clandestine intelligence gathering. That's it. On that minimal showing in an ex parte application to a secret court, with no showing even that the information is relevant to the investigation, the government can lawfully compel a doctor or hospital to release medical records, or a library to release circulation records. This is a truly breathtaking expansion of police power.

Let me turn to a final area of real concern about this legislation, which I think brings us full circle to the cautions I expressed on the day after the attacks. There are two very troubling provisions dealing with our immigration laws in this bill.

First, the Administration's original proposal would have granted the Attorney General extraordinary powers to detain immigrants indefinitely, including legal permanent residents. The Attorney General could do so based on mere suspicion that the person is engaged in terrorism. I believe the Administration was really over-reaching here, and I am pleased that Senator Leahy was able to negotiate some protections. The Senate bill now requires the Attorney General to charge the immigrant within seven days with a criminal offense or immigration violation. In the event that the Attorney General does not charge the immigrant, the immigrant must be released.

While this protection is an improvement, the provision remains fundamentally flawed. Even with this seven-day charging requirement, the bill would nevertheless continue to permit the indefinite detention in two situations. First, immigrants who win their deportation cases could continue to be held if the Attorney General continues to have suspicions. Second, this provision creates a deep unfairness to immigrants who are found not to be deportable for terrorism but have an immigration status violation, such as overstaying a visa. If the immigration judge finds that they are eligible for relief from deportation, and therefore can stay in the country because, for example, they have longstanding family ties here, the Attorney General could continue to hold them.

Now, I am pleased that the final version of the legislation includes a few improvements over the bill that passed the Senate. In particular, the bill would require the Attorney General to review the detention decision every six months and would allow only the Attorney General or Deputy Attorney General, not lower level officials, to make that determination. While I am pleased these provisions are included in the bill, I believe it still falls short of meeting even basic constitutional standards of due process and fairness. The bill continues to allow the Attorney General to detain persons based on mere suspicion. Our system normally requires higher standards of proof for a deprivation of liberty. For example, deportation proceedings are subject to a clear and convincing evidence standard. Criminal convictions, of course, require proof beyond a reasonable doubt.

The bill also continues to deny detained persons a trial or hearing where the government would be required to prove that the person is, in fact, engaged in terrorist activity. This is unjust and inconsistent with the values our system of justice holds dearly.

Another provision in the bill that deeply troubles me allows the detention and deportation of people engaging in innocent associational activity. It would allow for the detention and deportation of individuals who provide lawful assistance to groups that are not even designated by the Secretary of State as terrorist organizations, but instead have engaged in vaguely defined "terrorist activity" sometime in the past. To avoid deportation, the immigrant is required to prove a negative: that he or she did not know, and should not have known, that the assistance would further terrorist activity.

This language creates a very real risk that truly innocent individuals could be deported for innocent associations with humanitarian or political groups that the government later chooses to regard as terrorist organizations. Groups that might fit this definition could include Operation Rescue, Greenpeace, and even the Northern Alliance fighting the Taliban in northern Afghanistan. This provision amounts to "guilt by association," which I believe violates the First Amendment.

And speaking of the First Amendment, under this bill, a lawful permanent resident who makes a controversial speech that the government deems to be supportive of terrorism might be barred from returning to his or her family after taking a trip abroad.

Despite assurances from the Administration at various points in this process that these provisions that implicate associational activity would be improved, there have been no changes in the bill on these points since it passed the Senate.

Now here's where my cautions in the aftermath of the terrorist attacks and my concern over the reach of the anti-terrorism bill come together. To the extent that the expansive new immigration powers that the bill grants to the Attorney General are subject to abuse, who do we think is most likely to bear the brunt of that abuse? It won't be immigrants from Ireland, it won't be immigrants from El Salvador or Nicaragua, it won't even be immigrants from Haiti or Africa. It will be immigrants from Arab, Muslim, and South Asian countries. In the wake of these terrible events, our government has been given vast new powers and they may fall most heavily on a minority of our population who already feel particularly acutely the pain of this disaster.

When concerns of this kind have been raised with the Administration and supporters of this bill they have told us, "don't worry, the FBI would never do that." I call on the Attorney General and the Justice Department to ensure that my fears are not borne out.

The anti-terrorism bill that we consider in the Senate today highlights the march of technology, and how that march cuts both for and against personal liberty. Justice Brandeis foresaw some of the future in a 1928 dissent, when he wrote:

"The progress of science in furnishing the Government with means of espionage is not likely to stop with wire-tapping. Ways may some day be developed by which the Government, without removing papers from secret drawers, can reproduce them in court, and by which it will be enabled to expose to a jury the most intimate occurrences of the home. . . . Can it be that the Constitution affords no protection against such invasions of individual security?"

We must grant law enforcement the tools that it needs to stop this terrible threat. But we must give them only those extraordinary tools that they need and that relate specifically to the task at hand. . . .

We in this body have a duty to analyze, to test, to weigh new laws that the zealous and often sincere advocates of security would suggest to us. This is what I have tried to do with this anti-terrorism bill. And that is why I will vote against this bill when the roll is called.

Protecting the safety of the American people is a solemn duty of the Congress; we must work tirelessly to prevent more tragedies like the devastating attacks of September 11th. We must prevent more children from losing their mothers, more wives from losing their husbands, and more firefighters from losing their heroic colleagues. But the Congress will fulfill its duty only when it protects both the American people and the freedoms at the foundation of American society. So let us preserve our heritage of basic rights. Let us practice as well as preach that liberty. And let us fight to maintain that freedom that we call America.

I yield the floor.

Source: Senator Feingold, Russ. Statement during Consideration of HR 3162 USA PATRIOT Act of 2001, October 25, 2001. Congressional Record-Senate, pp. S11019–23.

2001: PRESIDENT BUSH SIGNS THE USA PATRIOT ACT

The USA PATRIOT Act was one of the longest, most complex, and most controversial bills ever passed by Congress. Crafted in the weeks directly following the horrific September 11, 2001, terrorist attacks via hijacked commercial airliners on New York City and Washington, D.C., the legislation granted sweeping new surveillance powers to the federal government.

The process by which the final bill called the USA PATRIOT Act was created was highly unusual. Normally, bills are drafted and approved in the appropriate Senate and House committees (usually the judiciary committees) and then reported out for debate, amendments, and a full vote. But the PATRIOT Act was created at breakneck speed. It relied heavily on "unofficial" drafts supplied by White House and Justice Department officials from the administration of President George W. Bush. In fact, both the Senate and House ended up holding separate and parallel negotiations with administration officials over the bill.

On September 19th, representatives of the White House, Department of Justice, and both houses of Congress met in the Capitol to exchange legislative proposals. Representing the White House were Attorney General John Ashcroft, Assistant Attorney General Viet Dinh, White House Counsel Alberto Gonzales, and the Justice Department entourage. Among the senators present were Orrin Hatch (R-UT), Richard Shelby (R-AL), and Patrick Leahy (D-VT). House Majority Leader Richard Armey (R-TX) and John Conyers (D-MI) were among the representatives from the House.

Viet Dinh opened the meeting by handing out copies of the Justice Department's draft of a PATRIOT Act bill that represented the administration's desire for increased antiterrorism authority. The draft called for such measures as indefinite detention of any noncitizen who may "further or facilitate acts of terrorism." It also authorized unchecked sharing of grand jury and eavesdropping data throughout the government, permitted Internet service providers to allow the FBI to tap e-mail, and lowered the FISA standard for surveillance authority.

Discussions on a compromise draft quickly emerged and continued for several days. On September 30, Leahy reached a deal with White House Deputy Counsel Timothy Flanigan, who was representing Attorney General Ashcroft. The deal included an agreement that the government could not use illegally obtained evidence against U.S. citizens and that a court must review information before it was shared among intelligence and law enforcement agencies. But when Ashcroft himself came to Leahy's office to sign off on the agreement, he told Leahy that the deal was off without significant expansion of governmental authority. Leahy felt betrayed, but he ultimately acceded to Ashcroft's demands.

The bill that reached the Senate was virtually the same as the draft the Viet Dinh had passed out at the September 19th meeting in the Capitol. It had been sent directly to the Senate floor without a committee vote. Meanwhile, the House Judiciary Committee developed a more balanced PATRIOT Act bill that authorized new national security measures without sacrificing fundamental civil liberties. Late on October 3rd, the Judiciary Committee passed its bill, H.R. 2975, unanimously. On October 11th, the Senate passed the much tougher version of the bill that had been written by Bush's Justice Department. That night, without warning, the House substituted the Senate language for the original House language. The House Judiciary Committee was unaware that its unanimously approved bill had been replaced, and when the Senate bill reached the House floor, few members had even read it, and there was no opportunity for amendments. Despite protests about this turn of events, however, House members felt enormous public pressure to pass a national security bill in the wake of 9/11. As a result, the bill was passed by the House on Friday, October 12th, by a vote of 337–79. "What you need to know is the Patriot Act that I sponsored is not the Patriot Act that was passed," Conyers later complained in a radio interview with the Marc Steiner Show. *"How, in a time of urgency and crisis, could the Attorney General decide to become a legislative member and replace all 43 members of the House Judiciary Committee? It was so arrogant, so uncalled for. . . . It was a usurpation of the congressional prerogative."*

President Bush signed the USA PATRIOT Act into law in a public ceremony on October 26, 2001. His comments at the event follow:

Good morning and welcome to the White House. Today we take an essential step in defeating terrorism, while protecting the constitutional rights of all Americans. With my signature, this law will give intelligence and law enforcement officials important new tools to fight a present danger.

I commend the House and Senate for the hard work they put into this legislation. Members of Congress and their staffs spent long nights and weekends to get this important bill to my desk. I appreciate their efforts and bipartisanship in passing this new law.

I want to thank the Vice President and his staff for working hard to make sure this law was passed. I want to thank the Secretary of State and the Secretary of Treasury for being here, both of whom lead important parts of our war against terrorism. I want to thank Attorney General John Ashcroft for spending a lot of time on the Hill to make the case for a balanced piece of legislation. I want to thank the Director of the FBI and the Director of the CIA for waging an incredibly important part on the two-front war, one overseas and a front here at home. I want to thank Governor Tom Ridge for his leadership.

I want to thank the Members of Congress who are here on the stage, the leaders, on this impressive effort: Senator Hatch and Senator Leahy and Senator Sarbanes and Senator Graham and Senator Reid. I also want to thank Representative Porter

Goss, LaFalce, Oxley, and Sensenbrenner for their hard work. And I want to welcome the men and women of law enforcement who are here in the White House with us today, as well.

The changes, effective today, will help counter a threat like no other our Nation has ever faced. We've seen the enemy and the murder of thousands of innocent, unsuspecting people. They recognize no barrier of morality. They have no conscience. The terrorists cannot be reasoned with. Witness the recent anthrax attacks through our Postal Service.

Our country is grateful for the courage the Postal Service has shown during these difficult times. We mourn the loss of the lives of Thomas Morris and Joseph Curseen, postal workers who died in the line of duty. And our prayers go to their loved ones.

I want to assure postal workers that our Government is testing more than 200 postal facilities along the entire eastern corridor that may have been impacted. And we will move quickly to treat and protect workers where positive exposures are found.

But one thing is for certain: These terrorists must be pursued; they must be defeated; and they must be brought to justice. And that is the purpose of this legislation. Since the 11th of September, the men and women of our intelligence and law enforcement agencies have been relentless in their response to new and sudden challenges.

We have seen the horrors terrorists can inflict. We may never know what horrors our country was spared by the diligent and determined work of our police forces, the FBI, ATF agents, Federal marshals, custom officers, Secret Service, intelligence professionals, and local law enforcement officials. Under the most trying conditions, they are serving this country with excellence and often with bravery.

They deserve our full support and every means of help that we can provide. We're dealing with terrorists who operate by highly sophisticated methods and technologies, some of which were not even available when our existing laws were written. The bill before me takes account of the new realities and dangers posed by modern terrorists. It will help law enforcement to identify, to dismantle, to disrupt, and to punish terrorists before they strike.

For example, this legislation gives law enforcement officials better tools to put an end to financial counterfeiting, smuggling, and money laundering. Secondly, it gives intelligence operations and criminal operations the chance to operate not on separate tracks but to share vital information so necessary to disrupt a terrorist attack before it occurs.

As of today, we're changing the laws governing information sharing. And as importantly, we're changing the culture of our various agencies that fight terrorism.

Countering and investigating terrorist activity is the number one priority for both law enforcement and intelligence agencies.

Surveillance of communications is another essential tool to pursue and stop terrorists. The existing law was written in the era of rotary telephones. This new law that I sign today will allow surveillance of all communications used by terrorists, including e-mails, the Internet, and cell phones. As of today, we'll be able to better meet the technological challenges posed by this proliferation of communications technology.

Investigations are often slowed by limit on the reach of Federal search warrants. Law enforcement agencies have to get a new warrant for each new district they investigate, even when they're after the same suspect. Under this new law, warrants are valid across all districts and across all States.

And finally, the new legislation greatly enhances the penalties that will fall on terrorists or anyone who helps them. Current statutes deal more severely with drug traffickers than with terrorists. That changes today. We are enacting new and harsh penalties for possession of biological weapons. We're making it easier to seize the assets of groups and individuals involved in terrorism. The Government will have wider latitude in deporting known terrorists and their supporters. The statute of limitations on terrorist acts will be lengthened, as will prison sentences for terrorists.

This bill was carefully drafted and considered. Led by the Members of Congress on this stage and those seated in the audience, it was crafted with skill and care, determination and a spirit of bipartisanship for which the entire Nation is grateful. This bill met with an overwhelming—overwhelming—agreement in Congress because it upholds and respects the civil liberties guaranteed by our Constitution.

This legislation is essential not only to pursuing and punishing terrorists but also preventing more atrocities in the hands of the evil ones. This Government will enforce this law with all the urgency of a nation at war. The elected branches of our Government and both political parties are united in our resolve to find and stop and punish those who would do harm to the American people.

It is now my honor to sign into law the USA PATRIOT ACT of 2001.

Source: Bush, George W. 2001. "Remarks on Signing the USA PATRIOT ACT of 2001." October 26, 2001. *Public Papers of the Presidents of the United States: George W. Bush (2001, Book II).* Washington, DC: Government Printing Office, pp. 1306–07.

2001: SECTION 213 AND SECTION 215 OF THE USA PATRIOT ACT

Many provisions of the USA PATRIOT Act have been condemned by civil rights and privacy advocates and critics of overzealous government surveillance. Among the provisions that have attracted the most opprobrium are Sections 213 and 215. Section 213 authorized law enforcement agencies to conduct searches without notifying the target of the search that it was taking place. These so-called "sneak and peek" warrants have been defended by law enforcement authorities as a valuable counterterrorism tool, but data on the execution of these special warrants indicate that only a tiny percentage of "sneak and peek" warrants were requested for terrorism investigations.

Section 215 granted the FBI authority to order any person or entity to turn over "any tangible things" that the FBI defines as relevant to official investigations into terrorism or other "clandestine intelligence activities." This provision has also been described by supporters in the law enforcement and national security communities as vital to protecting the nation, but opponents say that it gives the FBI a frightening level of authority to spy on U.S. citizens and permanent residents. These critics emphasize that under Section 215 the FBI is not required to show reasonable or probable grounds to believe that the person or persons they are investigating are engaging in criminal or terrorist activity. They also point out that Section 215 is the statute that the U.S. government relies on to defend the legality of the massive phone records collection programs carried out by the National Security Agency (NSA). On May 7, 2015, however, a federal appeals court ruled in ACLU v. Clapper *that the Section 215 statute did not give the government legal authority to carry out such bulk collection of telephone records. It is widely expected that the federal government will appeal this adverse ruling.*

Following are both sections as written in the USA PATRIOT Act.

Sec. 213. Authority for Delaying Notice of the Execution of a Warrant

Section 3103a of Title 18, United States Code, is amended—. . . .

"(b) DELAY—With respect to the issuance of any warrant or court order under this section, or any other rule of law, to search for and seize any property or material that constitutes evidence of a criminal offense in violation of the laws of the United States, any notice required, or that may be required, to be given may be delayed if—

"(1) the court finds reasonable cause to believe that providing immediate notification of the execution of the warrant may have an adverse result (as defined in section 2705);

"(2) the warrant prohibits the seizure of any tangible property, any wire or electronic communication (as defined in section 2510), or, except as expressly provided in chapter 121, any stored wire or electronic information, except where the court finds reasonable necessity for the seizure; and

"(3) the warrant provides for the giving of such notice within a reasonable period of its execution, which period may thereafter be extended by the court for good cause shown.'"

Sec. 215. Access to Records and Other Items Under the Foreign Intelligence Surveillance Act

Title V of the Foreign Intelligence Surveillance Act of 1978 (50 U.S.C. 1861 et seq.) is amended by striking sections 501 through 503 and inserting the following:

Sec. 501. Access to Certain Business Records for Foreign Intelligence and International Terrorism Investigations

"(a)(1) The Director of the Federal Bureau of Investigation or a designee of the Director (whose rank shall be no lower than Assistant Special Agent in Charge) may make an application for an order requiring the production of any tangible things (including books, records, papers, documents, and other items) for an investigation to protect against international terrorism or clandestine intelligence activities, provided that such investigation of a United States person is not conducted solely upon the basis of activities protected by the first amendment to the Constitution. . . .

"(b) Each application under this section—

"(1) shall be made to—

"(A) a judge of the court established by section 103 (a); . . .

"(c)(1) Upon an application made pursuant to this section, the judge shall enter an ex parte order as requested, or as modified, approving the release of records if the judge finds that the application meets the requirements of this section.

"(2) An order under this subsection shall not disclose that it is issued for purposes of an investigation described in subsection (a).

"(d) No person shall disclose to any other person (other than those persons necessary to produce the tangible things under this section) that the Federal Bureau of Investigation has sought or obtained tangible things under this section. . . .

Source: USA PATRIOT Act of 2001, Public Law 107–56 (October 26, 2001).

2002: SECRET FISA COURT REJECTS A JUSTICE DEPARTMENT SURVEILLANCE REQUEST

The proceedings of the secret Foreign Intelligence Surveillance Act (FISA) court had never been revealed to Congress or the public since its inception in 1979, but in August 2002 a conflict between the court and the Justice Department over the implementation of the PATRIOT Act was revealed to the Senate Judiciary Committee.

The clash came about on May 17, 2002, when the FISA court denied a Justice Department surveillance request on the grounds that it inappropriately combined criminal investigations with foreign intelligence investigations in violation of the FISA and the U.S. Constitution. Up until that moment, the FISA court had approved over 13,000 surveillance orders and, according to available records, had never refused an application for surveillance. The Justice Department appealed the unexpected rebuke (which is excerpted below), thus launching the first formal challenge to the court in its history.

The crux of the dispute centered on the provision in the PATRIOT Act that allows FISA surveillance orders to be issued if foreign intelligence gathering is "a significant purpose" of the investigation. Previously, FISA orders could only be approved in investigations whose "primary purpose" was foreign intelligence gathering. The Justice Department interpreted the PATRIOT Act provision to mean that a FISA order could now be issued even if its primary purpose was a criminal investigation, but the FISA court determined that this approach contradicted the intent of the FISA statute. In its May 17 opinion, the court scaled back the PATRIOT Act's information-sharing provisions. It allowed criminal prosecutors to consult with intelligence investigators, but ruled that they could not steer investigations to further prosecutions or to control or direct foreign intelligence investigations. The court also stated that the Justice Department had not complied with the FISA's minimization procedures (the process by which surveillance information inadvertently acquired on nontargeted individuals is isolated and destroyed), whose purpose is "to protect the privacy of Americans in these highly intrusive surveillances and searches, 'consistent with the need of the United States to obtain, produce, and disseminate foreign intelligence information.'"

In announcing its intention to appeal the FISA court's ruling, the Justice Department portrayed the court's action as one that would unacceptably limit the authority granted to it by the USA PATRIOT Act.

To what court did the Justice Department appeal the FISA ruling? By statute, there exists a United States Foreign Intelligence Surveillance Court of Review (FISCR), but in its 25 years of existence, it had never issued a ruling. This secret FISA Court of Review consisted of three semi-retired appeals court judges selected by Supreme Court Chief Justice William Rehnquist.

On November 18, 2002, the FISCR issued a ruling endorsing the government's claim that the PATRIOT Act allows it to obtain a FISA surveillance order even where its primary purpose is a criminal investigation. "After a careful review of the briefs filed by the government and amici," stated the FISCR, "we conclude that FISA, as amended by the Patriot Act, supports the government's position, and that the restrictions imposed by the FISA court are not required by FISA or the Constitution." The reasoning by which the FISCR reversed the FISA court seemed to be the notion that 9/11 had imposed a virtually permanent state of emergency on the American people: "FISA's general programmatic purpose, to protect the nation against terrorists and espionage threats directed by foreign powers, has from its outset been distinguishable from 'ordinary crime control.' After the events of September 11, 2001, though, it is hard to imagine greater emergencies facing Americans than those experienced on that date. . . . Even without taking into account the President's inherent constitutional authority to conduct warrantless foreign intelligence surveillance, we think the procedures and government showings required under FISA, if they do not meet the minimum Fourth Amendment warrant standards, certainly come close. We, therefore, believe firmly, applying the balancing test drawn from Keith, that FISA as amended is constitutional because the surveillances it authorizes are reasonable" (United States Foreign Intelligence Surveillance Court of Review, November 18, 2002, www.fas.org/irp/agency/doj/fisa/fisc111802.html*).*

Under normal circumstances, the public would have no knowledge of the FISCR ruling or its deliberations. But because the initial FISA case had been revealed to Congress, the FISCR reversal was, in part, made public. The extraordinary ex parte proceedings were particularly interesting—though disturbing to some legal scholars. Only the Justice Department representatives and the three judges were allowed to participate. Civil liberties groups were allowed to submit written "amicus" briefs, but the judges left it to the Justice Department to decide whether those briefs should be considered at all. Justice Department lawyers raised no objection to the introduction of the briefs, but some legal scholars assert that the absence of participation by any defender of the FISA Court decision indicated that the FISCR ruling was not rendered impartially.

Foreign Intelligence Surveillance Court Memorandum Opinion

The Department of Justice has moved this Court to vacate the minimization and "wall" procedures in all cases now or ever before the Court, including this court's adoption of the Attorney General's July 1995 intelligence sharing procedures, which are not consistent with new intelligence sharing procedures submitted for approval with this motion. The Court has considered the Government's motion, the revised intelligence sharing procedures, and the supporting memorandum of law as required by the Foreign Intelligence surveillance Act (hereafter the FISA or the Act) at 50 U.S.C. §1805(a)(4) and §1824(a)(4) (hereafter omitting citations to 50 U.S.C.) to determine whether the proposed minimization procedures submitted with the Government's motion comport with the definition of minimization procedures under §1801(b) and §1821(4) of the Act. The Government's motion will be GRANTED, EXCEPT THAT THE PROCEDURES MUST BE MODIFIED IN PART. . . .

THEREFORE, because

- the procedures implemented by the Attorney General govern the minimization of electronic surveillance searches of U.S. persons;
- such intelligence and criminal investigations both target the same U.S. person;
- the information collected through FISA surveillances and searches is both foreign intelligence information and evidence of crime, depending upon who is using it;
- there are pervasive and invasive techniques for electronic surveillances and physical searches authorized under the FISA;
- surveillances and searches may be authorized for extensive periods of time;
- notice of surveillances and searches is not given to the targets unless they are prosecuted;
- the provisions in FISA constrain discovery and adversary hearings and require ex parte, in camera review of FISA surveillances and searches at criminal trial;
- the FISA, as opposed to TITLE III and Rule 41 searches, is the only tool readily available in these overlapping intelligence and criminal investigations;
- there are extensive provisions in the minimization procedures for dissemination of FISA intercepts and seizures to criminal prosecutors and for consultation and coordination with intelligence officials using the FISA;
- criminal prosecutors would, under the proposed procedures, no longer be prohibited from "directing or controlling" counterintelligence investigations involving use of the FISA *toward law enforcement objectives;* and
- criminal prosecutors would, under the proposed procedures, be empowered to direct the use of FISA surveillances and searches *toward law enforcement objectives* by advising FBI intelligence officials on the initiation, operation, continuation and expansion of FISA authority from this Court.

The Court *FINDS* that parts of section II.B of the minimization procedures submitted with the Government's motion are NOT reasonably designed, in light of their purposes and technique, "consistent with the need of the United States to obtain, produce, or disseminate foreign intelligence information" as defined in §1801(h) and §1821(4) of the Act.

THEREFORE, pursuant to this Court's authority under §1805(a) and §1824(a) to issue *ex parte* orders for electronic surveillances and physical searches "*as requested or as* modified," the Court herewith grants the Government's motion BUT MODIFIES the pertinent provisions of sections II.B. of the proposed minimization procedures as follows:. . . .

"Notwithstanding the foregoing, law enforcement officials shall not make recommendations to intelligence officials concerning the initiation, operation, continuation or expansion of FISA searches or surveillances. Additionally, the FBI and the Criminal Division shall ensure that law enforcement officials do not direct or control the use of the FISA procedures to enhance criminal prosecution, and that advice intended to preserve the option of a criminal prosecution does not inadvertently result in the Criminal Division's directing or controlling the investigation using FISA searches and surveillances toward law enforcement objectives."

These modifications are intended to bring the minimization procedures into accord with the language used in the FISA, and reinstate the bright line used in the 1995 procedures, on which the Court has relied. The purpose of minimization procedures as defined in the Act, is not to amend the statute, but to protect the privacy of Americans in these highly intrusive surveillances and searches, "consistent with the need of the United States to obtain, produce, and disseminate foreign intelligence information."

Source: Foreign Intelligence Surveillance Court Memorandum Opinion, May 17, 2002. www.fas.org/irp/agency/doj/fisa/fisc051702.html. Accessed September 21, 2015.

2002: THE SUPREME COURT SANCTIONS SCHOOL DRUG TESTING

In March 2002, the U.S. Supreme Court heard the case of Board of Education of Pottawatomie County v. Earls. *This case pivoted around drug testing requirements that had been adopted by the Tecumseh, Oklahoma, School District for all middle and high school students who wanted to engage in school-affiliated extracurricular activities. This policy was quickly challenged by two high school students and their parents as a violation of the students' Fourth Amendment rights. A district court sided with the school district, but an appeals court reversed that judgment, agreeing that the policy violated the students' constitutional rights. The case then wound its way to the U.S. Supreme Court.*

In a closely contested 5–4 vote decided on June 27, 2002, the Supreme Court ruled on behalf of the school district. The majority asserted that the district's drug policy program was constitutional because it met the definition of a "reasonable" governmental search. The majority opinion, written by Justice Clarence Thomas, is excerpted below—as is the dissent written by Justice Ruth Bader Ginsberg. Both opinions made extensive references to Vernonia School District v. Acton (1995), *an earlier case in which the Supreme Court had sanctioned a school district program of random urinalysis of student athletes.*

JUSTICE THOMAS delivered the opinion of the Court.

Because this Policy reasonably serves the School District's important interest in detecting and preventing drug use among its students, we hold that it is constitutional. . . .

Searches by public school officials, such as the collection of urine samples, implicate Fourth Amendment interests. We must therefore review the School District's Policy for "reasonableness," which is the touchstone of the constitutionality of a governmental search.

In the criminal context, reasonableness usually requires a showing of probable cause. The probable-cause standard, however, "is peculiarly related to criminal investigations" and may be unsuited to determining the reasonableness of administrative searches where the "Government seeks to *prevent* the development of hazardous conditions.". . . .

Given that the School District's Policy is not in any way related to the conduct of criminal investigations, respondents do not contend that the School District requires probable cause before testing students for drug use. Respondents instead argue that drug testing must be based at least on some level of individualized suspicion. . . . But we have long held that "the Fourth Amendment imposes no irreducible requirement of [individualized] suspicion.". . . . Therefore, in the context of safety and administrative regulations, a search unsupported by probable cause may be reasonable "when 'special needs, beyond the normal need for law enforcement, make the warrant and probable-cause requirement impracticable.'"

Significantly, this Court has previously held that "special needs" inhere in the public school context. While schoolchildren do not shed their constitutional rights when they enter the schoolhouse, "Fourth Amendment rights . . . are different in public schools than elsewhere; the 'reasonableness' inquiry cannot disregard the schools' custodial and tutelary responsibility for children." In particular, a finding of individualized suspicion may not be necessary when a school conducts drug testing. In *Vernonia*, this Court held that the suspicionless drug testing of athletes was constitutional. The Court, however, did not simply authorize all school drug testing, but rather conducted a fact-specific balancing of the intrusion on the children's Fourth Amendment rights against the promotion of legitimate governmental interests. Applying the principles of *Vernonia* to the somewhat different facts of this case, we conclude that Tecumseh's Policy is also constitutional.

We first consider the nature of the privacy interest allegedly compromised by the drug testing. . . .

A student's privacy interest is limited in a public school environment where the State is responsible for maintaining discipline, health, and safety. Schoolchildren are routinely required to submit to physical examinations and vaccinations against disease. Securing order in the school environment sometimes requires that students be subjected to greater controls than those appropriate for adults.

Respondents argue that because children participating in nonathletic extracurricular activities are not subject to regular physicals and communal undress, they have a stronger expectation of privacy than the athletes tested in *Vernonia*. This distinction, however, was not essential to our decision in *Vernonia*, which depended primarily upon the school's custodial responsibility and authority.

In any event, students who participate in competitive extracurricular activities voluntarily subject themselves to many of the same intrusions on their privacy as do athletes. Some of these clubs and activities require occasional off-campus travel and communal undress. All of them have their own rules and requirements for participating students that do not apply to the student body as a whole. . . . This regulation of extracurricular activities further diminishes the expectation of privacy among schoolchildren.

Next, we consider the character of the intrusion imposed by the Policy. Urination is "an excretory function traditionally shielded by great privacy." But the "degree of intrusion" on one's privacy caused by collecting a urine sample "depends upon the manner in which production of the urine sample is monitored."

Under the Policy, a faculty monitor waits outside the closed restroom stall for the student to produce a sample and must "listen for the normal sounds of urination in order to guard against tampered specimens and to insure an accurate chain of custody." The monitor then pours the sample into two bottles that are sealed and placed into a mailing pouch along with a consent form signed by the student. This procedure is virtually identical to that reviewed in *Vernonia*, except that it additionally protects privacy by allowing male students to produce their samples behind a closed stall. Given that we considered the method of collection in *Vernonia* a "negligible" intrusion, the method here is even less problematic. In addition, the Policy clearly requires that the test results be kept in confidential files separate from a student's other educational records and released to school personnel only on a "need to know" basis. . . .

Moreover, the test results are not turned over to any law enforcement authority. Nor do the test results here lead to the imposition of discipline or have any academic consequences. Rather, the only consequence of a failed drug test is to limit the student's privilege of participating in extracurricular activities. Indeed, a student may test positive for drugs twice and still be allowed to participate in extracurricular activities. . . .

Given the minimally intrusive nature of the sample collection and the limited uses to which the test results are put, we conclude that the invasion of students' privacy is not significant.

Finally, this Court must consider the nature and immediacy of the government's concerns and the efficacy of the Policy in meeting them. This Court has already articulated in detail the importance of the governmental concern in preventing drug use by schoolchildren. The drug abuse problem among our Nation's youth has hardly abated since *Vernonia* was decided in 1995. In fact, evidence suggests that it has only grown worse. . . . The health and safety risks identified in *Vernonia* apply with equal force to Tecumseh's children. Indeed, the nationwide drug epidemic makes the war against drugs a pressing concern in every school. Additionally, the School District in this case has presented specific evidence of drug use at Tecumseh schools. Teachers testified that they had seen students who appeared to be under the influence of drugs and that they had heard students speaking openly about using drugs. A drug dog found marijuana cigarettes near the school parking lot. Police officers once found drugs or drug paraphernalia in a car driven by a Future Farmers of America member. And the school board president reported that people in the community were calling the board to discuss the "drug situation." . . .

Respondents consider the proffered evidence insufficient and argue that there is no "real and immediate interest" to justify a policy of drug testing nonathletes. We have recognized, however, that "[a] demonstrated problem of drug abuse . . . [is] not in all cases necessary to the validity of a testing regime," but that some showing does "shore up an assertion of special need for a suspicionless general search program." The School District has provided sufficient evidence to shore up the need for its drug testing program. Furthermore, this Court has not required a particularized or pervasive drug problem before allowing the government to conduct suspicionless drug testing. For instance, in [*National Treasury Employees Union v.*] *Von Raab* the Court upheld the drug testing of customs officials on a purely preventive basis, without any documented history of drug use by such officials. . . . Likewise, the need to prevent and deter the substantial harm of childhood drug use provides the necessary immediacy for a school testing policy. Indeed, it would make little sense to require a school district to wait for a substantial portion of its students to begin using drugs before it was allowed to institute a drug testing program designed to deter drug use. Given the nationwide epidemic of drug use, and the evidence of increased drug use in Tecumseh schools, it was entirely reasonable for the School District to enact this particular drug testing policy. We reject the Court of Appeals' novel test that "any district seeking to impose a random suspicionless drug testing policy as a condition to participation in a school activity must demonstrate that there is some identifiable drug abuse problem among a sufficient number of those subject to the testing, such that testing that group of students will actually redress its drug problem." Among other problems, it would be difficult to administer such a test. As we cannot articulate a threshold level of drug use that would suffice to justify a drug testing program for schoolchildren, we refuse to fashion what would in effect be a constitutional quantum of drug use necessary to show a "drug problem.". . .

We also reject respondents' argument that drug testing must presumptively be based upon an individualized reasonable suspicion of wrongdoing because such a testing regime would be less intrusive. In this context, the Fourth Amendment does not require a finding of individualized suspicion, and we decline to impose such a requirement on schools attempting to prevent and detect drug use by students. Moreover, we question whether testing based on individualized suspicion in fact would be less intrusive. Such a regime would place an additional burden on public school teachers who are already tasked with the difficult job of maintaining order and discipline. A program of individualized suspicion might unfairly target members of unpopular groups. The fear of lawsuits resulting from such targeted searches may chill enforcement of the program, rendering it ineffective in combating drug use. . . .

Finally, we find that testing students who participate in extracurricular activities is a reasonably effective means of addressing the School District's legitimate concerns in preventing, deterring, and detecting drug use. . . . In upholding the constitutionality of the Policy, we express no opinion as to its wisdom. Rather, we hold only that Tecumseh's Policy is a reasonable means of furthering the School District's important interest in preventing and deterring drug use among its schoolchildren. Accordingly, we reverse the judgment of the Court of Appeals. *It is so ordered.*

JUSTICE GINSBURG, with whom JUSTICE STEVENS, JUSTICE O'CONNOR, and JUSTICE SOUTER join, dissenting.

Seven years ago, in *Vernonia School Dist. 47J v. Acton,* this Court determined that a school district's policy of randomly testing the urine of its student athletes for illicit drugs did not violate the Fourth Amendment. In so ruling, the Court emphasized that drug use "increased the risk of sports-related injury" and that Vernonia's athletes were the "leaders" of an aggressive local "drug culture" that had reached "'epidemic proportions.'" Today, the Court relies upon *Vernonia* to permit a school district with a drug problem its superintendent repeatedly described as "not . . . major," to test the urine of an academic team member solely by reason of her participation in a nonathletic, competitive extracurricular activity—participation associated with neither special dangers from, nor particular predilections for, drug use. . . . The particular testing program upheld today is not reasonable, it is capricious, even perverse: Petitioners' policy targets for testing a student population least likely to be at risk from illicit drugs and their damaging effects. I therefore dissent. . . . This case presents circumstances dispositively different from those of *Vernonia*. True, as the Court stresses, Tecumseh students participating in competitive extracurricular activities other than athletics share two relevant characteristics with the athletes of *Vernonia.* First, both groups attend public schools. . . . Concern for student health and safety is basic to the school's caretaking, and it is undeniable that "drug use carries a variety of health risks for children, including death from overdose."

Those risks, however, are present for *all* schoolchildren. *Vernonia* cannot be read to endorse invasive and suspicionless drug testing of all students upon any evidence of drug use, solely because drugs jeopardize the life and health of those who use them. Many children, like many adults, engage in dangerous activities on their own time; that the children are enrolled in school scarcely allows government to monitor all such activities. If a student has a reasonable subjective expectation of privacy in the personal items she brings to school, surely she has a similar expectation regarding the chemical composition of her urine. Had the *Vernonia* Court agreed that public school attendance, in and of itself, permitted the State to test each student's blood or urine for drugs, the opinion in *Vernonia* could have saved many words.

The second commonality to which the Court points is the voluntary character of both interscholastic athletics and other competitive extracurricular activities. . . .

The comparison is enlightening. While extracurricular activities are "voluntary" in the sense that they are not required for graduation, they are part of the school's educational program; for that reason, the petitioner (hereinafter School District) is justified in expending public resources to make them available. Participation in such activities is a key component of school life, essential in reality for students applying to college, and, for all participants, a significant contributor to the breadth and quality of the educational experience. Students "volunteer" for extracurricular pursuits in the same way they might volunteer for honors classes: They subject themselves to additional requirements, but they do so in order to take full advantage of the education offered them. . . . .

Voluntary participation in athletics has a distinctly different dimension: Schools regulate student athletes discretely because competitive school sports by their nature require communal undress and, more important, expose students to physical risks that schools have a duty to mitigate. For the very reason that schools cannot offer a program of competitive athletics without intimately affecting the privacy of students, *Vernonia* reasonably analogized school athletes to "adults who choose to participate in a closely regulated industry." Interscholastic athletics similarly require close safety and health regulation; a school's choir, band, and academic team do not.

Vernonia initially considered "the nature of the privacy interest upon which the search [there] at issue intruded." The Court emphasized that student athletes' expectations of privacy are necessarily attenuated. . . . Competitive extracurricular activities other than athletics, however, serve students of all manner: the modest and shy along with the bold and uninhibited. Activities of the kind plaintiff-respondent Lindsay Earls pursued—choir, show choir, marching band, and academic team—afford opportunities to gain self-assurance, to "come to know faculty members in a less formal setting than the typical classroom," and to acquire "positive social supports and networks [that] play a critical role in periods of heightened stress."

On "occasional out-of-town trips," students like Lindsay Earls "must sleep together in communal settings and use communal bathrooms." But those situations are hardly equivalent to the routine communal undress associated with athletics; the School District itself admits that when such trips occur, "public-like restroom facilities," which presumably include enclosed stalls, are ordinarily available for changing, and that "more modest students" find other ways to maintain their privacy.

Finally, the "nature and immediacy of the governmental concern," faced by the Vernonia School District dwarfed that confronting Tecumseh administrators. Vernonia initiated its drug testing policy in response to an alarming situation: "[A] large segment of the student body, particularly those involved in interscholastic athletics, was in a state of rebellion . . . fueled by alcohol and drug abuse as well as the student[s'] misperceptions about the drug culture." Tecumseh, by contrast, repeatedly reported to the Federal Government during the period leading up to the adoption of the policy that "types of drugs [other than alcohol and tobacco] including controlled dangerous substances, are present [in the schools] but have not identified themselves as major problems at this time.". . .

Not only did the Vernonia and Tecumseh districts confront drug problems of distinctly different magnitudes, they also chose different solutions: Vernonia limited its policy to athletes; Tecumseh indiscriminately subjected to testing all participants in competitive extracurricular activities. Urging that "the safety interest furthered by drug testing is undoubtedly substantial for all children, athletes and nonathletes alike," the Court cuts out an element essential to the *Vernonia* judgment. Citing medical literature on the effects of combining illicit drug use with physical exertion, the *Vernonia* Court emphasized that "the particular drugs screened by [Vernonia's] Policy have been demonstrated to pose substantial physical risks to athletes." . . .

Notwithstanding nightmarish images of out-of-control flatware, livestock run amok, and colliding tubas disturbing the peace and quiet of Tecumseh, the great majority of students the School District seeks to test in truth are engaged in activities that are not safety sensitive to an unusual degree. . . .

Nationwide, students who participate in extracurricular activities are significantly less likely to develop substance abuse problems than are their less-involved peers. Even if students might be deterred from drug use in order to preserve their extracurricular eligibility, it is at least as likely that other students might forgo their extracurricular involvement in order to avoid detection of their drug use. Tecumseh's policy thus falls short doubly if deterrence is its aim: It invades the privacy of students who need deterrence least, and risks steering students at greatest risk for substance abuse away from extracurricular involvement that potentially may palliate drug problems. To summarize, this case resembles *Vernonia* only in that the School Districts in both cases conditioned engagement in activities outside the obligatory curriculum on random subjection to urinalysis. The defining characteristics of the two programs, however, are entirely dissimilar. The Vernonia district sought to test a subpopulation of students distinguished by their reduced expectation of privacy, their special susceptibility to drug-related injury, and their heavy involvement with drug use. The Tecumseh district seeks to test a much larger population associated with none of these factors. It does so, moreover, without carefully safeguarding student confidentiality and without regard to the program's untoward effects. A program so sweeping is not sheltered by *Vernonia;* its unreasonable reach renders it impermissible under the Fourth Amendment.

Source: Justice Thomas, Clarence. Opinion of the Court; Justice Ginsberg, Ruth Bader. Dissent. *Board of Education of Independent School District No. 92 of Pottawatomie County et al v. Earls,* 536 U.S. 822. Decided June 27, 2002. United States Reports, Volume 536, June–October 2002.

2002: PRESIDENT BUSH SIGNS THE HOMELAND SECURITY ACT

In the immediate aftermath of the September 11, 2001, terrorist attacks on the United States, the George W. Bush administration seized on the idea of forming a Department of Homeland Security to help guard against future attacks on American soil. The formation and authorization of this agency, which had actually been suggested by the U.S. Commission on National Security/21st Century several months before the attacks, became a top priority of the Bush administration.

Passage of legislation that would formally create the Homeland Security Department was contentious at times, as lawmakers and security experts debated the appropriate scope and reach. The inclusion of controversial riders that stripped thousands of government workers to be included under the DHS of some of their employment rights attracted fire as well. Ultimately, however, public support for the creation of the department, combined with intense lobbying from the Bush administration, was sufficient to assure passage. On November 25, 2002, Bush formally signed the Homeland Security Act authorizing the creation of the DHS. The legislation authorized the integration of all or part of 22 different agencies into a single cabinet-level department under the DHS banner, including divisions within the transportation, justice, energy, treasury, and agriculture departments. Prominent agencies that became part of the DHS included the Secret Service, Coast Guard, Customs Service, Immigration and Naturalization Service, Transportation Security Administration, and the Federal Emergency Management Agency. The DHS formally opened its doors on March 1, 2003, and it presently ranks as the third-largest cabinet department in the U.S. government in terms of employees, behind only the departments of Defense and Veterans Affairs.

Following is the text of President Bush's remarks upon signing the act into law on November 25, 2002.

Today we are taking historic action to defend the United States and protect our citizens against the dangers of a new era. With my signature, this act of Congress will create a new Department of Homeland Security, ensuring that our efforts to defend this country are comprehensive and united.

The new Department will analyze threats, will guard our borders and airports, protect our critical infrastructure, and coordinate the response of our Nation to future emergencies. The Department of Homeland Security will focus the full resources of the American Government on the safety of the American people. This essential reform was carefully considered by Congress and enacted with strong bipartisan majorities. . . .

From the morning of September the 11th, 2001, to this hour, America has been engaged in an unprecedented effort to defend our freedom and our security. We're fighting a war against terror with all our resources, and we're determined to win.

With the help of many nations, with the help of 90 nations, we're tracking terrorist activity; we're freezing terrorist finances; we're disrupting terrorist plots; we're shutting down terrorist camps; we're on the hunt, one person at a time. Many terrorists are now being interrogated. Many terrorists have been killed. We've liberated a country.

We recognize our greatest security is found in the relentless pursuit of these coldblooded killers. Yet, because terrorists are targeting America, the front of the new war is here in America. Our life changed and changed in dramatic fashion on September the 11th, 2001.

In the last 14 months, every level of our Government has taken steps to be better prepared against a terrorist attack. We understand the nature of the enemy. We understand they hate us because of what we love. We're doing everything we can to enhance security at our airports and power-plants and border crossings. We've deployed detection equipment to look for weapons of mass destruction. We've given law enforcement better tools to detect and disrupt terrorist cells which might be hiding in our own country.

And through separate legislation I signed earlier today, we will strengthen security at our Nation's 361 seaports, adding port security agents, requiring ships to provide more information about the cargo, crew, and passengers they carry. And I want to thank the Members of Congress for working hard on this important piece of legislation as well.

The Homeland Security Act of 2002 takes the next critical steps in defending our country. The continuing threat of terrorism, the threat of mass murder on our own soil, will be met with a unified, effective response. Dozens of agencies charged with homeland security will now be located within one Cabinet Department with the mandate and legal authority to protect our people. America will be better able to respond to any future attacks, to reduce our vulnerability and, most important, prevent the terrorists from taking innocent American lives.

The Department of Homeland Security will have nearly 170,000 employees, dedicated professionals who will wake up each morning with the overriding duty of protecting their fellow citizens. As Federal workers, they have rights, and those rights will be fully protected. And I'm grateful that the Congress listened to my concerns and retained the authority of the President to put the right people in the right place at the right time in the defense of our country.

I've great confidence in the men and women who will serve in this Department and in the man I've asked to lead it. As I prepare to sign this bill into law, I am pleased to announce that I will nominate Governor Tom Ridge as our Nation's first Secretary of Homeland Security. Americans know Tom as an experienced public servant and as the leader of our homeland security efforts since last year. Tom accepted that assignment in urgent circumstances, resigning as the Governor of Pennsylvania to organize the White House Office of Homeland Security and to develop a comprehensive strategy to protect the American people. He's done a superb job. He's the right man for this new and great responsibility.

We're going to put together a fine team to work with Tom. The Secretary of the Navy, Gordon England, will be nominated for the post of Deputy Secretary. And Asa Hutchinson of Arkansas, now the Administrator of the Drug Enforcement Administration, will be nominated to serve as Under Secretary for Border and Transportation Security.

The Secretary-designate and his team have an immense task ahead of them. Setting up the Department of Homeland Security will involve the most extensive reorganization of the Federal Government since Harry Truman signed the National Security Act. To succeed in their mission, leaders of the new Department must change the culture of many diverse agencies, directing all of them toward the principal objective of protecting the American people. The effort will take time and focus and steady resolve. It will also require full support from both the administration and the Congress. Adjustments will be needed along the way. Yet this is pressing business, and the hard work of building a new Department begins today.

When the Department of Homeland Security is fully operational, it will enhance the safety of our people in very practical ways. First, this new Department will analyze intelligence information on terror threats collected by the CIA, the FBI, the National Security Agency, and others. The Department will match this intelligence against the Nation's vulnerabilities and work with other agencies and the private sector and State and local governments to harden America's defenses against terror.

Second, the Department will gather and focus all our efforts to face the challenge of cyberterrorism and the even worse danger of nuclear, chemical, and biological terrorism. This Department will be charged with encouraging research on new technologies that can detect these threats in time to prevent an attack.

Third, State and local governments will be able to turn for help and information to one Federal domestic security agency, instead of more than 20 agencies that currently divide these responsibilities. This will help our local governments work in concert with the Federal Government for the sake of all the people of America.

Fourth, the new Department will bring together the agencies responsible for border, coastline, and transportation security. There will be a coordinated effort to safeguard our transportation systems and to secure the border so that we're better able to protect our citizens and welcome our friends.

Fifth, the Department will work with State and local officials to prepare our response to any future terrorist attack that may come. We have found that the first hours and even the first minutes after the attack can be crucial in saving lives, and our first-responders need the carefully planned and drilled strategies that will make their work effective.

The Department of Homeland Security will also end a great deal of duplication and overlapping responsibilities. Our objective is to spend less on administrators in offices and more on working agents in the field, less on overhead and more on protecting our neighborhoods and borders and waters and skies from terrorists.

With a vast nation to defend, we can neither predict nor prevent every conceivable attack. And in a free and open society, no Department of Government can completely guarantee our safety against ruthless killers who move and plot in shadows. Yet our Government will take every possible measure to safeguard our country and our people.

We're fighting a new kind of war against determined enemies. And public servants long into the future will bear the responsibility to defend Americans against terror. This administration and this Congress have the duty of putting that system into place. We will fulfill that duty. With the Homeland Security Act, we're doing everything we can to protect America. We're showing the resolve of this great Nation to defend our freedom, our security, and our way of life.

It's now my privilege to sign the Homeland Security Act of 2002.

Source: Bush, George W. 2002. "Remarks on Signing the Homeland Security Act of 2002." November 25, 2002. *Public Papers of the Presidents of the United States: George W. Bush (2002, Book II)*. Washington, DC: Government Printing Office, pp. 2128–31.

2003: THE AMERICAN LIBRARY ASSOCIATION ISSUES A RESOLUTION ON PRIVACY AND CIVIL LIBERTIES

Ever since the USA PATRIOT Act was signed into law by President George W. Bush in October 2001, the American Library Association (ALA) has expressed deep concerns about its impact on civil liberties and the sweeping powers it gave the federal government to conduct surveillance of private citizens. A long-time champion of privacy rights and the free and unfettered exchange of ideas and knowledge, the ALA believed that many provisions contained in the PATRIOT Act could and would be used in ways that violated constitutional protections. A representative summary of ALA sentiments about the PATRIOT Act can be found in its "Resolution on the USA Patriot Act and Related Measures That Infringe on the Rights of Library Users," which was adopted by the ALA Council on January 29, 2003.

WHEREAS, The American Library Association affirms the responsibility of the leaders of the United States to protect and preserve the freedoms that are the foundation of our democracy; and

WHEREAS, Libraries are a critical force for promoting the free flow and unimpeded distribution of knowledge and information for individuals, institutions, and communities; and

WHEREAS, The American Library Association holds that suppression of ideas undermines a democratic society; and

WHEREAS, Privacy is essential to the exercise of free speech, free thought, and free association; and, in a library, the subject of users' interests should not be examined or scrutinized by others; and

WHEREAS, Certain provisions of the USA PATRIOT Act, the revised Attorney General Guidelines to the Federal Bureau of Investigation, and other related measures expand the authority of the federal government to investigate citizens and non-citizens, to engage in surveillance, and to threaten civil rights and liberties guaranteed under the United States Constitution and Bill of Rights; and

WHEREAS, The USA PATRIOT Act and other recently enacted laws, regulations, and guidelines increase the likelihood that the activities of library users, including their use of computers to browse the Web or access e-mail, may be under government surveillance without their knowledge or consent; now, therefore, be it

RESOLVED, That the American Library Association opposes any use of governmental power to suppress the free and open exchange of knowledge and information or to intimidate individuals exercising free inquiry; and, be it further

RESOLVED, That the American Library Association encourages all librarians, library administrators, library governing bodies, and library advocates to educate their users, staff, and communities about the process for compliance with the USA

PATRIOT Act and other related measures and about the dangers to individual privacy and the confidentiality of library records resulting from those measures; and, be it further

RESOLVED, That the American Library Association urges librarians everywhere to defend and support user privacy and free and open access to knowledge and information; and, be it further

RESOLVED, That the American Library Association will work with other organizations, as appropriate, to protect the rights of inquiry and free expression; and, be it further

RESOLVED, That the American Library Association will take actions as appropriate to obtain and publicize information about the surveillance of libraries and library users by law enforcement agencies and to assess the impact on library users and their communities; and, be it further

RESOLVED, That the American Library Association urges all libraries to adopt and implement patron privacy and record retention policies that affirm that "the collection of personally identifiable information should only be a matter of routine or policy when necessary for the fulfillment of the mission of the library"; and, be it further

RESOLVED, That the American Library Association considers sections of the USA PATRIOT Act are a present danger to the constitutional rights and privacy rights of library users and urges the United States Congress to:

1. provide active oversight of the implementation of the USA PATRIOT Act and other related measures, and the revised Attorney General Guidelines to the Federal Bureau of Investigation;
2. hold hearings to determine the extent of the surveillance on library users and their communities; and
3. amend or change the sections of these laws and the guidelines that threaten or abridge the rights of inquiry and free expression; and, be it further

RESOLVED, That this resolution be forwarded to the President of the United States, to the Attorney General of the United States, to Members of both Houses of Congress, to the library community, and to others as appropriate.

Adopted by the ALA Council, January 29, 2003

Source: ALA Council. "Resolution on the USA PATRIOT Act and Related Measures That Infringe on the Rights of Library Users." January 29, 2003. Used by permission of the American Library Association.

2003: REPRESENTATIVE SANDERS INTRODUCES THE FREEDOM TO READ PROTECTION ACT

On March 6, 2003, Independent Congressman Bernie Sanders of Vermont (who since 2007 has served in Washington as one of the state's two U.S. senators), introduced the first major legislative attempt to roll back some of the vast powers granted to the executive branch in the 2001 USA PATRIOT Act.

The Freedom to Read Protection Act (H.R. 1157), which took special aim at Section 215 of the PATRIOT Act, was actually first drafted in response to an "open letter" signed by two-thirds of Vermont's independent booksellers and nearly 200 librarians from across the state. Thirty-two groups representing booksellers, librarians, book publishers, authors, and others joined several companies, including Barnes and Noble and Borders, in issuing a statement supporting H.R. 1157. Judith Krug, executive director of the American Library Association's (ALA) Office for Intellectual Freedom, said, "Protecting the confidentiality of one's use of the library is of primary concern to librarians. Rep. Sanders' bill would restore this core value of librarianship." Chris Finan, president of the American Booksellers for Free Expression (ABFFE), echoed that view: "The book community is united in believing that Section 215 of the Patriot Act threatens First Amendment freedom by making people afraid that their purchase or borrowing records may be monitored by the government."

The Sanders bill sought to modify Section 215 by returning to the standard under which the FBI had obtained library and bookstore records prior to the passage of the PATRIOT Act. The FBI would still have access to such records through the usual court-ordered search warrant or subpoena, but it would be required to provide "specific and articulable facts" supporting the belief that the target of the search was an agent of a foreign power. The PATRIOT Act had lowered that standard by allowing the FBI to seize "any tangible thing" from anyone, not just a foreign agent, and requiring the FBI to show only that the warrant was "relevant" to a counterintelligence investigation. Sanders explained in the Los Angeles Times *that his Freedom to Read Protection Act would ensure that FBI agents no longer had the authority to "engage in fishing expeditions to see what Americans read."*

Despite acquiring over 150 cosponsors, H.R.1157 languished in two different House committees for over a year. Finally, on July 8, 2004, Rep. Sanders tried an end run around hostile Republican chairmen by inserting language into a $39.8-billion appropriations bill that would bar the use of any of those funds to conduct surveillance under Section 215 of the PATRIOT Act. Despite a threatened White House veto, the Sanders provision, called the Freedom to Read Amendment, appeared to have broad support on the House floor, leading at one point in the voting by 219–210. But Republican leaders arbitrarily extended the allotted voting *time to allow them to reign in dissident party members. Irate Democrat members shouted in unison, "Shame, shame, shame," but the Republican leadership succeeded in bringing the vote down to a 210–210 tie, thus defeating the Sanders amendment. Afterwards, a disconsolate Sanders said that "I find it ironic that, on an amendment designed to protect American democracy and our constitutional rights, the Republican leadership in the House had to rig the vote and subvert the democratic process in order to prevail." Rep. Butch Otter, a conservative Republican from Idaho who cosponsored the amendment, said, "You win some, and some get stolen" ("House Rejects Effort to Curb PATRIOT Act's Section 215," American Libraries Online, July 9, 2004,* www.ala.org/ala/alonline/currentnews/newsarchive/alnews2004*).*

The defeat of the Freedom to Read Amendment foreshadowed a major battle in Congress during the 2005 debate on reauthorization of the PATRIOT Act's sunsetted provisions, including Section 215. When Sanders announced on March 9, 2005, that he would reintroduce the original Freedom to Read Protection Act, few thought that he could resurrect the support needed for passage. Yet, on June 15, 2005, the House approved the Sanders bill 238–187, with the support of 38 Republicans.

Sanders' victory was short-lived, however. As Congress began hearings on reauthorization of the full PATRIOT Act, defenders of Section 215 and other controversial PATRIOT Act provisions went on the offensive. On July 21, 2005, the House approved legislation that would make permanent 14 of the 16 expiring provisions of the PATRIOT Act. Section 215 was not made permanent in the House bill, but it was given a lengthy ten-year reauthorization, and none of the changes sought by Sanders were approved. This was essentially the end of the trail for the Freedom to Read Protection Act. The Senate would later make minor changes to the House bill, but the provisions of Section 215 that had been targeted by Sanders' bill remained untouched.

Following are remarks from a press conference that Sanders held on March 6, 2003, the day that he first unveiled his Freedom to Read Protection Act.

Good afternoon, and thank you for joining us here today to announce the introduction of the Freedom to Read Protection Act—legislation which will protect libraries, bookstores and their patrons from unjustified government surveillance into what books Americans are reading and buying, and what Web sites they may be visiting when using a library computer.

Let me begin by thanking the Members of Congress who have joined me here today. I also want to thank Chris Finan, president of the American Booksellers Foundations for Free Expression, and Emily Sheketoff, executive director of the American Library Association's Washington Office, for joining us. I am also delighted that Trina Magi—a librarian from the University of Vermont—and Linda Ramsdell, a bookstore owner from Hardwick, Vermont, who is the President of the New England Booksellers Association, are here with us today.

Let me also congratulate the 62 cities and towns all across this country that have passed resolutions on this issue—and that number is growing rapidly. That effort is being coordinated by the Bill of Rights Defense Committee, which understands that civil liberties and constitutional rights are not only a national issue, but also a local issue. I also want to thank the editorial boards of the many newspapers all over this country who have spoken out on this freedom to read issue—including the *Los Angeles Times*, the *Detroit Free Press*, the *Honolulu Observer*, the *Providence Journal-Bulletin*, the *Caledonia Record*, and the *Valley News*.

The tri-partisan legislation we are introducing today—called the Freedom to Read Protection Act—would protect the privacy and First Amendment rights of American citizens against unnecessary government intrusion. Specifically, this legislation will exempt libraries and bookstores from Section 215 of the so-called "Patriot Act." The Freedom to Read Protection Act is being introduced by 24 members of Congress including Republican Ron Paul of Texas, and Congressman John Conyers, the Ranking Member of the House Judiciary Committee. They are both unable to join us today, but I do want to recognize their support and leadership in protecting civil liberties. I am confident that in the days and weeks to come we will add many more cosponsors.

One of the cornerstones of our democracy is the right of Americans to criticize their government, and to read printed materials without fear of government monitoring and intrusion.

Yes, all of us are concerned about terrorism and all of us are determined to do all that we can to protect the American people from another terrorist attack. But, the threat of terrorism must not be used as an excuse by the government to intrude on our basic constitutional rights. We can fight terrorism, but we can do it at the same time as we protect the civil liberties that have made our country great.

Unfortunately, the Patriot Act has changed all that. Section 215 of the Patriot Act greatly expanded the FBI's ability to get records from all businesses, including libraries and booksellers, without meeting the traditional standard needed to get a search warrant in the United States.

This is a very dangerous situation. Today, all the FBI has to claim is that the information they want is somehow relevant to an investigation to protect against international terrorism. This is an extremely low threshold for government intrusion, and average Americans should be extremely concerned.

The reason they should care is that Section 215 does not just apply to terrorists, or even foreigners or agents of foreign powers. Under Section 215 of the Patriot Act, the person whose records are being searched by the FBI can be anyone. The

FBI doesn't even have to say that it believes the person is involved in criminal activity or that the person is connected to a foreign power.

Even more frightening, the FBI can investigate American citizens based in part on an American's exercise of his or her First Amendment rights, such as writing a letter to the editor of a newspaper or reading books the government may not approve of.

And the traditional legal protections, which have been embodied in our Constitution for hundreds of years, no longer apply. The government can gain access to our reading records through the secret FISA court, which was created by the Foreign Intelligence Surveillance Act in 1978, and which is off limits to the public. There's no way to know how many times the FBI has spied on library or bookseller records or whose records they have reviewed.

In fact, Section 215 prevents librarians and booksellers from telling their customers that their privacy has been violated. Who would have thought that in 21st century America, the government could gain access to library circulation records and bookseller customer records with no evidence that the person whose records they are getting is involved in any wrongdoing, that all of this would be handled through a secret government court, and that the librarians and booksellers would be compelled by the law not to let anyone know that the government had swooped in to get their records?

Now, some may ask how the federal government is using this new power. Members of Congress on both sides of the aisle are also interested in that question and have pressured the Justice Department to show how they are using these new powers. The information they have received after months of badgering the Department is inadequate. The Justice Department claimed most of the information regarding libraries and bookstores was "confidential," and could not be provided. This past October, several national organizations, including the American Booksellers Association, filed a Freedom of Information Act request to get statistical information, such as how many times the government has used its expanded surveillance authority under the Patriot Act. In January, a very limited amount of information was released to these groups, and they are continuing to push for a more complete disclosure.

Importantly, an anonymous survey done by the University of Illinois found that over 175 libraries across the county have been visited by federal authorities since the September 11 attacks. How is the Congress and the public supposed to make sure that these new powers are not being abused when we do not even know how often they are being invoked and the types of institutions that are being investigated?

For many people who cannot afford to buy books or have the Internet at home the library is critical to their ability to access information. Many librarians and booksellers now fear that patrons have begun to self-censor their library use and book purchases due to fears of government surveillance. We need to remove libraries and booksellers from Section 215 so that Americans know their freedom to access information won't be improperly scrutinized by federal agents.

Let us be clear. The FBI would still be able to gain access to library or bookseller records as part of an investigation into illegal activity. All our bill does is restore the traditional protections that Americans expect and deserve. If the FBI has probable cause to believe that information in a library or bookseller's records or computers is connected to an ongoing criminal investigation or terrorism investigation, they can go to court and get a search warrant.

In addition, the bill requires that the Justice Department provide more detailed information about its activities under Section 215 so we can determine how the FBI is using its new powers under Section 215.

Let me conclude by saying that all of us support protecting Americans from terrorism. But we do not win against terrorists by abandoning our most basic civil liberties. We cannot be an example of freedom for the world when our own government is spying on what Americans are reading.

Source: Remarks of Representative Bernie Sanders. *Congressional Record (House),* Volume 149, Number 40, March 12, 2003, pp. E441–42.

2003: ATTORNEY GENERAL ASHCROFT DEFENDS THE PATRIOT ACT ON CAPITOL HILL

On June 5, 2003, Attorney General John Ashcroft appeared before the House Committee on the Judiciary to defend the PATRIOT Act against charges that the FBI, the CIA, and other federal law enforcement agencies were violating basic American civil liberties under operations authorized by some of the act's provisions. His opening statement, excerpted below, relentlessly framed the PATRIOT Act as an essential weapon in the fight against terrorists and its use as a moral obligation to innocent victims of 9/11 and servicemen who had died in military operations in Iraq and Afghanistan. Ashcroft also insisted that federal authorities were not misusing their authority afforded by the PATRIOT Act to violate the constitutional protections of American citizens. Under questioning from committee members later in this same appearance, Ashcroft defended the use and legitimacy of a wide range of controversial activities carried out by the Justice Department under his watch, including the use of clandestine "sneak and peek" search warrants authorized by Section 213 of the PATRIOT Act—search warrants that, according to critics, rank as appalling violations of American civil liberties.

. . . During Operation Enduring Freedom, on the wind-swept plateaus of Afghanistan, some American military commanders read a list every morning to their troops—names of the men and women who died on September 11. It was a stark reminder of why they were there.

Joseph Maffeo
Diana M. Hale-McKinzy
Susan Ann Ruggiero
Manny Del Valle
Wanda Prince
Charles E. Sabin

To read every name of every victim who died at the hands of terrorists on September 11 would take three hours. To read all the names of sons and daughters, wives and husbands, friends and family affected by the loss of loved ones on that tragic day would be impossible.

I come before this Committee having not forgotten the promise made to those stolen from us by terrorism's ideology of hate. . . .

Twenty months ago President Bush pledged that al Qaeda and the terrorist network would not escape the patient justice of the United States—for we would remember the victims of terrorism.

Today, brave men and women in uniform abroad and at home answer our President's call for justice. Sworn to defend the Constitution and our liberties, and motivated by the memories of September 11, they live each day by a code of honor, duty, and country. And they know that they may die preserving the promise that terrorism will not reach this land of liberty again—for we are a nation locked in a deadly war with the evil of terrorism.

We will not forget that in Afghanistan, on the dusty road to Kandahar, Army Sgt. Orlando Morales was killed on reconnaissance patrol 70 in a town called Geresk. He leaves behind a wife and 17-month-old daughter. Sergeant Morales was in Afghanistan fighting to destroy the Taliban regime, terrorist operatives, and their training camps.

His sacrifice was not in vain. In this war, over half of al Qaeda's senior operatives have been captured or killed. Some of those captured were operatives, like Khalid Shaik Mohammed. Others, like military commander Mohammed Atef, are silenced forever. Overall, more than 3,000 foot soldiers of terror have been incapacitated.

We will not forget that in the battles in Iraq, Marine Lance Corporal David Fribley of Warsaw, Indiana, was killed near Nasiriyah by Iraqi soldiers who pretended to surrender—but then opened fire. Lance Corporal Fribley made the ultimate sacrifice to free the Iraqi people and to eliminate a key sponsor of terror.

We must not forget that this great fight for freedom did not end in Kabul. It will not end along the banks of the Tigris and Euphrates. The fight continues here—on America's streets, off our shores, and in the skies above.

Americans do not shy from danger or turn away from threats to liberty. On September 11, we saw our nation's finest ideals in action. Firefighters and police officers rushed to—not from—the World Trade Center. We saw Americans embrace duty, face danger, and sacrifice their lives for their fellow citizens and for freedom.

On that tragic day, 343 firefighters and 71 police officers died in the line of duty. Today, the Justice Department, agents of the Federal Bureau of Investigation, as well as state and local law enforcement officers, uphold the legacy of our fallen heroes.

From state troopers on the roads to cops on the beat, from intelligence analysts to FBI field agents, these are the sentinels serving with silent determination to protect America's citizens. They wage this defense with the tools you help provide them.

Twenty months ago, you understood what was needed to preserve freedom. You understood that our nation's success in this long war on terrorism demanded that the Justice Department continuously adapt and improve its capabilities to protect Americans from a fanatical, ruthless enemy.

That is why you worked with us to shape an anti-terrorism law housed in the framework of American freedom—the Constitution of the United States.

Congress overwhelmingly approved the USA PATRIOT Act. In the House, Representatives voted 357 to 66 for the measure, while the Senate supported the legislation by a near unanimous 98-to-1 vote.

The PATRIOT Act gave us the tools we needed to integrate our law enforcement and intelligence capabilities to win the war on terror.

It allowed the Department of Justice to use the same tools from the criminal process on terrorists that we use to combat mobsters or drug dealers. We use these tools to gather intelligence and to prevent terrorists from unleashing more death and destruction within our country. We use these tools to connect the "dots." We use these tools to save innocent lives.

The "Buffalo Cell" case shows how the PATRIOT Act and the criminal process can drive intelligence gathering. There, we learned of information about individuals who allegedly trained in an al Qaeda camp in Afghanistan and lived in the United States.

The Department used confidential informants to gather facts; we used subpoenas to collect travel information to track their movements; we deployed surveillance to record conversations; we used search warrants to locate weapons and jihad materials; and we used some of the best interrogators from the FBI to obtain critical admissions from some of the defendants.

The Department also used one of the most effective tools at the government's disposal—the leverage of criminal charges and long prison sentences. As is often the case with criminal defendants, when individuals realize that they face a long prison term like those under the PATRIOT Act, they will try to cut their prison time by pleading guilty and cooperating with the government.

In fact, since September 11, we have obtained criminal plea agreements, many under seal, from more than 15 individuals, who must—and will continue to—cooperate with the government in its terrorist investigations.

These individuals have provided critical intelligence about al Qaeda and other terrorist groups, safehouses, training camps, recruitment, and tactics in the U.S., and the operations of those terrorists who mean to do American citizens harm. . . .

With the PATRIOT Act and our prevention strategy, we can point to steady progress in America's war against terrorism.

We are targeting terrorists here at home, while developing detailed intelligence on terrorist threats:

- Hundreds of suspected terrorists have been identified and tracked throughout the U.S., with more than 18,000 subpoenas and search warrants issued;
- Our human sources of intelligence have doubled, as has the number of anti-terrorism investigations.

- In 2002, using Foreign Intelligence Surveillance Act tools, we targeted more than 1,000 international terrorists, spies and foreign powers, who threaten our country's security. We requested 170 emergency FISAs. This is more than three-times the total number of emergency FISAs obtained in the 23 years prior to September 11.

We are arresting and detaining potential terrorist threats:

- More than a dozen members of alleged terrorist cells in Buffalo, Seattle, Portland and Detroit, were arrested, along with more than 100 other individuals who were convicted or pled guilty to federal crimes as a result of our post-September 11 terrorism investigations;
- On Tuesday, we gained three convictions in the Detroit Cell case: two on terrorist conspiracy charges and the third on visa and document fraud charges; and

We are shutting down the terrorist financial infrastructure:

- As a result of 70 investigations into terror's money trail, more than $125 million in assets and over 600 accounts were frozen around the world.

We are building a long-term counter-terrorism capacity with:

- Over 1,000 new and redirected FBI agents dedicated to counter-terrorism and counter-intelligence;
- 250 new Assistant U.S. Attorneys; and
- 66 Joint Terrorism Task Forces, with a 337 percent increase in staffing.

Most important, no major terror attack has occurred on American soil since September 11.

Let me be clear. Al Qaeda is diminished, but not destroyed. Defeat after defeat has made the terrorists desperate to strike back.

Bombings in Tel Aviv, Israel, Bali, Indonesia, Casablanca, Morocco and Riyadh, Saudi Arabia are bitter reminders that the cold-blooded network of terror will continue to use the horror of their heinous acts to achieve their fanatical ends.

Innocent American and Saudi citizens died in the Riyadh compounds last month at the hands of al Qaeda.

We will not forget American Obadiah Abdullah, who converted to Islam and, after retiring from an 11-year career in the U.S. Army, took a job that would allow him to make a pilgrimage to Mecca.

Clifford Lawson retired as an Army staff sergeant in 1997. He had a talent for computers and electronics, and he loved his family. He was supposed to return home for his son's 13th birthday in July.

Todd Bair also served in the military. Just two weeks before he was murdered, he returned from a visit with his family. He was a man of faith, who leaves behind a wife and two sons, ages 11 and eight.

We must be vigilant and unrelenting. We must not forget that al Qaeda's primary terrorist target is the United States. Even though recent attacks were overseas, the terrorist network is committed to killing innocent Americans, including women and children, by the thousands or even the millions if they can. . . .

Despite the terrorist threat to America, there are some in Congress and across the country who suggest that we should not have a USA PATRIOT Act. Others, who supported the Act 20 months ago, now express doubts about the necessity of some of the Act's components.

Let me state this as clearly as possible.

Our ability to prevent another catastrophic attack on American soil would be more difficult, if not impossible, without the PATRIOT Act. It has been the key weapon used across America in successful counter-terrorist operations to protect innocent Americans from the deadly plans of terrorists.

Unfortunately, the law has several weaknesses which terrorists could exploit, undermining our defenses.

First, in pursuit of terrorist cells, current law makes it a crime to provide a terrorist organization with personnel or training. We must make it crystal clear that those who train for and fight with a designated terrorist organization can be charged under material support statutes.

Second, existing law does not consistently encourage cooperation by providing adequate maximum penalties to punish acts of terrorism. Some terrorist acts resulting in the death of citizens do not provide for the death penalty or even life imprisonment.

Third, terrorism offenses are not expressly included in the list of crimes that allow for pre-trial detention, even though it could prevent an attack. In criminal cases where public safety is of concern—such as drug dealing, organized crime, and gun crimes—defendants in federal cases are presumptively denied pretrial release.

As we weigh the Constitutional methods we will use to defend innocent Americans from terrorism, we must not forget the names that unite us in our cause:

Cherone Gunn
Ronald Scott Owens
Ronchester Santiago
Timothy Saunders
Lakiba Nicole Palmer

These are some of the brave men and women of the USS Cole who were murdered by al Qaeda in 2000. Weeks ago, when I met with the families of those who died on the Cole, they pleaded that we not forget them. I am committed to their families not being forgotten.

Cherone Gunn had been in the Navy less than a year and loved serving his country. He wanted to become a law enforcement officer. Ronchester Santiago planned to study electrical engineering at the University of Texas.

Ronald Scott Owens left behind his wife, Jamie, and a little girl named Isabella Marie. Lakiba Palmer died, leaving an 18-month-old daughter who will never know her mother. The two daughters of Timothy Saunders were ten and seven years old when they lost their father.

The names I have recalled today all bear silent, painful witness to the fact that the United States is a nation at war.

We must never forget that we are in a war to preserve life and liberty.

We must not forget that our enemies are ruthless fanatics, who seek to murder innocent men, women and children to achieve their twisted goals.

We must not forget that in the struggle between the forces of freedom and the ideology of hate, our challenge in this war against terrorism is to adapt and anticipate, to out-think and outmaneuver our enemies, while honoring our Constitution.

The United States Department of Justice has been called to defend America. We accept that charge.

We fight in the tradition of all great American struggles: with resolve, defiance, and honor.

We fight to secure victory over the evil in our midst.

We fight to uphold the liberties and ideals that define a free and brave people.

Every day the Justice Department is working tirelessly, taking this war to the hideouts and havens of our enemies, so that it never again touches the hearths and homes of America.

I thank you for the opportunity to testify today. I thank you for the Constitutional weapons that make the war for freedom a conflict whose end is not in doubt. And I thank the American people for their support and faith in the justice of our cause.

I would now be happy to answer your questions.

Source: Ashcroft, John. *Testimony before the House Committee on the Judiciary*. June 5, 2003. http://www.justice.gov/archive/ag/testimony/2003/060503aghouseremarks.htm.

2003: CONGRESS SHUTS DOWN "TOTAL INFORMATION AWARENESS" PROGRAM

In late 2002, the New York Times *published a story revealing that the Information Awareness Office (IAO), a relatively obscure department within the U.S. Department of Defense's Defense Advance Research Projects Agency (DARPA), had begun developing a sophisticated data mining system to track the "information signatures" of potential terrorists and criminals. The database system, dubbed Total Information Awareness (TIA), was being crafted to enable the warrantless capture and analysis of all manner of private data, including personal communications and medical, financial, and travel records.*

As the American public and lawmakers learned more about the proposed reach of the TIA program, concerns about its capacity to flout constitutional privacy protections rapidly increased. Critics from across the political spectrum declared their opposition to the program, and in September 2003, Congress formally eliminated funding for both the TIA and the Information Awareness Office that had sought to bring it to life. Following are excerpts from a House conference report on the provision, contained within a Department of Defense appropriations bill, that killed the IAO.

Sec. 8131.

(a) Notwithstanding any other provision of law, none of the funds appropriated or otherwise made available in this or any other Act may be obligated for the Terrorism Information Awareness Program: Provided, That this limitation shall not apply to the program hereby authorized for Processing, analysis, and collaboration tools for counterterrorism foreign intelligence, as described in the Classified Annex accompanying the Department of Defense Appropriations Act, 2004, for which funds are expressly provided in the National Foreign Intelligence Program for counterterrorism foreign intelligence purposes.

(b) None of the funds provided for Processing, analysis, and collaboration tools for counterterrorism foreign intelligence shall be available for deployment or implementation except for:

(1) lawful military operations of the United States conducted outside the United States; or

(2) lawful foreign intelligence activities conducted wholly overseas, or wholly against non United States citizens.

(c) In this section, the term "Terrorism Information Awareness Program" means the program known either as Terrorism Information Awareness or

> Total Information Awareness, or any successor program, funded by the Defense Advanced Research Projects Agency, or any other Department or element of the Federal Government, including the individual components of such Program developed by the Defense Advanced Research Projects Agency.

[. . .]

Joint Explanatory Statement

[. . .]

Terrorism Information Awareness (TIA)

The conferees agree with the Senate position which eliminates funding for the Terrorism Information Awareness (TIA) program within the Defense Advanced Research Projects Agency (DARPA). The conferees are concerned about the activities of the Information Awareness Office and direct that the Office be terminated immediately. The only research projects previously under the jurisdiction of the Information Awareness Office that may continue under DARPA are: Bio-Event Advanced Leading Indicator Recognition Technology, Rapid Analytic Wargaming, Wargaming the Asymmetric Environment, and Automated Speech and Text Exploitation in Multiple Languages (including Babylon and Symphony). The conferees find these programs are not components of TIA for the purposes of section 8131. The conference agreement does not restrict the National Foreign Intelligence Program from using processing, analysis and collaboration tools for counterterrorism foreign intelligence purposes.

Source: Conference Report on H.R. 2658, Department of Defense Appropriations Act, 2004 (House Report 108–283). *Congressional Record (House),* September 24, 2003, pp. H8500–50.

2004: A REPORT ON LAW ENFORCEMENT'S "LITTLE HELPERS"—DATA AGGREGATORS

In the summer of 2004, a young privacy law scholar named Chris Jay Hoofnagle wrote an influential article called "Big Brother's Little Helpers" that delineated the findings of an investigation carried out by the Electronic Privacy Information Center (EPIC) into American law enforcement's use of data aggregators, also known as commercial data brokers (CDBs). The article, which was first published in the North Carolina Journal of International Law and Commercial Regulation, *was seized on by privacy advocates calling for new restraints on government surveillance powers in the debate over reauthorization of the USA PATRIOT Act. The introduction from the article is excerpted below (with footnotes removed).*

Since this work was published, Chris Hoofnagle has become a prominent scholar at the University of California, Berkeley, where he teaches information privacy law, computer crime law, regulation of online privacy, and Internet law. He is also a leading scholar on the phenomenon of "Denialism," which he defines as "the systematic use of public relations tactics to manipulate scientific and regulatory debates by unprincipled, dangerous political movements."

I. Introduction

Traditionally, law enforcement officers obtained information by speaking with suspects' neighbors, employers, or friends. They would analyze paper arrest records and crime reports. In order to obtain personal information stored in private databases, they would have to call a variety of different vendors.

The shift to a digital environment has brought many changes to law enforcement's collection of information. Now, by visiting a single website, such as www.cpgov.com, law enforcement can obtain a comprehensive dossier on almost any adult. That website was custom-tailored for law enforcement by ChoicePoint, Inc. (Choicepoint), a commercial data broker (CDB).

CDBs make available a wide variety of information, from arrest and court records to notice that a suspect has opened a private mailbox. Access to private sector databases has significantly altered the balance of power between law enforcement and the individual. As one internal document from the United States Marshals Service (USMS) put it:

> With as little as a first name or a partial address, you can obtain a comprehensive personal profile in minutes. The profile includes personal identifying information (name, alias name, date of birth, social security number), all known addresses, drivers license information, vehicle information . . . telephone numbers, corporations,

> business affiliations, aircraft, boats, assets, professional licenses, concealed weapons permits, liens, judgments, lawsuits, marriages, worker compensation claims, etc.

This new power has been made possible by the confluence of fast network connections, the availability of public records, both electronic and paper, that are rich with personal information, and the alacrity of companies that have become very profitable from selling personal data to the government.

A number of risks to due process and privacy are raised by the collection and maintenance of information. The information could be used for political or personal purposes. Examples of police misuse of databases abound in the media, with violations found involving street-level local police officers to Federal Bureau of Investigation and Drug Enforcement Administration (DEA) officers. There is also a general risk that the collection of information on individuals will upset the balance between government and individuals, resulting in a shift of power that is oppressive. In a report mandated by the Privacy Act of 1974, the Privacy Protection Study Commission highlighted this risk:

> In a larger context, Americans must also be concerned about the long-term effect record-keeping practices can have not only on relationships between individuals and organizations, but also on the balance of power between government and the rest of society. Accumulations of information about individuals tend to enhance authority by making it easier for authority to reach individuals directly. Thus, growth in society's record-keeping capability poses the risk that existing power balances will be upset.

There is nothing inherently wrong with law enforcement buying access to CDBs. After all, the private sector provides law enforcement with many tools, including pistols and batons. But there are strict rules for the use of these police tools. There is training to help ensure that pistols are only fired with justification, and that batons are employed properly. If these tools are misused, there are serious repercussions, including the discipline or dismissal of the officer and section 1983 lawsuits. The Electronic Privacy Information Center (EPIC) is exploring whether similar substantive and procedural safeguards are in place for law enforcement officers who use CDBs to gain access to personal information. Specifically, EPIC is evaluating what, if any, safeguards are in place to protect individuals' privacy and due process rights.

To answer these questions, in June 2001, EPIC filed a series of requests under the Freedom of Information Act (FOIA) seeking access to government records regarding companies that sell personal information to the government. Almost three years and a lawsuit later, EPIC has obtained over 1,500 pages of material from nine agencies about ChoicePoint and other CDBs. In this article, findings are presented from the requests, and concerns are raised regarding law enforcement access to personal information. The conclusion sets forth a framework of privacy protections to address risks to due process and the Fourth Amendment posed by companies like ChoicePoint. Based on the findings, the Privacy Act of 1974 should be extended to CDBs, as they regularly serve as private escrows for information that the government could not otherwise collect legally. Furthermore, there should be broader protections for personal information in public records, as these sources form perhaps the greatest threat to the future of data privacy.

Determining agency practices from FOIA documents is difficult. There are few "smoking gun" FOIA documents. Rather, analysis requires viewing many different documents in context to determine agency action. Because of these limitations, documents are interpreted conservatively, and I have indicated in the text where there are ambiguities in the documents.

The analysis is also limited by the willingness of agencies to provide documents. Of the agencies covered by EPIC's request, the USMS released the largest number of unredacted documents. The FBI, on the other hand, had the greatest number of documents responsive to the FOIA request, but the substantial majority of this material was either heavily redacted or withheld in full. . . .

II. Findings from the FOIA Requests

On June 22, 2001, EPIC filed FOIA requests with seven agencies seeking access to records "concerning businesses that sell individuals' personal information." Several agencies initially rejected the request, arguing that EPIC needed to further specify the topic for the search of records. In those cases, EPIC specified that the request sought all records related to ChoicePoint, LexisNexis, Experian, Dun & Bradstreet, and Database Technologies Online.

In January 2002, EPIC filed suit in the United States District Court for the District of Columbia against all seven agencies for failure to comply with the FOIA's requirements. That litigation is still pending. EPIC continues to seek 5,000 pages of ChoicePoint contracting documents held by the FBI's Criminal Investigative Division. EPIC also seeks access to a Department of Justice (DOJ) memorandum from the agency's Office of Professional Responsibility. That document concerns an internal investigation regarding unauthorized disclosure of agency information. . . .

Since filing the requests, EPIC has received over 1,500 documents. The documents led to six major findings. First, the documents show that law enforcement can quickly obtain a broad array of personal information about individuals. Second, although EPIC filed a broad request for documents, there was almost no evidence of controls to prevent agency employees from misusing the databases. It appears as though auditing employee use of the databases is either impossible or simply not done. Third, the database companies are extremely solicitous to the government and actually design the databases for law enforcement use. Fourth, ChoicePoint expanded significantly in 2000 by starting to acquire and sell personal information of non-citizens. That discovery has led to strong international dissent. Fifth, many of the contracts with CDBs are sole-sources, meaning the contracts are not open to competitive bidding. Sixth, the FBI has a secret, sole-source contract with ChoicePoint to develop an information service prototype. . . .

Source: Hoofnagle, Chris Jay. 2004. "Big Brother's Little Helpers: How ChoicePoint and Other Commercial Data Brokers Collect and Package Your Data for Law Enforcement." *North Carolina Journal of International Law and Commercial Regulation* 29 (595), Summer: pp. 595–98. Used by permission.

2005: A BUSH ADMINISTRATION OFFICIAL URGES REAUTHORIZATION OF THE PATRIOT ACT

Even the constrained debate during the passage of the original Patriot Act produced expressions of concern over Section 215 orders and National Security Letters (NSLs), in part because of the fears that these provisions would be used to seize library and bookstore records. These concerns, muted during the 2001 congressional debate, emerged with new vigor during the 2005 PATRIOT Act reauthorization debates.

A reauthorization hearing held by the House Judiciary committee on June 8, 2005—excerpted below—produced both spirited criticism and resolute defense of Section 215 and NSLs. Representative Maxine Waters (D-CA) criticized Section 215's weak requirement of simple "relevance," saying it gave the government "too much secret surveillance power. . . . American citizens have the right to be eventually notified that they are under surveillance and Section 215 impedes that right by allowing the government to conduct surveillance, without the requirement of notice, for time periods that are unspecified and unchecked."

Representing the Bush administration, Deputy Attorney General James Comey responded that "Section 215 has been criticized by some because it does not exempt libraries and booksellers. The absence of such an exemption is consistent with criminal investigative practice. Prosecutors have always been able to obtain records from libraries and bookstores through grand jury subpoenas. Libraries and booksellers should not become safe havens for terrorists and spies . . . Concerns that Section 215 allows the government to target Americans because of the books they read or Web sites they visit are misplaced. The provision explicitly prohibits the government from conducting an investigation of a U.S. person based solely upon protected First Amendment activity."

Comey did not mention, however, that the prohibition against investigations based solely on activities protected by the First Amendment did not preclude investigations based partly or even predominantly on First Amendment activities. He was most steadfast in his defense of the simple relevance standard required for Section 215 orders. "The Department [of Justice] is very concerned by proposals currently pending before Congress which would require the government to show 'specific and articulable facts' that the records sought through a section 215 order pertain to a foreign power or agent of a foreign power. Such a requirement would disable the government from using a section 215 order at the early stages of an investigation, which is precisely when such an order is most useful."

In the end, Comey's arguments would carry the day in the House of Representatives, which passed a reauthorization bill that corresponded closely to the demands of the Justice Department and made no meaningful changes to Section 215 orders or NSLs.

The following excerpts from Deputy Inspector General James Comey's June 2005 testimony before the House Committee of the Judiciary illuminate many of the main criticisms and defenses of Section 215 that were made in the months leading up to the reauthorization vote.

Chairman Sensenbrenner: Mr. Comey, much of the criticism of the PATRIOT Act has been directed at section 215, which is the business records part of the PATRIOT Act. When the Attorney General was here a couple of months ago, he said he was going to propose some amendments to section 215 to address the concerns of the libraries and book stores. Could you detail what those changes are the AG proposes? And also, tell us how many times this section has been used relative to get library and book store records, if you can.

Mr. Comey: Yes, sir. section 215, as you said, has become known as the so-called "library provision"—something that remains a mystery to me. I tease some of my friends in journalism, to ask them to do an investigative piece to figure out how it came to be called that; because it never occurred to those of us in law enforcement, when we saw that we had a provision that we could obtain tangible things—which was defined as books, records, etcetera—that people would understand "books" to mean library books.

Regardless, it's become the "library provision." We've never used it in connection with a library or book store, as the Attorney General has said. But the Attorney General has also said that people have made some reasonable comments about section 215, and some constructive criticisms.

Among other things, they've said, "Look, you guys in Government understand it to be a relevance standard, but it doesn't say that in the statute." So the Attorney General has said that we will support adding a relevance standard. That's the way we've operated, and that's what we expect it to be.

Second, folks have said, "Look, it doesn't make it clear that we're able to talk to a lawyer, and to challenge if we believe the order is over-broad or abusive or something like that." And that's a very good point. And as the Attorney General has said, we support putting that in the statute. So, if someone receives a 215 order—most likely in the real world, a credit card issuer, a hotel company, or a travel record company—and they believe for some reason it's inappropriate, they can talk to a lawyer. And there are procedures in place, and the real power for them to challenge the court—before the court that issued that order. The substance of that order.

That's reasonable. That's appropriate.

But this is a very, very important tool, and it is a tool that offers far more oversight and involvement of the courts and Congress than our normal tool to obtain records, including records we could obtain from a book store or library; that is, grand jury process.

Section 215 requires that an FBI agent go to a Federal judge, nominated by the President, confirmed by the Senate, who sits on the Foreign Intelligence Surveillance Court, and make a written application for an order to obtain documents. So a Federal judge is involved. Then, requires us to report to Congress every 6 months on how we're using it precisely; what we're using it for; and how many times we've used it.

There is nothing like that oversight in the thousands and thousands of instances every day where we obtain records using the grand jury process. I think 215 strikes an important balance. It offers oversight and offers a very important tool to the FBI to obtain records in our most important investigations. . . .

Chairman Sensenbrenner: Thank you. The gentleman from Virginia, Mr. Scott [Bobby Scott, D-VA].

Mr. Scott: Thank you. Mr. Comey, it's good to see you again.

Mr. Comey: You, too.

Mr. Scott: You mentioned in your opening remarks that there is certain language that is not helpful in promoting an honest dialogue about this legislation. Would that include language such as, "To those who scare peace-loving people with phantoms of lost liberty, my message is this: Your tactics only aid terrorists; for they erode our national unity and diminish our Resolve"?

Mr. Comey: I may be a short-timer, Mr. Scott, but I would prefer not to focus on anybody's words in particular. Any words that chill aggressive questioning of Government authority I think are not helpful. As I said in my opening, I think people should demand to know—all points of the political spectrum. I think Republicans should have as big a problem with Government power as Democrats.

Mr. Scott: You recognize the words? [editor's note: The quote is from 2001 congressional testimony by Bush administration Attorney General John Ashcroft.]

Mr. Comey: I've heard them before, yes, sir.

Mr. Scott: You mentioned—you explained how in section 215, what we're calling the "library provision," you went to great lengths to explain how the judge was involved. Is that an important part of 215?

Mr. Comey: I believe it is, yes.

Mr. Scott: On roving wiretaps, when you have gotten probable cause, not that a crime has been committed, but the probable cause that the target is an agent of a foreign government—which means you can get the wiretap without probable cause of any crime, just that you're trying to get intelligence information which may not be criminal, just, you know, information on a trade deal, something, no crime as a predicate—and then you expand this as a roving wiretap, is it important that you ascertain before you start listening in that the target is actually in the location where you've placed the bug?

Mr. Comey: It may be important as a practical matter, because we don't want to waste time. But in intelligence investigations, given the nature of the people we're following and surveilling, both with spies and terrorists who are trained to look for us and to be very careful, I'm troubled by an ascertainment requirement; which would require us, as you said, Mr. Scott, as we do in the criminal context, to know that the target is the one on the phone or the target is the one near the bug.

Mr. Scott: Well, I say this because we've heard from witnesses before, like the Attorney General, that some of these—you know, we reduced the standard from the purpose of the wiretap being foreign intelligence to a significant purpose, which invites the question: If it wasn't the purpose, what was the purpose? And the answer, of course, is you're running a criminal investigation without probable cause.

Now, since you're running a criminal investigation, isn't it important that the people you're listening in are actually targets of the wiretap? I mean, you could put these all over town where the target may be using the phone. If he leaves, shouldn't you stop listening?

Mr. Comey: Well, you'd like to, because you don't want to waste the time, but the way——

Mr. Scott: Well, no, no. No, you're not wasting time. You're listening in to people you wanted to listen in to. I mean, because you're running the criminal investigation under the auspices of this less strict standard of foreign intelligence. Should you be able to take advantage of the criminal investigation with the lower standard by listening in, when the target isn't even there?

Mr. Comey: Well, first of all, you'd better not, if you work for me, be conducting an investigation to obtain criminal information using FISA unless the following is true: Significant purpose, as you said, Mr. Scott, is to obtain foreign intelligence. And if there is an additional purpose to obtain criminal information, it's only criminal information related to foreign intelligence crimes, terrorism crimes or espionage crimes. That's what the FISA court of review has told us is the law, and so we'd better—we are following the law.

Mr. Scott: Well, we changed the law under the PATRIOT Act.

Mr. Comey: Well, I've heard that said, but the court of appeals that governs this has said you may only collect information of foreign intelligence crimes if that's an additional purpose to the collection of foreign intelligence.

But the ascertainment—the way we collect intelligence information, we strike a balance. Because of the nature of the target, we stand off a little bit more. We collect, and don't necessarily review real-time what's being collected. And we account for that with the rules that govern the storage and dissemination of that information. And that's a balance that's been struck to recognize that criminal investigations are different, and I think it's a reasonable one.

When you drill down and look at the way we follow spies and follow terrorists, it would make it much more difficult to operate intelligence investigations if the agents were required to ascertain in every circumstance that the target is there at the bug or there on this particular phone.

Mr. Scott: Could you——

Mr. Comey: Rather than collecting and minimizing it later, and strictly controlling what you do with U.S. person information. I'm sorry, sir.

Chairman Sensenbrenner: The gentleman's time has expired. The gentleman from California, Mr. [Dan] Lungren [R-CA].

Mr. Lungren: I thank the Chairman. And I thank Mr. Comey for the open and forthright way with which you are facing this. And obviously, we wouldn't be here discussing the PATRIOT Act or the sunset provision, had it not been for 9/11. And sometimes we have to remind ourselves of that.

I was reminded of that today when, in my home district, we received news of a father and a son charged with lying to Federal agents about the son's alleged training at an al-Qaeda camp for a mission that the judge said was to "kill Americans whenever and wherever they can be found."

I'm not sure we've ever faced that before with a transnational organization that has indicated it is the duty of all those who have allegiance to the same beliefs they have to kill Americans—men, women, and children—wherever and whenever they can be found.

Having said that, there is this concern about the PATRIOT Act; whether it's real or imagined, whether it's perception or reality. And for that reason, I lean toward putting sunsets in this legislation; not because, Mr. Comey, I want to upset the cultural change that's trying to take place in the Justice Department. But I point to a cultural change that's needed in the Congress.

I think we're doing a tremendous job of oversight here, I think this Committee is. And I think that we have had good cooperation with the Department of Justice. But oversight has not been the strong suit of Congresses in the past. And I wonder whether we would be as vigorous if we didn't have the obligation of this. And some of us have a feeling that not only is it something necessary to effect the cultural change on the executive branch, but also the legislative branch.

Do you truly think that if we had sunset provisions for section 215, for instance, and some of the others, that that would be a real interference with what you're accomplishing and what you hope to accomplish in the future with the changes brought about by the PATRIOT Act?

Mr. Comey: The honest answer is I don't think it would be a disaster. But here's another reason why I don't think it makes sense. And I'm not in any position to talk about oversight, except that, as I said to the Chairman, we have seen, I think, remarkable oversight, as you noted, here. . . . the one thing I can tell you, though—and it's hard for me to put this into words without seeming small in my remarks—but we have devoted huge resources and time to this, as we should. But we have hundreds—"hundreds" is fair—of people working on what we've done over the last 6 months, and spending countless hours collecting information, responding, meeting.

That's an enormous drain. And it should be. But I hope it's a rare drain, and that we use it to establish that the base line is sound; that what Congress did in September—after September 11th was sound; and that what we can do going forward is rolling, and not in a way that makes everybody and his brother in the Department of Justice work on the effort.

We live in a bit of a myth, and that is that we have limitless resources. We don't. And it is a major challenge for us to do this. And we're happy to do it, because it ought to be done. I just—to be very frank, and I won't be here, it would be really hard to do this 3 years from now, or another 2 years from now, when we can substitute for it something that I think is as effective, which is rigorous oversight.

Mr. Lungren: Well, it sort of begs the question of whether we would have rigorous oversight——

Mr. Comey: Yes.

Mr. Lungren: —if we didn't have this requirement. And you have talked about the tremendous number of hours that have been put into it, precisely because the Department thinks it's important to have this reauthorized. And precisely because many of us think it's important to have it reauthorized, we are spending the time to do that. . . .

Chairman Sensenbrenner: The gentlewoman from California, Ms. Lungren [sic].

Ms. Lofgren: Actually, it's "Lofgren," not "Lungren."

Chairman Sensenbrenner: It's "Lofgren." [Laughter.]

I'm sorry. I should know better.

Ms. [Zoc] Lofgren (D CA): Thank you, Mr. Chairman. And thank you, Mr. Comey. I, to some extent, agree with the comments that we need to cool down the rhetoric on the PATRIOT Act. I think we're here, and it's important that we're here, to review the details not just of the sunsetting provisions of the act, but all of the act.

And yet, having said that, there are people in the country that everything they don't like they believe is because of the PATRIOT Act. And I constantly challenge, "Where in the act is this misbehavior?" There's things I don't like, too, but it's not all in the PATRIOT Act.

At the same time, I think it's a terrible mistake to criticize those, or to question the patriotism of those who are legitimately engaging in oversight to make sure if we have preserved the balance between our civil liberties and our need to have vigorous law enforcement; which is what we're doing here today.

Along those lines, I want to go back to section 215. In your testimony, you state that the FISA court has issued 35 orders, but that none were issued to a library. At the same time, you say if we exempt or change 215 relative to libraries, you know, it's the end of the world. The roof will fall in; terrorists will make libraries safe havens.

And I guess I'm skeptical of that. And I'm wondering if there isn't some intermediate provision that would assist with the anxiety that is afoot in the land. People are afraid that their reading habits are going to be interfered with. Their first amendment rights are in fact being chilled today, because of what people think is happening, even if it's not happening.

And so the question I have is, why not require that personally identifiable information be exempt from section 215?

It is true that anybody can go in and use a computer terminal in a library, and they can do good things or bad things. But the libraries I've been to don't keep track of who's on the terminals, and it's not personally identifiable. Could you answer that question?

Mr. Comey: Yes, I'd be happy to. Something is broken, but I think—and I may be impossibly naive—but I think it's people's understanding of 215, and not 215. And if what's broken is their understanding, I'm going to work till I have no more breath to try and fix that; rather than change 215 just because folks don't understand it.

Ms. Lofgren: What about the personally identifiable information exemption?

Mr. Comey: I don't know why we would do that, though, because that would—I don't think the sky would fall, but you would create a sanctuary in those particular places. Because a bad guy would know, "That's a place I can go."

Ms. Lofgren: Well, I mean, you can still get the information, if it's personally identifiable; just not through section 215.

Mr. Comey: If we couldn't use 215 to obtain information that we could tie to a particular person, say, we were following—again, this is the kind of thing that doesn't happen, but if we were following a terrorist, and he was sitting at a computer terminal, and we wanted to get the records, his records, and we had done something that made it impossible for us to obtain records that told us they were his, I don't know why we would do that. And I don't think librarians would want that.

Ms. Lofgren: Let me ask another question. And it goes back to our need to review the whole situation, not just what is being sunsetted. I guess in a way it goes back to the earlier comment about oversight and how much time and effort is being put into answering the questions that Congress has posed. And I assure you, I don't question that you are putting in a considerable amount of time.

. . . Finally, I just want to mention that we did not suspend habeas corpus in the PATRIOT Act. And yet, the detention of American citizens without charge, without access to counsel, has been referenced to the general action we took to authorize the invasion to enact the PATRIOT Act. Shouldn't we make it explicitly clear in any reauthorization that we are not suspending habeas corpus?

Mr. Comey: I don't know—certainly, no one that I know has argued that Congress has suspended habeas corpus, and in fact—

Ms. Lofgren: Then you wouldn't mind if we made that clear in the act?

Mr. Comey: Well, I suppose I wouldn't mind. I mean, I don't know how the legislative process works. But habeas corpus is alive and well in this country. And in fact, the litigation you're referring to is pursuant to the habeas corpus, the great writ, and being decided by the courts now, whether the Government has that authority.

Mr. Lungren: [Presiding.] The gentlelady's time has expired.

Source: Testimony of Deputy Attorney General James Comey. Reauthorization of the USA PATRIOT Act: Hearing before the Committee on the Judiciary, House of Representatives, One Hundred Ninth Congress, First Session, June 8, 2005. Washington, DC: U.S. Government Printing Office, 2005.

2005: THE SUPREME COURT RULES ON SEARCHES DURING TRAFFIC STOPS IN *ILLINOIS v. CABALLES*

After an Illinois state trooper stopped Roy Caballes for speeding, a second trooper, overhearing the radio transmission of the stop, drove to the scene with his narcotics detection dog and walked the dog around Caballes's vehicle while the first trooper wrote Caballes a warning ticket. When the dog alerted at the trunk of Caballes's vehicle, the officers searched the trunk, found marijuana, and arrested Caballes. The trial court determined that the dog's alerting provided sufficient probable cause to conduct the search. Caballes was convicted, but the Illinois Supreme Court reversed, finding that because there were no specific and articulable facts to suggest drug activity use of the dog unjustifiably enlarged a routine traffic stop into a drug investigation. The U.S. Supreme Court reversed the Illinois Supreme Court on January 24, 2005. The Court held in a 6–2 decision that a dog sniff conducted during a lawful traffic stop that revealed no information other than the location of a substance that no individual had any right to possess did not violate the Fourth Amendment.

Following are excerpts from the majority decision written by Justice John Paul Stevens and a dissenting opinion from Justice David Souter.

JUSTICE STEVENS delivered the opinion of the Court.

The question on which we granted certiorari is narrow: "Whether the Fourth Amendment requires reasonable, articulable suspicion to justify using a drug-detection dog to sniff a vehicle during a legitimate traffic stop." Thus, we proceed on the assumption that the officer conducting the dog sniff had no information about respondent except that he had been stopped for speeding. . . .

Here, the initial seizure of respondent when he was stopped on the highway was based on probable cause, and was concededly lawful. It is nevertheless clear that a seizure that is lawful at its inception can violate the Fourth Amendment if its manner of execution unreasonably infringes interests protected by the Constitution. A seizure that is justified solely by the interest in issuing a warning ticket to the driver can become unlawful if it is prolonged beyond the time reasonably required to complete that mission. . . .

[W]e accept the state court's conclusion that the duration of the stop in this case was entirely justified by the traffic offense and the ordinary inquiries incident to such a stop.

Despite this conclusion, the Illinois Supreme Court held that the initially lawful traffic stop became an unlawful seizure solely as a result of the canine sniff that occurred outside respondent's stopped car. That is, the court characterized the dog sniff as the cause rather than the consequence of a constitutional violation. In its view, the use of the dog converted the citizen–police encounter from a lawful traffic stop into a drug investigation, and because the shift in purpose was not supported by any reasonable suspicion that respondent possessed narcotics, it was unlawful. In our view, conducting a dog sniff would not change the character of a traffic stop that is lawful at its inception and otherwise executed in a reasonable manner, unless the dog sniff itself infringed respondent's constitutionally protected interest in privacy. Our cases hold that it did not. Official conduct that does not "compromise any legitimate interest in privacy" is not a search subject to the Fourth Amendment. We have held that any interest in possessing contraband cannot be deemed "legitimate," and thus, governmental conduct that only reveals the possession of contraband "compromises no legitimate privacy interest." . . . In *United States v. Place* (1983), we treated a canine sniff by a well-trained narcotics-detection dog as "sui generic" because it "discloses only the presence or absence of narcotics, a contraband item." . . .

Accordingly, the use of a well-trained narcotics-detection dog—one that "does not expose noncontraband items that otherwise would remain hidden from public view,"—during a lawful traffic stop, generally does not implicate legitimate privacy interests. In this case, the dog sniff was performed on the exterior of respondent's car while he was lawfully seized for a traffic violation. Any intrusion on respondent's privacy expectations does not rise to the level of a constitutionally cognizable infringement. This conclusion is entirely consistent with our recent decision that the use of a thermal-imaging device to detect the growth of marijuana in a home constituted an unlawful search [*Kyllo v. United States* (2001)]. Critical to that decision was the fact that the device was capable of detecting lawful activity. . . . The legitimate expectation that information about perfectly lawful activity will remain private is categorically distinguishable from respondent's hopes or expectations concerning the nondetection of contraband in the trunk of his car. A dog sniff conducted during a concededly lawful traffic stop that reveals no information other than the location of a substance that no individual has any right to possess does not violate the Fourth Amendment. The judgment of the Illinois Supreme Court is vacated . . .

It is so ordered.

JUSTICE SOUTER, dissenting.

I would hold that using the dog for the purposes of determining the presence of marijuana in the car's trunk was a search unauthorized as an incident of the speeding stop and unjustified on any other ground.

In . . . *Place* (1983), we categorized the sniff of the narcotics-seeking dog as "sui generic" under the Fourth Amendment and held it was not a search. The classification rests not only upon the limited nature of the intrusion, but on a further premise that experience has shown to be untenable, the assumption that trained sniffing dogs do not err. . . .

At the heart both of *Place* and the Court's opinion today is the proposition that sniffs by a trained dog are sui generis because a reaction by the dog in going alert is a response to nothing but the presence of contraband. Hence, the argument goes, because the sniff can only reveal the presence of items devoid of any legal use, the sniff "does not implicate legitimate privacy interests" and is not to be treated as a search.

The infallible dog, however, is a creature of legal fiction. [T]heir supposed infallibility is belied by judicial opinions describing well-trained animals sniffing and alerting with less than perfect accuracy, whether owing to errors by their handlers, the limitations of the dogs themselves, or even the pervasive contamination of currency by cocaine. In practical terms, the evidence is clear that the dog that alerts hundreds of times will be wrong dozens of times. Once the dog's fallibility is recognized, however, that ends the justification claimed in *Place* for treating the sniff as sui generis under the Fourth Amendment: the sniff alert does not necessarily signal hidden contraband, and opening the container or enclosed space whose emanations the dog has sensed will not necessarily reveal contraband or any other evidence of crime. This is not, of course, to deny that a dog's reaction may provide reasonable suspicion, or probable cause, to search the container or enclosure; the Fourth Amendment does not demand certainty of success to justify a search for evidence or contraband. The point is simply that the sniff and alert cannot claim the certainty that *Place* assumed, both in treating the deliberate use of sniffing dogs as sui generis and then taking that characterization as a reason to say they are not searches subject to Fourth Amendment scrutiny. . . .

It makes sense, then, to treat a sniff as the search that it amounts to in practice, and to rely on the body of our Fourth Amendment cases, including *Kyllo*, in deciding whether such a search is reasonable. As a general proposition, using a dog to sniff for drugs is subject to the rule that the object of enforcing criminal laws does not, without more, justify suspicionless Fourth Amendment intrusions. Since the police claim to have had no particular suspicion that Caballes was violating any drug law, this sniff search must stand or fall on its being ancillary to the traffic stop that led up to it. It is true that the police had probable cause to stop the car for an offense committed in the office's presence, which Caballes concedes could have justified his arrest. There is no occasion to consider authority incident to arrest, however, for the police did nothing more than detain Caballes long enough to check his record and write a ticket. As a consequence, the reasonableness of the search must be assessed in relation to the actual delay the police chose to impose . . .

The Court today does not go so far as to say explicitly that sniff searches by dogs trained to sense contraband always get a free pass under the Fourth Amendment, since it reserves judgment on the constitutional significance of sniffs assumed to be more intrusive than a dog's walk around a stopped car. For this reason, I do not take the [decision] as actually signaling recognition of a broad authority to conduct suspicionless sniffs for drugs in any parked car . . . or on the person of any pedestrian minding his own business on a sidewalk. But the Court's stated reasoning provides no apparent stopping point short of such excesses. For the sake of providing a workable framework to analyze cases on facts like these, which are certain to come along, I would treat the dog sniff as the familiar search it is in fact, subject to scrutiny under the Fourth Amendment.

Source: Justice Stevens, John Paul. Opinion of the Court; Justice Souter, David. Dissent. *Illinois v. Cabelles,* 543 U.S. 405. Decided January 24, 2005. United States Reports, Volume 543, November 2004.

2006: PRESIDENT BUSH DEFENDS THE NSA AND THE PATRIOT ACT

In December 2005, the New York Times *published the results of an investigation that had found that the National Security Agency (NSA) was carrying out secret and wide-ranging warrantless wiretapping and data mining of international telephone and Internet communication data at the behest of the Bush administration. The newspaper published the story despite heavy pressure from Bush administration officials, who insisted that revealing the NSA operation—which they asserted was perfectly legal—would deliver a terrible blow to the security and safety of the American people. The decision to publish "was critical in reflecting the media's shifting attitudes toward matters of national security—from believing the government to believing it less," wrote Eric Lichtblau, who coauthored the article with James Risen, in a 2008* Slate *magazine story. "The concerns about the program—in both its legal underpinnings and its operations—reached the highest levels of the Bush administration. There were deep concerns within the administration that the president had authorized what amounted to an illegal usurpation of power."*

Publicly, however, the Bush administration presented a united front in the wake of the controversial revelations about the NSA program. As President Bush does here in a January 11, 2006, press conference in Kentucky, administration spokespeople defended the NSA's warrantless wiretapping and data mining as both prudent and legal.

. . . Let me—I wish I didn't have to say this, but we're still at war, and that's important for the citizens of this Commonwealth to understand. You know, no President ever wants to be President during war. But this war came to us, not as a result of actions we took; it came to us as a result of actions an enemy took on September the 11th, 2001. And I vowed that day, starting when I was in Florida and got on the airplane to head across the country, that I would use everything in my power—obviously, within the Constitution—but everything in my power to protect the American people. That is the most solemn duty of Government, is to protect our people from harm.

And I vowed that we'd find those killers and bring them to justice, and that's what we're doing. We're on the hunt for an enemy that still lurks. I know because I'm briefed on a daily basis about the threats that face the United States of America. And my duty is to assess this world the way it is, not the way we'd like it to be. And there's a danger that lurks—and there's a danger that lurks because we face an enemy which cannot stand freedom. It's an enemy which has an ideology that does not believe in free speech, free religion, free dissent, does not believe in women's rights, and they have a desire to impose their ideology on much of the world.

Secondly, after September the 11th, not only did I vow to use our assets to protect the people by staying on the offense, by defeating an enemy elsewhere so we don't have to face them here at home, I also said that, "If you harbor a terrorist, if you provide safe haven to a terrorist, you're equally as guilty as the terrorist." And I meant it. And the Taliban in Afghanistan—a barbaric group of individuals who suppressed women, suppressed religious freedom, suppressed young girls—had harbored these terrorists. They provided safe haven. These folks were there plotting and planning a vicious attack against the United States of America in a safe haven called Afghanistan.

And so we took action. We took action because the Taliban refused to expel Al Qaida. And we took action because when an American President says something, he better mean it. In order to be able to keep the peace, in order to be able to have credibility in this world, when we speak, we better mean what we say, and I meant what we said. And we sent some brave souls into Afghanistan to liberate that country from the Taliban.

I also said, after September the 11th, that oceans no longer protected us. You know, when I was growing up, or other baby boomers here were growing up, we felt safe because we had these vast oceans that could protect us from harm's way. September the 11th changed all that. And so I vowed that we would take threats seriously. If we saw a threat, we would take threats seriously before they fully materialized, and I saw a threat in Saddam Hussein.

I understand that the intelligence didn't turn out the way a lot of the world thought it would be. And that was disappointing, and we've done something about it. We've reformed our intelligence services. But Saddam Hussein was a sworn enemy of the United States. He was on the nations-that-sponsor-terror list for a reason. I didn't put him on the list; previous Presidents put him on the list. And the reason why is because he was sponsoring terrorism. He was shooting at our airplanes. He had attacked his own people with chemical weapons. I mean, the guy was a threat.

I went to the United Nations; some of you were probably concerned here in Kentucky that it seemed like the President was spending a little too much time in the United Nations. But I felt it was important to say to the world that this international body that we want to be effective, spoke loud and clear not once, but 15-odd times to Saddam Hussein—said, "Disarm. Get rid of your weapons. Don't be the threat that you are, or face serious consequences." That's what the international body said. And my view is, is that in order for the world to be effective, when it says something, it must mean it.

We gave the opportunity to Saddam Hussein to open his country up. It was his choice. He chose war, and he got war. And he's not in power, and the world is better off for it.

The hardest decision I made as your President is to put troops into harm's way, because I understand the consequences. I see the consequences when I go to the hospitals. I see the consequences when I try to comfort the loved ones who have lost a son or a daughter in combat. I understand that full—firsthand: War is brutal. And so I didn't take the decision lightly. Now that I've made the decision, we must succeed in Iraq. I've tried to explain to my fellow citizens, I can understand folks who said, "I wish you hadn't done that. We don't agree with your decision." Now that we're there, in my humble opinion, we have got to succeed. . . .

***Q.* I'd like to ask, recently in the media, you've been catching a lot of flak about that National Security Agency thing.**

The President. Yes.

***Q.* There's people in our States and there's people that are in DC that will take and jeopardize what I feel is our national security and our troops' safety today for partisan advantage, for political advantage. They're starting an investigation in the Justice Department about the—looking into this, where these leaks came from. Is the Justice Department going to follow through and, if necessary, go after the media to take and get the answers and to shut these leaks up?**

The President. First, let me talk about the issue you brought up, and it's a very serious issue. I did say to the National—it's called the NSA, National Security Agency, that they should protect America by taking the phone numbers of known Al Qaida and/or affiliates and find out why they're making phone calls into the United States, and vice versa. And I did so because the enemy still wants to hurt us. And it seems like to me that if somebody is talking to Al Qaida, we want to know why.

Now, I—look, I understand people's concerns about Government eavesdropping, and I share those concerns as well. So obviously, I had to make the difficult decision between balancing civil liberties and, on a limited basis—and I mean limited basis—try to find out the intention of the enemy. In order to safeguard the civil liberties of the people, we have this program fully scrutinized on a regular basis. It's been authorized, reauthorized many times. We got lawyers looking at it from different branches of Government.

We have briefed the leadership of the United States Congress, both Republican and Democrat, as well as the leaders of the intelligence committees, both Republicans and Democrats, about the nature of this program. We gave them a chance to express their disapproval or approval of a limited program taking known Al Qaida numbers—numbers from known Al Qaida people—and just trying to find out why the phone calls are being made.

I can understand concerns about this program. Before I went forward, I wanted to make sure I had all the legal authority necessary to make this decision as your President. We are a rule—a country of law. We have a Constitution, which guides the sharing of power. And I take that—I put that hand on the Bible, and I meant it when I said I'm going to uphold the Constitution. I also mean it when I'm going to protect the American people.

I have the right as the Commander in Chief in a time of war to take action necessary to protect the American people. And secondly, the Congress, in the authorization, basically said the President ought to—in authorization of the use of troops—ought to protect us. Well, one way to protect us is to understand the nature of the enemy. Part of being able to deal with this kind of enemy in a different kind of war is to understand why they're making decisions they're making inside our country.

So I want to thank you for bringing that up. There will be a lot of hearings and talk about that, but that's good for democracy, just so long as the hearings, as they explore whether or not I have the prerogative to make the decision I made, doesn't tell the enemy what we're doing. See, that's the danger.

The PATRIOT Act is up for renewal. That's another piece of legislation which is important to protect. Do you realize that the PATRIOT Act has given our FBI and intelligence services the same tools of sharing information that we have given to people that are fighting drug lords? In other words, much of the authorities that we ask for in the PATRIOT Act to be able to fight and win the war on terror has already been in practice when it comes to dealing with drug lords. And I can't tell you how important it is to reauthorize the legislation.

There's a lot of investigation, you're right, in Washington, which is okay. That's part of holding people to account in a democracy. But at one point in time the Government got accused of not connecting the dots. You might remember that debate; we didn't connect the dots. And all of a sudden, we start connecting the dots through the PATRIOT Act and the NSA decision, and we're being criticized. Now, you know, I got the message early: Why don't you connect dots? And we're going to. And we're going to safeguard the civil liberties of the people. That's what you've got to know.

Source: Bush, George W. 2006. "Remarks on the War on Terror and a Question-and-Answer Session in Louisville, Kentucky." January 11, 2006. *Public Papers of the Presidents of the United States: George W. Bush (2006, Book I)*. Washington, DC: Government Printing Office, pp. 41–58.

2006: SENATOR LEAHY LAMBASTS REPUBLICAN OPPOSITION TO PATRIOT ACT REFORMS

On June 22, 2005, the Republican-led House of Representatives easily passed a bill reauthorizing the USA PATRIOT Act by a 257–171 vote. The Senate, on the other hand, embraced the need for PATRIOT Act reform in its own reauthorization bill, S.1389, introducing numerous civil liberties protections while retaining the PATRIOT Act's major antiterrorism powers. In an amazing show of common purpose and collegiality, the Senate Judiciary Committee unanimously *approved S.1389 and reported it out of committee, where it was* unanimously *approved by the full Senate.*

The differences between the House and Senate bills, though, necessitated the creation of a "conference committee" to merge the two bills into the final reauthorization legislation. As negotiations began, the Bush White House intervened, producing a one-sided conference report that did away with the civil liberties reforms. The report was promptly rejected by the Senate. The resulting chaos produced impassioned congressional debate on the administration-sanctioned conference report, with particular focus on Section 215 and National Security Letters (NSLs).

In an effort to get Senate Democrats back on board, Republicans presented a set of amendments specifically targeting Section 215 and NSLs, collectively titled the USA PATRIOT Act Additional Reauthorizing Amendments Act of 2006 (S.2271). Democratic critics charged, however, that the changes introduced in S.2271 were relatively minor, leaving most of the terms of the conference report unchanged. Russ Feingold (D-WI), the only senator who voted against the original PATRIOT Act, refused to accept S.2271. He explained: "What we are seeing, I regret to say, is quite frankly, a capitulation on the intransigent and misleading rhetoric of the White House that sees any effort to protect civil liberties as a sign of weakness. . . . We have come too far and fought too hard to agree to reauthorize the PATRIOT Act without fixing any of the major problems with the act. A few insignificant face-saving changes don't cut it" (Congressional Record—Senate, February 15, 2006, p. S1327.). Fierce criticism was also leveled by Senator Patrick Leahy (D-VT) in a January 31, 2006, floor speech, which is excerpted here.

Leahy ultimately joined with Feingold and seven other Democratic senators (along with Independent Bernie Sanders) to vote against the measure, but the Reauthorization and Improvement Act (H.R. 3199) easily passed by an 89–10 margin, with 35 Democrats joining 54 Republicans in support. Together H.R.3199 and S.2271 formed the full reauthorization package that would make 14 sections of the

PATRIOT Act permanent, sunset two others, and modify Section 215 and the NSLs authority. H.R.3199, the basic reauthorization law, made the following changes to Section 215 and NSLs:

- *Created a new sunset for Section 215 of December 31, 2009.*
- *Provided for greater congressional and judicial oversight of Section 215 and National Security Letters, including annual reports to Congress.*
- *Required personal approval by either the FBI Director, the FBI Deputy Director, or the Executive Assistant for Nation Security for Section 215 orders for library, bookstore, firearms, medical, tax, and educational records.*
- *Required the Inspector General of the Justice Department to conduct an audit for the years 2002–2006 to determine the effectiveness, and identify any abuses, with respect to the use of Section 215 or National Security Letters.*
- *Required the Attorney General to promulgate "minimization" standards to limit the retention and regulate the dissemination of information acquired concerning unconsenting U.S. persons.*
- *Required applications for Section 215 order to include a "statement of facts" showing reasonable grounds to believe that the materials sought are "relevant" to a terrorism or counterintelligence investigation. However, the materials sought are "presumptively relevant" if they pertain to a foreign power, an agent of a foreign power, or an individual in contact with a foreign power or agent.*
- *Allowed recipients of a Section 215 nondisclosure order to disclose its existence to their attorney.*
- *Allowed the recipient of a National Security Letter to petition a U.S. district court to modify or set aside the order.*
- *Prohibited service providers from disclosing the issuance of a NSL only if the investigative agency certifies that disclosure may endanger an individual or the national security of the United States; interfere with international relations or a criminal or intelligence investigation.*

The Additional Reauthorizing Amendments Act (S.2271) added the following restraints on Section 215 orders and NSLs:

- *Exempted the identity of attorneys sought for legal advice from Section 215 and NSL nondisclosure requirements.*
- *Established a judicial review procedure for Section 215 nondisclosure orders beginning one year after the issuance of the order.*
- *Exempted libraries operating in their "traditional role" from NSL orders.*

Remarks of Mr. Leahy on Improving the Patriot Act

Mr. President, those of us working constructively and in a bipartisan way to extend the USA PATRIOT Act with improvements have repeatedly offered to meet to work out the remaining differences. Sadly, the Senate leadership has not made the effort to work through the remaining concerns or brought us together.

I have continued meeting and talking with interested Republican and Democratic Senators. Senate staff has finally gotten together this week in a bipartisan meeting. I urge the majority leader to bring together key interested Senators to work out a bipartisan compromise that improves the failed conference report.

A majority of Senators—Republicans and Democrats, those who voted against cloture on the conference report that failed to pass the Senate and those who voted for it urged the Republican leader to act on a short-term, 3-month extension before the end of the last session.

Instead, he chose to proceed with a 6-month extension that Republicans in the House found objectionable. That led to the short extension that is about to expire this week. The President had said that he would not approve a short-term extension. House Republicans had said that they would not allow a short-term extension. But just before Christmas they demanded and enacted a shorter extension than anyone else had proposed.

As soon as it became apparent that the conference report filed by the Republican leadership would be unacceptable to the Senate, I joined on Thursday, December 8, in urging a 3-month extension to work out a better bill. On the first day the Senate was next in session, Monday, December 12, Senator Sununu and I introduced such a bill, S.2082. We sent out a "Dear Colleague" letter to other Senators on December 13 and that bipartisan bill was cosponsored by 46 other Senators. That bill would have extended the PATRIOT Act until March 31, 2006, to allow us all to work out the remaining differences and improve this reauthorization legislation in ways to better protect the rights of ordinary Americans. It proposed a commonsense solution to allow us to take a few more weeks to get this right for all Americans.

Contrary to the false claims and misrepresentations by some, there was no effort on either side of the aisle to do away with the PATRIOT Act. That is just not true. Along with others here in the Senate, I am seeking to mend and extend the PATRIOT Act, not to end it. There is no reason why the American people cannot have a PATRIOT Act that is both effective and that adequately protects their rights and their privacy.

The only people who were threatening an expiration of the PATRIOT Act were the President and House Republicans. As I noted on December 21, the administration and the Republican congressional leadership were the ones who were objecting to extending the act and threatening to have it expire. That was wrong. That made no sense. They came to their senses in the days that followed. But now, as we approach the expiration of the current extension this Friday, the Republican congressional leadership has taken no further action and we risk sections of the PATRIOT Act expiring, again.

Republican and Democratic Senators joined together last month to say we can do better to protect Americans' liberties while ensuring our national security is as strong as it can be. In the days after 9/11 we acted as Americans, not Democrats, not Republicans. The President's political adviser Karl Rove and the rest of those who are seeking to make the PATRIOT Act a partisan political issue should instead join with our bipartisan coalition and work with us to provide a better balance to protect the rights of Americans.

Every single Senator—Republican and Democratic—voted last July to mend and extend the PATRIOT Act. That bipartisan solution was cast aside by the Bush administration and Republican congressional leaders when they hijacked the conference report, rewrote the bill in ways that fell short in protecting basic civil liberties and then tried to ram it through Congress as an all-or-nothing proposition. I have joined with Senators of both parties in an effort to work to improve the bill. Some of us are working hard to protect the security and liberty of Americans. What is wrong is for the White House to manipulate this into partisan fight for its partisan political advantage. Instead of playing partisan politics, the Bush administration and Republican congressional leadership should join in trying to improve the law.

This is a vital debate. The terrorist threat to America's security is very real, and it is vital that we be armed with the tools needed to protect Americans' security. At the same time, however, the threat to civil liberties is also very real in America today. The question is not whether the Government should have the tools it needs to protect the American people. Of course it should. That is why I coauthored the PATRIOT Act 5 years ago, and that is why that Act passed with broad bipartisan support. When I voted for the PATRIOT Act, I did not think it was an ideal piece of legislation, and I knew that it would need careful oversight and, in due course, reform.

None of us wants the PATRIOT Act to expire, and those who threatened to let it expire rather than fix it play a dangerous game. This is about how to reconcile two shared and fundamental goals—ensuring the safety of the American people and protecting their liberty by means of a system of checks and balances that keeps the Government—their Government—accountable.

Those goals are not the goals of any particular party or ideology; they are shared American goals. How to balance security with liberty and Government accountability was the most fundamental dilemma with which the Framers of our Constitution wrestled, and how to adjust that balance in the post-9/11 world is a fundamental dilemma before this Congress.

Our Nation is a democracy, founded on the principles of balanced government. We need to restore checks and balances in this country to protect us all and all that we hold dear. Our Congress and our courts provide checks on the abuse of executive authority and should protect our liberties. Congress must write the law so it provides not just a check on Presidential power but also a clear role for the courts. All Americans need to take notice and need to demand that their liberties be maintained. We can do better and must do better for the American people.

Source: Senator Leahy, Patrick. 2006. "Improving the Patriot Act." *Congressional Record,* Volume 152, Number 9, January 31, 2006, pp. S362–63.

2006: PRESIDENT BUSH SIGNS A REAUTHORIZATION OF THE PATRIOT ACT

Although passage of legislation reauthorizing the PATRIOT Act had been fraught with false starts and political controversy, in the end Republican majorities in both the House and Senate—with some support from Democrats—were able to deliver the bill that the Bush administration had wanted all along. This legislation, the USA PATRIOT Improvement and Reauthorization Act, largely kept in place the surveillance authority and options that had been granted to the federal government with the first PATRIOT Act in 2001. The bill was signed into law by President George W. Bush on March 9, 2006. Following are excerpts from his remarks at the signing ceremony.

In a few moments I'll be signing the USA Patriot Improvement and Reauthorization Act. This is a really important piece of legislation. It is a piece of legislation that's vital to win the war on terror and to protect the American people.

The law allows our intelligence and law enforcement officials to continue to share information. It allows them to continue to use tools against terrorists that they used against—that they use against drug dealers and other criminals. It will improve our nation's security while we safeguard the civil liberties of our people. The legislation strengthens the Justice Department so it can better detect and disrupt terrorist threats. And the bill gives law enforcement new tools to combat threats to our citizens from international terrorists to local drug dealers.

It is an important piece of legislation. And I thank those here who helped get it passed. I particularly want to thank the Attorney General, Al Gonzales. It's good to see former Attorney Generals here, as well. I appreciate Secretary Mike Chertoff, Secretary John Snow, Ambassador Negroponte, Bob Mueller. Thank you all for coming. John Walters, appreciate you being here.

I particularly want to thank the members of the Congress who are up here, starting with the Speaker of the House, Denny Hastert. Mr. Speaker, thanks for your leadership on this important piece of legislation. I do want to pay special tribute to Senator Arlen Specter and Congressman Jim Sensenbrenner. These are the Chairmen of the Judiciary Committees that got this legislation to this desk. Thank you all for your hard work. I appreciate you being here.

I want to thank Pat Roberts, who's with us; John Boehner, Majority Leader; Roy Blunt, the Majority Whip. I want to thank all the other members of the Congress who have joined us, particularly Peter King, who is the Chairman of the House Homeland Security Committee.

I want to thank all the state and local officials who are here—Chief Ramsey, it's good to see you. Appreciate you coming. Always be good to the local police chief. (Laughter.)

America remains a nation at war. The war reached our shores on September the 11th, 2001. On that morning, we saw clearly the violence and hatred of a new enemy. We saw the terrorists' destructive vision for us when they killed nearly 3,000 men, women, and children.

In the face of this ruthless threat, our nation has made a clear choice: We will confront this mortal danger, we will stay on the offensive, and we're not going to wait to be attacked again. Since September the 11th, 2001, we have taken the fight to the enemy. We've hunted terrorists in the mountains of Afghanistan, cities of Iraq, the islands of Southeast Asia, and everywhere else they plot, plan, and train. Our men and women in uniform have brought down two regimes that supported terrorism. We liberated 50 million people. We've gained new allies in the war on terror.

As we wage the war on terror overseas, we're also going after the terrorists here at home, and one of the most important tools we have used to protect the American people is the Patriot Act. The Patriot Act closed dangerous gaps in America's law enforcement and intelligence capabilities, gaps the terrorists exploited when they attacked us on September the 11th.

The Patriot Act was passed with overwhelming bipartisan support. It strengthened our national security in two important ways: First, it authorized law enforcement and intelligence officers to share vital information. Before the Patriot Act, criminal investigators were often separated from intelligence officers by a legal and bureaucratic wall. The Patriot Act tore down the wall. And as a result, law enforcement and intelligence officers are sharing information, working together, and bringing terrorists to justice.

Secondly, the Patriot Act has allowed agents to pursue terrorists with the same tools they use against other criminals. Before the Patriot Act, it was easier to track the phone contacts of a drug dealer than the phone contacts of an enemy operative. Before the Patriot Act, it was easier to get the credit card receipts of a tax cheater than trace the financial support of an al Qaeda fundraiser. The Patriot Act corrected these double standards, and the United States is safer as a result.

Over the past four years, America's law enforcement and intelligence personnel have proved the Patriot Act works. Federal, state, and local law enforcement have used the Patriot Act to break up terror cells in Ohio, New York, Oregon and Virginia. We've prosecuted terrorist operatives and supporters in California and Texas, New Jersey, Illinois, Washington, and North Carolina.

The Patriot Act has accomplished exactly what it was designed to do. It has helped us detect terror cells, disrupt terrorist plots and save American lives. The bill I sign today extends these vital provisions. It also gives our nation new protections and added defenses.

This legislation creates a new position of Assistant Attorney General for National Security. This will allow the Justice Department to bring together its national security, counterterrorism, counterintelligence and foreign intelligence surveillance operations under a single authority. This reorganization fulfills one of the critical recommendations of the WMD Commission: It will help our brave men and women in law enforcement connect the dots before the terrorists strike. . . .

The Patriot Act has served America well, yet we cannot let the fact that America has not been attacked since September the 11th lull us into the illusion that the terrorist threat has disappeared. We still face dangerous enemies. The terrorists haven't lost the will or the ability to kill innocent folks. Our military, law enforcement, homeland security and intelligence professionals are working day and night to protect us from this threat. We're safer for their efforts, and we'll continue to give them the tools to get the job done.

And now, it's my honor to sign the USA Patriot Improvement and Reauthorization Act of 2005.

Source: Bush, George W. 2006. "Remarks on Signing the USA Patriot Improvement and Reauthorization Act of 2005." March 9, 2006. *Public Papers of the Presidents of the United States: George W. Bush (2006, Book I)*. Washington, DC: Government Printing Office, pp. 428–30.

2006: ROVING WIRETAPS AND "SNEAK AND PEEK" WARRANTS

Most of the contentious debate over reauthorization of the PATRIOT Act centered on Section 215 and National Security Letters (NSLs), but Section 213 of the PATRIOT Act (which authorized delayed notice search warrants, also known as "sneak and peek" warrants) and Section 206 (which authorized roving wire taps) received their share of attention as well. Democratic critics of these provisions such as Senator Russ Feingold (WI) were unable to garner enough support to place significant new limitations on these powers, but some modest changes were incorporated into the reauthorization bill.

On the "sneak and peek" provision, the Reauthorization Act required notice of a search warrant to be given no more than 30 days after the warrant's execution, a considerably longer period than the 7-day limit specified in the Senate's reauthorization bill, but considerably shorter than the 180-day limit in the House bill. In addition, the final reauthorization legislation removed the catch-all phrase "unduly delaying a trial" as a justification for delaying notice. Finally, the Reauthorization Act requires that no later than 30 days after the expiration or denial of such a warrant the issuing or denying judge must notify the Administrative Office of the U.S. Courts of the fact that the delayed notice was applied for, granted, modified, or denied; the length of time of the delay in giving notice; and the offense specified in the warrant or application.

On the "roving wiretap" provision, the Reauthorization Act required that if the government begins surveillance at a new site, the nature and location of which were unknown when the original order was issued, it must provide the FISA court with the facts and circumstances justifying the applicant's belief that each new site is or was being used, or is about to be used, by the target of the surveillance; an explanation of any proposed minimization procedures that differ from those contained in the original order, if such change is necessitated by the new site; and the total number of electronic surveillances that have been or are being conducted under the roving surveillance order. The act also added the Senate Judiciary Committee as a recipient of the semi-annual FISA reports and modified the FISA reporting requirements to include a description of the total number of applications made for roving electronic surveillance orders.

Following is the exact language of the Sections 108 and 114 of the Reauthorization Act; it shows how each section was modified from its original form in the 2001 USA PATRIOT Act.

(1) Section 108: Multipoint Electronic Surveillance

Sec. 108. Multipoint Electronic Surveillance Under Section 206 of the USA Patriot Act

(a) Inclusion of specific Facts in Application—

(1) APPLICATION—Section 104(a)(3) of the Foreign Intelligence surveillance Act of 1978 (50 U.S.C. 1804(a)(3)) is amended by inserting "specific" after "description of the".

(2) ORDER—Subsection (c) of Section 105 of the Foreign Intelligence surveillance Act of 1978 (50 U.S.C. 1805 (c)) is amended—

(A) in paragraph (1)(A) by striking "target of the electronic surveillance" and inserting "specific target of the electronic surveillance identified or described in the application pursuant to section 104(a)(3)"; and

(B) in paragraph (2)(B), by striking "where the Court finds" and inserting "where the Court finds, based upon specific facts provided in the application,".

(b) Additional Direction—Such subsection is further amended—

(1) by striking "An order approving" and all that follows through "specify" and inserting "(1) SPECIFICATIONS—An order approving an electronic surveillance under this section shall specify";

(2) in paragraph (1)(F), by striking "; and" and inserting a period;

(3) in paragraph (2), by striking "direct" and inserting "DIRECTIONS—An order approving an electronic surveillance under this section shall direct"; and

(4) by adding at the end the following new paragraph:

'(3) SPECIAL DIRECTIONS FOR CERTAIN ORDERS—An order approving an electronic surveillance under this section in circumstances where the nature and location of each of the facilities or places at which the surveillance will be directed is unknown shall direct the applicant to provide notice to the court within ten days after the date on which surveillance begins to be directed at any new facility or place, unless the court finds good cause to justify a longer period of up to 60 days, of—

"(A) the nature and location of each new facility or place at which the electronic surveillance is directed;
"(B) the facts and circumstances relied upon by the applicant to justify the applicant's belief that each new facility or place at which the electronic surveillance is directed is or was being used, or is about to be used, by the target of the surveillance;
"(C) a statement of any proposed minimization procedures that differ from those contained in the original application or order, that may be necessitated by a change in the facility or place at which the electronic surveillance is directed; and
"(D) the total number of electronic surveillances that have been or are being conducted under the authority of the order.".

(c) Enhanced Oversight—

(1) REPORT TO CONGRESS—Section 108(a)(1) of the Foreign Intelligence Surveillance Act of 1978 (50 U.S.C. 1808(a)(1)) is amended by inserting, "and the Committee on the Judiciary of the Senate," after "Senate Select Committee on Intelligence".
(2) MODIFICATION OF SEMIANNUAL REPORT REQUIREMENT ON ACTIVITIES UNDER FOREIGN INTELLIGENCE SURVEILLANCE ACT OF 1978—Paragraph (2) of section 108(a) of the Foreign Intelligence surveillance Act of 1978 (50 U.S.C. 1808(a)) is amended to read as follows:

"(2) Each report under the first sentence of paragraph (1) shall include a description of—

"(A) the total number of applications made for orders and extensions of orders approving electronic surveillance under this title where the nature and location of each facility or place at which the electronic surveillance will be directed is unknown;
"(B) each criminal case in which information acquired under this Act has been authorized for use at trial during the period covered by such report;
"(C) the total number of emergency employments of electronic surveillance under section 105(f) and the total number of subsequent orders approving or denying such electronic surveillance.".

(2) Section 114: Delayed Notice Search Warrants

Sec. 114. Delayed Notice Search Warrants

(a) Limitation on Reasonable Period for Delay—Section 3103a of title 18, United States Code, is amended—

(1) by striking subsection (b)(3) and inserting the following:

"(3) the warrant provides for the giving of such notice within a reasonable period not to exceed 30 days after the date of its execution, or on a later date certain if the facts of the case justify a longer period of delay.".

(2) by adding at the end the following:

"(c) Extensions of delay—Any period of delay authorized by this section may be extended by the court for good cause shown, subject to the condition that extensions should only be granted upon an updated showing of the need for further delay and that each additional delay should be limited to periods of 90 days or less, unless the facts of the case justify a longer period of delay.".

(b) Limitation on Authority to Delay Notice—Section 3103a(b)(1) of title 18 United States Code, is amended by inserting ", except if the adverse results consist only of unduly delaying a trial" after "2705".

(c) Enhanced Oversight—Section 3103a of title 18, United States Code, is further amended by adding at the end the following:

"(d) Reports—

"(1) REPORT BY JUDGE—Not later than 30 days after the expiration of a warrant authorizing delayed notice (including any extension thereof) entered under this section, or the denial of such warrant (or request for extension), the issuing or denying judge shall report to the Administrative Office of the United States courts—

"(A) the fact that a warrant was applied for;

"(B) the fact that the warrant or any extension thereof was granted as applied for, was modified, or was denied;

"(C) the period of delay in the giving of notice authorized by the warrant, and the number and duration of any extensions; and

"(D the offense specified in the warrant or application.

"(2) REPORT BY ADMINISTRATIVE OFFICE OF THE UNITED STATES COURTS—Beginning with the fiscal year ending September 30, 2007, the Director of the Administrative Office of the United States Courts shall transmit to Congress annually a full and complete report summarizing the data required to be filed with the Administrative Office by paragraph (1), including the number of applications for warrants and extensions of warrants authorizing delayed notice, and the number of such warrants and extensions granted or denied . . .

"(3) REGULATIONS—The Director of the Administrative Office of the United States Courts, in consultation with the Attorney General, is authorized to issue binding regulations dealing with the content and form of the reports required to be filed under paragraph (1)."

Source: USA PATRIOT Improvement and Reauthorization Act of 2005. 109th Congress Public Law 177. Washington, DC: Government Printing Office.

2006: DISTRICT COURT RULES NSL GAG ORDERS UNCONSTITUTIONAL

During the first few years following passage of the PATRIOT Act, librarians and booksellers complained that PATRIOT Act surveillance tools such as Section 215 and National Security Letters (NSLs) represented a threat to Americans' right to read. But Department of Justice spokespersons responded by claiming that they had never used such provisions against American citizens. PATRIOT Act critics could not prove otherwise, and in particular, librarians could provide no specific examples of PATRIOT Act intrusions. The inclusion of "gag rules" in Section 215 warrants and NSLs ensured that no librarian could publicly reveal PATRIOT Act surveillance without suffering heavy criminal penalties.

Eventually, however, two cases featuring anonymous plaintiffs challenged the use of NSLs and their accompanying gag orders. The first case, John Doe v. John Ashcroft, *arose when an Internet service provider (ISP) received a NSL that requested information on a subscriber and warned the ISP not to inform "any person" that the records were sought or obtained. The ACLU brought suit challenging §2709(c) of the PATRIOT Act on behalf of the ISP plaintiff, who was protected from criminal charges by using the anonymous name of "John Doe."*

*On September 28, 2004, U.S. District Judge Victor Marrero ruled that the FBI's use of NSLs and its enforcement of the accompanying gag order violated the First and Fourth Amendments to the Constitution. In particular, the written opinion defended the right of Internet subscribers to confidentiality and anonymity. Marrero categorically rejected the PATRIOT Act's use of open-ended gag orders, declaring: "[P]ublic knowledge secures freedom. Hence, an unlimited government warrant to conceal, effectively a form of secrecy per se, has no place in our open society. Such a claim is especially inimical to democratic values for reasons borne out by painful experience. Under the mantle of secrecy, the self-preservation that normally impels our government censorship may potentially be turned on ourselves as a weapon of self-destruction . . . [A] categorical and uncritical extension of nondisclosure may become the cover for spurious ends that the government may then deem too inconvenient, inexpedient, merely embarrassing, or illicit to expose to the light of the day" (*John Doe v. John Ashcroft, *Civil Action No. 04-Civ.-2614 (VM), United States District Court for the Southern District of New York, September 28, 2004).*

The U.S. government promptly appealed Marrero's decision, enforcement of which had been stayed in anticipation of just such an appeal. While Doe v. Ashcroft *awaited an appeals court hearing, a second anonymous case,* John Doe v. Alberto Gonzales, *arose to challenge the PATRIOT Act's gag order provision. The case was precipitated by an FBI visit to a Connecticut library in August 2005, during which two FBI agents delivered an NSL to library official George Christian, warning him to tell no one of the order. The letter directed Christian to surrender "all subscriber information billing information and access logs of any person" who used a specific computer at a library branch.*

Christian, who manages digital records for three dozen Connecticut libraries, refused to surrender these electronic records, and his employer, Library Connection Inc., filed suit for the right to publicly challenge and protest the order. As in the New York case, the threat of felony charges against the company if it went public made it necessary to file the suit anonymously. Hence, John Doe v. Alberto Gonzales *was born, with the plaintiff "John Doe" actually representing four Library Connection officials, George Christian, Peter Chase, Barbara Bailey, and Janet Nocek. George Christian, Library Connection's executive director, is identified in his affidavit as "John Doe 2," perhaps to distinguish him from the "John Doe" in the New York case.*

In September 2005, U.S. District Judge Janet Hall ruled that the NSL gag order violated the First Amendment rights of Christian and the other Library Connection officials. In particular, she concluded: "The defendants are hereby enjoined from enforcing 18 U.S.C. §2709(c) against the plaintiffs with regard to Doe's identity." Judge Hall's ruling prompted an almost immediate change in FBI behavior because she stayed enforcement of the order for just ten days.

Despite the fact that Hall's order freed the plaintiffs to identify only themselves, not the targets of the FBI investigation, the government quickly appealed, thus extending the silence imposed on the Connecticut librarians. The appeals court proceedings, which lasted until May 2006, were chaotic and often contradictory, as the Second Circuit sought to combine the New York and Connecticut cases while referring to the plaintiffs as "John Doe 1" and "John Doe 2."

The government continued to insist that the gag orders and the broader NSL authority were essential in the war on terror. Then, suddenly, during the first week of April 2006, the government filed a sealed letter brief with the court in which it unexpectedly stated that it "will not oppose" the lifting of the gag order on the Connecticut librarians. Still, the government reaffirmed its intent to pursue its appeal of the New York decision, which struck down the entire NSL provision as unconstitutional.

Meanwhile, the un-gagged Connecticut librarians and the broader library profession celebrated their victory over the PATRIOT Act's nondisclosure provision. "Imagine the government came to you with an order demanding that you compromise your professional and personal principles," said Janet Nocek, one of the librarians. "Imagine then being permanently gagged from speaking to your friends, your family or your colleagues about this wrenching experience" ("Tangled Web," NOW, PBS, June 2, 2006. www.pbs.org/now/shows/222/george-christian-interview.html).

*The actual decision of the Second Circuit Court of Appeals turned out to be anticlimactic, however. The ruling on "Doe I" (*John Doe v. Ashcroft*) was later "vacated and remanded" due to changes to the PATRIOT Act effected in the Reauthorization Act of 2006: "Because the Reauthorization Act added provisions permitting NSL recipients to challenge the issuance of NSLs in court, John Doe I no longer presses Fourth Amendment claims on this appeal. Therefore, we deem them abandoned, rendering this portion of the appeal moot." As for the First Amendment challenge in Doe I, the court remanded the case so that First Amendment issues could be re-examined at the lower court in light of changes wrought by the Reauthorization Act.*

*On the matter of "Doe II," the Second Circuit declared: "Given the concession of the Government on appeal that John Doe II can disclose its identity, the Government no longer opposes the relief granted by the District of Connecticut in its preliminary injunction ruling. Thus, the Government has effectively rendered this appeal moot by its own voluntary actions" (*John Doe I, John Doe II v. Alberto Gonzales, *United States Court of Appeals for the Second Circuit, May 23, 2006. Docket Nos. 05–0570-cv(L), 05–4896-cv(CON)).*

Following are excerpts from both the Doe v. Ashcroft *and* Doe v. Gonzales *rulings:*

John Doe v. John Ashcroft

Plaintiffs in this case challenge the constitutionality of 18 U.S.C. §2709 ("§2709"). That statute authorizes the Federal bureau of Investigation ("FBI") to compel communications firms, such as internet service providers ("ISPs") or telephone companies, to produce certain customer records whenever the FBI certifies that those records are "relevant to an authorized investigation to protect against international terrorism or clandestine intelligence activities." The FBI's demands under §2709 are issued in the form of national security letters ("NSLs"), which constitute a unique form of administrative subpoena cloaked in secrecy and pertaining to national security issues. The statute bars all NSL recipients from ever disclosing that the FBI has issued an NSL.

The lead plaintiff, called "John Doe" ("Doe") for purposes of this litigation, is described in the complaint as an internet access firm that received an NSL . . . Plaintiffs contend that §2709's broad subpoena power violates the First, Fourth and Fifth Amendments of the United States Constitution, and that the non-disclosure provision violates the First Amendment. They argue that §2709 is unconstitutional on its face and as applied to the facts of this case. Plaintiffs' main complaints are that, first §2709 gives the FBI extraordinary and unchecked power to obtain private information without any form of judicial process, and, second, that §2709's non-disclosure provision burdens speech categorically and perpetually, without any case-by-case judicial consideration of whether that speech burden is justified. The parties have cross-moved for summary judgment on all claims.

For the reasons explained below, the Court grants Plaintiffs' motion. The Court concludes that §2709 violates the Fourth Amendment because, at least as currently applied, it effectively bars or substantially deters any judicial challenge to the propriety of an NSL request. In the Court's view, ready availability of judicial process to pursue such a challenge is necessary to vindicate important rights guaranteed by the Constitution or by statute. On separate grounds, the Court also concludes that the permanent ban on disclosure contained in §2709(c), which the Court is unable to sever from the remainder of the statute, operates as an unconstitutional prior restraint on speech in violation of the First Amendment . . .

To summarize, the court concludes that the compulsory, secret, and unreviewable production of information required by the FBI's application of 18 U.S.C. §2709 violates the Fourth Amendment, and that the non-disclosure provision of 18 U.S.C. §2709(c) violates the First Amendment. The Government is therefore enjoined from issuing NSLs under §2709 or from enforcing the non-disclosure provision in this or any other case, but enforcement of the Court's judgment will be stayed pending appeal, or if no appeal is filed, for 90 days.

Source: John Doe v. John Ashcroft, Civil Action No. 04-Civ.-2614 (VM), United States District Court for the Southern District of New York, September 28, 2004.

John Doe v. Alberto Gonzales

On August 9, 2005, the plaintiffs filed suit challenging the constitutionality of 18 U.S.C. §2709. One of the plaintiffs is John Doe, the recipient of a National Security Letter ("NSL") issued pursuant to §2709. . . In this lawsuit, the plaintiffs claim, first, that §2709 violates the First Amendment by prohibiting any person from disclosing that the FBI has sought or obtained information with a NSL; second, that §2709 violates the First amendment by authorizing the FBI to order disclosure of constitutionally protected information without tailoring its demand to a demonstrably compelling need; third, that §2709 violates the First and Fourth Amendments because it fails to provide for or specify a mechanism by which a recipient can challenge the NSL's validity; fourth, that §2709 voilates the First, Fourth, and Fifth Amendments by authorizing the FBI to demand disclosure of constitutionally protected information without prior notice to individuals whose information is disclosed and without requiring that the FBI justify that denial of notice on a case-by-case basis; and fifth, that §2709 violates the Fifth Amendment because it is unconstitutionally vague. With respect to all five challenges, the plaintiffs claim that the statute is unconstitutional both on its face and as applied to them. They seek declaratory and injunctive relief.

Currently pending before the court is plaintiffs' motion for preliminary relief filed on August 16, 2005. The NSL in question tracks the language of the statute in advising the recipient "the Title 18, U.S.C., Section 2709(c), prohibits any officer employee or agent of yours from disclosing to any person that the FBI has sought or obtained access to information or records under these provisions [18 U.S.C. §2709]." . . .

The issue before the court in connection with the motion for preliminary injunction is whether the §2709(c) prohibition on the plaintiffs' disclosure of the identity of the recipient is unconstitutional as applied in this case such that enforcement of that prohibition ought to be enjoined pending resolution of the case on the merits . . .

For the reasons discussed above, the plaintiffs' motion for preliminary relief is GRANTED. The defendants are hereby enjoined from enforcing 18 U.S.C. §2709(c) against the plaintiffs with regard to Doe's identity.

Source: John Doe, et al. v. Alberto Gonzales, Civil Action No. 3:05-cv-1256 (JCH), September 9, 2005, U.S. District Court for the District of Connecticut.

2007: INSPECTOR GENERAL'S REPORT REVEALS FBI ABUSE OF NATIONAL SECURITY LETTERS

In March 2007, the Inspector General (IG) of the Department of Justice released a report that revealed massive FBI misuse of National Security Letters (NSLs). The FBI's record on NSLs was exposed as the result of a provision in the 2006 PATRIOT Act reauthorization that specifically required an IG audit of the agency's use of NSLs.

*The revelations of FBI abuse of NSLs brought calls for changes to the PATRIOT Act, with particular emphasis on tightening the loose "relevance standard" by which NSLs are authorized under the PATRIOT Act. But restricting the Justice Department's antiterrorism powers would prove much more difficult than reducing the Attorney General's authority to fire and replace DOJ employees. In his testimony before the Senate Judiciary Committee on March 28, 2007, FBI Director Mueller acknowledged the seriousness of the bureau's abuse of its NSL authority, but he firmly declared: "I do not believe, however, that the statute itself should be changed. The relevance standard established by the Patriot Act for the issuance of National Security Letters is unrelated to the problems identified by the Inspector General. As the Inspector General testified, the problems were generally the product o*f, and I quote, *'mistakes, carelessness, confusion, sloppiness, lack of training, lack of adequate guidance, and lack of adequate oversight.' In short, the statute did not cause the errors. The FBI's implementation of the statute did." ("Oversight of the Federal Bureau of Investigation," Senate Judiciary Committee, March 27, 2007, http://www.gpo.gov/fdsys/pkg/CHRG-110shrg38189/html/CHRG-110shrg38189.htm).*

Many Democratic members of Congress were not mollified by promises by the FBI and the Bush administration's Justice Department to clean up their record on NSLs. As Senator Patrick Leahy (D-RI), chairman of the Committee on the Judiciary stated, "This pattern of abuse and mismanagement causes me, and many others on both sides of the aisle, to wonder whether the FBI and Department of Justice have been faithful trustees of the great trust that the Congress and American people have placed in them to keep our Nation safe, while respecting the privacy rights and civil liberties of all Americans ("Oversight of the Federal Bureau of Investigation," Senate Judiciary Committee, March 27, 2007. http://judiciary.senate.gov/member_statement.cfm?id=2569&wit_id=2629).

Even Republican members of Congress were aggressive in their criticism of the FBI's use of NSLs. Rep. William Sensenbrenner (R-WI), the former Republican Chairman of the House Judiciary Committee that oversaw the use of the PATRIOT Act, declared, "I am shocked. I think that the Justice Department has overreached. There is something seriously wrong with the internal management of the Justice Department, and that better be fixed, because if it isn't, support for the internal part of the war upon terrorism is going to evaporate rapidly" ("Privacy Abuses: FBI Mistakes and Misuse of the Patriot Act," Lehrer Newshour, public television, March 9, 2007).

Conclusion and Recommendations

As required by the Patriot Reauthorization Act, this OIG review examined the FBI's use of national security letters from calendar years 2003 through 2005. The Act required the OIG to examine how many requests were issued by the FBI; any noteworthy facts or circumstances relating to such use, including any improper or illegal use of such authority; the importance of the information acquired to the intelligence activities of the Department of Justice or to others; the manner in which such information is collected, retained, analyzed, and disseminated by the Department; whether and how often the Department utilized such information to produce an analytical intelligence product for distribution within the Department of Justice, to the intelligence community, or to others; and whether and how often the Department provided such information to law enforcement authorities for use in criminal proceedings.

Our review found that the FBI's use of national security letter requests has grown dramatically since enactment of the Patriot Act in October 2001. The FBI issued approximately 8,5000 NSL requests in CY 2000, the last full year prior to passage of the Patriot Act. After the Patriot Act, the number of NSL requests increased to approximately 39,000 in 2003, approximately 56,000 in 2004, and approximately 47,000 in 2005. During the period covered by our review, the FBI issued a total of 143,074 NSL requests pursuant to national security letter authorities. . . .

We found that the use of NSL requests related to "U.S. persons" and "non-U.S. persons" shifted during our 3-year review period. The percentage of requests generated from investigations of U.S. persons increased from about 39 percent of all NSL requests issued in 2003 to about 53 percent of all NSL requests during 2005. . . .

It is important to note that these statistics, which were obtained from the FBI electronic database that tracks NSL usage, understate the total number of national security letter requests. We found that the OGC database is inaccurate and does not include all national security letter requests issued by the FBI.

Because of inaccuracies in the OGC database, we compared data in this database to a sample of investigative files in four FBI field offices that we visited. Overall, we found approximately 17 percent more national security *letters* and 22 percent more national security letter *requests* in the case files we examined in four field offices than were recorded in the OGC database. As a result, we believe that the total numbers of NSLs and NSL requests issued by the FBI are significantly higher than the FBI reported.

Further, we found the OGC database did not accurately reflect the status of investigative subjects or other targets of NSLs and that the Department's semiannual classified reports to Congress on NSL usage were also inaccurate. . . . [For example], we found that 12 percent of the case files we examined did not accurately report the status of the target of the NSL as being a U.S. person or a non-U.S. person. In each of these instances, the FBI database indicated that the subject was a non-U.S. person while the approval memoranda in the investigative file indicated the subject was a U.S. person or a presumed U.S. person.

With respect to the effectiveness of national security letters, FBI Headquarters and field personnel told us that they believe national security letters are indispensable investigative tools that serve as building blocks in many counterterrorism and counterintelligence investigations. National security letters have various uses, including obtaining evidence to support FISA applications for electronic surveillance, pen register/trap and trace devices, or physical searches; developing communication or financial links between subjects of FBI investigations and between those subjects and others; providing evidence to initiate new investigations, expand investigations, or enable agents to close investigations; providing investigative leads; and corroborating information obtained by other investigative techniques. . . .

As required by the Patriot Reauthorization Act, our review also examined instances of improper or illegal use of national security letters. First, our review examined national security letter violations that the FBI was required to report to the President's Intelligence Oversight Board (IOB). Executive Order 12863 directs the IOB to inform the President of any activities that the IOB believes "may be unlawful or contrary to Executive order or presidential directive." The FBI identified 26 possible violations involving the use of national security letter authorities from 2003 through 2005, of which 19 were reported to the IOB. These 19 involved the issuance of NSLs without proper authorization, improper requests under statutes cited in the national security letters, and unauthorized collection of telephone or Internet e-mail transactional records, including records containing data beyond the time period requested in the national security letters. Of these 26 possible violations, 22 were the result of FBI errors, while 4 were caused by mistakes made by recipients of the national security letters.

Second, in addition to the violations reported by the FBI, we reviewed documents relating to national security letters in a sample of FBI investigative files in four FBI field offices. In our review of 77 FBI investigative files, we found that 17 of these files—22 percent—contained one or more possible violations relating to national security letters that were not identified by the FBI. These possible violations included infractions that were similar to those identified by the FBI and considered as possible IOB violations, but also included instances in which the FBI issued national security letters for different information than what had been approved by the field supervisor. Based on our review and the significant percentage of files that contained unreported possible violations (22 percent), we believe that a significant number of NSL-related possible violations are not being identified or reported by the FBI.

Third, we identified many instances in which the FBI obtained telephone toll billing records and subscriber information from 3 telephone companies pursuant to more than 700 "exigent letters' signed by personnel in the Counterterrorism Division without first issuing national security letters. We concluded that the FBI's acquisition of this information circumvented the ECPA NSL statute and violated the Attorney General's Guidelines for FBI National Security Investigations and Foreign Intelligence Collection (NSI Guidelines) and internal FBI policy. These matters were compounded by the fact that the FBI used the exigent letters in on-emergency circumstances, failed to ensure that there were duly authorized investigations to which the requests could be tied, and failed to ensure that NSLs were issued promptly after the fact, pursuant to existing or new counterterrorism investigations. In addition, the exigent letters inaccurately represented that the FBI had already requested subpoenas for the information when, in fact, it had not.

Fourth, we determined that in circumstances during 2003 through 2005 FBI Headquarters Counterterrorism Division generated over 300 national security letters exclusive from "control files" rather than from "investigative files" in violation of FBI policy. In these instances, FBI agents did not generate and supervisors did not approve documentation demonstrating that the factual predicate required by the Electronic Communications Privacy Act, the Attorney General's Guidelines for FBI National Security Investigations and Foreign Intelligence Collection, and internal FBI policy had been established. When NSLs are issued from control files rather than from investigative files, internal and external reviews cannot determine whether the requests are tied to investigations that establish the required evidentiary predicate for issuing the national security letters.

Fifth, we examined FBI investigative files in four field offices to determine whether FBI case agents and supervisors adhered to FBI policies designed to ensure appropriate supervisory review of the use of national security letter authorities. We found that 60 percent of the investigative files we examined contained one or more violations of FBI internal control policies relating to national security letters. These included failures to document supervisory review of national security letter approval memoranda and failures to include required information such as the authorizing statute, the status of the investigative subject, or the number or types of records requested in NSL approval memoranda. Moreover, because the FBI does not retain copies of signed national security letters, we were unable to conduct a comprehensive audit of the FBI's compliance with its internal control policies and the statutory certifications required for national security letters. . . .

[I]n evaluating the FBI's use of national security letters it is important to note the significant challenges the FBI was facing during the period covered by our review and the major organizational changes it was undergoing. Moreover, it is also important to recognize that in most cases the FBI was seeking to obtain information that it could have obtained properly if it had followed applicable statutes, guidelines, and internal policies. We also did not find any indication that the FBI's misuse of NSL authorities constituted criminal misconduct.

However, as described above, we found that the FBI used NSLs in violation of applicable NSL statutes, Attorney General Guidelines, and internal FBI policies. In addition, we found that the FBI circumvented the requirements of the ECPA NSL statute when it issued at least 739 "exigent letters" to obtain telephone toll billing records and subscriber information from three telephone companies without first issuing NSLs. Moreover, in a few other instances, the FBI sought or obtained information to which it was not entitled under the NSL authorities when it sought educational records through issuance of an ECPA NSL, when it sought and obtained telephone toll billing records in the absence of a national security investigation, when it sought and obtained consumer full credit reports in a counterintelligence investigation, and when it sought and obtained financial records and telephone toll billing records without first issuing NSLs. . . .

Source: U.S. Department of Justice. Office of the Inspector General. 2007. *A Review of the Federal Bureau of Investigation's Use of National Security Letters.* March 2007, pp. 120–28.

2008: SECRET DOJ INSPECTOR GENERAL REPORT ON FBI USE OF SECTION 215 ORDERS

On December 24, 2014—Christmas Eve, when public interest in the news of the day is historically very low—the National Security Agency (NSA) finally responded to a Freedom of Information Act (FOIA) lawsuit from the New York Times *and other organizations by releasing a secret 2008 report produced by the Department of Justice's Office of the Inspector General (OIG). The report, called "A Review of the FBI's Use of Section 215 Orders for Business Records in 2006," was heavily redacted. But it still contained a number of criticisms of the employment and efficacy of Section 215 orders used by the FBI. The following excerpts from the declassified report question whether the agency was sufficiently respectful of preserving constitutional liberties in its use of Section 215 orders. It also indicated that in 2006, at least, "the evidence showed no instance where the information obtained from a Section 215 order described in the body of the report resulted in a major investigative development."*

OIG Analysis

As discussed above, because of a series of disagreements about how the FBI should retain and disseminate business records obtained pursuant to a Section 215 order, in September 2006 the Department issued "interim" minimization procedures for business records produced pursuant to Section 215 orders. These interim minimization procedures use general hortatory language stating that all activities conducted in relation to national security investigations must be "carried out in conformity with the Constitution." However, we believe this broad standard does not provide the specific guidance for minimization procedures that the Reauthorization Act appears to contemplate.

When discussing the issue raised by the Reauthorization Act of whether the minimization procedures "protect the constitutional rights of United States persons," OIPR [Office of Intelligence Policy and Review] and FBI attorneys asserted that most government requests for business records do not raise constitutional concerns. They noted that the Supreme court has held that individuals have no legitimate expectation of privacy for information voluntarily turned over to third parties. See e.g., *United States v. Miller,* 425 U.S. 435, 442–444 (1976); *Smith v. Maryland,* 442 U.S. 735 (1979); *Couch v. United States,* 409 U.S. 332, 335–336 (1973). Yet, not every business record obtainable through a Section 215 order falls under this rubric. For example, a request by the government for business records created and maintained by a sole proprietor may raise Fifth Amendment concerns. *Bellis v. United States,* 417 U.S. 85 (1974). Business record requests also may affect First Amendment rights of individuals. In addition, the Supreme Court also has not ruled on the appropriate privacy interest to be afforded to *{REDACTED}*____.

Moreover, the Reauthorization Act required the Department to adopt "specific procedures" reasonably designed "to minimize the retention, and prohibit the dissemination, of nonpublicly available information concerning unconsenting United States persons consistent with the need of the United States to obtain, produce and disseminate foreign intelligence information." We believe that the interim procedures do not adequately address this requirement, and we recommend that the Department continue its efforts to construct specific minimization procedures relating to Section 215 orders, rather than rely on general language in the Attorney General's NSI [National Security Investigation] Guidelines.

First, the interim procedures do not provide specific guidance regarding the retention of U.S. person information. The FBI acknowledged that its practice under the NSI Guidelines sections is to retain all information obtained in the course of a national security investigation for a period of *{REDACTED]*. However, the Reauthorization Act requires the Department to adopt "specific procedures" designed to minimize the retention of non-publicly available information concerning unconsenting United States persons, consistent with the need of the United States to obtain, produce, and disseminate foreign intelligence information. The Department's failure to distinguish the retention of U.S. person information from any other information obtained in the course of national security investigations appears inconsistent with the language of the Reauthorization Act. Moreover, while OIPR proposed retaining the business records *{REDACTED}*______ and the FBI recommended retaining them for *{REDACTED}* the interim guidelines simply follow general archives practices and allow the information to be retained without further evaluation for *{REDACTED}*.

Similarly, the interim procedures do not contain procedures that prohibit the dissemination of U.S. person information unless disclosure is necessary to understand or address the importance of the intelligence information. The FBI's assertion that agents can make this determination on a case-by-case basis conflicts with the statutory requirements that specific minimization procedures be developed to address this concern. *{REDACTED}*__________.

*{REDACTED}*_______ ignores the Reauthorization Act's statutory requirement that the Department adopt procedures "that are reasonably designed in light of the purpose and technique" of business records orders to minimize the retention and prohibit the dissemination of U.S. person information." We believe that standard procedures should be specifically adopted for *{REDACTED}*________________________ in accord with the requirements and intent of the Reauthorization Act.

As a result, we recommend that the FBI and OIPR continue to work to develop appropriate standard minimization procedures for business records. Pursuant to the Reauthorization Act, the Department should replace the interim procedures with final standard minimization procedures that provide specific guidance for the retention and dissemination of U.S. person information. In addition, we recommend that the FBI and OIPR monitor Section 215 requests to ensure that if a request implicates the rights of U.S. persons, that specific and particularized minimization procedures be included in the Section 215 application and implemented in a manner that protects the U.S. person's constitutional rights.

Conclusions

As required by the Reauthorization Act, the OIG conducted this review of the FBI's use of Section 215 requests for business records in 2006. The Reauthorization Act required the OIG to examine how many requests were prepared by the FBI; how many applications were approved, denied, or modified by the Foreign Intelligence Surveillance Act (FISA) Court; whether bureaucratic or other impediments hindered the FBI's use of Section 215; and the effectiveness of the FBI's use of Section 215. The Act also directed that the OIG examine any improper use of Section of 215 authority and identify any noteworthy facts or circumstances concerning Section 215 requests. Finally, the Act required the OIG to examine whether the minimization procedures adopted by the Department protect the constitutional rights of U.S. persons. As required by the Reauthorization Act, our review covered Section 215 requests processed in calendar year 2006.

We found that in 2006 the FBI and OIPR processed a total of 21 pure Section 215 applications and 32 combination applications. All but six of the pure Section 215 applications were formally submitted to the FISA Court. Each of the 47 Section 215 applications (15 pure requests and 32 combination requests) formally submitted to the FISA Court were approved.

The six pure Section 215 requests that were not formally presented to the FISA Court were withdrawn either while they were pending approval at the FBI's National Security Law Branch (NSLB) or at the Office of Intelligence and Policy Review (OIPR) because they lacked sufficient predicate or the provider did not maintain the records requested. The FBI obtained a wide variety of records using Section 215 orders in 2006, including credit card records, *{REDACTED}*______________________________.

Unlike in previous years *{REDACTED}*________________________.

We determined that when FBI agents submitted Section 215 requests processed in 2006, they encountered similar processing delays as those identified in our March 2007 report. These delays were caused by unfamiliarity with Section 215 orders, too few resources to handle requests expeditiously, the multi-layered review process, and substantive issues regarding whether the application met the statutory requirements. Overall, the average processing time for Section 215 orders in 2006 was 147 days, which was similar to the processing time for 2005. However, the FBI and OIPR were able to expedite certain Section 215 requests in 2006, and when the FBI identified two emergency requests the FBI and OIPR processed both Section 215 requests quickly.

We uncovered no evidence of harm to national security in any specific cases caused by the delay in obtaining Section 215 orders or by the FBI's inability to obtain information that was requested in Section 215 requests. However, agents expressed frustration about the amount of time and effort involved in obtaining a Section 215 order and stated that they would first pursue the information through other more efficient investigative techniques such as voluntary compliance and national security letters.

We again examined how the FBI in 2006 used information obtained through Section 215 orders in national security investigations. Aside from *{REDACTED}*______________________ Section 215 orders were used primarily to exhaust investigative leads, although in some instances the FBI obtained information to support additional FBI investigative requests and to assist foreign governments pursuing criminal investigations of non-U.S. persons. The evidence showed no instance where the information obtained from a Section 215 order described in the body of the report resulted in a major investigative development. However, *{REDACTED}*_______________________________.

We did not identify any illegal use of Section 215 authority. However, we identified two instances where the FBI received information inadvertently that was not authorized by the FISA Court order. In one instance, the FBI did not realize for 2 months that it was continuously receiving information that was not authorized by the FISA Court order. The FBI reported this matter to the IOB, and OIPR reported the matter to and sequestered the material with the FISA Court.

In the other instance the FBI recognized the matter quickly and took steps to immediately sequester the additional material. However, in this case, the FBI did not consider the matter to be reportable to the IOB because the records were not statutorily protected. OIPR has not made a decision regarding whether this is a compliance incident reportable to the FISA Court.

We recommend the FBI should develop procedures that require FBI employees to review materials received from Section 215 orders to ensure that the material they receive pursuant to a Section 215 is authorized by a Section 215 order.

Furthermore, we recommend that the FBI develop procedures for identifying and handling material that is produced pursuant to, but outside the scope of, Section 215 orders. The procedures should include the FBI's justification for handling any class of such material differently from other classes and should consider factors in addition to whether the material is or is not statutorily protected. For example, the procedures should also address such factors as whether the material contains non-public information about the U.S. persons who are not the subjects of FBI national security investigations, and whether the underlying Section 215 order included particularized minimization procedures. These procedures should be incorporated in the minimization procedures required by the Reauthorization Act.

We identified two other noteworthy items. The first involved a request *{REDACTED}*______________________________. We found the request *{REDACTED}*__________ to be noteworthy because the FISA Court twice refused to approve Section 215 applications for *{REDACTED}* citing First Amendment concerns *{REDACTED}*______________________________
____.

The second noteworthy item concerned *{REDACTED}*______________
____
____
____.

Finally, we examined whether the interim standard minimization procedures adopted by the Department for Section 215 orders are consistent with the requirements of the Reauthorization Act. Because of differences between the FBI and OIPR, the Department's interim procedures merely adopt the general language contained in the Attorney General's National Security Guidelines. However, these general standards do not provide specific guidance for minimization procedures that the Reauthorization Act appears to contemplate. We believe that these interim guidelines do not adequately address the intent and requirements of the Reauthorization Act for minimization procedures, and we recommend that the Department continue its efforts to develop specific standard minimization procedures relating to Section 215 orders.

Source: Office of the Inspector General, U.S. Department of Justice. 2008. *A Review of the FBI's Use of Section 215 Orders for Business Records in 2006.* March 2008, pp. 81–87. Declassified on December 11, 2014.

2008: PRESIDENT BUSH SIGNS THE FISA AMENDMENTS ACT (FAA)

One of the earliest important electronic surveillance laws in the United States was the Foreign Intelligence Surveillance Act (FISA) of 1978, which was passed by Congress with bipartisan support and signed into law by President Jimmy Carter. FISA authorized U.S. national security and law enforcement agencies to conduct surveillance of the activities and communications of "foreign powers" and "agents of foreign powers" on American soil.

In the aftermath of the Al Qaeda terrorist attacks on the United States on September 11, 2001, however, United States experienced a dramatic increase in public and political support for proposed expansions of surveillance powers, both in the United States and overseas. This support provided the momentum for the passage of the USA PATRIOT Act, the PATRIOT Act's reauthorization in 2005, and in 2008, the Foreign Intelligence Surveillance Act (FISA) Amendments Act (FAA) of 2008.

The FAA contained significant new powers to the U.S. government to conduct surveillance. It allowed both domestic and foreign warrantless surveillance, provided that the "intent" of the surveillance was to gather foreign intelligence. As a practical matter, this meant that warrantless surveillance could be carried out under FAA auspices against any American individuals, organizations, or businesses carrying out international communications to or about the foreign subject of an investigation. The FAA also provided retroactive immunity to all telecommunications companies that cooperated with the U.S. government's warrantless wiretapping program.

The FAA passed with broad political support. It passed the House on June 20, 2008, on a 293–129 vote, then sailed through the Senate on July 9 by a 69–28 tally. It was signed into law by President George W. Bush one day later. Following are excerpts from Bush's remarks at that signing ceremony.

In 2012, the FISA Amendments Act was renewed for another five years as various attempts to address civil liberties concerns by reducing its intelligence-gathering powers were beaten back. The measure passed Congress with bipartisan support, and it was signed into law by President Barack Obama on December 31, 2012.

Today I'm pleased to sign landmark legislation that is vital to the security of our people. The bill will allow our intelligence professionals to quickly and effectively monitor the communications of terrorists abroad while respecting the liberties of Americans here at home. The bill I sign today will help us meet our most solemn responsibility: to stop new attacks and to protect our people.

Members of my administration have made a vigorous case for this important law. I want to thank them and I also want to thank the members of the House and the Senate who've worked incredibly hard to get this legislation done. Mr. Vice President, welcome.

Respect the members of the Senate and the House who've joined us—Senate Republican Whip Jon Kyl; John Boehner, House Republican Leader; Roy Blunt, House Republican Whip. I do want to pay special tribute to Congressman Steny Hoyer, House Majority Leader, for his hard work on this bill. I thank so very much Senator Jay Rockefeller, Chairman of the Senate Select Committee on Intelligence, and Senator Kit Bond, Vice Chairman, for joining us. I appreciate the hard work of Congressman Silvestre Reyes, Chairman of the House Permanent Select Committee on Intelligence, and Congressman Pete Hoekstra, Ranking Member. I also welcome Congressman Lamar Smith, Ranking Member of the House Judiciary. I thank all the other members of the House and Senate who have joined us. I appreciate your very good work.

I welcome Attorney General Michael Mukasey, as well as Admiral Mike McConnell, Director of National Intelligence. I appreciate other members of the administration who have joined us. I want to thank the congressional staff who are here, and all the supporters of this piece of legislation.

Almost seven years have passed since that September morning when nearly 3,000 men, women and children were murdered in our midst. The attack changed our country forever. We realized America was a nation at war against a ruthless and persistent enemy. We realized that these violent extremists would spare no effort to kill again. And in the aftermath of 9/11, few would have imagined that we would be standing here seven years later without another attack on American soil.

The fact that the terrorists have failed to strike our shores again does not mean that our enemies have given up. To the contrary, since 9/11 they've plotted a number of attacks on our homeland. I can remember standing up here—I receive briefings on the very real and very dangerous threats that America continues to face.

One of the important lessons learned after 9/11 was that America's intelligence professionals lacked some of the tools they needed to monitor the communications of terrorists abroad. It is essential that our intelligence community know who our enemies are talking to, what they're saying, and what they're planning. Last year Congress passed temporary legislation that helped our intelligence community monitor these communications.

The legislation I am signing today will ensure that our intelligence community professionals have the tools they need to protect our country in the years to come. The DNI and the Attorney General both report that, once enacted, this law will provide vital assistance to our intelligence officials in their work to thwart terrorist plots. This law will ensure that those companies whose assistance is necessary to protect the country will themselves be protected from lawsuits from past or future cooperation with the government. This law will protect the liberties of our citizens while maintaining the vital flow of intelligence. This law will play a critical role in helping to prevent another attack on our soil.

Protecting America from another attack is the most important responsibility of the federal government—the most solemn obligation that a President undertakes. When I first addressed the Congress after 9/11, I carried a badge by the mother of a police officer who died in the World Trade Center. I pledged to her, to the families of the victims, and to the American people that I would never forget the wound that was inflicted on our country. I vowed to do everything in my power to prevent another attack on our nation. I believe this legislation is going to help keep that promise. And I thank the members who have joined us. And now it's my honor to sign the bill.

Source: Bush, George W. "Remarks by the President in the Signing of H.R. 6304, FISA Amendments Act of 2008." July 10, 2008. *Public Papers of the Presidents of the United States: George W. Bush (2008, Book II).* Washington, DC: Government Printing Office, pp. 1007–09.

2010: SUPREME COURT RULING IN *BERGHUIS v. THOMPKINS* NARROWS MIRANDA RIGHTS

In Miranda v. Arizona *(1966), the U.S. Supreme Court ruled that prior to police questioning people suspected of criminal actions must be informed of their constitutional rights to have an attorney and to remain silent and otherwise guard against self-incrimination. These so-called Miranda Rights subsequently became enshrined in the consciousness of the American public through years of recitation in films and on television.*

On June 1, 2010, however, the Roberts Court issued a 5–4 ruling in Berghuis v. Thompkins, *which significantly chipped away at the "right to remain silent" part of the Miranda Rights. The case of* Berghuis v. Thompkins *concerned a man arrested in Ohio for a murder in Michigan who subsequently underwent hours of questioning. The suspect was silent for much of that time, but he never formally asserted his constitutional right to remain silent, and he eventually made statements that were used by the prosecution to convict him.*

An appeal of the conviction was lodged on the basis that the suspect's Miranda rights had been violated by his interrogators. The Court, however, decided that in order to assert the right to remain silent a suspect must clearly state his wish not to speak to the police—remaining silent was not, in and of itself, sufficient for that right to be established. The Court further asserted that a suspect who begins talking even after hours of silence can reasonably be viewed as someone who is waiving his right to remain silent. Following are excerpts from the majority opinion penned by Justice Anthony Kennedy, as well as a sharply worded dissent from Justice Sonia Sotomayor.

Justice Kennedy's Opinion

Held

1. The state court's decision rejecting Thompkins' *Miranda* claim was correct under *de novo* review and therefore necessarily reasonable under AEDPA's more deferential standard of review, pp. 7–17.

    (a) Thompkins' silence during the interrogation did not invoke his right to remain silent. A suspect's *Miranda* right to counsel must be invoked "unambiguously." *Davis* v. *United States*, 512 U.S. 452, 459. If the accused makes an "ambiguous or equivocal" statement or no statement, the police are not required to end the interrogation, *ibid.*, or ask questions to clarify the accused's intent, *id.,* at 461–462. There is no principled reason to adopt different standards for determining when an accused has invoked the *Miranda* right to remain silent and the *Miranda* right to counsel at issue in *Davis*. Both protect the privilege against compulsory self-incrimination by requiring an interrogation to cease when either right is invoked. The unambiguous invocation requirement results in an objective inquiry that "avoid[s] difficulties of proof and . . . provide[s] guidance to officers" on how to proceed in the face of ambiguity. *Davis*, *supra*, at 458–459. Had Thompkins said that he wanted to remain silent or that he did not want to talk, he would have invoked his right to end the questioning. He did neither. Pp.8–10.

(b) Thompkins waived his right to remain silent when he knowingly and voluntarily made a statement to police. A waiver must be "the product of a free and deliberate choice rather than intimidation, coercion, or deception" and "made with a full awareness of both the nature of the right being abandoned and the consequences of the decision to abandon it." *Moran* v. *Burbine*, 475 U.S. 412, 421. Such a waiver may be "implied" through a "defendant's silence, coupled with an understanding of his rights and a course of conduct indicating waiver." *North Carolina* v. *Butler*, 441 U.S. 369, 373. If the State establishes that a *Miranda* warning was given and that it was understood by the accused, an accused's uncoerced statement establishes an implied waiver. The record here shows that Thompkins waived his right to remain silent. First, the lack of any contention that he did not understand his rights indicates that he knew what he gave up when he spoke. See *Burbine*, *supra*, at 421. Second, his answer to the question about God is a "course of conduct indicating waiver" of that right. *Butler*, *supra*, at 373. Had he wanted to remain silent, he could have said nothing in response or unambiguously invoked his *Miranda* rights, ending the interrogation. That he made a statement nearly three hours after receiving a *Miranda* warning does not overcome the fact that he engaged in a course of conduct indicating waiver. Third, there is no evidence that his statement was coerced. See *Burbine*, *supra*, at 421. He does not claim that police threatened or injured him or that he was fearful. The interrogation took place in a standard-sized room in the middle of the day, and there is no authority for the proposition that a 3-hour interrogation is inherently coercive. Cf. *Colorado* v. *Connelly*, 479 U.S. 157, 163–164, n. 1. The fact that the question referred to religious beliefs also does not render his statement involuntary. *Id.*, at 170. Pp. 10–15.

(c) Thompkins argues that, even if his answer to Helgert could constitute a waiver of his right to remain silent, the police were not allowed to question him until they first obtained a waiver. However, a rule requiring a waiver at the outset would be inconsistent with *Butler*'s holding that courts can infer a waiver "from the actions and words of the person interrogated." 441 U.S., at 373. Any waiver, express or implied, may be contradicted by an invocation at any time, terminating further interrogation. When the suspect knows that *Miranda* rights can be invoked at any time, he or she can reassess his or her immediate and long-term interests as the interrogation progresses. After giving a *Miranda* warning, police may interrogate a suspect who has neither invoked nor waived *Miranda* rights. Thus, the police were not required to obtain a waiver of Thompkins' *Miranda* rights before interrogating him. Pp. 15–17.

2. Even if his counsel provided ineffective assistance, Thompkins cannot show prejudice under a *de novo* review of this record. To establish ineffective assistance, a defendant "must show both deficient performance and prejudice." *Knowles* v. *Mirzayance*, 556 U.S. ___, ___. To establish prejudice, a "defendant must show that there is a reasonable probability that, but for counsel's unprofessional errors, the result of the proceeding would have been different," *Strickland* v. *Washington*, 466 U.S. 668, 694, considering "the totality of the evidence before the judge or jury," *id.*, at 695. Here, the Sixth Circuit did not account for the other evidence presented against Thompkins. The state court rejected his claim that he was prejudiced by evidence of Purifoy's earlier conviction. Even if it used an incorrect legal standard, this Court need not determine whether AEDPA's deferential standard of review applies here, since Thompkins cannot show prejudice under *de novo* review, a more favorable standard for him. *De novo* review can be used in this case because a habeas petitioner will not be entitled to relief if his or her claim is rejected on *de novo* review. See §2254(a). Assuming that failure to request a limiting instruction here was deficient representation, Thompkins cannot show prejudice, for the record shows that it was not reasonably likely that such an instruction would have made any difference in light of other evidence of guilt. The surviving victim identified Thompkins as the shooter, and the identification was supported by a surveillance camera photograph. A friend testified that Thompkins confessed to him, and the details of that confession were corroborated by evidence that Thompkins stripped and abandoned the van after the shooting. The jury, moreover, was capable of assessing Purifoy's credibility, as it was instructed to do. Pp. 17–19.

547 F. 3d 572, reversed and remanded.

Dissent of Justice Sotomayor

The Court concludes today that a criminal suspect waives his right to remain silent if, after sitting tacit and uncommunicative through nearly three hours of police interrogation, he utters a few one-word responses. The Court also concludes that a suspect who wishes to guard his right to remain silent against such a finding of "waiver" must, counterintuitively, speak—and must do so with sufficient precision to satisfy a clear-statement rule that construes ambiguity in favor of the police. Both propositions mark a substantial retreat from the protection against compelled self-incrimination that *Miranda* v. *Arizona*, 384 U.S. 436 (1966), has long provided during custodial interrogation. The broad rules the Court announces today are also troubling because they are unnecessary to decide this case, which is governed by the deferential standard of review set forth in the Antiterrorism and Effective Death Penalty Act of 1996 (AEDPA), 28 U.S. C. §2254(d). Because I believe Thompkins is entitled to relief under AEDPA on the ground that his statements were admitted at trial without the prosecution having carried its burden to show that he waived his right to remain silent; because longstanding principles of judicial restraint counsel leaving for another day the questions of law the Court reaches out to decide; and because the Court's answers to those questions do not result from a faithful application of our prior decisions, I respectfully dissent.

Source: Berghuis v. Thompkins, majority opinion of Justice Kennedy and dissent of Justice Sotomayor. 560 U.S. 370 (2010) (docket 08–1470).

2012: TWO DEMOCRATIC SENATORS DEBATE REAUTHORIZATION OF FISA

The Foreign Intelligence Surveillance Act (FISA), which was initially passed in 1978, is one of the major legal foundations for intelligence-gathering and surveillance activities of American intelligence agencies such as the National Security Agency and the Central Intelligence Agency. But in the 21st century, debates over reauthorizing, reforming, and remaking FISA to meet modern surveillance challenges and perennial civil liberties concerns have become particularly heated. In 2012, the FISA Amendments Act was renewed for another five years as lawmakers concerned about the extent of government surveillance under FISA auspices were unable to convince their opponents that FISA's intelligence-gathering measures were too dangerous to privacy. The law passed Congress with support from Republicans and Democrats, and it was signed into law by President Barack Obama on December 31, 2012.

The following exchange on the Senate floor in the run-up to the vote, however, shows how FISA reauthorization divided lawmakers that often agreed on other issues. In this excerpt, Senator Ron Wyden (D-OR), a member of the Senate Intelligence Committee, urges his colleagues not to pass the reauthorization bill without including significant new restraints and accountability measures on NSA surveillance. He is followed by fellow Democratic Senator and committee member Dianne Feinstein (CA), who insists that the reforms supported by Wyden are unnecessary and counterproductive. Particularly noteworthy is the section of Wyden's remarks in which he discusses how NSA Director Keith Alexander repeatedly insisted that it was impossible to know how many Americans had been subject to FISA intelligence-gathering measures; less than a year after Wyden's statement here, NSA whistle-blower Edward Snowden revealed, among other things, that NSA managed a program called Boundless Information that contained elaborate statistics about all calls and e-mails intercepted by the agency, including those made by Americans.

Mr. WYDEN: Also crucial to our country is the legislation before the Senate right now. Its name is a real mouthful.

Mr. President, I think you will recall this legislation from your days serving on the Senate Select Committee on Intelligence. The name of this is the Foreign Intelligence Surveillance Act Amendments Act. It also expires in a few days. Our job is to find a way to strike the best possible balance between protecting our country from threats from overseas and safeguarding the individual liberties of the law-abiding Americans we have cherished in this country for literally hundreds of years. This task of balancing security and liberty was one of the most important tasks defined by the Founding Fathers years and years ago, and it is no less important for the Congress today.

As I indicated earlier, the majority leader, Leader Reid, has accorded me the honor of beginning this debate. I will open with a very short explanation of what the FISA Amendments Act is all about. Of course, this is an extension of the law that was passed in 2008. It is a major surveillance law, and it is the successor to the warrantless wiretapping program that operated under the Bush administration, which gave the government new authorities to collect the communications of foreigners outside the United States. The bill before the Senate today would extend this law for another 5 years.

There is going to be a discussion of various issues, but all of them go to what I call the constitutional teeter-totter, which is basically balancing security, protecting our country at a dangerous time, and the individual liberties that are so important to all of us. I expect there will be amendments to strengthen protections for the privacy of law-abiding Americans.

I want to say to my colleagues and those who are listening that this is likely to be the only floor debate the Senate has on this law encompassing literally a 9-year period—from 2008 to 2017. So if we are talking about surveillance authority that essentially looks to a 9-year period, we ought to have an important discussion about it, and that is why I am grateful to the majority leader for making today's discussion possible. . . .

Our job here in the Congress is to make sure the laws we pass are in line with the vision of the Founding Fathers, which was to protect national security as well as the rights of individual Americans.

We all remember the wonderful comment by Ben Franklin. I will paraphrase it, but essentially Ben Franklin said: If you give up your liberty to have security, you really don't deserve either. We owe it to the hard-working men and women in the intelligence community to work closely with them. We need to find the balance Ben Franklin was talking about, and we can help them by conducting robust oversight over the work that is being done there so members of the public can have confidence in the men and women of the intelligence community. This will give the public the confidence to know that as we protect our security at a dangerous time, we are also protecting the individual liberties of our people.

The story with respect to this debate really begins in early America when the colonists were famously subjected to a lot of taxes by the British Government. The American colonists thought this was unfair because they were not represented in the British Parliament. They argued that if they were not allowed to vote for their own government, then they should not have to pay taxes.

We all remember the renowned rallying cry of the colonists. It was "no taxation without representation." Early revolutionaries engaged in protests against these taxes all over the country. Of course, the most famous of these protests was the Boston Tea Party in which colonists threw shiploads of tea into the Boston Harbor in protest of the tax on tea.

As we recall from our history books, there were a lot of taxes on items such as tea, sugar, paint, and paper. Because so many colonists believed these taxes were unjust, there was a lot of smuggling going on in the American Colonies. People would import things, such as sugar, and simply avoid paying the tax on them.

We all remember that the King of England didn't like this very much. He wanted the colonists to pay taxes whether they were allowed to vote or not. So the English authority began issuing what were essentially general warrants. They were called writs of assistance, and they authorized government officials to enter into any house or building they wanted in order to search for smuggled goods. These officials were not limited to only searching in certain houses, and they were not required to show any evidence that the place they were searching had any smuggled goods in it. Basically, government officials were allowed to say they were looking for smuggled goods and then would search any house they were interested in to see if the house had some of those smuggled goods.

An English authority's goal is to find smuggled goods. Letting constables and customs officers search any house or building is a pretty effective way to go out and find something. If they keep searching enough houses, eventually they will find some smuggled goods in one of them and seize those goods and arrest whoever lives in that house for smuggling. Of course, the problem is that if government officials can search any house they want, they are going to search through the houses of a lot of people who have not broken any laws. Mr. President, it is almost as if you decided you were going to search everybody in your State of Rhode Island. You could go in and turn them all upside down, shake them, and see if anything fell out. Obviously, you would find some people who had some things in their possession that they should not have, but that is not the way we do it in America. In America, there has to be probable cause in order to do something like that.

The American colonists had a huge problem with the idea that everybody's house was going to be checked for smuggled goods on the prospect that maybe somebody somewhere had engaged in smuggling. The colonists said it is not OK to go around invading people's privacy unless there is some specific evidence that they have done something wrong. That is how people in Rhode Island and Oregon feel today. One cannot just go out and check everybody in sight on the prospect that maybe there is someone who has done something wrong.

Back in the colonists' time, the law said that these writs of assistance were good until the King died. So when King George II died and the authorities had to get new writs, many colonists tried to challenge them in court.

In Boston, James Otis denounced this mass invasion of privacy by reminding the court that—and we remember this wonderful comment—a man's house is his castle. Mr. Otis described the writs of assistance as the power that places the liberty of every man in the hands of every petty officer. Unfortunately, the court ruled that these general orders permitting mass searches without individual suspicion were legal, and English authorities continued to use them. The fact that English officials went around invading people's privacy without any specific evidence against them was one of the fundamental complaints the American colonists had against the British Government. So naturally our Founding Fathers, with the wisdom they showed on so many matters, made it clear they wanted to address this particular complaint when they wrote the Bill of Rights.

The Bill of Rights ensures that strong protections of individual freedom would be included within our Constitution itself, and the Founding Fathers included strong protections for personal privacy in the fourth amendment. The fourth amendment states:

> The right of the people to be secure in their persons, houses, papers, and effects against unreasonable searches and seizures shall not be violated and no warrant shall issue but upon probable cause, supported by oath or affirmation, and particularly describing the place to be searched and the person or things to be searched.

This was a direct rejection of the authority the British had claimed to have when they ruled the American Colonies.

The Founding Fathers said our government does not have the right to search any house that government officials want to search even if it helps them to do their job. Government officials may only search someone's house if they have evidence that someone is breaking the law and they show the evidence to a judge to get an individual warrant.

For more than 200 years, this fundamental principle has protected Americans' privacy while still allowing our government to enforce the law and to protect public safety.

As time passed and we entered the 20th century, advances in technology—a whole host of technologies—gave government officials the power to invade individual privacy in a whole host of new ways—new ways the Founding Fathers never dreamed of—and all through those days, the Congress and the courts struggled to keep up.

Time and time again Congress and the courts were most successful when they returned to the fundamental principles of the fourth amendment. It is striking. If we look at a lot of the debates we are having today about the Internet—and the Presiding Officer has a great interest in this; we have talked often about it—certainly the Founding Fathers could never have envisioned tweeting and Twitter and the Internet and all of these extraordinary technologies. But what we have seen as technology has continued to bring us this treasure trove of information with all of these spectacular opportunities the Founding Fathers never envisioned is that time and time again the Congress and the courts were most successful when they returned to the fundamental principles of the fourth amendment. . . .

Justice Brandeis said that the right of the people to be left alone by their government is "the most comprehensive of rights"—the most comprehensive of rights, said Justice Brandeis—and, he said, "the right most valued by civilized men." And the Justice said that intrusions on individual privacy, "whatever the means employed, must be deemed a violation of the Fourth Amendment."

The reason I have outlined Justice Brandeis's views on this issue is that Justice Brandeis's views didn't prevail in 1928. Back in 1928 they thought they were dealing with high-tech surveillance. But suffice it to say that his views were eventually adopted by the full Supreme Court. That is why I believe it is so important that as we look to today's debate—really an opportunity to update the way in which that careful balance, the constitutional teeter-totter: security, well-being of all of us on this side and individual liberties on this side—it is so important to recognize what Justice Brandeis said about the value of getting it right when it comes to liberty, when it comes to individual freedom. . . .

When the Foreign Intelligence Surveillance Act, which is often known as FISA—Senators and those listening will hear that discussion almost interchangeably; the abbreviated name is FISA—when it was written in 1978, Congress applied Justice Brandeis's principles to intelligence gathering. The Congress, when they wrote the original FISA legislation in 1978, really said that Justice Brandeis got it right with respect to how we ought to gather intelligence. So the original FISA statute stated that if the government wants to collect an American's communications for intelligence purposes, the government must go to a court, show evidence that the American is a terrorist or a spy, and get an individual warrant. This upheld the same principle the Founding Fathers fought for in the revolution, it is the same principle enshrined in the Bill of Rights, and it said that government officials are not allowed to invade Americans' privacy unless they have specific evidence and an individual warrant.

After 9/11, the Bush administration decided it would seek additional surveillance authorities beyond what was in the original Foreign Intelligence Surveillance Act statute. To our great regret, instead of asking the Congress to change the law, the Bush administration developed a warrantless wiretapping program—let me repeat that, a warrantless wiretapping program—that operated in secret for a number of years. When this became public—as I have said on this floor before, these matters always do become public at some point—when it became clear that the Bush administration had developed this warrantless wiretapping program, there was a huge uproar across the land. I remember how angry many of my constituents were when they learned about the warrantless wiretapping program, and I and a lot of other Senators were very angry as well. . . .

There was a very heated debate. Congress passed the FISA Amendments Act of 2008, and that was to replace the warrantless wiretapping program with new authorities for the government to collect the phone calls and e-mails of those believed to be foreigners outside the United States.

The centerpiece of the FISA Amendments Act is a provision that is now section 702 of the FISA statute. Section 702 is the provision that gave the government new authorities to collect the communications of people who are believed to be foreigners outside the United States. This was different than the original FISA statute. Unlike the traditional FISA authorities and unlike law enforcement wiretapping authorities, section 702 of the FISA Amendments Act does not involve obtaining individual warrants. Instead, it allows the government to get what is called a programmatic warrant. It lasts for an entire year and authorizes the government to collect a potentially large number of phone calls and e-mails, with no requirement that the senders or recipients be connected to terrorism, espionage—the threats we are concerned about.

If that sounds familiar, it certainly should. General warrants that allowed government officials to decide whose privacy to invade were the exact sort of abuse that the American colonists protested over and led the Founding Fathers to adopt the fourth amendment in the first place. For this reason, section 702 of the FISA law contains language that is specifically intended to limit the government's ability to use these new authorities to spy on Americans.

Let me emphasize that because that is crucial to this discussion and the amendments that will be offered. It is never OK—never OK—for government officials to use a general warrant to deliberately invade the privacy of a law-abiding American. It was not OK for constables and Customs officials to do it in colonial days, and it is not OK for the National Security Agency to do it today. So if the government is going to use general warrants to collect people's phone calls and e-mails, it is extremely important to ensure that this authority is only used against foreigners overseas and not against law-abiding Americans.

Despite what the Acting President pro tempore and the Senate may have heard, this law does not actually prohibit the government from collecting Americans' phone calls and e-mails without a warrant. The FISA Amendments Act states—and I wish to quote because there have been a lot of inaccuracies and misrepresentations on this—the FISA Amendments Act states that acquisitions made under section

702 may not "intentionally target" a specific American and may not "intentionally acquire" communications that are "known at the time of acquisition" to be wholly domestic.

But the problem with that is, it still leaves a lot of room for circumstances under which Americans' phone calls and e-mails—including purely domestic phone calls and e-mails—could be swept up and reviewed without a warrant. This can happen if the government did not know someone is American or if the government made a technical error or if the American was talking to a foreigner, even if that conversation was entirely legitimate. . . .

When the Congress passed the FISA Amendments Act 4 years ago, it included an expiration date. The point of the expiration date was to ensure that Congress could review these authorities closely and the Congress could decide whether protections for Americans' privacy are adequate or whether they need to be modified. . . .

I am going to now spend a few minutes outlining the big questions I believe Americans deserve answers to. Certainly, the Congress has to have answers to these questions in order to do our job—our job of doing robust oversight over this law and over intelligence. . . .

First, if we want to know what kind of impact this law has had on Americans' privacy, we probably want to know roughly how many phone calls and e-mails that are to and from Americans have been swept up by the government under this authority. Senator Mark Udall, our distinguished colleague from Colorado and a great addition to the Intelligence Committee—he and I began the task of trying to ferret out this information some time ago. Over a year and a half ago, Senator Mark Udall and I asked the Director of National Intelligence how many Americans have had their communications collected under this law; in effect, swept up by the government under these authorities.

The response was it is "not reasonably possible to identify the number of people located in the United States whose communications may have been reviewed under the authority of the" FISA Amendments Act. That is how the government responded to Senator Udall and me.

If you are a person who does not like the idea of government officials secretly reviewing your phone calls and e-mails, you probably do not find that answer particularly reassuring. But suffice it to say, the situation got worse from there.

In July of this year, I and a tripartisan group of 12 other Senators . . . joined in writing another letter to the Director of National Intelligence asking additional questions about the impact of this law on Americans' privacy. . . .

The tripartisan group of Senators basically was just asking for a report, the kind of information that is a prerequisite to doing good oversight. Frankly, I think when we talk about oversight and we cannot even get a rough estimate of how many law-abiding Americans have had their communications swept up under this law, if they do not have that kind of information, oversight—the idea of robust oversight—it ought to be called toothless oversight if they do not have that kind of information.

The Director declined to publicly answer this question. So our tripartisan group and others continued. We asked the Director if anyone else has already done such an estimate. We did not ask about doing anything new. The intelligence community said: Oh, my goodness. It will be so hard to give even a rough estimate. So we said: OK. Just tell us if anyone else has already done such an estimate. The Director declined to publicly answer this question as well.

Right at the heart of this discussion is, if we are serious about doing oversight, the Congress ought to be able to get a straightforward answer to the question: Have any estimates been done already as to whether law-abiding Americans have had their communications swept up under the FISA authority?

Second, if we want to understand this law's impact on Americans' privacy, we probably want to know whether any wholly domestic communications have been collected under the FISA authorities. . . .

So our tripartisan group of Senators dug into this issue as well, and we asked the Director back in July if he knew whether any wholly domestic U.S. communications had been collected under the FISA Amendments Act. So here we are talking about wholly domestic communications from one American, for example, in Rhode Island, to another American in the home State of Senator Merkley and myself. I am disappointed to say the Director declined to answer this question as well.

That means the FISA Amendments Act involves the government going to a secret court on a yearly basis and getting programmatic warrants to collect people's phone calls and e-mails, with no requirement that these communications actually belong to people involved with terrorism or espionage. . . . The fact is, once the government has this pile of communications, which contains an unknown but potentially very large number of Americans' phone calls and e-mails, there are surprisingly few rules about what can be done with it.

If government officials wanted to search an American's house or read their e-mails or listen to their phone calls, they are supposed to show evidence to a judge and get an individual warrant. But this loophole in the law allowed government officials to make an end run around traditional warrant requirements and conduct backdoor searches for American's communications.

Now, let me be clear. If the government has clear evidence that an American is engaged in terrorism, espionage—serious crimes—I think the government ought to be able to read that person's e-mails and listen to that person's phone calls. I believe and have long felt that is an essential part of protecting public safety. But government officials ought to be required to get a warrant. As the Presiding Officer knows, there are even emergency provisions—and I support these strongly as well—that allow for an emergency authorization before you get the warrant, in order to protect the well-being of the American people.

So what we want to know at this point, if you are trying to decide whether the constitutional teeter-totter is being properly balanced or is out of whack, you want to know whether the government has ever taken advantage of this backdoor search loophole and conducted a warrantless search for the phone calls or e-mails of specific Americans. So when the tripartisan group wrote to the Director of National Intelligence, we asked him to state whether the intelligence community has ever deliberately conducted a warrantless search of this nature. The Director declined to respond to this as well . . .

If anybody is kind of keeping score on this, you will notice that the Director refused to publicly answer any of the questions that were asked in our letter. So if you are looking for reassurance that the law is being carried out in a way that respects the privacy of law-abiding American citizens, you will not find it in his response.

I should note that the Director did provide additional responses in a highly classified attachment to his letter. This attachment was so highly classified that I think of the 13 Senators who signed the letter of the tripartisan group, 11 of those 13 Senators do not even have staff who have the requisite security clearance to read it. So naturally that makes it hard for those Senators, let alone the public, to gain a better understanding of the privacy impact of the law. . . .

Intelligence officials do not deny the facts I have outlined this morning. They still insist they are already protecting innocent Americans' privacy. There is a lot of discussion about how this program is overseen by the secret FISA Court, how the court is charged with ensuring that all of the collections carried out under this program are constitutional.

To respond to those arguments, I would note that under the FISA Amendments Act, the government does not have to get the permission of the FISA Court to read particular e-mails or listen to particular phone calls. The law simply requires the court to review the government's collection and handling procedures on an annual basis. There is no requirement in the law for the court to approve the collection and review of individual communications even if government officials set out to deliberately read the e-mails of an American citizen.

Even when the court reviews the government's collection and handling procedures, it is important to note that the FISA Court's ruling are made entirely in secret. It may seem hard to believe, but the court's rulings that interpret major surveillance law and even the U.S. Constitution in significant ways—these are important judgments—the public has absolutely no idea what the court is actually saying. What that means is that our country is in effect developing a secret body of law so that most Americans have no way of finding out how their laws and their Constitution are being interpreted. That is a big problem. . . .

To put it another way, I think we understand that Americans know that intelligence agencies sometimes have to conduct secret operations, but the American people do not expect these agencies to rely on secret law. . . .

I do not take a backseat to any Member of this body in terms of protecting the sources and methods of those in the intelligence community doing their important work, but the law itself should never be secret. What Federal courts think the law and the fourth amendment to the Constitution actually mean should never be a secret from the American people, the way it is today. . . .

I was encouraged in 2009 when the Obama administration wrote to Senator Rockefeller and myself to inform us that they would be setting up a process for redacting and releasing those FISA Court opinions that contained significant interpretations of law. Unfortunately, over 3 years later, this process has produced literally zero results. Not a single redacted opinion or summary of FISA Court rulings has been released. I cannot even tell if the administration still intends to fulfill this promise. I often get the feeling they are hoping people will go away and forget that the promise was made in the first place. . . .

I have two last points. Beyond the fact that the programmatic warrants authorized by the FISA Amendments Act are approved by a secret court, the other thing that intelligence officials cite is that there are "minimization" procedures to deal with the issues that those of us who are concerned about privacy rights have raised. This is an odd term, but it simply refers to rules for dealing with information about Americans.

Intelligence officials will tell you that these are pretty much taking care of everything, and if there are not enough privacy protections in the law itself, minimization procedures provide all of the privacy protections any reasonable person could ever want or need.

These minimization procedures are classified, so most people are never going to know what they say. As someone who has access to the minimization procedures, I will make it clear that I think they are certainly better than nothing, but there is no way, colleagues, these minimization procedures ought to be a substitute for having strong privacy protections written into the law.

I will close with the reason I feel so strongly about this, which is that senior intelligence officials have sometimes described these handling procedures in misleading ways and make protections for Americans' privacy sound stronger than they actually are. I was particularly disappointed when the Director of NSA did this recently at a large technology conference.

In response to a question about the National Security Agency's surveillance of Americans, General Alexander referenced the FISA Amendments Act and talked in particular about the minimization procedures that applied to the collection of U.S. communications. Understand that this was at a big, open technology conference. General Alexander said that when the NSA sweeps up communications from a "good guy," which I think we all assume is a law-abiding American, the NSA has "requirements from the FISA court and the Attorney General to minimize that, which means nobody else can see it unless there is a crime that is being committed." Now, anybody who hears that phrase says: That is pretty good. I imagine that is what people in that technology meeting and the conference call wanted to hear. The only problem is that it is not true. It is not true at all. The privacy protections provided by these minimization procedures are simply not as strong as General Alexander made them out to be. . . .

So minimization procedures are not a bad idea, but the suggestion that we don't need privacy protections written into the law because of them is a bad idea. . . .

At this point, I close by way of saying I believe the FISA Amendments Act has enabled the government to collect useful intelligence information, and my goal is to reform the legislation. The two specific things I want to do are, first, require the intelligence community to provide more information about the impact of the FISA Amendments Act on Americans' privacy and, second, to make improvements to privacy protections so we can readily see where they are most needed.

So there will be several amendments that will be offered. The amendment I will be offering is sponsored by 15 Members of the Senate. It simply says the Director of the National Intelligence Agency should submit a report to the Congress on the privacy impact of the FISA Amendments Act. . . .

Additionally, the amendment would require the report to state whether any wholly domestic communications have been collected under the FISA Amendments Act and whether any government agencies have ever conducted any warrantless, backdoor searches. These are straightforward questions, and they are obviously relevant to understanding the scope of the law's impact on privacy. . . .

To me, at a minimum, if we don't pass a requirement that we get a rough accounting of whether there has even been an estimate done with respect to how many law-abiding Americans have been swept up under these FISA authorities, my view is that oversight becomes toothless, and that is not what our obligation over these issues is all about.

There will be other important amendments as well. Senator Merkley has one that I think is particularly important because it goes to this question of secret laws. Senator Leahy seeks to promote additional accountability as well with his important amendment. My colleague Senator Paul will be offering an amendment, an important amendment as well, with respect to reasonable searches and seizures under the fourth amendment. . . . striking the right balance between protecting our country and protecting our individual liberties is also important work. For that reason, I wanted to walk through the history of the FISA Amendments Act this morning, describe why it was so important, particularly for us to get even an accounting.

Remember, this doesn't disrupt any operations in the intelligence community. This is just an accounting of how many law-abiding Americans had their communications swept up under this law. That work is crucial too. . . .

Mrs. FEINSTEIN: Let me describe what these provisions do and why they are necessary to reauthorize.

What will expire on December 31 is title VII of FISA, which is called the FAA, the FISA Amendments Act. This authorizes the executive branch of the government to go to the FISA Court, which is a special court—and most people don't know this—of 11 Federal District Court judges appointed by the Supreme Court who review government requests for surveillance activities and obtain annual approval for a program to conduct surveillance on non-U.S. persons, in other words, surveillance on individuals who are not U.S. citizens or lawful permanent residents and who are located outside the United States.

Under current law, the Attorney General and the Director of National Intelligence may submit an application to the FISA Court. I call this a program warrant. It identifies the category of foreign persons against whom the government seeks to conduct surveillance. This application is accompanied by targeting and minimization procedures that establish how the government will determine that someone targeted for surveillance is located outside the United States; and, secondly, how it is going to minimize the acquisition and retention of any information concerning U.S. persons who are accidentally caught up in this.

If the FISA Court finds the procedures to be consistent with both law and the fourth amendment, they enter an order authorizing this kind of surveillance for 1 year—and the judges on the FISA Court have found both—and they have authorized the program to continue.

The process that follows allows the intelligence community to collect the communications of international terrorists and other non-U.S. persons who are located outside the country by, for example, acquiring electronic communications such as phone calls and e-mails sent to or from a phone number or an e-mail address known to be used by the person under surveillance.

Without this authority, the intelligence community would need to return to the process of going to the FISA Court in every individual case involving collection directed at a non-U.S. person and to prove in each case there is probable cause to believe the individual is part of or working for a foreign power or a terrorist group.

Now, here is the question: Can the government use section 702 of FISA to target a U.S. person? The answer to that is no. The law specifically prohibits the use of section 702 authorities to direct collection against—that means target—U.S. persons. So no one should think the targets are U.S. persons.

This prohibition is codified in section 702(b), which states that surveillance authorities may not be used—and let me quote the law—"to intentionally target any person known at the time of acquisition to be located in the United States or to intentionally target a United States person reasonably believed to be located outside the United States."

Now, if the government wants to engage in electronic surveillance targeting a U.S. person for foreign intelligence purposes, it must go back to the FISA Court and it must get a specific order from that court. In an emergency, the surveillance can commence before the court order is issued, but the government still must have probable cause to believe the U.S. person is an agent of a foreign power.

Let me take a few moments to address the principal concerns some of my colleagues have expressed about this legislation, which is the effect this one provision—Section 702—may have on the privacy and civil liberties of U.S. persons. And let me say that 13 members of the Intelligence Committee who have voted in favor of the extension of the FISA Amendments Act—and against previous amendments from Senator Wyden—do not believe privacy is being eliminated under the law this bill would reauthorize.

As I have discussed, section 702 establishes a framework for the government to acquire foreign intelligence by conducting electronic surveillance on non-U.S. persons who are reasonably believed to be located outside of the United States under a program that is annually approved by the court. The privacy concerns stem from the potential for intelligence collection directed at non-U.S. persons located abroad to result in the incidental collection of or concerning communications of U.S. persons. I understand these concerns, and I would like to explain why I believe the existing provisions are adequate to address them.

First, this section is narrowly tailored to ensure that it may only be used to target non-U.S. persons located abroad. It includes specific prohibitions on targeting U.S. persons or persons inside the United States and prohibitions on engaging in so-called reverse-targeting, which means targeting a non-U.S. person abroad when the real purpose is to obtain their communications with a person inside the United States. That is prohibited.

Anytime the intelligence community is seeking to collect the communications of an American, it has to demonstrate that it has probable cause and get an individual FISA Court order.

Second, Congress recognized at the time this amendments act was enacted that it is simply not possible to collect intelligence on the communications of a person of interest without also collecting information about the people with whom and about whom that person communicates, including, in some cases, non-targeted U.S. persons. The concern was addressed when the FAA was originally drafted.

Specifically, in order to protect the privacy and civil liberty of U.S. persons, Congress mandated that for collection conducted under 702, the Attorney General adopt and the FISA Court review and approve procedures that minimize the acquisition, retention, and dissemination of nonpublic information concerning unconsenting U.S. persons.

Third, numerous reports and assessments from the executive branch . . . provide the committee with extensive visibility into how these minimization procedures work and enable both the Intelligence and the Judiciary Committees to see how these procedures are effective in protecting the privacy and civil liberties of U.S. persons.

Oversight by the legislative, judicial, and executive branch of the government over the past 4 years has been very thorough. There are procedures and requirements in place under current law that provide protection for the privacy and civil liberties of U.S. persons. Those entrusted with the responsibility to collect the oversight, the committees of jurisdiction, the FISA Court, and the executive branch agencies together remain vigilant and continue to review the operations of these agencies.

Let me give a quick summary of the 702 reporting requirements under current law.

They include a semiannual assessment by the Attorney General and the DNI. Every 6 months the AG and the DNI are required to assess compliance with the targeting and minimization procedures and the acquisition guidelines adopted under Section 702. They are both further required to submit each assessment to the FISA Court and the congressional Intelligence and Judiciary Committees.

The inspector general of the Department of Justice and the inspector general of each element of the intelligence community are also authorized review compliance with Section 702. The IGs are required to provide copies of such reviews to the Attorney General, to the Director of National Intelligence, and the congressional Intelligence and Judiciary Committees. So we have the AG reviewing, we have the IGs reviewing, and then we have separate reviews by the agency heads.

The head of each element of the intelligence community must conduct an annual review which includes the following:

First, an accounting of the number of disseminated intelligence reports containing a reference to the U.S. person's identity. As a matter of fact, Members can go into a classified room at the offices of the Senate Intelligence Committee and review these reports. Any Member has access to that review.

Second, an accounting of the number of U.S. person identities subsequently disseminated by that element in response to requests for identities that were not referred to by name or title in the original reporting. Members can review that.

Third, the number of targets who were later determined to be located in the United States and, to the extent possible, whether communications of such targets were reviewed. Members can go in the Intelligence Committee offices and review that.

Fourth, a description of any procedures developed by the head of such element of the intelligence community and approved by the Director of National Intelligence to assess the extent to which acquisitions under 702 acquire communications of U.S. persons, and the results of any such assessment.

So you see, the reporting requirements go on and on.

Then there is a semiannual report. Every 6 months, the AG is required to fully inform the congressional Intelligence and Judiciary Committees concerning the implementation of Title VII of FISA, and there is a whole list of things that must be reviewed and recounted. Then there is a semiannual Attorney General review on FISA. There is also the provision for documents from the FISA Court relating to significant construction or interpretation of FISA. . . .

So, Mr. President, it is not a question of this oversight not being done. I must respectfully disagree with the Senator from Oregon on that point. There is clearly rigorous oversight, and we have done hearing after hearing, we have looked at report after report, and any Member of this body who so wishes can go and review this material in the offices of the Intelligence Committee.

Now, let me talk about a protection that does exist for privacy, but will expire if this bill is not passed. That is section 704. Under this section, the intelligence community is required to get a specific judicial order before conducting surveillance on a U.S. person located outside the United States.

Before this provision was enacted in 2008 as the product of Senators who were concerned—and they were listened to, and this was enacted—the intelligence community could conduct intelligence collection on U.S. persons outside the country with only the approval of the Attorney General but without a requirement of independent judicial review. Section 704 provides that judicial review by the special Foreign Intelligence Surveillance Court. This will only be preserved if title VII of this act is reauthorized. If it isn't, the privacy provision goes down with it.

Now, let me talk a bit more about the oversight that we have done. If you listen to some, there has been little oversight, but that is not the case. We have held numerous hearings with Directors of National Intelligence Dennis Blair and Jim Clapper; with the head of the NSA, General Alexander; and with Bob Mueller at the FBI. We have had Eric Holder appear before the committee to discuss this, and we have heard from intelligence community professionals involved in carrying out surveillance operations, the lawyers who review these operations, and, importantly, the inspectors general who carry out oversight of the program and have written reports and letters to the Congress with the results of that report.

The intelligence committee's review of these FAA surveillance authorities has included the receipt and examination of dozens of reports concerning the implementation of these authorities over the past 4 years, which the executive branch is required to provide by law. We have received and scrutinized all the classified opinions of the court that interpret the law in a significant way.

Finally, our staff has held countless briefings with officials from the NSA, the DOJ, the Office of the DNI, and the FISA Court itself, including the FBI. Collectively, these assessments, reports, and other information obtained by the Intelligence Committee demonstrate that the government implements the FAA surveillance authorities in a responsible manner, with relatively few incidents of noncompliance.

Let me say this. Where such incidents of noncompliance have arisen, they have been inadvertent. They have not been intentional. They have been the result of human error or technical defect, and they have been promptly reported and remedied. That is important. Through 4 years of oversight, from all these reports, from all the meetings, from all the hearings, we have not identified a single case in which a government official engaged in a willful effort to circumvent or violate the law. . . .

There is a view by some that this country no longer needs to fear attack. I don't share that view, and I have asked the intelligence committee staff to compile arrests that have been made in the last 4 years in America on terrorist plots that have been stopped. There are 100 arrests that have been made between 2009 and 2012. There have been 16 individuals arrested just this year alone. . . .

So I believe the FISA Amendments Act is important and these cases show the program has worked. As the years go on, I believe good intelligence is the most important way to prevent these attacks.

Information gained through programs such as this one—and through other sources as well—is able to be used to prevent future attacks. So, in the past 4 years, there have been 100 arrests to prevent something from happening in the United States, some of these plots have been thwarted because of this program. I think it is a vital program. We are doing our level best to conduct good oversight and keep abreast of the details of the program and to see that these reports come in. I have tried to satisfy Senator Wyden but apparently have been unable to do so.

I am hopeful the Senate Intelligence Committee's 13-to-2 vote to reauthorize this important legislation will be considered by all Members.

Source: FISA Amendments Act Reauthorization Act of 2012. *Congressional Record—Senate* 158, Number 168, December 27, 2012, pp. S8384–410.

2013: AN AMERICAN LIBRARIAN RECALLS RECEIVING A NATIONAL SECURITY LETTER

In November 2007, the Federal Bureau of Investigation (FBI) served Brewster Kahle, founder of the famed digital Internet Archive, with a National Security Letter (NSL), one of the most powerful items in the federal government's arsenal of surveillance and investigative tools. NSLs are essentially subpoenas for communications records and other private documents that the FBI and other agencies engaged in counterterrorism investigations may issue without formal approval from a judge. Penalties for defying NSLs—or even telling anyone of receiving an NSL—included potentially long prison sentences.

The NSL issued to Kahle mandated that he turn over information on an Internet Archive patron, including the user's name, address, and activity on the site. Kahle fought the subpoena, though, and after securing legal help from the Electronic Frontier Foundation (EFF), the FBI agreed in April 2008 to withdraw the letter it had issued to Kahle. In the following interview with The New Yorker, *Kahle recalls how he felt after receiving the NSL back in 2007.*

Please tell me about the national security letter you received.

The lawyers for the Internet Archive asked to have a private meeting, with no one else there but me. And they said, we've just received a national-security letter, to find out a lot of detailed information about a patron of the Internet Archive.

They were sort of grim: "Let's lock the doors, you'll be the only person who hears about this." They said that, according to the law, you have to give them the information they want, and you can only talk to people such that you can fulfill this request. Other than that, there's nothing else you can do, and then you can't ever mention it to anybody, ever.

So I asked, "Can I bring this up with my board?" And the answer is no. Could I discuss it with my wife? The answer is no, not without risking being put in prison for years.

How would that even go down? Say your wife wanted to turn you in: "He told me." Whom would she even tell?

Libraries have had a long history of dealing with authoritarian organizations demanding reader records—who's read what—and this has led to people being rounded up and killed. As a librarian, you take this very, very seriously. So, when you get demands for information about a patron's activities, there are things that sort of flash before your mind. Where am I? What century is this? What country am I in?

It was just somebody in the government, in the F.B.I., saying that they wanted this information. It wasn't a court order; it wasn't a subpoena. There are all sorts of ways that you ask a librarian questions. And this is not one of them! We're here to serve, and to answer questions!

Then the lawyers said the only thing you can do—and there's a risk to it—is to challenge it in court: sue the U.S. government. There is no appeals process; there is no discussion. The only thing you can do is to sue them. As I understand it, that leads to a delay, and that only makes you [look] more guilty of whatever it is they want to accuse you of, should you lose. You're going into risky territory, just by not complying and not shutting up about it.

How long did it take? Did the documents have to be prepared in secret? Were you scared?

Thank goodness that there are organizations like the Electronic Frontier Foundation. They took it up, [along with] the A.C.L.U. of Northern California. Again, they advised me to not even ask my board whether or not I can do this. So this is, in some sense, really putting myself at risk personally. Here I am, trying to make a decision as to whether or not we should sue the United States government over a secret demand for information, on my own.

Did you tell your wife?

No! I couldn't!

And is she now going, "What's wrong? Why are you white as a sheet?"

I did go home that night and over dinner with my family, I said, "Ask me what it was I did today, and remember my answer." So my son, who was, I don't know, nine, or something like that, asked me, "Daddy, what did you do today?" And I said, "I can't tell you." That was the only thing I said, and then months and months and months went by.

The Internet Archive has the fortune of having really good ties to the A.C.L.U. and the E.F.F. Can you imagine if you're some small company, or some small library? What do you do?

But the Internet Archive works closely with the National Archives and with the Library of Congress. What are they going to think? What does it mean, to sue the United States government? So we sued, and had to do it very fast, because the lawyers had to do it by the document-demand date. They filed suit, and then the government very quickly said that they wanted out. They didn't need this information after all.

How long did it take between the time you guys filed and the time they backed out?

Only a couple of months. But then the whole negotiation became that we wanted to tell people that this had happened. We wanted the gag order lifted. And to their credit, they were okay with this.

How long did that part take?

I think the whole process took about six or seven months.

What do you think about the people with whom you interfaced on the government side? Did they seem reasonable?

We've had lots of interactions with people from the government. These guys were reasonable. But, you know, the whole story in some sense started six months before this demand came in.

How so?

Six months before, we got a notice from the San Francisco F.B.I., saying they were going to give us a national-security letter. These guys in black suits come to the door, and they're talking to the office manager, who said, uh, you're talking to the wrong person. We scratched our heads. We called the E.F.F.

And we couldn't figure out why they would say they were going to give us this letter! Kind of an odd thing to do. You either do, or you don't; and they didn't. So we decided to tell them: if you give us one of these, we will fight it. And they didn't give us one, not at that time. It was later that they did.

A different one, or the same one, do you think?

I think it's probably a different one. The government is not one monolithic thing. It's a bunch of people, thinking they're doing their jobs.

We were a little bit psychologically prepared. Then when we got one of these things, it was like, "Well, this one's for real."

Eventually, we negotiated the release of documents. That way, when it came out, it would be a cookbook, for others in my position. Because this is really, really scary. If you're in my position, the only thing that you can really turn to is asking questions on the Internet—that you hope is not being spied upon. We wanted it such that people who looked this stuff up could basically get an idea of how one organization had dealt with it.

Do you encrypt all your own e-mail, as a result of this stuff?

No, that's really hard.

Source: Bustillos, Mary. "What It's Like to Get a National-Security Letter." *New Yorker* (June 27, 2013). http://www.newyorker.com/tech/elements/what-its-like-to-get-a-national-security-letter. Accessed April 21, 2015. Maria Bustillos/The New Yorker; © Condé Nast. Used by permission.

2013: THE SECRET FISA VERIZON ORDER

On June 6, 2013, the UK-based Guardian *newspaper published a story by journalist Glenn Greenwald revealing that the U.S. government had secured a top-secret court order from the Foreign Intelligence Surveillance Court requiring the Verizon telecommunications company to turn over the telephone records of millions of Americans to the National Security Agency. The order, which mandated that Verizon turn the records over on an "ongoing daily basis," covered numbers at both ends of the calls, as well as the duration, time, and location of the calls and various other identifying characteristics. The order included calls not only between the United States and other countries, but also those that took place entirely within the United States. According to Greenwald, "the document shows for the first time that under the Obama administration the communication records of millions of U.S. citizens are being collected indiscriminately and in bulk—regardless of whether they are suspected of any wrongdoing."*

TOP SECRET//SI//NOFORN

UNITED STATES
FOREIGN INTELLIGENCE SURVEILLANCE COURT
WASHINGTON, D.C.

IN RE APPLICATION OF THE
FEDERAL BUREAU OF INVESTIGATION
FOR AN ORDER REQUIRING THE
PRODUCTION OF TANGIBLE THINGS
FROM VERIZON BUSINESS NETWORK SERVICES,
INC. ON BEHALF OF MCI COMMUNICATION
SERVICES, INC. D/B/A VERIZON
BUSINESS SERVICES.

SECONDARY ORDER

This Court having found that the Application of the Federal Bureau of Investigation (FBI) for an Order requiring the production of tangible things from **Verizon Business Network Services, Inc. on behalf of MCI Communication Services Inc., d/b/a Verizon Business Services (individually and collectively "Verizon")** satisfies the requirements of 50 U.S.C. ? 1861,

IT IS HEREBY ORDERED that, the Custodian of Records shall produce to the National Security Agency (NSA) upon service of this Order, and continue production on an ongoing daily basis thereafter for the duration of this Order, unless otherwise ordered by the Court, an electronic copy of the following tangible things: all call detail records or "telephony metadata" created by Verizon for communications (i) between the United States and abroad; or (ii) wholly within the United States, including local telephone calls. This Order does not require Verizon to produce telephony metadata for communications wholly originating and terminating in foreign countries. Telephony metadata includes comprehensive communications routing information, including but not limited to session identifying information (e.g., originating and terminating telephone number, International Mobile Subscriber Identity (IMSI) number, International Mobile station Equipment Identity (IMEI) number, etc.), trunk identifier, telephone calling card numbers, and time and duration of call. Telephony metadata does not include the substantive content of any communication, as defined by 18 U.S.C.

§ 2510(8), or the name, address, or financial information of a subscriber or customer.

IT IS FURTHER ORDERED that no person shall disclose to any other person that the FBI or NSA has sought or obtained tangible things under this Order, other than to: (a) those persons to whom disclosure is necessary to comply with such Order; (b) an attorney to obtain legal advice or assistance with respect to the production of things in response to the Order; or (c) other persons as permitted by the Director of the FBI or the Director's designee. A person to whom disclosure is made pursuant to (a), (b), or (c) shall be subject to the nondisclosure requirements applicable to a person to whom an Order is directed in the same manner as such person. Anyone who discloses to a person described in (a), (b), or (c) that the FBI or NSA has sought or obtained tangible things pursuant to this Order shall notify such person of the nondisclosure requirements of this Order. At the request of the Director of the FBI or the designee of the Director, any person making or intending to make a disclosure under (a) or (c) above shall identify to the Director or such designee the person to whom such disclosure will be made or to whom such disclosure was made prior to the request.

IT IS FURTHER ORDERED that service of this Order shall be by a method agreed upon by the Custodian of Records of Verizon and the FBI, and if no agreement is reached, service shall be personal.

This authorization **requiring the production of certain call detail records or "telephony metadata" created by Verizon** expires on the 19th day of July, 2013, at 5:00 p.m., Eastern Time

ROGER VINSON
Judge, United States Foreign
Intelligence Surveillance Court

Source: Judge Vinson, Roger, April 25, 2013. "*In re Application of the Federal Bureau of Investigation for an Order Requiring the production of tangible things from Verizon Business Network Services, Inc. on behalf of MCI Communication Services, Inc. d/b/a Verizon Business Services*" (PDF). *Top Secret Order of the Foreign Intelligence Surveillance Court*. Electronic Privacy Information Center.

2013: PRESIDENTIAL TASK FORCE REPORT ON *LIBERTY AND SECURITY IN A CHANGING WORLD*

After the media and political firestorm that followed Edward Snowden's revelations about the extent of surveillance activities being carried out on U.S. and non-U.S. citizens by the National Security Agency (NSA), President Barack Obama created a presidential task force to analyze the nation's governmental surveillance activities and agencies. This group, called the Review Group on Intelligence and Communications Technology, was led by Richard Clarke, the former chief counter-terrorism advisor to the National Security Council in the George W. Bush administration; constitutional law scholars, Geoffrey Stone and Cass Sunstein; former CIA director Michael Morell; and privacy expert Peter Swire.

In December 2013, the group released its report, which included criticisms of Section 215, National Security Letters (NSLs), the FISA Court, and other key elements of the NSA security apparatus. It also included 46 recommended reforms to NSA operations, framing most of them as efforts to better protect the legitimate privacy rights and expectations of people in America and around the world. Some of the proposed changes, however, ran counter to the official positions of the Obama administration and were not implemented. The following is from the Executive Summary of the task force report.

Executive Summary

Overview

The national security threats facing the United States and our allies are numerous and significant, and they will remain so well into the future. These threats include international terrorism, the proliferation of weapons of mass destruction, and cyber espionage and warfare. A robust foreign intelligence collection capability is essential if we are to protect ourselves against such threats. Because our adversaries operate through the use of complex communications technologies, the National Security Agency, with its impressive capabilities and talented officers, is indispensable to keeping our country and our allies safe and secure.

At the same time, the United States is deeply committed to the protection of privacy and civil liberties—fundamental values that can be and at times have been eroded by excessive intelligence collection. After careful consideration, we recommend a number of changes to our intelligence collection activities that will protect these values without undermining what we need to do to keep our nation safe.

Principles

We suggest careful consideration of the following principles:

1. ***The United States Government must protect, at once, two different forms of security: national security and personal privacy.***

In the American tradition, the word "security" has had multiple meanings. In contemporary parlance, it often refers to *national security* or *homeland security*. One of the government's most fundamental responsibilities is to protect this form of security, broadly understood. At the same time, the idea of security refers to a quite different and equally fundamental value, captured in the Fourth Amendment to the United States Constitution: "The right of the people to be *secure* in their persons, houses, papers, and effects, against unreasonable searches and seizures, shall not be violated . . ." (emphasis added). Both forms of security must be protected.

2. ***The central task is one of risk management; multiple risks are involved, and all of them must be considered.***

When public officials acquire foreign intelligence information, they seek to reduce risks, above all risks to national security. The challenge, of course, is that multiple risks are involved. Government must consider all of those risks, not a subset, when it is creating sensible safeguards. In addition to reducing risks to national security, public officials must consider four other risks:

- Risks to privacy;
- Risks to freedom and civil liberties, on the Internet and elsewhere;
- Risks to our relationships with other nations; and
- Risks to trade and commerce, including international commerce.

3. ***The idea of "balancing" has an important element of truth, but it is also inadequate and misleading.***

It is tempting to suggest that the underlying goal is to achieve the right "balance" between the two forms of security. The suggestion has an important element of truth. But some safeguards are not subject to balancing at all. In a free society, public officials should never engage in surveillance in order to punish their political enemies; to restrict freedom of speech or religion; to suppress legitimate criticism and dissent; to help their preferred companies or industries; to provide domestic companies with an unfair competitive advantage; or to benefit or burden members of groups defined in terms of religion, ethnicity, race, and gender.

4. ***The government should base its decisions on a careful analysis of consequences, including both benefits and costs (to the extent feasible).***

In many areas of public policy, officials are increasingly insistent on the need for careful analysis of the consequences of their decisions, and on the importance of relying not on intuitions and anecdotes, but on evidence and data. Before they are undertaken, surveillance decisions should depend (to the extent feasible) on a careful assessment of the anticipated consequences, including the full range of relevant risks. Such decisions should also be subject to continuing scrutiny, including retrospective analysis, to ensure that any errors are corrected.

Surveillance of U.S. Persons

With respect to surveillance of U.S. Persons, we recommend a series of significant reforms. Under section 215 of the Foreign Intelligence Surveillance Act (FISA), the government now stores bulk telephony meta-data, understood as information that includes the telephone numbers that both originate and receive calls, time of call, and date of call. (Meta-data does not include the content of calls.). We recommend that Congress should end such storage and transition to a system in which such meta-data is held privately for the government to query when necessary for national security purposes.

In our view, the current storage by the government of bulk meta-data creates potential risks to public trust, personal privacy, and civil liberty. We recognize that the government might need access to such meta-data, which should be held instead either by private providers or by a private third party. This approach would allow the government access to the relevant information when such access is justified, and thus protect national security without unnecessarily threatening privacy and liberty. Consistent with this recommendation, we endorse a broad principle for the future: as a general rule and without senior policy review, the government should not be permitted to collect and store mass, undigested, non-public personal information about U.S. persons for the purpose of enabling future queries and data-mining for foreign intelligence purposes.

We also recommend specific reforms that will provide Americans with greater safeguards against intrusions into their personal domain. We endorse new steps to protect American citizens engaged in communications with non-U.S. persons. We recommend important restrictions on the ability of the Foreign Intelligence Surveillance Court (FISC) to compel third parties (such as telephone service providers) to disclose private information to the government. We endorse similar restrictions on the issuance of National Security Letters (by which the Federal Bureau of

Investigation now compels individuals and organizations to turn over certain otherwise private records), recommending prior judicial review except in emergencies, where time is of the essence.

We recommend concrete steps to promote transparency and accountability, and thus to promote public trust, which is essential in this domain. Legislation should be enacted requiring information about surveillance programs to be made available to the Congress and to the American people to the greatest extent possible (subject only to the need to protect classified information). We also recommend that legislation should be enacted authorizing telephone, Internet, and other providers to disclose publicly general information about orders they receive directing them to provide information to the government. Such information might disclose the number of orders that providers have received, the broad categories of information produced, and the number of users whose information has been produced. In the same vein, we recommend that the government should publicly disclose, on a regular basis, general data about the orders it has issued in programs whose existence is unclassified.

Surveillance of Non-U.S. Persons

Significant steps should be taken to protect the privacy of non-U.S. persons. In particular, any programs that allow surveillance of such persons even outside the United States should satisfy six separate constraints. They:

1) must be authorized by duly enacted laws or properly authorized executive orders;
2) must be directed exclusively at protecting national security interests of the United States or our allies;
3) must not be directed at illicit or illegitimate ends, such as the theft of trade secrets or obtaining commercial gain for domestic industries;
4) must not target any non-United States person based solely on that person's political views or religious convictions;
5) must not disseminate information about non-United States persons if the information is not relevant to protecting the national security of the United States or our allies; and
6) must be subject to careful oversight and to the highest degree of transparency consistent with protecting the national security of the United States and our allies.

We recommend that, in the absence of a specific and compelling showing, the U.S. Government should follow the model of the Department of Homeland Security and apply the Privacy Act of 1974 in the same way to both U.S. persons and non-U.S. persons.

Setting Priorities and Avoiding Unjustified or Unnecessary Surveillance

To reduce the risk of unjustified, unnecessary, or excessive surveillance in foreign nations, including collection on foreign leaders, we recommend that the President should create a new process, requiring highest-level approval of all sensitive intelligence requirements and the methods that the Intelligence Community will use to meet them. This process should identify both the uses and the limits of surveillance on foreign leaders and in foreign nations.

We recommend that those involved in the process should consider whether (1) surveillance is motivated by especially important national security concerns or by concerns that are less pressing and (2) surveillance would involve leaders of nations with whom we share fundamental values and interests or leaders of other nations. With close reference to (2), we recommend that with a small number of closely allied governments, meeting specific criteria, the U.S. Government should explore understandings or arrangements regarding intelligence collection guidelines and practices with respect to each other's citizens (including, if and where appropriate, intentions, strictures, or limitations with respect to collections).

Organizational Reform

We recommend a series of organizational changes. With respect to the National Security Agency (NSA), we believe that the Director should be a Senate-confirmed position, with civilians eligible to hold that position; the President should give serious consideration to making the next Director of NSA a civilian. NSA should be clearly designated as a foreign intelligence organization. Other missions (including that of NSA's Information Assurance Directorate) should generally be assigned elsewhere. The head of the military unit, U.S. Cyber Command, and the Director of NSA should not be a single official.

We favor a newly chartered, strengthened, independent Civil Liberties and Privacy Protection Board (CLPP Board) to replace the Privacy and Civil Liberties Oversight Board (PCLOB). The CLPP Board should have broad authority to review government activity relating to foreign intelligence and counterterrorism whenever that activity has implications for civil liberties and privacy. A Special Assistant to the President for Privacy should also be designated, serving in both the Office of Management and Budget and the National Security Staff. This Special Assistant should chair a Chief Privacy Officer Council to help coordinate privacy policy throughout the Executive branch.

With respect to the FISC, we recommend that Congress should create the position of Public Interest Advocate to represent the interests of privacy and civil liberties before the FISC. We also recommend that the government should take steps to increase the transparency of the FISC's decisions and that Congress should change the process by which judges are appointed to the FISC.

Global Communications Technology

Substantial steps should be taken to protect prosperity, security, and openness in a networked world. A free and open Internet is critical to both self-government and economic growth. The United States Government should reaffirm the 2011 International Strategy for Cyberspace. It should stress that Internet governance must not be limited to governments, but should include all appropriate stakeholders, including businesses, civil society, and technology specialists.

The U.S. Government should take additional steps to promote security, by (1) fully supporting and not undermining efforts to create encryption standards; (2) making clear that it will not in any way subvert, undermine, weaken, or make vulnerable generally available commercial encryption; and (3) supporting efforts to encourage the greater use of encryption technology for data in transit, at rest, in the cloud, and in storage. Among other measures relevant to the Internet, the U.S. Government should also support international norms or agreements to increase confidence in the security of online communications.

For big data and data-mining programs directed at communications, the U.S. Government should develop Privacy and Civil Liberties Impact Assessments to ensure that such efforts are statistically reliable, cost-effective, and protective of privacy and civil liberties.

Protecting What We Do Collect

We recommend a series of steps to reduce the risks associated with "insider threats." A governing principle is plain: Classified information should be shared only with those who genuinely need to know. We recommend specific changes to improve the efficacy of the personnel vetting system. The use of "for-profit" corporations to conduct personnel investigations should be reduced or terminated. Security clearance levels should be further differentiated. Departments and agencies should institute a Work-Related Access approach to the dissemination of sensitive, classified information. Employees with high-level security clearances should be subject to a Personnel Continuous Monitoring Program.

Ongoing security clearance vetting of individuals should use a risk-management approach and depend on the sensitivity and quantity of the programs and information to which individuals are given access.

The security of information technology networks carrying classified information should be a matter of ongoing concern by Principals, who should conduct an annual assessment with the assistance of a "second opinion" team. Classified networks should increase the use of physical and logical separation of data to restrict access, including through Information Rights Management software. Cybersecurity software standards and practices on classified networks should be at least as good as those on the most secure private-sector enterprises.

Source: President's Review Group on Intelligence and Communications Technologies. *Liberty and Security in a Changing World.* December 12, 2013, pp. 14–23.

2013: A PRIVACY RIGHTS GROUP EXAMINES GOVERNMENTAL USE OF COMMERCIAL DATA BROKERS

The World Privacy Forum (WPF) is a nonprofit and nonpartisan public interest research group with a self-described mission to protect privacy in the "digital era." In the fall of 2013, the WPF issued an analysis of the U.S. government's use of commercial data brokers for antiterrorist and anticrime surveillance and other activities. According to the group, the report showed that "if [the U.S. government] is going to outsource its data needs to commercial data brokers, it needs to attach the privacy standards it would have been held to if it had collected the data itself. Outsourcing is not an excuse for evading privacy obligations."

Much of the 2013 WPF report focused in particular on Office of Management and Budget (OMB) guidance for a so-called Do Not Pay Initiative providing privacy protection guidelines for federal agencies utilizing commercial data brokers. Following are excerpts from the report's Executive Summary and Recommendations sections.

Executive Summary

The U.S. federal government is one of the largest and most frequent customers of commercial data brokers. Instead of creating its own databases subject to privacy laws applicable to federal agencies, the federal government often outsources the collection of significant amounts of information to external companies where privacy laws do not apply. It is well-established that commercial data brokers have been and are widely used in this manner for government law enforcement activities. However, that is not their only use by government.

In April 2012, the U.S. Treasury launched a Do Not Pay portal designed to verify and check on the eligibility of individuals to receive government benefits and payments, such as those receiving food stamps, housing assistance, and survivor benefits. The scope of the people and vendors affected by the information in the portal is quite broad. The portal includes government-operated databases with information about individuals, databases that are usually subject to the Privacy Act of 1974. However, the Do Not Pay portal also includes information from a commercial database called The Work Number. The Work Number, owned by Equifax, is not a government-held database and is not subject to the Privacy Act.

This is important because The Work Number collects salary and other information on more than 190 million Americans. However, unlike most of the government-maintained databases in the portal, The Work Number is not subject to the privacy rules that apply standards of accuracy, relevance, timeliness, and completeness to federally-operated databases. This matters because eligible people whose Work

Number files contain errors may fail to pass verification to receive government benefits or payments for services provided to the government.

Few people know that their salary information is available commercially in this way, and few know that their salary information may be used to verify government benefits. If an individual is the victim of an identity thief who created fictitious or erroneous pay records, or if the Work Number data contains inadvertent or even intentional errors from participating employers, individuals will be harmed when the federal government relies on that information. In the case of the Do Not Pay portal, people may not receive government benefits for which they qualify. If the digital era has taught one lesson it has taught that errors in files and databases do not discriminate—errors, including identity errors—can happen to any file in any data base, and they can impact the most vulnerable people who need government assistance the most. Those with data errors may need to work through a long correction process before they can receive their benefits. However, finding and correcting errors is difficult, especially when no law grants access and correction rights for most private sector databases.

By using The Work Number, the Do Not Pay portal employs the increasingly popular model of government outsourcing its data needs to commercial data brokers that do not have to abide by the same privacy standards applicable to the government, a model which has been criticized for its privacy shortcomings. This is because commercial databases do not have to satisfy the same privacy standards as databases held by the government. If the federal government obtains personal information from commercial data brokers but keeps the information outsourced and does not maintain that information in a government system of records, then a key law—the Privacy Act of 1974—imposes few or no privacy constraints on federal agencies, and no constraints at all on the commercial data brokers supplying the information.

Being denied important government benefits is no small matter, and meaningful privacy protections must be in place to prevent harms from data errors and other problems. Recognizing the potential for harm and the shortcomings of using private databases, the Office of Management and Budget took the novel and long-requested step of issuing new guidance that establishes privacy standards for commercial data brokers used in the Do Not Pay Portal, such as The Work Number. The new standards extend some of the privacy requirements applicable to the federal government to commercial databases that the government uses.

Albeit only within the Do Not Pay Initiative, this is the first time the government's commercial data outsourcing model has been meaningfully altered to apply important privacy safeguards.

The positive news is that because of the new OMB requirements, information in commercial databases used in the Do Not Pay Initiative—including The

Work Number—must be sufficiently accurate, up-to-date, relevant, and complete to ensure fairness to the individuals who are the subject of those records. The other good news is that the OMB standard rejects using a commercial database that includes records about the exercise of rights protected by the First Amendment. Commercial data brokers that cannot meet these standards will not be able to sell their information for the Do Not Pay Initiative.

The guidance is new, and it is welcome, but it is just one step. There are still significant loopholes remaining in the OMB guidance. As discussed, the "data outsourcing" model that allows the government to evade Privacy Act protections can still exist almost everywhere else in government other than the Do Not Pay Initiative. OMB should act to provide guidance to establish privacy standards that are at least as good as those in the Do Not Pay Initiative **covering all government purchases of commercial databases containing personal information**, not just those in the Do Not Pay Initiative. This action would serve the rest of the government well—and citizens for that matter—by rejecting personal data from commercial sources that does not meet the same standards that the law imposes on that collected by federal agencies. Everyone benefits when better quality databases are used for decision-making about individuals. Programs will be more efficiently and more individuals will receive fair and appropriate treatment.

If this does not happen, and these standards are not created and applied to cover all government purchases of information from commercial databases, the model of government outsourcing its data needs while circumventing privacy protections will become a deeply entrenched norm across all levels of government. If the practice continues unabated, sloppy databases without the protection of federal standards can and will cause further harm to the millions of people who have been victims of identity theft and other forms of fraud, and the millions of people who unknowingly have erroneous, incomplete, or out of date information in their records.

When OMB wrote its new guidance, it only chose to use four of the much more complete set of Privacy Act standards to apply to the commercial databases in the Do Not Pay Initiative. (The four standards OMB used were that records must be accurate, up-to-date, relevant, and complete). OMB should not have cherry-picked some privacy standards while leaving others behind. At the earliest opportunity, OMB needs to expand the privacy standards for the Do Not Pay Initiative to require that participating commercial databases comply fully with all Fair Information Practices, including collection limitation, data quality, purpose specification, use limitation, security safeguards, openness, access and correction rights, and accountability. It is especially important that data subjects have meaningful, timely, and effective access and correction rights to any commercial databases used by federal agencies. OMB should take steps to expand the privacy standards at the earliest possible opportunity following a reasonable test of the new Do Not Pay procedures.

If the additional standards are not applied, then it could lead to a significant long-term weakening of privacy standards in government databases. A substantial reduction in privacy protections could be substituted as a new norm, which would be a negative consequence of truncating these protections in the long term.

Another issue in the OMB guidance is the allowance of a 6-month pilot period where the new rules do not apply. Currently, The Work Number is being used within this pilot program. Therefore, the information of the millions of people in this database is being tested and is available for viewing, although it is not supposed to be used for adverse actions during this period. The first substantive test of the new OMB guidance will be how the U.S. Treasury and other participants in the Do Not Pay Initiative apply the guidance to The Work Number as it moves out of the pilot phase.

Before permanent use of The Work Number database can happen, the OMB requirements call for public notice and comment. This is another novel feature of the OMB privacy standards for the Do Not Pay Initiative. OMB should provide ample and prominent public notice and comment opportunity. The public notice should include full documentation about the accuracy, timeliness, relevance, and completeness of The Work Number. An independent audit of The Work Number's compliance with these data standards would be especially useful. In addition, all of the data fields maintained by The Work Number must be published to allow the public to evaluate whether any of the data reflects on the exercise of First Amendment rights.

If the privacy protections OMB established are effective, it will be an important step forward. At least in the Do Not Pay Initiative, people would have more ability to challenge the information coming from databases such as The Work Number and get redress from problems when they occur. If the OMB guidance was then taken up widely across the federal government and by state governments, the result could be better quality commercial databases for use by governments and by others. There would be fewer errors, less fraud, less government waste, more redress for individuals, and a higher overall standard of modern fair information practices would be set. Data could be used in a fair way that helps, not hurts, people.

III. Recommendations

Recommendations for the Office of Management and Budget:

- OMB should establish privacy standards that are at least as good as those in and recommended for the Do Not Pay Initiative to cover ***all government purchases of commercial databases with personal information***. OMB should consider accomplishing an expansion by establishing a task force that includes representatives of consumer and privacy groups.

- In the near future, OMB should expand the privacy standards for the Do Not Pay Initiative to require that commercial databases comply fully with all Fair Information Practices, including collection limitation, data quality, purpose specification, use limitation, security safeguards, openness, access and correction rights, and accountability. [54] It is especially important that data subjects have meaningful, timely, and effective access and correction rights to any commercial databases used by federal agencies. OMB should take steps to expand the privacy standards at the earliest possible opportunity following a reasonable test of the new Do Not Pay procedures.
- Because The Work Number will be the first test of a pilot project under the Do Not Pay Initiative, OMB should ensure that it provides for ample and prominent notice and public comment opportunity if it proposes permanent adoption of The Work Number. This is essential so that there will be a fair test of the effectiveness of public oversight of the new private sector database standards. Public notice should include extensive documentation about the accuracy, timeliness, relevance, and completeness of The Work Number. An independent audit of The Work Number's compliance with data standards would be especially useful. In addition, all of the data fields maintained by The Work Number must be published to allow an evaluation whether any of the data reflects on the exercise of First Amendment rights.
- According to the OMB FAQ on the Initiative, Treasury is considering inclusion of state-level data. [55] Before expanding the Initiative to state data, OMB should apply to state databases the same privacy standards and procedures that the Do Not Pay memo applies to commercial databases.

Recommendations for the States

The states also use commercial data sources and have market power. Each state should follow the example policies established by OMB and require that any commercial databases containing personal information used for state activities meet privacy standards consistent with Fair Information Practices. Standards for state purchases might be established using executive rather than legislative authority. Governors or State Attorneys General might consider establishing uniform standards here so that all states impose the same standards.

Recommendations for Congress

Congress should request that the Government Accountability Office review the implementation of the OMB Do Not Pay Initiative to make sure that the privacy standards are fairly implemented.

If Congress is unwilling to legislate broadly applicable privacy standards consistent with Fair Information Practices for commercial databases containing personal information, Congress should nevertheless encourage, authorize, or direct OMB to establish standards for all government purchases of commercial databases containing personal information.

Recommendation for the Federal Trade Commission

The Federal Trade Commission has long had the ability to determine that the failure of a commercial database containing personal information to meet Fair Information Practices is an unfair trade practice. The Commission has not yet taken any meaningful step in that direction. Nevertheless, any partial action by the FTC toward the goal of broader implementation of Fair Information Practices would still be welcome.

Recommendation for the public, including consumer and privacy groups

The public as well as consumer and privacy groups should closely monitor the Do Not Pay Initiative and should actively participate in any opportunity for public comment about the use of commercial databases.

Source: Gellman, Robert and Pam Dixon. *Data Brokers and the Federal Government: A New Front in the Battle for Privacy Opens.* October 30, 2013. World Privacy Forum Web site. http://www.worldprivacyforum.org/2013/10/report-data-brokers-and-the-federal-government-a-new-front-in-the-battle-for-privacy-opens/. Accessed February 27, 2015. Used by permission of the World Privacy Forum.

2014: PRESIDENT OBAMA RESPONDS TO THE TASK FORCE REVIEW OF NSA OPERATIONS

On January 17, 2014, President Barack Obama gave a speech at the Justice Department in which he responded to a special White House task force report— Liberty and Security in a Changing World*—that had been ordered in the wake of revelations of secret domestic surveillance operations carried out by the National Security Agency (NSA). In his speech, Obama committed his administration to carrying out a number of reforms advocated by the task force and endorsed other recommendations for congressional implementation. He explained that many of these changes were being instituted via a special directive—Presidential Policy Directive 28.*

Defenders of the NSA's surveillance activities expressed relief that the administration stance was one of amending—rather than ending—the NSA's bulk telephone metadata collection program, which had been the centerpiece of Edward Snowden's revelations about the NSA. Meanwhile, some critics of U.S. surveillance practices in Congress said that the reforms would go a long way toward "rebuilding the public's trust" ("Senators Wyden, Udall, Heinrich Statement on President's Announcement on Surveillance Reform," January 17, 2014. http://*www.wyden.senate.gov/news/press-releases/senators-wyden-udall-heinrich-statement-on-presidents-announcement-on-surveillance-reform).*

At the dawn of our Republic, a small, secret surveillance committee borne out of the "The Sons of Liberty" was established in Boston. And the group's members included Paul Revere. At night, they would patrol the streets, reporting back any signs that the British were preparing raids against America's early Patriots.

Throughout American history, intelligence has helped secure our country and our freedoms. In the Civil War, Union balloon reconnaissance tracked the size of Confederate armies by counting the number of campfires. In World War II, code-breakers gave us insights into Japanese war plans, and when Patton marched across Europe, intercepted communications helped save the lives of his troops. After the war, the rise of the Iron Curtain and nuclear weapons only increased the need for sustained intelligence gathering. And so, in the early days of the Cold War, President Truman created the National Security Agency, or NSA, to give us insights into the Soviet bloc, and provide our leaders with information they needed to confront aggression and avert catastrophe.

Throughout this evolution, we benefited from both our Constitution and our traditions of limited government. U.S. intelligence agencies were anchored in a system of checks and balances—with oversight from elected leaders, and protections for ordinary citizens. Meanwhile, totalitarian states like East Germany offered a cautionary tale of what could happen when vast, unchecked surveillance turned citizens into informers, and persecuted people for what they said in the privacy of their own homes.

In fact, even the United States proved not to be immune to the abuse of surveillance. And in the 1960s, government spied on civil rights leaders and critics of the Vietnam War. And partly in response to these revelations, additional laws were established in the 1970s to ensure that our intelligence capabilities could not be misused against our citizens. In the long, twilight struggle against Communism, we had been reminded that the very liberties that we sought to preserve could not be sacrificed at the altar of national security.

If the fall of the Soviet Union left America without a competing superpower, emerging threats from terrorist groups, and the proliferation of weapons of mass destruction placed new and in some ways more complicated demands on our intelligence agencies. Globalization and the Internet made these threats more acute, as technology erased borders and empowered individuals to project great violence, as well as great good. Moreover, these new threats raised new legal and new policy questions. For while few doubted the legitimacy of spying on hostile states, our framework of laws was not fully adapted to prevent terrorist attacks by individuals acting on their own, or acting in small, ideologically driven groups on behalf of a foreign power.

The horror of September 11th brought all these issues to the fore. Across the political spectrum, Americans recognized that we had to adapt to a world in which a bomb could be built in a basement, and our electric grid could be shut down by operators an ocean away. We were shaken by the signs we had missed leading up to the attacks—how the hijackers had made phone calls to known extremists and traveled to suspicious places. So we demanded that our intelligence community improve its capabilities, and that law enforcement change practices to focus more on preventing attacks before they happen than prosecuting terrorists after an attack.

It is hard to overstate the transformation America's intelligence community had to go through after 9/11. Our agencies suddenly needed to do far more than the traditional mission of monitoring hostile powers and gathering information for policymakers. Instead, they were now asked to identify and target plotters in some of the most remote parts of the world, and to anticipate the actions of networks that, by their very nature, cannot be easily penetrated with spies or informants.

And it is a testimony to the hard work and dedication of the men and women of our intelligence community that over the past decade we've made enormous strides in fulfilling this mission. Today, new capabilities allow intelligence agencies to track who a terrorist is in contact with, and follow the trail of his travel or his funding. New laws allow information to be collected and shared more quickly and effectively between federal agencies, and state and local law enforcement.

Relationships with foreign intelligence services have expanded, and our capacity to repel cyber-attacks have been strengthened. And taken together, these efforts have prevented multiple attacks and saved innocent lives—not just here in the United States, but around the globe.

And yet, in our rush to respond to a very real and novel set of threats, the risk of government overreach—the possibility that we lose some of our core liberties in pursuit of security—also became more pronounced. We saw, in the immediate aftermath of 9/11, our government engaged in enhanced interrogation techniques that contradicted our values. As a Senator, I was critical of several practices, such as warrantless wiretaps. And all too often new authorities were instituted without adequate public debate.

Through a combination of action by the courts, increased congressional oversight, and adjustments by the previous administration, some of the worst excesses that emerged after 9/11 were curbed by the time I took office. But a variety of factors have continued to complicate America's efforts to both defend our nation and uphold our civil liberties.

First, the same technological advances that allow U.S. intelligence agencies to pinpoint an al Qaeda cell in Yemen or an email between two terrorists in the Sahel also mean that many routine communications around the world are within our reach. And at a time when more and more of our lives are digital, that prospect is disquieting for all of us.

Second, the combination of increased digital information and powerful supercomputers offers intelligence agencies the possibility of sifting through massive amounts of bulk data to identify patterns or pursue leads that may thwart impending threats. It's a powerful tool. But the government collection and storage of such bulk data also creates a potential for abuse.

Third, the legal safeguards that restrict surveillance against U.S. persons without a warrant do not apply to foreign persons overseas. This is not unique to America; few, if any, spy agencies around the world constrain their activities beyond their own borders. And the whole point of intelligence is to obtain information that is not publicly available. But America's capabilities are unique, and the power of new technologies means that there are fewer and fewer technical constraints on what we can do. That places a special obligation on us to ask tough questions about what we should do.

And finally, intelligence agencies cannot function without secrecy, which makes their work less subject to public debate. Yet there is an inevitable bias not only within the intelligence community, but among all of us who are responsible for national security, to collect more information about the world, not less. So in the absence of institutional requirements for regular debate—and oversight that is public, as well as private or classified—the danger of government overreach becomes more acute. And this is particularly true when surveillance technology and our reliance on digital information is evolving much faster than our laws.

For all these reasons, I maintained a healthy skepticism toward our surveillance programs after I became President. I ordered that our programs be reviewed by my national security team and our lawyers, and in some cases I ordered changes in how we did business. We increased oversight and auditing, including new structures aimed at compliance. Improved rules were proposed by the government and approved by the Foreign Intelligence Surveillance Court. And we sought to keep Congress continually updated on these activities.

What I did not do is stop these programs wholesale—not only because I felt that they made us more secure, but also because nothing in that initial review, and nothing that I have learned since, indicated that our intelligence community has sought to violate the law or is cavalier about the civil liberties of their fellow citizens.

To the contrary, in an extraordinarily difficult job—one in which actions are second-guessed, success is unreported, and failure can be catastrophic—the men and women of the intelligence community, including the NSA, consistently follow protocols designed to protect the privacy of ordinary people. . . .

Now, to say that our intelligence community follows the law, and is staffed by patriots, is not to suggest that I or others in my administration felt complacent about the potential impact of these programs. Those of us who hold office in America have a responsibility to our Constitution, and while I was confident in the integrity of those who lead our intelligence community, it was clear to me in observing our intelligence operations on a regular basis that changes in our technological capabilities were raising new questions about the privacy safeguards currently in place.

Moreover, after an extended review of our use of drones in the fight against terrorist networks, I believed a fresh examination of our surveillance programs was a necessary next step in our effort to get off the open-ended war footing that we've maintained since 9/11. And for these reasons, I indicated in a speech at the National Defense University last May that we needed a more robust public discussion about the balance between security and liberty. Of course, what I did not know at the time is that within weeks of my speech, an avalanche of unauthorized disclosures would spark controversies at home and abroad that have continued to this day.

And given the fact of an open investigation, I'm not going to dwell on Mr. Snowden's actions or his motivations; I will say that our nation's defense depends in part on the fidelity of those entrusted with our nation's secrets. If any individual who objects to government policy can take it into their own hands to publicly disclose classified information, then we will not be able to keep our people safe, or conduct foreign policy. Moreover, the sensational way in which these disclosures have come out has often shed more heat than light, while revealing methods to our adversaries that could impact our operations in ways that we may not fully understand for years to come.

Regardless of how we got here, though, the task before us now is greater than simply repairing the damage done to our operations or preventing more disclosures from taking place in the future. Instead, we have to make some important decisions about how to protect ourselves and sustain our leadership in the world, while upholding the civil liberties and privacy protections that our ideals and our Constitution require. We need to do so not only because it is right, but because the challenges posed by threats like terrorism and proliferation and cyber-attacks are not going away any time soon. They are going to continue to be a major problem. And for our intelligence community to be effective over the long haul, we must maintain the trust of the American people, and people around the world.

This effort will not be completed overnight, and given the pace of technological change, we shouldn't expect this to be the last time America has this debate. But I want the American people to know that the work has begun. Over the last six months, I created an outside Review Group on Intelligence and Communications Technologies to make recommendations for reform. I consulted with the Privacy and Civil Liberties Oversight Board, created by Congress. I've listened to foreign partners, privacy advocates, and industry leaders. My administration has spent countless hours considering how to approach intelligence in this era of diffuse threats and technological revolution. So before outlining specific changes that I've ordered, let me make a few broad observations that have emerged from this process.

First, everyone who has looked at these problems, including skeptics of existing programs, recognizes that we have real enemies and threats, and that intelligence serves a vital role in confronting them. We cannot prevent terrorist attacks or cyber threats without some capability to penetrate digital communications—whether it's to unravel a terrorist plot; to intercept malware that targets a stock exchange; to make sure air traffic control systems are not compromised; or to ensure that hackers do not empty your bank accounts. We are expected to protect the American people; that requires us to have capabilities in this field.

Moreover, we cannot unilaterally disarm our intelligence agencies. There is a reason why BlackBerrys and iPhones are not allowed in the White House Situation Room. We know that the intelligence services of other countries—including some who feign surprise over the Snowden disclosures—are constantly probing our government and private sector networks, and accelerating programs to listen to our conversations, and intercept our emails, and compromise our systems. We know that.

Meanwhile, a number of countries, including some who have loudly criticized the NSA, privately acknowledge that America has special responsibilities as the world's only superpower; that our intelligence capabilities are critical to meeting these responsibilities, and that they themselves have relied on the information we obtain to protect their own people.

Second, just as ardent civil libertarians recognize the need for robust intelligence capabilities, those with responsibilities for our national security readily acknowledge the potential for abuse as intelligence capabilities advance and more and more private information is digitized. After all, the folks at NSA and other intelligence agencies are our neighbors. They're our friends and family. They've got electronic bank and medical records like everybody else. They have kids on Facebook and Instagram, and they know, more than most of us, the vulnerabilities to privacy that exist in a world where transactions are recorded, and emails and text and messages are stored, and even our movements can increasingly be tracked through the GPS on our phones.

Third, there was a recognition by all who participated in these reviews that the challenges to our privacy do not come from government alone. Corporations of all shapes and sizes track what you buy, store and analyze our data, and use it for commercial purposes; that's how those targeted ads pop up on your computer and your smartphone periodically. But all of us understand that the standards for government surveillance must be higher. Given the unique power of the state, it is not enough for leaders to say: Trust us, we won't abuse the data we collect. For history has too many examples when that trust has been breached. Our system of government is built on the premise that our liberty cannot depend on the good intentions of those in power; it depends on the law to constrain those in power.

I make these observations to underscore that the basic values of most Americans when it comes to questions of surveillance and privacy converge a lot more than the crude characterizations that have emerged over the last several months. Those who are troubled by our existing programs are not interested in repeating the tragedy of 9/11, and those who defend these programs are not dismissive of civil liberties. . . .

Fortunately, by focusing on facts and specifics rather than speculation and hypotheticals, this review process has given me—and hopefully the American people—some clear direction for change. And today, I can announce a series of concrete and substantial reforms that my administration intends to adopt administratively or will seek to codify with Congress.

First, I have approved a new presidential directive [Presidential Policy Directive 28] for our signals intelligence activities both at home and abroad. This guidance will strengthen executive branch oversight of our intelligence activities. It will ensure that we take into account our security requirements, but also our alliances; our trade and investment relationships, including the concerns of American companies; and our commitment to privacy and basic liberties. And we will review decisions about intelligence priorities and sensitive targets on an annual basis so that our actions are regularly scrutinized by my senior national security team.

Second, we will reform programs and procedures in place to provide greater transparency to our surveillance activities, and fortify the safeguards that protect the privacy of U.S. persons. Since we began this review, including information being released today, we have declassified over 40 opinions and orders of the Foreign Intelligence Surveillance Court, which provides judicial review of some of our most sensitive intelligence activities—including the Section 702 program targeting foreign individuals overseas, and the Section 215 telephone metadata program.

And going forward, I'm directing the Director of National Intelligence, in consultation with the Attorney General, to annually review for the purposes of declassification any future opinions of the court with broad privacy implications, and to report to me and to Congress on these efforts. To ensure that the court hears a broader range of privacy perspectives, I am also calling on Congress to authorize the establishment of a panel of advocates from outside government to provide an independent voice in significant cases before the Foreign Intelligence Surveillance Court.

Third, we will provide additional protections for activities conducted under Section 702, which allows the government to intercept the communications of foreign targets overseas who have information that's important for our national security. Specifically, I am asking the Attorney General and DNI to institute reforms that place additional restrictions on government's ability to retain, search, and use in criminal cases communications between Americans and foreign citizens incidentally collected under Section 702.

Fourth, in investigating threats, the FBI also relies on what's called national security letters, which can require companies to provide specific and limited information to the government without disclosing the orders to the subject of the investigation. These are cases in which it's important that the subject of the investigation, such as a possible terrorist or spy, isn't tipped off. But we can and should be more transparent in how government uses this authority.

I have therefore directed the Attorney General to amend how we use national security letters so that this secrecy will not be indefinite, so that it will terminate within a fixed time unless the government demonstrates a real need for further secrecy. We will also enable communications providers to make public more information than ever before about the orders that they have received to provide data to the government.

This brings me to the program that has generated the most controversy these past few months—the bulk collection of telephone records under Section 215. Let me repeat what I said when this story first broke: This program does not involve the content of phone calls, or the names of people making calls. Instead, it provides a record of phone numbers and the times and lengths of calls—metadata that can be queried if and when we have a reasonable suspicion that a particular number is linked to a terrorist organization.

Why is this necessary? The program grew out of a desire to address a gap identified after 9/11. One of the 9/11 hijackers—Khalid al-Mihdhar—made a phone call from San Diego to a known al Qaeda safe-house in Yemen. NSA saw that call, but it could not see that the call was coming from an individual already in the United States. The telephone metadata program under Section 215 was designed to map the communications of terrorists so we can see who they may be in contact with as quickly as possible . . .

In sum, the program does not involve the NSA examining the phone records of ordinary Americans. Rather, it consolidates these records into a database that the government can query if it has a specific lead—a consolidation of phone records that the companies already retained for business purposes. The review group turned up no indication that this database has been intentionally abused. And I believe it is important that the capability that this program is designed to meet is preserved.

Having said that, I believe critics are right to point out that without proper safeguards, this type of program could be used to yield more information about our private lives, and open the door to more intrusive bulk collection programs in the future. They're also right to point out that although the telephone bulk collection program was subject to oversight by the Foreign Intelligence Surveillance Court and has been reauthorized repeatedly by Congress, it has never been subject to vigorous public debate.

For all these reasons, I believe we need a new approach. I am therefore ordering a transition that will end the Section 215 bulk metadata program as it currently exists, and establish a mechanism that preserves the capabilities we need without the government holding this bulk metadata.

This will not be simple. The review group recommended that our current approach be replaced by one in which the providers or a third party retain the bulk records, with government accessing information as needed. Both of these options pose difficult problems. Relying solely on the records of multiple providers, for example, could require companies to alter their procedures in ways that raise new privacy concerns. On the other hand, any third party maintaining a single, consolidated database would be carrying out what is essentially a government function but with more expense, more legal ambiguity, potentially less accountability—all of which would have a doubtful impact on increasing public confidence that their privacy is being protected.

During the review process, some suggested that we may also be able to preserve the capabilities we need through a combination of existing authorities, better information sharing, and recent technological advances. But more work needs to be done to determine exactly how this system might work.

Because of the challenges involved, I've ordered that the transition away from the existing program will proceed in two steps. Effective immediately, we will only pursue phone calls that are two steps removed from a number associated with a terrorist organization instead of the current three. And I have directed the Attorney General to work with the Foreign Intelligence Surveillance Court so that during this transition period, the database can be queried only after a judicial finding or in the case of a true emergency.

Next, step two, I have instructed the intelligence community and the Attorney General to use this transition period to develop options for a new approach that can match the capabilities and fill the gaps that the Section 215 program was designed to address without the government holding this metadata itself. They will report back to me with options for alternative approaches before the program comes up for reauthorization on March 28th. And during this period, I will consult with the relevant committees in Congress to seek their views, and then seek congressional authorization for the new program as needed.

Now, the reforms I'm proposing today should give the American people greater confidence that their rights are being protected, even as our intelligence and law enforcement agencies maintain the tools they need to keep us safe. And I recognize that there are additional issues that require further debate. For example, some who participated in our review, as well as some members of Congress, would like to see more sweeping reforms to the use of national security letters so that we have to go to a judge each time before issuing these requests. Here, I have concerns that we should not set a standard for terrorism investigations that is higher than those involved in investigating an ordinary crime. But I agree that greater oversight on the use of these letters may be appropriate, and I'm prepared to work with Congress on this issue.

There are also those who would like to see different changes to the FISA Court than the ones I've proposed. On all these issues, I am open to working with Congress to ensure that we build a broad consensus for how to move forward, and I'm confident that we can shape an approach that meets our security needs while upholding the civil liberties of every American.

Let me now turn to the separate set of concerns that have been raised overseas, and focus on America's approach to intelligence collection abroad. As I've indicated, the United States has unique responsibilities when it comes to intelligence collection. Our capabilities help protect not only our nation, but our friends and our allies, as well. But our efforts will only be effective if ordinary citizens in other countries have confidence that the United States respects their privacy, too. And the leaders of our close friends and allies deserve to know that if I want to know what they think about an issue, I'll pick up the phone and call them, rather than turning to surveillance. In other words, just as we balance security and privacy at home, our global leadership demands that we balance our security requirements against our need to maintain the trust and cooperation among people and leaders around the world.

For that reason, the new presidential directive that I've issued today will clearly prescribe what we do, and do not do, when it comes to our overseas surveillance. To begin with, the directive makes clear that the United States only uses signals intelligence for legitimate national security purposes, and not for the purpose of indiscriminately reviewing the emails or phone calls of ordinary folks. I've also made it clear that the United States does not collect intelligence to suppress criticism or dissent, nor do we collect intelligence to disadvantage people on the basis of their ethnicity, or race, or gender, or sexual orientation, or religious beliefs. We do not collect intelligence to provide a competitive advantage to U.S. companies or U.S. commercial sectors.

And in terms of our bulk collection of signals intelligence, U.S. intelligence agencies will only use such data to meet specific security requirements: counterintelligence, counterterrorism, counter-proliferation, cybersecurity, force protection for our troops and our allies, and combating transnational crime, including sanctions evasion.

In this directive, I have taken the unprecedented step of extending certain protections that we have for the American people to people overseas. I've directed the DNI, in consultation with the Attorney General, to develop these safeguards, which will limit the duration that we can hold personal information, while also restricting the use of this information.

The bottom line is that people around the world, regardless of their nationality, should know that the United States is not spying on ordinary people who don't threaten our national security, and that we take their privacy concerns into account in our policies and procedures. This applies to foreign leaders as well. . . .

Now let me be clear: Our intelligence agencies will continue to gather information about the intentions of governments—as opposed to ordinary citizens—around the world, in the same way that the intelligence services of every other nation does. We will not apologize simply because our services may be more effective. But heads of state and government with whom we work closely, and on whose cooperation we depend, should feel confident that we are treating them as real partners. And the changes I've ordered do just that.

Finally, to make sure that we follow through on all these reforms, I am making some important changes to how our government is organized. The State Department will designate a senior officer to coordinate our diplomacy on issues related to technology and signals intelligence. We will appoint a senior official at the White House to implement the new privacy safeguards that I have announced today. I will devote the resources to centralize and improve the process we use to handle foreign requests for legal assistance, keeping our high standards for privacy while helping foreign partners fight crime and terrorism.

I have also asked my counselor, John Podesta, to lead a comprehensive review of big data and privacy. And this group will consist of government officials who, along with the President's Council of Advisors on Science and Technology, will reach out to privacy experts, technologists and business leaders, and look how the challenges inherent in big data are being confronted by both the public and private sectors; whether we can forge international norms on how to manage this data; and how we can continue to promote the free flow of information in ways that are consistent with both privacy and security.

For ultimately, what's at stake in this debate goes far beyond a few months of headlines, or passing tensions in our foreign policy. When you cut through the noise, what's really at stake is how we remain true to who we are in a world that is remaking itself at dizzying speed. . . . So while the reforms that I have announced will point us in a new direction, I am mindful that more work will be needed in the future.

One thing I'm certain of: This debate will make us stronger. And I also know that in this time of change, the United States of America will have to lead. It may seem sometimes that America is being held to a different standard. And I'll admit the readiness of some to assume the worst motives by our government can be frustrating. No one expects China to have an open debate about their surveillance programs, or Russia to take privacy concerns of citizens in other places into account. But let's remember: We are held to a different standard precisely because we have been at the forefront of defending personal privacy and human dignity.

As the nation that developed the Internet, the world expects us to ensure that the digital revolution works as a tool for individual empowerment, not government control. Having faced down the dangers of totalitarianism and fascism and communism, the world expects us to stand up for the principle that every person has the right to think and write and form relationships freely—because individual freedom is the wellspring of human progress.

Those values make us who we are. And because of the strength of our own democracy, we should not shy away from high expectations. For more than two centuries, our Constitution has weathered every type of change because we have been willing to defend it, and because we have been willing to question the actions that have been taken in its defense. Today is no different. I believe we can meet high expectations. Together, let us chart a way forward that secures the life of our nation while preserving the liberties that make our nation worth fighting for.

Source: Obama, Barack. "Remarks by the President on Review of Signals Intelligence." January 17, 2014. White House Web site. http://www.whitehouse.gov/the-press-office/2014/01/17/remarks-president-review-signals-intelligence. Accessed January 27, 2015.

2014: PRIVACY AND CIVIL LIBERTIES OVERSIGHT BOARD CONDEMNS THE NSA'S SECTION 215 PROGRAM

In January 2014, an independent "watchdog" group within the federal executive branch known as the Privacy and Civil Liberties Oversight Board (PCLOB) issued its first-ever report. This report examined the efficacy, legality, and civil liberties implications of the National Security Agency's (NSA) metadata collection program, which is being carried out under the auspices of Section 215 of the USA PATRIOT Act. According to this board, which was made up of civil liberties and security experts appointed by the president and approved by the U.S. Senate, the NSA metadata program was not *authorized by Section 215. The PCLOB further asserted that the evidence showed that the Section 215 program's national security benefits had been broadly overstated by its defenders, that it would not have stopped 9/11 if it had been in place before those terrorist attacks, and that its continued existence posed serious "implications" for American civil liberties and privacy. This report, which was released only one week after President Barack Obama delivered a speech endorsing only modest reforms to the Section 215 program, was seized on by privacy advocates who had criticized Obama's proposals as inadequate.*

On May 7, 2015, the legality of the NSA's phone record surveillance programs carried out under Section 215 became further clouded. On that day, a federal appeals court ruled in ACLU v. Clapper *that the Section 215 statute did not give the government legal authority to carry out such bulk collection of telephone records.*

The excerpts below from the PCLOB report provide a brief description of the Section 215 program, summarize the program's record as a counterterrorism tool, assess whether it could have stopped 9/11 had it been in place at that time, and discuss its capacity to threaten basic American civil liberties.

Background: Description and History of the Section 215 Program

The NSA's telephone records program is operated under an order issued by the FISA court pursuant to Section 215 of the Patriot Act, an order that is renewed approximately every ninety days.

The program is intended to enable the government to identify communications among known and unknown terrorism suspects, particularly those located inside the United States. When the NSA identifies communications that may be associated with terrorism, it issues intelligence reports to other federal agencies, such as the FBI, that work to prevent terrorist attacks.

The FISC order authorizes the NSA to collect nearly all call detail records generated by certain telephone companies in the United States, and specifies detailed rules for the use and retention of these records. Call detail records typically include much of the information that appears on a customer's telephone bill: the date and time of a call, its duration, and the participating telephone numbers. Such information is commonly referred to as a type of "metadata." The records collected by the NSA under this program do not, however, include the content of any telephone conversation.

After collecting these telephone records, the NSA stores them in a centralized database. Initially, NSA analysts are permitted to access the Section 215 calling records only through "queries" of the database. A query is a search for a specific number or other selection term within the database.

Before any specific number is used as the search target or "seed" for a query, one of twenty-two designated NSA officials must first determine that there is a reasonable, articulable suspicion ("RAS") that the number is associated with terrorism. Once the seed has been RAS-approved, NSA analysts may run queries that will return the calling records for that seed, and permit "contact chaining" to develop a fuller picture of the seed's contacts. Contact chaining enables analysts to retrieve not only the numbers directly in contact with the seed number (the "first hop"), but also numbers in contact with all first hop numbers (the "second hop"), as well as all numbers in contact with all second hop numbers (the "third hop").

The Section 215 telephone records program has its roots in counterterrorism efforts that originated in the immediate aftermath of the September 11 attacks. The NSA began collecting telephone metadata in bulk as one part of what became known as the President's Surveillance Program. From late 2001 through early 2006, the NSA collected bulk telephony metadata based upon presidential authorizations issued every thirty to forty-five days. In May 2006, the FISC first granted an application by the government to conduct the telephone records program under Section 215.

The government's application relied heavily on the reasoning of a 2004 FISA court opinion and order approving the bulk collection of Internet metadata under a different provision of FISA.

On June 5, 2013, the British newspaper The Guardian published an article based on unauthorized disclosures of classified documents by Edward Snowden, a contractor for the NSA, which revealed the telephone records program to the public. On August 29, 2013, FISC Judge Claire Eagan issued an opinion explaining the court's rationale for approving the Section 215 telephone records program.

Although prior authorizations of the program had been accompanied by detailed orders outlining applicable rules and minimization procedures, this was the first judicial opinion explaining the FISA court's legal reasoning in authorizing the bulk records collection. The Section 215 program was reauthorized most recently by the FISC on January 3, 2014. . . .

IV. Demonstrated Efficacy of the NSA's Bulk Collection of Telephone Records

Clearly, the NSA's bulk acquisition of telephone records provides the government with certain capabilities that would otherwise be lacking in the endeavor to combat terrorism. But the question remains whether those capabilities have demonstrably enhanced the government's efforts to safeguard the nation. . . .

Any attempt to assess the value of the NSA's telephone records program must be cognizant of a few considerations. First, the information that the NSA obtains through Section 215 is not utilized in a vacuum. Rather, it is combined with information obtained under different legal authorities. . . . Moreover, what the Section 215 program yields is the identification of telephone numbers of potential interest, or the revelation of connections between telephone numbers of interest, which must be passed on to the FBI or other agencies as leads for further investigation. Any assessment of the program's value, and any expectations about what it can be expected to accomplish, must bear this consideration in mind.

Finally, an intelligence-gathering tool like the NSA's Section 215 program can provide value that materially enhances the safety of the nation even if it never provides the single critical piece of insight enabling the government to thwart an imminent terrorist attack. Because the work of intelligence gathering and analysis is cumulative, it is rare that any particular technique or legal authority can be identified as the key component without which a terrorist plot would have succeeded. Intelligence-gathering tools can provide value in more indirect ways, by helping to advance investigations and focus efforts in ways that are sometimes more difficult to measure.

That being said, in the Board's view, an intelligence-gathering tool with significant ramifications for privacy and civil liberties cannot be regarded as justified merely because it provides *Some* value in protecting the nation from terrorism. Particularly when an intelligence program reaches as broadly as the NSA's bulk collection of telephone records—potentially touching the lives of nearly every American, and in the process investing considerable power in the hands of the government to monitor the communication patterns of its citizens—we believe it is necessary to measure the value provided by the program by considering whether comparable results could be achieved through less intrusive means and whether any unique value offered by the program outweighs its implications for privacy and civil liberties. . . .

In our effort to carry out this balancing task with respect to the NSA's Section 215 program, we have examined a wealth of classified materials regarding the operation of the program. . . . In particular, we have closely scrutinized the specific cases cited by the government as instances in which telephone records obtained under Section 215 were useful in counterterrorism investigations. . . .

We have examined those incidents in depth, attempting to discern precisely what was accomplished in each case through the use of Section 215 records and whether similar results could have been achieved using more tailored means of gathering telephone records. . . .

Our analysis suggests that where the telephone records collected by the NSA under its Section 215 program have provided value, they have done so primarily in two ways. The first is by offering additional leads regarding the contacts of terrorism suspects already known to investigators, which can help investigators confirm suspicions about the target of an inquiry or about persons in contact with that target. But our review suggests that the Section 215 program offers little unique value here, instead largely duplicating the FBI's own information-gathering efforts. The second is by demonstrating that known foreign terrorism suspects do not have U.S. contacts or that known terrorist plots do not have a U.S. nexus. This can help the intelligence community focus its limited investigatory resources by avoiding false leads and channeling efforts where they are needed most. But the value of this benefit must be kept in perspective. . . .

Based on the information provided to the Board, we have not identified a single instance involving a threat to the United States in which the telephone records program made a concrete difference in the outcome of a counterterrorism investigation. Moreover, we are aware of no instance in which the program directly contributed to the discovery of a previously unknown terrorist plot or the disruption of a terrorist attack. And we believe that in only one instance over the past seven years has the program arguably contributed to the identification of an unknown terrorism suspect. In that case, moreover, the suspect was not involved in planning a terrorist attack and there is reason to believe that the FBI may have discovered him without the contribution of the NSA's program.

Even in those instances where telephone records collected under Section 215 offered additional information about the contacts of a known terrorism suspect, in nearly all cases the benefits provided have been minimal—generally limited to corroborating information that was obtained independently by the FBI. And in those few cases where some information not already known to the government was generated through the use of Section 215 records, we have seen little indication that the same result could not have been obtained through traditional, targeted collection of telephone records. . . . In other words, we see little evidence that the unique capabilities provided by the NSA's bulk collection of telephone records actually have yielded material counterterrorism results that could not have been achieved without the NSA's Section 215 program. . . .

9/11

Some have suggested that if the NSA's calling records program were in place before 9/11, it could have alerted the government that one of the future airplane hijackers was in the United States, and perhaps have led to the prevention of the attacks. For several years, beginning in the late 1990s, the NSA intercepted telephone calls to and from a prominent Al Qaeda safe house in Yemen. A number of calls were made in early 2000 between this safe house and a person named Khalid, who after 9/11 was identified as hijacker Khalid al-Mihdhar. Although the NSA was able to listen to these conversations, it did not have the telephone number that was calling the safe house, and thus it did not know that Mihdhar made the calls from San Diego, California. Had the NSA known this information, it is argued, the government could have identified Mihdhar as the caller and been aware of his presence in the United States, perhaps leading to his apprehension and the identification and detention of other hijackers.

For two reasons, we do not believe the Mihdhar example supports continuance of the NSA's Section 215 program. First, the failure to identify Mihdhar's presence in the United States stemmed primarily from a lack of information sharing among federal agencies, not of a lack of surveillance capabilities. As documented by the 9/11 Commission and others, this was a failure to connect the dots, not a failure to collect enough dots.

Second, in order to have identified the San Diego telephone number from which Mihdhar made his calls, it was not necessary to collect the entire nation's calling records. As explained by the 9/11 Commission Report, the joint inquiry into the 9/11 attacks by the House and Senate intelligence committees, and a Department of Justice Inspector General report, the government had ample opportunity before 9/11 to pinpoint Mihdhar's location, track his activities, and prevent his 2001 reentry into the United States. By early 2000, the CIA was aware of Mihdhar and knew that he had a visa enabling him to travel to the United States. Yet despite having information that Mihdhar and fellow hijacker Nawaf al-Hazmi "were traveling to the United States," the CIA "missed repeated opportunities to act based on the information in its possession." The agency did not advise the FBI of what it knew or "add their names to watch lists."

Furthermore, at the time that Mihdhar and Hazmi were in San Diego in early 2000, when the calls to Yemen were made, they were living with "a long-time FBI asset."

Mihdhar left the United States in June 2000, and he was able to return in 2001 because he still had not been placed on any watchlists. And "[o]n four occasions in

2001, the CIA, the FBI, or both had apparent opportunities to refocus on the significance of Hazmi and Mihdhar and reinvigorate the search for them." Yet these opportunities were missed.

It is argued, however, the NSA's bulk telephone records program could have made up for these intelligence lapses and failures of information sharing. Knowledge that the telephone calls from "Khalid" to the Yemen safe house were made from San Diego theoretically could have led the government to discover Mihdhar's presence in the United States. But obtaining this knowledge did not require a bulk telephone records program. The NSA knew the telephone number of the Yemen safe house. If the telephone calls with Mihdhar were deemed suspicious at the time, the government could have used existing legal authorities to request from U.S. telephone companies the records of any calls made to or from that Yemen number. Doing so could have identified the San Diego number on the other end of the calls. Thus we do not believe that a program that collects all telephone records from U.S. telephone companies was necessary to identify Mihdhar's location in early 2000, nor that such a program is necessary to make similar discoveries in the future.

Finally, in the absence of evidence that the NSA's Section 215 program has made any significant contribution to counterterrorism efforts to date, some officials have suggested to us that the program should be preserved because it might do so in the future. Like a burglar alarm or a fire insurance policy, under this reasoning, the program is valuable even if it has not yet been triggered by a break-in or a fire. Yet, it is worth noting that the program supplied no advance notice of attempted attacks on the New York City subway, the failed Christmas Day airliner bombing, or the failed Times Square car bombing. Given the limited value this program has demonstrated to date, as outlined above, we find little reason to expect that it is likely to provide significant value, much less essential value, in safeguarding the nation in the future.

V. Privacy and Civil Liberties Implications of the NSA's Bulk Collection of Telephone Records

Having described what we believe to be the value of the NSA's telephone records program in combating terrorism, we now turn to the implications of that program for privacy and civil liberties. We believe those implications are serious. The design of the NSA's program shows that the government recognizes the privacy concerns raised by the collection and analysis of telephone calling records. The government has responded to those concerns by imposing rules that limit the NSA's use of telephone records after their collection by the agency. These rules offer many valuable safeguards designed to curb the intrusiveness of the program. But in our view, they cannot fully ameliorate the implications for privacy, speech, and association that follow from the government's ongoing collection of virtually all telephone records of every American.

Because telephone calling records can reveal intimate details about a person's life, particularly when aggregated with other information and subjected to sophisticated computer analysis, the government's collection of a person's entire telephone calling history has a significant and detrimental effect on that person's privacy. Beyond such individual privacy intrusions, permitting the government to routinely collect the calling records of the entire nation fundamentally shifts the balance of power between the state and its citizens. Moreover, as outlined below, this practice can be expected to have a chilling effect on the free exercise of speech and association, because law-abiding individuals and groups engaged in sensitive or controversial work cannot trust in the confidentiality of their relationships as revealed by their calling patterns. Finally, for the reasons explained below, we do not believe that these concerns are eliminated by the detailed rules placed on the NSA's use of telephone calling records after their collection.

A. The Revealing Nature of Telephone Calling Records

Telephone calling records, which indicate who called whom, at what time, and for how long, but do not include the contents of any conversations, are a form of "metadata." Like the address on the outside of an envelope, which announces the envelope's destination but does not reveal the content of the letter inside, telephone calling records provide information about the existence and details of a call without revealing what was said.

But while telephone calling records are distinct from the spoken content of any conversation, they can be highly revealing nonetheless. As Justice Stewart noted over thirty years ago, the telephone numbers that a person dials "easily could reveal the identities of the persons and the places called, and thus reveal the most intimate details of a person's life." Because the circumstances of a particular call can be highly suggestive of its content, the mere record of a call potentially offers a window into the caller's private affairs. Some illustrative examples cited by a privacy advocacy organization include the following: calling a suicide prevention hotline; calling a telephone sex service at 2:30 a.m.; calling an HIV testing service, then one's doctor, then one's health insurance company within the same hour; receiving a call from the local NRA office during a campaign against gun legislation, then calling one's congressional representatives immediately afterward; and calling one's gynecologist, speaking for half an hour, then calling the local Planned Parenthood number later that day.

At bottom, telephone metadata is information about a person's conduct. Just as it reveals something about a person to know that he or she visited the doctor's office, likewise it reveals something about that person to know that he or she called the doctor's office on the telephone. When the government collects metadata about its citizens, therefore, it is collecting information about its citizens' activity.

Moreover, when the government collects all of a person's telephone records, storing them for five years in a government database that is subject to high-speed digital searching and analysis, the privacy implications go far beyond what can be revealed by the metadata of a single telephone call. The frequency with which two numbers are in contact with each other, along with the timing and duration of their calls, provides insight into the nature of the relationship between the two callers. When both of those numbers are in contact with a third number, the pattern of calls among these three numbers adds to the story that can be gleaned from their communications records. Thus, aggregation of numerous calling records over an extended period of time can paint a clear picture of an individual's personal relationships and patterns of behavior. This picture can be at least as revealing of those relationships and habits as the contents of individual conversations—if not more so. The power of such communications metadata to illustrate a person's social connections with stark accuracy has been illustrated vividly by technology researchers.

Based on our consideration of this issue, the Board is convinced that telephone calling records, when collected in bulk and subjected to powerful analytic tools, can reveal highly sensitive personal information. The government acknowledges as much, arguing that "sophisticated analytic tools" can reveal "chains of communication" and "connections between individuals." As one former general counsel of the NSA recently was quoted as saying: "Metadata absolutely tells you everything about somebody's life. . . . [It's] sort of embarrassing how predictable we are as human beings. . . . . If you have enough metadata you don't really need content."

There is a paradox here. We have concluded, based on the evidence provided by the government, that the NSA's Section 215 program has not proven useful in identifying unknown terrorists or terrorist plots, in part because the program often merely corroborates information about connections among individuals that have already been obtained independently through other means. Yet we also conclude that telephone calling records, if used in more expansive ways than the government currently employs them, can reveal a great deal about an innocent person's habits, private affairs, and network of social, familial, and professional connections. This capability is magnified when calling records are aggregated across customers and carriers and over a long period of time.

The very power that inheres in the analysis of telephone calling records—a power that the government has emphasized in defending the intelligence value of the NSA's Section 215 program—illustrates the depth of the privacy implications entailed by the program without proving its effectiveness as a counterterrorism tool.

B. Privacy Implications of Bulk Collection of Telephone Calling Records

Given the ability of telephone calling records to reveal intimate details of a person's life, significant privacy interests are at stake when the government collects all of a person's calling records, particularly when it retains this information for years in a database that enables swift mapping of one's pattern of communications and network of contacts.

At the most basic level, routine government collection of telephone records defeats the core concept of information privacy—the ability of individuals to control information about themselves. This loss of control is heightened when it is the government collecting personal records. With its powers of compulsion and criminal prosecution, the government poses unique threats to privacy when it collects data on its own citizens. Allowing it to gather vast quantities of information about the conduct of individuals as a routine matter where those individuals are not suspected of any crimes affects the balance of power between the state and its people.

Collection and analysis of information on the scale of the NSA's Section 215 program also heightens the risk of the types of mistakes that often accompany the implementation of large information systems. Indeed, privacy violations, including the inadvertent collection of unauthorized personal data, improper use of the data collected, or dissemination of that data to persons or entities not approved to receive it, may be inevitable. . . .

Since the NSA began collecting telephone and Internet metadata under the supervision of the FISA court, there have been repeated instances of precisely these sorts of violations. Government collection of personal information on such a massive scale also courts the ever-present danger of "mission creep." At the moment, telephone records obtained by the NSA under Section 215 may exclusively be used in furtherance of clearly defined counterterrorism efforts, and only in the manner prescribed by the FISA court's orders.

Once collected, however, information is always at risk of being appropriated for new purposes. Thus, when the government assembles a database containing the calling histories of millions of individuals, proposals to make this information available for other important governmental functions may be inevitable. Already, it has been reported in the press, officials from numerous federal agencies have exerted pressure on the NSA to share its data and surveillance tools for investigations into "drug trafficking, cyberattacks, money laundering, counterfeiting and even copyright infringement."

An even more compelling danger is that personal information collected by the government will be misused to harass, blackmail, or intimidate, or to single out for scrutiny individuals or groups adhering to minority religions or holding unpopular views. To be clear, the Board has seen no evidence suggesting that anything of the sort is occurring at the NSA. But while the danger of such abuse may seem remote, it is more than merely theoretical. The government's rampant misuse of its surveillance authority during the twentieth century to squelch domestic dissent in the name of national security was amply documented by the reports of the Church Committee, and was in fact the impetus for passage of the Foreign Intelligence Surveillance Act. . . .

Prudence cautions against assuming that abuse of surveillance powers is a problem that will never reoccur, and any decision to invest the government with a broad surveillance power must duly take into account the abuse that this power could enable, whether or not such abuse is evident today. Regardless of the good faith with which it may be wielded today, the immense power afforded the government by routine collection of all telephone records enables significant abuse and intrusion into Americans' privacy.

C. Chilling of Free Speech and Association

The NSA's bulk collection of telephone records also directly implicates freedom of speech and association. The readiness with which individuals engage in certain political and social activities understandably may be chilled by knowledge that the government collects a record of virtually every telephone call made by every American. Inability to expect privacy vis-à-vis the government in one's telephone communications means that people engaged in wholly lawful activities—but who for various reasons justifiably do not wish the government to know about their communications—must either forgo such activities, reduce their frequency, or take costly measures to hide them from government surveillance. Among the important freedoms that may be threatened by this chilling effect are the rights to participate in political activism, communicate with and benefit from the press, and promote novel or unpopular ideas. . . .

Source: Privacy and Civil Liberties Oversight Board. *Report on the Telephone Records Program Conducted under Section 215 of the USA PATRIOT Act and on the Operations of the Foreign Intelligence Surveillance Court*. Washington, DC: PCLOB, January 23, 2014, pp. 8–9, 144–48, 153–61.

2014: SENATOR FEINSTEIN REACTS TO REVELATIONS OF CIA SPYING ON THE SENATE

In 2009, the U.S. Senate Intelligence Committee launched an investigation into the detention and interrogation activities of the Bush administration's Central Intelligence Agency (CIA) after 9/11. The investigation's focus included waterboarding and other brutal interrogation methods approved and employed by the CIA and other government agencies as counterterrorism tools, even though some of these methods were historically understood to constitute forms of torture.

In response to the Senate investigation, the CIA created a secure computer system separate from other CIA networks where Senate aides could review agency documents related to the investigation. In September 2009, however, Republican unhappiness with a separate Justice Department investigation into Bush-era detention and interrogation practices led GOP committee members to withdraw from the Senate review.

In the first half of 2010, more than 900 secret documents mysteriously disappeared from the computer system being used by the Senate staffers to carry out their review. Later that same year, Senate investigators discovered excerpts from a secret internal report called the Panetta Review (named after former CIA director Leon Panetta) that acknowledged problems with the CIA detention program. But the Panetta Review was never intended to be made available to investigators, and when CIA officials learned that it was in the hands of Senate staffers, they secretly penetrated the computer system used by the Senate investigators to spy on its activities.

In December 2012, the Senate Intelligence Committee submitted its final report to the White House and CIA for comment. This report was highly critical of CIA interrogation and detention programs. Over the course of the next several months, CIA Director John Brennan (who had been confirmed in March 2013) oversaw the development of an official rebuttal. This top-secret response heavily criticized the committee and insisted that it had reached many erroneous conclusions. The Senate Intelligence Committee countered, however, by noting that the CIA's official response did not match its own findings in the Panetta Review.

Tensions between the Senate Intelligence Committee and the CIA continued to rise over the ensuing months, driven by CIA displeasure with the committee's stated intention to eventually release the report publicly, the CIA's refusal to hand over a complete version of the Panetta Review to committee investigators, and growing evidence that the CIA had secretly been spying on the Senate Intelligence Committee and its staffers. On March 5, 2014, Brennan flatly denied the "spurious allegations" about CIA spying on the Senate, dismissing such accusations as "wholly unsupported by the facts." This denial so angered Senate Intelligence

Committee Chairman Dianne Feinstein (D-CA)—generally known as a staunch supporter of America's intelligence community—that on March 11, 2014, she took to the Senate floor to excoriate the agency for violating "the Fourth Amendment, the Computer Fraud and Abuse Act, as well as Executive Order 12333, which prohibits the C.I.A. from conducting domestic searches or surveillance." The full text of Feinstein's speech, which went into considerable detail about the dispute, is reprinted below.

Four months later, an internal investigation by the CIA's Office of the Inspector General (OIG) revealed that Feinstein's accusations were correct. Brennan issued an apology to Feinstein and the committee's ranking Republican, Senator Saxby Chambliss (R-GA), and promised to take steps to prevent a recurrence of its spying on the Senate. These revelations prompted some demands for Brennan to be fired, but the Obama White House defended the CIA chief. Meanwhile, Senators on both sides of the aisle expressed shock at the CIA's actions, which they described as a grave and illegal violation of the U.S. Constitution's separation of power provisions. "How do we do our oversight," Senator Angus King (I-ME) told the New York Times, *"if we can't believe what is being represented to us in our committee?"*

Meanwhile, the results of the Senate Intelligence Committee's investigation into the Bush administration's detention and interrogation programs were finally released to the public in an executive summary on December 9, 2014. This summary concluded that the CIA misled the American public and its elected officials—including the White House—about both the severity and effectiveness of its torture techniques.

Statement of Senator Dianne Feinstein

Over the past week, there have been numerous press articles written about the Intelligence Committee's oversight review of the Detention and Interrogation Program of the CIA, specifically press attention has focused on the CIA's intrusion and search of the Senate Select Committee's computers as well as the committee's acquisition of a certain internal CIA document known as the Panetta Review.

I rise today to set the record straight and to provide a full accounting of the facts and history.

Let me say up front that I come to the Senate Floor reluctantly. Since January 15, 2014, when I was informed of the CIA's search of this committee's network, I have been trying to resolve this dispute in a discreet and respectful way. I have not commented in response to media requests for additional information on this matter. However, the increasing amount of inaccurate information circulating now cannot be allowed to stand unanswered.

The origin of this study: The CIA's detention and interrogation program began operations in 2002, though it was not until September 2006, that Members of the Intelligence Committee, other than the Chairman and Vice Chairman, were briefed. In fact, we were briefed by then-CIA Director Hayden only hours before President Bush disclosed the program to the public.

A little more than a year later, on December 6, 2007, a *New York Times* article revealed the troubling fact that the CIA had destroyed videotapes of some of the CIA's first interrogations using so-called "enhanced techniques." We learned that this destruction was over the objections of President Bush's White House Counsel and the Director of National Intelligence.

After we read about the tapes' destruction in the newspapers, Director Hayden briefed the Senate Intelligence Committee. He assured us that this was not destruction of evidence, as detailed records of the interrogations existed on paper in the form of CIA operational cables describing the detention conditions and the day-to-day CIA interrogations.

The CIA director stated that these cables were "a more than adequate representation" of what would have been on the destroyed tapes. Director Hayden offered at that time, during Senator Jay Rockefeller's chairmanship of the committee, to allow Members or staff to review these sensitive CIA operational cables given that the videotapes had been destroyed.

Chairman Rockefeller sent two of his committee staffers out to the CIA on nights and weekends to review thousands of these cables, which took many months. By the time the two staffers completed their review into the CIA's early interrogations in early 2009, I had become chairman of the committee and President Obama had been sworn into office.

The resulting staff report was chilling. The interrogations and the conditions of confinement at the CIA detention sites were far different and far more harsh than the way the CIA had described them to us. As result of the staff's initial report, I proposed, and then-Vice Chairman Bond agreed, and the committee overwhelmingly approved, that the committee conduct an expansive and full review of CIA's detention and interrogation program.

On March 5, 2009, the committee voted 14–1 to initiate a comprehensive review of the CIA Detention and Interrogation Program. Immediately, we sent a request for documents to all relevant executive branch agencies, chiefly among them the CIA.

The committee's preference was for the CIA to turn over all responsive documents to the committee's office, as had been done in previous committee investigations.

[CIA] Director [Leon] Panetta proposed an alternative arrangement: to provide literally millions of pages of operational cables, internal emails, memos, and other documents pursuant to the committee's document requests at a secure location in

Northern Virginia. We agreed, but insisted on several conditions and protections to ensure the integrity of this congressional investigation.

Per an exchange of letters in 2009, then-Vice Chairman Bond, then-Director Panetta, and I agreed in an exchange of letters that the CIA was to provide a "stand-alone computer system" with a "network drive" "segregated from CIA networks" for the committee that would only be accessed by information technology personnel at the CIA—who would "not be permitted to" "share information from the system with other [CIA] personnel, except as otherwise authorized by the committee."

It was this computer network that, notwithstanding our agreement with Director Panetta, was searched by the CIA this past January, and once before which I will later describe.

In addition to demanding that the documents produced for the committee be reviewed at a CIA facility, the CIA also insisted on conducting a multi-layered review of every responsive document before providing the document to the committee. This was to ensure the CIA did not mistakenly provide documents unrelated to the CIA's Detention and Interrogation Program or provide documents that the president could potentially claim to be covered by executive privilege.

While we viewed this as unnecessary and raised concerns that it would delay our investigation, the CIA hired a team of outside contractors—who otherwise would not have had access to these sensitive documents—to read, multiple times, each of the 6.2 million pages of documents produced, before providing them to fully-cleared committee staff conducting the committee's oversight work. This proved to be a slow and very expensive process.

The CIA started making documents available electronically to the committee staff at the CIA leased facility in mid-2009. The number of pages ran quickly to the thousands, tens of thousands, the hundreds of thousands, and then into the millions. The documents that were provided came without any index, without organizational structure. It was a true "document dump" that our committee staff had to go through and make sense of.

In order to piece together the story of the CIA's detention and interrogation program, the committee staff did two things that will be important as I go on:

First, they asked the CIA to provide an electronic search tool so they could locate specific relevant documents for their search among the CIA-produced documents—just like you would use a search tool on the Internet to locate information.

Second, when the staff found a document that was particularly important or that might be referenced in our final report, they would often print it or make a copy of the file on their computer so they could easily find it again. There are thousands of such documents in the committee's secure spaces at the CIA facility.

Now, prior removal of documents by CIA. In early 2010, the CIA was continuing to provide documents, and the committee staff was gaining familiarity with the information it had already received.

In May of 2010, the committee staff noticed that [certain] documents that had been provided for the committee's review were no longer accessible. Staff approached the CIA personnel at the offsite location, who initially denied that documents had been removed. CIA personnel then blamed information technology personnel, who were almost all contractors, for removing the documents themselves without direction or authority. And then the CIA stated that the removal of the documents was ordered by the White House. When the committee approached the White House, the White House denied giving the CIA any such order.

After a series of meetings, I learned that on two occasions, CIA personnel electronically removed committee access to CIA documents after providing them to the committee. This included roughly 870 documents or pages of documents that were removed in February 2010, and secondly roughly another 50 were removed in mid-May 2010.

This was done without the knowledge or approval of committee members or staff, and in violation of our written agreements. Further, this type of behavior would not have been possible had the CIA allowed the committee to conduct the review of documents here in the Senate. In short, this was the exact sort of CIA interference in our investigation that we sought to avoid at the outset.

I went up to the White House to raise this issue with the then-White House Counsel, in May 2010. He recognized the severity of the situation, and the grave implications of Executive Branch personnel interfering with an official congressional investigation. The matter was resolved with a renewed commitment from the White House Counsel, and the CIA, that there would be no further unauthorized access to the committee's network or removal of access to CIA documents already provided to the committee.

On May 17, 2010, the CIA's then-director of congressional affairs apologized on behalf of the CIA for removing the documents. And that, as far as I was concerned, put the incident aside.

This event was separate from the documents provided that were part of the "Internal Panetta Review," which occurred later and which I will describe next.

At some point in 2010, committee staff searching the documents that had been made available found draft versions of what is now called the "Internal Panetta Review."

We believe these documents were written by CIA personnel to summarize and analyze the materials that had been provided to the committee for its review. The Panetta review documents were no more highly classified than other information we had received for our investigation—in fact, the documents appeared to be based on the same information already provided to the committee.

What was unique and interesting about the internal documents was not their classification level, but rather their analysis and acknowledgement of significant CIA wrongdoing.

To be clear, the committee staff did not "hack" into CIA computers to obtain these documents as has been suggested in the press. The documents were identified using the search tool provided by the CIA to search the documents provided to the committee.

We have no way to determine who made the Internal Panetta Review documents available to the committee. Further, we don't know whether the documents were provided intentionally by the CIA, unintentionally by the CIA, or intentionally by a whistle-blower.

In fact, we know that over the years—on multiple occasions—the staff have asked the CIA about documents made available for our investigation. At times, the CIA has simply been unaware that these specific documents were provided to the committee. And while this is alarming, it is also important to note that more than 6.2 million pages of documents have been provided. This is simply a massive amount of records.

As I described earlier, as part of its standard process for reviewing records, the committee staff printed copies of the Internal Panetta Review and made electronic copies of the committee's computers at the facility.

The staff did not rely on these Internal Panetta Review documents when drafting the final 6,300-page committee study. But it was significant that the Internal Panetta Review had documented at least some of the very same troubling matters already uncovered by the committee staff—which is not surprising, in that they were looking at the same information.

There is a claim in the press and elsewhere that the markings on these documents should have caused the staff to stop reading them and turn them over to the CIA. I reject that claim completely.

As with many other documents provided to the committee at the CIA facility, some of the Internal Panetta Review documents—some—contained markings indicating that they were "deliberative" and/or "privileged." This was not especially noteworthy to staff. In fact, CIA has provided thousands of internal documents, to include CIA legal guidance and talking points prepared for the CIA director, some of which were marked as being deliberative or privileged.

Moreover, the CIA has officially provided such documents to the committee here in the Senate. In fact, the CIA's official June 27, 2013, response to the committee study, which Director Brennan delivered to me personally, is labeled "Deliberative Process Privileged Document."

We have discussed this with the Senate Legal Counsel who has confirmed that Congress does not recognize these claims of privilege when it comes to documents provided to Congress for our oversight duties.

These were documents provided by the executive branch pursuant to an authorized congressional oversight investigation. So we believe we had every right to review and keep the documents.

There are also claims in the press that the Internal Panetta Review documents, having been created in 2009 and 2010, were outside the date range of the committee's document request or the terms of the committee study. This too is inaccurate.

The committee's document requests were not limited in time. In fact, as I have previously announced, the committee study includes significant information on the May 2011 Osama bin Laden operation, which obviously postdated the detention and interrogation program.

At some time after the committee staff identified and reviewed the Internal Panetta Review documents, access to the vast majority of them was removed by the CIA. We believe this happened in 2010 but we have no way of knowing the specifics. Nor do we know why the documents were removed. The staff was focused on reviewing the tens of thousands of new documents that continued to arrive on a regular basis.

Our work continued until December 2012, when the Intelligence Committee approved a 6,300-page committee study of the CIA's Detention and Interrogation Program and sent the report to the executive branch for comment. The CIA provided its response to the study on June 27, 2013.

As CIA Director Brennan has stated, the CIA officially agrees with some of our study. But, as has been reported, the CIA disagrees and disputes important parts of it. And this is important: Some of these important parts that the CIA now disputes in our committee study are clearly acknowledged in the CIA's own Internal Panetta Review.

To say the least, this is puzzling. How can the CIA's official response to our study stand factually in conflict with its own Internal Review?

Now, after noting the disparity between the official CIA response to the committee study and the Internal Panetta Review, the committee staff securely transported a printed portion of the draft Internal Panetta Review from the committee's secure room at the CIA-leased facility to the secure committee spaces in the Hart Senate Office Building.

And let me be clear about this: I mentioned earlier the exchange of letters that Senator Bond and I had with Director Panetta in 2009 over the handling of information for this review. The letters set out a process whereby the committee would provide specific CIA documents to CIA reviewers before bringing them back to our secure offices here on Capitol Hill.

The CIA review was designed specifically to make sure that committee documents available to all staff and members did not include certain kinds of information, most importantly the true names of non-supervisory CIA personnel and the names of specific countries in which the CIA operated detention sites.

We had agreed up front that our report didn't need to include this information, and so we agreed to redact it from materials leaving the CIA's facility.

Keeping with the spirit of the agreements, the portion of the Internal Panetta Review at the Hart Building in our safe has been redacted. It does not contain names of non-supervisory CIA personnel or information identifying detention site locations. In other words, our staff did just what the CIA personnel would have done had they reviewed the document.

There are several reasons why the draft summary of the Panetta Review was brought to our secure spaces at the Hart Building.

Let me list them:

The significance of the Internal Review given disparities between it and the June 2013 CIA response to the committee study. The Internal Panetta Review summary now at the secure committee office in the Hart Building is an especially significant document as it corroborates critical information in the committee's 6,300-page Study that the CIA's official response either objects to, denies, minimizes, or ignores.

Unlike the official response, these Panetta Review documents were in agreement with the committee's findings. That's what makes them so significant and important to protect.

When the Internal Panetta Review documents disappeared from the committee's computer system, this suggested once again that the CIA had removed documents already provided to the committee, in violation of CIA agreements and White House assurances that the CIA would cease such activities.

As I have detailed, the CIA has previously withheld and destroyed information about its Detention and Interrogation Program, including its decision in 2005 to destroy interrogation videotapes over the objections of the Bush White House and the Director of National Intelligence. Based on the information described above, there was a need to preserve and protect the Internal Panetta Review in the committee's own secure spaces.

Now, the Relocation of the Internal Panetta Review was lawful and handled in a manner consistent with its classification. No law prevents the relocation of a document in the committee's possession from a CIA facility to secure committee offices on Capitol Hill. As I mentioned before, the document was handled and transported in a manner consistent with its classification, redacted appropriately, and it remains secured—with restricted access—in committee spaces.

In late 2013, I requested in writing that the CIA provide a final and complete version of the Internal Panetta Review to the committee, as opposed to the partial document the committee currently possesses.

In December, during an open committee hearing, Senator Mark Udall echoed this request. In early January 2014, the CIA informed the committee it would not provide the Internal Panetta Review to the committee, citing the deliberative nature of the document.

Shortly thereafter, on January 15, 2014, CIA Director Brennan requested an emergency meeting to inform me and Vice Chairman Chambliss that without prior notification or approval, CIA personnel had conducted a "search"—that was John Brennan's word—of the committee computers at the offsite facility. This search involved not only a search of documents provided to the committee by the CIA, but also a search of the "stand alone" and "walled-off" committee network drive containing the committee's own internal work product and communications.

According to Brennan, the computer search was conducted in response to indications that some members of the committee staff might already have had access to the Internal Panetta Review. The CIA did not ask the committee or its staff if the committee had access to the Internal Review, or how we obtained it.

Instead, the CIA just went and searched the committee's computers. The CIA has still not asked the committee any questions about how the committee acquired the Panetta Review. In place of asking any questions, the CIA's unauthorized search of the committee computers was followed by an allegation—which we have now seen repeated anonymously in the press—that the committee staff had somehow obtained the document through unauthorized or criminal means, perhaps to include hacking into the CIA's computer network.

As I have described, this is not true. The document was made available to the staff at the offsite facility, and it was located using a CIA-provided search tool running a query of the information provided to the committee pursuant to its investigation.

Director Brennan stated that the CIA's search had determined that the committee staff had copies of the Internal Panetta Review on the committee's "staff shared drive" and had accessed them numerous times. He indicated at the meeting that he was going to order further "forensic" investigation of the committee network to learn more about activities of the committee's oversight staff.

Two days after the meeting, on January 17, I wrote a letter to Director Brennan objecting to any further CIA investigation due to the separation of powers constitutional issues that the search raised. I followed this with a second letter on January 23 to the director, asking 12 specific questions about the CIA's actions—questions that the CIA has refused to answer.

Some of the questions in my letter related to the full scope of the CIA's search of our computer network. Other questions related to who had authorized and conducted the search, and what legal basis the CIA claimed gave it authority to conduct the search. Again, the CIA has not provided answers to any of my questions.

My letter also laid out my concern about the legal and constitutional implications of the CIA's actions. Based on what Director Brennan has informed us, I have grave concerns that the CIA's search may well have violated the separation of powers principles embodied in the United States Constitution, including the Speech and Debate clause. It may have undermined the constitutional framework essential to effective congressional oversight of intelligence activities or any other government function.

I have asked for an apology and a recognition that this CIA search of computers used by its oversight committee was inappropriate. I have received neither.

Besides the constitutional implications, the CIA's search may also have violated the Fourth Amendment, the Computer Fraud and Abuse Act, as well as Executive Order 12333, which prohibits the CIA from conducting domestic searches or surveillance.

Days after the meeting with Director Brennan, the CIA inspector general, David Buckley, learned of the CIA search and began an investigation into CIA's activities. I have been informed that Mr. Buckley has referred the matter to the Department of Justice given the possibility of a criminal violation by CIA personnel.

Let me note: because the CIA has refused to answer the questions in my January 23 letter, and the CIA inspector general review is ongoing, I have limited information about exactly what the CIA did in conducting its search.

Weeks later, I was also told that after the inspector general referred the CIA's activities to the Department of Justice, the acting general counsel of the CIA filed a crimes report with the Department of Justice concerning the committee staff's actions. I have not been provided the specifics of these allegations or been told whether the department has initiated a criminal investigation based on the allegations of the CIA's acting general counsel.

As I mentioned before, our staff involved in this matter have the appropriate clearances, handled this sensitive material according to established procedures and practice to protect classified information, and were provided access to the Panetta Review by the CIA itself. As a result, there is no legitimate reason to allege to the Justice Department that Senate staff may have committed a crime. I view the acting general counsel's referral as a potential effort to intimidate this staff—and I am not taking it lightly.

I should note that for most, if not all, of the CIA's Detention and Interrogation Program, the now acting general counsel was a lawyer in the CIA's Counterterrorism Center—the unit within which the CIA managed and carried out this program.

From mid-2004 until the official termination of the detention and interrogation program in January 2009, he was the unit's chief lawyer. He is mentioned by name more than 1,600 times in our study.

And now this individual is sending a crimes report to the Department of Justice on the actions of congressional staff—the same congressional staff who researched and drafted a report that details how CIA officers—including the acting general counsel himself—provided inaccurate information to the Department of Justice about the program.

Mr. President, let me say this. All Senators rely on their staff to be their eyes and ears and to carry out our duties. The staff members of the Intelligence Committee are dedicated professionals who are motivated to do what is best for our nation.

The staff members who have been working on this study and this report have devoted years of their lives to it—wading through the horrible details of a CIA program that never, never, never should have existed. They have worked long hours and produced a report unprecedented in its comprehensive attention to detail in the history of the Senate.

They are now being threatened with legal jeopardy, just as the final revisions to the report are being made so that parts of it can be declassified and released to the American people.

Mr. President, I felt that I needed to come to the floor today, to correct the public record and to give the American people the facts about what the dedicated committee staff have been working so hard for the last several years as part of the committee's investigation.

I also want to reiterate to my colleagues my desire to have all updates to the committee report completed this month and approved for declassification. We're not going to stop. I intend to move to have the findings, conclusions and the executive summary of the report sent to the president for declassification and release to the American people. The White House has indicated publicly and to me personally that it supports declassification and release.

If the Senate can declassify this report, we will be able to ensure that an un-American, brutal program of detention and interrogation will never again be considered or permitted.

But Mr. President, the recent actions that I have just laid out make this a defining moment for the oversight of our Intelligence Community. How Congress responds and how this is resolved will show whether the Intelligence Committee can be effective in monitoring and investigating our nation's intelligence activities, or whether our work can be thwarted by those we oversee.

I believe it is critical that the committee and the Senate reaffirm our oversight role and our independence under the Constitution of the United States.

Source: Senator Feinstein, Dianne. "Statement on Intel Committee's CIA Detention, Interrogation Report [press release]." March 11, 2014. Office of Senator Dianne Feinstein Web site. http://www.feinstein.senate.gov/public/index.cfm/2014/3/feinstein-statement-on-intelligence-committee-s-cia-detention-interrogation-report. Accessed February 12, 2015.

2014: WORLD PRIVACY FORUM URGES STRONGER PRIVACY PROTECTIONS FOR MEDICAL RECORDS

The Universal Periodic Review (UPR) is a regularly scheduled program, first established by the United Nations General Assembly in 2006 and subsequently conducted through the UN's Human Rights Council, to review the human rights records of each of the United Nations' 193 Member States. The United States has described itself as a "strong supporter of the UPR process, which provides a unique avenue for the global community to discuss human rights around the world." Under the UPR process, individual nations come up for review every four and a half years. In anticipation of the United States' second scheduled review in May 2015, the U.S. government invited "civil society" organizations to comment on various civil liberties and human rights issues and developments in the United States. The following "UPR comment" statement, from the privacy rights group World Privacy Forum (WPF), expressed grave concern about the vulnerability of private health records to U.S. intelligence agencies, and it urged the U.S. government to take steps to shore up the privacy protections afforded to medical records of American citizens.

Civil Society Consultation on the Universal Periodic Review Recommendations on National Security Supported by the U.S.

The Right to Health Privacy: Human Rights and the Surveillance and Interception of Medical and Health Records by Security Agencies

Comments on Universal Periodic Review Recommendations on National Security supported by the U.S.

The World Privacy Forum respectfully submits these comments to the Civil Society Consultation on the Universal Periodic Review Recommendations on National Security supported in whole or in part by the U.S. The World Privacy Forum is a 501 (c)(3) non-profit public interest research group based in the United States. We focus exclusively on privacy and security issues and have substantive expertise in health privacy.

1. Our comments focus on the issue of the U.S. National Security Agency's (NSA) interception of, acquisition of, and access to the health (including physical and mental health) records held by health care providers, health insurers, and health care clearinghouses located in the United States or otherwise subject to U.S. health privacy law.
2. The Universal Declaration of Human Rights, in Article 12 and 25, provides that individuals should be free to seek health care without intrusion

by their government. The United Nations General Assembly adopted resolution 68/167 in December 2013, which expresses concern regarding the negative impact that surveillance and interception of communications may have on human rights. The United States in the 2010 UPR supported the right to privacy, and the goal of legislation or regulations that would work to prevent the violations of individual privacy, including "constant intrusion," by its intelligence and security organizations. Specifically, the U.S. supported in part:

- § **59:** Legislate appropriate regulations to prevent the violations of individual privacy, constant intrusion in and control of cyberspace as well as eavesdropping of communications, by its intelligence and security organizations.
- § **187:** Guarantee the right to privacy and stop spying on its citizens without judicial authorization.

3. The World Privacy Forum acknowledges that there are lawful reasons for access to health records for investigations.
4. We are, however, most concerned that non-transparent access to patient health files by national security agencies occurs in two circumstances: 1.) When the files are held by health care providers, and 2.) When the files are in transmission between providers, insurers, and other lawful users. In these comments, we discuss the issue of a lack of transparency and oversight regarding the acquisition and use of health records by federal agencies with national security functions and, in particular, by the NSA.

I. The Lack of Transparency Regarding U.S. Security Agency Acquisition of Health Records When Held by Health Care Providers and Other Entities Covered Under Health Privacy Legislation

5. There are no meaningful procedures or protections established by federal law governing the acquisition or interception of patient health records by national security agencies from a health care provider, insurer, or clearinghouse.
6. U.S. health care providers are regulated under the federal health privacy rule. Federal law includes a broad national security exemption that offers no effective restrictions on the disclosure of health records by health care providers for national security and intelligence activities. The exemption [45 CFR 164.512(k)(2)] states:

(2) *National security and intelligence activities.* A covered entity may disclose protected health information to authorized federal officials for the

conduct of lawful intelligence, counter-intelligence, and other national security activities authorized by the National Security Act (50 U.S.C. 401, *et seq.*) and implementing authority (*e.g.*, Executive Order 12333). [45 CFR 164.512(k)(2)].

7. Because of the breadth of this exemption, it is lawful for health care providers and other entities covered by the law to disclose health records to national security agencies without any procedural standards, any formal judicial request, any showing of relevance or importance, any probable cause, or any reasonable cause. The law does not require a written—or indeed any—request for it to be lawful for a covered entity to hand over patient health files. Further, there are no adequate procedures under which a record keeper or record subject can challenge a request for the records as unlawful, inappropriate, or as not in accordance with statutory procedures.

II. The Lack of Transparency Regarding the U.S. Security Agency Acquisition of Health Records in Transmission Outside of the Health Care Provider Context

8. Events since 2010 have better informed the public and the world about health record privacy and national security investigation activities, including interception of health records in bulk collections. We are most concerned about examples regarding the NSA's activities.
9. The NSA has broken the encryption that in the past has protected health records. (New York Times, *Top Secret NSA Program Cracks Most Internet Encryption Tools*, Sept. 05, 2013.) While this does not prove that the NSA is deliberately intercepting health records, it does indicate that traditional means of making health files private are no longer reliable against intrusion, particularly during transmission, even when the security meets the requirements set out in the federal health security rule. We certainly have no confidence that standard encryption protocols protect health records against NSA capabilities.
10. Health records of individuals, including non-targeted individuals, have been routinely intercepted by the NSA. A reporter at the Washington Post who received copies of intercepted files from former NSA contractor Edward Snowden documented this issue, noting the presence of health files. He wrote: "About 16,000 of the data files contained the text of intercepted conversations. The rest were photographs or documents such as **medical records,** travel vouchers, school transcripts and marriage contracts." (Barton Gellman, The Washington Post, *How 160,000 intercepted communications led to our latest NSA story*, July 11, 2014.

<http://www.washingtonpost.com/world/national-security/your-questions-answered-about-the-posts-recent-investigation-of-nsa-surveillance/2014/07/11/43d743e6-0908-11e4-8a6a-19355c7e870a_story.html>.

11. The U.S. Executive Branch acknowledged in 2013 that the business records provision of the USA PATRIOT ACT had been re-interpreted to allow the U.S. government to collect the private records of large numbers of ordinary Americans via bulk collection. A bi-partisan group of U.S. Senators wrote to the Director of National Intelligence on June 27, 2013 requesting answers to issues regarding interception of health records:

    "We are troubled by the possibility of this bulk collection authority being applied to other categories of records. The bulk collection authority could potentially be used to supersede bans on maintaining gun owner databases, or laws protecting the **privacy** of **medical records,** financial records, and records of book and movie purchases. These other types of bulk collection could clearly have a significant impact on Americans' privacy and civil liberties as well." <http://www.wyden.senate.gov/download/?id=87b45794-0fa4-4b1a-b3a6-e659a91a5042&download=1>.

12. No existing legal mechanisms provide appropriate standards, transparency, or oversight in the use of health records for national security investigations.

III. The Importance of Health Privacy as a Human Right and Value Worth Protecting

13. We are concerned that individuals may be chilled from seeking necessary and even life-saving health treatment due to legitimate privacy concerns regarding their health records. As health records become increasingly digitized, routine access to patients' electronic health records by U.S. intelligence and security agencies becomes more likely. We include remote electronic access to this assessment.

14. The goals of UPR § 59 are that countries "Legislate appropriate regulations to prevent the violations of individual privacy, constant intrusion in and control of cyberspace as well as eavesdropping of communications, by its intelligence and security organizations. These goals are not being met in the United States with respect to disclosure and interception of health records by national security agencies.

IV. Recommendations

5. The World Privacy Forum recommends the following steps be taken:

Recommendation 1. Change U.S. law so there are more accountability and better procedures for national security requests, demands, and interceptions. Specifically, we recommend the following changes to U.S. law with respect to access by or disclosure of health records to U.S. national security agencies:

1. Health information should only be disclosed for national security purposes pursuant to a judicial warrant.
2. There must be procedures under which record keepers can challenge national security demands for health records that are unlawful or inappropriate.

If there is no requirement for a judicial warrant, then we offer these further recommendations:

1. Requests for health information by all national security agencies must meet standards of reasonable or probable cause.
2. Formal requests by all national security agencies for health records should be subject to the supervision of the federal courts.

Recommendation 2. The U.S. should accept the letter and spirit of §59 and §187 and should take immediate corrective action.

6. The lack of sufficient human rights protections for health privacy and health records in the U.S. erodes the values expressed in the Universal Declaration of Human Rights, in Article 12 and 25.

Thank you for your attention to this matter.
Respectfully submitted,
Pam Dixon, Executive Director, World Privacy Forum

Source: Dixon, Pam. "The Right to Health Privacy: Human Rights and the Surveillance and Interception of Medical and Health Records by Security Agencies." October 7, 2014. World Privacy Forum Web site. http://www.worldprivacyforum.org/2014/10/wpf-universal-periodic-review-comments-the-right-to-health-privacy-human-rights-and-the-surveillance-and-interception-of-medical-and-health-records-by-security-agencies/. Accessed February 25, 2015. Used by permission of the World Privacy Forum.

2014: FBI DIRECTOR COMEY DISCUSSES THE DANGERS OF "GOING DARK"

On October 16, 2014, FBI Director James B. Comey delivered the following speech at the Brookings Institution in Washington, D.C. In this address, Comey talked at length about concerns in the FBI and elsewhere in the U.S. intelligence community that decisions by high-tech companies to encrypt digital communications—while an understandable response to heightened concerns about consumer privacy—posed a potentially serious threat to law enforcement efforts to combat crime and uncover terrorist threats. Comey described this phenomenon as "going dark," and he warned that it would have serious negative consequences if left unaddressed. He urged Congress to head off this trend by passing laws that would require high-tech firms to build systems and services with gateways that would enable intelligence agencies, armed with the necessary legal authority, to examine encrypted information.

The Challenge of Going Dark

Technology has forever changed the world we live in. We're online, in one way or another, all day long. Our phones and computers have become reflections of our personalities, our interests, and our identities. They hold much that is important to us.

And with that comes a desire to protect our privacy and our data—you want to share your lives with the people you choose. I sure do. But the FBI has a sworn duty to keep every American safe from crime and terrorism, and technology has become the tool of choice for some very dangerous people.

Unfortunately, the law hasn't kept pace with technology, and this disconnect has created a significant public safety problem. We call it "Going Dark," and what it means is this: Those charged with protecting our people aren't always able to access the evidence we need to prosecute crime and prevent terrorism even with lawful authority. We have the legal authority to intercept and access communications and information pursuant to court order, but we often lack the technical ability to do so.

We face two overlapping challenges. The first concerns real-time court-ordered interception of what we call "data in motion," such as phone calls, e-mail, and live chat sessions. The second challenge concerns court-ordered access to data stored on our devices, such as e-mail, text messages, photos, and videos—or what we call "data at rest." And both real-time communication and stored data are increasingly encrypted.

Let's talk about court-ordered interception first, and then we'll talk about challenges posed by different means of encryption.

In the past, conducting electronic surveillance was more straightforward. We identified a target phone being used by a bad guy, with a single carrier. We obtained a court order for a wiretap, and, under the supervision of a judge, we collected the evidence we needed for prosecution.

Today, there are countless providers, countless networks, and countless means of communicating. We have laptops, smartphones, and tablets. We take them to work and to school, from the soccer field to Starbucks, over many networks, using any number of apps. And so do those conspiring to harm us. They use the same devices, the same networks, and the same apps to make plans, to target victims, and to cover up what they're doing. And that makes it tough for us to keep up.

If a suspected criminal is in his car, and he switches from cellular coverage to Wi-Fi, we may be out of luck. If he switches from one app to another, or from cellular voice service to a voice or messaging app, we may lose him. We may not have the capability to quickly switch lawful surveillance between devices, methods, and networks. The bad guys know this; they're taking advantage of it every day.

In the wake of the Snowden disclosures, the prevailing view is that the government is sweeping up all of our communications. That is not true. And unfortunately, the idea that the government has access to all communications at all times has extended—unfairly—to the investigations of law enforcement agencies that obtain individual warrants, approved by judges, to intercept the communications of suspected criminals.

Some believe that the FBI has these phenomenal capabilities to access any information at any time—that we can get what we want, when we want it, by flipping some sort of switch. It may be true in the movies or on TV. It is simply not the case in real life.

It frustrates me, because I want people to understand that law enforcement needs to be able to access communications and information to bring people to justice. We do so pursuant to the rule of law, with clear guidance and strict oversight. But even with lawful authority, we may not be able to access the evidence and the information we need.

Current law governing the interception of communications requires telecommunication carriers and broadband providers to build interception capabilities into their networks for court-ordered surveillance. But that law, the Communications Assistance for Law Enforcement Act, or CALEA, was enacted 20 years ago—a lifetime in the Internet age. And it doesn't cover new means of communication. Thousands of companies provide some form of communication service, and most are not required by statute to provide lawful intercept capabilities to law enforcement.

What this means is that an order from a judge to monitor a suspect's communication may amount to nothing more than a piece of paper. Some companies fail to comply with the court order. Some can't comply, because they have not developed interception capabilities. Other providers want to provide assistance, but they have to build interception capabilities, and that takes time and money.

The issue is whether companies not currently subject to the Communications Assistance for Law Enforcement Act should be required to build lawful intercept capabilities for law enforcement. We aren't seeking to expand our authority to intercept communications. We are struggling to keep up with changing technology and to maintain our ability to actually collect the communications we are authorized to intercept.

And if the challenges of real-time interception threaten to leave us in the dark, encryption threatens to lead all of us to a very dark place.

Encryption is nothing new. But the challenge to law enforcement and national security officials is markedly worse, with recent default encryption settings and encrypted devices and networks—all designed to increase security and privacy.

With Apple's new operating system, the information stored on many iPhones and other Apple devices will be encrypted by default. Shortly after Apple's announcement, Google announced plans to follow suit with its Android operating system. This means the companies themselves won't be able to unlock phones, laptops, and tablets to reveal photos, documents, e-mail, and recordings stored within.

Both companies are run by good people, responding to what they perceive is a market demand. But the place they are leading us is one we shouldn't go to without careful thought and debate as a country.

At the outset, Apple says something that is reasonable—that it's not that big a deal. Apple argues, for example, that its users can back-up and store much of their data in "the cloud" and that the FBI can still access that data with lawful authority. But uploading to the cloud doesn't include all of the stored data on a bad guy's phone, which has the potential to create a black hole for law enforcement.

And if the bad guys don't back up their phones routinely, or if they opt out of uploading to the cloud, the data will only be found on the encrypted devices themselves. And it is people most worried about what's on the phone who will be most likely to avoid the cloud and to make sure that law enforcement cannot access incriminating data.

Encryption isn't just a technical feature; it's a marketing pitch. But it will have very serious consequences for law enforcement and national security agencies at all levels. Sophisticated criminals will come to count on these means of evading detection. It's the equivalent of a closet that can't be opened. A safe that can't be cracked. And my question is, at what cost?

Correcting Misconceptions

Some argue that we will still have access to metadata, which includes telephone records and location information from telecommunications carriers. That is true. But metadata doesn't provide the content of any communication. It's incomplete information, and even this is difficult to access when time is of the essence. I wish we had time in our work, especially when lives are on the line. We usually don't.

There is a misconception that building a lawful intercept solution into a system requires a so-called "back door," one that foreign adversaries and hackers may try to exploit.

But that isn't true. We aren't seeking a back-door approach. We want to use the front door, with clarity and transparency, and with clear guidance provided by law. We are completely comfortable with court orders and legal process—front doors that provide the evidence and information we need to investigate crime and prevent terrorist attacks.

Cyber adversaries will exploit any vulnerability they find. But it makes more sense to address any security risks by developing intercept solutions during the design phase, rather than resorting to a patchwork solution when law enforcement comes knocking after the fact. And with sophisticated encryption, there might be no solution, leaving the government at a dead end—all in the name of privacy and network security.

Another misperception is that we can somehow guess the password or break into the phone with a so-called "brute force" attack. Even a supercomputer would have difficulty with today's high-level encryption, and some devices have a setting whereby the encryption key is erased if someone makes too many attempts to break the password, meaning no one can access that data.

Finally, a reasonable person might also ask, "Can't you just compel the owner of the phone to produce the password?" Likely, no. And even if we could compel them as a legal matter, if we had a child predator in custody, and he could choose to sit quietly through a 30-day contempt sentence for refusing to comply with a court order to produce his password, or he could risk a 30-year sentence for production and distribution of child pornography, which do you think he would choose?

Case Examples

Think about life without your smartphone, without Internet access, without texting or e-mail or the apps you use every day. I'm guessing most of you would feel rather lost and left behind. Kids call this FOMO, or "fear of missing out."

With Going Dark, those of us in law enforcement and public safety have a major fear of missing out—missing out on predators who exploit the most vulnerable among us . . . missing out on violent criminals who target our communities . . . missing out on a terrorist cell using social media to recruit, plan, and execute an attack.

Criminals and terrorists would like nothing more than for us to miss out. And the more we as a society rely on these devices, the more important they are to law enforcement and public safety officials. We have seen case after case—from homicides and car crashes to drug trafficking, domestic abuse, and child exploitation—where critical evidence came from smartphones, hard drives, and online communication.

Let's just talk about cases involving the content of phones.

In Louisiana, a known sex offender posed as a teenage girl to entice a 12-year-old boy to sneak out of his house to meet the supposed young girl. This predator, posing as a taxi driver, murdered the young boy and tried to alter and delete evidence on both his and the victim's cell phones to cover up his crime. Both phones were instrumental in showing that the suspect enticed this child into his taxi. He was sentenced to death in April of this year.

In Los Angeles, police investigated the death of a 2-year-old girl from blunt force trauma to her head. There were no witnesses. Text messages stored on her parents' cell phones to one another and to their family members proved the mother caused this young girl's death and that the father knew what was happening and failed to stop it. Text messages stored on these devices also proved that the defendants failed to seek medical attention for hours while their daughter convulsed in her crib. They even went so far as to paint her tiny body with blue paint—to cover her bruises—before calling 911. Confronted with this evidence, both parents pled guilty.

In Kansas City, the DEA investigated a drug trafficking organization tied to heroin distribution, homicides, and robberies. The DEA obtained search warrants for several phones used by the group. Text messages found on the phones outlined the group's distribution chain and tied the group to a supply of lethal heroin that had caused 12 overdoses—and five deaths—including several high school students.

In Sacramento, a young couple and their four dogs were walking down the street at night when a car ran a red light and struck them—killing their four dogs, severing the young man's leg, and leaving the young woman in critical condition. The driver left the scene, and the young man died days later. Using "red light cameras" near the scene of the accident, the California Highway Patrol identified and arrested a suspect and seized his smartphone. GPS data on his phone placed the suspect at the scene of the accident and revealed that he had fled California shortly thereafter. He was convicted of second-degree murder and is serving a sentence of 25 years to life.

The evidence we find also helps exonerate innocent people. In Kansas, data from a cell phone was used to prove the innocence of several teens accused of rape. Without access to this phone, or the ability to recover a deleted video, several innocent young men could have been wrongly convicted.

These are cases in which we had access to the evidence we needed. But we're seeing more and more cases where we believe significant evidence is on that phone or a laptop, but we can't crack the password. If this becomes the norm, I would suggest to you that homicide cases could be stalled, suspects could walk free, and child exploitation might not be discovered or prosecuted. Justice may be denied, because of a locked phone or an encrypted hard drive.

My Thoughts

I'm deeply concerned about this, as both a law enforcement officer and a citizen. I understand some of this thinking in a post-Snowden world, but I believe it is mostly based on a failure to understand why we in law enforcement do what we do and how we do it.

I hope you know that I'm a huge believer in the rule of law. But I also believe that no one in this country should be above or beyond the law. There should be no law-free zone in this country. I like and believe very much that we need to follow the letter of the law to examine the contents of someone's closet or someone's cell phone. But the notion that the marketplace could create something that would prevent that closet from ever being opened, even with a properly obtained court order, makes no sense to me.

I think it's time to ask: Where are we, as a society? Are we no longer a country governed by the rule of law, where no one is above or beyond that law? Are we so mistrustful of government—and of law enforcement—that we are willing to let bad guys walk away . . . willing to leave victims in search of justice?

There will come a day—and it comes every day in this business—where it will matter a great deal to innocent people that we in law enforcement can't access certain types of data or information, even with legal authorization. We have to have these discussions now.

I believe people should be skeptical of government power. I am. This country was founded by people who were worried about government power—who knew that you cannot trust people in power. So they divided government power among three branches, with checks and balances for each. And they wrote a Bill of Rights to ensure that the "papers and effects" of the people are secure from unreasonable searches.

But the way I see it, the means by which we conduct surveillance through telecommunication carriers and those Internet service providers who have developed lawful intercept solutions is an example of government operating in the way the founders intended—that is, the executive, the legislative, and the judicial branches proposing, enacting, executing, and overseeing legislation, pursuant to the rule of law.

Perhaps it's time to suggest that the post-Snowden pendulum has swung too far in one direction—in a direction of fear and mistrust. It is time to have open and honest debates about liberty and security.

Some have suggested there is a conflict between liberty and security. I disagree. At our best, we in law enforcement, national security, and public safety are looking for security that enhances liberty. When a city posts police officers at a dangerous playground, security has promoted liberty—the freedom to let a child play without fear.

The people of the FBI are sworn to protect both security and liberty. It isn't a question of conflict. We must care deeply about protecting liberty through due process of law, while also safeguarding the citizens we serve—in every investigation.

Where Do We Go from Here?

These are tough issues. And finding the space and time in our busy lives to understand these issues is hard. Intelligent people can and do disagree, and that's the beauty of American life—that smart people can come to the right answer.

I've never been someone who is a scaremonger. But I'm in a dangerous business. So I want to ensure that when we discuss limiting the court-authorized law enforcement tools we use to investigate suspected criminals that we understand what society gains and what we all stand to lose.

We in the FBI will continue to throw every lawful tool we have at this problem, but it's costly. It's inefficient. And it takes time.

We need to fix this problem. It is long past time.

We need assistance and cooperation from companies to comply with lawful court orders, so that criminals around the world cannot seek safe haven for lawless conduct. We need to find common ground. We care about the same things. I said it because I meant it. These companies are run by good people. And we know an adversarial posture won't take any of us very far down the road.

We understand the private sector's need to remain competitive in the global marketplace. And it isn't our intent to stifle innovation or undermine U.S. companies. But we have to find a way to help these companies understand what we need, why we need it, and how they can help, while still protecting privacy rights and providing network security and innovation. We need our private sector partners to take a step back, to pause, and to consider changing course.

We also need a regulatory or legislative fix to create a level playing field, so that all communication service providers are held to the same standard and so that those of us in law enforcement, national security, and public safety can continue to do the job you have entrusted us to do, in the way you would want us to.

Perhaps most importantly, we need to make sure the American public understands the work we do and the means by which we do it.

I really do believe we can get there, with a reasoned and practical approach. And we have to get there together. I don't have the perfect solution. But I think it's important to start the discussion. I'm happy to work with Congress, with our partners in the private sector, with my law enforcement and national security counterparts, and with the people we serve, to find the right answer—to find the balance we need.

Source: Comey, James. Remarks at Brookings Institution, Washington, DC, October 16, 2014. Federal Bureau of Investigation (FBI) Web site. http://www.fbi.gov/news/speeches/going-dark-are-technology-privacy-and-public-safety-on-a-collision-course. Accessed January 30, 2015.

2014: THREE SENATORS SPEAK OUT IN SUPPORT OF THE USA FREEDOM ACT

In the wake of the public uproar that surrounded Edward Snowden's June 2013 leaks of classified National Security Agency (NSA) documents revealing the NSA's extensive secret surveillance programs and the forced participation of telecommunications companies in those programs, lawmakers in Washington, D.C., scrambled to respond.

Long-standing critics of the USA PATRIOT Act and NSA practices expressed determination to rein in the federal government's surveillance authority. "Congress has a crucial opportunity to reassert constitutionally guaranteed liberties by reforming the N.S.A.'s overbroad collection of Americans' personal data," wrote Democratic senators Ron Wyden (OR), Mark Udall (CO), and Martin Heinrich (NM). Public trust in United States' intelligence agencies, they charged, "has been undermined by the N.S.A.'s domestic surveillance programs, as well as by senior officials' misleading statements about surveillance. Only by ending the dragnet collection of ordinary Americans' private information can this trust be rebuilt" ("End the NSA Dragnet, Now." New York Times, *November 25, 2013).*

An NSA reform bill called the USA Freedom Act was introduced in both houses of Congress on October 29, 2013. One of the cosponsors was conservative Representative Jim Sensenbrenner (R-WI), who had actually been principal author of the original PATRIOT Act and civil liberties groups, expressed hope that bipartisan concern about the NSA activities would result in passage. As the bill made its way through the House Judiciary Committee, however, defenders of the PATRIOT Act in general and the NSA surveillance programs in particular were able to weaken or eliminate many of the bill's proposed changes. This compromise House version ultimately passed by a 303–121 vote on May 22, 2014.

In the Senate, meanwhile, a stronger version of the USA Freedom Act was introduced. But a November 18 vote to permit the bill to move forward to the floor of the Senate for debate fell two votes short of the 60 votes necessary to end a Republican-led filibuster of the legislation. Only four Republicans voted to move the legislation forward—Ted Cruz (TX), Mike Lee (UT), Dean Heller (NV), and Lisa Murkowski (AK).

Following are excerpts from the floor remarks of three supporters of the USA Freedom Act during the November 18 Senate showdown over the legislation. The three senators are conservative Republican Mike Lee of Utah and progressive Democratic senators Patrick Leahy of Vermont and Richard Blumenthal of Connecticut.

Mr. LEE. Madam President, in 2013, the country learned that the government, specifically the NSA, had been collecting and storing enormous amounts of information about American citizens, and that the data collection at issue was not limited to those who were actually suspected of terrorist activity or even necessarily to those who were connected to those suspected of engaging in terrorist activity. Many were understandably very concerned about how much and what kind of data was being collected and whether this information could be or had been abused by government officials.

Today proponents of the metadata program claim it cannot be used to identify ordinary American citizens. But earlier this year researchers at Stanford University proved that the very type of metadata collected under Section 215 of the PATRIOT Act could be used to uncover a lot of information, including information about a person's politics, what kind of medications they might be taking, about where they go to church, and so on and so forth.

The USA FREEDOM Act is a bipartisan piece of legislation that would end bulk collection of metadata currently gathered by the NSA, and it would help address the problem of the American government spying on its own citizens without cause. It also would improve transparency for the data that NSA does collect. It has the support of leaders in our intelligence community, the Department of Justice, civil liberties groups, the National Rifle Association, and several tech companies.

Opponents of this bill say it will impair our national security. They say the bill will keep our intelligence community from protecting us. But what opponents of this bill fail fully to appreciate is that most Americans are deeply concerned about the collection of their own personal information. This bill is an opportunity to strike a reasonable commonsense balance between protecting Americans' privacy and at the same time protecting our national security.

While I believe there are honest, decent people working in our intelligence community, and while I think this has been overwhelmingly the norm, it is important to heed a warning given to us centuries ago by James Madison. In *Federalist 51,* Madison wrote:

> If men were angels, no government would be necessary. If angels were to govern men, neither external nor internal controls on government would be necessary. In framing a government which is to be administered by men over men, the great difficulty lies in this: you must first enable the government to control the governed; and in the next place oblige it to control itself.

Congress should address this issue now. The provision of the PATRIOT Act authorizing this kind of data collection expires just after Memorial Day this coming year, and it is important to adopt a compromise well ahead of this deadline that all interested parties can accept.

The PRESIDING OFFICER (Mr. Donnelly). The Senator from Vermont.

Mr. LEAHY. I thank the junior Senator from Utah who has worked so hard on this.

It has been more than a year since Americans first learned that the government had been secretly sweeping up the telephone records of innocent Americans, regardless of whether there was any connection whatsoever to terrorism or criminal activity. I introduced the original USA FREEDOM Act last October with Republican Congressman Jim Sensenbrenner, and the Senate Judiciary Committee held six public hearings to address these issues.

During those hearings, we learned that the bulk phone records collection program had not, as previously advertised, thwarted 54 terrorist plots, or even dozens, or even a few. In fact, we learned through our public hearings that after all the talk about why we needed this program, we learned that the number was maybe one. That is an important fact for these who argue that the NSA's bulk phone records program is somehow essential to our fight against ISIL or other terrorists. It did nothing to stop ISIL from starting in the first place.

Our bill protects Americans. It enhances privacy protections and ends indiscriminate data collection by the NSA, but also keeps the essential tools our intelligence community needs to protect our Nation. That is the simple truth and important to remember. That is why our intelligence community strongly supports this bill.

As someone who worked in law enforcement, and as a native of Vermont where the right of privacy is cherished, I know we can have both liberty and security. The USA FREEDOM Act provides for commonsense reforms to government surveillance, and promotes greater accountability and transparency of the government's surveillance programs, and it improves the FISA Court.

This is a carefully crafted bill that builds on the work of the House of Representatives. It has the unprecedented support of the Director of National Intelligence, the Attorney General, the Director of the NSA, American technology companies, and privacy and civil liberties groups across the political spectrum, ranging from the ACLU and EFF to the NRA and TechFreedom. Lawmakers from all parts of the political spectrum, from the right to left, support the USA FREEDOM Act. They know it is a reasonable and responsible compromise. There is no reason why we should not proceed to a debate on this important bill.

I understand that there are some Members who want votes on parts of it, and that is fine. Let's have the votes. Let's not block this bill and say: Well, we want something better. That means you don't vote yes, you don't vote no, you vote maybe. Let's have some relevant amendments, and let's vote on them. Don't let this get bogged down in procedural nonsense that the American public hates. Senators should allow us to get onto this bill and help us reach an agreement on a limited list of germane amendments to be considered. Let's have germane amendments and vote them up or down. If we work together, we can finish the bill by the end of the week.

We cannot afford to delay action on these reforms until next year. As both the ACLU and the NRA pointed out yesterday in a joint op-ed in the Washington Times, "every day that the Senate fails to vote on these reforms is a day in which law-abiding citizens have reason to fear that the constitutional protections so dear to the Founders and so crucial to the functioning of a free society no longer apply.'"

I echoed the words we heard from the Senator from Utah. Every day that we fail to act is another day that American businesses are harmed. One conservative think tank estimated that the "mistrust engendered by the NSA's programs could cost the U.S. technology industry between $35 billion and $180 billion over the next three years."' That is a staggering amount.

Senators should listen to the intelligence community professionals who protect our nation every day, and who are calling for swift passage of this bill. Ask the Director of National Intelligence. Ask the Attorney General. They will tell you that it is better for our national security, and better for our fight against terrorism if we pass the USA FREEDOM Act.

This is a reasonable compromise that all Senators should support, and I thank the Majority Leader for bringing this bill to the floor. And I thank Senators Dean Heller, Mike Lee, Dick Durbin, Al Franken, and Richard Blumenthal for their steadfast work on this bill.

Our bill is good for privacy and civil liberties, and upholds our Constitution. It is good for American business. It is good for national security. And most importantly, it is the right thing to do on behalf of Vermonters and the rest of the American people. I urge all Senators to vote in favor of the cloture motion pending before us.

Mr. BLUMENTHAL. Mr. President, I wish to begin by thanking our very esteemed colleague, the chairman of the Judiciary Committee, Senator Leahy, for his leadership on this issue and my colleagues whom he has named who have helped in drafting and crafting this very important piece of legislation.

I also wish to thank my friends and colleagues across the aisle, such as the Senator from Utah, who have supported and helped to make clear that this bill advances the cause of safeguarding our Nation without in any way detracting from its essential operational intelligence capabilities.

In fact, National Intelligence Director Clapper said:

> The bill will retain the essential operational capabilities of the existing bulk telephone metadata program while eliminating bulk collection.

This bill increases trust and confidence and credibility of our intelligence system. It advances that trust and confidence in the capability of government surveillance to do its job but at the same time protect our vital privacy interests. It advances the cause of constitutional liberty and the appearance and perception of trust in that system. It does so by making the Foreign Intelligence Surveillance Court look and function like the courts we are accustomed to seeing issue search warrants in the criminal process and protect essential liberties. It does it by strengthening and, in fact, installing an adversarial process so that more than just the government's version of the facts and law are presented to the Foreign Intelligence Surveillance Court. It does it by providing for appellate review, just as we have in normal civilian court. It does it by increasing the transparency and accountability of the FISA Court system.

Our Founders would have been astonished and appalled to learn that we permit warrants to be issued by a court that is operating in secret, issuing secret opinions, and making secret law much like the Star Chamber did, and that is why this reform is so profoundly and historically important—because we made the FISA Court one that we can more aptly and abundantly trust and one that will have credibility and confidence.

I support this bill. I thank my colleagues for showing that we can work together in a bipartisan way to safeguard the essential rights of Americans at the same time we protect and preserve our national security.

Source: "USA Freedom Act—Motion to Proceed." *Congressional Record,* November 18, 2014 113th Congress, 2nd Session Issue: Vol. 160, No. 141—Daily Edition.

2014: THREE SENATORS SPEAK OUT AGAINST THE USA FREEDOM ACT

In the wake of the public uproar that surrounded Edward Snowden's June 2013 leaks of classified National Security Agency (NSA) documents revealing the NSA's extensive secret surveillance programs and the forced participation of telecommunications companies in those programs, lawmakers in Washington, D.C., scrambled to respond.

Long-standing critics of the USA PATRIOT Act and NSA practices expressed determination to rein in the federal government's surveillance authority. Defenders of the programs, however, vowed to fight back against many of the proposed reforms, saying that they would make Americans more vulnerable to terrorist attacks.

An NSA reform bill called the USA Freedom Act was introduced in both houses of Congress on October 29, 2013. One of the cosponsors was conservative Representative Jim Sensenbrenner (R-WI), who had actually been principal author of the original PATRIOT Act and civil liberties groups, expressed hope that bipartisan concern about the NSA activities would result in passage. As the bill made its way through the House Judiciary Committee, however, defenders of the PATRIOT Act in general and the NSA surveillance programs in particular were able to weaken or eliminate many of the bill's most sweeping proposals. This compromise House version ultimately passed by a 303–121 vote on May 22, 2014.

In the Senate, meanwhile, a stronger version of the USA Freedom Act was introduced. But a November 18 vote to permit the bill to move forward to the floor of the Senate for debate fell two votes short of the 60 votes necessary to end a Republican-led filibuster. Only four Republicans voted to move the legislation forward—Ted Cruz (TX), Mike Lee (UT), Dean Heller (NV), and Lisa Murkowski (AK).

Following are excerpts from the floor remarks of three critics of the USA Freedom Act during the November 18 Senate showdown over the legislation. The three senators are Republicans Marco Rubio of Florida, Susan Collins, of Maine, and Saxby Chambliss of Georgia.

Mr. RUBIO. God forbid tomorrow morning we wake up to the news that a member of ISIL is in the United States and Federal agencies need to determine who this person is coordinating with to carry out a potential attack within the homeland. One of the tools they will use is a tool that allows them to see the people they have been calling and interacting with so we can disrupt that cell before they carry out a horrifying attack that could kill millions of American people.

Today we are able to do that because of a program that collects those records and keeps them—not in the hands of anyone who is looking at them on a regular basis but keeps them readily available for the government so the government can access those records and disrupt that plot. What this bill would do is take that apart. In essence, it would ask the companies to keep those records—at least in the hopes that they would. Under this plan, if this were to pass, if suddenly we were to go target these members of ISIL and find out whom they are coordinating with, those records may not be there and that plot may indeed go forward. That would be a horrifying result.

Here is why this doesn't make sense. First of all, we are rushing this to the floor of the Senate in a lameduck session, on an issue that doesn't even expire until next year, on a bill that was not listened to or heard in a committee, and they cannot cite a single example of this program ever being abused—not one simple example of this specific program being abused by anybody intentionally. So we are dealing with a theoretical threat.

The second thing is that even as we speak, law enforcement agencies investigating a common crime don't even need to go to a court to access these very same records. They can just issue an administrative subpoena and get ahold of them. We are actually making it harder to go after a terrorist than it will be to go after a common criminal. This is happening at a time when homegrown violent extremism is the single fastest growing threat to the United States, people here at home who have been radicalized—even on the Internet—and people who have traveled to the Middle East and been radicalized in the hopes of returning and carrying out attacks here.

I hope this body would take more time to study an issue of this magnitude because this program was specifically designed to address the intelligence gaps that existed after the 9/11 attacks. I promise you, if, God forbid, any horrifying event like that were to happen, the first question we will be asked is why didn't we know about it and why didn't we prevent it. If this program is gutted, we potentially will not be able to know about it, and we will not be able to prevent it.

Ms. COLLINS. Mr. President, we need reform of the NSA program but not in this manner. Let's remember why this intelligence tool was put into place. It was enacted in the wake of the worst terrorist attack in our country that took the lives of nearly 3,000 people. We have testimony from the former Director of the FBI and from the former Deputy Director of the CIA telling us that had this tool been in place, it is likely—most likely—that the plot that killed nearly 3,000 people would have been uncovered. Why would we weaken the ability of our intelligence community at a time when the threats against this country have never been greater?

Let me address to my colleagues the privacy issue that has been raised—an issue that all of us care about. These data are far more safe, far more subject to privacy protections if they are held by the Federal Government where only 22 vetted and trained government employees have access to them instead of nearly 150 telecommunications companies that employ thousands of workers, and the government is going to have to go to those companies and ask for the data. That greatly exposes the privacy of individual Americans far more than the current system.

So for both of those reasons, I urge my colleagues to oppose the bill of the distinguished Senator from Vermont. It is a mistake. It would make us less safe, and we have expert testimony telling us that. Thank you, Mr. President.

Mr. CHAMBLISS. Mr. President, in closing, let me say there are any number of reasons why the substance of this bill is totally flawed. We live in a dangerous world today. We all know and understand that. While the provisions in this bill wouldn't have prohibited ISIL from being formed—it didn't prevent ISIL from being formed—the provisions in the underlying FISA bill give the Intelligence Committee all the tools they need to make sure that when ISIL recruits individuals to go to Syria to fight, if they are trying to recruit Americans, we can find out about that. We have under surveillance today any number of individuals, whom we think have been committed to jihad, who live in America.

Secondly, there is another part of their recruiting that is even more dangerous than asking young men and women to come to Syria to fight for ISIL. They want people to go into the Parliament in Canada and start killing people. They want people to walk the streets of New York and pull out a gun or a hatchet or whatever it may be and start killing people.

If we eliminate this program—and that is basically what the Leahy amendment does—then we are going to take a tool away from our intelligence community that is not going to allow them to be able to interrupt and disrupt those types of terrorist attacks.

Now, with respect to our privacy, folks, gosh, we need to be really protective of privacy issues in this country. We live under a Constitution that has survived for in excess of 200 years. It has lots of privacy protections in it, and all of us want to see that happen.

But let me tell my colleagues what is going to happen if this amendment comes to the floor and should happen to pass today. The metadata that is collected by the NSA can be accessed by 22 individuals—22. That means there is an opportunity for leaks to occur or for individual privacy rights to be breached by 22 people. If this amendment ever became law, all of a sudden, all of the telecoms are going to be holding this metadata information as opposed to the NSA holding it. All of those telecoms have thousands of employees, lots of whom have access—will have access to this metadata. So instead of having the potential for 22 people to breach the privacy rights of American citizens, all of a sudden we are going to have thousands of opportunities for the privacy rights of Americans to be breached.

Let me close by saying that this program has been criticized an awful lot simply because of the leaks that Mr. Snowden made because of his theft of government property. But the fact is there cannot be one single case pointed to by anybody who can show that as a result of the collection of metadata under 215, any American has had their privacy rights breached. It simply has not happened. It will not happen if we keep this program in place.

Do we need to modify it? You bet. And Senator Feinstein and I did a good job of that, considering 10 amendments within our committee, voting on all 10 of them. Some of them passed. Some of them didn't. The bill came out of our committee on a bipartisan vote.

The Leahy amendment has not even gone to the Judiciary Committee to give the members of the Judiciary Committee the opportunity to review it, to file amendments on it, to debate it in committee, and vote on it. That is not the way this institution has ever worked, and it is not the way it should work here in a lameduck session with time running out, and particularly on a controversial and sensitive and important program as is the 215 FISA amendment program.

Source: "USA Freedom Act—Motion to Proceed." *Congressional Record,* November 18, 2014 113th Congress, 2nd Session Issue: Vol. 160, No. 141—Daily Edition.

2015: REVELATIONS OF SIM CARD SPYING BY THE NSA AND GCHQ

On February 19, 2015, The Intercept, *an investigative news publication created by Glenn Greenwald, Laura Poitras, and Jeremy Scahill to report on whistle-blower Edward Snowden's revelations of National Security Agency's (NSA) surveillance activities, released a blockbuster report that stunned privacy rights advocates around the world. The online magazine reported that in 2010 and 2011 the NSA and its British counterpart, the Government Communications Headquarters (GCHQ), worked together to hack into the computer network of Gemalto, the largest manufacturer of SIM cards in the world. Gemalto operates in 85 countries, and its clientele of 400 wireless network providers includes such telecommunications giants as AT&T, T-Mobile, Verizon, and Sprint. The following is an excerpt from* The Intercept's *explosive story.*

American and British spies hacked into the internal computer network of the largest manufacturer of SIM cards in the world, stealing encryption keys used to protect the privacy of cellphone communications across the globe, according to top-secret documents provided to *The Intercept* by National Security Agency whistleblower Edward Snowden.

The hack was perpetrated by a joint unit consisting of operatives from the NSA and its British counterpart Government Communications Headquarters, or GCHQ. The breach, detailed in a secret 2010 GCHQ document, gave the surveillance agencies the potential to secretly monitor a large portion of the world's cellular communications, including both voice and data.

The company targeted by the intelligence agencies, Gemalto, is a multinational firm incorporated in the Netherlands that makes the chips used in mobile phones and next-generation credit cards. Among its clients are AT&T, T-Mobile, Verizon, Sprint and some 450 wireless network providers around the world. The company operates in 85 countries and has more than 40 manufacturing facilities. One of its three global headquarters is in Austin, Texas, and it has a large factory in Pennsylvania.

In all, Gemalto produces some 2 billion SIM cards a year. Its motto is "Security to be Free."

With these stolen encryption keys, intelligence agencies can monitor mobile communications without seeking or receiving approval from telecom companies and foreign governments. Possessing the keys also sidesteps the need to get a warrant or a wiretap, while leaving no trace on the wireless provider's network that the communications were intercepted. Bulk key theft additionally enables the intelligence agencies to unlock any previously encrypted communications they had already intercepted, but did not yet have the ability to decrypt.

As part of the covert operations against Gemalto, spies from GCHQ—with support from the NSA—mined the private communications of unwitting engineers and other company employees in multiple countries.

Gemalto was totally oblivious to the penetration of its systems—and the spying on its employees. "I'm disturbed, quite concerned that this has happened," Paul Beverly, a Gemalto executive vice president, told *The Intercept*. "The most important thing for me is to understand exactly how this was done, so we can take every measure to ensure that it doesn't happen again, and also to make sure that there's no impact on the telecom operators that we have served in a very trusted manner for many years. What I want to understand is what sort of ramifications it has, or could have, on any of our customers." He added that "the most important thing for us now is to understand the degree" of the breach.

Leading privacy advocates and security experts say that the theft of encryption keys from major wireless network providers is tantamount to a thief obtaining the master ring of a building superintendent who holds the keys to every apartment. "Once you have the keys, decrypting traffic is trivial," says Christopher Soghoian, the principal technologist for the American Civil Liberties Union. "The news of this key theft will send a shock wave through the security community."

Beverly said that after being contacted by *The Intercept*, Gemalto's internal security team began on Wednesday to investigate how their system was penetrated and could find no trace of the hacks. When asked if the NSA or GCHQ had ever requested access to Gemalto-manufactured encryption keys, Beverly said, "I am totally unaware. To the best of my knowledge, no."

According to one secret GCHQ slide, the British intelligence agency penetrated Gemalto's internal networks, planting malware on several computers, giving GCHQ secret access. We "believe we have their entire network," the slide's author boasted about the operation against Gemalto.

Additionally, the spy agency targeted unnamed cellular companies' core networks, giving it access to "sales staff machines for customer information and network engineers machines for network maps." GCHQ also claimed the ability to manipulate the billing servers of cell companies to "suppress" charges in an effort to conceal the spy agency's secret actions against an individual's phone. Most significantly, GCHQ also penetrated "authentication servers," allowing it to decrypt data and voice communications between a targeted individual's phone and his or her telecom provider's network. A note accompanying the slide asserted that the spy agency was "very happy with the data so far and [was] working through the vast quantity of product."

The Mobile Handset Exploitation Team (MHET), whose existence has never before been disclosed, was formed in April 2010 to target vulnerabilities in cellphones. One of its main missions was to covertly penetrate computer networks of corporations that manufacture SIM cards, as well as those of wireless network providers. The team included operatives from both GCHQ and the NSA.

While the FBI and other U.S. agencies can obtain court orders compelling U.S.-based telecom companies to allow them to wiretap or intercept the communications of their customers, on the international front this type of data collection is much more challenging. Unless a foreign telecom or foreign government grants access to their citizens' data to a U.S. intelligence agency, the NSA or CIA would have to hack into the network or specifically target the user's device for a more risky "active" form of surveillance that could be detected by sophisticated targets. Moreover, foreign intelligence agencies would not allow U.S. or U.K. spy agencies access to the mobile communications of their heads of state or other government officials.

"It's unbelievable. Unbelievable," said Gerard Schouw, a member of the Dutch Parliament, when told of the spy agencies' actions. Schouw, the intelligence spokesperson for D66, the largest opposition party in the Netherlands, told *The Intercept*, "We don't want to have the secret services from other countries doing things like this." Schouw added that he and other lawmakers will ask the Dutch government to provide an official explanation and to clarify whether the country's intelligence services were aware of the targeting of Gemalto, whose official headquarters is in Amsterdam.

Last November, the Dutch government proposed an amendment to its constitution to include explicit protection for the privacy of digital communications, including those made on mobile devices. "We have, in the Netherlands, a law on the [activities] of secret services. And hacking is not allowed," Schouw said. Under Dutch law, the interior minister would have to sign off on such operations by foreign governments' intelligence agencies. "I don't believe that he has given his permission for these kind of actions."

The U.S. and British intelligence agencies pulled off the encryption key heist in great stealth, giving them the ability to intercept and decrypt communications without alerting the wireless network provider, the foreign government or the individual user that they have been targeted. "Gaining access to a database of keys is pretty much game over for cellular encryption," says Matthew Green, a cryptography specialist at the Johns Hopkins Information Security Institute. The massive key theft is "bad news for phone security. Really bad news."

As consumers began to adopt cellular phones en masse in the mid-1990s, there were no effective privacy protections in place. Anyone could buy a cheap device from RadioShack capable of intercepting calls placed on mobile phones. The shift from analog to digital networks introduced basic encryption technology, though it was still crackable by tech savvy computer science graduate students, as well as the FBI and other law enforcement agencies, using readily available equipment.

Today, second-generation (2G) phone technology, which relies on a deeply flawed encryption system, remains the dominant platform globally, though U.S. and European cellphone companies now use 3G, 4G and LTE technology in urban areas. These include more secure, though not invincible, methods of encryption, and wireless carriers throughout the world are upgrading their networks to use these newer technologies.

It is in the context of such growing technical challenges to data collection that intelligence agencies, such as the NSA, have become interested in acquiring cellular encryption keys. "With old-fashioned [2G], there are other ways to work around cellphone security without those keys," says Green, the Johns Hopkins cryptographer. "With newer 3G, 4G and LTE protocols, however, the algorithms aren't as vulnerable, so getting those keys would be essential."

The privacy of all mobile communications—voice calls, text messages and Internet access—depends on an encrypted connection between the cellphone and the wireless carrier's network, using keys stored on the SIM, a tiny chip smaller than a postage stamp, which is inserted into the phone. All mobile communications on the phone depend on the SIM, which stores and guards the encryption keys created by companies like Gemalto. SIM cards can be used to store contacts, text messages, and other important data, like one's phone number. In some countries, SIM cards are used to transfer money. As *The Intercept* reported last year, having the wrong SIM card can make you the target of a drone strike.

SIM cards were not invented to protect individual communications—they were designed to do something much simpler: ensure proper billing and prevent fraud, which was pervasive in the early days of cellphones. Soghoian compares the use of encryption keys on SIM cards to the way Social Security numbers are used today. "Social security numbers were designed in the 1930s to track your contributions to your government pension," he says. "Today they are used as a quasi national identity number, which was never their intended purpose."

Because the SIM card wasn't created with call confidentiality in mind, the manufacturers and wireless carriers don't make a great effort to secure their supply chain. As a result, the SIM card is an extremely vulnerable component of a mobile phone. "I doubt anyone is treating those things very carefully," says Green. "Cell companies probably don't treat them as essential security tokens. They probably just care that nobody is defrauding their networks." The ACLU's Soghoian adds, "These keys are so valuable that it makes sense for intel agencies to go after them."

As a general rule, phone companies do not manufacture SIM cards, nor program them with secret encryption keys. It is cheaper and more efficient for them to outsource this sensitive step in the SIM card production process. They purchase them in bulk with the keys pre-loaded by other corporations. Gemalto is the largest of these SIM "personalization" companies.

After a SIM card is manufactured, the encryption key, known as a "Ki," is burned directly onto the chip. A copy of the key is also given to the cellular provider, allowing its network to recognize an individual's phone. In order for the phone to be able to connect to the wireless carrier's network, the phone—with the help of the SIM—authenticates itself using the Ki that has been programmed onto the SIM. The phone conducts a secret "handshake" that validates that the Ki on the SIM matches the Ki held by the mobile company. Once that happens, the communications between the phone and the network are encrypted. Even if GCHQ or the NSA were to intercept the phone signals as they are transmitted through the air, the intercepted data would be a garbled mess. Decrypting it can be challenging and time-consuming. Stealing the keys, on the other hand, is beautifully simple, from the intelligence agencies' point of view, as the pipeline for producing and distributing SIM cards was never designed to thwart mass surveillance efforts.

One of the creators of the encryption protocol that is widely used today for securing emails, Adi Shamir, famously asserted: "Cryptography is typically bypassed, not penetrated." In other words, it is much easier (and sneakier) to open a locked door when you have the key than it is to break down the door using brute force. While the NSA and GCHQ have substantial resources dedicated to breaking encryption, it is not the only way—and certainly not always the most efficient—to get at the data they want. "NSA has more mathematicians on its payroll than any other entity in the U.S.," says the ACLU's Soghoian. "But the NSA's hackers are way busier than its mathematicians." . . .

Source: Scahill, Jeremy and Josh Begley. "The Great SIM Heist: How Spies Stole the Key to the Encryption Castle." *The Intercept* (February 19, 2015). https://firstlook.org/theintercept/2015/02/19/great-sim-heist/. Accessed February 27, 2015. Used by permission of First Look Media, Inc.

Bibliography

Aid, Matthew. 2009. *The Secret Sentry: The Untold History of the National Security Agency*. New York: Bloomsbury.

Altheide, David L. 2006. *Terrorism and the Politics of Fear*. New York: AltaMira Press.

Angwin, Julia. 2014. *Dragnet Nation: A Quest for Privacy, Security, and Freedom in a World of Relentless Surveillance*. New York: Times Books.

Ashcroft, John. 2006. *Never Again: Securing America and Restoring Justice*. New York: Center Street.

Ball, Kirstie, and Laureen Snider, eds. 2013. *The Surveillance-Industrial Complex: A Political Economy of Surveillance*. New York: Routledge.

Bamford, James. 1982. *The Puzzle Palace: Inside the National Security Agency, America's Most Secret Intelligence Organization.* Boston, MA: Houghton Mifflin.

Bamford, James. 2001. *Body of Secrets: Anatomy of the Ultra-Secret National Security Agency.* New York: Anchor Books.

Bamford, James. 2008. *The Shadow Factory: The Ultra-Secret NSA from 9/11 to the Eavesdropping on America.* New York: Anchor Books.

Boghosian, Heidi. 2013. *Spying on Democracy: Government Surveillance, Corporate Power, and Public Resistance.* San Francisco: City Lights Books.

Cate, Fred H., et al. 2003. *Financial Privacy, Consumer Prosperity, and the Public Good.* Washington, DC: Brookings Institute.

Cole, David, and James X. Dempsey. 2006. *Terrorism and the Constitution: Sacrificing Civil Liberties in the Name of National Security,* Third Edition. New York: New Press.

Cole, Simon A. 2001. *Suspect Identities: A History of Fingerprinting and Criminal Identification.* Cambridge, MA: Harvard University Press.

Darmer, M. Katherine, Robert M. Baird, and Stuart E. Rosenbaum, eds. 2004. *Civil Liberties vs. National Security in a Post 9/11 World.* Amherst, NY: Prometheus Books.

Diffie, Whitfield, and Susan Landau. 1999. *Privacy on the Line: The Politics of Wiretapping and Encryption.* Cambridge, MA: MIT Press.

Engelhardt, Tom. 2014. *Shadow Government: Surveillance, Secret Wars, and a Global Security State in a Single-Superpower World.* Chicago: Haymarket Books.

Farber, Daniel. 2008. *Security vs. Liberty: Conflicts between National Security and Civil Liberties in American History.* New York: Russell Sage Foundation.

Fried, Albert. 1996. *McCarthyism: The Great American Red Scare: A Documentary History.* Oxford: Oxford University Press.

Goldstein, Justin Robert. 2001. *Political Repression in Modern America from 1870 to 1976.* Chicago: University of Illinois Press.

Greenwald, Glen. 2014. *No Place to Hide: Edward Snowden, the NSA, and the Surveillance State.* New York: Metropolitan Books.

Horton, Scott. 2015. *Lords of Secrecy: The National Security Elite and America's Stealth Warfare.* New York: Nation Books.

Kutulas, Judy. 2006. *The American Civil Liberties Union and the Making of Modern Liberalism, 1930–1960.* Chapel Hill: University of North Carolina Press.

Landau, Susan. 2010. *Surveillance or Security? The Risks Posed by New Wiretapping Technologies.* Cambridge, MA: MIT Press.

Maclin, Tracy. 2013. *The Supreme Court and the Fourth Amendment's Exclusionary Rule.* New York: Oxford University Press.

Miller, Russell A. 2008. *U.S. National Security, Intelligence and Democracy: From the Church Committee to the War on Terror.* London: Routledge.

Mills, Jon L. 2015. *Privacy in the New Media Age.* Gainesville: University Press of Florida.

Moore, Adam D. 2010. *Privacy Rights: Moral and Legal Foundations.* University Park, PA: Penn State University Press.

Moyer, Bruce. 2015. "The Most Powerful Court You Have Never Heard Of." *Washington Watch, Federal Bar Association*, March. http://www.fedbar.org/Advocacy/Washington-Watch/WW-Archives/2015/March-2015-The-Most-Powerful-Court-You-Have-Never-Heard-Of.aspx. Accessed September 22, 2015.

Murphy, Paul L. 1979. *World War I and the Origin of Civil Liberties in the United States.* New York: W.W. Norton.

Nissenbaum, Helen. 2009. *Privacy in Context: Technology, Policy, and the Integrity of Social Life.* Palo Alto, CA: Stanford University Press.

Reuter, Dean, and John Yoo, eds. 2011. *Confronting Terror: 9/11 and the Future of American National Security.* New York: Encounter Books.

Risen, James. 2006. *State of War: The Secret History of the CIA and the Bush Administration.* New York: Free Press.

Risen, James. 2014. *Pay Any Price: Greed, Power, and Endless War*. New York: Houghton Mifflin Harcourt.

Rotenberg, Marc, Jeramie Scott, and Julia Horwitz. 2015. *Privacy in the Modern Age: The Search for Solutions*. New York: New Press.

Schneier, Bruce. 2015. *Data and Goliath: The Hidden Battles to Collect Your Data and Control Your World*. New York: Norton.

Schulhofer, Stephen J. 2012. *More Essential than Ever: The Fourth Amendment in the Twenty-First Century*. New York: Oxford University Press.

Solove, Daniel J. 2002. "Digital Dossiers and the Dissipation of the Fourth Amendment Privacy." *Southern California Law Review* 75: 1083–167.

Solove, Daniel J. 2011. *Nothing to Hide: The False Tradeoff between Privacy and Security*. New Haven, CT: Yale University Press.

Solove, Daniel J., Marc Rotenberg, and Paul M. Schwartz. 2006. *Privacy, Information, and Technology*. New York: Aspen Publishing.

Stephens, Otis H., Jr., and Richard A. Glenn. 2006. *Unreasonable Searches and Seizures: Rights and Liberties under the Law*. Santa Barbara, CA: ABC-Clio.

Sullivan, E. Thomas, and Toni M. Massaro. 2013. *The Arc of Due Process in American Constitutional Law*. New York: Oxford University Press.

Tanner, Adam. 2014. *What Stays in Vegas: The World of Personal Data—Lifeblood of Big Business—and the End of Privacy as We Know It*. New York: Public Affairs.

Theoharis, Athan G. 1998. *Culture of Secrecy: The Government Versus the People's Right to Know*. Lawrence: University Press of Kansas.

Tushnet, Mark, ed. 2005. *The Constitution in Wartime: Beyond Alarmism and Complacency*. Durham, NC: Duke University Press.

Vile, John M., and David L. Hudson Jr. 2012. *Encyclopedia of the Fourth Amendment*. Santa Barbara, CA: ABC-CLIO.

Wallace, Robert, H. Keith Melton, and Henry R. Schlesinger. 2008. *Spycraft: The Secret History of the CIA's Spytechs, from Communism to al-Qaeda*. New York: Dutton.

About the Contributors

LAWRENCE W. BAKER is an independent publishing professional with more than three decades of experience in reference, academic, and trade publishing. He has been a project editor, writer, copyeditor, proofreader, and indexer for hundreds of books in his career.

MAYA A. BERNSTEIN is the privacy advocate of the Internal Revenue Service (IRS). She previously served as Privacy Advocate of the U.S. Department of Health and Human Services and as Senior Policy Analyst at the Office of Management and Budget (OMB). During her time at the OMB, she helped government agencies implement the Privacy Act of 1974.

DAVID J. BROWN is the managing attorney of the law offices of David J. Brown, LC, in Lawrence, Kansas. He is also an adjunct faculty member of the University of Kansas School of Law.

MIHAEL COLE is a Crown prosecutor in Ottawa, Canada. He received his JD from the University of Ottawa Law School.

SIMON A. COLE is Professor of Criminology, Law, and Society at the University of California, Irvine. He is the author of *Suspect Identities: A History of Fingerprinting and Criminal Identification*, which was awarded the 2003 Rachel Carson Prize by the Society for Social Studies of Science. He is also a coauthor (with Michael Lynch, Ruth McNally, and Kathleen Jordan) of *Truth Machine: The Contentious History of DNA Fingerprinting*.

PAM DIXON is the founder and executive director of the internationally recognized World Privacy Forum, a nonprofit, nonpartisan public interest research group, www.worldprivacyforum.org. There she focuses on in-depth research of emerging privacy issues. She has testified before Congress and state legislators on various privacy and technology issues and has written numerous books and articles on privacy issues.

GREGORY M. DUHL is Professor of Law at William Mitchell College of Law. He previously taught law at Southern Illinois University and the University of Tulsa. He earned his JD from Harvard Law School.

LARKIN R. EVANS holds bachelor's degrees in English and in Studio Art from Southern Methodist University. She received her JD from the University of Kansas in 2004.

LOUIS FISHER is Scholar in Residence at the Constitution Project. Previously he worked for four decades at the Library of Congress as Senior Specialist in Separation of Powers (Congressional Research Service, from 1970 to 2006) and Specialist in Constitutional Law (the Law Library, from 2006 to 2010). Fisher has taught at Queens College, Georgetown University, American University, Catholic University Law School, Indiana University, Catholic University, the College of William and Mary Law School, and Johns Hopkins University. Currently he is a Visiting Professor at the William and Mary Law school.

ROBERT GELLMAN is a privacy and information policy consultant in Washington, D.C. A graduate of the Yale Law School, Gellman has worked on privacy matters for more than 35 years. He served half of that time on the staff of the House of Representatives Subcommittee responsible for the Privacy Act of 1974. He also served a term as a member of the Department of Health and Human Service's National Committee on Vital and Health Statistics. Gellman has testified as a privacy expert before several state legislatures and has been an expert witness in court cases.

RICHARD A. GLENN is Professor of Government and Political Affairs at Millersville University.

MARGARET HAERENS is a writer and researcher who has written extensively on the intersection of social policy and technology.

KEVIN HILLSTROM is an independent scholar who has published numerous works on subjects related to American politics, policy, and history.

CHRIS JAY HOOFNAGLE is Lecturer in Residence and Director, Information Privacy Programs, at the Berkeley Center for Law & Technology. He is also Senior

Staff Attorney at the Samuelson Law, Technology and Public Policy Clinic. Hoofnagle has written extensively in the fields of information privacy, the law of unfair and deceptive practices, consumer law, and identity theft.

KEVIN M. KEENAN is an attorney with the Wheeler Upham law firm in Grand Rapids, Michigan. He earned his JD from the Thomas M. Cooley Law School in 2008. Keenan is the author of *Invasion of Privacy: A Reference Handbook.*

SUSAN LANDAU is Professor of Cybersecurity Policy at Worcester Polytechnic Institute's Department of Social Science and Policy Studies, where her research focuses on communications security and surveillance, critical infrastructure protection, identity, and privacy. Landau is the author of *Surveillance or Security? The Risks Posed by New Wiretapping Technologies* and the coauthor, with Whitfield Diffie, of *Privacy on the Line: The Politics of Wiretapping and Encryption.*

CHRISTOPHER P. LATIMER is chair of the Department of Political Science at Framingham State University. He has also served as Assistant Dean of Social Science and Associate Professor of Political Science at Endicott College and Associate Professor of Political Science at the State University of New York at Cortland. He earned a PhD at the University of Albany, SUNY, and a JD from American University: Washington College of Law.

MARY LE ROUGE is an independent scholar who has written widely on American and international politics, policy, and history.

WILLIAM C. LOWE is Dean of Ashford University's College of Liberal Arts and Professor of History.

GARY T. MARX is Professor Emeritus of Sociology at MIT. His research has focused on race and ethnicity, social movements, law and society, and surveillance.

DEBRA MILLER is a writer and lawyer who has written and edited numerous books and anthologies on historical, political, and policy topics.

STEVE MUNCH is a candidate for a law degree and a doctoral degree in sociology at Northwestern University. He received his bachelors of arts in history and sociology from the University of Kansas in 2006 and received a master's in sociology at Northwestern.

JAMES P. NEHF is Professor, Cleon H. Foust Fellow, and John S. Grimes Fellow at the Indiana University Robert H. McKinney School of Law.

PATRICIA OSLUND is a research economist for the Institute for Policy and Social Research at the University of Kansas.

MARCY E. PEEK is Assistant Professor of Law at Whittier Law School. Peek earned her JD from Harvard Law School.

SEAN M. PEEK is the founder of the Peek Family Law practice in Denver, Colorado. Peek graduated cum laude from Thomas M. Cooley Law School in Lansing, Michigan, in 2008. He attended the University of Washington and graduated in 2004 with a degree in political science.

MARK PERRY is Professor on the Faculty of Law and the Faculty of Science at the University of Western Ontario. He is a barrister and solicitor of the Law Society of Upper Canada, a Faculty Fellow at IBM's Center for Advanced Studies, and a correspondent for the Computer Law and Security Report.

MICHAEL PETRUNIK is a former Associate Professor of Criminology at the University of Ottawa.

NEIL M. RICHARDS is Professor of Law at Washington University in St. Louis. Richards is an internationally recognized expert in the fields of privacy, First Amendment, and information law. His recent work explores the complex relationships between free speech and privacy in cyberspace.

JOHN M. SCHEB was a longtime judge (1974–1992) on Florida's Second District Court of Appeals. Upon retiring from the bench, he became a lecturer with the Stetson University College of Law. In addition to teaching, Judge Scheb coauthored numerous professional articles as well as college and law school textbooks on criminal law, administrative law, and appellate practice.

JOHN M. SCHEB II is Professor in the Department of Political Science at the University of Tennessee at Knoxville and Faculty Fellow at the Howard H. Baker, Jr. Center for Public Policy.

AARON SCHWABACH is Professor of Law at Thomas Jefferson School of Law in San Diego.

RIC SIMMONS is the Chief Justice Thomas J. Moyer Professor for the Administration of Justice and Rule of Law at the Moritz College of Law in the Ohio State University. He is a former prosecutor in New York City and has written numerous articles exploring the relationship between the Fourth Amendment and emerging technologies.

ANTHONY SIMONES is Manager of Judicial Education and Programming for the Office of State Courts Administrator in Missouri. He was formerly Associate Professor of Criminal Justice and Political Science at Dalton State College.

DANIEL J. SOLOVE is the John Marshall Harlan Research Professor of Law at the George Washington University Law School. He is a Senior Policy Advisor at Hogan Lovells. He is also the founder of TeachPrivacy, which provides privacy and data security training programs to businesses, schools, health care institutions, and other organizations.

DAVID E. SORKIN is Associate Professor of Law at The John Marshal Law School in Chicago, Illinois, and is affiliated with the school's Center for Information Technology and Privacy Law.

THOMAS G. STACY is a Professor of Law at the University of Kansas. Stacy's teaching and research focus on criminal law, constitutional law, and health law.

OTIS H. STEPHENS JR. became the Resident Scholar of Constitutional Law at the University of Tennessee, Knoxville College of Law, in 2000. He retired in 2012. Professor Stephens has authored, coauthored, or edited six books on the U.S. Constitution and Supreme Court and published numerous articles, book reviews, and professional papers. He held a postdoctoral fellowship at Harvard Law School, and in addition to UT, he has taught at Johns Hopkins University and Georgia Southern College.

ATHAN THEOHARIS is Professor Emeritus of History at Marquette University in Wisconsin.

GRACE VANDEMARK is an independent scholar who writes about American history and U.S. politics.

JOHN WILSON WELLS is Associate Professor of Political Science at Carson Newman College. He is coeditor of *American National Security and Civil Liberties in an Era of Terrorism.*

BRIAN L. ZIRKLE is Associate Professor of Sociology at Johnson County Community College in Overland, Kansas.

Index

Note: Page numbers in **bold** indicate main entries.